THE SAGE DICTIONARY
OF CRIMINOLOGY

THE SAGE DICTIONARY OF CRIMINOLOGY

Compiled and edited by
Eugene McLaughlin and John Muncie

SAGE Publications
London • Thousand Oaks • New Delhi

SAGE Publications Ltd
6 Bonhill Street
London EC2A 4PU

SAGE Publications Inc
2455 Teller Road
Thousand Oaks, California 91320

SAGE Publications India Pvt Ltd
32, M-Block Market
Greater Kailash – I
New Delhi 110 048

British Library Cataloguing in Publication data

A catalogue record for this book is available
from the British Library

ISBN 0 7619 5907 6
ISBN 0 7619 5908 4 (pbk)

Library of Congress control number available

Typeset by Mayhew Typesetting, Rhayader, Powys
Printed in Great Britain by The Cromwell Press Ltd,
Trowbridge, Wiltshire

CONTENTS

LIST OF CONTRIBUTORS

EDITORS

Eugene McLaughlin, The Open University, UK

John Muncie, The Open University, UK

ADMINISTRATIVE SUPPORT

Pauline Hetherington, The Open University, UK

Sue Lacey, The Open University, UK

INTERNATIONAL ADVISORY BOARD

Pat Carlen, University of Bath, UK

Stuart Henry, Wayne State University, Michigan, USA

Tony Jefferson, University of Keele, UK

Victor Jupp, University of Northumbria, UK

Pat O'Malley, La Trobe University, Melbourne, Australia

Joe Sim, Liverpool John Moores University, UK

Elizabeth Stanko, Royal Holloway, University of London, UK

René van Swaaningen, Erasmus University Rotterdam, The Netherlands

AUTHORS

Robert Agnew, Emory University, Atlanta, USA

Bruce Arrigo, School of Professional Psychology, Fresno, California, USA

Gregg Barak, Eastern Michigan University, USA

Piers Beirne, University of Southern Maine, USA

Ben Bowling, University of London, UK

Trevor Bradley, Victoria University, Wellington, New Zealand

Eamonn Carrabine, Essex University, UK

Geertrui Cazaux, University of Southern Maine, USA

Kathryn Chadwick, Edge Hill University College, Ormskirk, UK

John Clarke, The Open University, UK

Roy Coleman, Liverpool John Moores University, UK

Iain Crow, University of Sheffield, UK

Kathleen Daly, Griffith University, Brisbane, Australia

Julia Davidson, Westminster University, UK

Anna Duncan, Victoria University, Wellington, New Zealand

Paul Ekblom, Home Office, UK

Clive Emsley, The Open University, UK

Jeff Ferrell, Northern Arizona University, USA

Loraine Gelsthorpe, University of Cambridge, UK

Peter Gill, Liverpool John Moores University, UK

David Greenberg, New York University, USA

Nic Groombridge, St Mary's College, London, UK

Willem de Haan, University of Groningen, The Netherlands

Keith Hayward, University of East London, UK

Frances Heidensohn, Goldsmiths College, University of London, UK

Stuart Henry, Wayne State University, Michigan, USA

Paddy Hillyard, University of Ulster at Jordanstown, Northern Ireland

Clive Hollin, University of Leicester, UK

Barbara Hudson, University of Central Lancashire, UK

Gordon Hughes, The Open University, UK

Ruth Jamieson, Keele University, UK

Tony Jefferson, Keele University, UK

Victor Jupp, University of Northumbria, UK

Roger Kern, Eastern Michigan University, USA

Maggy Lee, Essex University, UK

Eugene McLaughlin, The Open University, UK

Dragan Milovanovic, Northeastern Illinois University, USA

Wayne Morrison, Queen Mary and Westfield College, University of London, UK

John Muncie, The Open University, UK

Karim Murji, The Open University, UK

Pat O'Malley, La Trobe University, Melbourne, Australia

Ken Pease, University of Huddersfield, UK

Hal Pepinsky, Indiana University, USA

Mike Presdee, University of Sunderland, UK

Jill Radford, University of Teesside, UK

Joseph Rankin, Eastern Michigan University, USA

Roger Sapsford, University of Teesside, UK

Esther Saraga, The Open University, UK

Phil Scraton, Edge Hill University College, Ormskirk, UK

James Sheptycki, University of Durham, UK

Joe Sim, Liverpool John Moores University, UK

Richard Sparks, Keele University, UK

Elizabeth Stanko, Royal Holloway, University of London, UK

Colin Sumner, University of East London, UK

Maggie Sumner, Westminster University, London, UK

René van Swaaningen, Erasmus University Rotterdam, The Netherlands

Mark Thornton, Victoria University, Wellington, New Zealand

Steve Tombs, Liverpool John Moores University, UK

Tonia Tzannetakis, University of Athens, Greece

Claire Valier, Lancaster University, UK

Sandra Walklate, Manchester Metropolitan University, UK

Reece Walters, Victoria University, Wellington, New Zealand

Louise Westmarland, Scarman Centre, University of Leicester, UK

Nicole Westmarland, University of Stirling, UK

Dick Whitfield, Probation Office, Kent, UK

Dave Whyte, Liverpool John Moores University, UK

David Wilson, University of Central England, Birmingham, UK

Anne Worrall, Keele University, UK

Jock Young, Middlesex University, UK

PREFACE

The compilation of the dictionary has been a truly collective endeavour and could not have been developed without the generous help, support and suggestions of many different people. From the outset the editors have been supported by an international advisory board with representatives from the USA, Australia and the Netherlands as well as the UK. They provided invaluable advice in drawing up an initial list of key terms which had international and universal significance and furnished the editors with the names of specialist academics world-wide. As a result the dictionary has been immeasurably enhanced by contributions from criminological researchers and authors, of whom many are the leading scholars in their field. With more than 250 entries written by 69 academics and practitioners from Europe, USA, Australia and New Zealand, never before has the work of so many criminologists – often with widely differing perspectives – been brought together in a single endeavour. We are indebted to them all.

A work of this nature has also been a necessarily lengthy and complex exercise in collaboration, collation, formatting, timetabling and processing. Without the formidable administrative and secretarial skills of Sue Lacey and Pauline Hetherington of the Social Policy Department at the Open University it would not have been possible at all. Last but not least we express sincere thanks to Gillian Stern and Miranda Nunhofer and the team at Sage for their invaluable support, assistance and care for this project.

EDITORS' INTRODUCTION

The Sage Dictionary of Criminology explores the categories of thought, methods and practices that are central to contemporary criminological study. Unlike many other dictionaries or encyclopaedias in this area, its starting point is not to elucidate particular legal powers or criminal justice procedures but to unravel issues of theoretical and conceptual complexity.

The dictionary was constructed on the principle that criminology is a contested interdisciplinary discourse marked by constant incursion, interactions, translations and transgressions. Competing theoretical perspectives meet and sometimes they are able to speak to, listen to and understand each other, at others they appear not to share any common discourse. There is, therefore, no one definition of criminology to be found in this dictionary but a multitude of noisy argumentative criminological perspectives which in themselves often depend and draw upon knowledges and concerns generated from elsewhere. As a result, the dictionary deliberately includes pieces that depart from traditional agendas, transgress conventional boundaries and suggest new points of formation and avenues for cross-discipline development. Many of the entries will be of vital importance in understanding criminology in terms of what it is discursively struggling to become. A canonical closure or discursive unification of criminology is no more possible at the beginning of the twenty-first century than it was at the beginning of the twentieth century. New modes of information exchange and the unprecedented mobility of ideas rule out disciplinary parochialism and assertion of authoritative positions. This is what will give criminology its intellectual strength and ensure that the field of criminological studies remains dynamic and relevant for future generations of students.

The rationale of the dictionary can best be explained by way of a detailing of its scope and structure. In compiling this dictionary every effort has been made to ensure that it is broadly representative and inclusive in tone, reflecting the field of criminology in its diverse and expansive dimensions. Though they appear in alphabetical order, the choice of entries has been guided by four organizing principles. Each entry concerns one of the following:

- a major theoretical position;
- a key theoretical concept;
- a central criminological method; *or*
- a core criminal justice philosophy or practice.

Each entry is central to the field, standing either as an intellectual benchmark, or as an emergent thematic in the shifting and expanding field of criminological studies. As a result, the dictionary provides a comprehensive introduction to criminological theory, its diverse frames of reference and its expansive modes of analysis.

Throughout, the dictionary aims to be fully international and deliberately avoids legal terms and cases which are specific to particular criminal justice jurisdictions. For the same reason it also deliberately avoids legally defined acts of crime – such as theft, burglary, murder and so on – but does include those 'crimes' which are either emergent – such as cybercrime and animal abuse – or those with a wider theoretical resonance – such as corporate crime, serial killing, hate crime and so on.

In selecting these entries we have been particularly concerned to help students to think through and utilize key concepts, methods and practices and to complement as well as supplement the teaching materials already used in university and college-based criminology and related courses. It is designed as an accessible learning resource for undergraduate students in the fields of criminology, criminal justice studies, the sociology of crime and deviance, socio-legal studies, social policy, criminal law and social work.

To ensure maximum accessibility each entry is headed by a short statement or *definition* which sets out the basic parameters of the concept itself. From here any comparability with an orthodox dictionary ends. The following section – *distinctive features* – is more encyclopaedic in style and allows for some detailed comment on the concept's origins, development and general significance. Throughout, we have encouraged authors to reflect critically and freely on criminology's historical knowledge base and on potential future developments. We have ensured that a final section – *evaluation* – has been included for all major theoretical positions. This allows for some initial considered and critical assessment of how they have been or can be debated, challenged and reworked. Evaluation sections also appear in many of the other entries, but at the discretion of the individual authors. As a guide, we have encouraged entries of up to 1500 words each for major theoretical positions and up to 1000 words each for theoretical concepts, methods and criminal justice concepts. Each entry is also cross-referenced to those other *associated concepts* included in the dictionary to facilitate a broader and in-depth study. Finally, each entry concludes with a list of up to six *key readings* to reinforce the aim of the dictionary as a learning resource to be built upon by the reader. We are also aware that for many students an initial entry into criminological study is as much through the names of particular authors as it is through a particular key concept. To this end, the dictionary concludes with both a *subject index* and a *name index* to further enhance its accessibility. All these features are designed to facilitate the dictionary's use as a study guide for introductory courses in the field, as a source of reference for advanced study, as a supplement to established textbooks and as a reference guide to the specialized language of theoretical and conceptual criminology. Patient reading will uncover the full range of connections to be made across the entries and their associated concepts.

There is one final point we wish to make. This dictionary originated in a series of conversations between ourselves and Gillian Stern in London and Milton Keynes in 1997 and 1998. We finally committed ourselves to the dictionary when we realized that it fitted in with the criminological project we had embarked upon at the Open University. We continue to view this dictionary as part of our ongoing dialogue with/in criminology and we intend to produce a second edition which will enable us to reflect on the framework we have constructed and expand upon the range of theoretical perspectives, concepts, methodologies and emergent issues. We will persist with our efforts to be as inclusive and internationalist as possible and to emphasize the importance of a theory-led criminology. To this end we would welcome feedback as well as any possible future contributions.

Eugene McLaughlin
John Muncie
Milton Keynes, UK
December 2000

A

ABOLITION

Definition

In criminology and criminal justice, the term 'abolition' currently refers to the attempt to do away with punitive responses to criminalized problems. It is the first step in the abolitionist strategy, followed by a plea for dispute settlement, redress and social justice. In more general terms it refers to the abolition of state (supported) institutions which are no longer felt to be legitimate. Historically, the term abolition has been used in the fight against slavery, torture, prostitution, capital punishment and prison.

Distinctive Features

Though the literal meaning of the verb 'to abolish' suggests differently, penal abolition should not be interpreted in absolute terms. Abolitionists do not argue that the police or courts should be abolished. The point is that crime is not to be set apart from other, non-criminalized, social problems and that the social exclusion of 'culprits' seldom solves problems. Instead, crime problems should be treated in the specific context in which they emerge and reactions should be oriented around reintegration, rather than exclusion. Neither do abolitionists argue against social control in general terms. It is indeed hard to imagine social co-existence without any form of social control. The problem is the top-down, repressive, punitive and inflexible character of formal social control systems. It is these specific characteristics of penal control which are to be abolished (Bianchi and van Swaaningen, 1986).

Abolitionists question the ethical calibre of a state that intentionally and systematically inflicts pain upon other people. They point out that, because generally accepted goals of general and special prevention cannot be supported with empirical data, the credibility of the whole penal rationale is at stake. Depenalization (pushing back the punitive character of social reactions) and decriminalization (against the labelling of social problems as crimes) are the central strategies of abolition. Stan Cohen (1988) has identified five other 'destructuring moves' which are part of the politics of abolition: decarceration (away from prison), diversion (away from the institution), decategorization (away from offender typologies), delegalization (away from the state) and deprofessionalization (away from the expert). In a next, positive or reconstructive phase, a distinction is made between abolitionism as a way of thinking (an alternative way of understanding the problem of crime and punishment), and as a way of acting (a radical approach to penal reform).

In their attempts at depenalization, abolitionists first pointed their arrows at the prison system. This struggle has its roots in prisoners' movements or a religiously inspired penal lobby (Mathiesen, 1974; van Swaaningen, 1997). During the early 1980s, the attention shifted to the pros and cons of non-custodial measures as alternatives to prison. Warnings against the net-widening effects were contrasted with their potential value in the attrition of the penal system. The recognition that sanctioning-modalities at the end of the penal chain do not change its punitive, excluding character, focused attention on the diversion of cases in preliminary phases, with the aim of preventing the stigmatizing effects of both trial and punishment. This phase was followed by the advocacy of a whole alternative procedural rationale, in which non-punitive responses to social problems were promoted, including forms of social crime prevention designed to address the structural contexts of crime (de Haan, 1990).

Notably, Nils Christie's and Louk Hulsman's abolitionist perspectives contain many implicit references to Habermas's idea of the 'colonization of the lifeworld'. The 'decolonization' of criminal justice's 'system rationality' is another object of abolition. Though the tension Habermas observes between systems and lifeworlds does not lead him directly to a rejection of the criminal justice system, he does argue against the degeneration of criminal justice into a state-instrument of crime control in which the critical dimension of power is ignored. Thus, penal instrumentalism is another object of abolition which can be derived from Habermas.

A further aim of abolition is related to the constitution of moral discourse. In Western, neo-liberal societies values like care and empathy are delegated to the private sphere and are thereby excluded from public, or political, ethics. These latter ethics are dominated by abstract, so-called 'masculine' notions such as rights, duties and respect, which outrule more subjective, contextually determined 'feminine' notions such as care and empathy. The dominance of abstract approaches of rights results in a morality oriented at a generalized other, whereas a feminist approach is oriented at a concrete other. Thus, abolitionism also implies the abolition of the 'masculine', individualistic, neo-liberal values upon which our penal systems are built (van Swaaningen, 1989).

René van Swaaningen

Associated Concepts: abolitionism, community justice, critical criminology, deconstruction, redress, the state

Key readings
Bianchi, H. and van Swaaningen, R. (eds) (1986) *Abolitionism: Towards a Non-Repressive Approach to Crime.* Amsterdam, Free University Press.
Cohen, S. (1988) *Against Criminology.* New Brunswick, NJ, Transaction.
de Haan, W. (1990) *The Politics of Redress: Crime, Punishment and Penal Abolition.* London, Unwin Hyman.
Mathiesen, T. (1974) *The Politics of Abolition.* London, Martin Robertson.
Van Swaaningen, R. (1989) 'Feminism and abolitionism as critiques of criminology', *International Journal for the Sociology of Law,* 17 (3), pp. 287–306.
Van Swaaningen, R. (1997) *Critical Criminology – Visions From Europe.* London, Sage.

ABOLITIONISM

Definition

A sociological and political perspective that analyses criminal justice and penal systems as social problems that intensify rather than diminish crime and its impact. On this basis prisons (the initial focus of study) reinforce dominant ideological constructions of crime, reproduce social divisions and distract attention from crimes committed by the powerful. Abolitionists advocate the radical transformation of the prison and punishment system and their replacement with a reflexive and integrative strategy for dealing with these complex social phenomena.

Distinctive Features

Liberal approaches to the study of the prison are built on a number of often competing and contradictory goals: rehabilitation, general prevention, incapacitation, punishment and individual and collective deterrence. Abolitionism, which emerged out of the social movements of the late 1960s challenges these liberal perspectives by arguing that the criminal justice system and prisons in practice contribute little to the protection of the individual and the control of crime. In the words of the Dutch abolitionist Willem de Haan, the prison 'is counter productive, difficult to control and [is] itself a major social problem'. Crime is understood as a complex, socially constructed phenomenon which 'serves to maintain political power relations and lends legitimacy to the crime control apparatus and the intensification of surveillance and control' (de Haan, 1991, pp. 206–7). At the same time abolitionists are critical of the unquestioning acceptance by liberals of prison reform. For abolitionists like Thomas Mathiesen liberal reform can never have a positive effect because it reinforces and bolsters the system, thus perpetuating processes of brutalization for the confined. Alternatively, 'negative reforms' are supported for their potential to challenge and undermine the system leading eventually to the demise of prisons. Abolitionists advocate a system that deals with crime as a socially constructed phenomenon. Crime should be responded to not by the negativity of a system built on punitive exclusion but on a reflexive and participatory system of inclusion built on redress, social policy, mutuality and solidarity. 'The aim is compensation rather than retaliation; reconciliation rather than blame allocation. To this end, the criminal justice system needs to be decentralized and neighbourhood courts established as a complement or substitute' (de Haan, 1991, pp. 211–12). Abolitionism therefore 'implies a negative critique of the fundamental shortcomings of the criminal law to realize social justice' while simultaneously offering both an alternative way of thinking about crime and a 'radical approach to penal reform' (van Swaaningen, 1997, p. 117).

It is also important to note that abolitionism is not a homogeneous theoretical and political movement but varies across cultures. Not only has it been principally a European phenomenon (Davies, 1998), but within Europe there have been different strands to the movement with some pointing to the distinct differences between European and British movements. In Europe early abolitionists such as Mathiesen, Christie, Bianchi and Hulsman advocated an alternative vision for criminal justice politics. Second generation abolitionists, neo-abolitionists, accept many of the abolitionist principles, including the rejection of both the concept of crime and 'penality as the ultimate metaphor of justice' (van Swaaningen, 1997, pp. 116 and 202). However, British neo-abolitionists such as Box-Grainger, Ryan, Ward, Hudson and Sim also advocated engaging in more interventionist work to develop a 'criminology from below', which

> In utilizing a complex set of competing, contradictory and oppositional discourses, and providing support on the ground for the confined and their families, has challenged the hegemony around prison that has united state servants, traditional reform groups and many academics on the same pragmatic and ideological terrain. In a number of areas . . . such as deaths in custody, prison conditions, medical power, visiting, censorship and sentencing these groups have conceded key points to the abolitionist argument and have moved onto a more radical terrain where they too have contested the construction of state-defined truth around penal policy. (Sim, 1994, pp. 275–6)

Evaluation

In the light of the huge increase in prison populations around the globe and the continuing rise in both reported crimes and crimes audited in victimization and self-report studies, abolitionism offers an impor-

tant series of insights into the role of the prison and its failures at the beginning of the twenty-first century. The perspective continues to pose the key question: is prison the answer to the problem of crime even allowing for an expanded definition to include crimes committed by the powerful?

There have been a number of issues raised and criticisms made of the abolitionist position. Most have come from those who, like abolitionists, would see themselves as part of a theoretical and political tradition that was on the critical wing of politics and social science. Left realists would criticize abolitionists for their idealism and for their 'anarcho communist position' which is 'preoccupied with abolishing or minimizing state intervention rather than attempting to make it more effective, responsive and accountable' (Matthews, cited in Sim, 1994, p. 265).

Abolitionists would reject the charge of idealism and as noted above would point to the influence that they have had on a number of political debates and social policies in terms of making the state more accountable. For example, the issue of deaths in custody which became a major political debate in the UK in the 1980s and 1990s involved not only individuals who were part of the abolitionist movement but had a significant hegemonic impact on liberal reform groups by pulling them onto a more radical and critical terrain in terms of demanding political action to deal with the devastating impact of these deaths on the family and friends of the deceased (Sim, 1994). Abolitionists would also say that the problem with criminology is that it suffers from too little utopian and idealistic thought rather than too much.

Feminist writers have also drawn attention to the problem of violent men and what should be done to protect women from the predations of, for example, men who rape. This raises the broader question of dangerousness and the nature of the response that is needed to deal with dangerous individuals. What, for example, do we do with those who engage in serial killing and who are overwhelmingly men? Abolitionists would agree that violence against women is a major issue across societies which should be taken and responded to seriously but would maintain that simply confining violent men inside can often only mean detaining them in institutions where the pervasive culture of masculinity is likely to reinforce misogynist views around male power and women (Sim, 1994). Therefore they would say that the nature of the institutions and the broader culture which objectifies women and equates heterosexuality with domination and power needs to be addressed.

They would argue further that dangerousness is a social construction in that there are a range of behaviours that can have immense implications for individual and group safety but which are rarely, if ever, labelled dangerous. The non-implementation of health and safety laws would be an example of this point. Finally, abolitionists would argue that the distinction between normal and abnormal, which lies at the heart of positivist thought, and which dominates debates about violence and dangerousness, is also problematic. They would point to the killings carried out by, and the non-prosecution of, the 'normal' men who murdered hundreds of innocent men, women and children in Vietnam in 1968 as an example of the social construction of dangerousness. This crime took place 15 months before the infamous Manson murders in the USA. This latter case has become deeply embedded in popular and political consciousness while the former case has largely been forgotten.

At another level, Angela Davies (1998, pp. 102–3) has argued that while the European abolitionist tradition has offered many important insights into the nature of the prison 'there is no sustained analysis of the part anti-racism might play in the theory and practice of abolitionism'. This is particularly important when it is recognized that prison populations around the world contain a disproportionate number of people drawn from ethnic minority backgrounds.

For the future, abolitionists have increasingly connected with the emerging discourses and debates around human rights and social justice which they see as mechanisms for developing negative reforms, thereby promoting a response to social harm that is very different from the destructive prison and punishment systems that currently exist.

Joe Sim

Associated Concepts: abolition, critical criminology, hegemony, left idealism, redress, social constructionism, social justice, the state

Key Readings

Bianchi, H. and van Swaaningen, R. (eds) (1986) *Abolitionism: Towards a Non-Repressive Approach to Crime.* Amsterdam, Free University Press.
Davies, A. (1998) 'Racialized punishment and prison abolition', in J. James (ed.), *The Angela Y. Davies Reader.* Oxford, Blackwell.

De Haan, W. (1991) 'Abolitionism and crime control: a contradiction in terms', in K. Stenson and D. Cowell (eds), *The Politics of Crime Control.* London, Sage.
Mathiesen, T. (1990) *Prison on Trial.* London, Sage.
Sim, J. (1994) 'The abolitionist approach: a British perspective', in A. Duff, S. Marshall, R.E. Dobash and R.P. Dobash (eds), *Penal Theory and Practice: Tradition and Innovation in Criminal Justice.* Manchester, Manchester University Press.
Van Swaaningen, R. (1997) *Critical Criminology: Visions From Europe.* London, Sage.

ACTION RESEARCH

Definition

Action research is a form of research, often evaluative in nature, which has the intention of influencing the future direction of practice and policy.

Distinctive Features

The origins of action research are generally traced to the work of Kurt Lewin (1943), who envisaged that social research should seek to address certain goals. In many forms of enquiry the researcher seeks to distance himself or herself from the topic being researched, and from the parties to social action. The action researcher, in contrast, enters into a dialogue with the parties to social action, transmitting results at certain points during the investigation so that the parties involved can make changes to the ways in which they are proceeding, and sometimes to the aims they are seeking to achieve. The consequences of these changes are then studied in turn, and further feedback and change may take place in an iterative process. Such a process can also have consequences for the research design and methods originally adopted by the researcher(s), which may have to change in order to accommodate new developments in social action. Action research is therefore a dynamic model of research, which requires time for reflection and review.

Action research has been used in community-based initiatives, such as community development projects and crime prevention programmes, in order to inform the future progress of social intervention. An example of action research in practice can be found in an evaluation of a domestic violence project where 'regular feedback was given to the project in order that this could inform subsequent developments'. Here the difficulties of achieving 'longer term reflections and change' when beset by shorter term 'operational' issues were noted (Kelly, 1999).

Evaluation

Action research has also been employed where participants and researchers share a commitment to achieving a particular end, such as anti-racist action, feminist approaches to working, and the pursuit of human rights (see, for example, Mies, 1993). Action research raises questions about the extent to which the researcher can remain aloof and detached from social action; the researcher may be regarded more as an actor with a particular set of skills and experience. Action research can also have the aim of empowering participants in social action. This may be achieved by enabling participants to have more control over their lives and communities, or by increasing the research skills of participants so that they have a greater ability to monitor, evaluate and reflect on their activities themselves, or both of the foregoing. One such development has been the attempt to empower user interests in public service evaluations. 'User' research has a 'commitment to changing the balance of power between those who provide and those who receive services', the interests of service users being enhanced through the research process (Barnes, 1993).

Iain Crow

Associated Concepts: evaluation research, praxis, reflexivity

Key Readings

Barnes, M. (1993) 'Introducing new stakeholders: user and researcher interests in evaluative research – a discussion of methods used to evaluate the Birmingham Community Care Special Action Project', Policy and Politics, 21 (1), pp. 47–58.

Everitt, A. and Hardiker, P. (1996) Evaluating for Good Practice. Basingstoke, Macmillan.

Greenwood, D.J. and Levin, M. (1998) Introduction to Action Research: Social Research for Social Change. London, Sage.

Kelly, L. (1999) Domestic Violence Matters: An Evaluation of a Development Project. Home Office Research Study No. 193, Research, Development and Statistics Directorate, London, HMSO.

Lewin, K. (1943) 'Forces behind food habits and methods of change', Bulletin of the National Research Council, 108, pp. 35–65.

Mies, M. (1993) 'Towards a methodology for feminist research', in M. Hammersley (ed.), Social Research: Philosophy, Politics and Practice. London, Sage.

ACTUARIALISM

Definition

Actuarialism refers to the suite of risk calculation techniques that underpin correctional policies.

Distinctive Features

Actuarialism is most closely associated with the 'new penology' writings of Malcolm M. Feeley and Jonathan Simon. The term the 'new penology' had been floating around American criminal justice circles for several years before Feeley and Simon finally pulled the various components together. They argue that in response to the need for more accountability and rationality a radical shift took place in correctional policy in the USA during the 1980s. The old transformative rationales for the correctional system were replaced by the actuarial language of probabilistic calculations and statistical distributions applicable to populations. Rather than concentrating on individuals, the system shifted to targeting and managing specific categories and sub-populations. Management was to be realized through the application of increasingly sophisticated risk assessment technologies and practices. This shift also enabled the system to construct its own measures of success and failure and to predict its own needs. In many respects Feeley and Simon viewed actuarialism as both the logical consequence of the original utilitarian penal reform project and a radical departure in that the system had moved beyond any interest in reform or rehabilitation. The correctional system under actuarialism becomes a hyper-rational processing system that fulfils the mandate that it has been given. For them actuarialism logically connected with neo-liberal socio-economic policies that produced surplus populations that had to be contained and controlled. In the UK actuarialism is most closely associated with the work of the probation service, whose professional task is risk assessment of the likelihood of re-offending and the threat posed to the community.

Eugene McLaughlin

Associated Concepts: managerialism, prediction studies, rational choice theory, risk, situational crime prevention

Key Readings

DiLulio, J. (1987) *Governing Prisons: A Comparative Study of Correctional Management*. New York, The Free Press.

Feeley, M. and Simon, J. (1992) 'The new penology: notes on the emerging strategy of corrections and its implications', *Criminology*, 30 (4), pp. 452–74.

Simon, J. (1988) 'The ideological effect of actuarial practices', *Law and Society Review*, 22, pp. 771–800.

Simon, J. and Feeley, M. (1995) 'True crime: the new penology and public discourse on crime', in T. Blomberg and S. Cohen (eds), *Punishment and Social Control*. New York, Aldine de Gruyter.

ADMINISTRATIVE CRIMINOLOGY

Definition

A term coined by Jock Young in the 1980s to refer to the reconstitution of establishment criminology in the UK and USA in the aftermath of the demise of positivist inspired correctionalist theory and practice and the emergence of radical criminology. Administrative criminology concentrates on the nature of the criminal event and the setting in which it occurs and assumes that offenders are rational actors who attempt to weigh up the potential costs and benefits of their actions. The goal of administrative criminology is to make crime less attractive to offenders.

Distinctive Features

The term 'administrative criminology' encompasses a large number of writers from a variety of academic backgrounds involved in a wide range of research sites. They are united by: acceptance of dominant definitions of what constitutes the problem of crime; a lack of interest in the social causes of crime; acceptance of the need for their research to be applied to aid policy development and decision-making; support for rational choice or 'opportunity' approaches to specific offenders and specific

offences; advocacy of 'what we know' and 'what works' criminal justice policies; proposing modesty and realism in making claims about what can be achieved; and being either employed within the criminal justice system or acting as paid advisers to criminal justice officials.

For Jock Young, the work of James Q. Wilson (in the USA) and Ronald V. Clarke (in the UK) has been vital to the emergence of a fully fledged administrative criminology. Administrative criminology's starting point is that despite the massive investment in welfare in the 1960s and a sustained period of prosperity, crime rates escalated to unprecedented levels in many Western societies. James Q. Wilson took this startling fact as proof that social democratic theorizing on the causes of and solutions to crime was seriously flawed. He argued that it was time to go back to basics on criminal justice policy. Criminologists should concentrate their efforts on producing policies that addressed what the public was afraid of, that is 'predatory' street crimes such as muggings, assaults, robberies, burglaries and so on, carried out by strangers. Crime reduction rather than social engineering should be the focus of criminal justice policies. The importance of engaging in focused research and evaluated pilot studies was to produce rigorous knowledge and avoid costly mistakes. Scepticism about the role of the criminal justice system in crime control also meant that policy-makers needed to think about how to integrate practical crime control into other aspects of public policy.

In the UK, Ronald V. Clarke, a senior researcher at the Home Office, reached similar conclusions to Wilson and began to formulate an approach to 'commonplace crime' that was not hindered by what he viewed as the limitations of mainstream criminological theorizing, particularly its failure to develop realistic and practical policy recommendations. From Clarke's perspective, criminal justice policy-makers cannot do much about the desire of some young men to become involved in delinquency and criminal activity. However, most offenders are involved in a rational choice structuring process that consists of evaluating the perceived risks in the commission of a particular offence, the rewards that are likely to be realized and the skills and resources required to execute a criminal act successfully. As a consequence, criminal justice policy-makers should concentrate their efforts on reducing the physical opportunities for offending and increasing the chances of offenders being caught and punished. The focus on how a criminal's decision-making in a given situation is influenced by her/his perception of risk, effort and reward led to the development of a suite of opportunity reduction techniques to: increase the effort associated with committing a crime; multiply the risks of crime; reduce the rewards of crime; and remove the excuses for crime. The techniques and strategies chosen must be appropriate to the specifics of the crime committed and their setting.

Evaluation

Such situational crime prevention policy initiatives lend themselves to evaluation for effectiveness and this enabled administrative criminologists to develop evidence-based, problem-solving approaches to crime reduction. Administrative criminology's other concern is to re-organize the state's crime control efforts to make them as efficient, effective and focused as possible. It has no particular sentimental attachment to the criminal justice system and is willing to advocate managerialization, actuarialization and privatization.

By the end of the 1990s administrative criminologists had become increasingly sophisticated in formulating and defending their perspective, going so far as to present 'opportunity' as a 'root cause' of crime. To date there has been no adequate response from either critical criminology or left realism.

Eugene McLaughlin

Associated Concepts: actuarialism, managerialism, rational choice theory, routine activity theory, situational crime prevention

Key Readings

Clarke, R.V. (ed.) (1997) *Situational Crime Prevention: Successful Case Studies*, 2nd edn. New York, Harrow and Heston.

Cornish, D. and Clarke, R.V. (eds) (1996) *The Reasoning Criminal: Rational Choice Perspectives on Offending*. New York, Springer-Verlag.

Felson, M. and Clarke, R.V. (1998) *Opportunity Makes the Thief: Practical Theory for Crime Prevention*. London, Home Office, Police Research Group Paper 98.

Newman, G., Clarke, R.V. and Shoham, S. (eds) (1997) *Rational Choice and Situational Crime Prevention*. Aldershot, Ashgate.

Sherman, L., Gottfredson, D., MacKenzie, D., Eck, J., Reuter, P. and Bushway, S. (1997) *Preventing Crime: What Works, What Doesn't, What's Promis-*
ing: A Report to The United States Congress, http://www.ncjrs.org/works/index.htm.
Wilson, J.Q. (1983) *Thinking about Crime*. New York, Basic Books.

AETIOLOGY

See Causation

ANARCHIST CRIMINOLOGY

Definition

Anarchism is one of the most difficult political ideologies to conceptualize and define, primarily because there is no one anarchist ideology and because of the degree of misrepresentation by its political opponents. It is a meeting place for a bewildering number of philosophies, belief systems and practices and originated as a reaction to the emergence of the nation state and capitalism in the nineteenth century. Anarchists are united, first and foremost, by the belief that the state is coercive, punitive, exploitative, corrupting and destructive. Alternative forms of mutual aid and voluntary organization that are non-authoritarian, non-coercive, non-hierarchical, functionally specific and decentralized are advocated.

Distinctive Features

A number of specifically anarchist principles have been developed from the work of Max Stirner (1806–56), Pierre Joseph Proudhon (1809–65), Mikhail Bakunin (1814–76) Peter Kropotkin (1842–1921) and Emma Goldman (1869–1940). In general, these principles do not conceive of a disorderly or chaotic society but rather a more expansive form of social order without the state. This social order will maximize individual freedoms and encourage voluntary association and self-regulation. A broad spectrum of anarchist thought also wishes to replace monopoly forms of capitalism and private property with collectivist forms of ownership. According to sympathetic criminologists such as Jeff Ferrell, there cannot be fully fledged anarchist criminology because it would be a contradiction in terms. However, Peter Kropotkin's writings on law and state authority still stand as a key reference point for any emergent anarchist criminology. Kropotkin argues that law is useless and harmful, sustaining mass criminality and generating social pathologies. Laws protecting private property and the interests of the state are responsible for generating between two-thirds and three-quarters of all crime. The body of criminal law that is geared towards the punishment and prevention of 'crime' does not prevent crime and degrades society because it fosters the worst human instincts and obedience to the status quo and bolsters state domination.

Kropotkin insists that the majority of crime will disappear the day private property ceases to exist and human need and cooperation rather than profits and competition become the organizing principle of social life. Alternative forms of social solidarity and inclusive notions of social justice, rather than state-run systems of criminal justice and the fictional 'rule of law', can contain anti-social behaviour. Here, there are obvious links to the core principles underpinning abolitionism, left idealism and peacemaking criminologies.

Anarchists deny that their vision relies on disorder, violence and lawlessness. However, the belief that anarchism originates in everyday struggle rather than abstract theorizing leads to the advocacy of direct or creative action and 'propaganda by deed'. The resultant protest and resistance tactics and set-piece confrontations which are vital to the renewal of theory and practice bring anarchist groups into confrontation with the forces of law and order and they thus risk potential criminalization. It is in this moment that the stereotypical representation of the nihilistic anarchist is conjured up in the news media.

Evaluation

Anarchist theory provides criminologists with:

- an uncompromising critique of law, power and the state;
- the promise of un-coercive social relationships;
- the possibility of alternative forms of dispute settlement and harm reduction;
- a form of political intervention that may be appropriate to an increasingly complex and fragmented world where conventional forms of politics are increasingly redundant;
- the basis to develop both libertarian and communitarian criminologies.

Jeff Ferrell (1995, p. 106) sums up the possibilities of anarchist criminology: 'At its best, anarchism and the process of justice that flows from it constitute a sort of dance that we make up as we go along, an emerging swirl of ambiguity, uncertainty, and pleasure. Once you dive into the dance, there are no guarantees – only the complex rhythms of human interaction and the steps that you and others invent in response. So, if you want certainty or authority, you might want to sit this one out. As for the rest of us: start the music.'

Eugene McLaughlin

Associated Concepts: abolitionism, left idealism, peacemaking criminology, the state

Key Readings
Ferrell, J. (1995) 'Anarchy against the discipline', *Journal of Criminal Justice and Popular Culture*, 3 (4), pp. 86–106.
Ferrell, J. (1999) 'Anarchist criminology and social justice', in B.A. Arrigo (ed.), *Social Justice/Criminal Justice*. Belmont, CA, Wadsworth.
Kropotkin, P. (1996) 'Law and authority', in J. Muncie, E. McLaughlin and M. Langan (eds), *Criminological Perspectives: A Reader*. London, Sage.
Tifft, L.L. (1979) 'The coming re-definitions of crime: an anarchist perspective', *Social Problems*, 26, pp. 392–402.

ANIMAL ABUSE

Definition

Animal abuse is any act that contributes to the pain, suffering or unnatural death of an animal or that otherwise threatens its welfare. Animal abuse may be physical, psychological or emotional, may involve active maltreatment or passive neglect or omission, and may be direct or indirect, intentional or unintentional.

Distinctive Features

Species-specific indicators indicate the impact on the psychological and physical welfare of animals. Specific health, physiological, ethological and production indicators (when the animals are incorporated in production processes, e.g. animal husbandry) can be determined, from which a violation of animals' welfare can be assessed. Reduced life expectancy, impaired growth, impaired reproduction, body damage, disease, immunosuppression, adrenal activity, behaviour anomalies and self-narcotization are indicators of poor welfare. Welfare thus depends not solely on an animal's subjective experiences. Although poor welfare and suffering often occur together, suffering is no prerequisite for poor welfare. When an act or omission entails negative effects on an animal's welfare – to be assessed using these species-specific indicators – it can be classified as animal abuse. But scientific uncertainty about many aspects of animals' mental state or emotional life requires the use of a precautionary principle: an act should be regarded as animal abuse if we are unsure if it has a detrimental effect on the welfare of an animal. Following the descriptions of the 'battered child syndrome' and the 'battered woman syndrome', attempts should also be made to identify the clinical signs and pathology of physical abuse of companion animals, as specified in the 'battered pet syndrome'.

Evaluation

The apparent importance of animal abuse has recently been highlighted through its complex relationship with child abuse and domestic violence (Lockwood and Ascione, 1998). One line of research has examined the supposed links between animal abuse and other expressions of family violence, for example, child abuse and woman abuse. It has been found that several forms of violence often co-exist with different categories of victim. The presence of animal abuse might indicate that other family members are also potential victims; acknowledging this connection can help in the prevention of human interpersonal violence. Other research has examined the correlation between animal abuse committed by children and the development of aggressive or violent behaviour at later stages in life. Here, it has been found that children abusing animals are more likely subsequently to exhibit aggressive and violent tendencies towards humans. Animal abuse in childhood is thus seen to signify the need for intervention by a variety of social and human service agencies.

The importance of detecting and preventing animal abuse has tended to become a justifiable and legitimate field of research, action and intervention, precisely because of its connection with expressions of human interpersonal violence. However, this is an anthropocentric or speciesist approach to animal abuse. Several philosophers have established the moral significance of animals in their own right. Because animals are sentient living beings, with interests and desires, and are 'subjects-of-a-life', animals are taken into the circle of moral consideration (Regan and Singer, 1989). Speciesism thus stands for a prejudice or biased attitude favouring the interests of the members of one's own species against those of members of other species. As with other systems of discrimination like racism and sexism, speciesism rests on the domination and subordination of others, here solely based on the fact that animals are not human (Adams and Donovan, 1995). A non-speciesist and more sensitive definition of animal abuse focuses on the interests of animals and the consequences of animal abuse for their welfare (Beirne, 1995; Cazaux, 1999). It rests not on an exhaustive enumeration of possibly abusive acts or omissions (e.g., burning, poisoning, assault, neglect, etc.) but on the effects of practices on animals' physical and psychological welfare.

Henceforth, this definition of animal abuse invalidates the distinction between animal cruelty and animal abuse. The effects of abuse on animals' welfare are independent of offenders' sadistic, malicious or benign propensities. Nor should the definition of animal abuse include the anthropocentric phraseology 'unnecessary suffering' – often inscribed in animal welfare laws – since it lends legitimacy to animal suffering deemed necessary for economic, political or scientific reasons. For example, from a non-speciesist viewpoint, bestiality is not an offence of decadence or of sexual indecency but, because of its similarity to the sexual assault of women and children, it should be named interspecies sexual assault (Beirne, 1997).

Animal abuse refers not only to individual cases of socially unacceptable practices, such as the abuse of companion animals, but also to several institutionalized systems founded on the exploitation and subordination of animals which are by many viewed as socially acceptable. These include the abuse of animals in agriculture, hunting, fishing, trapping, entertainment and sports and in experimental research.

What is classified as animal abuse is thus independent of human intention or ignorance, socially sanctioned or socially rejected norms, and labels of necessary or unnecessary suffering. It is also independent of whether the animal victim is categorized as a companion animal, a wild animal, as livestock or as an experimental animal, and covers both single and repeated or institutionalized incidents of animal abuse.

Geertrui Cazaux and Piers Beirne

Associated Concepts: family crime, hidden crime, violence

Key Readings

Adams, C.J. and Donovan, J. (eds) (1995) *Animals and Women*. London, Duke University Press.

Beirne, P. (1995) 'The use and abuse of animals in criminology: a brief history and current review', *Social Justice*, 22 (1), pp. 5–31.

Beirne, P. (1997) 'Rethinking bestiality: towards a concept of interspecies sexual assault', *Theoretical Criminology*, 1 (3), pp. 317–40.

Cazaux, G. (1999) 'Beauty and the Beast: animal abuse from a non-speciesist criminological perspective', *Crime, Law & Social Change*, 31 (2), pp. 105–25.

Lockwood, R. and Ascione, F.R. (eds) (1998) *Cruelty to Animals and Interpersonal Violence*. Indiana, Purdue University Press.

Regan, T. and Singer, P. (eds) (1989) *Animal Rights and Human Obligations*. London, Prentice–Hall.

ANOMIE

Definition

A state of ethical normlessness or deregulation, pertaining either to an individual or a society. This lack of normative regulation leaves individuals without adequate ethical guidance as to their conduct and undercuts social integration.

Distinctive Features

Anomie is one of the foundational concepts of modern criminological thought. Its prominence in American theorizing (where it forms the basis of 'strain' theory) is largely due to the interpretation given to anomie in the work of Robert Merton. His 1938 article 'Social Structure and Anomie' is one of the most influential articles in the history of sociology. Whilst Merton's theory is now seen as reductionist and somewhat mechanistic in the view it offers of human agency, fertile ground is still seen in Durkheim's original late nineteenth-century formulation of anomie. This is largely due to the scope of Durkheim's questioning. Along with fellow Europeans Marx, Nietzsche

and Weber, Durkheim was concerned with grappling with the new problems of modernity and sought to identify the key features underlying social change. With modernity human desires and passions seemed freer, the pace of change was dramatic: how then was 'social solidarity' or social cohesion possible? Durkheim did not pose the question so much in terms of 'what are the forces driving us apart?', but rather asked 'what is it that keeps us together?' How is society itself possible? What are the roles and 'functions' of humans and social institutions? And how are we to learn about it in order that we may adapt to change?

Durkheim located the driving force of modernity in the twin factors of the division of labour and the freeing of desire. Society is to be conceived as a 'moral milieu' which positions and constitutes the individual. Individuals experience social reality through their differential positioning in the social division of labour. Humans are motivated by the pursuit of pleasure and the satisfaction of desire and they attain happiness when their possibilities for satisfying desire are not at odds with the social realities of the division of labour. But what happens when the cultural regulation of desire breaks down and desire is released as a mobile, infinite capacity transcending the limitations on satisfaction inherent in any division of labour?

In his doctoral thesis, first published in 1893, Durkheim argued that the consequences of anomie, or the failure of moral regulation, were clear in

> the continually recurring conflicts and disorders of every kind, of which the economic world offers so sorry a spectacle. For, since nothing restrains the forces present from reacting together, or prescribes limits to them that they are obliged to respect, they tend to grow beyond all bounds, each clashing with the other, each warding off and weakening the other . . . Men's passions are stayed only by a moral presence they respect. If all authority of this kind is lacking, it is the law of the strongest that rules, and a state of warfare, either latent or acute, is necessarily endemic. (Durkheim, 1984, pp. xxxii–xxxiii)

Durkheim thus explicitly reversed Hobbes's picture of 'the war of all against all' inherent in the state of nature. Whereas for Hobbes this is the purely natural or pre-social state, which humans overcome by creating a powerful sovereign to lay down definitions of meaning (laws) and enforce obedience, Durkheim places this state of social war and crime as a product of society, a result of the breakdown of moral regulation. Modernity is characterized by increasing individualism, by autonomy of thought and action, but this autonomy is dependent upon greater interdependency in the division of labour and increased complexity within the collective consciousness: 'liberty itself is the product of regulation'. The task for 'advanced societies' was to achieve a balance between the functions of the division of labour, law and culture, 'the conditions that dominate social evolution'. With the old certainties disappearing, the individual finds him/herself without secure footing upon reality; anomie threatens. In times of economic crisis, either dramatic increases in prosperity or disasters, anomie may become the normal state of being: 'greed is aroused without knowing where to find its ultimate foothold. Nothing can calm it, since its goal is far beyond all it can attain. Reality seems valueless by comparison with the dreams of fevered imaginations; reality is therefore abandoned, but so too is possibility when it in turn becomes reality: A thirst for novelties, unfamiliar pleasures, nameless sensations, all of which lose their savour once known' (Durkheim, 1984, p. 254).

What was the solution to the state of anomie? While Durkheim personally argued that the solution to the normative deregulation causing anomie could not be the imposition of normative restructuring through violence and the manipulation of cultural symbols – the solution that both Fascism and state Stalinism were later to offer – he bequeathed few theoretical tools for integrating studies of culture, class and perceptions of social 'reality'. The understanding of anomie which was to be developed within criminology was constrained by its centrality to the middle range theorizing of Robert Merton (1938).

Writing shortly after the social democratic compromise of the 'new deal', Merton identified the key cultural message of modernist American culture as the 'success' goal, in particular 'money-success'. A 'strain to anomie' resulted from a disjuncture between cultural goals and legitimate means of achievement. Specifically, the new technologies of advertising put forward a cultural goal of economic affluence and social ascent, but individuals, differentially positioned in the social structure, understood that the institutionally available means may or may not enable personal success. Whilst the majority of Americans may 'conform', others may 'innovate', accepting the cultural goal but rejecting the institutionally available means. Particularly for those 'located in the lower reaches of the social structure' crime could, therefore, be a reaching for the American dream, albeit sought through illegitimate channels. Merton's theory was further developed with the 'differential opportunity' theorizing of Cloward and Ohlin (1960) and anomie has proved a fertile, if somewhat elusive concept to build upon, recently informing Agnew's (1992) 'positive' strain theory.

Evaluation

Merton's theory struck a deep chord with many. It seemed to offer a way of constraining crime by improving the legitimate life chances of those who otherwise may make the choice to innovate deviantly. However, the positivist tendencies of American sociology meant that any concept difficult to operationalize into survey questions or mathematically inscribable data remained elusive rather than accepted, and always open to the charge of weak sociology.

Anomie is thus a highly suggestive concept, but difficult to operationalize. What are we to make of this? Perhaps the intellectual history of anomie reflects the impossibility of achieving a 'transparent' sociology, capturing the true 'experience' of the subject. Durkheimian sociology had a normative element; it was for modern society to arrive at a state of scientific self-consciousness. This would aid the creation of moral individualism in that mankind would attain an objective knowledge of how things stood, of the functional interdependency of all upon all. But this dream of happiness as attunement to our shared knowledge of the state of reality has been undercut by the relentless division of labour, by 'reality' in 'late-modern' 'Western' societies being characterized by oscillation, plurality and perspectivism, rather than stability. The technological intensification of cultural reproduction – via the advent of generalized communication, the mass media, the Internet – gives us a sea of information, rendering 'our' experience communicable to a trans-local set of 'fellow-feelers' while appearing inconsistent and superficial to our 'others'. Few would see the function of modern 'art' as to offer representations of the 'absolute' or gateways into the eternal truths of the human condition; rather it is designed to 'shock' or draw the observer into the experience of ambiguity and ambivalence. Within criminology, understanding anomie offered the hope that criminological theorists could demonstrate particular policy recommendations, namely that crime could be averted by reconciling the means available to agents through the goals offered by culture. If agents could be assured that they could achieve the cultural goals through legitimate or 'normal' means (education, employment etc.), then the strain to deviance would lessen. But in the globalized capitalism of the late-modern condition, at least within Western societies, multiple goals and fractured and overlapping identities appear the norm. The very concept of deviance loses its grip. Moreover, the range of candidates available as cultural goals, not just consumerism but the enhancement of power or the creation of personal identity as a life choice, render the technological fix of adjusting 'means to ends' a mirage. The concept of anomie may take on the role of an existential prop, never quite fitting within any criminological theory, but always hinting at something of fundamental importance in the human condition.

Wayne Morrison

Associated Concepts: differential association, functionalism, relative deprivation, social control theory, strain theory, subculture

Key Readings

Agnew, R. (1992) 'Foundation for a general strain theory of crime and delinquency', *Criminology*, 30 (1), pp. 47–87.

Cloward, R. and Ohlin, L. (1960) *Delinquency and Opportunity*. New York, The Free Press.

Downes, D. and Rock, P. (1998) 'Anomie', in *Understanding Deviance: A Guide to the Sociology of Crime and Rule Breaking*, 3rd edn. Oxford, Oxford University Press.

Durkheim, E. (1970) *Suicide* (trans. S.A. Solovay and J.H. Mueller, ed. G.E.G. Catlin), New York, The Free Press.

Durkheim, E. (1984) *The Division of Labour in Society* (trans. W.D. Halls). Basingstoke, Macmillan.

Merton, R.K. (1938) 'Social structure and anomie', *American Sociological Review*, 3, pp. 672–82.

APPRECIATIVE CRIMINOLOGY

Definition

An approach that seeks to understand and appreciate the social world from the point of view of the individual, or category of individual, with particular reference to crime and deviance.

Distinctive Features

The designation 'appreciative criminology' owes much to use of the term 'appreciative studies' by Matza (1969) to refer to specific studies of deviant subcultures such as those of the hobo, the juvenile gang, the drug-taker. Such studies are characterized by observing, sometimes by participation, the social world of deviants with a view to producing an appreciative account of the deviant's own story in his or her own terms. Theoretically, appreciative criminology is influenced by the interactionist perspective which developed in social psychology and sociology in the 1930s and which received further impetus in the 1960s and 1970s, for example in connection with new deviancy theory. Interactionism offers an alternative to positivist ways of thinking about crime and criminality. Amongst other things, positivism started from assumptions such as: there are categories of individuals who are criminal and who have characteristics which clearly distinguish them from non-criminals; the explanations for criminality lie in individual pathologies; such pathologies are the causes and determinants of criminality. Instead, interactionism offers a framework which emphasizes human choice and free will rather than determinism; a view of crime and deviance as something which is generated in interactions rather than as a characteristic of individual backgrounds; and an assumption that social action and the social world are flexible, changing and dynamic rather than fixed, objective and external. Above all, appreciative studies took from interactionism the notion that there can be variability of meanings in social contexts and in society in general, rather than consensus. The aim of appreciative studies was, and is, to describe, understand and appreciate the social meanings and interpretations which categories of individuals attribute to events, contexts and others' actions. Such studies are epitomized in the title of Howard Parker's (1974) book *View from the Boys*, a study of male juvenile gangs in Liverpool based on the perspectives of the gang members themselves.

Methodologically, appreciative studies have been influenced by the ethnographic tradition in social research. Ethnography, which liberally means description ('graphy') of cultures ('ethno'), has its roots in social anthropology and the study of pre-industrial societies.

Subsequently it has been adapted to the examination of subcultures in complex society. Ethnography has a number of methodological commitments which make it especially appropriate to appreciative studies of deviant subcultures using an interactionist framework. First, there is a commitment to studying the social world from the point of view of the individuals being studied. Secondly, it is assumed that there can be a multiplicity of perspectives rather than just one, and also that each is equally valid for the people who hold them. Thirdly, social perspectives (and the social meanings, definitions, labels and stereotypes which comprise them) cannot be separated from social interactions. Therefore, particular attention should be paid to the ways in which people interact in specific social contexts. Fourthly, there is a belief that such observation should be naturalistic, that is individuals should be studied behaving as they would normally and naturally do so. It is for this reason that ethnographers often rely on participant observation although that is not the only form of data collection used.

The Chicago School of Sociology of the 1920s and 1930s was a source of classic appreciative studies. Researchers adapted some of the techniques of social anthropologists to study the subcultures of crime within their city (in addition to statistical analysis of crime rates to map zones of the city). They produced books with titles such as *The Jack Roller* (Shaw, 1930), *The Hobo* (Anderson, 1923), and *The Gang* (Thrasher, 1927). There was particular emphasis on the transitional zone of the city with indicators of social disorganization such as high turnover of population, poor housing and high incidence of crime.

Appreciative studies captured the culture of crime in this zone and also the mechanisms by which this culture was transmitted. In doing so, the Chicago sociologists emphasized the distinctiveness of the deviant subcultures and their separation from mainstream society. In the 1960s and 1970s there was a resurgence of ethnographic studies, linked to an interactionist framework, but with a particular slant towards the process of labelling. For example, Howard Becker's (1963) study of marijuana smokers was influential in generating a greater concern with the ways deviant and non-deviant worlds meet and interact rather than with their separation. This was part of the emergence of labelling theory as a radical response to the predominance of positivist conventional criminology. Becker was not interested in asking questions about the causes of smoking marijuana; instead he focused on the question of how and why marijuana users come to be defined and labelled as deviant. This involved looking at interactions between the would-be deviant and the agencies of social control.

Evaluation

The critiques that can be levelled at appreciative criminology are those which, in terms of theory, can be levelled at interactionism and which, in terms of methodology, can be directed at ethnography. For example, explanations of crime and deviance that are grounded in interactions in small-scale contexts run the risk of neglecting wider social structural dimensions of power, inequality and oppression (although for some a synthesis based on theorizing at different levels is feasible). Methodologically, ethnographic studies endure the criticisms that they lack generalizability to wider contexts and – being reliant on the deviants themselves for data – are not scientific or objective. There is also the possibility that taking an appreciative stance is synonymous with glorifying the criminal. This does not find sympathy with those who emphasize the need to face up to the reality of crime and the consequences of it for victims.

Such criticisms apart, appreciative studies have provided a rich vein within criminology and have described and explained criminal and deviant subcultures which would not otherwise have been made visible by other theoretical and methodological approaches.

Victor Jupp

Associated Concepts: Chicago School of Sociology, cultural criminology, ethnography, interactionism, labelling, new deviancy theory, participant observation, subculture

Key Readings
Anderson, N. (1923) *The Hobo: The Sociology of the Homeless Man*. Chicago, University of Chicago Press.

Becker, H. (1963) *Outsiders: Studies in the Sociology of Deviance*. New York, The Free Press.

Matza, D. (1969) *Becoming Deviant*. Englewood Cliffs, NJ, Prentice–Hall.

Parker, H. (1974) *View from the Boys*. Newton Abbot, David and Charles.

Shaw, C.R. (1930) *The Jack Roller*. Chicago, University of Chicago Press.

Thrasher, F.M. (1927) *The Gang*. Chicago, University of Chicago Press.

AUTHORITARIAN POPULISM

Definition

Conceptualized as an essential aspect of how social democratic states and their institutions respond to crises within advanced capitalist political economies, authoritarian populism explains how increasingly repressive punitive laws and sanctions gain popular legitimacy. This mobilization of state power aims to manage consent, organize regulation and secure hegemony through an increasingly authoritarian political agenda derived from political disaffection and discontent. It reaffirms reactive and reactionary discourses established around the 'collapse' of democracy, the 'breakdown' in law and order, the 'militancy' of the unions, the 'decline' in moral values and so on. These discourses are exploited through political and media 'campaigns', thus generating 'moral panics' within popular discourse and social reaction.

Distinctive Features

Basing his analysis on the proposition that 'state-monopolized physical violence permanently underlies the techniques of power and mechanisms of consent' within Western capitalist democracies, Poulantzas (1978, p.81) claimed that during the 1970s a new *form* of state had emerged: 'authoritarian statism . . . intensified state control over every sphere of socio-economic life *combined with* radical decline of the institutions of political democracy and with draconian and multiform curtailment of so-called "formal" liberties' (1978, pp. 203–4). Repressive measures depended on the actual exercise of state-sanctioned violence and, significantly, on its internationalization through ideological acceptance or, for those who opposed the rise of authoritarianism, through *mechanisms of fear*.

For Stuart Hall, Poulantzas had made a defining contribution to the critical analysis of the 'exceptional shifts' towards authoritarianism within Western social democracies. Yet he felt that Poulantzas had misread the strategy of anti-statism prevalent within the radical right – a strategy representing itself as anti-

statist to win popular support while disguising the reality of honing state centralism. More importantly, Poulantzas had neglected the purposeful and orchestrated construction and manipulation of popular consent. Herein lay the essence of Hall's claim for authoritarian populism: 'harness[ing] . . . support [of] some popular discontents, neutraliz[ing] opposing forces, disaggregat[ing] the opposition and incorporat[ing] *some* strategic elements of popular opinion into its own hegemonic project' (Hall, 1985, p. 118).

Hall's response to, and development of, Poulantzas's thesis emerged from his work with colleagues at the Centre for Contemporary Cultural Studies, Birmingham, UK during the 1970s. In their exhaustive analysis of the 'crisis' in the UK political economy, Hall et al. (1978, p. 303) identified 'deep structural shifts' which had resulted in 'the extension of the law and the courts at the level of political management of conflict and the class struggle'. As the state had become more directly interventionist within the economy, establishing the foundation for capitalist reconstruction through the libertarianism of the 'free-market', it became both necessary and 'legitimate' for 'public opinion to be actively recruited in an open and explicit fashion in favour of the "strong state" . . . [characterized as] the ebb and flow of authoritarian populism in defence of social discipline' (1978, pp. 304–5).

For Hall et al. (pp. 317–20) the 'crisis' that was 'policed' through the gradual development of *legitimate coercion* comprised four distinct elements: a crisis of and for British capitalism; a crisis of the 'relations of social forces' derived in the economic crisis; a crisis of the state in mobilizing popular consent for potentially unpopular socio-economic strategies; a crisis in political legitimacy, in social authority, in hegemony; the imposition of 'social authority' and societal discipline. The authors identified the collapse of postwar social-democratic consensus and the consolidation of New Right ideology as a fundamental shift in the balance of social forces – from consent to coercion – inherent within social democracies; a shift they characterized as the emergence of an exceptional form of the capitalist state.

Further expanding the thesis, Hall (1979, p. 19) proposed that the 'language of law and order is sustained by moralisms . . . where the great syntax of "good" versus "evil", of civilized and uncivilized standards, of the choice between anarchy and order constantly divides the world up and classifies it into its appointed stations'. By appealing to 'inherent' social values and evoking an overarching moral imperative, law and order rhetoric appealed to a collective common sense; 'welding people to that "need for authority" . . . so significant for the Right in the construction of consent to its authoritarian programme'. Populism, however, was not simply a 'rhetorical device', it operated on 'genuine contradictions' and reflected a 'rational and material core' (1979, p. 20).

Hall (1980, p. 3) considered the 'drive' towards a 'more disciplinary, authoritarian kind of society' to be 'no short-term affair'. It embodied a 'regression' to a stone-age morality' promoted by politicians, together with, in popular discourse, 'a blind spasm of control: the feeling that the *only* remedy for a society which is declared to be "ungovernable" is the imposition of order, through a disciplinary use of law by the state'. Thus, the 'shift "from above" [was] pioneered by, harnessed to and, to some extent, legitimated by a popular groundswell below'; a populism exemplified by 'a sequence of "moral panic"' (Hall, 1985, p. 116).

Evaluation

The most strident critique of authoritarian populism came from Jessop et al. (1988). Concentrating on its application to the rise and consolidation of Thatcherism in the UK they argued it over-emphasized the significance of ideology and downplayed structural relations of political economy. It was too concerned with the 'relative autonomy' of language and discourse, neglected the political economy of the New Right (preferring instead to focus on its 'hegemonic project') and 'generate[d] an excessive concern with the mass media and ideological production at the expense of political and economic organization . . .' (1988, p. 73). They rejected the idea that Thatcherism had secured hegemony and achieved a new expression of collective 'common-sense'; the New Right had neither broad consensus nor political legitimacy for its objectives. Further, Hall was criticized for idealizing the gains of postwar social democracy and for failing to address the political economic determinants of global economic restructuring.

The ensuing debate was severe. Hall denied that authoritarian populism had been conceived as a *comprehensive* analysis of Thatcherism. It was 'preposterous' to claim that he had suggested that Thatcherism had secured hegemony. Rather, it constituted a politics,

shared by Western capitalist states, hegemonic in 'conception and project', whose 'dominance' had become 'self-evident' by the mid-1980s (Hall, 1985, p. 119). Returning to Gramsci, he concluded it was 'impossible to conceptualize or achieve' hegemony without accepting the economy as the 'decisive nucleus' around which civil society consolidated (1985, p. 120).

As academic hostilities cooled it became clear that the significance of authoritarian populism conceptually lay in its contribution to theorizing the political and ideological dimensions of the authoritarian shift and its populist appeal for stronger laws, imposed order and tightening discipline. What remained unexplored was the foundation of popular authoritarianism within the wider society, given – as Hall and others recognized – that people are not mere 'dupes'. Historically, an authoritarian streak can be detected within the collective psyche which appears to transcend cultural and regional differences. Further, authoritarian responses to orchestrated moral panics, not derived in economic crises or which occur during periods of relative economic expansionism, require consideration.

Yet Hall's analysis – combining Gramsci, Laclau and Poulantzas – demonstrated that advanced capitalism is served, serviced, but rarely confronted, by state institutions whose decision-makers share its ends, if not always its means, in a coincidence of interests expressed in a common and dominant ideology. In functioning, the state – exemplified by the rule of law, its derivation and administration – tutors and guides the broad membership of society. State institutions are sites for the regeneration and reconstruction of ideas as well as policies. This process, sensitive to and informing of popular discourses, serves to defend the structural contradictions and inequalities of advanced capitalism whether in recession (crisis) or in growth (reconstruction). In this climate, authoritarian populism serves as a poignant reminder that if consensus cannot be forged, it will be forced.

Phil Scraton and Kathryn Chadwick

Associated Concepts: criminalization, critical criminology, hegemony, moral panic, the state

Key Readings
Hall, S. (1979) 'The Great Moving Right Show', *Marxism Today*, January, pp. 14–20.
Hall, S. (1980) *Drifting into a Law and Order Society*. London, The Cobden Trust.

Hall, S. (1985) 'Authoritarian populism: a reply to Jessop et al.', *New Left Review*, 151, pp. 115–24.

Hall, S., Critcher, C., Jefferson, T., Clarke, J. and Roberts, B. (1978) *Policing the Crisis: Mugging, the State and Law and Order*. London, Macmillan.

Jessop, B., Bennett, K., Bromley, S. and Ling, T. (1988) *Thatcherism*. Cambridge, Polity Press.

Poulantzas, N. (1978) *State, Power, Socialism*. London, Verso.

B

BEHAVIOUR MODIFICATION

Definition

Early theories of learning gave rise to a range of strategies, termed behaviour modification, aimed at changing behaviour. These practical techniques were widely used with a range of groups, including offenders. As theories of learning became more sophisticated and their research base grew, so their application, in the associated methods of behaviour change, developed accordingly.

Distinctive Features

The early learning theorists maintained that behaviour is functionally related both to its setting (i.e., the antecedent conditions), and to its consequences (via reinforcement and punishment). It follows from this position that a given behaviour can be changed by modifying both the setting events and the outcomes for the behaviour.

The strategy of bringing about behavioural change through modification of the environment is called *stimulus control* and is a standard technique in behaviour modification (Martin and Pear, 1992). This strategy is evident in situational crime prevention where the aim is to reduce offending by, say, reducing opportunity or increasing the chances of detection. Similarly, behaviour change can be attempted by modifying the consequences that follow a given behaviour. There is a range of established methods that focus on control of reinforcement and punishment contingencies to bring about behavioural change. Token economy programmes are one such method, in which optimal behaviours are strengthened by the reward of tokens or points which can later be exchanged for tangible rewards. Token economies were used in the American prison system for a period of time but were discontinued for ethical reasons.

As well as bringing about behavioural change through modification of antecedents and consequences, the focus can be on the behaviour itself. The rationale underpinning this particular strategy is that changing behaviour will elicit different outcomes from the environment. In turn, these new outcomes will then reinforce and strengthen the new behaviour, thereby bringing about behavioural change. Strategies that focus explicitly on overt behaviour are often termed *behaviour therapy*, although the basic theory is the same as that informing behaviour modification. In the 1970s the notion of skills training in health services was developed and quickly became widespread in the form of assertion, life and social skills training. Skills training with offenders became popular and was used with a range of types of offender, including sex offenders and violent offenders (Hollin, 1990a).

As behavioural theory developed to produce social learning theory, behaviour modification and behaviour therapy evolved into cognitive-behavioural therapy. A number of particular techniques have become associated with cognitive-behavioural practice: these techniques include self-instructional training, thought stopping, emotional control training, and problem-solving training (Sheldon, 1995). The method of change underpinning this approach is that by bringing about change of internal (psychological and/or physiological) states and process, this covert change will, in turn, mediate change at an overt behavioural level. Changes in overt behaviour will then elicit new patterns of reinforcement from the environment and so maintain behaviour change. Cognitive-behavioural methods have been widely used with offender groups, particularly with young offenders (Hollin, 1990b).

In practice, behaviour change techniques are seldom used in isolation: it is more common to see amalgams of techniques in the form of *multimodal programmes*. Such multimodal programmes might include elements such as problem-solving skills training, social skills training and emotional control training. Given the complexity of many of the problems for which cognitive-behavioural therapy has been used, including offending, it is appropriate that change is sought by attending to a range of aspects of an individual's functioning. If the cognitive-behavioural model has several inter-related constituents, then attempts at change will be well served by attending to a range of those aspects rather than one in isolation. There are several multimodal programmes designed for offender groups, including Reasoning and Rehabilitation (Ross et al., 1988) and Aggression Replacement Training (Goldstein et al., 1998).

One of the main concerns lies in the abuse of behavioural methods. First, when these powerful methods are used inappropriately by untrained personnel; second, when they are used with people, such as prisoners, who are not in a position to give free consent.

Clive Hollin

Associated Concepts: conditioning, differential reinforcement, situational crime prevention, social learning theory,

Key Readings

Goldstein, A.P., Glick, B. and Gibbs, J.C. (1998) *Aggression Replacement Training: A Comprehensive Intervention for Aggressive Youth*, 2nd edn. Champaign, IL, Research Press.

Hollin, C.R. (1990a) 'Social skills training with delinquents: a look at the evidence and some recommendations for practice', *British Journal of Social Work*, 20, pp. 483–93.

Hollin, C.R. (1990b) *Cognitive-Behavioural Interventions with Young Offenders*. Elmsford, NY, Pergamon Press.

Martin, G. and Pear, J. (1992) *Behaviour Modification: What It Is and How To Do It*, 4th edn. Englewood Cliffs, NJ, Prentice–Hall.

Ross, R.R., Fabiano, E.A. and Ewles, C.D. (1988) 'Reasoning and rehabilitation', *International Journal of Offender Therapy and Comparative Criminology*, 32, pp. 29–35.

Sheldon, B. (1995) *Cognitive-Behavioural Therapy: Research, Practice and Philosophy*. London, Routledge.

BEHAVIOURISM

See Conditioning

BIFURCATION

Definition

Bifurcation is a concept – built on the 'just deserts' premise – which seeks to reserve incarceration solely for those offenders who pose a risk to the community, whilst finding community-based penalties for less serious offenders.

Distinctive Features

Bifurcation is a reaction to at least two different forces within transnational criminal systems. First it is a reaction to the expansion of the penal estates of several Western democracies, which has seen the prison populations of, for example, the USA quadruple since the early 1980s, with a corresponding growth in expenditure on maintaining the penal estate. This expansion is in turn partly a reaction to the neo-conservativism of Republicans in the USA and the Conservatives in England and Wales, the latter coming to power in 1979 and the former with the election of Ronald Reagan in 1980.

With increasing numbers of people being incarcerated, politicians came under increasing pressure to reduce the amount of money being spent on maintaining the infrastructure of the penal estate. One way of doing this was to reserve imprisonment only for those people who posed a risk to the public, and to find alternative punishments for largely non-violent offenders. By adopting this policy a government could appear to be 'tough and soft simultaneously' (Pitts, 1988, p. 29) This has been described as 'penal pragmatism' (Cavadino and Dignan, 1992), and further interpreted as a reaction to the 'penal crisis'.

In England and Wales bifurcation is most commonly associated with the Criminal Justice Act of 1991. In the words of the White Paper which preceded the Act – *Crime, Justice and Protecting the Public* – for most offenders, imprisonment has to be justified in terms of public protection, denunciation and retribution. Otherwise it can be an expensive way of making bad people worse. The prospects of reforming offenders are usually much better if they stay in the community, provided the public is properly protected (Home Office, 1990).

The passage of the 1991 Act did reduce the prison population significantly; it fell from 45,835 in October 1992 to 41,561 in January 1993. This downward trend continued until expansionist policies re-appeared in the wake of the murder of 2-year-old James Bulger by two 10-year-olds in 1993, and the 'prison works' speech of the then Home Secretary, Michael Howard, in the same year (Wilson and Ashton, 1998).

The second force at the heart of bifurcation is the theoretical concept of just deserts. Put simply this is a return to elements of classical criminology which suggests that 'the punishment should fit the crime'. As such, prisons should not be filled with minor property offenders – who in fact fill most prisons in Western democracies – but with offenders who pose a risk to the public, and who would be dangerous if not incarcerated. Just deserts is therefore also a recognition that prisons do not rehabilitate offenders, but often stigmatize them, making it more difficult for them to re-integrate into society.

Evaluation

Bifurcation showed limited success in England and Wales in that the passage of the 1991 Criminal Justice Act did reduce the prison population significantly. However, it is of relevance that it was a concept that was unable to withstand popular, 'common sense' clamour to increase prison numbers, largely as a reaction to a tragic but atypical murder, and when political expediency determined a different course of action. In short, when it was in the government of Britain's interests to appear 'tough' on criminals as well as crime, bifurcation became politically irrelevant.

David Wilson

Associated Concepts: classicism, just deserts, neo-conservative criminology

Key Readings

Bottomley, A.K. (1980) 'The "Justice Model" in America and Britain: development and analysis,' in A. Bottoms and R. Preston (eds), *The Coming Penal Crisis: A Criminological and Theological Exploration*. Edinburgh, Scottish Academic Press, pp. 25–52.

Cavadino, M. and Dignan, J. (1992) *The Penal System: An Introduction*. London, Sage.

Home Office (1990) *Crime, Justice and Protecting the Public*. London, HMSO, cm 965.

Pitts, J. (1988) *The Politics of Juvenile Crime*. London, Sage.

Wilson, D. and Ashton, J. (1998) *What Everyone in Britain Should Know About Crime and Punishment*. London, Blackstone's.

BIOLOGICAL CRIMINOLOGY

Definition

The basic premise of biological criminology is that certain people are born to be criminal through the inheritance of a genetic or physiological predisposition to crime. Environmental conditions are not ignored but viewed as potential triggers of the biological force. As behaviour is viewed as reflecting a prewritten, often inherited, code, criminality lies beyond individual control. Accordingly biological criminology is overwhelmingly positivist in nature.

Distinctive Features

Early positivists such as Lombroso, Ferri and Garafalo identified the criminal in terms of physical stigmata. Physical anomalies with hereditary origins (such as large cheekbones, flat nose and thick eyebrows) were thought to mark out a criminal propensity. The notion of the criminal as defective reworks Darwin's theory of evolution. As humans develop they learn how to adapt to their environment. Those who do not are viewed as an atavistic throwback to an earlier stage of evolution as pre-social and more criminally inclined. In his later work Lombroso placed less emphasis on the atavistic nature of all criminality. By 1897 he claimed that the 'born criminal' applied to only a third of all criminals. To this he added the categories of the epileptic, the insane and the 'occasional criminal'. The latter exhibited no inbred anomalies, but turned to crime as a result of a variety of environmental conditions. His later work also attempted to measure the effect of climate, rainfall, price of grain, banking practices, poor education and the structure of government, Church and religion on occasional criminality. However, he never totally abandoned the notion that criminals were abnormal. He never allowed for the possibility that criminality could be 'normal'.

Several attempts have subsequently been made to test biological and genetic theories. A study of 3,000 prisoners in London in the 1910s discovered high correlation between the criminality of spouses, between parents and their children and between brothers. Poverty, education and broken homes were poor correlates. It was argued that criminality was passed down through inherited genes. Accordingly, in order to reduce crime, it was increasingly recommended that people with such inherited characteristics should not be allowed to reproduce. This logic was fertile ground for the growth of *eugenics*, a doctrine concerned with 'improving' the genetic selection of the human race. Evidence from the Cambridge Study in Delinquent Development established in the 1960s also continues to suggest that crime does indeed run in families. From a base of 397 families, half of all convictions were concentrated in just 23. Convictions of one family member were strongly related to convictions of each other family member. Three-quarters of convicted mothers and convicted fathers had a convicted child.

Further, more sophisticated research directed at isolating 'a genetic factor' has been carried out with twins and adoptees. These have attempted to test two key propositions:

1 That identical (monozygotic or MZ) twins have more similar behaviour patterns than fraternal (dizygotic or DZ) twins.
2 That children's behaviour is more similar to that of their biological parents than to that of their adoptive parents.

In a review of research carried out between 1929 and 1961, Mednick and Volavka (1980) noted that, overall, 60 per cent of MZ twins shared criminal behaviour patterns compared to 30 per cent of DZ twins. More recent work has found a lower, but still significant, level of association. Christiansen's (1977) study of 3,586 twin pairs in Denmark found a 52 per cent concordance for MZ groups and a 22 per cent concordance for the DZ groups. The evidence for the genetic transmission of some behaviour patterns thus appears quite strong. However, telling criticisms have also been made of this line of research. For example, a tendency to treat identical twins more alike than fraternal twins may account for the greater concordance. Thus the connection between criminality and genetics may be made through environmental conditions, derived from the behaviour of parents or

from twins' influence on each other's behaviour.

As a result, Mednick, Gabrielli and Hutchings (1987) proposed that the study of adoptions would be a better test of a relative genetic effect, particularly if it could be shown that the criminality of biological parent and child was similar even when the child had grown up in a completely different environment. Using data from over 14,000 cases of adoption in Denmark from 1924 to 1947, Mednick et al. concluded that some factor *is* transmitted by convicted parents to increase the likelihood that their children – even after adoption – will be convicted for criminal offences. As a result, this type of research continues to attract research funding and publicity. In 1994 the Centre for Social, Genetic and Development Psychiatry was established at the Maudsley Hospital in South London to examine what role genetic structures play in determining patterns of behaviour (including crime). In 1995 a major international conference was held behind closed doors to discuss the possibility of isolating a criminal gene – the basis of which rested on the study of twins and adoptees (Ciba Foundation, 1996). In one of the best selling social science books of the decade, *The Bell Curve* (New York, Basic Books, 1994), Herrnstein and Murray claimed that American blacks and Latinos are disproportionately poor not because of discrimination, but because they are less intelligent. Further, they suggested that IQ is mainly determined by inherited genes and that people with low IQ are more likely to commit crime because they lack foresight and are unable to distinguish right from wrong. Such theory indeed remains politically and popularly attractive because it seems to provide *scientific* evidence, which clearly differentiates 'us' from 'them'. If certain people are inherently 'bad' then society is absolved of all responsibility. Such reasoning is, of course, most characteristic of totalitarian regimes whether in Nazi Germany or the former USSR or in programmes of forced therapy practised in the USA.

Further research has examined the effect of a wide range of biochemical factors These have included: hormone imbalances; testosterone, vitamin, adrenalin and blood sugar levels; allergies; slow brain-wave activity; lead pollution; epilepsy; and the operation of autonomic nervous system. None of the research has, as yet, been able to establish any direct causal relationships. While some interesting associations have been discovered – for example between male testosterone levels and verbal aggression, between vitamin B deficiency and hyperactivity, and between stimulation of the central portion of the brain (the limbic) and impulsive violence – it remains disputed that such biological conditions will automatically generate anti-social activities, which in turn will be translated into criminality.

Evaluation

Most critical commentaries on this work – notwithstanding the question of its ethical position – have argued that each fails to recognize the potential effect of a wide range of environmental factors. The high correlation in the criminality of family members could be explained by reference to poor schooling, inadequate diet, unemployment, common residence or cultural transmission of criminal values. In other words, criminality may not necessarily be an inherited trait, but be learned or generated by a plethora of environmental factors. The usual comparative controls of criminal and non-criminal are doubly misleading. Offenders in custody are not representative of criminals in general, but constitute a highly selected sub-set of those apprehended, charged and convicted. Control groups of the non-criminal are almost certain to include some individuals who have committed crimes but whose actions have remained undetected. Indeed most current research in this tradition would not claim that biological make-up *alone* can be used as a sufficient explanation of crime. The question of exactly *what* is inherited remains unanswered. Rather, some biological factors may generate criminality, but only when they interact with certain other psychological or social factors. Whilst correlational analysis may suggest that criminality is transmitted in certain families, it is now acknowledged that it does not allow us to distinguish the relative importance of genetic and environmental factors. Characteristics that are linked to offending (e.g. intelligence, impulsivity, aggressiveness) could be genetically transmitted, but not criminality *per se*.

It is now more common to find biology considered as but one element within *multiple factor* explanations. For example, Wilson and Herrnstein (1985) argue that individuals have the free will to choose criminal actions when they believe that the rewards will outweigh any negative consequences. Such a decision (freely made) is, however, influenced by inherited constitutional factors. Low IQ, abnormal body type and an impulsive personality, it is argued, will predispose a person to make criminal decisions, but criminality is not a matter of nature versus nurture, but of nature *and* nurture. This approach is a defining characteristic of *socio-biology*, developed in the 1970s and heralded by its advocates as a way forward in unifying the social and natural sciences. Generally, it is argued that some people carry with them the potential to be violent or anti-social and that environmental conditions can sometimes trigger anti-social responses. Socio-biologists view biology, environment and learning as mutually interdependent factors. Sociopathy may not be inherited, but a biochemical preparedness for such behaviours is present in the brain, which, if given a certain type of environment, will produce anti-social behaviour (Jeffery, 1978).

Nevertheless, the search for biological, physiological or genetic correlates of criminality is continually hampered because it is practically impossible to control for environmental and social influences and thus to be able to measure precisely the exact influence of a genetic effect.

John Muncie

Associated Concepts: determinism, dispositional theories, genetics, individual positivism, somatotyping

Key Readings

Christiansen, K.O. (1977) 'A review of studies of criminality among twins', in S. Mednick and K.O. Christiansen (eds), *Biosocial Bases of Criminal Behaviour*. New York, Gardner.

Ciba Foundation Symposium 194 (1996) *Genetics of Criminal and Antisocial Behaviour*. Chichester, Wiley.

Jeffery, C.R. (1978) 'Criminology as an interdisciplinary behavioural science', *Criminology*, 16 (2), pp. 149–69.

Mednick, S. and Volavka, J. (1980) 'Biology and crime', in N. Morris and M. Tonry (eds), *Crime and Justice*, vol. 2. Chicago, University of Chicago Press.

Mednick, S.A., Gabrielli, W. and Hutchings, B. (1987) 'Genetic factors in the etiology of criminal behaviour', in S. Mednick, T. Moffit and S. Stack (eds), *The Causes of Crime: New Biological Approaches*. Cambridge, Cambridge University Press.

Wilson, J.Q. and Herrnstein, R.J. (1985) *Crime and Human Nature*. New York, Simon and Schuster.

'BROKEN WINDOWS'

Definition

'Broken Windows' is arguably one of the most influential and widely cited articles in North American criminology. It was published originally by James Q. Wilson and George Kelling in 1982 and updated by Kelling and Coles (1996). Using a mixture of research findings on policing and self-proclaimed 'common sense', Wilson and Kelling produced a working theory about the role of the police in promoting neighbourhood safety through reducing the fear of crime.

Distinctive Features

The image of 'broken windows' is used to explain how neighbourhoods descend into incivility, disorder and criminality if attention is not paid to their maintenance. An un-repaired broken window signals to law-abiding and criminals alike that no one cares. Gradually other windows in the building will be smashed and this will reinforce the sense that the local community and the authorities have relinquished ownership and that disorder is tolerated. For them, petty disorderly acts, which are not necessarily breaches of the criminal law, trigger a chain reaction that undermines community safety and paves the way for serious criminality. If a neighbourhood or a street is perceived to be increasingly disorderly and unsafe people modify their behaviour accordingly. People, fearful of being harassed, will avoid or withdraw from these areas or move through them as quickly as possible and respectable residents, aware that things will deteriorate, will move out or fortify their homes. Because only the weak and vulnerable are left behind this leaves the neighbourhood open to colonization by drug dealers, pimps and prostitutes and other 'street criminals'. It is they who then lay claim to ownership of the streets and who set the appropriate norms of behaviour. The human equivalents of the 'broken windows' are down and outs, rowdy teenagers and importuning beggars: 'The unchecked pan-handler is, in effect, the first broken window.' Thus, policy-makers should pay attention to the policing of these disorderly and disreputable individuals because they create the conditions within which more serious forms of criminality can flourish.

According to Wilson and Kelling, shifts in policing styles also leave certain neighbourhoods and streets exposed to such a chain reaction. The authors step back to ask why the public is so supportive of foot patrols even though this particular policing style has been discredited as a method of effective crime control. For them it is because foot patrolling heightens the sense of public safety and the impression of social order. Experienced foot patrol officers with a sense of duty and an aura of authority, intuitively recognize that their primary role is 'order maintenance' and 'community safety' rather than crime fighting or law enforcement. This form of police work enables officers to become intimately acquainted with the law-abiding and respectable as well as criminals and the disreputable. They also notice indicators of routine normality and the out of the ordinary. Their task is to order social relations and activities on the streets and use their discretionary powers to regulate disorderly tendencies through reinforcement of communal norms and informal social controls. As a consequence, the police enjoy the confidence and support of the community because they are effective in responding to and dealing with the 'quality of life' matters that exasperate people on a daily basis. In a neighbourhood where policing is defined as a collaborative effort between patrol officers and the community, there is considerably less likelihood of disorder and incivilities going unchecked and fewer opportunities to break windows with impunity.

However, from the 1970s onwards the nature of police–community relations changed as a result of: the police claiming that the fight against high profile, serious crime was their priority; deploying officers in patrol cars; concentrating resources in high-crime areas; the bureaucratization and professionalization of police work; the emergence of a strident civil rights culture; and the decriminalization of victimless crimes. As a result police officers became more distant from local communities and less able and willing to intervene in petty 'non-police' matters. In neighbourhoods at risk of tipping over into disorder, 'de-policing' had a disastrous effect because it meant that respectable residents had no support from the authorities.

Wilson and Kelling (1982, p. 36) thus argue for a *return* to old-fashioned, community-oriented 'order maintenance' police work and to employ such methods in neighbourhoods where they will make a qualitative difference. The primary police task should be to protect areas and support communities where 'the public order is deteriorating but not unreclaimable, where the streets are used frequently but by apprehensive people, where a window is likely to be broken at any time, and must quickly be fixed if all are not to be shattered'. It is a waste of police resources to concentrate on crime-ravaged neighbourhoods that are beyond redemption.

Evaluation

The compelling analysis underpinning 'Broken Windows' fed into policy discussions about the need for new approaches to urban policing. What is significant is that it lends itself to both benign and authoritarian policy responses and mission statements. It could be argued that 'problem oriented policing' strategies are premised on a similar type of understanding of the role of the police in stabilizing urban communities and how police legitimacy can be secured through responding to 'quality of life issues' and prioritizing crime prevention. However, its core argument has also been adapted to justify aggressive street policing tactics such as those practised in New York in the 1990s. NYPD's 'zero tolerance' crime fighting strategy returned officers to street patrolling and mandated them to target the broad spectrum of low level misconduct and widespread anti-social behaviours which made the city feel unsafe and disorderly.

There is considerable disagreement over how much of the remarkable improvement in the New York crime rate could be attributed to the 'broken windows' strategy. However, what is beyond dispute is that Wilson and Kelling reopened a debate on what the core role of the police should be and how policing should be organized.

Eugene McLaughlin

Associated Concepts: defensible space, problem oriented policing, zero tolerance

Key Readings

Bratton, W.J. (1997) 'Crime is down in New York: blame the police', in N. Dennis (ed.), *Zero-Tolerance Policing: Policing a Free Society*. London, Institute of Economic Affairs.

Goldstein, H. (1990) *Problem-Oriented Policing*. New York, McGraw–Hill.

Kelling, G.L. and Coles, C.M. (1996) *Fixing Broken Windows: Restoring Order and Reducing Crime in Our Communities*. New York, Touchstone Books.

Skogan, W. (1990) *Disorder and Decline: Crime and the Spiral of Urban Decline in American Neighborhoods*. New York, The Free Press.

Wilson, J.Q. and Kelling, G. (1982) 'Broken windows', *Atlantic Monthly*, 249 (3), pp. 29–38.

Young, J. (1997) 'Zero tolerance: back to the future', in A. Marlow and J. Pitts (eds), *Planning Safer Communities*. London, Russell House Publishing.

C

CAPITAL PUNISHMENT

Definition

Capital punishment is punishment by execution – either by hanging, electrocution, firing squad, gas chamber, lethal injection, or beheading. Capital punishment can be imposed for a range of offences, but in Western countries, except in exceptional circumstances, is usually reserved for murder.

Distinctive Features

Capital punishment by hanging was used in England and Wales between 1016 and 1964, and between 1900 and 1949 751 people were hanged, of whom 87 were women. The purpose of capital punishment seems to have been both retributive and deterrent. Until 1868 hangings were public affairs. The last public execution was of the Irish nationalist Michael Barrett in May 1868, with some 2,000 people attending (Potter, 1993, p. 94). These public events were usually drunken affairs, with spectators often using the occasion as an opportunity to commit further crimes, thus turning what was intended as a solemn state ritual – which was supposed to reflect the power of the law – into a shambles (Ignatieff, 1978, pp. 21–4). After May 1868 executions took place behind the prison's walls with increasing standardization in the process of death, so that a uniform scaffold apparatus was adopted, a standard length and thickness of rope, and tables of 'drops' were published so that executioners – a profession itself which became increasingly specialized – could judge the execution in relation to the condemned's height and weight. Although executions were private, selected members of the public were allowed to attend. For example, in August 1868 at the hanging of Thomas Wells in Maidstone Gaol – the first person to be executed in prison – 16 reporters were present so as to be able to describe the final moments of the death of the condemned man for the morning papers (Potter, 1993, p. 95). The 1965 Murder (Abolition of the Death Penalty) Act ended capital punishment except in exceptional circumstances – such as treason, arson in HM Dockyards, and piracy – for a trial period of five years. Actual abolition occurred in England and Wales in December 1969.

This trend towards the abolition of public executions, and thereafter capital punishment itself, has been a process most obviously observed in Western Europe. There has been a tendency to treat capital punishment as a somewhat closed policy issue, especially as those former Warsaw Pact countries which have applied to join the Council of Europe have signalled their intention to move to abolition. Indeed Russia has also reduced the number of offences for which the death penalty can be imposed. However, the abolitionist cause has not had much impact on several regions of the world. So, for example, as Hood (1996) advises, most of the Middle East and North African states have expressed strong support for the continued use of capital punishment, which reflects their Islamic beliefs and law; China continues to use capital punishment enthusiastically; and only one Caribbean country has abolished the death penalty since 1965.

By far the most vocal and visible retentionist advocate of capital punishment is the United States of America. In 1999, for example, there were some 3,000 people on 'death row' awaiting execution in the 37 states that have retained the death penalty. Of note, concern has been expressed that blatant racial discrimination operates in the application of capital punishment in the USA. So, for example, the killers of white people were eleven times more likely to be condemned to death than the murderers of African Americans. However, discrimination in the application of the death penalty can be seen most obviously by focusing on the race of the victim of the murder. In Georgia, for example, prosecutors sought the death penalty in 70 per cent of the cases where the murderer was African American and the victim was white, but when there was a white murderer and the victim was African American the same prosecutors sought the death penalty in only 15 per cent of cases (Donziger, 1996). Others have drawn attention to how politicians use the issue of capital punishment symbolically for electoral advantage. So, for example, it has been suggested that Bill Clinton scheduled the execution in Arkansas of a brain-damaged black man – Rickey Ray Rector – during his Presidential campaign bid in 1992 so as to demonstrate his toughness on crime and punishment. On the eve of his execution Mr Rector is reported to have been barking like a dog, laughing inappropriately, and on being offered his last meal, asked to save his dessert 'until later'.

The most consistently debated question about capital punishment is whether it has a deterrent effect, and this remains the most common justification for the death penalty by retentionist countries. However, comparative studies of neighbouring abolitionist and retentionist states in the USA have suggested that abolition is not associated with higher murder rates in general, or with higher murder rates of police or prison officers in particular (Hood, 1996, p. 166). Even where a deterrent effect has been detected critics would still debate whether the decision to murder is a matter of rational choice, and whether data on executions and murder are reliable. In his comprehensive study, undertaken on behalf of the United Nations Committee on Crime Prevention and Control, Hood (1996, p. 167) concludes that 'research has failed to provide scientific proof that executions have a greater deterrent effect than life imprisonment. Such proof is unlikely to be forthcoming. The evidence as a whole still gives no positive support to the deterrent hypothesis.'

David Wilson

Associated Concepts: deterrence, retribution

Key Readings

Bedau, A.H. (1998) *The Death Penalty in America: Current Controversies*. New York, Oxford University Press.

Donziger, S. (ed.) (1996) *The Real War on Crime: The Report of the National Criminal Justice Commission*. New York, Harper Collins.

Gatrell, U.A.C. (1994) *The Hanging Tree: Execution and the English People 1770–1868*. Oxford, Clarendon Press.

Hood, R. (1996) *The Death Penalty: A World-Wide Perspective*. Oxford, Clarendon Press.

Ignatieff, M. (1978) *A Just Measure of Pain: The Penitentiary in the Industrial Revolution, 1750–1850*. Harmondsworth, Penguin Books.

Potter, H. (1993) *Hanging in Judgement: Religion and the Death Penalty in England*. London, SCM Press.

Sarat, A. (ed.) (1998) *The Killing State*. New York, Oxford University Press.

CARCERAL SOCIETY

Definition

The concept of the emergence and existence of a carceral society was first suggested by Michel Foucault (1977) in his book *Discipline and Punish: The Birth of the Modern Prison*. In this book not only does Foucault attack the idea that prisons have somehow become more enlightened and humanitarian – that they have progressed – but he also tries to unmask the disciplinary nature of modern society, of which prison is but one manifestation.

Distinctive Features

Discipline and Punish opens with a description of the gruesome torture of the regicide Damiens in 1757, and is almost immediately counterbalanced in the text by the detailed plans for a young offender institution some 70 years later. However, the reader is not meant to infer from these descriptions that somehow punishment has become more humane or enlightened – the book stands as a full-frontal attack on modernism – but rather how prisons punish in other ways, which might be less public and individualized, but which are equally gruesome. Moreover, punishment is no longer intended to alter individual behaviour, but rather becomes the basis on which physical and social structures are created within society – not just within prisons – and which thus alters the behaviour of everyone. For Foucault the key words are inspection, surveillance and power, which in relation to prison were symbolized by Bentham's Panopticon.

What is of interest is that Foucault saw these 'carceral impulses' swarming outside of the Panopticon and other penal institutions: 'their mechanisms have a certain tendency to become de-institutionalized, to emerge from the closed fortresses in which they once functioned and to circulate in a "free" state' and thus 'infecting' schools, hospitals and factories. Their purpose was to observe, inspect and ultimately control the general population, a disciplinary impulse that he saw at work in a variety of locations, and within a variety of organizations – from religious and charity groups, to the development of a centralized police force in France.

Evaluation

The concept can be applied within a variety of Western societies that have sought to control the behaviour of their inhabitants, not on the basis of controlling the behaviour of individual members of that society but rather of the population as a whole. So many more areas of social life are being subjected to categorization, surveillance, prevention, organized forms of control and 'compliance systems' of both a formal and informal nature. Inevitably this has also meant that the number of people who come to be managed by the criminal justice system has increased, and the massive growth of, for example, the prison populations of the USA and England and Wales is testimony to this expansion. Hand in glove we have also seen, for example, the increased use of CCTV, airport security checks, and random urine checks at work. At another level there is greater awareness of 'lifestyle controls' in the form of no smoking zones, or evidence that some businesses may not hire people who are overweight.

Foucault's work is filled with rich historical insight, and has re-emerged as a powerful tool with which to analyse more contemporary concepts such as risk management, actuarialism and population control which are often incorrectly presented as 'theory neutral'.

David Wilson

Associated Concepts: actuarialism, governmentality, net widening, panopticism, penality, situational crime prevention, social control, target hardening

Key Readings

Bogard, W. (1996) *The Simulation of Surveillance: Hypercontrol in Telematic Societies.* Cambridge, Cambridge University Press.

Driver, F. (1984) 'Power, space and the body: a critical reassessment of Foucault's *Disipline and Punish'*, *Society and Space*, 3, pp. 425–46.

Foucault, M. (1977) *Discipline and Punish: The Birth of the Modern Prison.* London, Allen Lane.

Gandy, O. (1993) *The Panoptic Sort.* Boulder, Westview Press.

CARNIVAL (OF CRIME)

Definition

A description and analysis of popular festive behaviour as a necessary act of irrational excess and excitement in opposition to the dominant accepted values of the restraint, sobriety and rationality of modern industrial life. Transgression and crime are understood as an integral part of the performance of carnival no longer restricted to festivals but as an enjoyable part of popular everyday life and as a site of resistance to rationality.

Distinctive Features

The most important analysis of the nature of carnival is that of the work of Mikhail Bakhtin (1984), who stressed that the structure and imagery of carnival seeks to legitimate its participants' behaviour making it a period of licensed misrule. A characteristic of carnivalesque transgression is the open defiance of dominant authority structures and values, thereby putting the transgressor in a position of power as their behaviour turns the social world 'upside down'. Such social behaviour is full of irrational, senseless, offensive acts performed in a time of disorder, transgression and doing wrong in an otherwise ordered world where such acts would be considered criminal.

Contemporary theorists of popular culture (Docker, 1996) have analysed the place of carnival in popular pleasure including media entertainment, whilst cultural criminologists have looked at the pleasure of doing wrong (Katz, 1988; Presdee, 2000). The latter highlight the notion that carnival functions as a playful and pleasurable resistance to authority where those normally excluded from the discourse of power celebrate their anger at their exclusion. Cultural criminologists maintain that, through the dual processes of the scientific rationality and containment of contemporary everyday life, carnival has shattered and its fragments and debris are now to be found not in the pleasure and excitement of organized carnival but in acts of transgression and crime (Presdee, 2000). Without a partly licensed and organized carnival 'form', the carnivalesque emerges more unrehearsed and unannounced and often in a more violent and criminal way. Lyng (1990) has described such performance as 'edgework' – intense and often ritualised moments of pleasure and excitement which accompany the risk, danger and skill of transgression and which come to play a key part in the construction of shared subcultural meaning.

Many pleasurable activities such as rave culture, drug taking, body modification, the use of the internet, joy riding and SM activities, contain both elements of the carnivalesque and of crime whilst the political demonstration 'the Carnival against Capitalism' that erupted at the 30 November 1999 meeting of the World Trade Organization in Seattle, USA, evidenced a global carnival of crime and pleasure, partially organized through the Internet, that showed that practical politics (such as the demonstrations by 'Reclaim the Streets' and 'Tree Dwellers' in the UK) can cause widespread disruption; can be criminal yet immensely pleasurable to the participants.

The carnival as analysed by Bakhtin resulted in a return to law and order and led to reintegration into the existing structures of social life. Now, as carnival explodes into everyday life there is no longer an inevitable return to law and order. The expectation has grown that crime as carnival will be continually performed without shame and without social reintegration.

Mike Presdee

Associated Concepts: anarchist criminology, cultural criminology, cybercrime, hedonism

Key readings

Bakhtin, M. (1984) Rabelais and His World. Bloomington, Indiana University Press.
Docker, J. (1996) Postmodernism and Popular Culture: A Cultural History. Cambridge, Cambridge University Press.
Ferrell, J. and Sanders, C.R. (1995) Cultural Criminology. Boston, MA, Northeastern University Press.
Katz, J. (1988) Seductions of Crime: Moral and Sensual Attractions in Doing Evil. New York, Basic Books.
Lyng, S. (1990) 'Edgework: a social psychological analysis of voluntary risk taking', American Journal of Sociology, 95, pp. 851–86.
Presdee, M. (2000) Cultural Criminology and the Carnival of Crime. London, Routledge.

CAUSATION

Definition

The key proposition of causal analysis is that certain antecedent individual and social factors will invariably and unconditionally have a certain effect.

Distinctive Features

To establish that one factor is the cause of another, we have at least to show that the supposed cause precedes the supposed effect in time and, ideally, that the effect occurs always and only when the cause occurs. (Social causation is generally complex, however, and it may take a combination of causes to produce an effect. We may also find that a cause does not determine an effect absolutely, but only probabilistically: the cause may make the effect more likely but not always and inevitably produce it.) We should note that association between the supposed cause and the effect is a *necessary* condition for causation but not a *sufficient* one. To demonstrate causation beyond argument it is necessary to establish the mechanism by which the cause brings about the effect.

In social and criminological research we seldom speak absolutely of 'causes', but rather of 'antecedents' or 'influences' or 'predisposing factors'. Rarely is it possible, even in theory, to argue that an antecedent factor leads deterministically to its effect; we are more likely to want to say that it renders a behaviour more likely or influences the way in which events and actions are interpreted. The exception is when treatments or ways of handling offenders or crimes are being evaluated. Here we shall want to show that the treatment or form of handling *does* have the desired effect and is the only reasonable explanation for the effect's occurrence.

The essence of casual analysis, in criminological as in all other research, is control of alternative explanations. In an *experiment* this control is delivered as part of the design of the study: a treatment or manipulation is shown to lead to the effect, and the study is so designed that all other explanations for the effect can be ruled out. Where experiments are not possible or ethical – i.e. in most criminological research – then statistical control is used to rule out alternative explanations.

Roger Sapsford

Associated Concepts: correlational analysis, determinism, experiments, multivariate analysis, positivism, prediction studies

Key Readings

Belson, W.A. (1975) *Juvenile Theft: The Causal Factors.* London, Harper and Row.

Glueck, S. and Glueck, E. (1950) *Unravelling Juvenile Delinquency.* Cambridge, MA, Harvard University Press.

Sapsford, R. and Jupp, V. (eds) (1996) *Data Collection and Analysis.* London, Sage.

CHAOS THEORY

Definition

Chaos theory, sometimes referred to as complexity theory, and one of the emerging perspectives in postmodern criminology, is the study of orderly disorder. Chaos theory is the study of dynamic systems that exhibit both 'determinism' and 'free will'. Modernist thought has constructed determinism and free will as dualities; chaos theory argues both can be at work in complex, dynamic systems.

Distinctive Features

Chaos theory had already been anticipated by Nietzsche (cited in Babich, 1996, p. 109): 'the total character of the world . . . is in all eternity chaos'. Order appears only as an imposition or as 'aesthetic anthropomorphisms', as 'semiotic fictions' according to Nietzsche. In the early 1990s a number of theorists in America (Bruce Arrigo, Dragan Milovanovic, Hal Pepinsky, Robert Schehr, T.R. Young) began applying chaos theory to criminology, law and sociology (Milovanovic, 1997). Chaos theory includes several key conceptualizations:

Attractors Four types of attractors have been identified: point, cyclic/periodic/limit, torus,

and strange. Each lives in 'phase space', a map portraying dynamic systems in movement in their various phases. Attractors are regions in phase space toward which dynamic systems move. The point attractor reflects movement toward a point in phase space. A swinging pendulum (the dynamic systems) eventually comes to rest at a point. This 'point' attracts trajectories to it. The periodic, cyclic or limit attractor is seen as a circle with each point on the circle depicting at least two dimensions simultaneously. A swinging pendulum, with no frictional forces, will move back and forth traversing space and changing momentum. This could be depicted in phase space as a circle with the two axes marked position and momentum. Hence, any point on this circle represents simultaneously its location and momentum. For both the point and periodic attractor, modernist thought would have no problem in the determinacy involved.

The next two attractors become increasingly 'fuzzy'; one sees both order and disorder existing. Modernist thought is hard pressed to explain them. A torus attractor looks very much like an inflated inner tube. If our pendulum was connected with a worn hinge it would wobble as it moved in its trajectory. Hence this introduces the third degree of freedom. To depict this we would include movement in the form of a line winding itself around the outside of the torus. In other words, the torus depicts two coupled cyclic attractors. Where the two coupled systems repeat frequencies in a ratio way we have a periodic torus; where they don't, we have a quasiperiodic torus. The shape of the torus itself does indicate there is overall order in the system (read 'determinism' or stability); however, within the torus, or at any moment, accurate prediction escapes us (thus a degree of instability, or if you will 'free will'). The strange attractor combines order and disorder (orderly disorder), and is the most indeterminate of the four attractors. The most celebrated strange attractor is the butterfly attractor, which looks very much like a pair of butterfly wings. Each wing represents an 'outcome basin', or a region toward which trajectories move. These attractors both exhibit a form (i.e., the shape of a butterfly wing), or order, stability, or can even be interpreted as having a degree of determinism, and also disorder (i.e., within the wings, indeterminacy prevails). Thus within each wing are trajectories portraying the dynamic system in movement in its various phases, but no accurate prediction can exist, hence we have instability, disorder, indeterminacy, or 'free will'.

Bifurcation diagram (logistic mapping) This phase map was developed in early studies of gypsy moth populations. It was found that rather than linear development, non-linear movement appears in the form of 'period doubling'. Here, with increasing input of some major variable, results do not follow neat predictable outcomes. Rather, initially periodic attractors develop as solutions to the question of what size population, but with additional proportional input, bifurcations or splitting exists, where first two solutions (periodic attractors) then 4, then 8, 16, 32 and so on emerge. In other words, proportional inputs did not produce proportional results, and various attractors appear: first, point, then periodic, then torus, and then strange attractors. After that, deep chaos is experienced where prediction escapes us. However, within these latter regions, called far-from-equilibrium conditions, order spontaneously arises out of disorder. These pockets of order are called 'dissipative structures'.

Far-from-equilibrium conditions Modernist thought privileges order, stability, homeostasis, equilibrium, structural functionalism. Chaos theory argues for inherent instabilities. Thus disorder, instability and far-from-equilibrium conditions are privileged. Within these regions both order and disorder live side by side, not as dualisms. Within these regions 'structures' are extremely sensitive to perturbations. Even very small inputs can produce disproportionate effects. Thus contrary to the privileging of bureaucratic structures as is assumed in homeostatic systems, 'dissipative structures' appear which are only temporary structures of stability.

Dissipative structures These 'structures' are characterized as always in process; they are both 'structures' and also dissipating – are in constant reconfiguring modes of being. They offer only temporary stability points. They exist in far-from-equilibrium conditions. Unger's (1987) blueprint for a 'superliberal' society entails the emergence of these dissipative structures (without him naming them as such).

Iteration This is a process by which one begins with a simple algorithm, plugs in an initial value, solves, takes the result, plugs it back into the algorithm, solves, plugs in the solution into the initial algorithm and so on. It is feedback. What one finds is that even a very slight variance can, with a number of subsequent iterations, produce large, disproportional effects. In empirical criminology

rounding and dismissing 'minor' variables in calculating 'variance explained' may overlook important factors once iterated. One of the classic forms produced by a simple algorithm and iteration is the Mandelbrot set.

Sensitivity to initial conditions Chaos theory shows that especially in far-from-equilibrium conditions, even with small perturbations, or with even some small change in initial starting values in iterations, large, unintended, and disproportional results occur: 'a butterfly flapping its wings in Southeast Asia produces a hurricane in Florida'. A school crossing guard taking interest in a child in the ghetto may, upon iteration, produce a person transcending his/her adverse environment.

Non-linearity Modernist thought privileges linear developments. Perhaps best expressed in syllogistic reasoning and deductive logic in legal reasoning. Chaos theory indicates that complex systems often exhibit 'jumps', singularities, and unintended consequences. Even beginning with a deterministic mathematical formula can produce unexpected, non-linear changes.

Fractals and fractal geometry Modernist thought privileges Euclidean geometry with its whole integer dimensions (0,1,2,3, etc.). Chaos theory indicates that within these integer dimensions an infinite number of others exist. The classic question of how long is the coast of England is answered by: it's infinite; it depends on the measuring device; use a yardstick and one gets one result, use a footstick, one gets another result, use an 'inch stick' and yet another result. With each measurement the distances increase. Fractals are useful in getting away from Boolean logic, as in yes–no answers privileged in legal logic. Truth is always somewhere in between. Fractal geometry opens up 'space' in which alternative visions may appear.

Evaluation

Chaos theory has been applied in criminology (see generally, Milovanovic, 1997) to explain rural crime, banditry, property crime, gender and racial violence, organized crime, corporate crime, white collar crime; in modelling Richard Quinney's critical theory in criminology; in developing a 'chaos of violence'; and in juvenile delinquency research. In law, several applications have developed: it has been integrated with semiotic analysis; it has been applied to explain the role of the American legal system; it has been shown relevant in forensic psychology to explain the insane defendant; it has been shown how law imposes coordinates on the body and language by which reality gets constructed in restricted ways; it has been shown that law operates much like an 'autopoeitic' system (e.g., dissipative structure); and it has been applied in decision-making in law. In social justice it has been used to explain models of a more just society (Henry and Milovanovic, 1996); to explain the spontaneous development of new forms of organization in single room occupancy areas; used in the development of new models of society that are more sensitive to being human; applied to a critique of existing mediation programs (Schehr and Milovanovic, 1999); and used as the basis of a new approach in social movement theory.

The methodological thrust of doing chaos theory involves:

1   locating the attractors hidden in complex data sets.
2   determining how many attractors exist in that data set.
3   finding the change point(s) at which new attractors are produced (for purposes of social control).
4   identifying the key parameters which drive the system into ever more uncertainty (for purposes of developing humanistic social policy).
5   determining which setting of those key parameters is acceptable to the whole society.

Chaos theory is one of the perspectives within postmodern criminology. It continues to find wide application areas in criminology and law. Several theorists have integrated chaos theory with other perspectives within postmodern analysis in developing a model that draws from the innovative conceptual tools offered. Perhaps the greatest influence has been on those who are eager to develop novel ways of approaching old problems.

Dragan Milovanovic

Associated Concepts: constitutive criminology, postmodernism, post-structuralism

Key Readings
Babich, B. (1996) 'The order of the real: Nietzsche and Lacan', in D. Pettigrew and F. Raffaoul (eds),

Disseminating Lacan. Albany, NY: State University of New York Press.
Henry, S, and Milovanovic, D. (1996) Constitutive Criminology. London, Sage.
Milovanovic, D. (1996) 'Postmodern criminology', Justice Quarterly, 13 (4), pp. 567–609.
Milovanovic, D. (ed.) (1997) Chaos, Criminology, and Social Justice: The New Orderly (Dis)Order. Westport, CT, Praeger.
Schehr, R. and Milovanovic, D. (1999) 'Conflict mediation and the postmodern: chaos, catastrophe, and psychoanalytic semiotics', Social Justice, 26 (1), pp. 208–32.
Unger, R. (1987) False Necessity. New York, Cambridge University Press.

CHICAGO SCHOOL OF SOCIOLOGY

Definition

A school of sociological enquiry renowned for establishing links between environmental factors and crime.

Distinctive Features

To understand the Chicago School it helps to know something of Chicago itself. In a little over a century – largely as a result of its significant geographical location – Chicago grew from an obscure frontier trading-post to become one of the world's greatest cities with a population that, by 1930, had exceeded 3 million. One of the striking features of this phenomenal expansion was the extent to which Chicago became home to a panoply of ethnic groups: not only was the city a point of gravitation for migrating African Americans keen to escape the poverty and repression of the rural South, but it was also a destination point for large numbers of European immigrants. Consequently, by 1900 Chicago was an amalgam of disparate social worlds and conflicting identities. Against this socially turbulent background, a new school of sociological enquiry emerged.

The starting point for the Chicago School was Robert Park's 'theory of human ecology'. Derived from the observations of early plant ecologists, Park postulated that human communities were closely akin to any natural environment in that their spatial organization and expansion was not the product of chance, but instead was patterned and could be understood in terms analogous to the basic natural processes that occur within any biotic organism. Thus, Park maintained that the city could be thought of as a super-organism; an amalgamation of a series of subpopulations differentiated either by race, ethnicity, income group or spatial factors. Accordingly, each of these groups acted 'naturally' in that they were underpinned by a collective or organic unity. Furthermore, not only did each of these 'natural areas' have an integral role to play in the city as a whole, but each community or business area was interrelated in a series of 'symbiotic relationships'. Close observation of these relationships enabled Park to conclude that just as is in any natural ecology, the sequence of 'invasion–dominance–succession' was also in operation within the modern city.

Park's thoughts on the social ecology of the city were developed by his colleague, Ernest Burgess (Park et al., 1925), whose *concentric zone theory* contended that modern cities expanded radially from their inner-city core in a series of concentric circles. Burgess identified five main zones within Chicago, each two miles wide. At the centre was the business district, an area of low population and high property values. This in turn was encircled by the 'zone in transition'; a place characterized by run-down housing, high-speed immigration, and high rates of poverty and disease. Surrounding that zone, in turn, were zones of working-class and middle-class housing, and ultimately the affluent suburbs. Of greatest importance to the Chicagoans, however, was the zone in transition. This was the oldest residential section of the city and was comprised primarily of dilapidated, ghetto housing that was unlikely to be renovated because of its proximity to the busy commercial core. The affordability of accommodation in these neighbourhoods ensured that the zone served as a temporary home for thousands of immigrants too poor to afford lodgings elsewhere in Chicago. A pattern quickly emerged whereby immigrant families only remained in the zone for as long as it took them to become sufficiently economically established to move out and 'invade' an area further from the business district. Consequently, this was an area of great flux and restlessness – a place in which communal ties were lost, traditional shared folkways were undermined, and impersonal relations prevailed. Such neighbourhoods were sometimes described as 'socially disorganized', and it was within these un-integrated urban spaces that the members of the Chicago School sought to unearth the substantive causes of crime and deviance.

The Chicagoans set about assiduously researching the city's many social problems. Taking their lead from Park, they proceeded from the premise that the best way to identify the causes of social problems such as crime was by close observation of the social processes intrinsic to urban existence. To facilitate this task the School developed innovative new research methods such as *participant observation* and the *focused interview*. Such techniques enabled the Chicagoans to 'enter the world of the deviant' and compile ethnographic data on hobos and taxi-dancers, racketeers and street-gang members. The result was a series of stunning qualitative and appreciative studies (e.g. Anderson, 1923; Shaw, 1930) that not only provided great insight into many diverse urban subcultures, but also went a long way to establishing a theorized methodology for studying social action.

Arguably, it is the findings that emerged from the School's empirical work that remain its most enduring legacy. Clifford Shaw and Henry McKay (1942) set about statistically testing the assumption that crime was greater in disorganized areas than elsewhere in the city by plotting juvenile delinquency court statistics onto Burgess's concentric circle model. Their findings had immense implications for criminology. Simply stated, they found that delinquency rates were at their highest in run-down inner-city zones and progressively declined the further one moved out into the more prosperous suburbs. Of critical importance, they also identified that this spatial patterning of juvenile crime remained remarkably stable (often over very long periods of time) irrespective of the neighbourhood's racial or national demographic composition. These findings allowed Shaw and McKay to conclude that delinquency was a product of sociological factors within the zone of transition rather than individual pathology or any inherent ethnic characteristics. This was a momentous breakthrough that did much to dispel earlier criminological theories, that located the root cause of crime within the individual. Having established this important position, Shaw and McKay went on to claim that socially disorganized neighbourhoods perpetuate a situation in which delinquent behaviour patterns are *culturally transmitted*. In contrast to orderly neighbourhoods where community integration is strong and 'conventional values' are deeply ingrained, in disorganized environments – because of the paucity of supervision and the collapse of community provisions – the prevailing value-system is likely to be both conducive to, and supportive of delinquent behaviour. In other words, criminal conventions and delinquent traditions are 'transmitted down through successive generations of boys, in much the same way that language and other social forms are transmitted' (1942, p. 166). This observation, along with Edwin Sutherland's (1939) related theory of *differential association*, was an important strand in subsequent criminological theories that attempted to account for crime by reference to deviant subcultures.

Evaluation

The work of the Chicago School has had a considerable influence on the development of criminological theory. In particular, it helped crystallize thinking and give structure to the nascent and very disparate movements within the then fledgling discipline of sociology.

By developing innovative research methodologies, the School laid the foundations for a new type of 'appreciative', reflexive, qualitative analysis. More importantly, by identifying the important relationship between environmental factors and crime, the School greatly compromised the (then still popular) belief that criminality was a product of innate biological or pathological factors. Vitally, it established the importance of detailed appreciation of the social lifeworlds of individuals for understanding the meaningfulness of their behaviour. Despite its many achievements however, the School has not been without its critics.

A common criticism, challenging the usefulness of the ecological model, is that the theory of human ecology contained certain fallacious assumptions – not least that the work of the Chicagoans (in particular that of Shaw and McKay) implied that *individual* action can be explained *solely* by the larger environment in which that individual resided. This later famously became known as the 'ecological fallacy'. Similarly, the key concept of 'social disorganization' has been questioned on the grounds that it was held by the Chicagoans to be both the cause of delinquency *and* the proof that it existed. This tautological 'like-causes-like' fallacy today is recognized as fundamentally flawed.

Major reservations have also been expressed about the wisdom of basing empirical research into juvenile delinquency upon official statistics. Aside from the obvious criticism that Shaw and McKay consistently failed to acknowledge that crime rates are always the product of *social construction*, the 'delinquency areas' scrutinized in their research were often locations in which delinquents *resided* and thus not necessarily the same neighbourhoods in which they committed their crimes.

A further criticism concerns the failure of the Chicagoans to place the everyday world of crime and deviance into the wider economic or political context. So concerned were Park and his followers with the day-to-day processes of urban life and the ways in which these concerns impinged upon and contributed to crime in the city, that they neglected to consider fully the underlying forces of capitalist development that also played a major role in shaping social life and determining patterns of urban segregation in Chicago.

Keith Hayward

Associated Concepts: appreciative criminology, community crime prevention, geographies of crime, participant observation, social ecology

Key Readings

Anderson, N. (1923) *The Hobo: The Sociology of the Homeless Man*. Chicago, University of Chicago Press.

Faris, R.E.L. (1967) *Chicago Sociology, 1920–1932*. Chicago, University of Chicago Press.

Park, R.E., Burgess, E.W. and McKenzie, R.D. (eds) (1925) *The City*. Chicago, University of Chicago Press.

Shaw, C.R. (1930) *The Jack-Roller: A Delinquent Boy's Own Story*. Chicago, University of Chicago Press.

Shaw, C.R. and McKay, H.D. (1942) *Juvenile Delinquency and Urban Areas*. Chicago, University of Chicago Press.

Sutherland, E. (1939) *Principles of Criminology*, 3rd edn, Philadelphia, J.B. Lippincott.

CHILD ABUSE

See Family crime; Violence

CLASSICISM

Definition

An approach to the study of crime and criminality which is underpinned by the notion of rational action and free will. It was developed in the late eighteenth and early nineteenth centuries by reformers who aimed to create a clear and legitimate criminal justice system based upon equality. At its core is the idea that punishment should be proportionate to the criminal act and should be viewed as a deterrent. Further assumptions include the notion of individual choice within a consensual society based upon a social contract and the common interest.

Distinctive Features

One of the central features of the classical perspective within criminology is the emphasis upon voluntarism and hedonism. Individualism and self-interest are placed at the forefront of explanations about why some people commit crime and how they should be punished. One of the first proponents of this approach was the Italian philosopher Cesare Beccaria, with his work on the right to punish and methods to prevent crime, first published in 1764. He argued that society should create laws that may infringe upon the personal liberty of a few, but result in the greater happiness of the majority. His approach to the prevention of crime was that the pain of punishment should be greater than the potential pleasure resulting from the act. Hence, the punishment should be proportionate to the harm it causes society.

Another early advocate of this utilitarian approach was the philosopher and penal reformer Jeremy Bentham, who argued that punishment should be calculated to inflict pain in proportion to the damage to the public interest. As this philosophy was developed into criminological and legal definitions of crime, formal equality before the law and the similarity of criminals and non-criminals was emphasized in penal policy. In contrast to positivist approaches, which were developed in the late nineteenth century by Lombroso and Ferrero (1895) and Ferri (1901), for example, classicists maintained that the reasoning individual had simply made an error of judgement in committing a criminal act – a violation of the social contract. To prevent this recurring the individual must be sure of swift, sharp and certain punishment, so that, according to Beccaria, crime and punishment are associated in the human mind.

Evaluation

As an alternative to the apparently cruel, harsh system based on terror, absolute control

and paternal benevolence which had preceded Beccaria and Bentham's ideas, leading to reforms to the legal system, classicism appears to offer a reasonably fair and more transparent philosophy of punishment. It provides a benchmark by which other theories can be compared and an important philosophical underpinning for anti-positivistic paradigms that emphasize free will. What it fails to take into account, however, are the reasons or causes of societal inequality or conditions within which individuals are said to be propelled to commit certain acts that may violate legal codes. Classical criminologies assume that there is an agreed collective set of values or goals, ignoring the possibility of conflicting groups or aims. Although Beccaria conceded that there are pre-rational individuals (children) and sub-rational people (the mentally insane), he failed to acknowledge that social conditions may affect 'rational' judgement. Furthermore, unlike later neo-classicists, Beccaria did not view crime as a rational response to certain social conditions such as poverty, although he did concede that the poor may have to be deterred more forcefully than other members of society.

Critiques offered by positivist criminologists also suggest that social and individual forces, such as biology, physiology and environment create situations which may lead individuals to commit certain acts. Early theorists, mentioned above, proposed that some particular bodily difference, such as skull size, could identify and predict propensity to crime (see for example Lombroso and Ferrero, 1895). Later, psychologists working within positivist frameworks argued that there could be an individual explanation in terms of personality characteristics which might predispose some people to commit crime. In contrast, classicism maintains that although hedonistic, pleasure-seeking principles may lead some people to make errors of judgement, they are essentially similar to those who do not commit such acts. Furthermore, in terms of gender this perspective fails to take into account the disparity between rates of offending between men and women. One of the questions this type of critique raises is the inability to explain these differences in terms of offending as an irrational act or individual error.

Another difficulty with the classical school is that it assumes a rational, legal and 'just' system ignoring functionalist arguments regarding the necessary and beneficial aspects of crime. It seems unable to account for white collar and corporate crime or the 'dark' figure of crime because, if self-report studies are to be believed, 'crime' is a regular and common occurrence. This questions the extent to which the majority of individuals in society can be argued to be acting in an 'irrational' manner, if this is the case.

Louise Westmarland

Associated Concepts: free will, functionalism, neo-conservative criminology, positivism, rational choice theory

Key Readings

Beccaria, C. (1764) *On Crimes and Punishments* (reprinted 1963). New York, Bobbs–Merrill.
Beirne, P. (1993) *Inventing Criminology: Essays on the Rise of Homo Criminalis*. Albany, SUNY Press.
Bentham, J. (1791) *Collected Works of Jeremy Bentham* (reprinted 1843). London, J. Bowring.
Ferri, E. (1901) 'Causes of criminal behavior', reprinted 1968 in S.E. Grupp (ed.), *The Positive School of Criminology: Three Lectures by Enrico Ferri*. Pittsburgh, University of Pittsburgh Press.
Lombroso, C. and Ferrero, W. (1895) *The Female Offender*. London, Fisher Unwin.
Roshier, B. (1989) *Controlling Crime: The Classical Perspective in Criminology*. Milton Keynes, Open University Press.

COGNITIVE-BEHAVIOURAL THERAPY

See Behaviour modification; Social learning theory

COHORT STUDIES

Definition

Cohort studies involve the collection of data from the same group of respondents over a period of time. Research employing the cohort approach can be either qualitative or quantitative. Researchers adopting a qualitative approach might seek to conduct in-depth interviews with a group of respondents on a longitudinal basis, whilst researchers employing a more quantitative approach might survey the same sample of respondents over a period of time. Cohort studies are a form of longitudinal study.

Distinctive Features

Cohort studies are employed where there is a desire to explore patterns of behaviour over time or, where there is an interest in following life events and increasingly they are used in evaluation research, where there is a desire to observe the impact of rehabilitative programmes upon recipients. The aims of cohort-based research are to identify what motivates groups of people to behave as they do, to describe life events and sometimes to explore the impact of programmes or policies.

The form that cohort research takes will be dependent upon the methodological techniques employed within a particular study. Typically a sample of respondents is selected at the outset of a study on the basis of some defining characteristic. The respondents may, for example, share the same birthday or the same interest or may have been convicted of a particular offence at a given time. This group of respondents or participants are asked to participate in the research over a specified time period and are contacted at regular intervals, in order to participate in interviews or to complete questionnaires.

Some cohort studies are based upon the analysis of secondary data. In the case of criminological research such data may have been collected by criminal justice agencies in the conduct of their work. As the data already exist the researcher may select a cohort of individuals and attempt to trace their criminal histories. One such study was conducted by Peter Marshall (1998), in which he aimed to estimate the number of men in England and Wales who had received convictions for a variety of sexual offences. The work was based upon data from the Home Office Offender Index, a database which stores information on all convictions from 1963 to the present. Marshall calculated estimates on the basis of five cohort samples of men born between 1953 and 1973. The men's criminal histories were compiled by 'sampling one in thirteen records from each year – based upon all birthdays in four weeks of each year' (1998, p. 2). Marshall was able to estimate the number of men convicted of sexual offences in England and Wales, and found that at least 260,000 men aged 20 or over had been convicted of a sexual offence in the 1993 population, 110,000 of whom had committed a sexual offence against a child. Of his cohort of men born in 1953, approximately one in 60 had a conviction by age 40 for some type of sexual offence (this does include less serious forms of sexual offending).

Evaluation

The value of quantitative cohort research lies in its ability to provide a great deal of data regarding respondents' lives and motivations, over a long period of time. As the work is not conducted in a retrospective fashion, problems associated with respondent recall of past events are also diminished. The advantages are similar in qualitative work, except that in addition rich, detailed data may be collected on an ongoing basis, providing a fuller picture of respondents' lives rather than simply a snapshot.

Relatively few cohort studies have been conducted by social researchers given the resources associated with the design and management of such projects. Another key problem arises in attempting to retain the original sample over time. Some respondents may be inaccessible as the study progresses or may wish to withdraw from the research. A great deal of effort is involved in retaining the cooperation of respondents. A further problem arises in that the production of findings is slow, given the long-term nature of cohort research.

Julia Davidson

Associated Concepts: longitudinal study, social survey, time series design

Key Readings

Marshall, P. (1998) *The Prevalence of Convictions for Sexual Offending*. Home Office Research Findings Briefing, No. 55, London, HMSO.
Sapsford, R. and Jupp, V.R. (eds) (1996) *Data Collection and Analysis*. London, Sage.

COMMUNITARIANISM

Definition

The broad philosophical and sociological tradition in which there is an emphasis on the centrality of informal, communal bonds and networks for the maintenance of social order. It is critical of individualistic, liberal theories of social behaviour and 'society', invoking notions of 'social beings' and 'community' rather than 'atomized individuals'. It has both conservative and radical variants.

Distinctive Features

The intellectual pedigree of this body of ideas/perspective is one of a decidedly mixed 'parentage'. Apart from the important connections back to Aristotelian notions of civic republicanism and Judaeo-Christian ideas of communion, the expression of communitarian aspirations is also associated with socialist and anarchist thinking. Furthermore, communitarian philosophy may also be linked to a conservative sociological tradition in which a critique of Enlightenment's project may be discerned. As a result of this heterodox pedigree, communitarianism may be said to 'break' with traditional ideas of right and left. Thus, for example, within much communitarian thought, both the market and the (welfare) state are viewed as dangers to the vibrant, organic community.

Liberalism's emphasis on individual rights and freedoms and abstract notions of 'enlightened self-interest' is subject to a critique for its neglect of the inherently social nature of humans. In contrast, communitarians point to the collective character of human existence in which obligation and mutual dependency are to the fore. Questions about solidarity and belonging are central to communitarianism in all its versions. Social compliance in turn derives primarily from informal cultural controls built into everyday relations. Much of its appeal then is to real people in specific, morally bounded communities rather than through abstract notions of liberty and individual rights. Herein lies its strong conservative appeal.

The sociologist and populist 'guru' Amitai Etzioni (1994) is the most prominent contemporary proponent of the conservative communitarian project to undertake a 'remoralization' of society. In Etzioni's words, 'Communitarians call to restore civic virtues, for people to live up to their responsibilities and not to merely focus on their entitlements, and to shore up the moral foundations of society.' At times Etzioni is quite explicit in harking back to a vision of a more stable, orderly and lawful past based on an idealized image of small-town America. Accepting that there was discrimination against women and ethnic minorities in the past, Etzioni nevertheless expresses concern that the assumed, previous bedrock of moral consensus has not been replaced by anything of substance other than 'a strong sense of entitlement and a weak sense of obligation'. The contemporary weakness of community is identified as both the cause of most of our ills (including crime and disorder) but also its potential saviour, when 're-moralized'.

Quite specific suggestions are put forward by conservative communitarians on law and order which further reinforce the dominant motifs of obligation and the shoring up of our moral foundations. Apart from support for vigilant 'self-policing' in the community, this communitarian agenda appears to lend support to a draconian and public version of 'shaming' offenders. The bottom line for authors like Etzioni, however, in their diagnosis of the problem and solution of crime and disorder, always appears to be the existence of a tight and homogeneous community.

There is also a radical variant of communitarianism in which the principles of spontaneous solidarity, rules of reciprocity and small-scale communities with participatory democracy are to the fore. Bill Jordan captures the working definition of 'community' adopted in this body of work as follows: it is 'the voluntary exchanges within systems of mutual obligation that include members through reciprocity, sharing and redistribution' (Jordan, 1996, p. 186). In contrast to moral authoritarian communitarianism, radical communitarians are keen to emphasize that individual moral autonomy needs to be assured and realized through specific projects and commitments. The good society is defiantly pluralistic and mutual tolerance is a crucial feature of it.

According to radical communitarians, recent years in neo-liberal societies have witnessed a deterioration in social relations due to the denial of access for the poor to majority goods and thus their experience of majority power as unjust. As a consequence, both the autonomy of poor people as citizens and the quality of life in the community have been jeopardized. Such processes of social exclusion and polarization do not necessarily destroy communities in any simple sense but radical communitarian commentators recognize that new forms of particularistic communities do emerge in the absence of any notion of a shared, common good. It is argued that marginalization, inequality and exclusion lie at the root of much crime and anti-social activities. As a consequence, the radical communitarian agenda on crime prevention gives ethical priority to decisions over *redistribution and reintegration* which in turn allows all members to participate both in the decisions themselves and, crucially, in the shared life of their communities. Unless such developments take place, it is suggested, the decay in consent and in allegiance to democracy and civil order will continue and with it the growth of more coercive and authoritarian methods of government and social control. The politics of enforcement will gather greater force.

A major contribution to the radical communitarian debate on crime, disorder and the decline of communities in the USA is found in the work of Elliot Currie (1997). Currie contends that the most serious problem facing contemporary USA is that its most disadvantaged communities are sinking into a permanent state of terror and disintegration. Radical communitarian commentators like Currie argue that behind the growth of crime is a *cultural* as well as a *structural* transformation of poor communities. In this regard, there are some common themes to both the conservative and radical communitarians. The connecting points are around the concern with cultural deprivation and morality. However, there are also important breaks between the two variants of communitarianism, as exemplified in the radical version's concern with structural inequalities, promotion of diversity and the key and positive role of the state in addressing social 'wounds'.

Evaluation

Moral authoritarian or conservative communitarianism has been widely criticized for the following reasons:

- a normative emphasis on one moral community at the expense of a sociological recognition of the plurality and diversity of actually existing communities;
- a desire to return to a traditional and nostalgic past;
- a neglect of power structures in human societies or at least a naturalization of hierarchical relations;
- a critique of personal rights and a call for duties but a failure to critique property rights;
- a glorification of past solidaristic communities together with a failure to conceptualize the crucial importance of struggles versus oppression in the creation of collectivist communities;
- finally, a naive and exclusivist call for a return to the 'traditional' family as the means to prevent social ills, including crime.

Within the popular conservative variant of communitarianism, there is a vision of a unitary, homogeneous community sustained by strongly held moral certainties, celebrating in turn mono-culturalism and setting; and, albeit at times implicitly, a morally prescriptive agenda for the social exclusion of marginalized and 'deviant' categories of people.

The extent to which the aspirations for a radical communitarian agenda are realizable in the face of both the authoritarian penal populism and the fragmentation of communities in neo-liberal societies remains open to further debate. There remains a lack of empirical substantiation for its participatory democratic visions of civil society and vibrant, expansive and tolerant communities. Furthermore, the key question remains as to what might create the more redistributive economic strategies upon which these radical communitarian visions of crime prevention and social reconstruction are dependent.

Community remains a deeply problematic word which is often derided by social scientists and yet it is hard to live without. It may be a necessary fiction, evoking as it does the fundamentally collective, shared and interdependent quality of our existence and the pull of the local on most of our lives (and especially those of the poor and disadvantaged).

Gordon Hughes

Associated Concepts: abolitionism, community crime prevention, community safety, left realism, restorative justice, shaming

Key Readings

Currie, E. (1997) 'Market, crime and community', *Theoretical Criminology*, 1 (2), pp. 147–72.

Etzioni, A. (1994) *The Spirit of Community: The Reinvention of American Society*. New York, Touchstone.

Hughes, G. (2000) 'Communitarianism and law and order', in T. Hope (ed.), *Perspectives on Crime Reduction*. Dartmouth, Ashgate.

Jordan, B. (1996) *A Theory of Poverty and Social Exclusion*. Cambridge, Polity Press.

COMMUNITY CORRECTIONS

Definition

A catch-all term for the range of correctional strategies and programmes for dealing with the punishment, treatment or supervision of offenders without recourse to penal custody.

Distinctive Features

Community corrections are generally viewed as being synonymous with 'alternatives to custody' and may range from the use of supervisory probation orders, community service orders, rehabilitation programmes, half-way houses, electronic tagging and home curfews to even more draconian, shaming corrections in the community. There is a marked diversity of programmatic activities which have a 'community-based' label. Across the world, such strategies and programmes still generally exist on the 'borderlands' of criminal justice and social welfare, in which a mix of the principles of punishment, care and treatment is evident. They are particularly associated with the work of the probation or correction services in most Western jurisdictions (Hamai et al., 1995). Community corrections have been popularly perceived as 'soft options' when compared with custodial sentences and widespread debate continues to rage over their 'effectiveness', however defined. They have also been popularly viewed as marginal to the 'real work' of criminal justice, namely custody, despite the use of community penalties outnumbering those sentenced to custody in most countries. In the USA, for example, there were 1.5 million adults sentenced to penal custody as against 3 million on parole in 1994.

The changing nature of community corrections and sentences has been driven by a heady mix of populist political motives, pragmatic managerial and economic concerns as well as philosophical and moral principles. As Tim May (1994, p. 860) notes, 'attempts therefore to improve an evolutionary theoretical scheme on the spread of community-based sentences must be treated with caution'.

A recent shift in the wake of dominant New Right thinking across many neo-liberal societies has seen the move from 'welfare' to 'punishment' models of community corrections and the populist punitive political call for such community sentences to be 'tough'. Indeed, in the USA the use of the term 'corrections' rather than 'treatment' itself is indicative of the sullied reputation of treatment models of rehabilitation (National Advisory Commission on Criminal Justice Standards and Goals, in Carter and Wilkins, 1976). More generally, since the 1980s the 'professional-therapeutic' rationale has been replaced by a 'punishment-administrative' rationale of community sentences (May, 1994). Apart from the shift to make community sanctions 'tougher', the other key, related shift is that of concentrating on the administrative and managerial technicalities of such corrections, with particular emphasis placed on cost and effectiveness.

Evaluation

The contemporary picture of community penalties and treatment programmes across many societies is confusing and messy. Many of these programmes are currently overlaid with contradictory objectives and concerns, including the issues of managerialist effectiveness, value for money, public protection, victim satisfaction, responsibility of the offender, as well as the vestiges of rehabilitation and restoration. And this situation is not helped by 'community' being such a slippery and promiscuous word. According to critics of the appeal to community in criminal justice practices, the rise of community-based, non-incarcerative sanctions is particularly dangerous due to their potential for widening the net of social control from inside the prison and out into the community (Cohen, 1985). However, such sweeping, if seductive, generalizations are open to question from existing trends (Bottoms, 1983). There is also the danger that criticisms of community-based programmes may serve to vacate the political space to those forces who want to increase the profile of retributive and incarcerative penalties yet further.

Like probation, community corrections are always practised in 'the shadow of prison'. We seem incapable of conceptualizing other penalties except in terms of their relationship to imprisonment. This is perhaps why non-incarcerative sanctions and programmes attract such popular suspicion. Across the world, it would seem that non-incarcerative measures are increasingly concerned with the 'punitive' restriction of liberty, surveillance and monitoring rather than treatment and welfare. An alternative vision is put forward by Ann Worrall to this depressing scenario in her argument that such measures should be viewed as constituting a sphere of social control which is quite separate from that of the prison, based on self-government and normalizing instruction. This would result in a widening of the net of inclusion (Worrall, 1997, p. 151).

Gordon Hughes

Associated Concepts: bifurcation, managerialism, neo-conservative criminology, net widening, probation, rehabilitation, social control

Key Readings

Bottoms, A. (1983) 'Neglected features of contemporary penal systems', in D. Garland and P. Young (eds), *The Power to Punish*. London, Heinemann.

Carter, R. and Wilkins, L. (1976) *Probation, Parole and Community Corrections*. New York, John Wiley.

Cohen, S. (1985) *Visions of Social Control*. Cambridge, Polity Press.

Hamai, F., Ville, R., Harris, R., Hough, M. and Zvedic, U. (eds) (1995) *Probation Around the World*. London, Routledge.

May, T. (1994) 'Probation and community sanctions' in M. Maguire, R. Morgan and R. Reiner (eds), *Oxford Handbook of Criminology*. Oxford, The Clarendon Press.

Worrall, A. (1997) *Punishment in the Community*. London, Longman.

COMMUNITY CRIME PREVENTION

Definition

The strategy which prioritizes the participation of members of the community in the active prevention of crime and related incivilities. It is also associated with explanations which look for the causes of crime and disorder in the fabric of the community and the wider social environment.

Distinctive Features

The strategy was most famously pioneered by the Chicago School of Sociology in the early twentieth century, which focused on the communal 'pathology' behind high rates of crime and delinquency in urban environments. Its enduring legacy is the rationale of community development. Key individuals of the Chicago School, such as Shaw and McKay (1969), were at pains to develop practical ways of modifying those aspects of socially disorganized community life which fostered delinquency and criminal careers among its members. The strategy which emerged, and is now often termed 'community crime prevention', was one which targeted specific problem neighbourhoods and sought to compensate poor communities for their lack of 'normal' institutional infrastructure by initiating programmes of community development. The success of the Chicago School's own programmes has been widely questioned but it has nevertheless influenced subsequent community interventions across the globe (Hope, 1995).

Appeals to community in crime prevention initiatives remain popular among both practitioners and politicians. This is in no small part due to the seductive rhetoric of 'community' in a world where traditional, tightly knit and cohesive communities appear to be the exception rather than the rule. It is also linked to the perceived growing problem of policing the most deprived and marginalized urban communities and the recognition that the solution to problems may require the participation of the involved communities themselves. In practice, many researchers have noted that the active role of the community is often limited to rhetoric rather than practice. Contemporary strategies of community crime prevention – increasingly termed 'community safety' – are generally multi-agency in character and involve both situational techniques (such as CCTV) and some limited social initiatives, such as the 'self-help policing' of Neighbourhood Watch schemes. Overall, such strategies are generally 'top-down' in character with limited 'bottom-up' participation.

Evaluation

Despite the lack of tangible, measurable successes, by the 1990s multi-agency community crime prevention appeared to be a phenomenon whose 'time had come' on the global stage. However, for some critics, the appeal to community sits more comfortably at the level of rhetoric than practice. According to other critical commentators, the idea that the solution to neighbourhood crime problems can be achieved primarily through the self-help efforts of residents is fundamentally flawed. Tim Hope (1995, p. 78), for example, argues that instead of communitarian self-help, disintegrating urban communities may need significant investment in their institutional infrastructure to offset the powerful tendencies of destabilization of poor communities within the urban free-market economy.

There are some important conceptual and political questions with regard to the popular appeal to 'community' in crime control discourses. For example, the nature of the community to which such appeals in dominant political discourses on law and order are made is itself often a highly selective rhetorical device. Crawford (1997) has noted that it is assumed (wrongly) in the dominant discourse that the lack of community necessarily leads to decline and thus crime, whereas 'more'

community equals less crime. Furthermore, community is assumed to be a defence against 'outsiders' and that community will be characterized by homogeneity rather than diversity. In accord with a long tradition of sociological scepticism on the use of this slippery word, Crawford alerts us to the exclusionary and bounded 'majoritarian' mode of legitimation which is likely to result from the particular effects of the dominant discourse on multi-agency 'community' crime prevention and community safety; not least leading to the demonization of the labelled 'other' and 'outsider'.

Most contemporary sociologists and criminologists are deeply sceptical about the use of appeals to community in crime control 'talk' and practice. According to Garland (1996), appeals to, and use of, community as a new means of 'governing' crime may again be best understood as part of the wider adaptation to the realization of high crime rates as a normal 'social fact' in late modernity. More than this, they are part of a 'responsibilization strategy' by means of which the state devolves responsibilities for crime prevention onto agencies, organizations, groups and individuals outside of the state and persuades them to act appropriately. According to this logic, the sources of crime and also the means of its control and prevention are viewed as lying in the behaviour and attitudes of individual citizens and their local communities.

However, this grand theoretical critique may be guilty of neglecting countervailing forces at work on the wider social fabric and of underplaying the possibility of 'unsettlements' of the state's dominant agenda on crime control. We may, for example, ask what of mobilization around community as symbolic of new resistances and solidarities in opposition to the central state's programme of popular penalism and 'privatized prudentialism'?

Despite the criticisms noted above, the idea that communities *do* have a key role to play in crime prevention remains influential in criminological circles. The argument that community 'breakdown' is a key contributing factor in patterns of rising crime and delinquency and claims that some communities are being excluded from 'mainstream' social life in a period of increased social polarization and greater social inequality remains a powerful one. Again, it is wise to be wary about the novelty of such ideas. The Chicago School in the USA in the 1920s and 1930s claimed to have identified a crucial link between the disorganized and disadvantaged community and the growth and sustenance of criminality.

Thus similar claims and arguments about community tend to re-occur in different historical contexts, highlighting the continuing potency of community ideas.

Gordon Hughes

Associated Concepts: Chicago School of Sociology, communitarianism, community justice, community safety, crime prevention, left realism, self-policing, social exclusion

Key Readings

Crawford, A. (1997) *The Local Governance of Crime.* Oxford, The Clarendon Press.

Garland, D. (1996) 'The limits of the sovereign state: strategies of crime control in contemporary society', *British Journal of Criminology*, 33 (4), pp. 445–71.

Hope, T. (1995) 'Community crime prevention' in M. Tonry and D. Farrington (eds), *Building a Safer Society: Strategic Approaches to Crime.* Chicago, University of Chicago Press.

Shaw, C. and McKay, H. (1969) *Juvenile Delinquency and Urban Areas.* Chicago, University of Chicago Press.

COMMUNITY JUSTICE

Definition

The term is deployed generally to describe a range of conflict resolution strategies, usually associated with informal, popular or restorative forms of justice.

Distinctive Features

The term 'community justice' has begun to enter the vocabulary of those who work with offenders and victims, although few are sure what it means (Nellis, 2000). That noted, the word has a long tradition in criminological thought, having been deployed in analyses of popular and informal justice. It is also particularly associated with abolitionist and communitarian perspectives/traditions in criminology (see Christie, 1977). The current, growing popularity of the term among practitioners and policy-makers is in part linked to the recognition that state-administered systems of justice are expensive, unduly bureaucratic and slow, individualized in their response to offenders and neglectful of the needs of victims and the wider community.

Abolitionists have long shared these misgivings but the main impulse of the abolitionist critique of traditional formal criminal justice is based on the criminalizing consequences of disintegrative shaming and retributive punishment and the failures of contemporary criminal justice policy owing to its overbearing reliance on imprisonment. Communitarians of different varieties share the abolitionist bias towards informal, reintegrative and educational solutions. However, they also openly accept that punishment is the inevitable concomitant of law enforcement with censure as a mostly legitimate response to wrong-doing; and with denunciation in the name of the victim and the common good as morally appropriate (Nellis, 2000).

The claims of community justice are also evident in populist law and order interpretations of the limitations of the formal and legalistic system of criminal justice. Vigilantism and public shaming are common expressions of this variant of the movement for community justice.

However, the contemporary appeal to community justice in criminal justice systems and for policy-makers and practitioners is based on less extreme criticisms of, and organizational departures from, formal, adversarial justice than that associated with either abolitionism or populist punitiveness. In effect, the practice of community justice is for the most part aimed at organizational reform of parts of the justice system which are viewed as failing due to high costs, poor coordination and lack of participation and involvement of lay actors in the process. There are clear parallels with the emergence of the strategy of multi-agency community safety and crime reduction. The actual claims for returning justice to the community (however defined) appear to have more to do with rhetoric and legitimation than actual practice. Instead, community justice as realized in specific criminal justice and social welfare systems tends to be a not so new or radical strategy based on multi-agency work with relatively low tariff offenders in which the active involvement of the victim, offender and other relevant members of the community is encouraged. Among the most influential examples of such institutional practices in contemporary societies are the 'reintegrative shaming' initiatives such as Family Group Conferences and sentencing circles and the widely used penalties such as community service orders for 'shallow end' offenders. Is it then mostly a 'rebranding' of the status quo? According to proponents of community justice, it offers to open up further possibilities, in ways that other terms and ideas do not. In particular, there is the hope that over time new practices might develop which will tilt the centre of gravity away from imprisonment and mass social exclusion and towards the creation of inclusive communities which would also be freer from crime (Nellis, 2000). Prime among these new possibilities are initiatives in restorative justice, such as reparation and compensation schemes and victim–offender mediation initiatives.

Evaluation

There are some important reservations to be made about the contemporary appeal to community and communal participation in criminal justice. Community justice initiatives have tended to define community loosely if at all and critics have noted the wide variety of forms that these initiatives often take. In particular, the dangers of populist appeals to a 'participatory' politics of enforcement in crime control are evident. The 'off-loading' by central government of crime control practices onto communities, however 'represented', does have its dangers for the central state, not least in the creation of volatile new spaces such as vigilantism. The rise of vigilantism is evident in the examples of 'communities' taking the law into their own hands against 'paedophiles' and 'persistent' offenders. We need to be wary of opening up criminal justice issues to democratic participation at precisely the moment when relations of trust between groups of citizens and between citizens and government have been at their weakest. In order to counteract the dangers of a reactionary and exclusivist moral majoritarian backlash against the criminalized, Jordan and Arnold (1995, p. 180) argue that 'balanced democratic governance may require the public power to repair social conflicts through actions in other spheres before attempting to open up criminal justice policy for public participation'. In other words, there may be a key role to be played by the state in healing the wounds in the social fabric by measures of social justice before 'the community' can be allowed to participate in an inclusive politics of crime control and social justice.

Gordon Hughes

Associated Concepts: abolitionism, communitarianism, community crime prevention, community safety, governmentality, redress, restorative justice, shaming

Key Readings

Christie, N. (1977) 'Conflicts as property', *British Journal of Criminology*, 17 (1), pp. 1–19.

Galaway, B. and Hudson, J. (1996) *Restorative Justice: International Perspectives.* Monsey, NY, Criminal Justice Press.

Jordan, B. and Arnold, J. (1995) 'Democracy and criminal justice', *Critical Social Policy*, 44/45, pp. 171–80.

Nellis, M. (2000) 'Creating community justice', in K. Pease, S. Ballintyne and V. McLaren (eds), *Key Issues in Crime Prevention, Crime Reduction and Community Safety.* London, IPPR.

COMMUNITY POLICING

Definition

A policing philosophy that promotes community-based problem-solving strategies to address the underlying causes of crime and disorder and the fear of crime. The stated intention of community policing is to enhance the quality of life of local communities.

Distinctive Features

Community policing is one of the most popular contemporary approaches to police work and has emerged in response to evidence that indicated that the police could not fight crime by themselves and increasingly conflictual relationships with minority ethnic communities. There is no general consensus as to what community policing actually entails and it can take various forms, for example 'team policing', 'foot patrol', 'problem oriented policing', 'neighbourhood policing', 'service-based policing', 'policing by consent'. It recognizes that effective police work is a collaborative effort between the police and the community and involves identifying the problems of crime and disorder that concern the community and attempts to include all sections of the community in the search for solutions to these problems. At the centre of community policing initiatives are localized policing, community partnerships and problem oriented approaches.

- Localized policing requires a process of organizational decentralization. Officers need to be assigned to the same beat and same shifts so that they can establish the trust and confidence of local people and secure an intimate day-to-day knowledge of local conditions. Officers also need to be given more operational freedom and uncommitted patrol time to tailor their work to local demands and optimize contact with the community.

- Forging meaningful partnerships with the community necessitates a degree of de-professionalization on the part of the police. Active community involvement in deliberations about police priorities obliges the police to be open about issues such as strategies and resourcing.
- Problem oriented policing identifies the underlying causes of crime and disorder that the community feels most strongly about and constructs tailor-made strategies that have the support of the community. It also enables police officers and communities to alter the conditions and circumstances that encourage criminal and disorderly behaviour.

Community policing holds out the promise of reduced levels of crime and disorder, improved quality of life for the community, enhanced relationships between the police and the community, a supportive environment for police operations and greater job satisfaction for police officers. The long-term aim is to produce strong self-sufficient communities that have the ability to protect themselves from crime and disorder. There is no single recipe for successful community policing but for it to work it requires the entire police force to shift to a broader conceptualization of police work and the transformation of the mindset of police officers of all ranks. The production of genuine community policing is not possible unless it is constructed within a framework of democratic accountability that necessitates service to communities rather than the state or the police bureaucracy. The radical implications of such a move mean that many police forces will continue to opt for a 'spray on', token version of community policing that leaves the hegemonic position of the police bureaucracy intact.

Eugene McLaughlin

Associated Concepts: 'broken windows', governmentality, problem oriented policing

Key Readings
Greene, J.R. and Mastrofski, S.D. (1991) *Community Policing: Rhetoric or Reality?* New York, Praeger Press.
Lyons, W. (1997) 'Reflections on power relations in community policing', in A. Sarat and S. Silbey (eds), *Studies in Law, Politics and Society*, Vol. 16, pp. 103–38. London, JAI.
McLaughlin, E. (1994) *Community, Policing and Accountability.* Aldershot, Gower.
Skogan, W.G. and Hartnet, S.M. (1997) *Community Policing: Chicago Style.* Oxford, Oxford University Press.
Trojanowiz, R.C. (1998) *Community Policing: A Contemporary Perspective.* New York, Anderson Publishing Co.
Watson, E.M., Stone, A. and Deluca, S.M. (1997) *Strategies for Community Policing.* New York, Prentice–Hall.

COMMUNITY SAFETY

Definition

The strategy which seeks to move beyond a police-driven crime prevention agenda, to involve other agencies and generate greater participation from all sections of the 'community'. It has been particularly associated with local 'partnership' strategies of crime and disorder reduction from local authorities. However, it is a capacious phrase which may also refer to strategies aimed at improving community safety from harms from all sources, not just those acts classifiable as 'crimes'.

Distinctive Features

By the 1990s community safety could be viewed as the 'rising' star of crime prevention. The use of this referent, rather than crime prevention, may reflect a diminished confidence in formal criminal justice agencies which, compared to the networks of civil society, have limited impact on patterns of crime. It also involves an expanded role to be played by an array of voluntary and commercial organizations and responsible ('responsibilized') individuals in 'partnership' with statutory agencies, all of which now represent a key feature of the politics of social defence in increasingly fearful and divided societies. The subtext of community safety then is that of a holistic, managerialist approach allied to the promotion of community activism and of a logic of responsibilization – with the consequence that blame is placed on fellow citizens rather than the wider social arrangements that generate harms. Multi-agency strategies of community safety are most pronounced in the UK, where they have become a statutory feature of local crime and disorder reduction policies. As legislated in the UK, it is merely a style of crime reduction/prevention – 'a synonym of crime prevention with fluffy overtones added' (Pease and Wiles, 2000).

More generally across the world, community safety also often appears to be a means by which many powerful sectional interests within civil society are able to 'lock', 'light' and 'zone' themselves out of harm's way, whilst areas blighted by de-industrialization and acute levels of victimization are least likely to have the material resources, political connections and the civic associations that meaningful community safety presupposes (Hope, 1995).

Viewed more broadly, community safety refers to the absence of likely or serious harms, whether caused by human agency or otherwise (Pease and Wiles, 2000). This pan-hazard paradigm offers a challenge to dominant, compartmentalized thinking about harms in which each agency seeks to reduce the harms traditionally central to its compartmental function. It is concerned with dangers from whatever source, not just crime but also, for example, traffic and transport, housing and working conditions. This approach to harm reduction and the promotion of public safety is not as yet common, necessarily involving what is often termed 'joined-up thinking'. It also necessitates sustained, multi-agency coordinated attention to access to, and delivery of, welfare and health services, educational and employment opportunities, as well as confronting institutionalized discrimination and vested power interests. But there are potential advantages of rethinking community safety as strategies aimed at the minimization of the number and seriousness of harms rather than focusing on crime prevention alone: not least so that serious harms caused by non-human agency may take their rightful place among reasons to be fearful (Pease and Wiles, 2000).

Evaluation

The debate on whether community safety and crime prevention amount to the same thing or whether they carry different connotative baggage is still nascent and unfinished. As Pease and Wiles note, community safety is a phrase to be preferred (over crime prevention and crime and disorder reduction) only if

safety refers to the likely absence of harms (particularly serious harms) from all sources, and not just from human acts classifiable as crimes. In particular this requires a shift of focus from that of the harming person to that of the harming circumstance. If used narrowly we are likely to see the emergence of double standards – whereby some of us are protected from attack by others while others of us choke on polluted air or are victimized as a result of inadequate protective building design.

Many academic commentators have sought to debunk the idea of community, on various counts (for being nebulous, nostalgic, intrinsically oppressive and so forth). According to many academic commentators, 'community safety' is at best a 'feel good' word marked by an extreme vagueness. It is generally seen to exist more happily at the level of rhetoric rather than practice where it is limited by some serious structural constraints (Gilling, 1997). Critics of community safety have also alerted us to the dangers of appeals to community in the politics of criminal justice and crime prevention, not least for the tendency to produce intolerance towards those viewed as 'outsiders'. But the idea of community also has a long association with the solidarity struggles of the weak and the poor. If it did not exist then it would need to be invented.

Community safety remains a 'wicked issue', not just for the challenges it raises for not easily compartmentalized practices and policies about harm reduction, but also for the theoretical, moral and political challenges associated with its nascent and contested agenda in the new governance of crimes and harms (Hughes, 2000).

Gordon Hughes

Associated Concepts: communitarianism, community crime prevention, community justice, left realism, multi-agency crime prevention, self-policing, social crime prevention, social harm

Key Readings

Hope, T. (1995) 'Community crime prevention', in M. Tonry and D. Farrington (eds), *Building a Safer Society*. Chicago, University of Chicago Press.
Hughes, G. (2000) 'In the shadow of crime and disorder: the contested politics of community safety', *Crime Prevention and Community Safety*, 2 (4), pp. 47–60.
Crawford, A. (1997) *Local Governance of Crime*. Oxford, The Clarendon Press.

Gilling, D. (1997) *Crime Prevention: Theory, Policy and Practice*. London, UCL Press.

Pease, K. and Wiles, P. (2000) 'Crime prevention and community safety: Tweedledum and Tweedledee?', in K. Pease, S. Ballintyne and V. McLaren (eds), *Key Issues in Crime Prevention, Crime Reduction and Community Safety*. London, IPPR.

COMMUNITY SENTENCES

Definition

Penalties, imposed on offenders by criminal courts, that do not involve imprisonment. These include various forms of reprimand, financial penalties, supervision and unpaid work and are sometimes referred to as 'non-custodial' sentences or 'alternatives to prison'.

Distinctive Features

Although community sentences vary around the world, it is possible to classify them in three ways: self-regulatory, financial and supervisory (Worrall, 1997). Self-regulatory penalties involve some form of public admonition or reprimand which is assumed to be sufficiently shaming of itself to deter the offender from further law-breaking. Financial penalties are of two kinds: fines are both retributive and deterrent in purpose and are generally paid to the central administration of a criminal justice system; compensation is paid (through the courts) to the victim of a crime and is intended to provide reparation. Supervisory sentences are imposed when courts believe that the offender is unable to stop committing crimes without support or surveillance and they may contain one or more of three elements: rehabilitation (through education, therapeutic programmes, counselling and welfare advice), reparation (through unpaid work for the community) and incapacitation (through curfews and electronic monitoring).

Some community sentences have long histories, while others have been introduced more recently. For example, in many countries, the origins of probation (the main form of supervision) can be traced back to the late nineteenth century, whereas community service (unpaid work) was introduced in the 1960s and 1970s and electronic monitoring in the 1980s.

Expansion in the use of supervisory sentences since the 1970s has been due to the desire of many governments to be seen to be finding less expensive, but equally demanding, alternatives to imprisonment. This has been termed the 'decarceration' debate and resulted from a loss of confidence in the 1950s and 1960s in the 'rehabilitative ideal' (based on the discredited therapeutic possibilities of institutions). In reality, such expansion has been an accompaniment, rather than an alternative, to a rising prison population.

Evaluation

Community sentences have many advantages over imprisonment. They allow offenders to retain family, work and social ties while, at the same time, giving them the opportunity to repair the damage they have done to the community and resolve the personal and social problems which may have led to their offending in the first place. They enable the offender to avoid the stigma of imprisonment and the risk of becoming embedded in a criminal culture as a result of constant association with other criminals in prison. Community sentences are also far less costly to administer than imprisonment.

Despite these advantages, community sentences have an 'image' problem. Although many more offenders receive some form of community sentence than are imprisoned, penal debates and policies focus overwhelmingly on prisons and neglect other forms of punishment. Attempts to raise the profile of community sentences encounter a number of obstacles.

First, and of most significance, is the public and media perception that community sentences are but a poor substitute for the 'real punishment' of prison. Viewed as 'soft options', community sentences are often represented in policy documents as weak and undemanding 'let offs', which do not command public confidence. There is, therefore, a constant search among advocates of community sentences to include more and more demanding conditions which distinguish 'intermediate sentences' (as they are sometimes called) from traditional welfare-oriented supervision (Byrne et al., 1992; Petersilia, 1998). Second is the obstacle of unfair and inconsistent sentencing. Despite increasingly sophisticated guidelines on the use of community sentences, there remain concerns that certain groups of offenders are over-represented in prison for reasons that may have little to do with the seriousness of their offences. Community sentences tend to be available only to the relatively advantaged socially – those with sufficient money to pay a fine, those who are employed and those who are perceived to be able to 'benefit' from supervision. Third is the obstacle of 'net-widening', a term which entered criminal justice vocabulary in the 1960s in the wake of labelling theory. With the proliferation of alternatives to custody comes the danger that instead of keeping people out of prison, community sentences will simply draw more and more people into the 'net' of the criminal justice system and thereby increase the likelihood that they will eventually end up in prison. With 'net-widening' comes the concept of the 'dispersal of discipline' (Cohen, 1985) which proposes that community sentences extend the restrictions of liberty experienced in prison to the community outside the prison walls. The electronic monitoring of offenders in their own homes is a concrete example of this concept. The fourth obstacle is that of enforcement. Ensuring compliance with community sentences is notoriously difficult and courts have the right to send to prison any offender who fails to pay a fine or who breaches the conditions of a supervisory order. In this way, community sentences always function 'in the shadow' of imprisonment.

Anne Worrall

Associated Concepts: community justice, decarceration, electronic monitoring, incapacitation, net widening, probation, rehabilitation, reparation, restorative justice, shaming

Key Readings

Brownlee, I. (1998) *Community Punishment: A Critical Introduction*. Harlow, Addison Wesley Longman.

Byrne, J.M., Lurigio, A.J. and Petersilia, J. (1992) *Smart Sentencing: The Emergence of Intermediate Sanctions*. London, Sage.

Cohen, S. (1985) *Visions of Social Control*. Cambridge, Polity Press.

Mair, G. (1997) 'Community penalties and the probation service', in M. Maguire, R. Morgan and R. Reiner (eds), *The Oxford Handbook of Criminology*, 2nd edn. Oxford, Oxford University Press.

Petersilia, J. (ed.) (1998) *Community Corrections*. Oxford, Oxford University Press.

Worrall, A. (1997) *Punishment in the Community: The Future of Criminal Justice*. Harlow, Addison Wesley Longman.

COMPARATIVE METHOD

Definition

The selection and analysis of cases which are similar in known ways and which differ in other ways, with a view to formulating or testing hypotheses.

Distinctive Features

The types of cases which are the basis for comparison can vary and can include individuals, groups, institutions, situations, cultures, geographical areas and time periods. Where different societies or cultures are compared it is common to refer to cross-cultural comparison. Comparison can be used both to develop and to test hypotheses.

One way of developing hypotheses is by the process of theoretical sampling, which is closely associated with qualitative, ethnographic research. This process involves the selection of cases for analysis (such as settings, groups or individuals) with a view to forming generalizations about how and why such cases differ. For example, it could involve the observation of beat police officers and criminal investigation officers in order to form generalizations about the differing ways in which they take decisions and the factors that influence decision-taking. Often comparison takes place by maximizing and minimizing differences, for example by ensuring that all the officers are of the same age, sex, social class and ethnic background whilst they differ in terms of the nature of their police role and police training. The process can be continuous as the researcher seeks out new cases and maximizes and minimizes other differences in order to modify and extend hypotheses. For example, this could involve comparing decision-making by beat and criminal investigation officers in both urban and rural areas. When no extra insight can be gained by further comparisons the stage of theoretical saturation has been reached. Another way of developing research questions or hypotheses is by the examination of 'deviant' or 'critical' cases in comparison with cases that are close to the norm. For example, this could involve the comparison of a geographical area that has an extremely high level of crime with areas that are close to the average in order to formulate generalizations about factors that can account for these differences of extreme.

Using comparison for hypothesis testing can be illustrated by forms of statistical analysis (although qualitative research also tests hypotheses, by using a process known as analytic induction). Assume that a researcher wishes to test a hypothesis that the level of crime in geographic areas is associated with levels of unemployment. This can be done by grouping areas according to their level of unemployment (high, medium, low). Each of the three categories of area will be measured in terms of their average level of crime and statistical tests can be applied in order to provide evidence as to whether differences between the areas are so substantial and significant that levels of crime must be associated with levels of unemployment (or vice versa).

The comparative method is reflected in different research styles. For example, the use of quasi-experimental or evaluative designs to assess policy initiatives involves the comparison of the two groups or areas, one of which receives the policy initiative whilst the other does not. The two groups are compared before and after the introduction of the initiative with regard to the feature at which the policy is aimed. This two-way comparison (of two groups on a before–after basis) facilitates some evaluation of the effectiveness of the policy initiative. The comparative method in social surveys is illustrated by the way in which categories of people in a sample (for example, men and women; old and young) are compared in terms of their having or not having an attribute (for example, a scale that measures 'fear of crime'). Qualitative, ethnographic work emphasizes the development of generalizations and of 'grounded theory' by the systematic comparisons of cases in terms of their similarities and their differences. The cases that are compared include interactions, social meanings, contexts, social actions and cultural groups. Because this is a continuous, rather than once and for all activity, it is sometimes referred to as the constant comparative method. Other methods to use comparison include content analysis (the comparison of documents), historical research (the comparison of historical periods) and analysis of official statistics (comparison of areas, groups or time period in terms of social indicators).

Comparison permeates different stages of research. For example, in research design it is illustrated in the ways in which samples are selected for study so as to compare subsets on some variables while holding others constant. At the analysis stage different areas or social groups can be compared on a variable at the same point in time (cross-sectional analysis) or the same areas or groups can be compared on a variable at different points in time (longitudinal analysis). Sometimes comparison takes place after publication of results from several researchers working independently, for example, in examining the conclusions of projects from different parts of the world to consider how different societies deal with domestic disputes. In other cases researchers from different countries collaborate to produce inter-societal comparisons (see, for example, Van Dijk et al., 1990: Mawby and Kirchoff, 1996).

Evaluation

Comparison is an essential part of research methodology. It involves deliberately seeking or anticipating comparisons between sets of observations. Without comparison with a baseline or against a control group it is not possible to reach plausible and credible conclusions. However, this requires the clear establishment of a baseline and the ability to control for factors the researcher does not wish to vary.

Victor Jupp

Associated Concepts: content analysis, ethnography, evaluation research, social survey

Key Readings
Mawby, R. and Kirchoff, G. (1996) 'Coping with crime: a comparison of victims' experiences in England and Germany', in P. Davies, P. Francis and V. Jupp (eds), *Understanding Victimization*. Newcastle, University of Northumbria Press.
May, T. (1997) *Social Research: Issues, Methods and Process*. Buckingham, Open University Press.
Van Dijk, J.J.M., Mayhew, P. and Killias, M. (1990) *Experiences from across the World: Key Findings of the 1989 International Crime Survey*. Deventer, Netherlands, Kluwer.

CONDITIONING

Definition

The processes by which an organism's behaviour is related to, or conditioned by, the environment; often used to mean *learning*.

Distinctive Features

In the history of psychology, the term conditioning is most closely associated with the Russian Nobel prizewinner Ivan Pavlov (1849–1936). Pavlov was a physiologist whose work was concerned with the canine digestive system: it was in the course of this experimental work that he observed an unusual pattern of salivation in dogs. Dogs naturally salivate at the sight of food (a reflex or *unconditioned response*), but Pavlov also observed that his dogs salivated at cues such as the sound of the food pails in the laboratory. Clearly, dogs are not born with the capacity to salivate at the sound of clanking metal, so there must be another explanation for their behaviour. In a series of famous experimental studies Pavlov established that it was the close temporal pairing of sound and the appearance of food that elicited the wayward salivation. In other words, the sound became associated with the food, so that the sound elicited the animal's behaviour. Thus, the salivation had become conditional to the sound and so could be thought of as a *conditioned response*. This process of learning by association is called *classical conditioning*.

The concept of classical conditioning is fundamentally important in advancing the position that the origins of behaviour lie not within the organism but are located in the environment. Thus, the way in which a person behaves can be understood by reference to that person's environment rather than the person's inner world.

The discovery of the phenomenon of learning by association surfaced alongside the emergent discipline of psychology in American universities in the early 1900s. At that time psychology in Europe was dominated by Freudian theory, so perhaps it is not surprising that the emerging New World departments of psychology searched for a fresh theoretical paradigm. The key figure in the struggle for this new paradigm was the academic researcher John B. Watson (1878–1958). Watson rejected the non-scientific theories prevalent in Europe and looked to formulate a new basis for psychology. In Watson's vision the task would be to understand behaviour, not by drawing on the ghost in the machine of psychodynamic forces and the niceties of philosophical debate, but by producing empirical evidence firmly based within a scientific tradition. Such an experimental approach to psychology would be informed by evolutionary biology, neuroscience and the principles of conditioning.

The focus of this endeavour would be behaviour, and the work of Pavlov and his contemporaries would be the starting point. Watson's position, expounded in a classic paper published in 1913, *Psychology as the Behaviorist Views It*, finally gave behaviourism to the academic world.

Can behaviour really be viewed as a string of classically conditioned responses? B.F. Skinner (1904–90) took Watson's vision and developed behaviourism into a dominant force in psychological method and thought. Acknowledging the role of learning by association, Skinner's significant contribution was to cultivate the notion of learning through the consequences of behaviour, and hence to the unfolding of *radical behaviourism*. Simply, Skinner's experimental work demonstrated that as behaviour acts upon the environment, the resultant environmental consequences of that behaviour then act to increase or decrease the probability of future instances of such behaviour. A behaviour that produces consequences that the individual finds rewarding and increase the rate of behaviour is said to be *reinforced*; a behaviour that produces consequences that the individual finds aversive and decrease the rate of behaviour is said to be *punished*. (In the technical sense used here, punishment simply means that a behaviour decreases in frequency.) Further, the organism learns that the environmental conditions, or setting events, signal the likelihood that a certain behaviour will produce certain consequences. The relationship between a setting event, the behaviour and its consequences is called a three-term contingency. The process of learning through consequences is referred to as *operant* (or *instrumental*) *conditioning*.

In operant conditioning, behaviour is understood in terms of an interaction between the person and the environment. The environment influences the person and the person influences the environment. The range of environmental influences on our behaviour is vast: the list would encompass political, economic, educational and legal systems, images in the popular media, and the words and actions of friends, peers, and parents. All of these environmental forces, to a greater or lesser extent, shape our behaviour; our behaviour, to a greater or lesser extent, moulds the world in which we live.

Evaluation

The notion of conditioning received a bad press in novels such as *Brave New World* and

Clockwork Orange, which to some extent influenced popular views of the motives of advocates of theories of conditioning. Indeed, several academic and professional commentators have dismissed theories of learning by impugning the characters of their proponents. It is noticeable that since Skinner's death several texts have attempted to give a more rounded picture of behaviourism (Nye, 1992; O'Donohue and Kitchener, 1999).

There are two critical lines to consider in the evaluation of conditioning. First, the rejection of mentalism as an explanatory concept, with the associated forsaking of free will as a vehicle for accounting for human actions. Second, the gap in understanding, at a psychological and physiological level, of the way in which conditioning takes place.

Clive Hollin

Associated Concepts: behaviour modification, differential association, free will, opportunity theory, personality theory, rational choice theory, social learning theory

Key Readings

Bjork, D.W. (1993) *B.F. Skinner: A Life*. New York, Basic Books.
Davey, G. (ed.) (1981) *Applications of Conditioning Theory*. London, Methuen.
Lee, V.L. (1988) *Beyond Behaviorism*. Hillsdale, Lawrence Erlbaum.
Nye, R.D. (1992) *The Legacy of B.F. Skinner: Concepts and Perspectives, Controversies and Misunderstandings*. Belmont, Wadsworth.
O'Donohue, W. and Kitchener, R. (eds) (1999) *Handbook of Behaviorism*. San Diego, Academic Press.
Watson, J.B. (1913) 'Psychology as the behaviorist views it', *Psychological Review*, 20, pp. 158–77.

CONFLICT THEORY

Definition

Conflict theory is usually contrasted with positivism or those theories that assume that a basic consensus exists in society. It has taken three major forms. *Culture conflict* theory focuses on clashes between conduct norms. *Group conflict* theory relates such clashes directly to the position of elites and the wielding of political power. *Class conflict* theory views power differentials in the context of the systematic generation of structured inequalities in capitalist societies. All stress that to understand crime we must also understand the interests served by criminal law and the way in which those in authority use their power.

Distinctive Features

According to consensus theory, society is held together by a common acceptance of such basic values as right and wrong. Because of this common agreement social order is largely harmonious and predictable. On the other hand, conflict theory argues that there is little agreement on basic values. Society is composed of many competing groups, each of which promotes different interests. Conflict, rather than stability, is the fundamental characteristic of social order. Power and authority are reflections of social, economic and political inequality. Law is a means the powerful use to enforce their own interests at the expense of others.

Thorsten Sellin (1938) was the first to argue that conflict causes crime. He noted that modern societies were characterized by social anonymity, poorly defined personal relationships and the existence of a wide variety of competing groups, which meant that however certain groups behaved they would always violate the norms of some other group. Crime occurs when the law of one group is extended to cover the domain of another (as in cultural migration) and when differentiation occurs within one group (as in disputes over law enforcement). The conduct which the state denotes as criminal is related directly to the decisions of those who wield political power and control the legislative and judicial manifestations of authority. George Vold (1958) extended this analysis through the concepts of 'group conflict' and 'political organization'. He argued that groups conflict with each other when the goals of one can be achieved only at the expense of others. Each of many interest groups attempts to secure its own interests by lobbying the legislature to enact laws in their favour. Groups that are able to do so curb the behaviour of competing groups. As a result the process of law-making, law-breaking and law enforcement is a direct reflection of fundamental conflicts between interest groups and the relative power that they hold. Patterns of criminalization reflect the different degrees of political power wielded by different social groups. Criminality becomes a normal and natural response of groups struggling to maintain their own way of life.

During the 1960s several criminologists, also influenced by labelling, further refined criminological conflict theory. In the USA Austin Turk (1969) developed the thesis by accounting for specific processes of criminalization in societies based on relationships of conflict, domination and subordination between authorities and subjects. Richard Quinney's early work (1970) set out a number of propositions to establish the social reality of crime. Crime was defined as human conduct created by authorized agents in a politically organized society. Criminal definitions describe behaviours that conflict with the interests of those with the power to shape public policy. The social reality of crime is constructed by the formulation and application of criminal definitions by 'certain social segments', their diffusion within the rest of society, the development of behaviour patterns related to criminal definitions and the construction of criminal conceptions. As such, the defining quality of crime lies not in criminal behaviour but in the power to criminalize. The greater the social conflict the more likely that the powerful will criminalize the behaviour of those who challenge their interests.

Chambliss (1975) and Quinney in his later work (1974) subsequently developed conflict theory by relating such pluralist notions as 'social segments' to specific class divisions and specific modes of economic production. Class conflict theory, derived from Marxism, included the premises that:

- Acts are defined as criminal because it is in the interest of the ruling class to define them as such.
- The ruling class will violate laws with impunity while members of the subject classes will be punished.
- Criminal behaviour is a consequence of the repression and brutalization of capitalism.
- Criminal law is an instrument of the state to maintain the existing social order.
- Crime diverts the working class's attention from the exploitation they experience; it contains their resistance.
- Crime will persist in capitalist societies because of the fundamental tendency of such societies to promote inequality and class conflict.

In these ways, conflict theory has produced a series of complex analyses of why certain behaviours are criminalized by the state while others are not, and how a capitalist economic system itself is capable of generating certain patterns of crime.

Evaluation

Conflict theory has taken many forms within the rubric that conflict is natural to society. Initial formulations adopted an interactionist or pluralist view of conflicting interest groups; later formulations, influenced by Marxism or political anarchism, have emphasized the centrality of structured class inequalities and ruling class power. The heyday of conflict theory was in the political turmoil of 1960s and 1970s America. By the mid-1970s it was largely superseded by the New Criminology and critical criminology developed in the UK. Its key propositions that law always arises from conflict and that criminalization always serves the interests of the ruling class have been severely tested. Such a priori generalizations have either been outrightly rejected by neo-conservative criminology or critiqued by critical criminology as one-dimensional and deterministic. Conflict theory tends to view the relationship between power and consciousness as relatively simple. It suggests that crime only exists when it is recognized by the powerful or when one is in a position of disadvantage in an unequal society. It fails to grasp adequately the fluidity and negotiation of class relations, whilst more or less ignoring those of 'race' and gender. But whatever its limitations its lasting legacy is to have started the process of politicizing criminology; turning attention to the fact that the study of crime cannot adequately proceed in isolation from the study of criminal law.

John Muncie

Associated Concepts: criminalization, critical criminology, interactionism, labelling, Marxist criminologies, new criminology, radical criminologies, the state

Key Readings

Chambliss, W. (1975) 'Toward a political economy of crime', *Theory and Society*, 2, pp. 149–70.

Quinney, R. (1970) *The Social Reality of Crime*. Boston, Little, Brown.

Quinney, R. (1974) *Critique of the Legal Order*. Boston, Little, Brown.

Sellin, T. (1938) *Culture Conflict and Crime*. New York, Social Science Research Council.

Turk, A. (1969) *Criminality and Legal Order*. Chicago, Rand McNally.

Vold, G. (1958) *Theoretical Criminology*. New York, Oxford University Press.

CONFORMITY

See Social control theory

CONSTITUTIVE CRIMINOLOGY

Definition

Constitutive criminology is a postmodernist theoretical perspective that draws on several critical social theories, most notably symbolic interactionism, phenomenology, social constructionism, structural Marxism, structuration theory, semiotics, chaos theory and affirmative postmodernism. The core of the constitutive argument is that crime and its control cannot be separated from the totality of the structural and cultural contexts in which it is produced, nor can it lose sight of human agents' contribution to those contexts (Henry and Milovanovic, 1994, 1996).

Distinctive Features

Constitutive theory rejects the argument of traditional modernist criminology that crime and offenders can be separated from social processes of societal production and analysed and corrected in isolation from the whole. Nor is crime understandable as a determined product of cultures and structures. Instead of setting out to identify factors that 'cause' offending, constitutive criminology seeks to examine the relations that co-produce crime.

Constitutive criminology is founded on the proposition that humans are responsible for actively creating their world with others. They do this by transforming their surroundings through interaction with others, not least via discourse. Through language and symbolic representation humans identify differences, construct categories, and share a belief in the reality of that which is constructed that orders otherwise chaotic states. It is towards these social constructions of reality that humans act.

In the process of investing energy in their socially constructed, discursively organized categories of order and reality, human subjects not only shape their social world, but are also shaped by it. They are co-producers and co-productions of their own and others' agency. Constitutive criminology is about how some of this socially constructed order, as well as some of the human subjects constituted within it, can be harmed, impaired and destroyed by both the process, and by what is built during that process: ultimately by each other as fellow subjects.

Constitutive theorists argue that the co-production of harmful relations occurs through society's structure and culture, as these are energized by active human subjects – not only as offenders, but also as the social categories such as victims, criminal justice practitioners, academics, commentators, media reporters and producers of film and TV crime shows, and most generally, as investors, producers and consumers in the crime business. They look at what it is about the psycho-socio-cultural matrix (the cloth of crime) that provides the discursive medium through which human agents construct 'meaningful' harms to others. The approach taken, therefore, shifts the criminological focus away from narrow dichotomized issues focusing either on the individual offender or on the social environment. Instead, constitutive criminology takes a holistic conception of the relationship between the 'individual' and 'society' which prioritizes neither one nor the other, but examines their mutuality and interrelationship.

According to constitutive criminologists, a major source of harmful relations emanates from structures of power. Unequal power relations, built on the constructions of difference, provide the conditions that define crime as harm. Constitutive criminology defines crime as the harm resulting from humans investing energy in harm-producing relations of power. Humans suffering such 'crimes' are in relations of inequality. Crimes are nothing less than people being disrespected. People are disrespected in numerous ways but all have to do with denying or preventing us becoming fully social beings. What is human is to make a difference to the world, to act on it, to interact with others and together to transform environment and ourselves. If this process is prevented we become less than human; we are harmed. Thus constitutive criminologists define crime as 'the power to deny others their ability to make a difference' (Henry and Milovanovic, 1996, p. 116).

Constitutive criminology also has a different definition of criminals and victims from that of modernist criminological theories. The offender is viewed as an 'excessive investor' in the power to dominate others. Such 'investors' put energy into creating and magnifying differences between themselves and others. This investment of energy disadvantages, disables and destroys others' human potentialities. The victim is viewed as a 'recovering subject', still with untapped human potential but with a damaged faith in humanity. Victims are more entrenched, more disabled, and suffer loss. Victims 'suffer the pain of being denied their own humanity, the power to make a difference. The victim of crime is thus rendered a non-person, a non-human, or less complete being' (Henry and Milovanovic, 1996, p. 116).

This reconception of crime, offender and victim thus locates criminality not in the person, nor in the structure or culture but in the ongoing creation of social identities through discourse and leads to a different notion of crime causation. To the constitutive theorist crime is not so much *caused* as *discursively constructed* through human processes of which it is one. Consciously striving to reconstruct the discourse of the excessive investor at both a societal and a systemic level, crime feeds off itself, expanding and consuming the energies intended to control it. Put simply, crime is the co-produced outcome, not only of humans and their environment, but of human agents and the wider society through its excessive investment, to the point of obsession, in crime, through crime shows, crime drama, crime documentaries, crime news, crime books, crime films, crime precautions, criminal justice agencies, criminal lawyers and criminologists. All are parasitic of the crime problem, but as constitutive criminology suggests, they also contribute to its ongoing social and cultural production and ongoing reproduction.

Evaluation

The implications of constitutive theory are, first that crime must be deconstructed as a recurrent discursive process, and second, that conscious attempts must be made at reconstruction with a view to preventing recurrence. Given this interrelated nature of social structures and human agents and their social and cultural productions in the co-production of crime, constitutive criminology calls for a justice policy of reconstruction. This is achieved through *replacement discourse* which 'is directed toward the dual process of deconstructing prevailing structures of meaning and displacing them with new conceptions, distinctions, words and phrases, which convey alternative meanings . . . Replacement discourse, then, is not simply critical and oppositional, but provides both a critique and an alternative vision' (Henry and Milovanovic, 1996, pp. 204–5). The new replacement constructions are designed to displace crime as moments in the exercise of power and as control. They offer an alternative medium by which social constructions of reality can take place. This is not a unitary medium but, as Smart (1990, p. 82) has argued, refers instead to 'subjugated knowledges, which tell different stories and have different specificities' and which aim at 'the deconstruction of truth' and the power effects of claims to truth. Instead of replacing one truth with another, replacement discourse invokes a 'multiplicity of resistances' to the ubiquity of power (1990, p. 82). Beyond resistances, the concept of replacement discourse offers a celebration of unofficial, informal, discounted and ignored knowledges through its discursive diversity. In terms of diminishing the harm experienced from all types of crime (street, corporate, state, hate etc.), constitutive criminology talks of 'liberating' replacement discourses that seek transformation of both the prevailing political economies and the associated practices of crime and social control. Constitutive criminology thus simultaneously argues for ideological as well as materialistic change; one without the other renders change only in part. In short, constitutive criminology argues for a transpraxis which is deconstructive, reconstructive and sensitive to the dialectics of struggle.

Stuart Henry and Dragan Milovanovic

Associated Concepts: chaos theory, crime, deconstruction, Marxist criminologies, newsmaking criminology, postmodernism, praxis, social harm

Key Readings

Barak, G. (1994) *Media Process and the Social Construction of Crime: Studies in Newsmaking Criminology*. New York, Garland.

Henry, S. and Milovanovic, D. (1994) 'The constitution of constitutive criminology', in D. Nelken (ed.), *The Futures of Criminology*. London, Sage.

Henry, S. and Milovanovic, D. (1996) *Constitutive Criminology: Beyond Postmodernism*. London, Sage.

Henry, S. and Milovanovic, D. (eds) (1999) *Constitutive Criminology at Work: Applications to Crime and Punishment*. New York, State University of New York Press.

Smart, C. (1990) 'Feminist approaches to criminology, or postmodern woman meets atavistic man', in L. Gelsthorpe and A. Morris (eds), *Feminist Perspectives in Criminology*. Milton Keynes, Open University Press, pp. 70–84.

CONTAINMENT THEORY

Definition

Developed by Walter Reckless in the 1950s, this social-psychological approach to understanding the causes of crime and conformity falls under the more general heading of social control theories. The main assumption is that strong inner controls (especially a positive self-concept) and outer controls (particularly the family) act to insulate or buffer adolescents from delinquency.

Distinctive Features

Containment theory is one of a number of related social control explanations that depict how social-psychological factors as well as social institutions restrain individuals from violating societal norms. Reckless (1967) is credited with developing this theoretical approach during the 1950s and 1960s. As one of the earlier social control theorists, he was curious as to why some boys in high crime neighbourhoods did not break the law. He speculated that a positive self-concept or attitude (inner containment) was the key variable that could explain why some boys did not turn to crime even in the face of outside or external pressures, especially delinquent peers.

Reckless divided explanatory factors into two general categories: those that are either 'inner' or 'outer' to the individual psyche, and those variables that act as either criminogenic or controlling behavioural influences. Inner containment and pushes are internal social-psychological influences, whereas outer containments, pressures and pulls are external to the individual. Inner and outer containments act as defences against deviation, thus insulating or buffering a youth from the criminogenic influences of society's pushes and pulls.

Inner pushes are social-psychological states and include such factors as a need for immediate gratification, hostility, restlessness, discontent, alienation and frustration. *External pressures and pulls* include deviant companions, membership in criminal subcultures, poverty, unemployment, limited occupational opportunities, minority status, and other inequalities.

Outer containments are external to the individual psyche or personality and act as buffers or insulators, encouraging conformity to community and legal norms. External controls include effective parental supervision and discipline, conforming or positive peer influences, memberships in organizations interested in the activities of their members, etc. *Inner containments* are self-controls that develop during socialization and include such components as a good self-concept, goal directedness, a well-developed superego, and high frustration tolerance. Inner containment is also generally seen as a product of favourable external socializing agencies such as teachers, peers and especially parents.

Although both inner and outer containments comprise defences against deviance, inner containments (especially a positive self-concept) received the most theoretical and empirical attention from Reckless and his associate Dinitz (1967). Together they spent over a decade investigating the effects of inner containment, concluding that a precondition of conforming behaviour is a positive self-concept which acts as an insulator against delinquency. Indeed, they argued that youths growing up even in the most criminogenic areas can insulate themselves against deviance through the maintenance of what they considered to be the strongest defence against delinquency – a positive self-concept.

If a youth's outer containments are weak, the internal and external pressures and pulls must be controlled by the inner control system. On the other hand, if the outer buffers are strong and effective, the inner containment system does not have to play such a significant role. Thus, Reckless believed that strong inner containments could compensate for weak outer containments, and vice versa. Reckless's 'Prediction Model' specified that deviance is greatest when both inner and outer controls are weak and lowest when both control systems are strong. In those instances in which one is weak and the other strong, he believed that weak inner containment has a higher probability of criminality than weak outer containment.

Evaluation

Despite claims by Reckless that containment theory explains most forms of delinquency, that it is both social and psychological in nature, and that unlike most other (macro) theories it can be used to explain individual case histories, the theory has been harshly criticized. Many consider its concepts too vague and the theory too broad to produce testable hypotheses. No conceptual information is offered concerning the interrelations among delinquency and the various combinations of inner and outer containment and environmental pressures, pushes and pulls. Accordingly, no interactions are hypothesized among inner and outer containments, pushes and pulls. Jensen (1970) points out that, other than his rather vaguely stated 'prediction model', Reckless's theory appears to be little more than an inadequate classification scheme, since apparently there is no rationale for classifying its variables as pushes, pulls, or inner and outer containments other than in terms of the behaviours to be explained.

Although differential involvement in delinquency is explained somewhat differently by the various social control theories, there is much conceptual overlap between Reckless and subsequent theorists such as Hirschi (1969). For example, 'delinquent companions' (environmental pulls or attachments), 'conventional activities' (outer containment or involvement), 'educational expectations' (inner containment or commitment), and 'attitudes toward the law' (inner containment or belief) are variables and concepts that are integral to both theories (Rankin, 1977).

Nevertheless, Reckless's theory has been criticized as conceptually vague, with little empirical evidence that a positive self-concept or self-esteem is negatively related to crime and delinquency. In addition, Reckless did not explain *why* a negative self-concept makes adolescents vulnerable to delinquency – nor could he account for those adolescents with bad self-concepts who were not delinquent. A number of research studies found little association between self-esteem and delinquency – a finding contrary to the key containment hypothesis. Thus, the main flaw of containment theory is the lack of empirical evidence linking this concept to crime and delinquency. This has led to containment theory being superseded by subsequent social control theories, especially Hirschi's (1969) theory of the social bond.

Joseph Rankin and Roger Kern

Associated Concepts: neutralization (techniques of), social control theory

Key Readings

Hirschi, T. (1969) *Causes of Delinquency.* Berkeley, CA: University of California Press.
Jensen, G. (1970) 'Containment and delinquency: analysis of a theory', *University of Washington Journal of Sociology,* 2, pp. 1–14.
Rankin, J. (1977) 'Investigating the interrelations among social control variables and conformity', *Journal of Criminal Law and Criminology,* 67, pp. 470–80.
Reckless, W. (1967) *The Crime Problem.* New York, Appleton–Century–Crofts.
Reckless, W. and Dinitz, S. (1967) 'Pioneering with self-concept as a vulnerability factor in delinquency', *Journal of Criminal Law, Criminology and Police Science,* 58, pp. 515–23.

CONTENT ANALYSIS

Definition

Content analysis is a strategy of research which stresses the objective, systematic and quantitative approach to the analysis of documents. Typically, it is concerned with the manifest content and surface meaning of a document rather than with deeper layers of meanings or with differing interpretations which can be placed on the same content.

Distinctive Features

In its widest sense, content analysis can refer to the analysis of the content of all types of document by whatever means. The range of documents examined by criminologists can include diaries, letters, newspapers, magazines, stories, essays, official documents, memoranda and research reports. Here, content analysis is used in a specific sense to refer to the positivist approach to documentary analysis which, according to Holsti (1969), has the following features. First, the procedures should be objective in that each step in the research process should be carried out on the basis of explicitly formulated rules so that different researchers following the same procedures will get the same results. Secondly, procedures must be systematic, that is, rules must be applied with consistency. Thirdly, content analysis should have generality, by which is meant that findings must have theoretical relevance. Fourthly, content analysis should be quantitative and include counting the frequency with which certain words or themes appear in documents. Finally, content analysis should be concerned with the manifest content and surface meaning of a text rather than with deeper layers of meaning.

Typically, research designs cluster around one or more of the following questions: What are the characteristics of the content? What inferences can be made about the causes and generation of content? What inferences can be made about the effects of content on readers or viewers? For example, in characterizing the films watched by adolescents the researcher may categorize them as 'high', 'medium' or 'low' in terms of violence by counting the number of actions in each film which s/he defines as 'violent'. Or research on the images of youth portrayed by popular newspapers may categorize and count the number of articles which portray a 'positive', 'negative' or 'neutral' image. In such cases, the definition of the relevant categories comes from the researcher. Once the categories are delineated, the analysis of content is often a technical process and may be carried out by appropriate computer software.

Evaluation

The positivist approach to content analysis emphasizes the manifest contents of documents which are subsequently categorized according to definitions provided by the researcher. The latent meanings of the content and the possibility of differing interpretations by 'producers' and 'receivers' are not treated as problematic nor as a prime focus of interest. By way of contrast, an interpretative (or interactionist) approach places social meanings at the centre of any analysis, that is, meanings attributed to the contents of documents by producers and by the variety of audiences. In doing so, the interpretative tradition is at odds with the positivist assumptions of a correspondence between intent, content and effect on different audiences and also at odds with the belief that there is a common universe of meanings uniting all relevant parties. What the interpretative tradition brings to the research agenda is a focus on the ways in which meanings are assigned both by authors and audiences, and the subsequent consequences. It would, for example, be interested in the ways in which the same documents placed before a court of law can be interpreted differently by defendants, prosecutors, jurors and judge. The interpretative approach to documents is very close to the ethnographic tradition in social research.

Whilst accepting the possibility of a multiplicity of meanings and interpretations, the critical tradition adds further dimensions, for example by examining the ways in which the contents of documents come to be treated as 'knowledge' and also the role of such knowledge in the exercise of power. This could be at a societal level, by analysing the ways in which official reports define certain forms of action as illegitimate and thereby justify the exercise of state power against certain sections of society; or it can be at a micro level, by analysing the ways in which police and probation records result in the ways in which an individual is dealt with in the criminal justice system.

Victor Jupp

Associated Concepts: documentary analysis, ethnography, interactionism, positivism

Key Readings

Holsti, O.R. (1969) *Content Analysis for the Social Sciences and Humanities*. Reading, MA, Addison–Wesley.

Jupp, V.R. and Norris, C. (1993) 'Traditions in documentary analysis', in M. Hammersley (ed.), *Social Research: Philosophy, Politics and Practice*. London, Sage.

Scott, J. (1990) *A Matter of Record*. Cambridge, Polity Press.

CONTROL THEORY

See Social control theory

CONVERSATIONAL ANALYSIS

Definition

A research methodology in the social sciences which analyses naturally occurring conversation systematically, using tape recordings and transcripts. It aims to 'describe people's methods for producing orderly social interaction' (Silverman, 1993, p. 120).

Distinctive Features

Conversational analysis is one particular research technique associated with the broader research perspective of ethnomethodology, which emerged in the 1960s as a reaction against the 'grand theorizing' and 'abstracted empiricism' of earlier sociologists such as Talcott Parsons (Heritage, 1984). Ethnomethodology emphasizes the importance of studying the ways in which people routinely ascribe meaning to daily events in specific, local social contexts. Consequently, the ways in which people talk to each other become worthy of study in their own right. This emphasis on naturally occurring speech counteracted previous preferences for researcher-dominated methods such as structured interviews, observation or experimental manipulation of behaviour. All these approaches, it was argued, produced only 'glossed' or idealized interpretations of how research subjects presented themselves within a pre-conceived theoretical framework and denied the researcher access to the genuinely 'raw' data of mundane social interaction.

The underlying assumptions of conversational analysis are that spoken interaction is organized in identifiable, stable structural patterns and that its meaning is dependent on its context. Therefore, it is not possible to engage in a priori theoretical construction or interpretation of motives or meaning, in the absence of detailed examination of actual conversation. It is also important that no aspect of the conversation (for example, pauses or overlapping speech) should be dismissed as irrelevant. For this reason, conversations must be tape recorded and later transcripts must include every detail of the process, rather than being 'tidied up' versions of interviews. Analysis of transcripts involves close attention to sequencing, timed intervals and the characteristics of speech production such as volume, emphasis and intonation. These features are indicated by the use of written symbols which constitute the agreed conventions of conversational analysis (Ten Have, 1999).

The core tool of conversational analysis is the concept of the 'adjacency pair', a term used by Harvey Sacks (Heritage, 1984) to describe a sequence of two utterances which are adjacent, produced by different speakers, ordered as a first and second part and in such a way as the first part requires a particular second part. Examples of common adjacent pairs are 'question–answer', 'greeting–greeting', 'offer–acceptance/refusal'. The concept of the 'adjacency pair' is a template not only for describing conversational action but also for interpreting it. It can be used to demonstrate how the first speaker uses his or her action as the basis for interpreting the second speaker's

response – and how the second speaker then continues the process. This sequencing leads on to the other key aspect of conversational analysis which concerns the obligations of participants to listen, understand and turn-take. Turn-taking is viewed as the mechanism by which actors display to each other that they are engaged in social interaction. Violation of turn-taking (for example by interrupting, 'talking over' someone or failing to respond to an invitation to speak) indicates a failure of social competence. Conversational analysis is also interested in 'lexical choice' – the words and descriptive terms which speakers select in differing contexts – and in 'interactional asymmetries'. Heritage (1997) identifies four potential sources of asymmetry which may exist between participants in institutional talk – inequalities of status, 'know-how' (that is, understanding of the institution), knowledge and rights to knowledge. All these factors would shape, and would be detectable in, any conversation between, for example, a magistrate, a solicitor and a defendant in court.

Evaluation

Although conversational analysis is a useful tool for studying ordinary interactions in a variety of criminologically relevant situations, it may be of particular value in the study of 'institutional talk'. Here, an understanding of the basic structures and sequences of conversation can be extended to an understanding of how criminal justice institutions, such as courts and prisons, function (Atkinson and Drew, 1979). Of particular interest are the ways in which professionals routinely legitimate, or account for their actions. However, conversational analysis is a highly technical methodology which is not readily accessible to novice researchers. Of more practical use may be the similar, but broader and less technical approach of discourse analysis.

Anne Worrall

Associated Concepts: discourse analysis, ethnography

Key Readings
Atkinson, J.M. (1982) 'Understanding formality: the categorization and production of "formal" interaction', British Journal of Sociology, 33, pp. 86–117.
Atkinson, J.M. and Drew, P. (1979) Order in Court: The Organization of Verbal Interaction in Judicial Settings. London, Macmillan.

Heritage, J. (1984) *Garfinkel and Ethnomethodology*. Cambridge, Polity Press.

Heritage, J. (1997) 'Conversation analysis and institutional talk', in D. Silverman (ed.), *Qualitative Research: Theory, Methods and Practice*. London, Sage.

Silverman, D. (1993) *Interpreting Qualitative Data: Methods for Analysing Talk, Text and Interaction*. London, Sage.

Ten Have, P. (1999) *Doing Conversation Analysis: A Practical Guide*. London, Sage.

CORPORATE CRIME

Definition

Illegal acts or omissions, punishable by the state under administrative, civil or criminal law, which are the result of deliberate decision-making or culpable negligence within a legitimate formal organization. These acts or omissions are based in legitimate, formal, business organizations, made in accordance with the normative goals, standard operating procedures, and/or cultural norms of the organization, and are intended to benefit the corporation itself.

Distinctive Features

Attention to corporate crime has a long tradition traceable back to the work of Bonger in Western Europe and Ross in the USA in the early 1900s. With Sutherland's pathbreaking work in the 1940s, the phenomenon of corporate crime received greater prominence, but also came to be conflated with the concept of white collar crime, a conflation which remains problematic (Nelken, 1994). A recent, significant stage in conceptual clarification was the distinction between 'occupational' and 'organizational' crimes (Slapper and Tombs, 1999, pp. 15–18).

Much research into corporate crime has sought to overcome the absence of utilizable official statistics in almost all national jurisdictions by documenting the scale of such offending. Further, quantitative corporate crime research using large data sets, typically focusing upon the largest corporations such as the Fortune 500 in the USA (Sutherland, 1983; Clinard and Yeager, 1980), has sought to isolate empirical correlates of offending, such as industry, size, profitability and so on. Findings from such empirical efforts remain

contentious, save for the overwhelming conclusion that offending is widespread and pervasive. Various strands of qualitative work have also been undertaken around corporate crime. One focus has been case studies of a particular event, very often with a view to determining via social science that a particular corporate activity constitutes illegality in the absence of any successful legal action. Much academic work has also been devoted to specific types or categories of crime, most notably around financial crimes, crimes committed directly against consumers, crimes arising directly out of the employment relationship and crimes against the environment. Finally, there have been several industry-specific case studies, notably in the car, chemicals, financial services, oil, and pharmaceuticals sectors. Taken together, these bodies of work demonstrate the scale and pervasiveness of corporate crimes across societies, and support the now almost universally accepted claim that the economic (not to mention physical and social) costs of corporate offending far outweigh those associated with 'conventional' or 'street' offending.

Much of this work has proceeded either at the margins of, or beyond, criminology. This is partially explained by the fact that criminology remains wedded to state-defined crime and criminal law, each of which are largely understood in individualistic and inter-personal terms; it is little surprise that much work around corporate crime has hailed from critical criminologies, which are based upon a commitment to a critique of dominant definitions of crime and criminal law, while at the same time examining processes of criminalization (and, by implication, noncriminalization). Corporate crime research also faces enormous methodological difficulties, may be relatively unattractive to the funders of research and is unlikely to produce immediately utilizable policy proposals: all of which may further explain its relative omission from dominant criminological agendas.

Evaluation

Conceptual disputes as to what constitutes corporate crime continue, many pursuing classic disputes as to the 'proper' domain of criminology. One consequence of the relative marginality of corporate crime research to criminology remains theoretical underdevelopment around this concept. Moreover, the field of corporate crime has constantly suffered from problems of legitimacy, not least because of its extensions of the term 'crime' to those acts or omissions punishable beyond the criminal law and, secondly, its desire to include as 'crimes' acts or omissions that have never been defined as such through any criminal justice process. These shifts beyond both the criminal law and formal legal processes have frequently opened up corporate crime researchers to charges of moralizing. Other conceptual disputes can be understood as necessary responses to changing social phenomena, such as the seemingly increasingly complex relationships between legitimate and illegitimate organizations.

There are good reasons why corporate crime research – leading to both empirical and theoretical development – should, and may well, proliferate. These include: the spread of the corporate form, as privatization has been championed across nation-states; diversification in the nature of corporate structures and organization; the apparent internationalization of much corporate activity; associated claims regarding the growing power of corporations *vis-à-vis* national governments and populations, and resistance associated with these trends; the dogged persistence of so-called 'quality of life' issues such as environmental protection which emerged to prominence in the Western capitalist states from the 1960s onwards; and the increasing exposure of the active role of corporations in human rights atrocities. Against these trends, and militating against corporate crime research, should be noted the power of corporations to secure, via their political allies, the decriminalization of their activities through the introduction of various forms of self-regulation or through simple deregulation, each of which are significant trends in contemporary capitalist nation-states (Snider, 2000).

Corporate crime research remains crucial to critical agendas within and around criminology. For a focus upon corporate crime entails continual scrutiny of the coverage and omissions of legal categories, the presences and absences within legal discourses, the social constructions of these categories and discourses, their underpinning of, treatment within and development through criminal justice systems and the ways in which particular laws are enforced (or not enforced), interpreted, challenged and so on.

Steve Tombs and Dave Whyte

Associated Concepts: criminalization, critical criminology, critical research, deviance, hidden crime, human rights, Marxist criminologies, organized crime, radical criminologies, the state, state crime, transnational organized crime, white collar crime

Key Readings

Clinard, M. and Yeager, P. (1980) *Corporate Crime*. New York, The Free Press.

Nelken, D. (1994) 'White-collar crime', in D. Nelken (ed.), *White-Collar Crime*. Aldershot, Dartmouth.

Slapper, G. and Tombs, S. (1999) *Corporate Crime*. London, Longman.

Snider, L. (2000) 'The sociology of corporate crime: an obituary. (Or, Whose knowledge claims have legs?)', *Theoretical Criminology*, 4 (2), pp. 169–206.

Sutherland, E. (1983) *White-Collar Crime. The Uncut Version*. New Haven, CT, Yale University Press.

CORRELATIONAL ANALYSIS

Definition

Correlation is the association of two variables – the predictability of the values of one from the values of another. We speak of *positive* correlation when high values on one variable predict high values on the other, and *negative* correlation when high values on one variable predict low values on another. Examples would be height and weight (positive correlation) and fitness and exhaustion after exercise (negative correlation).

Distinctive Features

The degree of correlation is generally expressed as a *correlation coefficient* (Pearson's product-moment coefficient being the most commonly used), which varies between +1 (perfect positive correlation) and −1 (perfect negative correlation). A value of zero would mean no correlation whatsoever, with the value on one variable offering no help at all in predicting the value on another. The correlation coefficient expresses the extent to which the values on the two variables can be fitted to a joint prediction line, with a high value of the coefficient indicating a very good fit and a low value a very poor one (see Figure 1). Correlational analysis usually deals with linear relationships – ones that can be fitted by a straight line – and other related methods are needed for predicting non-linear relationships. Figure 2 illustrates linear and non-linear relationships.

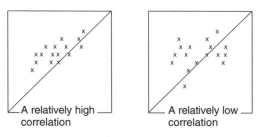

Figure 1: Good and Poor Correlation

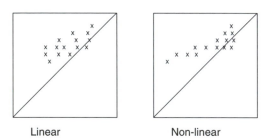

Figure 2: Linear and Non-linear relationships

Figure 3: Multiple Correlation

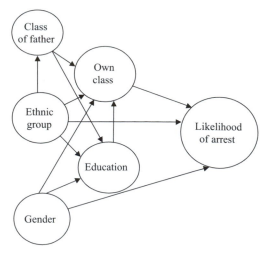

Figure 4: Path analysis

More than one variable can be combined via multiple regression into a *multiple correlation coefficient* (Figure 3), estimating how well a dependent variable can be predicted from an array of possible causal influences. The analysis will also generally permit the researcher to determine which variables are necessary for the prediction and which can be discarded as not adding anything further. An elaboration of this method, *path analysis*, permits the testing of hypotheses about chains of influence by taking into account relationships between the possible causes as well as relationships with the dependent variable. Paths on the diagram which turn out not to be statistically significant are deleted to leave a clear indication of the direct and indirect influences on the dependent variable suggested by the data (see Figure 4).

The technique of *partial correlation* is one of the ways in which we may control for alternative explanations by statistical means. A partial correlation coefficient expresses the relationship between a dependent and an independent variable with the effect of a third variable removed. For example, in an analysis of the effects of age on offending behaviour we might control for extent of previous criminal behaviour by partialling out (removing) the effects of previous convictions.

Evaluation

Correlational analysis is used to assess the degree of influence of one variable on another – for example, the extent to which social circumstances, childhood experiences and personality characteristics may provide explanations for subsequent criminal behaviour. The old maxim, however, is that 'correlation does not prove causation'. Correlation is a necessary condition for establishing causal influence – if one variable influences another, it must be correlated with it – but it is not a sufficient one. It is always possible that a third variable, not present in the analysis, may be an explanation both for the effect and for the apparent cause.

Roger Sapsford

Associated Concepts: causation, multivariate analysis

Key Readings

Hood, R. (1992) *Race and Sentencing*. Oxford, The Clarendon Press.

Sapsford, R.J. (1999) *Survey Analysis*. London, Sage.

CRIME

Definition

Crime is not a self-evident and unitary concept. Its constitution is diverse, historically relative and continually contested. As a result an answer to the question 'what is crime?' depends upon which of its multiple constitutive elements is emphasized. This in turn depends upon the theoretical position taken by those defining crime.

Distinctive Features

Key elements in determining crime are: (1) harm; (2) social agreement or consensus; and (3) official societal response. 'Harm' includes the nature, severity and extent of harm or injury caused and the kind of victim harmed. 'Consensus' refers to the extent of social agreement about whether victims have been harmed. 'Official societal response' refers to the existence of criminal laws specifying under what conditions (such as intent and knowledge of the consequences) that an act resulting in harm can be called crime, and the enforcement of such laws against those committing acts that harm. These dimensions have emerged from and been differently emphasized by six basic theoretical traditions: legal, moral consensus, sociological positivism, rule-relativism, political conflict, power-harm.

In early formulations, a simple relationship was assumed between each of the three key dimensions, such that if an action caused harm, people would be outraged and enact laws that the state would enforce to penalize the perpetrator. Thus emerged what became known as the moral or consensus position on crime that states that crimes are acts, which shock the common or collective morality, producing intense moral outrage among people. In founding this view Durkheim stated that, 'an act is criminal when it offends the strong, well-defined states of the collective consciousness' (1984 [1893], p. 39). Specifically, crime was a term used, 'to designate any act, which, regardless of degree, provokes against the perpetrator the characteristic reaction known as punishment' (1984 [1893], p. 31). As a result, the basic definition of crime became behaviour defined and sanctioned by criminal law. Thus there is no crime without law, and law is based on the 'injury' or 'harm done'. In a seminal statement reflecting the Durkheimian consensus view, Michael and Adler (1933, p. 5) asserted that 'criminal law gives behaviour its quality of criminality' and that 'the character of the behaviour content of criminal law will be determined by the capacity of behaviour to arouse our indignation' (1933, p. 23).

Evaluation

Several flaws in the legal consensus view of crime led to various critical challenges that stemmed from those holding different theoretical positions. The first problematic is the issue of what harm has been caused and what counts as harm. Even classical thinkers of the eighteenth century disagreed about this. The concept of 'harm' according to Cesare Beccaria refers to restrictions on the freedom of individuals to accumulate wealth. Beccaria identified three categories of crimes based upon the seriousness of their harm *to society*. The most serious of these crimes were those against the state, followed by crimes that injure the security and property of individuals; last in importance, were crimes disruptive to the public peace. But for Jeremy Bentham, harms were behaviours that caused 'pain' rather than restrictions of freedom to accumulate wealth. Bentham discusses twelve categories of pain whose measurement was necessary in order to give legislators a basis on which to decide whether to prohibit an act. He believed that no act ought to be an offence *unless* it was detrimental to the community. An act is detrimental if it harms one or more members of the community. Bentham elaborated a list of offence categories that he considered to be of five classes: public offences, semi-public offences, self-regarding offences (offences detrimental only to the offender), offences against the state, multiform or anomalous offences. Each should carry a punishment determined by the circumstances. Bentham declared that only harms to others should be criminal offences; cases of public morality and transactional crimes where 'consent has been given' should not be subject to the criminal law. In considering crime as defined in law therefore, the concern is not with those who commit crime, only with those acts that harm others.

A related issue is who should determine whether a consensus of outrage exists on whether harm has been committed. Those who have been termed 'sociological positivists' argued that the measure of such consensus or outrage was the purview of social scientists. Thorsten Sellin (1938), for example, advocated a science of criminal behaviour free from the politics of criminal law, legislators and lawyers. Instead scientists should employ their own value-neutral techniques to measure independently whether harm had been caused and to establish whether outrage existed and through these means establish scientific definitions of crime (1938, pp. 20–1). Sellin proposed to do this based on studying naturally existing 'conduct norms' rather than using legally constructed laws. Such study 'would involve the isolation and classification of norms into universal categories, transcending political and other boundaries, a necessity imposed by the logic of science' (Sellin, 1938, p. 30). The problem here is the assumption that science, and the scientific process itself, is any more free of influence than law (Schwendinger and Schwendinger, 1970).

Rule-relativists further argued that the meaning of what is defined in law or in moral consensus is not fixed but varies. They argued that what is defined as crime in law is historically, temporally and culturally relative. Their insight highlights the role of changing rather than absolute values about crime. Their challenge to the strict legal view of crime has been developed further by social constructionist arguments that show how what is harm depends on social context and situational meaning, itself shaped by the interaction between interest groups, such as offender, victim, community organizations, police agencies in the local setting. The emergence of an act as an 'offence' depends how these groups negotiate and honour claims that harm has been created.

The legal consensus position is also criticized because it ignores the politics of law-making. Radical conflict theorists claim that what gets defined as crime depends on having the power to define and the power to resist criminalizing definitions. Indeed, if interests influence the law creation process, then not all acts causing indignation or outrage will be legislated against. Only those harms that powerful interests deem worthy will be subject to criminalization. As Edwin Suther-

land (1940) first stated, this would mean that many harms, particularly those perpetrated by powerful corporations, remain outside the criminal law, even though they may be subject to civil regulation. For Sutherland, an adequate definition of crime should be based on an expanded definition of harm that includes 'social injury'. Similarly, Quinney (1977) wanted to expand the definition of crime to include not only the legal harms resulting from economic domination in a capitalist society, but also the crimes of government and of their agencies of social control. However, legalists such as Paul Tappan (1947) vigorously disagreed with expanding the legal definition, arguing that without adhering strictly to law, the concept of crime was open-ended and meaningless.

But for those taking a critical conflict perspective an adequate definition of crime must be based on a definition of harm tied neither to law nor consensus but to an independent notion of 'human rights'. Without such independent anchoring of the definition of crime those victimized are subject to the tyranny of moral majorities or the bias of powerful interests who determine the law. Because of this the harms that result from racism, sexism, ageism, or from 'insidious injuries' perpetrated by corporations through harmful work conditions, or harmful products, were for years neither acknowledged in society nor in law (Schwendinger and Schwendinger, 1970).

Postmodernist criminologists have also developed the idea that harm must be related to a concept of humanity and they argue for a dynamic conception of the different ways that humanity can be harmed. The postmodernist constitutive approach to defining crime goes beyond powerful groups and classes to the total context of powerful relations in situational and global contexts. For example, Henry and Milovanovic (1996, p. 104) state that 'crimes are nothing less than moments in the expression of power such that those who are subjected to these expressions are denied their own contribution to the encounter and often to future encounters'. They argue that crime 'is the power to deny others . . . in which those subject to the power of another, suffer the pain of being denied their own humanity, the power to make a difference'. Henry and Milovanovic (1996, p. 103) distinguish between 'harms of reduction' and 'harms of repression'. Harms of reduction occur when an offended party experiences a loss of some quality relative to their present standing that results from another's action. Harms of repression (or oppression) result from the actions of another that limit or restrict a person from achieving a future desired position or standing, though one achieved without harming others. Harms of repression have also been described as crimes against human dignity: 'acts and conditions that obstruct the spontaneous unfolding of human potential' (Tifft, 1995, p. 9).

The idea of criminalizing the use of power to reduce or suppress another is particularly important in order to expose the previously hidden crimes of gender oppression, sexual harassment, hate crime and racism that critical theorists have long complained are neglected in the legal and consensus definitions. It is also central to the unveiling of white collar, corporate and state crimes. Indeed, the analysis of power relations in the creation of crime highlights the intersecting forces of class, race and gender relations which coalesce in law and social institutions to legitimize harm and thereby render legalized relations, relations of harm. It follows, therefore, that law itself can create crime, not merely by definition but by its use of power over others and its concealment of the harms of others within the protection of law (Tifft, 1995).

Finally, there has been an increased recognition of the need to integrate each of the different dimensions of crime. This began explicitly with John Hagan's (1985) notion of the pyramid of crime which was further developed by Henry and Lanier (1998) in their notion of the 'prism of crime'. The aim of these approaches is to capture the multiple dimensions of crime simultaneously, rather than emphasizing any one element as predominant. Henry and Lanier's prism, for example, affords a way of incorporating individual and social harm; crimes of the powerful and those of the powerless; crimes that are invisible as well as those that are highly visible; and crimes that are selectively enforced as well as those more consistently enforced. In this way they aim for a more comprehensive definition that transcends the politics of the lawmaking process.

Stuart Henry

Associated Concepts: conflict theory, constitutive criminology, corporate crime, crimes against humanity, hate crime, hidden crime, integrative criminology, labelling, organized crime, political crime, social harm, state crime, transnational organized crime, war crimes

Key Readings

Durkheim, E. (1984) [1893] *The Division of Labor in Society*. New York, The Free Press.

Hagan, J. (1985) *Modern Criminology*. New York, McGraw–Hill.

Henry, S. and Lanier, M. (1998) 'The prism of crime: arguments for an integrated definition of crime', *Justice Quarterly*, 15 (4), pp. 609–27.

Henry, S. and Milovanovic, D. (1996) *Constitutive Criminology: Beyond Postmodernism*. London, Sage.

Michael, J. and Adler, M.J. (1933) *Crime, Law and Social Science*. New York, Harcourt Brace and Jovanovich.

Quinney, R. (1977) *Class, State, and Crime*. New York, David McKay.

Schwendinger, H. and Schwendinger, J. (1970) 'Defenders of order or guardians of human rights?', *Issues in Criminology*, 5, pp. 123–57.

Sellin, T. (1938) *Culture, Conflict and Crime*. New York, Social Science Research Council.

Sutherland, E.H. (1940) 'White-collar criminality', *American Sociological Review*, 5, pp. 1–12.

Tappan, P.R. (1947) 'Who is the criminal?', *American Sociological Review*, 12, pp. 96–102.

Tifft, L.L. (1995) 'Social harm definitions of crime', *The Critical Criminologist*, 7, pp. 9–13.

CRIME CONTROL MODEL

Definition

A crime control perspective or model which stresses that the primary function of the criminal courts is to punish offenders and, by so doing, to control crime.

Distinctive Features

The 'crime control' model involves a system of criminal justice which has as its primary aim the need to repress criminal conduct. The courts are thus more guardians of law and order than upholders of impartial justice. The failure of law enforcement to bring criminal conduct under tight control is viewed as leading to the breakdown of public order and thence to the disappearance of an important condition of human freedom. That is, whilst crime and disorder remain inadequately checked then the law-abiding citizen may become the victim of all sorts of unjustifiable invasions of his or her interests. The security of person and property is diminished and therefore the liberty to function as a member of society. The inherent claim is that the criminal justice process is a positive guarantor of social freedom. In order to achieve this high purpose, the crime control model requires that primary attention is given to the efficiency with which the criminal process operates to screen suspects, determine guilt and secure appropriate punishment (Packer, 1964).

While 'due process' values prioritize civil liberties in order to ensure that the innocent are acquitted (even at the risk of acquitting some who are guilty), 'crime control' values stress the goal of convicting the guilty (even at the risk of convicting some who are innocent, or of infringing some civil liberties). In a 'crime control' model, formal rules of procedure are often seen as obstacles standing in the way of securing a defendant's conviction. As the ultimate aim is to punish offenders and to deter future crime, the criminal justice system cannot afford a high acquittal rate; the system must work efficiently and speedily to apprehend and convict offenders. Packer (1964) likens the crime control model to an assembly line or a conveyor belt which, beginning with a presumption of guilt, moves the offender to workers at fixed stations who perform on each case to bring it one step closer to being a finished product, or a closed file.

It is argued that the main tool of the pre-modern model of crime control was the spectacular, public, bloody punishment of the offender who had offended sovereign power. The 'Bloody Code' of crime control, as criminal justice was popularly referred to in eighteenth-century England, was however supplemented by more traditional, communitarian mechanisms of social control (custom and informal means) which had survived from the feudal era. Following criticisms from classical reformers there was new interest in rationality, formalism and legality. The lasting philosophical influence of classicist views on crime and its prevention are perhaps to be found in utilitarianism and what has been called social contract theory (Hughes, 1998). According to this perspective the punishment of the offender is only justifiable in terms of its contribution to the prevention of future infringements on the well-being and happiness of others. Social contract theory derives from the idea that the power and authority of government to control crime (through punishment amongst other means) stems from an unwritten but none the less binding contract entered into by members of society whereby they agree to certain measures in order to secure freedom against the invasive actions of others. Following this, Garland (1996) refers to 'sovereign crime control', meaning that the state is there to provide security, law and order and crime control within its territorial boundaries.

A key meaning of the 'crime control model', therefore, relates to a wide range of mechanisms employed by the state, from the introduction of the police to control disruptive behaviour, to the developing institutions of criminal justice and corrections, and from situational crime prevention to multi-agency crime prevention work and other sophisticated modes of community control, to achieve crime control ends.

Evaluation

There are strong criticisms that the adoption of a 'crime control model' leads to harsh penalties and unnecessarily intrusive measures (Hudson, 1996). It is clearly associated with 'get tough', 'prisons work' and 'zero tolerance' policies. Yet such movements in criminal justice do not reflect unalloyed scientific endeavour; rather, they reflect political concerns (Stenson and Cowell, 1991).

Some radicals view the crime control measures of the criminal justice system as largely ineffective and even criminogenic. Many concerned with justice for juveniles, for instance, have argued that there should be as little intervention in young offenders' lives as possible on the basis that criminal justice interventions might well exacerbate their offending. Others would argue that the most effective forms of crime control are those that relate to deep social and economic structures, which seemingly contribute to the onset of crime in the first place.

In a deeply pessimistic but important review of crime control, Nils Christie (1993) has argued that it has become an industry with unlimited potential for growth and which presents very real danger for the value of human life.

Loraine Gelsthorpe

Associated Concepts: crime prevention, criminal justice, deterrence, due process model, governmentality, social control, zero tolerance

Key readings
Christie, N. (1993) *Crime Control As Industry.* London, Routledge.
Garland, D. (1996) 'The limits of the sovereign state: strategies of crime control in contemporary society', *British Journal of Criminology*, 36 (4), pp. 445–71.

Hudson, B. (1996) *Understanding Justice*. Buckingham, Open University Press.

Hughes, G. (1998) *Understanding Crime Prevention*. Buckingham, Open University Press.

Packer, H. (1964) 'Two models of the criminal process', *University of Pennsylvania Law Review*, 113, pp. 1–68.

Stenson, K. and Cowell, D. (eds) (1991) *The Politics of Crime Control*. London, Sage.

CRIME MAPPING

See Geographies of crime

CRIME PREVENTION

Definition

Any action taken or technique employed by private individuals or public agencies aimed at the reduction of damage caused by acts defined as criminal by the state. Given that crimes are events proscribed only by legal statute, it is not surprising that there is a great plethora of activities and initiatives associated with the term 'crime prevention'.

Distinctive Features

Crime prevention in its broadest sense has a long history, stretching back to the first use of locks and bolts to protect persons and property. However, it was only during the last three decades of the twentieth century that it emerged as a key institutional feature of criminal justice systems and related sites of social control across most contemporary societies. It is also during this recent period that we have seen a massive output of criminological writing aimed at classifying different types of crime prevention. Crime prevention is a chameleon concept which cannot be neatly or unproblematically defined. There continue to be many different meanings to crime prevention and in turn divergent policies and practices associated with the notion.

There is no consensus among criminologists with regard to how best to define the phenomenon of crime prevention. Instead, there are competing models and typologies, often of a limited theoretical nature, and seemingly driven by rather narrow technical concerns

about the measurement and evaluation of 'success' or 'failure'. One of the leading experts on the evaluation of crime prevention initiatives, Ken Pease, has recommended caution towards any attempt to look for universality in the techniques of prevention since, when we consider the prevention of crime, we are in fact looking at a set of events joined only in their proscription by statute (Pease, 1997, p. 659).

A popular means of defining crime prevention in criminology in the late twentieth century has been in terms of the distinction between situational and social strategies of prevention (to complicate matters further, the social strategies are often termed 'community' crime prevention). Situational crime prevention chiefly concerns opportunity reduction, such as the installation of surveillance technology in public spaces to reduce the opportunities for the theft of vehicles or crimes against victims. Social crime prevention is focused chiefly on changing social environments and the motivations of offenders. Social crime prevention measures thus often tend to focus on the development of schemes to deter potential or actual offenders from future offending. Both situational and social crime prevention approaches tend to be what is termed 'multi-agency' in orientation, rather than being driven by one agency alone, such as the police. Common to both elements of this distinction is the claim to be less damaging than traditional (retributive) justice approaches. Also common to both situational and social prevention is a narrow focus on 'street crime' and specific categories of offender (young, working-class males) rather than other social harms and offenders.

Another approach to classifying types of crime prevention is that there are three major models of crime prevention, borrowed from theorizing in medical epidemiology (Weiss, 1987). First, there is 'primary' crime prevention involving the reduction of criminal opportunities without reference to criminals. In primary crime prevention attention is turned to the crime event rather than the motivated offender. In the second type of crime prevention, termed 'secondary', the focus is on changing people before they do something criminal. Here then attention is on the prevention of criminality. Finally, 'tertiary' crime prevention focuses on the truncation of the criminal career, or reduction of the seriousness of offending, for example through the treatment of known offenders.

Another attempt to provide a comprehensive typology of crime prevention strategies is found in Tonry and Farrington (1995). These authors distinguish four major strategies of crime prevention (law enforcement, developmental, communal and situational). According to law enforcement strategy, criminal laws exist and are enacted so that fewer of the proscribed acts take place and general prevention in turn is the primary justification for maintaining a system of criminal punishment. This traditional law enforcement approach to both crime prevention and punishment operates chiefly through deterrence, incapacitation and rehabilitation. Developmental preventive interventions are designed to prevent the development of criminal potential in individuals, especially targeting the risk and protective factors discovered in studies of human development. Community prevention is designed to change the social conditions that influence offending in residential communities. And situational prevention involves interventions designed to prevent the occurrence of crimes, especially by reducing opportunities and increasing risks.

Evaluation

Despite the plethora of activities and definitional distinctions noted above, there remains a continuing dominance of a narrow focus in administrative criminology on 'what works' as crime prevention techniques (most associated with situational crime prevention 'fixes'). Viewed critically, this technicist focus is limiting and runs the risk of missing the broader sociological and political context in terms of which trends in crime prevention need to be understood. It may be noted that the concern with evaluating policies and intiatives for reducing or managing crimes may mean that crime prevention experts lose sight of the wider levers of crime, disorder and harms in contemporary societies.

According to critical authors, the 'growth industry' around crime prevention, crime reduction and community safety – which includes the academic criminological community – reflects important wider social transformations in contemporary societies (Crawford, 1997; Hughes, 1998; O'Malley, 1992). This insight is crucial to the recognition that developments in crime prevention are not just well-intentioned, technical solutions or responses to specific new crime events but reflect broad trends in social control and the governance of diverse and often fragmented populations. In particular, the increasing emphasis on (at best) crime reduction and

(more pragmatically) risk management associated with an 'actuarialist' model of justice may reflect the decline of the nation state's claims to sovereignty over crime control and may further accentuate trends towards social exclusion and with 'safety' increasingly becoming the 'club'-like privilege of the privileged and affluent.

Gordon Hughes

Associated Concepts: administrative criminology, community safety, crime control model, fear of crime, governmentality, multi-agency crime prevention, realist criminologies, situational crime prevention, social crime prevention, surveillance

Key Readings

Crawford, A. (1997) *The Local Governance of Crime.* Oxford, The Clarendon Press.

Hughes, G. (1998) *Understanding Crime Prevention: Social Control, Risk and Late Modernity.* Buckingham, Open University Press.

O'Malley, P. (1992) 'Power, risk and crime prevention', *Economy and Society*, 21 (3), pp. 251–68.

Pease, K. (1997) 'Crime prevention', in M. Maguire, R. Morgan and R. Reiner (eds), *The Oxford Handbook of Criminology*, 2nd edn. Oxford, The Clarendon Press.

Tonry, M. and Farrington, D. (1995) *Building a Safer Society: Strategic Approaches to Crime.* Chicago, University of Chicago Press.

Weiss, R. (1987) 'Community and crime prevention', in E. Johnson (ed.), *Handbook on Crime and Delinquency*, New York, Greenwood Press.

CRIMES AGAINST HUMANITY

Definition

The International Military Tribunal at Nuremberg impressed the concept of crimes against humanity into international law. These crimes were defined as the 'murder, extermination, enslavement or deportation, and other inhumane acts committed against any civilian population, before or during the war or persecutions on political, racial or religious grounds in the execution of or in connection with any crime within the jurisdiction of the Tribunal, whether or not in violation of the domestic law of the country in question'. The international criminal tribunals for the former Yugoslavia and Rwanda added the crimes of rape and torture to the inventory of crimes against humanity. By the time the International Criminal Court is established there will be new crimes against humanity to append to the register. Crimes against humanity are different from genocide because they do not require the intention to eradicate, or attempt to eradicate, a national, ethnic, racial or religious group by mass murder. They are distinguishable from war crimes in that they apply in times of peace as well as war.

Eugene McLaughlin

Associated Concepts: genocide, hate crime, torture, war crimes

Key Readings

Bassiouni, M.C. (1999) *Crimes Against Humanity in International Law*. The Hague, Kluwer Law.

Gutman, R. and Rieff, D. (eds) (1999) *Crimes of War: What the Public Should Know*. New York, W.W. Norton and Co.

Ratner, S.R. and Abrams, J.S. (1997) *Accountability for Human Rights*. Oxford, The Clarendon Press.

Robertson, G. (2000) *Crimes Against Humanity*. Harmondsworth, Penguin.

CRIMINAL CAREERS

Definition

Ordered sequences of criminal law violations. An important difference between occupational and criminal careers is that the positions in occupational careers are usually legitimate, are often established by formal organizations, and frequently follow a standard pattern. Criminal law violations are less widely approved and usually do not involve organizationally defined positions. The concept is distinct from the linguistically similar phrase, 'career criminals'.

Distinctive Features

A criminal career has a beginning and an end; its trajectory is characterized by age of onset, age of desistance, frequency of violations of each type of crime, and the probabilities of switching between offence categories. Individuals, organizations and places may have criminal careers. Most research and theorizing has concerned the criminal careers of individuals.

Criminal career research confronts a number of methodological issues. Some of the most important are:

- The validity of different types of data (official records, self-reports, reports of others). Often the trajectories derived from different sources are similar, but in some cases, those constructed from official records differ from those based on non-official sources. Arrest statistics show aggregate levels of violence rising to a peak in late adolescence and early adulthood, and then declining. Observations of children, however, suggest that aggressive behaviour may be highest at ages 1 or 2, and declines gradually with age. Because small children are weak, do little damage, and are not considered fully responsible for their actions, small children's aggression is handled informally, and is often neglected in studies of criminal careers.

- Aggregate data or individual-level data? A good deal of theorizing has been based on aggregate-level data. For a number of different offences, in different times and places, rates of aggregate involvement in crime rise with age and then decline. Quite different patterns of individual starts, stops and frequencies can yield the same aggregate pattern. To distinguish among these different patterns, data on individual careers are required.

- Cross-sectional or longitudinal analyses? In a one-shot, cross-sectional study, information about crime is collected from individuals of different ages at a single time. This design cannot distinguish age effects from cohort effects. Longitudinal research following one or more cohorts over time cannot distinguish the effects of age from period. No design can disentangle the linear effects of age, period and cohort. Researchers have typically dealt with this issue by assuming that one or more of these effects is zero.

Research on aggregate patterns has established that the age distribution of involvement in crime has changed dramatically over the past 200 years, that it differs from country to country, and is offence-specific. Studies of individual careers show trajectory shapes to be person-specific. There is a substantial degree of continuity in individual criminal involvement: those with high levels of involvement at one time tend to have high levels at later times. Yet change occurs, with many careers ending in adolescence or early adulthood.

Research has identified numerous antecedents of early onset of criminality in early childhood traits and family characteristics. Subsequent trajectories are influenced by marriage, employment, changing patterns of peer association, imprisonment and participation in treatment programmes. Studies differ on whether offences tend to become more serious as careers progress.

Most offenders are not specialists. Superimposed on a pattern of random switching between crimes is a modest degree of specialization. Specialization is somewhat greater for white collar criminals and sex offenders.

Evaluation

The strength of the criminal career perspective is that it directs attention to changes in patterns of criminal behaviour over the life course and to the dependence of age, or stage of career, on factors that influence criminal behaviour.

Thus far, research on criminal careers has tended to be individualistic: little attention has been paid to the possible mutual dependence of career trajectories of co-offenders. Statistical analyses have tended to lump offences of different kinds together, possibly obscuring differences among offences. Studies of crime switching have tended not to examine the temporal shape of trajectories.

Career research has concentrated on the 'common' crimes of interpersonal violence, theft, vandalism, illegal drug use, status offences and public order offences. Little research has been done on careers in consumer fraud, stock market fraud, insurance fraud, price-fixing, insider trading, tax evasion, offering and soliciting bribes, embezzlement, espionage, money laundering, arms trafficking, child molesting, perjury, making and distributing pornography, war crimes, police and prison guard violence, and genocide. Some of these offences can be carried out only by those who meet advanced educational standards and who hold office in legitimate organizations. For these offenders, onset is expected to be late, and involvement to occur at older ages. Predictors of common criminality (for example, impulsive personality, childhood aggressiveness, inadequate parental supervision in childhood, school difficulties and low socio-economic status) may not predict involvement for these offences. Marriage and employment may not promote desistance, as they do for routine violence and property offences. Late initiators of

careers in 'common' crimes have also been little studied.

David Greenberg

Associated Concepts: cross-sectional design, deterrence, deviance, deviancy amplification, labelling, longitudinal study, recidivism

Key Readings

Blumstein, A., Cohen, J., Roth, J.A. and Visher, C.A. (eds) (1986) *Criminal Careers and 'Career Criminals'*, 2 vols. Washington, DC, National Academy Press.

Farrington, D.P. (1997) 'Human development and criminal behaviour' in Mike Maguire, Rod Morgan and Robert Reiner (eds), *The Oxford Handbook of Criminology*, 2nd edn. Oxford, The Clarendon Press.

Greenberg, D.F. (ed.) (1996) *Criminal Careers*, 2 vols. Aldershot, and Brookfield, VT, Dartmouth.

Le Blanc, M. and Fréchette, M. (1989) *Male Criminal Activity from Childhood through Youth: Multilevel and Developmental Perspective*. New York, Springer-Verlag.

Thornberry, T. (ed.) (1997) *Developmental Theories of Crime and Delinquency*. New Brunswick, NJ, Transaction.

Tonry, M., Ohlin, L. and Farrington, D.P. (eds) (1991) *Human Development and Criminal Behavior*. New York, Springer-Verlag.

CRIMINAL JUSTICE

Definition

The process through which the state responds to behaviour that it deems unacceptable. Criminal justice is delivered through a series of stages: charge; prosecution; trial; sentence; appeal; punishment. These processes and the agencies which carry them out are referred to collectively as *the criminal justice system*.

Distinctive Features

The framework of criminal justice is laid down by legislation specifying the penalties available in consequence of various crimes; and the powers, rules and procedures for each process and agency. In the UK, legislation has generally prescribed maximum penalties, leaving considerable discretion to courts in deciding the actual penalty in individual cases. The life sentence for murder has traditionally been the only mandatory sentence.

Other countries have more prescriptive penal codes, with less discretion available to courts. In recent years, the UK has followed other jurisdictions, especially the USA, in introducing more mandatory sentences. Discretion has been reduced at all points in the system. Under the slogan 'truth in sentencing', politicians have decreed that offenders should serve the sentence pronounced by the court, or at least a fixed percentage of it, rather than have the length of sentence actually served determined by prison governors or probation officers through decisions about early release or early termination of community orders.

Life imprisonment is the most severe punishment in most Western countries. The important exception is the USA, where use of the death penalty has increased during the 1990s; several states which did not have it have introduced or re-introduced the death penalty. In most years, Texas carries out the highest number of executions. Eastern European countries seeking membership of the European Union have abolished the death penalty, as part of moves to bring their criminal justice systems into line with the European Convention on Human Rights.

In the 1980s, several high-profile cases in England and Wales were shown to have resulted in wrongful convictions. Concern with these miscarriages of justice led to a Royal Commission on Criminal Justice in 1993. Some changes in procedures resulted, among the most important of which was the requirement upon prosecutors to disclose evidence more fully to the defence before trial. Gradually, however, these concerns have faded and by the mid-1990s widespread perception that too many guilty people were being acquitted has led to further changes which swing the balance of advantage back towards the prosecution.

Theoretical analysis of criminal justice has focused on the tension between the objective of crime control, and the values of due process. Although crime control, or crime reduction, is obviously the overall aim of criminal justice, it is limited by rights accorded to defendants. Crime control and due process were represented as alternative models of criminal justice by Herbert Packer (Sanders and Young, 1994). If crime control is the dominant consideration, severe penalties may be imposed: penalties designed to ensure protection of the public through removal or incapacitation of the offender, so that there is no chance of a further offence. Establishing guilt 'beyond reasonable doubt' may seem less important than demonstrating the conse-

quences of crimes. Due process values emphasize fairness and equality in criminal justice, and respect the rights of offenders, so that there should be proper safeguards through representation, rules of evidence, and the prosecution having to establish guilt according to rigorous standards of proof. Due process models also expect punishment to be proportionate to the seriousness of the offence, and not to be degrading or inhumane. The 1980s are said to be characterized by dominance of due process values, while there has been a marked swing towards crime control in the 1990s.

Criminologists have been interested in the possibility and extent of discrimination in criminal justice. Unemployment, race and gender have been shown to influence criminal justice decision-making. High unemployment rates correlate with high imprisonment rates; black offenders have been found to be more likely than their white counterparts to be imprisoned; being female is associated with receiving probation where male offenders might receive a fine or other non-interventive sentence. There is some disagreement among criminologists about whether the criminal justice treatment of women is more or less severe than that of males, but general agreement that it is different. Conversely, consensus about the extent of different treatment due to race has been harder to establish, but there is general agreement that if there is any difference, it is in the direction of greater severity for black offenders.

Barbara Hudson

Associated Concepts: crime control model, discretion, discrimination, disparity, disproportionality, due process model, penality, probation, social justice

Key Readings

Ashworth, A. (1994) *The Criminal Process*. Oxford, Oxford University Press.

Ashworth, A. and Wasik, M. (eds) (1998) *Fundamentals of Sentencing Theory*. Oxford, The Clarendon Press.

Davies, M., Croall, H. and Tyrer, J. (1995) *Criminal Justice: An Introduction to the Criminal Justice System in England and Wales*. Harlow, Longman.

Hood, R. (1992) *Race and Sentencing: A Study in the Crown Court*. Oxford, The Clarendon Press.

Lacey, N. (1994) *Criminal Justice*. Oxford, Oxford University Press.

Sanders, A. and Young, R. (1994) *Criminal Justice*. Oxford, Butterworths.

CRIMINALIZATION

Definition

Crime is a status conferred on and ascribed to certain non-approved acts legislated against and, through the due process of law, punished. Derived in social reaction theory, criminalization is the institutionalized process through which certain acts and behaviours are labelled as 'crimes' and 'outlawed'. It reflects the state's decision to regulate, control and punish selectively. Critical theorists have developed this analysis further, arguing that criminalization does not occur in a vacuum. It is influenced by contemporary politics, economic conditions and dominant ideologies and is contextualized by the determining contexts of social class, gender, sexuality, 'race' and age.

Distinctive Features

While it is clear that certain acts and behaviours receive widespread disapproval and condemnation transcending time, place and culture, much that is declared 'unlawful' and defined as 'crime' is derived in social and societal reaction. Not all harmful acts are defined as crimes and not all crimes are necessarily harmful. Criminalization represents the technical process through which acts are defined as crimes, legislated against, regulated through law enforcement and, via the courts, punished. Further, however, it is a political, economic and ideological process through which individuals and identifiable groups are selectively policed and disciplined.

Reflecting on postwar USA, Spitzer (1975) argued that criminalization specifically targets those whose 'behaviour, personal qualities, and/or position threaten the social relations of production', challenging the established economic order, the 'process of socialization for productive and non-productive roles' and the 'ideology which supports the functioning of capitalist society'. The deviant status ascribed to such 'problem populations' is the product of a process of social categorization. For Spitzer, critical analysis 'must examine where these images and definitions came from' and 'what they reflect about the structure of and priorities in specific class societies . . .' (1975).

Although criticized for economic reductionism, Spitzer placed class and marginalization firmly on the labelling and social reaction

agenda. In other words, crime and criminalization were inextricably, although not always, linked to subordination and oppression within advanced capitalist societies. This discussion reasserted the importance of Marx's analysis of the relative surplus population within developing capitalism and its threat to social order and economic conditions. The political management of the relative surplus population, of the marginalized, relies on the rule of law and its selective enforcement to discipline oppositional forces embodying strategies of surveillance, regulation and control.

Within the UK, Box (1983) demonstrates how contemporary economic crises have impacted on the criminalization of subordinate groups. Ideological constructions derived in nineteenth-century social conditions were mobilized in the 1980s, best illustrated by the continua which dichotomize the rough and the respectable, the undeserving and deserving poor, the subversive and the conforming. The rough, undeserving and dangerous 'underclass' – the 'enemy within' – necessitate hardline policing, tougher sentencing and secure containment. The implication was that imprisonment is used to control and regulate problem populations, particularly during economic recession.

Critical analysis, however, contests the simplistic claim that rising unemployment and increased poverty lead inevitably to crime and thus a swelling prison population. Box and Hale (1982, p. 22) record a more complex picture in which imprisonment is 'not a direct response to any rise in crime, but is an ideologically motivated response to the perceived threat posed by the swelling population of economically marginalized persons'. They contend that increases in street crime, for example, managed by the rhetoric and practices of authoritarian 'law and order' responses, is a myth constructed with the political objective of strengthening criminal justice control agencies.

In the USA Currie (1998, p. 185) reflects that in 1967 the Kerner Commission on Urban Disorders brought the USA to a law and order crossroads. He notes a common agreement that 'we could never imprison our way out of America's violent crime problem', that tackling violent crime meant 'attacking social exclusion' and 'making a real rather than rhetorical commitment' to defeating the material realities of crime and exclusion. The USA took another road, and at the end of century 'bursting prisons, devastated cities and [a] violent crime rate unmatched in the "developed" world' was the result. According to Parenti (1999), a right-wing cultural back-lash provided the foundation for the ideolo-gical reaffirmation of the 'underclass' as marginals by choice rather than circumstance.

Marginalization and criminalization together protect, reinforce and reproduce established order interests whether political, economic or both. Coercive intervention, however, requires not only authority but also legitimacy: 'The power to criminalize is not derived necessarily in consensus politics but is implicitly a political act. Criminalization [reflects] ideologies associated with margin-alization and it is within these portrayals that certain actions are named, contained and regulated . . . a powerful process because it mobilizes popular approval and legitimacy in support of powerful interests within the state' (Scraton and Chadwick, 1991, pp. 172–3). Thus popular support has to be won for state policies and law reforms that are essentially authoritarian, including the normalization of 'special powers'. It is the political manage-ment of negative reputations and violent identities – developed, consolidated, trans-mitted and reproduced through ideologies of 'other' – which underwrites a hardening process of criminalization.

Evaluation

The radical critique at the heart of critical analysis within criminology in 1970s USA, UK and Europe was criticized for economic reductionism and false universalism. It was accused of over-simplification regarding its proposed close association of class, margin-alization and criminalization. The critique noted that crime, deviance and social conflict were complex and could not be reduced to material causation (unemployment, poverty, poor housing and so on).

Neo-classical, conservative criminologists considered concepts such as criminalization to be little more than justifications for crimes committed by individuals who had made informed choices and should be held respon-sible for their acts. As conservative analysis reasserted its position through the consolida-tion of 'underclass theory', it was matched by the emergence of 'ethical socialists' who also emphasized 'dismembered families', 'lone mothers', lack of civic responsibility and life-style choice as the primary causes of poverty and violent crime. Taken together, these critiques reaffirmed individual and social pathologies as underlying conditions in which much crime is rooted.

From their roots within radicalism the self-styled UK 'left realists' argued that critical analysis had been flawed by economic reductionism. Leading to 'left idealism' and a failure to 'take crime seriously'. This created a heated debate in which critical criminologists argued that the associated structural processes of marginalization and criminalization could not be confined to the relations of production and distribution. They emphasized the signifi-cance of patriarchy, heterosexuality, 'race' and age as institutionalized and oppressive con-structs, subordinating and marginalizing people at the political-ideological as well as political-economic level.

Conceptually, criminalization explains the structural conditions in which certain acts are defined as crimes, and subsequently policed and punished. It explores the creation and political management of identities in the determining contexts of societal power rela-tions. And it provides an understanding of the criminal justice clampdown, the rise in puni-tive legislation and the authoritarian shift within social democratic states. This clamp-down is exemplified in the UK by the mantra 'tough on crime, tough on the causes of crime' which underpins a multi-agency or matrix approach to social discipline: zero tolerance and 'quality of life' policing; increased surveillance, targeting and hardline interven-tions. With the criminal justice 'net' widening to include 'anti-social' behaviour, to regulate children at a very early age, the criminalizing context has been further extended.

Kathryn Chadwick and Phil Scraton

Associated Concepts: authoritarian populism, crime, critical criminology, emergency legisla-tion, labelling, left realism, net widening, racialization, radical feminism, risk, social harm, social reaction, surveillance, underclass

Key Readings

Box, S. (1983) *Power, Crime and Mystification.* London, Tavistock.

Box, S. and Hale, C. (1982) 'Economic crisis and the rising prisoner population in England and Wales', *Crime and Social Justice*, no.17.

Currie, E. (1998) *Crime and Punishment in America.* New York, Metropolitan Books.

Parenti, C. (1999) *Lockdown America: Police and Prisons in the Age of Crisis.* London, Verso.

Scraton, P. and Chadwick, K. (1991) 'Challenging the new orthodoxies: the theoretical imperatives and political priorities of critical criminology', in K.

Stenson and D. Cowell (eds), *The Politics of Crime Control*. London, Sage.

Spitzer, S. (1975) 'Towards a Marxian theory of deviance', *Social Problems*, 22, pp. 368–401.

CRITICAL CRIMINOLOGY

Definition

Critical criminology applies critical analysis to the 'discipline' of criminology, the study of crime and the administration of criminal justice. It emphasizes the contextualizing relationship of structure and agency, locating the 'everyday', routine world within structural and institutional relations. It locates 'crime', 'deviance' and 'social conflict' within their *determining contexts* rather than being obsessed with *causation*. It endeavours to broaden the scope of analysis to a consideration of *harm* rather than crime, *social justice* rather than criminal justice, *treatment* rather than punishment and discourses of *human rights* rather than discipline and control. The structural relations of production and distribution, reproduction and patriarchy, and neo-colonialism are identified as the primary determining contexts within which the inter-relationships and mutual dependencies of structural forms of oppression can be understood.

Distinctive Features

Breaking with traditional, academic criminology which prioritized liberalism, pluralism and reformism, radical criminology emerged in the early 1970s. In Britain, the National Deviancy Conference (NDC) was formed, uniting academics, practitioners and campaigners in the pursuit of a radical alternative to mainstream criminology. From the NDC developed the 'New Criminology' which set the radical agenda via the proposal for a 'fully social theory' of deviance. This involved establishing theoretical connections between the law, the state, legal and political relations and the functions of crime. Its objective was to evolve a Marxist perspective prioritizing a political-economic focus on class and class relations. Implicit in this analysis was the connection between class, crime and the state with 'crime control' providing the coercive means through which

threats to the established social and economic order are identified and regulated. It is the state, through its legislation, that establishes official means of crime control. Hence, the state's role to guarantee *continuity*, to manage *conflict* and to *reproduce* the dominant social and economic order.

In responding to this 'radical' direction in criminology, critics targeted its implied economic reductionism. They suggested that within critical analysis the rule of law and its relations were reduced to functional subsidiaries of the political economy. In European societies, notably Scandinavia, Holland and West Germany, the development of radical criminology was more inclined towards abolitionism; 'the product of the same counter-cultural politics of the 1960s which gave rise to the cultural radicalism of the "new" or "critical" criminology' (Cohen, 1996, p. 3).

Throughout the 1980s profound differences emerged within critical criminology, experienced most acutely in Britain. Key proponents of 'New Criminology' redefined themselves as 'left realists'. The primary proposition was that 'crime' needs to be 'taken seriously' and 'confronted' by politicians, policy-makers and academics. Emphasizing crime, crime prevention and civil disorder, the left realist solution to the problem of crime proposes a democratic, multi-agency approach geared to a more equal distribution of resources and a reformed system of legal justice. Central to the work of left realism has been the labelling and rejection of 'idealism' in radical criminology, exposing the political and theoretical weaknesses of 'left idealism' as economically reductionist and deterministic. Critical criminology, however, cannot be so lightly dismissed.

According to Scraton and Chadwick (1991) a 'second phase' in the development of critical criminology can be identified. Established theoretical principles have not been rejected but refined, redeveloped and extended. The initial call from new criminology to locate the world of everyday life within broader structural relations remains a defining principle, setting the agenda for the consolidation of critical analysis within criminological theory. Significant here is the relationship between 'structure' and 'agency'. Agency refers to the experiential, everyday world of diverse social relations and interaction. Structure encompasses the world of institutions and structural relations – and their histories – which set the boundaries to social interaction and personal opportunity within society, containing and regulating social relations.

Moreover, while critical analysis remains committed to an economic analysis focusing on the relations of production and distribution – emphasizing class relations and the dynamics and consequences of advanced capitalism and globalization – other inter-related centres of power and their institutional relations also are prioritized. These include the structural relations of reproduction and dependency, emphasizing global domination of women and the complexities, yet universality, of contrasting patriarchies. Also significant are the structural relations of neo-colonialism, emphasizing the pervasiveness of institutional racism and its imperialist legacy; connecting slavery, colonization, immigration and migration. Scraton (1991, p. 93) identifies these structural relations as the 'determining contexts' of social action and human potential. These are relations embodying exploitation, oppression and subordination. They are relations of power, both economic and political, underpinned by deep ideological traditions and their contemporary manifestation.

A further important dimension of critical criminology is the relationship between power and knowledge. For Foucault (1980), power is not unidimensional but is dispersed throughout society, not resting with one dominant state, sovereign or class. Power and knowledge imply each other. Crucially, the power–knowledge axis permeates and sustains official discourses. For critical theorists, official discourses are developed and reproduced through the primary determining contexts of class, 'race' and gender. Discrimination resulting from these determining contexts is experienced daily, interpersonally, at the level of agency. Yet they also have a structural significance in that classism, racism, sexism and heterosexism are institutionalized and oppressive constructs. They inform legislation, policy and practice throughout institutions, organizations and professions. It is through the process of institutionalization that the relations of domination and subordination gain their legitimacy and achieve structural significance.

The processes of marginalization and criminalization are central in explaining and analysing the relationship between the law, crime, punishment and the state. Critical theorists argue that there is a direct relationship between economic crises and political responses of the state and judiciary, leading to the marginalization and criminalization of certain groups. While economic changes bring political responses, through state action, when such action is coercive or involves the use of force and violence, it has to be legitimated. This is the dichotomy between coercion and consent. Critical criminology demonstrates that the process of criminalization protects, reinforces and reproduces the political, economic and social interests of an established order. The process requires institutional legitimacy and also the winning of popular consent for state policies and legal shifts that are essentially authoritarian. Negative reputations, stereotyped images and collective, violent identities – the stuff of 'folk devils' – are transmitted through ideologies. The state institutional response relies heavily on winning 'hearts and minds' in pursuing this ideological appeal through popular discourse. Political, economic and ideological forces, then, are intricately connected in the creation, maintenance and portrayal of the process of criminalization.

Evaluation

Critical criminology contests and rejects the knowledge base, theoretical traditions and imperatives of administrative criminology. It also challenges the emphases of left realist analyses, arguing that this approach remains locked into – and constrained by – definitions, policies and practices shaped and administered within the criminal justice priorities of social democratic states. While taking 'crime' seriously, it retains a commitment to the location of 'crime', 'deviance' and 'conflict' within the determining contexts of power and their institutionalized relations.

Critical criminology also incorporates a human rights discourse and agenda. This development reaffirms that 'advanced' democracies, whatever their claims for upholding the principles of equality and liberty, embody and reproduce the structural inequalities of global capitalism, patriarchy and neo-colonialism. These inequalities are woven into the fabric of the state and civil society; hegemonic rather than ideological. They are supported and reproduced through what Foucault calls 'regimes of truth'. Critical analysis has focused on the structure, procedures and appropriateness of the criminal justice process (from the derivation of laws to the administration of punishments) in identifying their specific and cumulative deficit in revealing 'truth' and delivering 'justice'. A human rights discourse, agenda and process, provide a processual and procedural alternative to the administration of the law and criminal justice

(Cohen, 1993, 1996). It is also a priority for critical criminology in challenging the context and consequences of state-sanctioned regimes of truth.

Kathryn Chadwick and Phil Scraton

Associated Concepts: abolitionism, authoritarian populism, criminalization, critical research, human rights, left idealism, Marxist criminologies, new criminology, post-colonial criminology, radical criminologies, radical feminism, the state

Key Readings

Cohen, S. (1993) 'Human rights and crimes of the state: the culture of denial', *Australian and New Zealand Journal of Criminology*, 26 (2), pp. 97–115.

Cohen, S. (1996) 'Crime and politics: spot the difference', *British Journal of Sociology*, 47 (1), pp. 1–21.

Foucault, M. (1980) *Power/Knowledge: Selected Interviews and Other Writings, 1972–1977* (ed. C. Gordon). Brighton, Harvester Wheatsheaf.

Scraton, P. (1991) 'Recent developments in criminology: a critical overview', in M. Haralambos (ed.), *Developments in Sociology: An Annual Review No. 7.* Ormskirk, Causeway Press.

Scraton, P. and Chadwick, K. (1991) 'Challenging the new orthodoxies: the theoretical imperatives and political priorities of critical criminology', in K. Stenson and D. Cowell (eds), *The Politics of Crime Control.* London, Sage.

Sim, J., Scraton, P. and Gordon, P. (1987) 'Crime, the state and critical analysis', in P. Scraton (ed.), *Law, Order and the Authoritarian State: Readings in Critical Criminology.* Milton Keynes, Open University Press.

CRITICAL RESEARCH

Definition

Critical social research begins with the premise that 'knowledge', including the formalized 'domain assumptions' and boundaries of academic disciplines, is neither value-free nor value-neutral. Rather, knowledge is derived and reproduced, historically and contemporaneously, in the structural relations of inequality and oppression that underpin established social orders. Challenging the quantitative foundations of positivism and the interpretive foundations of phenomenology, critical research endeavours to locate the experiential realities of individuals and communities (agency) within their historical, structural and reproductive contexts (structure).

Distinctive Features

Writing in the late 1950s, and demonstrating a growing scepticism for mainstream social science and its application within the USA, Wright Mills (1959, p. 20) criticized the 'bureaucratic techniques which inhibit sociological inquiry by "methodological" pretensions', its 'obscurantist conceptions' and its trivializing of 'publicly relevant issues' by an overstated 'concern with minor problems'. Such 'inhibitions, obscurities and trivialities' had created a crisis for a form of state-supported social research which decontextualized people's lives, their experiences and their opportunities. For Wright Mills, researching and teaching at the height of McCarthyism, sociology had 'lost its reforming push' and its 'tendencies towards fragmentary problems and scattered causation' had been 'conservatively turned to the use of the corporation, army and the state'.

Throughout the 1960s in the USA and Western Europe the radical critique of social sciences consolidated. It proposed that commissioned research was conceptualized and designed to further the material interests of the powerful, in political and economic institutions, at the expense of the powerless. Of particular concern was how social research was used to serve and service the military–industrial complex and its international, expansionist objectives. The radical critique claimed that crime and other social problems which were the consequence of structural inequality, economic deprivation and cultural discrimination were reconstructed through mainstream social research as the inevitable outcomes of individual or community pathologies.

Central to the critique was the assertion that social science, far from being constituted by 'value-free', 'objective' or 'scientific' disciplines independent of each other and distinct from societal relations, was directly implicated in the maintenance and reproduction of social order. In its applications and interventions social science was a part of, rather than apart from, the political, economic and social developments geared to regulating conflict and managing change. Thus its emphases and methodologies reflected its purpose and utility.

Within criminology the radical critique emphasized the significance of social conditions and structural inequalities in the creation of 'crime', 'deviance', disorder and conflict. Challenging the traditions of criminality, causation, pathologization and correction, critical research switched the emphasis to socio-legal definitions, social and societal reactions and the structural contexts of daily interaction within communities. As Wright Mills had proposed: the 'most fruitful distinction with which the sociological imagination works' operates 'between the *personal troubles* of the milieu and the *public issues* of social structure' (1959, p. 8; emphases added).

Thus, critical social research 'is underpinned by a critical-dialectical perspective' committed to 'dig[ging] beneath the surface of historically specific, oppressive social structures' (Harvey, 1990, p. 1). Initially critical research was concerned with class-based oppression but the emergence of second-wave feminist analyses and anti-racist research extended critical methodologies to all structural forms of oppression and their integration. Critical research 'delv[es] beneath ostensive and dominant conceptual frames in order to reveal the underlying practices, their historical specificity and structural manifestations' (1990, p. 4). In this context critical research is not only historically grounded, it is concerned with the political-ideological context as well as the political-economic determinants which shape and legitimate the social conditions of structural inequality. This includes the institutional arrangements through which official discourse and academic knowledge are produced and confers legitimacy on existing social arrangements.

As Hudson (2000, p. 177) notes, 'of all the applied social sciences, criminology has the most dangerous relationship to power: the categories and classifications, the labels and diagnoses and the images of the criminal produced by criminologists are stigmatizing and pejorative'. Such conceptions and their application inform 'strategies of control and punishment' and impact individually and collectively on 'rights and liberties'. Thus it is through critical social research that the power–knowledge axis, at the heart of Foucault's discussion of the material reality of societal 'regimes of truth', is exposed and deconstructed.

The search for knowledge and truth – epistemology – has been central to research traditions. Critical social research challenges the academic knowledge base which serves to reproduce dominant power relations and their

structural inequalities. Of particular significance is official discourse, reflecting and reinforcing the 'view from above', conferring legitimacy on political and economic institutions and their operation. As regimes of truth are constructed they become the institutionalized and professionalized manifestations of knowledge. Thus 'knowledge' becomes 'institutionally appropriate', exercised and delivered through the interventions of professional 'experts'. Through mobilizing the politics of reputation and representation, those 'knowledges' considered inappropriate, non-legitimate or oppositional are marginalized and disqualified. Critical social research challenges official discourses and the power, authority and legitimacy of state institutions. Within criminology the 'object of investigation is the cluster of theories, policies, legislation, media treatments, roles and institutions that are concerned with crime, and with the control and punishment of crime' (Hudson, 2000, p. 177).

Connected to the *object* and *substance* of critical research is *reflexivity*, through which 'myths' and 'hidden truths' are revealed and people are helped 'to change the world for themselves' (Neuman, 1994, p. 67). The objective of reflective, qualitative action research in revealing 'the underlying mechanisms that account for social relations' is to 'encourage dramatic social change from grass-roots level' (1994, p. 67). As Stanley (1990, p. 15) comments in her discussion of feminist praxis, 'succinctly the point is to change the world, not only to study it'. Unpopular with governments and state institutions, criticized for reductionism and over-simplification and deprived of significant funding, critical research has been a highly successful antidote to the functional, self-serving apologism of administrative criminology and the decontextualized relativism – particularly regarding power – of postmodernist discourses on crime and punishment.

Phil Scraton and Kathryn Chadwick

Associated Concepts: action research, criminalization, critical criminology, discourse analysis, feminist research, reflexivity

Key Readings

Harvey, L. (1990) *Critical Social Research*. London, Sage.

Hudson, B. (2000) 'Critical reflection as research methodology', in V. Jupp, P. Davies and P.

Francis (eds), *Doing Criminological Research*. London, Sage.

Neuman, W. (1994) *Social Research Methods: Qualitative and Quantitative Approaches*. Boston, MA, Allyn and Bacon.

Scraton, P. (ed.) (1987) *Law, Order and the Authoritarian State: Readings in Critical Criminology*. Milton Keynes, Open University Press.

Stanley, L. (ed.) (1990) *Feminist Praxis*. London, Routledge.

Wright Mills, C. (1959) *The Sociological Imagination*. New York, Oxford.

CROSS-SECTIONAL DESIGN

Definition

A design in which a cross-section of the population is selected for study and data are collected from or about each selected case at one particular point in time.

Distinctive Features

The term cross-sectional design often refers to a type of social survey in which subsets of a population are selected to be part of a sample. Where the subsets are represented in direct proportion to their existence in the population it is common to refer to proportionate cross-sectional designs. Where subsets are not selected in proportion to their presence in the population – perhaps to give greater weight to the views of minority groups – the term disproportionate cross-sectional design is used. Because data are collected from sample members at one single point in time cross-sectional surveys are sometimes also known as one-shot designs.

One-shot cross-sectional surveys are appropriate to obtaining representative 'snap shots' of the population in terms of basic attributes (such as class, age, ethnicity) and also in terms of subjective variables (such as opinions and attitudes). In the United Kingdom police forces are required by legislation to carry out crime audits of their area, including a survey of the general public's views on the ways in which the community is policed. One-shot cross-sectional surveys are well suited to this purpose. Sometimes cross-sectional surveys are also used to collect retrospective data, for example observations about what sample members did in the past or had done to them. At the analysis stage an attempt is made to correlate past actions, behaviours or events with contemporary attributes, attitudes or other subjective feelings. For example, crime surveys seek to connect respondents' previous victimization of crime with current fears about the possibility of further victimization.

The term cross-sectional design also relates to the use of official statistics and other social indicators to describe geographical areas at any given point in time. For example, the Chicago School of urban sociology used delinquency rates (amongst others) to 'map' the city of Chicago in the 1930s. This was the basis for a concentric circle theory of urban development and the mapping of the city in terms of such rates resembled a cross-section of an onion. Such statistical analysis was used alongside detailed ethnographic accounts of the 'underside' of life within different concentric circles.

Evaluation

Cross-sectional designs provide a relatively cheap and quick means of describing populations on a number of variables at any point in time. They also facilitate the search for patterns of relationships between variables, for example various indicators of social exclusion (such as unemployment, poor housing standards, low educational standards) and levels of criminal and disorderly actions.

As indicated earlier, cross-sectional surveys sometimes collect retrospective data – about past experiences, perhaps – with a view to correlating past experiences with present actions or attitudes. Such correlations subsequently form the basis for causal inferences suggesting, say, that previous experience of victimization engenders present fears of crime. There are, however, difficulties with this. For example, there are doubts about the reliability of respondents' memories of past experiences. More crucially, correlations indicating potential relationships between past experiences and current attitudes and feelings do not by themselves provide sufficient evidence of causality. What is also needed is direct evidence of time-ordering and of causal forces. Sometimes this can be provided by longitudinal surveys, in which a sample of individuals is studied over a long period of time (sometimes a life-time).

A further problem with cross-sectional studies is related to one of the strengths, namely that they provide snapshots at a particular point in time. However, this means that such studies are not useful vehicles for examining social change in society or for mapping social trends over time. One way of overcoming this is by taking equivalent samples at different points in time and collecting data on the same variables with a view to examining changes or trends. This is known as a trend or a time series design, an example of which is the British Crime Survey which seeks to examine changes and trends in victimization.

Victor Jupp

Associated Concepts: Chicago School of Sociology, longitudinal study, official criminal statistics, sampling, social survey, time series design, victim surveys

Key Readings

Jupp, V.R. (1996) *Methods of Criminological Research.* London, Routledge.

Mayhew, P. (1996) 'Researching crime and victimization: the BCS', in P. Davies, P. Francis and V. Jupp (eds), *Understanding Victimization.* Newcastle, University of Northumbria, Social Sciences Press.

CULTURAL CRIMINOLOGY

Definition

An emergent theoretical orientation that investigates the convergence and contestation of cultural, criminal and crime control processes. Cultural criminology emphasizes the role of image, style, representation and meaning both within illicit subcultures, and in the mediated construction of crime and crime control.

Distinctive Features

As developed by Ferrell (1999), Ferrell and Sanders (1995) and other theorists, cultural criminology incorporates a number of orientations regarding the cultural construction of crime and crime control. At its most basic, cultural criminology seeks to import the insights of cultural studies into criminology, building especially from the pioneering work of the Birmingham Centre for Contemporary Cultural Studies in the 1970s on subcultural symbolism and mediated social control. Similarly, cultural criminology operates from

the postmodern propositions that style is substance, that meaning resides in representation, and that crime and crime control can therefore only be understood as an ongoing spiral of intertextual, image-driven 'media loops' (Manning, 1998). Undergirding the use of these contemporary perspectives in cultural criminology are somewhat more traditional projects: the expansion of existing interactionist understandings, and the sharpening of critical analysis in criminology. Cultural criminologists attempt to develop the 'symbolic' in 'symbolic interaction' by exploring the stylized dynamics of illicit subcultures and the representational universes of the mass media. Similarly, they seek to unravel the complex circuitry through which the meaning of crime and crime control is constructed, enforced and resisted.

These theoretical orientations inform the methodologies favoured by cultural criminologists. As employed within cultural criminology, ethnographic research draws on sociological, anthropological and cultural studies traditions to investigate nuances of meaning developed within particular cultural milieux, and to explore the situated dynamics of illicit subcultures. At its extreme, such research is designed to develop a form of criminological *verstehen* whereby the researcher approaches an empathic, appreciative understanding of the meanings and emotions associated with crime and crime control. Alternatively, other cultural criminologists utilize methods of media and textual analysis to develop critical, scholarly readings of mediated crime and crime control accounts. Such scholarship investigates both historical and contemporary texts, ranging from newspapers, film and television to popular music, comic books and cyberspace. Recently cultural criminologists have also begun to integrate these two methodological frameworks in exploring the ongoing confluence of illicit subcultures, media constructions and public meanings.

Framed by these theoretical and methodological orientations, cultural criminological analysis has developed in a number of areas. First, cultural criminology conceptualizes crime as a subcultural phenomenon organized around symbolic communication, shared aesthetics and collective identity. Given this, cultural criminologists focus especially on the dynamics of subcultural style as defining both the internal characteristics of illicit subcultures and external, mediated constructions of them (Hebdige, 1979). In addition, cultural criminologists highlight the intensities of collective experience and emotion within illicit subcultures, as embodied in moments of edgework and adrenalin, and as given meaning within shared vocabularies of motive.

If cultural criminologists in this sense conceptualize crime as culture, they also explore the ways in which culture comes to be reconstructed as crime. Focusing on 'culture wars' fought around issues of art and obscenity, alternative musical forms like punk and rap, and the allegedly criminogenic effects of television and film, researchers reveal the looping, reflexive process by which such media-generated popular culture forms are in turn criminalized by campaigns of moral enterprise themselves fought in the mediated realm of sound bites, press conferences and newspaper headlines. In this sense, 'cultural criminalization' occurs – that is, the mediated representation of popular culture forms as criminal or criminogenic, with or without attendant legal proceedings. Significantly, this process also embodies contemporary political dynamics, as moral entrepreneurs and cultural reactionaries utilize mediated channels to delegitimate alternative or illicit subcultures.

Cultural criminologists likewise explore the broader mediated construction of crime and crime control. Research in this area focuses not only on everyday media texts, but on the complex, reciprocal interconnections between the criminal justice system and the mass media that shape such texts. Much of this work builds from, and in some cases reconceptualizes, Cohen's (1972) classic model regarding the invention of folk devils and the generation of moral panic around issues of crime and deviance. In this sense, this work examines the cultural dynamics by which certain activities come to be constructed as crime and threat, while others are left 'unconstructed'. It further emphasizes the ironies inherent in the marketing of crime as both threat and entertainment.

Threaded through all these areas of enquiry is a concern with relations of power, control and resistance. Cultural criminologists emphasize the new and often insidious forms of coercion and control that emerge within mediated 'wars' on crime and within the everyday consumption of crime as drama and entertainment. At the same time, they highlight forms of resistance that emerge as audiences remake and reverse mediated meanings, and as illicit subcultures embody their insubordination in stylized identities and collectively meaningful experience. Moreover, cultural criminology itself is designed to operate as a form of intellectual resistance, as a counter-discourse on contemporary crime issues that through 'newsmaking criminology' (Barak, 1994) and other public practices can generate alternative images of crime and crime control.

Evaluation

Despite a common focus on representation and meaning in the investigation of crime and crime control, much of the work in cultural criminology has remained divided between the study of illicit subcultures on the one hand, and mass media texts on the other. Yet such a sharp disjunction misses a number of key dynamics regarding crime and culture, including the reconstruction of mass media texts by various subcultures and audiences; the production of localized, situated media by illicit subcultures and crime control agencies alike; and the subsequent appropriation of these situated images and symbols by the mass media. As noted previously, some recent work in cultural criminology has in fact begun to address this problem, by linking subcultural dynamics, organizational imperatives and situated media to broader, mass media constructions of crime and crime control, and by highlighting the reflexive process by which each party to public crime controversies remakes and recontextualizes the meanings of the other. Less promising is the ability of cultural criminologists to address issues of audience and audience meanings; as is the case with much media analysis and criticism, the epistemic activities of audiences remain more imagined than investigated.

Cultural criminologists are also just beginning to explore a number of key domains in which culture, crime and crime control converge. Contemporary policing is coming to be conceptualized as a set of semiotic practices entangled with 'reality' television programmes, everyday public surveillance, and the symbolism and aesthetics of police subcultures themselves. Public controversies regarding homeless populations, street gangs, graffiti crews, and other marginalized groups are beginning to be investigated as conflicts over the construction of meaning and identity in public domains, and thus over ownership of 'cultural space'. Numerous investigations of embodied emotions – of pleasure, fear and excitement as the affective forces driving both crime and crime control – continue to emerge. Perhaps most importantly, cultural criminology is beginning to move beyond its British and US roots to explore the contested convergence of cultural and criminal dynamics in a variety of world settings, and to investigate the migration of illicit meanings across real and imagined borders.

Finally, as a nascent theoretical perspective, cultural criminology perhaps constitutes to this point less a completed, definitive paradigm than an eclectic constellation of critiques linked by sensitivities to image and representation in the study of crime and crime control. Oriented as they are to the multiplicity of meanings and indeterminacy of images continually developing around crime and crime control, though, cultural criminologists themselves would likely embrace cultural criminology as an always unfinished project, open to emerging configurations of culture, crime and crime control, and to emerging critiques of them.

Jeff Ferrell

Associated Concepts: appreciative criminology, carnival (of crime), constitutive criminology, critical criminology, discourse analysis, ethnography, interactionism, newsmaking criminology, postmodernism, social constructionism, subculture

Key Readings

Barak, G. (ed.) (1994) *Media, Process, and the Social Construction of Crime: Studies in Newsmaking Criminology.* New York, Garland.
Cohen, S. (1972) *Folk Devils and Moral Panics.* London, MacGibbon and Kee. (New edition Oxford, Martin Robertson, 1980.)
Ferrell, J. (1999) 'Cultural criminology', *Annual Review of Sociology*, no. 25, pp. 395–418.
Ferrell, J. and Sanders, C.R. (eds) (1995) *Cultural Criminology.* Boston, MA, Northeastern University Press.
Hebdige, D. (1979) *Subculture: The Meaning of Style.* London, Methuen.
Manning, P.K. (1998) 'Media Loops', in F. Bailey and D. Hale (eds), *Popular Culture, Crime, and Justice.* Belmont, CA, West/Wadsworth.

CYBERCRIME

Definition

The use of electronic communication for criminal and transgressive activities that involve the internet and web-based information and communication technologies (ICTs).

Distinctive Features

Cybercrimes are computer-mediated activities that have been defined as illegal or illicit and are acted out through global electronic networks. By the 1990s, cyberspace had become established as one of the fastest growing sites of crime and transgression (Thomas and Loader, 2000). The internet not only offers its users access to global markets and the diffuse networks and links that support illegal and legal markets but also provides the means to traverse the state boundaries of national legal systems and controls. The internet offers the possibility of invisibility and anonymity to transgressors through the use of encryption, passwords, digital compression, steganography and remote storage and as a result has become a major site of action for organized crime, petty crime, state crime and hate crime. It has been used in activities involving drugs, the moving of illegal money, oil trafficking and arms trafficking as well as other sanction-breaking businesses. State and commercial secrets have been stolen and sold through the internet. Potentially harmful political ideas have also been promulgated and disseminated with the aim of inciting violence against ethnic and minority groups. The Internet has also facilitated the development of a global market for pornography and illegal sexual activities.

Cybercrime involves illegal activities that are aimed at national and international economies as well as political and social relations and structures, thereby jeopardizing and putting at risk not only political and economic life but also personal everyday life. Cybercrime often involves cyberviolence that puts the personal safety of citizens at risk through, for example, the manipulation of the emotions of vulnerable individuals by chat room activities and noticeboard communications. Violent acts can be planned and set up hidden from the gaze of CCTV and other security measures.

Anti-social acts on the Internet have led to the World Wide Web becoming an important site for the carnival of crime where protest and disruption can be organized and practised. The use of e-mail carnivalesque to disrupt state and commercial organization has become commonplace, whilst the organizing of illegal popular pleasures, such as bare knuckle fighting or cock, quail and dog fighting, has meant that law enforcement agencies must now counteract such transgressions through their own development of cyber technology (Presdee, 2000).

Mike Presdee

Associated Concepts: Carnival (of crime), corporate crime, hidden crime, state crime, transnational organized crime

Key Readings

Grabosky, P.N. and Smith, R.G. (1998) *Crime in the Digital Age: Controlling Telecommunications and Cyberspace Illegalities.* NSW and New Brunswick, NJ, Federation Press.

Presdee, M. (2000) *Cultural Criminology and the Carnival of Crime.* London, Routledge.

Thomas, D. and Loader, B.D. (eds) (2000) *Cybercrime: Law Enforcement, Security and Surveillance in the Information Age.* London and New York, Routledge.

Wall, D. (1997) 'Policing the virtual community: the internet, cybercrimes and the policing of cyberspace', in P. Francis, P. Davies and V. Jupp (eds), *Policing Futures.* London, Macmillan.

Wall, D. (1999) 'Cybercrimes: new wine, no bottles?', in P. Davies, P. Francis and V. Jupp (eds), *Invisible Crimes.* London, Macmillan.

D

DECARCERATION

Definition

The process that refers to a deliberate move away from the use of imprisonment as the central and predominant penal sanction, usually towards the use of alternative sanctions in the community.

Distinctive Features

Although criticisms against the form and level of prison use and the search for alternatives can be traced back at least to the nineteenth century, decarceration as a distinct process is a contemporary phenomenon. As part of what Cohen (1985) has termed the destructuring impulse in the 1960s, the decarceration movement grew in popularity at a time when the very idea of institutional response to deviance was subject to sustained critique. The prison system and total institutions in general were condemned as degrading, ineffective in terms of their stated goals (they neither deter nor rehabilitate), counter-productive (they cement deviant careers), and as part of the crime problem rather than its solution. Many proponents of decarceration have since argued for displacing the use of specific parts of the prison system (for example, juvenile detention); others have concentrated on advocating alternative sanctions. Community-based corrections and treatments are regarded as more humane, less stigmatizing, and more effective than institutional measures in the control of criminals and other problem populations. Intervention should be aimed at reintegration rather than segregation.

From a Marxist perspective, the prison system represents the symbol *par excellence* of a class society and of class justice. By inflicting coerced discipline and incarcerating predominantly young people, unemployed and ethnic minorities, it reproduces hegemonic power relations in the society. Critical studies on the association between imprisonment and unemployment, the repression of political dissent, human rights violations by the prison system, and overcrowding and inhumane prison conditions which have led to deaths and revolts, have served to highlight the role of the prison system as a repressive and ideological state apparatus. In this sense, decarceration is to be fought for as part of the class struggle.

Decarceration has also been closely associated with the abolitionist social movements and the radical penal lobby in Western Europe, Scandinavia and North America. Thomas Mathiesen (1986) advocated the principle of the 'unfinished' character of alternatives to prison and campaigned for 'negative' reforms that would ultimately lead to prison abolition. As academic involvement increased and the focus widened from the prison system to the penal system, abolitionism developed as a new paradigm in criminology and as an alternative approach to crime and crime control.

Evaluation

Most Western criminal justice systems have witnessed some form of reduction in the use of custody at various times, but decarceration has not had a profound effect in decentring the prison system both in terms of actual prison population and its position in penal thinking. Critics have also pointed to the unintended and perverse consequences of decarceration. Scull (1984) argued that treatment in the community often amounted to benign neglect, leaving people to fend for themselves without the care and supervision that they required. In his seminal work on the transformations in social control strategies, Cohen (1979, 1985) suggested that the extension of community corrections seemed to fit Foucault's model of 'dispersed discipline'. In the case of the decarceration of delinquents and criminals, old institutions remain while new community sanctions and supervisory punishments intended as 'alternatives' to custody are used as supplements to custody, thereby widening the net of social control. More, rather than fewer, deviants are drawn in to the correctional continuum. The network of control agencies expands both physically and territorially. Boundaries between liberty and confinement have been blurred through the development of home curfews, tracking, and tagging.

Whilst the decarceration critique continues to be influential, it does not necessarily reflect the current diverging control trends. In the case of the mentally ill, for example, the state-sponsored closing down of hospitals and asylums has continued to take place but mainly as a response to the retrenchment of welfare policies and fiscal pressures. Vass (1990) also warned that an uncritical acceptance of the decarceration critique can lead to impasse and a paralysis of inventive thought and praxis.

Maggy Lee

Associated Concepts: abolition, abolitionism, diversion, penality, penology, radical non-intervention, social control, transcarceration

Key Readings
Cohen, S. (1979) 'The punitive city: notes on the dispersal of social control', in *Contemporary Crises*, no. 3, pp. 83–93.

Cohen, S. (1985) *Visions of Social Control: Crime, Punishment, and Classification*. Cambridge, Polity Press.

Mathiesen, T. (1986) 'The politics of abolition', *Contemporary Crises*, no. 10, pp. 81–94.

Scull, A. (1984) *Decarceration: Community Treatment and the Deviant – A Radical View*, rev. edn. Englewood Cliffs, NJ, Prentice–Hall.

Vass, A. (1990) *Alternatives to Prison – Punishment, Custody and the Community*. London, Sage.

DECONSTRUCTION

Definition

A literary and social scientific method of analysis most closely linked to postmodernism. Deconstructionists identify communication, whether spoken or written, as the construction of a 'text' that can be endlessly interpreted and re-interpreted, where meaning is always a departure from, rather than arrival at, ultimate truths. Deconstructionists recognize that texts convey multiple, contradictory and hidden meanings that can only be provisionally examined and decoded. Thus, as a method of enquiry, deconstructionism reveals some of the hidden assumptions and embedded values (i.e., ideology) conveyed, knowingly or not, through the construction of a given text.

Distinctive Features

Deconstruction has been popularized chiefly by Jacques Derrida. In part, as a response to the objectivistic, absolutistic and positivistic sciences, Derrida's critique of Western epistemology and intellectual thought (i.e., 'logocentrism') reveals the hidden contradictions in which truth claims are asserted. Termed 'the metaphysics of presence', Derrida examines how any value can be placed in relation to its corresponding binary term (e.g., white vs. black, straight vs. gay, objective vs. subjective, male vs. female). The value of the first term stems, in part, from the value of the second term; however, the value of the second term stems, in part, from the value of the first term. What this mutual interdependence demonstrates is that neither value can be privileged, despite the fact that we do this all the time in our constructed texts. Indeed, the first term becomes dominant, and the second repressed. The metaphysics of presence shows us how, through communication, the first value is identified as presence, active, privileged, while the second value is rendered an absence, passive, dismissed. The task of deconstruction is to show how these 'hierarchies' are basic to all phenomena and to demonstrate the way in which the texts that constitute these hierarchies can be decoded. Thus, the aim of deconstruction is to transform that which is absent into that which is felt and made present.

The deconstructionist strategy to decode existing power relations conveyed through a text is termed the 'reversal of hierarchies'. By turning the terms in binary opposition 'on their heads', so to speak, the implied and unspoken tension is revealed and their interdependence is made manifest. Further, deconstructionists like Derrida explain this mutual interdependence through the concept of *differance* (with an 'a'). *Differance* implies three meanings: (1) that the two terms in binary opposition 'differ' from one another to maintain their meaning; (2) that the two terms in binary opposition 'defer' to one another in the sense of implying the other term; and (3) that the two terms in binary opposition 'defer' to one another to maintain their interdependence.

Relatedly, deconstruction advocates the 'free play of the text'. Once a text (e.g., a legal narrative) is constructed, it is liberated, to some significant degree, from its author. That is to say, the narrative has meaning beyond what was intended by the author – even if the author could exhaust his/her own intended meaning. For example, our understanding of homosexuality, the death penalty, mental illness, homelessness, abortion, drug addiction, politics, art, the presidency, and so on, today is considerably different from what it was 25 years ago. Deconstructionists tell us that this is because the meaning of each of these texts is historically situated; that is, different contexts create different meanings, and these various meanings are never exhaustible. This logic gives rise to the deconstructionist claim of 'foundationless' knowledge (i.e., truths absent from original, structured, anchored realities). Nihilist deconstructionists conclude that if all is relative, why bother to effect any change. Affirmative deconstructionists conclude that there are positional, provisional, relational truths (i.e., contingent universalities) that warrant attention where the voices of and ways of knowing for those most silenced (i.e., the metaphysics of presence) necessitate wholesale support and recognition.

Evaluation

Modernity's quest for exactness, precision and ultimate truths finds considerable critique in the face of deconstructionism. As a method for uncovering hidden assumptions and values, deconstruction reveals how all texts (e.g., legal, criminological) are informed by ideology. The Critical Legal Studies Movement has relied heavily on deconstructionism to advance this position in relation to legal doctrines, the Constitution and statutory law.

Criminology, although more slow in applying the tools of deconstruction, has raised similar questions in relation to criminological theory, criminal law and criminal behaviour. Postmodern critical criminology has been the leading exponent of this deconstructionist agenda.

Bruce Arrigo

Associated Concepts: critical criminology, discourse analysis, postmodernism, post-structuralism

Key Readings

Caputo, J. (ed.) (1997) *Deconstruction in a Nutshell: A Conversation with Jaques Derrida*. New York, Fordham University Press.

Cornell, D., Rosenfeld, M. and Carlson, D. (eds) (1992) *Deconstruction and the Possibility of Justice*. New York, Routledge.

Derrida, J. (1973) *Speech and Other Phenomena*. Evanston, IL, Northwestern University Press.

Derrida, J. (1976) *Of Grammatology*. Baltimore, MD, Johns Hopkins University Press.

Derrida, J. (1978) *Writing and Differance*. Chicago, University of Chicago Press.

Derrida, J. (1981) *Positions*. Chicago, University of Chicago Press.

DECRIMINALIZATION

Definition

A process that refers to the removal of labelling of social problems or deviant behaviours as crimes.

Distinctive Features

Decriminalization grew out of the abolitionist critique of penal responses to criminalized problems. It is based on a rejection of the penal reconstruction of reality (with its associated concepts such as crime, guilt and punishment) and its paralysing effect on attempts to address underlying social problems and circumstances. Abolitionists pointed to the top-down, repressive, punitive and inflexible character of penal control, the appropriation of conflicts from their owners, and the fundamental shortcomings of criminal law to realize social justice, and argued that criminal law sanction should be replaced by dispute settlement and redress. In policy terms, decriminalization means that social policy instead of crime policy is needed in dealing with the social problems and conflicts that are currently singled out as the problem of crime. Hulsman (1986) and de Haan (1990) even argued for the abandoning of the very notion of 'crime' in criminology and for criminologists to talk and think about problematic events, troubles, harms, conflicts or mistakes instead.

Decriminalization has also been closely associated with a labelling approach to crime and deviance. If, as labelling theorists suggested, social reaction does not reduce offending but confirms deviant careers, then the reach of reaction should be reduced. In the narrowest sense, decriminalization involves taking certain offences (such as minor drug use and offences against public morality) out of the realm of criminal law. For example, proponents of decriminalization of drugs generally point to the costly, counter-productive and unsuccessful efforts of law enforcement as a response to drug use. Next to a full, *de iure* decriminalization, many proponents also advocate a *de facto* decriminalization. This means that certain acts will not be prosecuted even though they will formally remain illegal. Opponents, however, often argue that decriminalization would increase use, thereby increasing serious costs to society.

Evaluation

Decriminalization has been used as a measure in penal reform in most Western criminal justice systems with varying degrees of success in halting the trend of criminalization and challenging the crime control and punishment nexus. Wider developments of managerialism in criminal justice have meant that decriminalization is sometimes used as an attractive label for the state to clean up the criminal justice system's caseload and to transfer petty offences to alternative modes of control that offer the involved person less protection against arbitrary measures than a criminal law suit would. Critics have also argued that a *de facto* decriminalization of certain offences often involves an expansion of the policy discretions of the prosecution and the police (as in the use of police cautioning for minor drug-related offences). Mass settlements of offences by administrative or financial means are presented as forms of decriminalization, whereas their punitive character is retained.

Maggy Lee

Associated Concepts: abolition, abolitionism, criminalization, decarceration, diversion, labelling, redress

Key Readings

de Haan, W. (1990) *The Politics of Redress: Crime, Punishment and Penal Abolition*. London, Unwin Hyman.

Hulsman, L. (1986) 'Critical criminology and the concept of crime', in H. Bianchi and R. van Swaaningen (eds), *Abolitionism: Towards a Non-repressive Approach to Crime*. Amsterdam, Free University Press, pp. 25–41.

DEFENSIBLE SPACE

Definition

The use of a range of architectural and environmental measures designed to reduce crime by encouraging communities to protect their public and private spaces from external intrusion.

Distinctive Features

From the 1920s researchers at the University of Chicago had begun to record how rates of crime persisted in certain areas of cities even when the composition of their populations had changed. Such observations led to the conclusion that it was not the nature of individuals, but the nature of particular neighbourhoods that determined levels of disorder. By the 1960s a school of architectural determinism emerged (Jacobs, 1961) in which features of the built environment were viewed as intrinsically criminogenic. The control of crime and disorder, it was argued, would best be achieved by restructuring residential environments so that they were controlled by local communities empowered to mark out and defend their own territories. The most famous exponent of such work was the American architect Oscar Newman (1972). He defined defensible space as a range of mechanisms, real and symbolic barriers, strongly defined areas of influence, and improved opportunities for surveillance that combine to bring an environment under the control of its residents.

Newman argued that poorly designed buildings, such as the high-rise tower block, housing large low income families, produced crime rates as much as three times higher than adjacent lower-rise buildings with socially identical residents and with a similar population density. For Newman a combination of indifferent architects, land speculators, corporate financiers and city planning departments had contrived to build the maximum of housing space at the lowest cost and without consideration of the social consequences. The high-rise double-loaded corridor apartment tower has no 'defensible space' other than the interior of the apartment itself. Everything else – the lobby, stairs, elevators and corridors – is a 'nether world of fear and crime'. Newman's solution to create secure environments was fourfold:

- *Enhance territoriality* – the sub division of places into zones of influence to discourage outsiders and to encourage residents to defend their areas.
- *Increase surveillance* – the positioning of windows so that residents can survey the exterior and the interior public areas of their environment.
- *Improve image* – the redesign of buildings to avoid the stigma of low-cost or public housing.
- *Enhance safety* – the placing of public housing projects within urban areas perceived to be safe.

Whilst Newman's approach has been critiqued as over-general and neglectful of social factors, it has been influential in a number of ways. Certain design features, such as improving external lighting, reducing anonymous open spaces, increasing pedestrian access and the resetting of windows to allow for greater surveillance have been implemented in numerous housing projects world-wide. For example, in the late 1970s new models of spatial segregation appeared in the USA with the emergence of 'common interest communities'. Affluent Americans were opting to lock themselves away in carefully screened cooperative housing schemes and defended residential enclaves.

The most obvious way of reducing opportunities for crime lies in the use of physical barriers. This target hardening, involving locks, bolts, gates, guard dogs, security screens and so on appears to be highly effective. Improving access and windows security on public housing estates is known to reduce the incidence of burglaries. Controlling access – historically evident in the moats and portcullises of medieval castles – finds its contemporary form in entry phones, electronic personal identification measures, fencing

around apartment blocks and street closures. The key paradox which surrounds the effectiveness of 'defensible space' and other situational crime prevention measures is generally referred to as the problem of displacement. The possible displacement effects are:

- *temporal* – the movement of crime/disorder to a different time;
- *tactical* – the continual committal of crime, but by more sophisticated means;
- *target* – the movement of crime to different targets;
- *spatial* – the movement of criminal activity to different places.

Early empirical work appeared to support the premise of spatial displacement in particular. Increasing the police presence in one area of New York brought about a reduction in street crime, but also seemed to increase the level of crime in surrounding precincts. However Clarke (1991) argued that even when such displacement occurs it is unlikely ever to be complete. If the displacement is to crimes of lesser seriousness or to areas where the burden of victimization is more evenly spread, then it may be considered 'benign' rather than 'malign' (Barr and Pease, 1990). As a result, the issue of displacement remains unresolved. Nevertheless, the concept of defensible space has also come to be linked with two other unwelcome developments. First, continual surveillance suggests the emergence of a fortress society in which fear of crime and distrust stimulate a forever expanding network of barricades. Secondly, the growth in the capacity and penetration of electronic surveillance (such as CCTV) conjures up images of a totalitarian 'Big Brother' state.

John Muncie

Associated Concepts: Chicago School of Sociology, panopticism, situational crime prevention, social control, surveillance

Key Readings

Barr, R. and Pease, K. (1990) 'Crime placement, displacement and deflection', in N. Morris and M. Tonry (eds), *Crime and Justice: A Review of Research*, vol. 12. Chicago, University of Chicago Press.

Blakely, E.J. and Snyder, M. (1997) *Fortress America*. Washington, Brookings Institution.

Clarke, R.V. (1991) *Situational Crime Prevention:*

Successful Case Studies. New York, Harrow and Heston.

Davis, M. (1994) *Beyond Blade Runner: Urban Control and the Ecology of Fear*. Westfield, NJ, Open Magazine Pamphlet Series.

Jacobs, J. (1961) *The Death and Life of Great American Cities*. Harmondsworth, Penguin.

Newman, O. (1972) *Defensible Space: People and Design in the Violent City*. London, Architectural Press.

DELINQUENCY

Definition

A term, loosely used, to refer to any kind of youthful misbehaviour.

Distinctive Features

Criminologists frequently use the concepts of 'crime' and 'delinquency' interchangeably, especially when their object of study is young people. However, there are crucial differences. Whilst a legal definition of crime refers to behaviour prohibited by criminal law, delinquency is also applied to all manner of behaviours that are deemed to be undesirable. It is capable of capturing the legally proscribed, but also waywardness, misbehaviour, incorrigibility, the 'anti-social' and that believed to constitute the 'pre-criminal'. Much of this ambiguity derives from the establishment of separate systems of juvenile justice designed to punish and treat offenders but also to protect the vulnerable and neglected. All Western jurisdictions stipulate that under a certain age young people cannot be held fully responsible for their actions. It is widely assumed that juveniles are *doli incapax* (incapable of evil), but how certain age groups – child, juvenile, young person, adult – are perceived and constituted in law is not universally agreed upon. Taking Europe as an example, in Scotland the age of criminal responsibility is 8, in England and Wales 10, in France 13, in Germany 14, in Spain 16 and in Belgium 18. Each is a socially and historically specific concept and as such is liable to review and change. For example, in England and Wales in the late 1990s the presumption that had been enshrined in law since the fourteenth century that those under 14 were incapable of criminal intent was abolished.

In the USA under the statutes of various states delinquency is in part specifically defined, but retains a series of vague and imprecise standards that rest on the need to intervene early to prevent future offending or tackle assumed family or psychological problems. Determinations of what might constitute reprehensible behaviour extend a court's jurisdiction to establish conduct rather than purely legal norms. These are often referred to as status offences – that is, the violation of formal or informal rules which are applied only to certain sections of society. The focus is less on the offence itself and more on who commits it. In the USA such status offences as being incorrigible, truant or sexually precocious apply only to children.

Most historians agree that delinquency was first identified as a major social problem in the early nineteenth century. Social surveys and empirical investigations permitted a problem to be identified but they presupposed existing conceptions of how youth should behave, what relation should exist between different age groups and what should be the appropriate role of the family. In the early nineteenth century, with the rapid growth of industrial capitalism, factory production and high density urban populations, the condition of the labouring classes became the object of considerable middle class concern – whether this was fear of their revolutionary potential, disgust at their morality or alarm at their impoverishment and criminal tendencies. In England, these fears galvanized around dramatic images of gangs of 'naked, filthy, roaming, lawless and deserted children'. Accurate estimations of the extent of 'delinquency' were impossible, not least because of its ill-defined nature. Susan Magarey (1978) contends that there may have been some justification for these growing fears, particularly in the newly recorded prison statistics of the 1830s. The number of under 17s imprisoned increased from some 9,500 in 1838 to some 14,000 in 1848. However she finds that this rise is explicable less with reference to 'increased lawlessness' and more with changes in the position of children in relation to the criminal law and the subsequent criminalization of behaviour for which previously there may have been no official action. In particular, the Vagrancy Act 1824 and the Malicious Trespass Act 1827 considerably broadened legal conceptions of 'criminality' to include, for example, suspicion of being a thief, gambling on the street and scrumping apples from orchards and gardens. Previous nuisances were transformed into criminal offences. Moreover, the remit given to the Metropolitan Police in 1829 included apprehension of 'all loose, idle and disorderly persons not giving good account of themselves'. This alone made many more street children liable to arrest. In these ways juvenile delinquency was 'legislated into existence'.

John Muncie

Associated Concepts: crime, deviance, subculture

Key Readings

Magarey, S. (1978) 'The invention of juvenile delinquency in early nineteenth century England', *Labour History* (Sydney), 34, pp. 11–25.

May, M. (1973) 'Innocence and experience: the evolution of the concept of juvenile delinquency in the mid-nineteenth century', *Victorian Studies*, 17 (1), pp. 7–29.

Tappan, P. (1949) *Juvenile Delinquency*. New York, McGraw–Hill.

West, D. and Farrington, D. (1973) *Who Becomes Delinquent?* London, Heinemann.

West, D. and Farrington, D. (1977) *The Delinquent Way of Life*. London, Heinemann.

DEMONIZATION

Definition

The act of condemning or denouncing evil that is attributed to demonic influence or powers.

Distinctive Features

Demonology refers to possession by evil spirits, as well as to the construction of a catalogue of enemies. In both cases the object of demonization is an 'other', an out-group to which blame for misfortune is attributed, and its purpose is to erect and reaffirm certain moral and social boundaries. In terms of attribution theory the argument would be that bad events require explanation or causes and that demonization is a method of assigning blame or guilt. Denunciation fosters a dichotomization of 'us' and 'them' that serves to shore up the moral barricades of society. Historically, witchcraft has been a key source for demonology. Witches were connected to wicked acts prompted by the devil. The strongly sexualized and gendered dimension in this should not be ignored, such as the 'insatiable' sexual appetite attributed to

women. The nature and scale of reaction in such events has been seen as a defensive reaction by religious groups seeking to maintain moral boundaries, particularly at times of rapid social change. For Erikson (1966) deviance manifests itself in the form that is most feared, suggesting that demons are defined by psychic needs.

In modern times the objects of demonization have been ideological and political deviants whose 'wickedness' is attributed to some shadowy and ambiguous force that enables them to perform feats beyond ordinary human capabilities – sometimes this is connected with a conspiracy theory. Thus, the subversion myth is a narrative that explains why things have gone wrong by attributing blame or demonizing certain groups or individuals by holding them responsible for bad events or occurrences (Goode and Ben-Yehuda, 1994). The cast list of demonized groups is extensive, including Jews under the Third Reich, the Soviet show trials, and the McCarthy era in the USA. These state crimes are instances of the mass production – or fabrication – of deviance that signify the need for society to take exceptional measures to protect itself, connecting the concept of demonization to scapegoating and moral panics. Homosexuals, abortionists, drug users, migrants and asylum seekers, as well as counter-cultural movements, have all been objects of scapegoating and demonization. Furthermore, countries have also been demonized, for instance the reputation of some 'terrorist' Islamic states has been linked to Islamaphobia and Eurocentrism.

In more mundane terms the identification of folk devils such as particular youth cultures has been the basis for labelling outsiders who are then treated as legitimate targets of self-righteous anger and deserving of punishment. A folk devil is treated as the embodiment of evil and, as such, is stripped of all positive characteristics and ascribed negative ones. This occurs through a symbolization process in which 'images are made much sharper than reality' (Cohen, 1972, p. 43). New folk devils are placed into and connected with a gallery of contemporary folk devils that may underlie a moral panic. The identification of groups and their characteristics are listed in stereotypical manner by the media and reaffirm their negative characteristics and may set in process deviancy amplification. Goode and Ben-Yehuda (1994) have emphasized the need for careful attention to the specific social context of demonization – particularly its timing, content and targets.

Evaluation

Like scapegoating, the term demonization is loosely used in a generalized way that makes it difficult to assess its usefulness, unless there is some attention to the details of the discursive process of attribution. Historical work on witchcraft has connected demonization to a cosmology that invokes and attributes evil to some people or groups. Modern instances of demonization seem to focus on conservative moral rhetorics reacting to the erosion of a 'way of life', linking demonization to moral enterprise and symbolic crusades to bolster moral barricades.

Karim Murji

Associated Concepts: deviancy amplification, folk devil, moral panic, racialization, scapegoating, social censure, stereotyping

Key Readings

Cohen, S. (1972) *Folk Devils and Moral Panics*. London, MacGibbon and Kee (new edition, Oxford, Martin Robertson, 1980).

Erikson, K. (1966) *Wayward Puritans*. New York, Wiley.

Goode, E. and Ben-Yehuda, N. (1994) *Moral Panics: The Social Construction of Deviance*. Oxford, Blackwell.

Pfohl, S. (1985) *Images of Deviance and Social Control: A Sociological History*. New York, McGraw–Hill.

DENIAL

Definition

The various processes by which individual actors, social groups or states either 'block, shut out, repress or cover up certain forms of disturbing information [about wrong doing] or else evade, avoid or neutralize' its consequences (Cohen, 1995, p. 19).

Distinctive Features

Classic accounts of the denial of responsibility would include Sykes and Matza's (1957) seminal work on 'techniques of neutralization', which identified five major techniques for denying or deflecting blame for wrongdoing away from the perpetrator. These were: denial of responsibility for the act; denial of the injury caused; denial of the victim; condemnation of the condemners and appeal to higher loyalties. Somewhat later, Scott and Lyman (1968) made the crucial distinction between 'excuses', in which the perpetrator admits the act in question was wrong, but denies full responsibility for it; and 'justifications', in which the perpetrator accepts responsibility for the act, but denies that it was wrong.

Denial may be either conscious or unconscious. Conscious denial is a rhetorical rejection or evasion of the truth or its consequences. As Mary Douglas has argued, it is a 'forensic' strategy in the sense that the accounts in question are aimed at manipulating or deflecting attributions of 'responsibility' or blame away from the person, group or entity doing the denying (Douglas, 1992). Stanley Cohen (1995) later developed the argument that, what is being denied may be matters of *'fact'* (for example, how many people were 'disappeared' by the Pinochet regime); matters of *interpretation* (whether certain actions constitute torture or 'moderate physical pressure'); or the *implications* or consequences of the acts in question (for example, the acknowledgement of the harm done to the victim).

In contrast to these rhetorical forms of denial (lying to others), unconscious forms of denial are the expressions of the psychological processes (or 'defence mechanisms') that enable a person to evade or distort the 'claims of external reality' – a form of *lying to one's self*. This denial or disavowal of an external truth is only one element in a larger psychological repertoire for dealing with extreme threat or social injury. Other defences include psychic *numbing*, a form of dissociation involving the diminished capacity or inclination to feel; and *doubling*, the formation of a separate self, specific to the context of atrocity (Lifton and Markusen, 1990). For psychoanalysts, there is an important distinction to be made between this form of unconscious denial or disavowal of *external reality* and the psychological process whereby the demands of *internal* desires are 'repressed' from a person's consciousness.

Evaluation

Stanley Cohen's recent work on denial sharpens the distinction between conscious 'rhetorical' forms of denial and the forms of denial that involve unconscious processes that serve to disavow or block out the claims of external reality. An additional focus of

Cohen's work on the denial of responsibility is the extension of the analysis of denial by individuals to include collective forms of denial, such as denial of human rights violations by *representatives of the state*. In principle, there is no reason why this approach to 'denial' could not be applied to the analysis of the motivational accounts offered by perpetrators of other forms of crime – for example, the white collar crime of insider trading or the corporate criminality of transnational corporations involved in the dumping of toxic waste. Researchers working in these areas will confront the problem of accounts that are driven by economic and other interests rather than personal deceits. Criminologists and criminal lawyers working on issues of denial in the future will face the continuing challenge of avoiding reducing the issue to the play of discourses rather than the expression of specific interests and personal responsibility.

Ruth Jamieson

Associated Concepts: corporate crime, human rights, neutralization (techniques of), state crime

Key Readings

Cohen, S. (1995) *Denial and Acknowledgement: The Impact of Information About Human Rights Violations*. Jerusalem, The Hebrew University of Jerusalem, Centre for Human Rights.

Douglas, M. (1992) *Risk and Blame*. London, Routledge.

Lifton, R.J. and Markusen, E. (1990) *The Genocidal Mentality*. London, Macmillan.

Scott, M. and Lyman, S. (1968) 'Accounts', *American Sociological Review*, 33 (10), pp. 46–62.

Sykes, G.M. and Matza, D. (1957) 'Techniques of neutralization: a theory of delinquency', *American Sociological Review*, 22, pp. 664–70.

DETERMINISM

Definition

There is no easy definition of the term 'determinism'. Honderich (1993) describes three meanings of the term, each with its own subtle shifts and variations. Alongside its use with reference to small particles in physics, determinism can be used as an opposite to free will, or it can be used in a more restricted sense to mean that human action is subject to causal laws. In a more general sense, as used here, determinism can be taken in the sense of inevitability: once the antecedents to an event are understood, so prediction of future similar events becomes possible.

Distinctive Features

Bertrand Russell's (1961) *A History of Western Philosophy* traces the concept of determinism back to 440 BC and the philosophers Leucippus and Democritus. As the basis of their philosophical stance, known as atomism, they argued that nothing happens by chance, that everything is explicable by natural laws. In a position akin to much modern science, the atomists said that science should be empirical, seeking to discover the natural laws by which to understand the universe. Not all philosophers agreed with this view and, from Socrates, Plato, and Aristotle onwards, the debate has continued.

In the field of human behaviour, including criminal behaviour, the match is made between, on the one hand, determinism, and free will on the other. If determinism holds that behaviour is predictable (once the laws governing behaviour are eventually understood), so free will takes the contrary stance: no matter what the antecedents might be at the point of acting, individuals could, had they wished, have acted differently than they did.

What might determine human behaviour? There are many levels of explanation, ranging through genetic, psychological, social and political theories. Regardless of whether the antecedents are said to be inside the person or in the environment (or a combination of the two), human action is a function of its antecedent conditions. Such antecedent conditions may be unique to the individual, none the less it is these conditions that determine behaviour. Explanations of behaviour then move beyond the concepts of freedom and dignity (Skinner, 1971).

In thinking about criminal behaviour, the issue of determinism is of importance. If behaviour is determined, then this directly challenges the principles of free will, responsibility and choice, the principles upon which many systems of justice are based. At both a philosophical and scientific level the issues are complex (Alper, 1998): it seems unlikely that the debate started by the atomists is likely to be resolved in the foreseeable future.

Clive Hollin

Associated Concepts: biological criminology, free will, individual positivism, positivism, prediction studies, sociological positivism

Key Readings

Alper, J.S. (1998) 'Genes, free will, and criminal behavior', *Society, Science, and Medicine*, 46, pp. 1599–1611.

Honderich, T. (1993) *How Free Are You? The Determinism Problem*. Oxford, Oxford University Press.

Russell, B. (1961) *A History of Western Philosophy*, 2nd edn. London, George Allen and Unwin.

Skinner, B.F. (1971) *Beyond Freedom and Dignity*. New York, Knopf.

DETERRENCE

Definition

A philosophy of punishment that aims to prevent criminal activity through the development and application of effective and efficient sanctions. It involves demonstrating to both the citizenry and the reasoning criminal that the pains and losses associated with apprehension and punishment will overshadow the possibility of criminal gain or profit.

Distinctive Features

Utilitarian or rational choice theories of human nature posit that individuals are responsible for their actions and will naturally indulge in behaviours that bring them maximum benefits and goods and minimize risks and costs. For Cesare Beccaria (1738–94) and Jeremy Bentham (1748–1832) the over-riding purpose of their work was to provide the criminal justice system with a unified philosophy. They concluded that the role of the criminal law was to promote the well-being of the community and it did so when it deterred the commission of crime and minimized the severity of the crimes committed. Because it is natural that human beings will violate the law if they are allowed to do so, to prevent crime society must make the punishments for criminal behaviour greater than the pleasures derived from the successful completion of criminal acts. Deterrence requires three key elements:

- The certainty of apprehension, conviction and punishment.

- The severity of the punishment to be greater than the potential benefits of the criminal act.
- The clarity of punishment to ensure that the offender is in a position to make the link between her/his punishment and her/his criminal behaviour.

Deterrence assumes two principal forms and both are supposed to make it clear that crime does not pay. General deterrence is aimed at influencing the total population with future or potential criminal activity being prevented by the universal threat and fear of punishment. Specific deterrence is targeted at the known offender to ensure that this individual is deterred from further involvement in criminal activity. The ultimate form of individual deterrence is the death penalty. Although positivism replaced deterrence theory during the first half of the twentieth century, it re-emerged in the aftermath of 'nothing works' in the form of rational choice and routine activity approaches to crime control.

Critics of deterrence focus on its limited conception of human beings and human action. They argue that we need to develop a considerably more sophisticated theory of human behaviour which explores the internal and external checks on why people do or do not engage in criminal activity. This theory must also recognize that there are a bewildering number of motivational states, rational and irrational, that lead to the commission of criminal acts. We also need to research the complexities of communication and understanding. It is evident that many petty criminals are not capable of accurately balancing the costs and benefits of crime before the commission of the act. It is also the case that many young males who get involved in street fights with other young men do not think about the consequences of their actions either for themselves or others. Deterrence theory has also been criticized because it fails to think through the consequences of what it is proposing for offenders. Many offenders are driven to re-offending because, as a result of being processed by the criminal justice system, they have no alternative. The labelling process and 'naming and shaming' effectively close off the possibility of 'going straight'.

Eugene McLaughlin

Associated Concepts: rational choice theory, routine activity theory, situational crime prevention

Key Readings

Grasmick, H. and Bursik, R. (1990) 'Conscience, significant others and rational choice: extending the deterrent model', *Law and Society Review*, 24, pp. 837–61.

Klepper, S. and Nagin, D. (1989) 'The deterrent effect of perceived certainty and severity of punishment revisited', *Criminology*, 27, pp. 721–46.

Matravers, M. (ed.) (1999) *Punishment and Political Theory*. Oxford, Hart Publishing.

Piliavin, I., Gartner, R., Thornton, C. and Matsueda, R. (1986) 'Crime, deterrence and rational choice', *American Sociological Review*, 51, pp. 101–19.

Scarre, G. (1996) *Utilitarianism*. London, Routledge.

DEVIANCE

Definition

Deviance is a twentieth-century sociological concept intended to designate the aggregate of social behaviours, practices, acts, demeanours, attitudes, beliefs, styles or statuses which are culturally believed to deviate significantly from the norms, ethics, standards and expectations of society. It emerged in the USA around 1937, within the context of Roosevelt's New Deal, as a solution to the problem of how sociologists in an emergent welfare state were to summarize categorically such matters as delinquency, mental and physical disability, criminal behaviour, drug abuse, cultural rebellion, sustained dependency upon state benefits, street-level political opposition, intellectual and artistic radicalism, homosexuality, and the behaviour of native American populations – without insulting but yet implying the value of both psychiatric and sociological explanations of these phenomena as forms of sociopathy. Social deviance refers to that which is censured as deviant from the standpoint of the norms of the dominant culture. It is an effect of the bio-politics of social-democratic welfare capitalism.

Distinctive Features

Social deviance is a broader concept than criminal behaviour, referring to a range of social phenomena which the dominant culture has stood against either in principle or in practice. As such, it is intertwined with the dominant culture – the very identity and historical formation of which are defined, driven and sustained by what it censures as social deviance. As a defining feature of a dominant culture and a reflection of divisions in a political economy, social deviance is a pivotal aspect in the constitution of society. Society's norms and virtues are defined, partly, by their opposition to its enemies' sins and vices. It is therefore seen as legitimate for the agencies of social control, and the state as a whole, to violate the liberty of those who are held by those agencies to violate the rights and principles of others or of the state itself.

Without that differential in authoritative backing, there is often little in the physics of the respective behaviours which would differentiate them. It is the significance we attribute to behaviours which locates them within the moral order of virtue, deviance, criminality, insanity or evil. How an act, such as a killing, for example, is perceived within the dominant culture depends more upon our historically shaped principles of morality and the circumstances of its execution than upon any behavioural feature. Killing could be described as a heroic act in war, a sign of evil or madness when perpetrated upon a stranger, a crime of passion in a domestic relationship, an act of mercy in the case of euthanasia, or as tortious negligence in industrial situations.

The concept of deviance is distinct from that of mere difference in that the former contains the implicit likelihood of possible authoritative intervention or sanction. Difference in modern society is respected as a right: deviance is always liable to be penalized or regulated. Deviance is a culturally unacceptable level of difference which is subject to constant suspicion and surveillance from social control agencies. Difference is seen to contribute to the vitality and creativity of modern capitalist society, whereas deviance always holds a threat to the social fabric.

Evaluation

Many social scientists today feel that the concept of deviance has run its historical course or at least has lost its cutting edge. Until the 1970s, the sociology of deviance focused on the social processes whereby certain acts, individuals or groups were targeted for social censure, stigmatization, exclusion or punishment. That study advanced criminology away from the naive idea that crimes were unambiguous acts of evil committed by born criminals. It served a social-democratic movement which highlighted the social roots of misbehaviour, thus placing the blame more upon society than the individual and raising important questions about dominant social norms, the dangers of criminalization, the impartiality of policing, the neutrality of justice, and the counter-productiveness of punishment.

At the beginning of the new millennium, however, social scientists cynically believe that moral judgements are always made from a standpoint of partisan interest as well as general principle and that they are therefore profoundly relative to the culture or period within which they are embedded. Events of the twentieth century, such as the Holocaust, have given many an awareness of the horrors that can be involved in scapegoating censured social groups. In addition, globalization, mass communications, travel and mobility have resulted in a greater moral tolerance in a highly differentiated, multicultural, world – who is to say what is now deviant? Consequently, all moral judgements are now seen as questionable in principle, not just those pertaining to areas of ambiguity. Indeed, any lack of ability to challenge a moral judgement would be taken as a negative sign regarding its authority. In a depoliticized age, the power of authority to define and control popular morality and culture has been reduced. Deviance could be anything within a multi-cultural pluralism and has therefore lost its significance as a social issue. Society has advanced to the point where condescending sensitivity to insulting the urban poor has been supplanted by critiques of social censure and of political authority itself. The core meaning and purpose of the concept of social deviance has thus been eroded. When norms lose their authority, authority loses its norms.

What concerns politicians and social scientists at the beginning of a new century are two issues that co-exist and interrelate in a constant tension: (1) to locate, understand and create areas of social agreement which might constitute the basis of social censure and control for a more healthy, secure and peaceful society, and (2) to expose, criticize and explain social norms and systems of social control which are discriminatory, hypocritical and oppressive in order to enable a society where its members are allowed to develop their positive capacities to the full. Authority is trying to regain its moral power and moral critique is trying to expose authority. The continuing harsh reality of poverty, inequality, oppression, misinformation and ill-health on a global scale means that both these utopian concerns face massive challenges.

Colin Sumner

Associated Concepts: crime, delinquency, governmentality, labelling, moral panic, penality, penology, social censure, social control, social exclusion, stigma

Key readings
Becker, H. (1963) *Outsiders*. New York, Free Press.
Goffman, E. (1968) *Stigma*. Harmondsworth, Penguin.
Lemert, E. (1951) *Social Pathology*. New York, McGraw–Hill.
Matza, D. (1969) *Becoming Deviant*. Englewood Cliffs, NJ, Prentice–Hall.
Sumner, C.S. (1994) *The Sociology of Deviance: An Obituary*. Buckingham, Open University Press.
Young, J. (1999) *The Exclusive Society: Social Exclusion, Crime and Difference in Late Modernity*. London, Sage.

DEVIANCY AMPLIFICATION

Definition

The process whereby media, police, public and political reaction to non-conformity acts not to control deviancy but has the obverse reaction of increasing it.

Distinctive Features

Leslie Wilkins (1964) first used the term 'deviation amplification' to explore the relationship between levels of tolerance/intolerance and the reinforcement of deviant identities. He noted how societies that had developed an intolerant response to deviancy tended to define more acts as criminal and took more formal action against criminals. This in turn led to the increased alienation of deviants, more crime by deviant groups and a corresponding affirmation of intolerance of deviants by conforming groups. The production of intolerance is subject to a 'positive feedback loop', in which the identification of and reaction to deviancy becomes self-perpetuating. The further an individual is defined as having moved away from the cultural norm the more they are likely actually to behave in a non-conformist fashion. As a result Wilkins argued that deviancy control is best achieved by building social systems that can tolerate difference and minimize the number of persons who are defined as deviant.

The concept of deviancy amplification has clear resonances with many of the propositions of a labelling approach in which the key factor in deviancy creation is believed to be social reaction, rather than individual behaviour. In Britain, Jock Young (1971b) applied the concept in his participant observation study of marijuana users in Notting Hill, London in the late 1960s. He showed how the relatively harmless social activity of marijuana smoking was transformed into a serious social problem through the combined reaction of the mass media, the police and the public. Through sensational reporting, users were portrayed by the media as sick, promiscuous and dangerous outsiders. During 1967 such stereotypes inflamed popular indignation. Media pressure forced the police to take more direct action by increasing surveillance and rates of arrest. For the drug users what was once a peripheral activity became a symbol of their difference and a key part of their defiance of perceived social injustices. Police activity acted to amplify the extent and symbolic importance of drug usage for the users themselves. Moreover as drug taking was driven underground it moved from being a low key, low profit activity to one organized by a 'criminal underworld' and practised in an even more secretive fashion. In this way social reaction amplifies deviance in both mythical and actual terms. A vicious spiral of escalation ensues.

The concept has also been used by Stan Cohen (1972) in his study of the moral panic associated with the Mods and Rockers in Britain in the mid 1960s. Here again it was argued that relatively minor scuffles between groups of youths were exaggerated by media reportage and magnified by subsequent police and judicial targeting. Again their deviance was initially amplified through social reaction which in turn produced an actual amplification in real levels of deviancy as the Mods and Rockers took on aspects of their new publicly defined personas.

Evaluation

Together with the labelling approach, the concept of deviancy amplification draws attention to the unintended consequences of public perceptions, police actions and social reaction in general. It reveals how processes of reaction are also processes of invention and creation. The concept has been most commonly applied to explain escalations in expressive forms of deviancy. Its wider applicability to other less publicized forms of rule-breaking are less clear. It may remain the case that in other instances (for example, domestic violence) it is a *lack* of negative social reaction (intolerance) which provides a climate for its continuation. The extent to which a real amplification of deviance is driven by its public identification also remains questionable (and probably unknowable). A complex of motivations may underlie the development of deviant careers, of which social reaction might play a relatively small part.

John Muncie

Associated Concepts: deviance, labelling, moral panic, social reaction

Key Readings

Cohen, S. (1972) *Folk Devils and Moral Panics.* London, MacGibbon and Kee.

Wilkins, L.T. (1964) *Social Deviance.* London, Tavistock.

Young, J. (1971a) 'The role of the police as amplifiers of deviancy, negotiators of reality and translators of fantasy', in S. Cohen (ed.), *Images of Deviance.* Harmondsworth, Penguin.

Young, J. (1971b) *The Drug Takers: The Social Meaning of Drug Use.* London, Paladin.

DIFFERENTIAL ASSOCIATION

Definition

Initially developed by Edwin H. Sutherland (1883–1950), the concept of differential association is an attempt to account for the acquisition and maintenance of criminal behaviour in terms of contact, or association, with particular environments and social groups.

Distinctive Features

Much of the very early research and theory concerned with the causes of crime had focused attention on the individual characteristics of the offender: these individual factors included genetic and biological functioning, psychological factors and psychiatric status. During the 1920s and 1930s a group of researchers, including Clifford R. Shaw and Henry D. McKay, at the University of Chicago began to challenge the view that explanations for crime were to be found at an individual level. The significant contribution of the

Chicago School was the advancement of the thesis that crime was brought about not by individual factors, but was a product of social forces.

As the attention of criminologists turned to social factors, the particular role of social organization and disorganization in explaining crime came to prominence. A broad position evolved that people, perhaps particularly young people, living in parts of cities that are characterized by social disadvantage and disorganization were at a greatly increased risk of participating in delinquency. Further, once a neighbourhood becomes a focus for a delinquent culture, then the possibility arises that through cultural transmission of delinquent values other young people will be drawn into that crime. In a sense, these emerging sociological theories shifted pathology from the individual to the social structure.

During the 1930s Sutherland spent part of his academic career at the University of Chicago, working alongside the researchers who developed a sociological theory of crime. However, Sutherland's own contribution was in part driven by a strain that was evident in the data collected by the Chicago researchers. While formulating a cogent theoretical perspective based on social disorganization, the data also spoke of a social cohesion and organization at the centre of criminal activity. For example, it was difficult to argue that white collar crime was a product of social disorganization.

Sutherland took a broad perspective, advocating that crime itself is a socially defined construct, with the power to define crime held by certain influential sections of society. It was therefore not the case that he ascribed to a view of crime as a product of individual psychopathology. However, he did not lose sight of the individual: he was concerned to understand how crime was transmitted through generations, and how a given individual was drawn into crime. The mechanism for cultural transmission was seen to be learning, such that criminal behaviour is learned in the same way that any other behaviour is learned. Sutherland argued that the answer to the next question, how criminal behaviour is learned, lies in understanding how social influences impact on the individual. Specifically, each individual has a *differential association* with other people more or less disposed to delinquency.

As an explanatory concept of the impact of differential associations, Sutherland invoked the notion of a 'definition': those individuals with more contact with other people favourably disposed towards crime would themselves develop definitions favourable to crime, and vice versa. A definition towards crime would indicate learning not only of the skills to commit an offence, but would also incorporate the attitudes and moral values that supported criminal activity. It is important to note that Sutherland is not suggesting that the association has to be with criminals, rather that the association is with people who might either encourage crime or fail to censure criminal acts.

As the theory developed in sophistication, Sutherland set out a number of postulates:

1 Criminal behaviour is learned.
2 Learning takes place through association with other people.
3 The main setting for learning is within close personal groups.
4 Learning includes techniques to carry out certain crimes and attitudes and motives supportive of committing crime.
5 Learning experiences – differential associations – will vary in frequency and importance for each individual.
6 The processes involved in learning criminal behaviour are no different from the learning of any other behaviour.

Evaluation

With the articulation of this position as Differential Association Theory, Sutherland offered perhaps the first integrated social psychological account of crime. Sutherland continued to refine his ideas throughout his writings, and after his death his colleague Donald Cressey continued the work (e.g. Sutherland, 1939, 1947; Sutherland and Cressey, 1974). Sutherland's views are remarkable in that they anticipate much of what is to follow in both psychology and criminology. The theory is clearly sociological in its portrayal of powerful social forces as defining the nature of crime. However, with its concern for the individual, it is also psychological in orientation. The proposition that learning takes place through associations within social groups and intimate relationships is evident in contemporary social learning theory and in social structure theories in criminology. The view that each individual's unique learning experiences lead to the acquisition of specific skills and cognitions fits with contemporary learning theory. Indeed, offenders' cognitions in the form of rational choice and decision-making have become a focus for much debate in the recent literature. Finally, Sutherland's view of the normality of the learning that leads to criminal behaviour is in accord with the many contemporary theorists who reject explanations of crime based on individual psychopathology.

Sutherland's theory does leaves many questions to be answered. How does learning occur? What exactly are the social conditions that lead to learning criminal skills and attitudes? At an individual level, how do skills and attitudes function? Sutherland did not have the empirical base from which he could begin to answer such questions but he set an agenda for future generations of researchers.

Clive Hollin

Associated Concepts: appreciative criminology, Chicago School of Sociology, conditioning, differential reinforcement, interactionism, rational choice theory, social learning theory

Key Readings
Sutherland, E.H. (1939) *Principles of Criminology*. Philadelphia, Lippincott.
Sutherland, E.H. (1947) *Principles of Criminology*, 5th edn. Philadelphia, Lippincott.
Sutherland, E.H. and Cressey, D.R. (1974) *Principles of Criminology*, 9th edn. Philadelphia, Lippincott.

DIFFERENTIAL REINFORCEMENT

Definition

In learning theory the concept of reinforcement refers to the relationship between a behaviour and the outcomes it produces. Attempts to understand criminal behaviour in terms of its outcomes are called differential reinforcement.

Distinctive Features

Sutherland's concept of differential association highlights the importance of learning in attempts to understand criminal behaviour. In the 1950s such ideas were being developed in criminology, whilst within mainstream psychology there were significant advances in the development of theories of learning. In particular, B.F. Skinner's work on the principles of operant conditioning had demonstrated the relationship between behaviour and its consequences (Skinner, 1938, 1969). Skinner's experimental research showed that the environmental consequences that follow a specific behaviour act either to increase or decrease the probability of that behaviour happening again in the future. When behaviour produces consequences that the individual finds rewarding and the frequency of that behaviour is increased, it is said to be *reinforced*. Alternatively, a behaviour that produces outcomes that the individual finds aversive and which therefore act to decrease the rate of behaviour is said to be *punished*. (In language of operant conditioning, the term 'punishment' simply means that a behaviour decreases in frequency.)

The principles of reinforcement were applied to criminal behaviour, as an extension of differential association theory. They offered a means, consistent with learning theory, to account for the way in which offending could be both acquired and maintained (Burgess and Akers, 1966). Jeffery (1965) suggested that criminal behaviour can be viewed as operant behaviour: that is, within the context of the associations that an individual experiences, criminal behaviour is acquired and maintained by its reinforcing consequences. Further, extending the principles of operant learning, criminal behaviour will occur when the environment signals that a criminal act is likely to produce rewards. To understand why a person commits a crime, it is necessary to understand that individual's learning history. The task of understanding an individual's learning history means understanding the rewarding (and punishing) consequences of the criminal behaviour for the individual concerned. It is necessary, therefore, to understand not only the person but also their environment which provides the setting for criminal acts.

The setting conditions for crime operate at two levels: first, conditions of the type known to be precursors to persistent offending; second, the immediate situational cues that signal that a criminal act is likely to produce rewarding consequences. With regard to the former, this might include individual factors such as poor school attainment, family and peer relationships, and social disadvantage such as low family income and poor housing.

The importance of immediate setting events has been increasingly recognized over the past few years. For example, houses may be targeted for burglary because they offer an easy opportunity, such as an unlocked door or an open window; or because of design features, such as thick trees or high hedges, that hide the criminal from observation and detection; or that goods such as televisions and video recorders are easily observed, making the property an attractive target. This situational analysis of the environment in which crimes occur has informed both understandings of criminal behaviour and situational crime prevention strategies to reduce crime.

Moving to the consequences of criminal behaviour, in acquisitive crimes such as burglary and embezzlement, the rewards are plainly financial and material gain. Such gains can be *positively reinforcing* in that they produce material outcomes that the offender finds rewarding. Alternatively, the gains can be *negatively reinforcing* in that they allow the offender to avoid the aversive situation of having no money. The link between unemployment and crime would serve as a broad example of how offending might be related to the need to avoid an unwanted financial and social situation. As well as tangible, material rewards, criminal behaviour can also produce social rewards such as peer group status and esteem.

Jeffery also noted that criminal behaviour can produce aversive consequences, such as loss of liberty and disrupted intimate relationships, that can have a punishing (in the learning theory sense of the word) effect on behaviour. Overall, for each and every individual it is the historical balance of reinforcement and punishment that determines the likelihood of criminal behaviour when the opportunity presents itself. (For a case study applying behavioural analysis to a complex set of criminal behaviours see Gresswell and Hollin, 1992.)

Evaluation

As the research on processes of learning matured two crucial issues emerged. First, the complexity of people's lives means that it is impossible to know their full learning history. Thus, there can never really be a complete understanding of any behaviour, criminal or otherwise. A behavioural analysis of an individual's criminal behaviour will always be limited by the boundaries of the available information. Secondly, in adopting operant conditioning as an explanatory framework, differential reinforcement falls prey to the criticism that it does not consider what happens inside the individual.

Clive Hollin

Associated Concepts: conditioning, differential association, rational choice theory, situational crime prevention, social learning theory

Key Readings

Burgess, R. and Akers, R. (1966) 'A differential association-reinforcement theory of criminal behavior', *Social Problems*, 14, pp. 128–47.

Gresswell, D.M. and Hollin, C.R. (1992) 'Towards a new methodology for making sense of case material: An illustrative case involving attempted multiple murder', *Criminal Behaviour and Mental Health*, 2, pp. 329–41.

Jeffery, C.R. (1965) 'Criminal behavior and learning theory', *Journal of Criminal Law, Criminology, and Police Science*, 56, pp. 294–300.

Skinner, B.F. (1938) *The Behavior of Organisms: An Experimental Analysis*. New York, Appleton–Century–Crofts.

Skinner, B.F. (1969) *Contingencies of Reinforcement: A Theoretical Analysis*. Englewood Cliffs, NJ, Prentice-Hall.

DISASSOCIATION

See Neutralization (techniques of); Subculture

DISCOURSE ANALYSIS

Definition

A generic term covering a heterogeneous range of social science research methods which are concerned with the activities present in recorded talk and their relationship to other texts (for example, official statements of policies and practices). It is concerned with 'the way versions of the world, of society, events and inner psychological worlds are produced in discourse' (Potter, 1997, p. 146).

Distinctive Features

Discourse analysis is a perspective on social life which combines theoretical ideas and analytical orientations from different disciplines such as linguistics, psychology and sociology. It shares many of the features of conversational analysis in that it is concerned with the ways in which people ascribe meaning to routine social interactions through talk. However, discourse analysis differs from conversational analysis in a number of ways (Silverman, 1993). It deals with a wider range of social science concerns (such as gender relations and social control) and, consequently, does not eschew the use of theoretical frameworks. It uses a variety of written, as well as spoken, 'utterances', especially in relation to the analysis of institutional talk. Finally, it does not require the same degree of mechanistic precision in the analysis of transcripts.

The concept of 'discourse' developed as a reaction against both positivistic epistemologies seeking scientific 'truths' and relativistic perspectives on knowledge which claimed that the process of knowing is ineluctably contradictory, uncertain and contingent (Worrall, 1990). It sought to identify the mechanisms whereby 'truths' are socially constructed through talk and, despite (or because of) underlying incoherence, become the accepted (and, therefore, powerful) version of events. According to Foucault (1972) discourse is the key to power. Power, he argues, is not the overt domination of one group by another but the acceptance by all that there exists a reliable, smooth and coherent 'text' underlying all the apparent paradoxes of life. This process of reconstructing paradox as coherence is the fundamental project of discourse.

Analysis of discourse involves the deconstruction of coherence to reveal the underlying paradox and expose the absence of that which is represented as being present. For example, one way of ensuring the continuity of discourse is to demarcate its boundaries by employing 'practices of exclusion'. Such practices might include the prohibition of certain topics or explanations on grounds of 'irrelevance' (for example, poverty as an explanation of crime), the disqualification of certain individuals from being authorized speakers (for example, victims of crime in the courtroom) and the rejection of certain statements as illegitimate (for example, a sex offender claiming that his offence 'just happened').

In order to analyse discourse one has to ask questions not just about the content of discourse but also about its author (who says it?), its authority (on what grounds?), its audience (to whom?), its object (about whom?) and its objective (in order to achieve what?). Discourse analysis is particularly interested in the way in which rhetoric and argument are organized in talk and texts so as to undermine alternative or oppositional versions.

Evaluation

Potter (1997, p. 147) says that 'a large part of doing discourse analysis is a craft skill, more like bike riding or chicken sexing than following the recipe for a mild chicken rogan josh'. The main difficulty in defining discourse analysis is that it covers a wide range of activities from linguistic analysis (akin to conversational analysis) to postmodern analysis of the relationship between the construction of knowledge and power (Lyon, 1999). In some of its variations it would not be recognized as a research 'method' at all by many social scientists. Despite these criticisms, discourse analysis has played an important role in encouraging a reflexive and critical approach to the conventional wisdom, which passes for knowledge in penal policy and the criminal justice system. It has exposed the inconsistencies and contradictions which are rendered coherent in institutional and routine talk about crime and criminals.

Anne Worrall

Associated Concepts: conversational analysis, deconstruction, documentary analysis, postmodernism

Key Readings
Burton, F. and Carlen, P. (1979) *Official Discourse.* London, Routledge and Kegan Paul.

Foucault, M. (1972) *The Archaeology of Knowledge.* London, Tavistock.

Lyon, D. (1999) *Postmodernity,* 2nd edn. Buckingham, Open University Press.

Potter, J. (1997) 'Discourse Analysis as a way of analysing naturally occurring talk', in D. Silverman (ed.), *Qualitative Research: Theory, Methods and Practice.* London, Sage.

Silverman, D. (1993) *Interpreting Qualitative Data: Methods for Analysing Talk, Text and Interaction.* London, Sage.

Worrall, A. (1990) *Offending Women: Female Lawbreakers and the Criminal Justice System.* London, Routledge.

DISCRETION

Definition

The power conferred on criminal justice professionals to use their judgement to decide what action to take in a given situation.

This includes the decision to take no action. Discretion is officially delegated within the criminal justice system and it is not limited to one decision point. Because it extends to all points of decision-making and encompasses procedures and working methods, flows back and forth through all parts of the criminal justice system.

Distinctive Features

Discretion is one of the most contentious issues in criminal justice because the professionals involved at each stage of the criminal justice process enjoy a considerable degree of mandated flexibility in the decisions they can make about the processing of individual cases. It is the day-to-day discretionary actions of police officers, prosecutors, defence lawyers, judges and prison and probation officers that lubricate the criminal justice system and ensure that 'justice' is discharged. Discretion provides criminal justice professionals with the space both to engage in discriminatory activities and to subvert policies that they do not agree with.

There is wide agreement that the establishment of consistent criminal justice policies and the fair and equal treatment of all individuals, irrespective of class, gender or race, requires the regulation of discretionary powers.

Particular attention has focused on the discretionary powers of police officers because they are the 'gatekeepers' to the criminal justice system, and unlike many other organizations, discretionary power is located primarily with the lowest-ranking employees. The police role requires discretionary power because officers are required to deal with a vast range of laws, incidents and forms of behaviour and make critical decisions. The source of police discretion lies with the legal powers they are given, the nature of the criminal law they have to enforce, the context within which policework takes place and limitations on resources. However, the location of a considerable degree of unregulated autonomy at the bottom of the organization poses serious problems for supervisors. Police officers can use their discretion to discriminate for or against sections of the community either through under- or over-enforcement of the law. The injudicious, provocative and abusive application of police powers triggered serious confrontations between the police and minority ethnic communities in the USA and UK during the 1990s.

As a result of judicial judgements, commu-nity complaints about misconduct, miscar-riages of justice and an increasing number of expensive civil actions, police forces have paid considerably more attention to structuring the discretionary powers of officers. This has resulted in:

- Training programmes to equip officers to use discretion in a more professional manner.
- The creation of ethical principles and guidelines governing the whole organiza-tion.
- Codes of practice and internal circulars to limit and/or guide stop and search, interrogation, use of deadly force and response to domestic violence and racist violence.
- Strategies to raise the visibility of officers' work practices.
- The establishment of internal and external reviews bodies.

These strategies are premised on the prin-ciple that discretion is an inescapable part of police work. However, there are many who believe that the problem of police discretion will not be resolved until discretionary powers such as stop and search are abolished or meaningful complaints systems and modes of democratic accountability are implemented.

Eugene McLaughlin

Associated Concepts: 'broken windows', crim-inal justice, discrimination, disparity, dispro-portionality, net widening, social control, zero tolerance

Key Readings

Galligan, D.J. (1990) Discretionary Powers: A Legal Study of Official Discretion. Oxford, The Clarendon Press.

Hawkins, K. (ed.) (1992) The Uses of Discretion. Oxford, The Clarendon Press.

Ohlin, L.E. and Remington, F.J. (1993) Discretion in Criminal Justice: The Tension Between Individualiza-tion and Uniformity. Albany, State University of New York Press.

Walker, S. (1993) Taming the System: The Control of Discretion in Criminal Justice 1950–90. Oxford, Oxford University Press.

Vizant, J.C. and Crothers, L. (1998) Street-Level Leadership: Discretion and Legitimacy in Front-Line Public Service. Washington, DC, Georgetown University Press.

DISCRIMINATION

Definition

Discrimination consists of unfavourable treatment based on a person's sex, gender, 'race', ethnicity, culture, religion, language, class, sexual preference, age, physical disability or any other improper ground. It limits the economic, social and political opportunities of the individual or group discriminated against. In some contexts discrimination has been legally enforced (for example, *apartheid* in South Africa). In many other contexts discrimination exists *de facto*, in spite of laws intended to prevent its occurrence.

Distinctive Features

Discrimination includes behaviour ranging in severity from aversion and avoidance to harassment and violence. It includes insulting, patronizing or disrespectful behaviour, refusal to offer employment (or pay fair wages), to provide housing or medical treatment, or to provide a commercial or social service. Discrimination directly restricts civil liberties such as freedom of movement and association. It can also take the form of harassment, attack, exclusion and expulsion. In its most extreme form, discrimination has led to mass murder. Some theorists emphasize an investigation of the 'life form' of discrimination and its roots in local histories. Others emphasize the effects of discrimination in creating disadvantage and limiting the life chances of those discriminated against. Poverty, unemployment, ignorance, crime, increased infant mortality and a shortened life expectancy have all been shown to be consequences of discrimination. Racial discrimination has been one of the most prominent explanations for the over-representation of black people among arrestees and in-prison populations.

A distinction can be made between direct and indirect discrimination. Among the best examples of *direct discrimination* are those that have been enshrined in national or state legislation such as the Jim Crow laws in the USA. These laws enforced segregation in education and public transport and also prohibited sexual relationships across the 'colour-line'. In some places African Americans were denied the right to vote and, as a consequence, to serve on juries or gain equal access to justice. In South Africa, until the *apartheid* regime ended in 1990, blacks were

not allowed to vote or travel without restriction. Similarly, restrictions on women's ability to own property, to vote and so on have been in place in many countries. An explicit ban on the employment of openly homosexual people in the police or military is another example of direct discrimination. Such legal restrictions have obvious and wide-ranging consequences for fairness and social justice.

These *de jure* forms of discrimination are easy to identify and criticize as unjust. Even when there are no laws promoting or requiring discrimination, however, people are often directly excluded or singled out for unfavourable treatment. In many criminal justice agencies (including police, prisons and the courts) explicit, overt and direct discrimination has led to informal restrictions on the recruitment and promotion of women, ethnic minorities and other social groups. Discrimination also contributes to explaining why there are often marked inequalities in service provision (Brown, 1997). Sometimes discriminatory practices persist even in the face of laws or policies designed to eliminate discrimination. This *de facto* discrimination can be the result of covert activity – that which is intentional, but hidden – but can also result from indirect discrimination.

Indirect discrimination refers to treatment that might be described as 'equal' in a formal sense between different groups, but is discriminatory in its *actual effect* on a particular group. The 'minimum height' requirement for police officers in some jurisdictions is an example of indirect discrimination. Women and people from some ethnic groups are less likely to be able to meet the minimum requirement while height is irrelevant to the job of being a police officer. This requirement, irrespective of its intent, clearly has the *effect* of restricting job opportunities for some groups, and may, therefore, be considered discriminatory.

Sometimes indirect discrimination occurs knowingly, but covertly to exclude women, homosexuals or people from ethnic minority communities, but there are many other instances where such exclusion appears to be neither conscious nor deliberate. For example, few criminal justice agencies provide services for non-English speakers in the UK or USA. Although it is probably not the intent of these organizations specifically to exclude non-English speakers, this is, in fact, what happens and can be seen as having an indirect discriminatory effect.

Discrimination is closely tied to the concept of *prejudice*: ideas that identify particular groups as 'inferior' or 'a problem'. The expression of prejudiced opinions and the use of negative stereotypes are often found to accompany discriminatory practice. Such prejudices (as racism, sexism and homophobia) are frequently explicit. In some criminal justice occupations, women and people from ethnic and other minorities are seen by the dominant group of white men as inferior, less able to do the job (in both front-line and managerial contexts) and find their employment prospects affected as a result. For example, in Britain, male police officers have strongly resisted the idea of women joining the police service in numbers. When they were employed, some men felt that women should be kept 'in their proper place', and away from 'real' police-work (Brown, 1997). The experience of abusive and discriminatory practices in the workplace and the so-called 'glass ceiling' to career advancement has led to many employees taking legal action against employers in criminal justice agencies.

Evaluation

Studies of discrimination in action in the criminal justice process have suggested that it occurs under certain conditions. Where the law is permissive, individual discretion wide, and where there is a lack of guidelines as to how a decision should be taken, decision-making is often based on subjective judgements. For example, police officers have the power to stop and search a person of whom they have 'reasonable suspicion', an ambiguous and ill-defined concept. In such instances of wide discretion and autonomy, and where cultural norms support particular kinds of stereotypes and prejudices, the results are frequently discriminatory. It has been shown that police officers use colour as a criterion for stop and search and that black people are much more likely to be stopped than would be expected given their numbers in the general population. Where decisions, and how they are reached are not monitored and where accountability is weak, discrimination can go unchecked.

The right to equality before the law and protection against discrimination has been central to conceptions of basic human rights that underpin the formation of the United Nations and the European Union. Protection against discrimination is recognized in Article 7 of the Universal Declaration of Human Rights, and in Article 14 of the European Convention on Human Rights. These call for fundamental rights and freedoms to be secured 'without discrimination on any grounds such as sex, race, colour, language, religion, political or other opinion, national or social origin, association with a national minority, property, birth or other status'. The international conventions on the elimination of all forms of discrimination against women and against racial discrimination are more stringent. These require governments to review national and local policies, and to 'amend, rescind or nullify' any laws or regulations which have the effect of creating or perpetuating discrimination and also a duty to promote tolerance and equality of opportunity (Banton, 1996).

Legislation based on these international principles can be found in many countries. These focus on the concepts of anti-discrimination (for example, anti-racism/anti-sexism/anti-homophobia), equal opportunities, or affirmative action. In the USA, the Civil Rights Act 1963 prohibited discrimination against blacks and other minorities in respect of voting, employment and the use of public accommodations. The Fair Housing Act 1968 prohibited property companies from discriminating when seeking buyers for houses. Similarly, in Britain, Race Relations Acts of 1965 and 1968 prohibited direct discrimination on the grounds of 'race' and ethnicity, and the 1976 Race Relations Act extended the law to prohibit indirect discrimination. Similar legislation prohibits discrimination against disabled people and against women. The Race Relations (Amendment) Act 2000 will apply these principles for the first time to public services, including the police.

The concept of discrimination is helpful to understand the processes by which the life chances of less powerful individuals and groups are shaped by the responses to them by the powerful. It contributes to understanding how, for example, women and people from ethnic minority communities make up a disproportionately small number of the ranks of criminal justice professions (especially those at the top, such as chiefs of police and judges). It helps to explain why the culture of these professions is often hostile – in both language and practice – to particular groups (such as women, gay people, disabled people and those from ethnic minority communities). It also helps to explain why the protections of the criminal justice process are so often described as unsatisfactory by members of these excluded groups.

The notion of anti-discriminatory practice is a perspective that acknowledges the existence and impact of 'race', gender and homophobic stereotyping, prejudice and their echo in direct and indirect discrimination. From this perspective, positive action is required actively to eliminate discrimination and promote equality of opportunity.

Ben Bowling

Associated Concepts: criminal justice, criminalization, discretion, disparity, disproportionality, human rights, social justice

Key Readings

Banton, M. (1996) *International Action Against Racial Discrimination*. Oxford, The Clarendon Press.

Bowling, B. and Phillips, C. (2000) *Racism, Crime and Justice*. London, Pearson.

Brown, J. (1997) 'Equal opportunities and the police service in England and Wales: past, present and future possibilities', in P. Francis, P. Davies and V. Jupp (eds), *Policing Futures*. London, Macmillan.

Kleg, M. (1993) *Hate, Prejudice and Racism*. Albany, NY, State University of New York Press.

DISPARITY

Definition

The concept of 'disparity' is most clearly associated with sentencing and the practice of giving different sentences for similar offences, but it also has wider relevance in terms of offenders and victims being treated differently or unequally throughout the criminal justice system when their circumstances are similar.

Distinctive Features

Discoveries of disparity in the treatment of offenders in the criminal justice system strike at the heart of the ideal that justice is abstract and that all are equal before the law. Whilst disparity is concerned more with differences in process than differences in outcome, it is often used interchangeably with 'discrimination' and most pointedly concerns 'equal treatment'. Indeed, most people appear to believe that fairness necessarily involves treating 'like cases alike'. But equal treatment involves at one extreme the impartial application of existing rules and procedures, regardless of the outcome (procedural justice), and at the other, the idea that any policies or procedures that have the effect of punishing a higher proportion of one social group than another

are unjust, and that law and policy should be adjusted so as to achieve equal outcomes (substantive justice). Techniques for reducing disparity include: judicial self-regulation (with courts of appeal and the like), statutory sentencing principles (as in penal codes), numerical guideline systems (as in the Minnesota system – with clear classifications of offences and categories of relative gravity), and mandatory sentences (prescribed maximum and minimum penalties) (Ashworth, 1998).

Calls to eradicate disparity have included calls for equal treatment, but this is not unproblematic. Following critiques of the sentencing of women for example, both in principle and practice, 'equal' has come to~mean 'like men'. As punishment has become increasingly more severe in England and Wales, the USA and elsewhere, 'equal treatment' with men is far from desirable (let alone 'just' some would argue) and so the quest for equal treatment is increasingly questioned.

In the USA, Tonry (1996) has revealed that the success of sentencing guidelines in various states has led to increased imprisonment of women as the disparities between sentencing females and males have been reduced. Indeed, this process of 'levelling-up' in order to reduce sentencing disparities is not uncommon. The 'split the difference' policy of California is rather unusual, however, involving a lowering of sentences for men and a raising of sentences for women.

In jurisdictions where there are sentencing guidelines rather than rigid systems of mandatory sentencing, the move towards consistency, equality and proportionality of punishment to crime has meant that mitigating circumstances, such as child care or family responsibilities, have ceased to be available. Thus the call for 'equal treatment' has been replaced by a call for 'appropriateness'. That is, it is argued that what is required is that circumstances appropriate to each person should be considered regardless of assumptions about gender-based and other stereotypical perceptions of 'needs' (Hudson, 1996).

Evaluation

The concept of disparity is often confused with and used interchangeably with 'discrimination'. Whereas disparity concerns the consistency with which criteria are applied to cases, discrimination, properly understood, refers to the use of illegitimate criteria. For instance, race is a prime example of a criterion that has been recognized as illegitimate. However, the concepts are closely intertwined. A good deal of research has been carried out to measure both disparity and discrimination, though much of this has been statistical in nature with obvious limitations. First, there is an assumption that disparity or discrimination can be proved or dismissed through sophisticated statistical analysis. Secondly, it ignores the more dynamic aspects of decision-making – the significance of appearance and demeanour, prejudices revealed in attitude rather than in specific decision, and the interaction between defendants and officials. Thirdly, such research has often focused on a single process or moment in decision-making, and on a single factor (for example, race or gender), when a number of factors may be relevant in combination. Equally, treating 'like cases alike' in terms of outcomes (sentencing outcomes for instance) can mask processual differences. But the real problem is that 'disparity' is an empty category that can be filled only by reference to some standard, and in principle the standard could be set by any criteria.

Loraine Gelsthorpe

Associated Concepts: discrimination, disproportionality, racialization

Key Readings

Ashworth, A. (1998) 'Four techniques for reducing disparity', in A. von Hirsch and A. Ashworth (eds), *Principled Sentencing: Readings on Theory and Policy*. Oxford, Hart Publishing.

Daly, K. (1994) *Gender, Crime and Punishment*. New Haven, CT, Yale University Press.

Hudson, B. (1996) *Understanding Justice*. Buckingham, Open University Press.

Tonry, M. (1996) *Sentencing Matters*. New York, Oxford University Press.

DISPLACEMENT

See Defensible space; Rational choice theory; Repeat victimization; Situational crime prevention; Surveillance.

DISPOSITIONAL THEORIES

Definition

An alternative means of describing positivist and some interactionist theories. Its key characteristic is to argue that because of certain biological, psychological or sociological conditions some people are born with or come to acquire a *disposition* to behave in a criminal manner. A 'dispositional bias' is at its strongest in positivism but is also present in those interactionist and labelling theories which maintain that the labelling of people as deviant cements a deviant identity and predisposes them to commit further criminal acts. An alternative to dispositional theory can be found in rational choice theory.

John Muncie

Associated Concepts: criminal careers, deviancy amplification, individual positivism, labelling, positivism, sociological positivism

DISPROPORTIONALITY

Definition

The extent to which something appears to be inappropriate or 'out of proportion' in relation to something else. The term has been used in criminology to describe a disparity, or imbalance, in patterns of crime and the administration of criminal justice.

Distinctive Features

It is common to describe a situation where an individual or a group is privileged or disadvantaged in comparison to another as disproportionate. Five examples illustrate the usage of the term.

1 *Disproportionality in punishment*. The penological notion of proportionality is central to just desert theories of sentencing (von Hirsch, 1998). A sentence of the court could be described as disproportionate if a person convicted of a minor offence were sentenced to a long prison term or if a judge or magistrate failed to take into account mitigating circumstances. Disproportionality in sentencing can also be identified at the group level. For example, Hood's (1992) study of Crown Courts in the English Midlands found that black people were disproportionately given custodial sentences in comparison to whites, even once all legally relevant variables had been taken into account. This study also indicated that where a custodial sentence was given, the average sentence length was longer

for black and Asian defendants, in comparison with their white counterparts.

2 *Disproportionality in the use of police powers*. The use of a power – such as that to stop and search under s.1 of the Police and Criminal Evidence Act in the UK – can be described as disproportionate if it is used excessively on specific social groups. For example, police statistics show that black people in London are about five times as likely to be stopped and searched in comparison with white people. The term has also been used in human rights jurisprudence to describe an imbalance in the intrusiveness of a police power – such as planting a listening device – in comparison with the seriousness of the crime being investigated.

3 *Disproportionality in imprisonment*. There are a disproportionately large number of black people in the prison population in Britain, in comparison with their numbers in the general population: while there are 176 white people in prison per 100,000, there are 1,245 black people in prison per 100,000 (cf Tonry, 1994). The obvious question that arises from these statistics is why the British criminal justice system imprisons so much greater a proportion of the black population than the white population. Among the possible explanations are a disproportionate risk of being arrested, convicted or sentenced to custody, or disproportionately long prison sentences. Disproportionate rates of imprisonment could also reflect rates of offending among the black population.

4 *Disproportionality in victimization and offending*. Evidence from victimization surveys indicating that people from ethnic minorities suffer a level of victimization that exceeds that of white people can be described as 'disproportionate victimization'. The term can also be used to describe unexpectedly high actual or supposed 'crime rates' among, for example, black people. In this usage, 'disproportionality in offending' is a rival explanation to 'discrimination in criminal justice' for disproportionate imprisonment rates (Russell, 1998: 46).

5 *Disproportionality in employment in the criminal justice professions*. Statistical evidence shows that many fewer women and people from ethnic minority groups are employed in criminal justice agencies, especially in more senior ranks, than would be expected on the basis of their numbers in the population. This appears – on the face of it – to be the result of discrimination on the part of employers, and there is certainly evidence that such discrimination does occur. However, this imbalance may also be explained by legitimate factors – such as a lack of suitably qualified applicants, or an unwillingness to apply for reasons of preference for other occupations.

Evaluation

Disproportionality is a slippery concept, not least because it has subtly different meanings depending on the context in which it is used. The example of the 'race and crime debate' – where the term is frequently used – can serve as an illustration of the various competing definitions.

There is more or less universal agreement that black people are more likely than white people to be stopped, searched, arrested and imprisoned. The question on which the 'race and crime' debate has turned is whether this disproportionality – found in the 'outcomes' of the criminal justice process – is the result of discrimination (at one or more points in the process), disproportionate involvement of black people in offending, or a combination of both. Further questions are also raised of how the disproportionately high rates of unemployment, poverty, exclusion from school and the concentration of black people into urban areas impacts on their experiences of crime and criminal justice. These uses of the term are subtly distinct from the penological notion of proportionality, referring to the extent to which punishment and crime are commensurate. The definitions coincide when it can be shown that the punishment of black people is not only disproportionate in comparison to their numbers in the population, but also unduly harsh given the nature of their offending.

Identifying disproportionate outcomes of the criminal justice process is a necessary, but not sufficient step towards establishing discrimination. In civil rights jurisprudence, disparities in the treatment of women, people from ethnic and other minorities can be taken as *prima facie* evidence of discrimination which can be tested by assessing the extent to which differences can be explained by legitimate factors. Where disparities are shown to be unjustified, the discriminatory practices that create and sustain them may be ruled unlawful and complainants entitled to redress.

Ben Bowling

Associated Concepts: discrimination, disparity, just deserts, penology, victimology

Key Readings

Bowling, B. and Phillips, C. (2001) *Racism, Crime and Justice*. London, Pearson.

von Hirsch, A. (1998) 'Proportionate sentences: a desert perspective', in A. von Hirsch and A. Ashworth (eds), *Principled Sentencing: Readings on Theory and Policy*, 2nd edn. London, Hart Publishing.

Hood, R. (1992) *Race and Sentencing*. Oxford, Oxford University Press.

Russell, K. (1998) *The Color of Crime*. New York and London, New York University Press.

Tonry, M. (1994) 'Racial disproportion in US prisons', *British Journal of Criminology*, 34, pp. 97–115.

DISPUTE SETTLEMENT

See Informal justice; Redress; Restorative justice

DIVERSION

Definition

The process of keeping offenders and other problem populations away from the institutional arrangements of criminal justice or welfare.

Distinctive Features

Diversion has its roots in what Stanley Cohen (1985) termed the 'destructuring moves' of the 1960s. Its orientation toward an alternative procedural rationale grew out of a radical critique of the penal welfare strategy and was closely associated with measures of decarceration (away from prison), delegalization (away from the state) and deprofessionalization (away from the expert). Diversion subsequently emerged as a dominant trend in juvenile justice reform. Short of rejecting penal sanctions completely, proponents of diversion in juvenile justice advocated the development of initiatives to keep juveniles out of court, custody and residential care. Their general aim was to remove or minimize the juveniles' penetration into the justice system. For critics of treatment-type interventions, increased professional services were seen as either failing to reform the delinquent or were morally unacceptable. Social work professionals redefined their mission in terms of 'leaving the kids alone'. In the process, social sciences arguments (especially from the labelling perspective) suggesting that the process of arrest, trial and conviction can have potentially damaging effects of stigmatization, were rediscovered.

In a parallel debate, diversion fitted in with the demands for a 'return to justice' from the liberal justice lobby (Morris et al., 1980). Their central arguments are that due process safeguards have been undermined by the rise of individualized treatment in juvenile justice. The expectation is that, by re-establishing values of proportionality, procedural justice and predictability of legal administration, the extent of penal intervention would also be reduced. Similar 'just deserts' arguments have since been used to support the use of police cautioning outside the formal court system as the proportionate response to minor forms of law-breaking or to offences committed by persons of low culpability (such as the old and the mentally ill).

Evaluation

Diversionary initiatives (especially alternatives to formal court processing) have proliferated in most Western juvenile justice systems. They are frequently state-sponsored and administered or controlled either by officials (such as the police) or community-based agencies. Because of its definitional ambiguity, diversion has developed in different directions at different times and came to have a variety of meanings in terms of policies and programmes. In particular, the distinction between 'diversion from' and 'diversion to' has been a major concern in juvenile justice literature. In this latter version of diversion as a referral to alternative programmes, the paradox is that more, rather than fewer, juveniles ended up being subject to new forms of community-based intervention.

Diversion can also mean keeping the younger and less delinquent population away from a career of crime through early identification and treatment. The expansion of delinquency prevention initiatives can thus generate an inflationary spiral in the processing of delinquency cases, leading to greater regulation in the lives of young people and their families (Klein, 1979). Furthermore, critics argued that diversion has sometimes been conflated with a crime control ideology. In the United States, intensive programmes such as 'boot camps', which were originally promoted as an alternative measure to divert offenders who would otherwise be sentenced to long-term incarceration, are increasingly being used as a sentencing option in their own right for less serious offenders.

Wider developments of managerialism in criminal justice in the 1990s have meant that criminal justice officials supported diversion out of the practical need for a rationalization of resources and the establishment of an efficient crime management apparatus. Diversion of cases in preliminary phases is now part of the state's strategy of 'defining deviance down' to adapt to high crime rates and increased caseloads in most Western criminal justice systems (Garland, 1996).

Maggy Lee

Associated Concepts: bifurcation, community sentences, crime prevention, decarceration, decriminalization, just deserts, labelling, managerialism, net widening, radical non-intervention, social control

Key Readings

Cohen, S. (1985) *Visions of Social Control: Crime, Punishment, and Classification*. Cambridge, Polity Press.

Garland, D. (1996) 'The limits of the sovereign state – strategies of crime control in contemporary society', *British Journal of Criminology*, 36 (4), pp. 445–71.

Klein, M. (1979) 'Deinstitutionalization and diversion of juvenile offenders: a litany of impediments', in N. Morris and N. Tonry (eds), *Crime and Justice: An Annual Review of Research*, vol. 1. Chicago, University of Chicago Press.

Morris, A., Giller, H., Szwed E. and Geach, H. (1980) *Justice for Children*. London, Macmillan.

Pratt, J. (1986) 'Diversion from the juvenile court', *British Journal of Criminology*, 24 (2), pp. 81–92.

DOCUMENTARY ANALYSIS

Definition

The detailed examination of documents with a view to making assertions about some aspect of the social world, for example, the social or historical context in which the documents were produced, the social meanings which they transmit, the effects of such meanings on social groups and the social control function of documents.

Distinctive Features

A wide range of documents has been used in social research including life histories, diaries, newspapers and magazines, stories, essays, official documents and records, web pages and research reports. Such documents may be made up exclusively of the written word or they may include statistics, as in a report of crime trends.

The life history is similar to a biography or autobiography and is a means by which an individual provides a written record of his or her own life in his or her own terms. It can include a descriptive summary of life events and experiences and also an account of the social world from the subject's point of view. The use of newspapers has been central in what is usually referred to as media analysis. Media analysis has several interests, one of which is an examination of the way in which stereotypes of categories of people or types of action are created, reinforced and amplified with wide-ranging consequences for those people and actions. For example, newspapers have been used to examine the portrayal of folk devils and also the creation and career of the label and stereotype of the 'mugger' in the British press.

Researchers can make use of essays or other writings which are already in existence or can solicit such writings as part of their research design. For example, Cohen and Taylor's (1972) examination of the subjective experiences of imprisonment and strategies of psychological survival among long-term prisoners was in part founded on an analysis of essays and poems and topics suggested by Cohen and Taylor themselves. Official documents, for example reports of public inquiries, provide valuable data for the analysis of official definitions of what is defined as problematic (for example, public disorder), what is viewed as the explanation of the problem and what is deemed as the preferred solution. Apart from documents at a societal or macro level, there are other official documents at an institutional or micro level which can be just as important to the disposal and destination of individuals, for example, offenders. These are organizational records, such as probation reports, which define what is, or is not, problematic about individuals, which put forward explanations for behaviour and actions and which record decisions relating to outcomes. Such individual records are not insulated from official documents operating at a societal level in so far as there is often a close connection between the formulation of concepts, explanations and solutions at one level and such formulation and application at another.

Evaluation

The validity of any document is dependent on its authenticity (whether it is original and genuine), its credibility (whether it is accurate), its representativeness (whether it is representative of the totality of documents in its class) and its meaning (what it is intended to say) (Scott, 1990). What is more, any evaluation of documentary analysis must consider the way in which it is influenced by broad theoretical approaches and the types of research questions posed by these approaches. For example, the positivist approach to documents – sometimes also known as content analysis – assumes that there is a correspondence between the manifest content of documents and their meaning: documents are representations of what they mean. Researchers using this approach analyse the manifest content of documents to ask questions such as: What are the characteristics of content? What inferences can be made about the causes and generation of content? What inferences can be made about the effects of communication?

By way of contrast, the interpretative approach starts from the assumption that different meanings can be attributed by different individuals to the same manifest content. It would, for example, be interested in the varying ways in which defendants, prosecutors, judges and jurors make sense of documents placed before a court of law and with what consequences.

A critical approach to documentary analysis is concerned with how and when certain kinds of documents come to be treated and accepted as 'knowledge' and with the social control functions of such knowledge. In this way, critical analysis emphasizes the close connection between documents and the exercise of power. One variant of this critical approach to documents is discourse analysis, associated with Michel Foucault.

Victor Jupp

Associated Concepts: content analysis, discourse analysis, folk devil, positivism, stereotyping

Key Readings

Cohen, S. and Taylor, L. (1972) *Psychological Survival: The Experience of Long-term Imprisonment.* Harmondsworth, Penguin.

Jupp, V. and Norris, C. (1993) 'Traditions in documentary analysis', in M. Hammersley (ed.), *Social Research: Philosophy, Politics and Practice.* London, Sage.

Scott, J. (1990) *A Matter of Record: Documentary Sources in Social Research.* Cambridge, Polity Press.

DOMESTIC VIOLENCE

See Family crime; Violence; Victimology.

DRIFT

See Subculture

DUE PROCESS MODEL

Definition

A 'due process' model or perspective emphasizes the need to administer justice according to legal rules and procedures which are publicly known, fair and seen to be just.

Distinctive Features

In a 'due process' model of criminal justice the main function of the criminal courts is to act as an impartial arbitrator of conflicts arising between the state and its citizens. Central to this perspective are the presumption of innocence, the restraints of arbitrary power and the inviolability of legal rules and procedures. Such procedures do not weight the process against the accused or in favour of those in power, but rather seek to guarantee a measure of judicial equality to all parties: hence the absolute need to abide by strict and formal procedures, to ensure that adherence to 'due process' results in a smooth-running, fair and impartial system. Other key elements (legal safeguards) in a 'due process model' might be described as follows: arrested persons must be informed as to what the charges are and, where relevant, why they are going to court; there are clear standards of proof (with the plaintiff or prosecution bearing the onus of proof); there are extensive rules which determine what is allowable or not as legal evidence (with 'hearsay evidence', crudely translated as 'gossip', being admissible only under certain conditions), and with each party being given the opportunity to tender evidence before the court (and jury) to cross examine the other party so as to clarify matters or raise objections. In addition, within a 'due process model' judicial proceedings are normally conducted in open court so as to avoid situations like the Inquisition, where 'justice' is arrived at behind closed doors with few public checks and balances upon judicial power. Herbert Packer, who offered an incisive account of both a 'due process' model and a 'crime control' model in 1964, suggests that whilst the crime control model resembles an assembly line, the due process model looks very much like an obstacle course – with successive stages being designed to present formidable impediments to carrying the accused any further along the process. Whilst 'justice must be seen to be done' though, in the case of minors there may be some limitations on this procedure, with special 'juvenile' or 'youth courts' being held behind closed doors so as to protect them from public gaze. Also, there may be exceptions to the rule of 'open court' when it is thought appropriate, especially in sensitive or difficult situations, to hear testimony 'in camera' (behind closed doors, with bans on publishing the proceedings). Broadly speaking, however, the institutional processes associated with 'due process' are designed to protect a citizen's rights.

The concept of 'due process' has its origins in the Classical School of criminology, which itself was reacting against punishment under the *ancien régime* of eighteenth-century Europe which was both arbitrary and harshly retributive, dominated by capital and corporal penalties. As a protagonist of the Classical School, jurist and philosopher Cesare Beccaria (1738–94) published *Dei Delitta e delle Pene* (1764) (On Crimes and Punishments), which provided a thorough and searching critique of the criminal justice systems of Europe. Beccaria, along with others in the Classical School called for reform, for clarity in the law and 'due process' in criminal procedure, combined with certainty and regularity of punishment.

In England, the due process approach is often associated with the attitudes of the legal profession, particularly those involved in defence work, and with the aims of such organizations as Liberty. The concept has been brought to bear in a number of areas within the criminal justice system where there has been concern about a lack of fairness and openness in decision-making processes. For example, there have been criticisms of the lack of 'due process' safeguards associated with the system of parole ever since its inception. By this is meant that there have been criticisms about the secretive nature of the decision-making processes, a lack of accountability, and a lack of attention to offenders' rights in the whole process. The concept has been similarly employed to describe procedural irregularities in decision-making processing affecting cautions and prosecutions, with evidence to suggest that some people might be given cautions where there is insufficient evidence to convict or where there is no admission of guilt (see Wasik et al., 1999, chapter 2).

Evaluation

The concept of 'due process' has been usefully employed in critiques of criminal justice practice in recent years, particularly in England with regard to the lack of procedural safeguards in police interviews, the use of cautions, legal representation, parole decisions, prisoners' rights and the use of the Crown Court (with adult style criminal proceedings) for juveniles.

Whilst the concept of due process may be useful as a representation of 'the ideal', setting out how the system *ought to be*, there are those who would argue that 'the reality', that is *how the system is*, may be so far removed that the 'ideal' becomes increasingly difficult to achieve with the result that the criminal justice process finds it harder and harder to function efficiently. In this case, complexity and high standards may militate against justice.

It has also been argued that procedural justice (due process) is a far cry from substantive justice and that really it is substantive justice (that is, justice which relates to specific human rights aims or to penological aims such as abolitionism, restorative justice, rehabilitation and deterrence) which should be of central importance. Formal legalism – mere adherence to rules and adoption of legal safeguards – does not in itself make a system just.

Loraine Gelsthorpe

Associated Concepts: classicism, crime control model, disproportionality, just deserts

Key Readings

Hudson, B. (1996) *Understanding Justice.* Buckingham, Open University Press.

Packer, H. (1964) 'Two models of the criminal process', *University of Pennsylvania Law Review,* 113, pp. 1–68.

Wasik, M., Gibbons, T. and Redmayne, M. (1999) *Criminal Justice. Text and Materials,* London, Longman.

E

EDGEWORK

See Carnival (of crime); Cultural criminology;
Postmodernism

ELECTRONIC MONITORING

Definition

The process by which offenders' movements
or whereabouts may be checked for the
purpose of enforcing a curfew or court order.
Most systems in current use involve the fitting
of a small electronic device, or 'tag' on the
ankle or wrist of the offender and checking
compliance with the conditions of a curfew or
house arrest by using a static monitoring unit
at the offender's home. Developing systems
include computer aided voice recognition to
allow checks from different locations, GMS
locator systems using the mobile telephone
infrastructure and GPS (ground position by
satellite) technology to provide continuous
checks on movement and location. These last
two are as yet untested except in small-scale
projects. All have the same aim – to offer some
spatial control short of the total separation
imposed by custody.

Distinctive Features

Electronic monitoring in criminal justice
systems started in 1984 in the USA as a
means of enforcing house arrest. Early pilot
projects grew fairly rapidly – there were thirty
within two years – and by 1988 over 3,000

offenders were being tagged. The early years
were, however, dogged by technical problems,
unrealistic expectations and poor outcomes.
Although designed to reduce both prison
populations and criminal justice costs, the
generally low risk offenders on whom they
were made, coupled with the ability to detect
breaches of the order at any time, led to
significant net widening. A 10-year summary
of experience by the National Institute of
Justice in Washington concluded that, all too
often, both costs and prison populations had
risen.

Nevertheless, continued experimentation
and development covered bail enforcement,
'front door' schemes (as a sentencing option
for the courts, either on its own or in
conjunction with another community penalty)
and 'back door' schemes (as a condition of
early release from prison). Canada, Australia
and Singapore (where it was extensively used
as part of a home release programme for
drug addicts) were all early users; England
and Wales, Sweden and the Netherlands
started different types of applications in 1995.
Much of Western Europe now has, or is
planning for, pilot projects to test its usefulness.

England and Wales is set to be one of the
largest users. A 'back door' home detention
curfew scheme for prisoners serving up to 4-
year sentences started in January 1999 and
curfew orders as a sentence of the courts
became available from December 1999.
Jointly, they should produce about 35,000
orders per year. They followed a substantial
pilot project over 4 years (Mortimer and May,
1997). In most jurisdictions, though, tagging
remains a small-scale sentencing option – the
USA had about 77,000 monitored offenders at
any one time in 1998 compared with 1.7
million in prison and 3.6 million on probation
or parole.

Evaluation

Providing electronic monitoring to low risk offenders has been found to increase recidivism rates and further increase costs. It is cost effective when used on moderate and high risk offenders and coupled with appropriate interventions that target specific criminogenic factors. The evidence is that electronic monitoring is more effective when combined with other rehabilitative programmes (Evans, 1996). It is also most effective as a short-term option, 'buying time' for other community options, including treatment programmes, to take effect. Compliance rates have been found to fall steeply after 3 months (Whitfield, 1997).

The most successful outcomes have been demonstrated in Sweden, where a carefully targeted 'front door' scheme to replace prison sentences of up to 3 months has, over 3 years, reduced the prison population by 25 per cent and saved an estimated 150m kroner. Targeting remains the key issue if electronic monitoring is to develop, long term, as a viable community-based sentencing option – although its future as a device for controlling prison numbers through 'back door' schemes is probably more certain. All too often, electronic monitoring has been used as a simple punishment or for offenders other than those for whom it was designed – people whose movements are linked to their offending. Critics see it as redolent of excessive state control and part of the increasingly stringent apparatus of criminal sanctions; supporters, as a way of reducing prison populations and costs without increasing risks. The dangers, as well as the opportunities offered by new technologies, will continue to need careful assessment.

Dick Whitfield

Associated Concepts: community sentences, net widening, social control, surveillance

Key Readings

Evans, D. (1996) 'Electronic monitoring: APPA testimony to Ontario Standing Committee on Administration and Justice', *Perspectives*, Fall 1996, pp. 8–10 (Lexington, KY; APPA).

Mortimer, E. and May, C. (1997) *Electronic Monitoring in Practice*, Research Study no. 177. London, Home Office.

Whitfield, D. (1997) *Tackling the Tag – the Electronic Monitoring of Offenders*. Winchester, Waterside Press.

EMERGENCY LEGISLATION

Definition

Laws introduced following the suspension of, or departure from, legal normality when either a state of emergency is declared or is assumed to exist. They typically involve the pervasive violation of human rights.

Distinctive Features

States of emergency occur with remarkable frequency throughout the world and at any one time a large proportion of the world population is subject to emergency legislation. Once introduced, it often has a permanency which belies its nomenclature. International law, in particular human rights law, however, lays down standards to govern the use of emergency legislation. Generally, for example, where such standards apply, the threat must be proximate and the use of the powers limited spatially, but these criteria are largely ignored.

Both totalitarian and democratic regimes resort to this form of law (see, for example, Amnesty International, 1999), notwithstanding that they may be signatories of international human rights treaties. In totalitarian or military regimes the introduction of emergency powers and the suspension of the legal safeguards for the protection of the citizen have frequently permitted the security forces to resort to anonymous arrests, secret detentions, torture, disappearances and extra-judicial killings. In democratic regimes the violation of human rights is generally less but nevertheless involves fundamental derogation from the rule of law permitting arbitrary arrest, detention without trial and widespread restrictions on the freedom of movement and expression. For example, the United Kingdom – a signatory of international human rights treaties – introduced emergency legislation in Northern Ireland in 1973 replacing other special powers (Farrell, 1986) which had been in existence since the state was established in 1921. It involved expanded powers of arrest, detention without trial and jury-less courts (Ni Aolain, 1996). Emergency legislation, even in democratic regimes, is often accompanied by 'dirty tricks' and secret wars and the use of state directed or 'independent' pro-state death squads (McLaughlin, 1996, p. 287). States that resort to emergency legislation typically deny that any abuses have occurred and devise a number of techniques of denial (Cohen, 1993). In addition, the appearance of legitimacy and justification can be lent to the laws concerned and the violations of rights they allow by an explicit declaration of a state of emergency in accordance with specific human rights law instruments which the state concerned has ratified.

Evaluation

Emergency legislation is an important concept because of its prevalence throughout the world. It has, however, been little studied by criminologists. Political crimes committed under it have largely been ignored in traditional texts. In addition, there has been very little analysis of the form of criminal justice which is established by emergency legislation or the patterns of abuse which occur. As a result, generalizations about criminal justice systems have, at best, been partial, or, at worst a caricature of the reality.

Paddy Hillyard

Associated Concepts: human rights, political crime, the state

Key Readings

Amnesty International (1999) *Annual Report 1999.* London, Amnesty International Publications.

Cohen, S. (1993) 'Human rights and crimes of the state: the culture of denial', *Australian and New Zealand Journal of Criminology*, 28 (1), pp. 87–115.

Farrell, M. (1986) *The Apparatus of Repression: Emergency Legislation.* Derry, Field Day Publications.

International Commission of Jurists (1983) *States of Emergency: Their Impact on Human Rights.* Geneva, International Commission of Jurists.

McLaughlin, E. (1996) 'Political violence, terrorism and crimes of the state', in J. Muncie and E. McLaughlin (eds), *The Problem of Crime.* London, Sage.

Ni Aolain, F. (1996) 'The fortification of an emergency regime', *Albany Law Review*, 59 (4), pp. 1353–87.

ENVIRONMENTAL CRIMINOLOGIES

See Chicago School of Sociology; Geographies of crime; Social ecology

ESSENTIALISM

Definition

This concept has been used in various ways in the philosophy of the social sciences. Essentialists believe that it is possible to establish the truth of a scientific theory and arrive at total explanations by identifying the essence or the reality that lies behind the appearance of a phenomenon. The concept also refers to the assumption that human beings possess indispensable qualities or characteristics which classify their true nature. An essence is a reality fixed in an originating moment and applies to both the inherent, innate properties of an individual human being and the abstract universal governing the type to which all examples conform.

Distinctive Features

In criminology there has been a remarkable tendency to essentialize crime and the relationship between class and crime; gender and crime; race and crime and social structure and crime. Essentialism also has a critical place in common sense conversations about crime and criminality and provides the basis for the construction of stereotypes and the marking out of differences such as criminal and noncriminal; normal and abnormal; and deviant and non-deviant.

Essentialist ways of thinking are challenged by post-structuralists and postmodernists who stress that 'truth' and 'reality' are contingent, contestable, historical, relational, provisional and plural in nature and demand that we interrogate the power relations inherent in the act of naming. In criminology, it was interactionist or labelling approaches that first challenged essentializing theories.

Eugene McLaughlin

Associated Concepts: biological criminology, interactionism, Marxist criminologies, personality theory, positivism, postmodernism, poststructuralism, stereotyping

ETHNIC CLEANSING

See Genocide

ETHNOGRAPHY

Definition

The study of small groups of people and of micro social situations and contexts. The emphasis is usually on explanations based on understanding the ways in which individuals interpret and socially construct their world.

Distinctive Features

Ethnography has its roots in the social anthropology of the late nineteenth century and early twentieth century and literally means the description (graphy) of cultures (ethno). Social anthropologists studied the institutions, beliefs and customs of pre-industrial societies, mainly in Africa, the Pacific and the Americas. The main forms of fieldwork were observation of cultural groups in their natural habitat and 'talking' to members of these groups. The commitments and the methods of social anthropologists were adapted by sociologists to the study of subcultural groups within the fast advancing industrial, urban society of the twentieth century. For example, the Chicago School of urban sociology advocated the detailed examination of small groups and subcultures within a complex urban context by seeking to examine actions and events as if they were 'anthropologically strange'. They produced detailed qualitative accounts of the underside of Chicago, for example a delinquent boy's own story: *The Jack Roller* (Shaw, 1930). Such accounts stood alongside quantitative analyses of the city, usually in the form of 'mappings' of its social ecology, for example by using indices such as delinquency rates. Ethnographic accounts provided description of the subcultures within particular ecological areas or 'zones'.

Ethnography continues to play an important role in criminological research, especially when linked to theoretical perspectives such as new deviancy, interactionism, labelling and appreciative criminology. As a research style it is especially suited to such perspectives because of their emphasis on interactions, social meanings and constructions, labelling, stereotyping, and to explanations based on these.

A number of methodological commitments are associated with ethnographic research. First, there is a focus on studying the social world from the perspectives of the individuals being studied. It is emphasized that social scientific explanations should be based or 'grounded' (Glaser and Strauss, 1967) in the everyday perspectives of everyday people rather than in the pre-constituted and abstract theories of social scientists. Secondly, it is assumed that different individuals and categories of individuals can have different perspectives. A social context comprises several perspectives, each of which is equally valid for the people who hold them. There is, then, no single objective reality: rather there is a multiplicity of realities and the role of the ethnographer is to capture and describe these. Thirdly, social perspectives (and the social meanings, definitions, labels and stereotypes which comprise them) cannot be separated from social interactions. Indeed they are the very substance of interactions. For this reason ethnographers pay particular attention to observing the ways in which people interact in social contexts. Fourthly, there is a belief that such observation should be naturalistic, that is, that everyday people should be studied interacting in what for them are everyday situations, and as they would normally and naturally do so. Therefore, ethnographic research is often covert rather than overt, so as not to disturb the social context which is being examined.

The ethnographic tradition has refused to link itself to any particular form of data collection. It rejects fixed protocols as to how data should be collected and analysed. However, the main sources of data include unstructured interviews (for example, life histories and narrative interviews), documents and forms of observation. Participant observation is often cited as being central to ethnographic research, although other forms of unstructured observation are used. Participant observation involves the collection of findings by participating in the social world of those being studied: taking on some role in the social group, or on its margins, and observing, reflecting upon and interpreting the actions of individuals in the group.

The close involvement of the researcher in what he or she is studying can mean that the researcher has a major impact on the findings and the conclusions derived from them. Therefore, in order to assess their validity it is important for the researcher to reflect upon and report his or her role in all stages of the research. This is known as reflexivity.

Evaluation

There are key issues regarding the validity of criminological research based on ethnography. One concerns whether a researcher can provide an accurate account of a social context as opposed to a personal interpretation. Related to this is the issue of reliability, that is, whether different researchers would produce the same account and reach the same conclusions. Further, there is the danger that the emphasis on small-scale contexts inhibits the extent to which conclusions can be generalized from such contexts. Much depends on their representativeness and typicality.

These issues apart, ethnography has made an important contribution to criminology in terms providing an appreciative and humanistic dimension, opening up explanations based on empathy and subjective understanding and in making visible the 'underside' of the social world in a way that would not be made possible by the more formal methods of social surveys and experimentation.

Victor Jupp

Associated Concepts: appreciative criminology, Chicago School of Sociology, cultural criminology, interactionism, labelling, new deviancy theory, participant observation, reflexivity

Key Readings

Ferrell, J. and Hamm, M. (eds) (1998) *Ethnography at the Edge: Crime, Deviance and Field Research*. Boston, Northeastern University Press.

Glaser, B. and Strauss, A.L. (1967) *The Discovery of Grounded Theory*. Chicago, IL, Aldine.

Hammersley, M. (1992) *What's Wrong With Ethnography?* London, Routledge.

Hammersley, M. and Atkinson, P. (1995) *Ethnography: Principles in Practice*, 2nd edn. London, Routledge.

Hobbs, D. and May, T. (eds) (1983) *Interpreting the Field: Accounts of Ethnography*. Oxford, Oxford University Press.

Shaw, C.R. (1930) *The Jack Roller*. Chicago, University of Chicago Press.

EUGENICS

See Genetics

EVALUATION RESEARCH

Definition

The form of policy research devoted to assessing the consequences (intended and unintended) of either a set of existing policies or a new policy programme. It has a particular focus on the measurement of the extent to which stated goals and objectives of policies and programmes are being, or have been, met.

Distinctive Features

This is a broad body of research findings which is focused on testing and measuring 'what works' in terms of the outputs and outcomes of initiatives and programmes of intervention and policy innovation in criminal justice and crime control. Most evaluative research is sponsored by the bodies who themselves are responsible for the particular programme or innovation. It is often 'in-house' in character and is generally based on short-term funding. By the end of the twentith century the evaluation industry had grown substantially. The question of the effectiveness of the myriad of measures employed to reduce crime and criminality came to occupy the centre of policy debates in many Western criminal justice jurisdictions. And yet the problem remains as to how the meaning of effectiveness can be adequately pinned down. The development of a renewed interest in 'what works' is for some heartening following the years of pessimism in criminology engendered by Martinson's influential evaluation that 'nothing works' in rehabilitation programmes for offenders (Martinson, 1974).

Evaluation

Much evaluation research has been criticized by criminologists for being compromised by its dependency on the sponsorship of the very agencies whose work it is asked to evaluate. However, it should not be inferred from such criticisms that independent, academic evaluation research is flawed *per se* and insignificant to both criminology and the policy process. In Tilley's (2000) view, 'What evaluations can offer is a way of winnowing over a period of time what works in producing varying outcomes, at least for a while, for whom and in what circumstances.'

At its worst, much evaluation research is short-term in character, poorly funded, often undertaken by inadequately trained employees of one of the agencies implicated in the programme concerned and characterized by severe technical difficulites. The lack of adequate and proper evaluations in criminal justice and crime reduction is widely recognized and remarked on by academic commentators. As Nick Tilley (2000) notes, there are many areas of uncertainty in this body of work. In particular, the 'industry' around evaluation is described by Tilley as an 'evaluation jungle' in which there are dangers, pitfalls and difficulties, and risks of becoming lost in the thickets. The rhetorical power of evaluation is substantial and hard(-looking) evidence can be effective in eliciting resources. Most commissioners of evaluation research want the 'facts' but facts do not speak for themselves in research and they are often contested. As noted earlier, much evaluative research is tied to the 'apron strings' of the sponsor, is often 'in-house' in character and based normally on short-term funding. All these factors mitigate against its success as academically credible research.

It is important to distinguish 'in-house' audits from detached and 'scientific' research-based evaluations. Other difficulties are associated with independent evaluations of programmes. Most of those involved in the programme (bar the independent evaluator) are characterized by a strong success imperative and will be looking for good news. And independent and objective evaluation is attractive not least for the external credibility it brings. Negative or sober findings and uncertain and nuanced narratives of achievement from academic evaluations – which has been the norm – are likely to result in tears for those committed to the programme in question. To add to the potentially tangled terrain of evaluation research, it important to recognize that academic evaluators also have their own agendas which may not serve the policy and practice purposes of evaluation (such as pursuing their own academic research interests rather than those of the commissioning agency).

The attractions of evaluation research to both the public and policy-makers lie in its concern with discovering just what works and what doesn't in specific contexts and processes. Indeed, the case for systematic evaluations of crime control and reduction initiatives may be said to be taken as given. It is difficult to argue with efforts to reduce crime in the most efficient, effective and economical fashion. Indeed, all those engaged professionally in criminal justice and crime prevention doubtless wish to know whether their work is having a real impact. None of those involved in the work of crime reduction and criminal justice wishes to spend time, money, effort and indeed whole careers achieving little or nothing. Furthermore, given the broader backdrop of a managerialized 'audit culture' increasingly at work in criminal justice systems, with its emphasis on the monitoring of measurable outputs, it is unlikely that the pressure on public agencies to measure effectiveness through evaluation audits will diminish.

It is important to note that both crime and crime control are not 'closed systems'; instead there are both exogenous and endogenous sources of change in these 'open systems' which undermine the predictability of future effectiveness on the basis of past effectiveness (Tilley, 2000). Modesty in what evaluation research may offer policy-makers and practitioners in criminal justice would appear necessary. It is widely recognized by criminologists that, however objective, academic evaluations cannot provide the sole basis for deciding on policy and practice. Policy and practice are necessarily the site for contested value positions about which the evaluator has no authoritative opinion.

Gordon Hughes

Associated Concepts: action research, actuarialism, administrative criminology, experiments, managerialism

Key Readings

Martinson, R. (1974) 'What works? Questions and answers about prison reform', *Public Interest*, 35, pp. 22–54.
Pawson, R. and Tilley, N. (1997) *Realistic Evaluation*. London, Sage.
Sherman, L., Gottfredson, D., MacKenzie, D., Eck, J., Reuter, P. and Bushway, S. (1997) 'Preventing Crime: What Works, What Doesn't, What's Promising'. A Report to the US Congress, http://www.ncjrs.org/works/index.htm
Tilley, N. (2000) 'The evaluation jungle', in K. Pease, S. Ballintyne and V. McLaren (eds), *Key Issues in Crime Prevention, Crime Reduction and Community Safety*. London, IPPR.

EXPERIMENTS

Definition

An experiment is a research study in which the researcher makes a measured intervention or treatment – a manipulation of the independent variable(s) – and observes its effect on a dependent variable, with (ideally) every other possible source of variation in the dependent

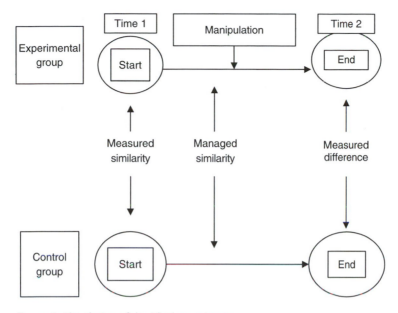

Figure 1: The design of the ideal experiment

variable controlled by the design of the study. Where literally *every* other possible source of variation has been controlled, any observed change in the dependent variable *must* be due to the manipulation of the independent variable.

Distinctive Features

Figure 1 illustrates a typical two-group experiment. The upper line represents a group who receive the treatment or intervention, and we shall assume that their experience between time 1 and time 2 is carefully controlled. Their state at time 1 and time 2 is carefully measured, and any change is recorded. A change at time 2 might not be due to the manipulation, however, it might have happened in any case simply from maturation (growing older). We therefore have a second group who are as similar as possible to the first at time 1 and whose experience between time 1 and time 2 is as near as possible the same, except that they do not receive the treatment. If Group 1 differs from Group 2 at time 2, having been similar at time 1, then the difference must logically be due to the treatment, which is the only difference in the two group's experiences.

One further check that is generally made is on the operation of chance itself. Because effects are normally probabilistic rather than absolute, a *small* difference between the two

groups may not signify more than the operation of chance. That is, if the manipulation had no effect whatsoever, we would still expect group scores not to come out exactly identical but to vary a little. The question is, how large is 'small' or 'very slightly'? In other words, how big does a difference have to be before we pay attention to it? As a decision rule we use statistical techniques based on the mathematics of probability which can specify, given certain assumptions, how likely a given size of difference is to be obtained by chance alone. Arbitrarily we tend to reject the 'null hypothesis' of only chance variation when the odds on obtaining our result by chance alone are as long as one in twenty ($p < 0.05$) or one in a hundred ($p < 0.01$). If the observed result is sufficiently unlikely on one of these criteria it is described as *statistically significant* and accepted as probably reflecting a real underlying difference. (Statistical mathematics is complex but the application of statistical tests is relatively easy, given computer packages to do the calculations for us.)

One use of experimental designs is in the evaluation of treatments, policies and institutional changes. To evaluate the effectiveness of a new way of running a prison, for example, one might institute the new regime in one setting and refrain from instituting it in another. If the two settings are very similar, and the inmate groups are also very similar to each other, then differences in inmate behaviour between the two might be taken as probably the result of the innovation (but with considerable reservations, discussed below). Experimental research is seldom used for the study of crime and the causes of crime, because it is generally impossible and always unethical to institute a manipulation of some people's lives and refrain from doing so with others, at random, in order to make observable changes in their behaviour or attitudes. The gross factors known to be linked to crime and disorder – gender, class, material deprivation and unemployment, membership of particular groups or subcultures, perhaps personality variables – are not susceptible to manipulation by the experimenter.

Evaluation

The logic of experimentation is impeccable, but its preconditions can seldom be met. For the experiment to prove causation conclusively, every extraneous factor must be controlled and every variable precisely measured. It is very difficult to control every extraneous factor outside the laboratory (or at all, with human subjects). Real-life experimental evaluations tend to founder on the difficulty of measuring the intervention (the treatment): when something is 'shown to work' it is generally very difficult indeed to specify precisely what that 'something' is.

Roger Sapsford

Associated Concepts: causation, evaluation research

Key Readings

Fowles, A.J. (1978) *Prison Welfare: An Account of an Experiment at Liverpool*. Home Office Research Study No. 35. London, HMSO.

Haney, C., Banks, C. and Zimbardo, P.G. (1973) 'Interpersonal dynamics in a simulated prison', *International Journal of Criminology and Penology*, 1, pp. 69–97.

Jupp, V. (1989) *Methods of Criminological Research*. London, Unwin Hyman.

EXTRATERRITORIAL LAW ENFORCEMENT

Definition

Law enforcement activity which extends outwith the boundaries of the state in which the law enforcement agency so engaged is officially headquartered.

Distinctive Features

There are a number of legal principles that give meaning to the idea of 'extraterritorial law enforcement'. The most important is the 'territorial principle', which is a concept that reflects an important aspect of sovereignty. Under this principle the state has the authority to act as the sovereign power within its territory. According to Shaw (1997, p. 458), this 'is the indispensable foundation for the application of the series of legal rights a state possesses'. In the criminological domain it is well accepted that a state should be able to prosecute offences committed, or allegedly committed, on its soil, since territoriality is a logical manifestation of the international state-system which vests power in the authorities representing the individual state's sovereign power. The logical corollary of this is that other states do not have the right to exercise law enforcement powers within the territory of another sovereign state. To do so is to undertake 'extraterritorial law enforcement'. Unless states affected by extraterritorial law enforcement consent to such it may be considered a violation of state sovereignty.

It is the state's authorities who are responsible for the conduct of law and the maintenance of good order within its territory. Thus all crimes committed (or alleged to have been committed) within the territorial jurisdiction of a state may come before the municipal courts and the accused, if convicted, may be sentenced. This is so even if the accused is a foreign national (with the possible exception of persons who have diplomatic immunity who are normally protected from such actions).

The territorial concept has been modified in certain ways in order that certain anomalies can be answered. Thus territoriality has been extended so as to include crimes where only part of the offence has occurred on a given state's territory. A classic illustrative example would be where a person fires a weapon across an international frontier resulting in someone's death. In such situations both the state where the gun was fired and the state where the death takes place may exercise jurisdiction, but the actual exercise of such powers often depends on where the offender is apprehended. A similar logic might also be applied in cases involving criminal conspiracy where criminal activities are alleged to have occurred in each of two or more countries. This instance is, however, complicated by the fact that 'criminal conspiracy' is not recognized in every jurisdiction.

Advances in communications and travel have transformed the context in which these principles are applied. For example, in Europe the Protocol concerning Frontier Controls and Policing, Co-operation in Criminal Justice and Mutual Assistance relating to the Channel Fixed Link (1991) was established to facilitate joint French-British policing of the Channel Tunnel. Under this Protocol police, customs and immigration officers may carry out their duties in specified 'control zones' in one another's territory, and on board through trains and at international railway stations. In effect, the Protocol creates a 'reciprocal constitution of sovereign territory in the domain of the other' (Sheptycki, 1998, p. 62). Under these arrangements each state can claim jurisdiction and can apply its own law when it cannot be ascertained with certainty where precisely an offence has been committed. However, it is also the case that the state that first receives the person suspected of having committed such an offence has priority in exercising jurisdiction. Thus, although jurisdiction is primarily territorial it is not exclusively so. States may enter into arrangements whereby jurisdiction is exercised outside the national territory and whereby jurisdiction by other states is exercised within the territory.

The 'nationality principle' also may affect states' view of criminal jurisdiction. For example, Germany claims jurisdiction over crimes committed by German nationals, notwithstanding that the offence may have been committed abroad. The nationality principle may be useful in proceeding in instances where it is alleged that persons have undertaken foreign travel for the purposes of engaging in criminal activity, for example illicit sexual activity with under-age persons. In the German case, charges may be brought in the 'tourist's' home country and is, in fact, the only way to proceed since Germany will not extradite its own nationals. According to Shaw (1997), English courts usually limit such actions to serious cases; treason, murder and bigamy have provided the case law.

The 'passive personality principle' asserts that states may exercise jurisdiction in order to try individuals for alleged offences committed abroad which affect the nationals of the state so claiming. The International Convention Against the Taking of Hostages (1979) allows states to claim jurisdiction in hostage incidents on the basis of the passive personality principle, 'if the state considers it appropriate'. Further, the Comprehensive Crime Control Act (1982) extends the jurisdiction of the USA to include '[a]ny place outside the jurisdiction of any nation with respect to an offence by or against a national of the United States' (Shaw, 1997, p. 468). It seems likely that, as the global fight against terrorism and transnational organized crime develops, so will applications of the passive personality principle.

The 'protective principle' or the 'state security principle' allows states to exercise jurisdiction over 'aliens' (i.e. non-nationals) who have committed, or have allegedly committed, an act abroad that is prejudicial to the security of the state concerned. This principle is justified on the basis that it allows for the protection of the 'vital interests' of the state concerned. However, this is a complicated matter since the alleged perpetrator may not be committing an offence under the law of the country of residence and an extradition request may be refused on the grounds that the alleged offence is 'political'. The classic case in UK law is *Joyce v Director of Public Prosecutions*, which pertained to the infamous pro-Nazi Second World War propagandist Lord Haw Haw, who was convicted of treason.

In the wake of the *Achille Lauro* incident, the Omnibus Diplomatic Security and Anti-Terrorism Act (1986) provided for jurisdiction over homicide and physical violence outside the USA where an American national is the victim. This legislation combines aspects of both the passive personality principle and the state security principle. Article 6 provides that jurisdiction may be claimed over an offence when a US national has been seized, threatened, injured or killed; or if the offence has been committed in an attempt to compel the US government to do or abstain from doing any act.

On the 'high seas' criminal law enforcement is exclusive to the flag-state of the vessel concerned. The flag-state may give permission to another state's vessels to exercise criminal law jurisdiction, or the captain of a vessel may invite officers aboard, but in the absence of such permission, no vessel may be boarded on the high seas by another country's personnel. Notable exceptions are in cases of piracy and when a vessel has engaged in 'hot pursuit' from a place within territorial waters.

Evaluation

Extraterritorial law enforcement is frequently contested, even when one of the above principles can be invoked. There are instances where apprehension of a suspect and the exercise of criminal law jurisdiction might be considered illegal, especially when extradition treaties provide for the legal transfer of alleged criminals. The case *US* v *Alvarez-Machain* is one example. The Supreme Court decision in this case suggests that, notwithstanding the existence of an extradition treaty between the USA and Mexico, unlawful apprehension of a suspect by state agents acting in the territory of another state would not, under American law, be considered a bar to the exercise of jurisdiction. In the UK, the case of *R.* v *Horseferry Road Magistrates Court* ex parte *Bennet*, the House of Lords declared that, where an extradition treaty exists with the relevant country, 'our courts will refuse to try him if he has forcibly been brought within our jurisdiction in disregard of those procedures by a process to which our own police, prosecuting or other executive authority have been a knowing party' (Shaw, 1997, p. 480).

James Sheptycki

Associated Concepts: the state, transnational organized crime, transnational policing

Key Readings

Shaw, M.N. (1997) *International Law*, 4th edn. Cambridge, Cambridge University Press.
Sheptycki, J.W.E. (1998) 'The global cops cometh', *British Journal of Sociology*, 49 (1), pp. 57–74.

EXTROVERSION/INTROVERSION

Definition

Extroversion may be taken as meaning 'outward turning', as in turning one's thoughts to the world; introversion as 'inward turning', as in self-contemplation.

Distinctive Features

Carl Jung (1875–1961) used the terms to refer to an outward (extroverted) or inward (introverted) turning of psychic energy. Jung suggested that this distinction was, indeed, one of the most fundamental aspects of human personality. Sigmund Freud (1856–1939) also drew on the notion of extroversion and introversion in his theories of psychopathology. Freud saw an outward approach to life as

beneficial, contraindicative of psychopathology; while introversion was seen to be a sign of not at all healthy psychic functioning.

Personality theory, most prominent in mainstream psychology from the 1940s through to the 1970s, also used the notion of extroversion/introversion. However, the terms extroversion and introversion were often used to refer to social behaviour, rather than psychic functioning. In particular, the psychometric approach to the measurement of personality identified outgoing, sociable behaviour and inward-looking, withdrawn behaviour as opposite poles of a basic personality type. This personality type was described in detail in the work of Hans Eysenck (1916–97), with Extroversion (E), alongside Neuroticism (N) and Psychoticism (P), as the three basic dimensions of personality (Eysenck, 1959).

Eysenck's work is important because he attempted to connect his basic personality types to other areas of research and theory so as to produce a more complete account of human functioning. In particular, Eysenck made connections between physiological functioning (primarily the central and autonomic nervous systems), conditionability in Pavlovian terms, and social development. Simply, Eysenck argued that a personality type which combined High E and High N would condition least well; while a Low E–Low N combination would condition most effectively. Eysenck developed this theme to give an account of criminal behaviour based on his theory of personality (Eysenck, 1964, 1977).

The force of Eysenck's contribution was to present a testable theory of antisocial behaviour. The evidence testing the theory is mixed, with some studies indicating support for Eysenck's position. However, psychological theories have moved on to become much more environmental in nature, placing a greater emphasis on the role of the social and physical environment in explaining behaviour.

Clive Hollin

Associated Concepts: conditioning, individual positivism, personality theory

Key Readings

Eysenck, H.J. (1959) *Manual of the Maudsley Personality Inventory*. London, University of London Press.
Eysenck, H.J. (1964) *Crime and Personality*. London, Routledge and Kegan Paul.
Eysenck, H.J. (1977) *Crime and Personality*, 3rd edn. London, Routledge and Kegan Paul.

F

FAMILY CRIME

Definition

An emergent generic term which draws attention to the extent and range of violence and abuse in 'private' domestic life.

Distinctive Features

Historically, one of the major consequences of representing crime as part of the public sphere is that events occurring within the private sphere of the family have been considered to be less serious than 'real crime' and as something distinct from crises of law and order. For example, domestic violence, child abuse and elder abuse have rarely been discussed as part of political and public concerns about the 'problem of crime'. This partiality is also reflected in academic criminology. Relatively few texts discuss child abuse and elder abuse, in particular, except in the context of victimization.

Family violence, understood primarily in terms of cruelty to children, but also involving what was described as conjugal violence, was first identified as a social problem in the late nineteenth century. The public concern at the time was short-lived, and did not re-emerge until the second half of the twentieth century. Events outside the family which might be identified as criminal have tended, except in 'extreme' cases, to be seen as normal if they occur within the confines of family relationships. For example, if an adult assaults another in the street, it is likely to be considered a criminal act; but if a man hits his wife at home this is more likely to be seen as a domestic argument. Equally, if parents hit a child, this may be seen as normal discipline, an under-standable reaction to a difficult child, or at worst cruelty, yet infant murders are more common than murders in any other age group.

Since the 1960s different forms of family violence have come to be identified and made more visible: physical abuse and neglect of children in the 1960s, domestic violence in the 1970s, child sexual abuse in the 1980s and elder abuse in the 1990s. As a result it has been argued that the family is the predominant setting for every form of physical violence: from slaps to torture and murder. Some form of physical violence in the life cycle of family members is so likely that it can be said to be 'almost universal' (Hotaling and Straus, 1980).

By the end of the twentieth century domestic violence in particular assumed a new visibility. In the UK evidence from victimization surveys revealed that:

- one woman in four experiences domestic violence at some stage in their life;
- two women are killed by current or former partners every week;
- thousands of children witness cruelty and violence everyday;
- domestic violence accounts for one-quarter of all violent crime.

In contrast, child abuse does not typically appear in victim surveys; estimates of its extent are usually taken from the numbers of children whose names have been placed on child protection registers, but even then they number tens of thousands every year.

Evaluation

As a result there now appears to be a greater agreement that family crime not only exists but is extensive. But there remains little consensus on how such violence and abuse should be understood and tackled. Historically the issue has been seen as primarily a private, a welfare or a civil, rather than a criminal, matter. It remains significant that the first Society for the Protection of Children was only set up in New York in 1871 when a child who was being treated cruelly by her adoptive parents could only be 'rescued' when a judge interpreted that the word 'animal', in the laws against cruelty to animals, might also include children. Similarly from the earliest record, many, if not most, societies have given the patriarch of the family the right to use force against women and children under his control. The issue of 'legitimate chastisement' is most strikingly illustrated by the 'rule of thumb', which is reputedly derived from the ancient right of a husband to beat his wife with a stick no thicker than his thumb.

Since the 1970s feminist research and campaigning have been pivotal in providing resources for women survivors of male violence and in ensuring that, first, rape and domestic violence and, latterly, child sexual abuse have been firmly placed on the political agenda. Gordon (1989) challenged the idea that state intervention was an intrusion into private matters by asking 'whose privacy' and 'whose liberties' were being violated. Many jurisdictions now recognize domestic violence as a crime and as a police priority. However, the state response to violence against children has been more ambivalent and clouded in notions of child protection, rather than criminalizing abusers. Although corporal punishment of children has been condemned by many Western jurisdictions and by international conventions of human rights, the constitution of 'reasonable chastisement' remains contested. In the UK, for example, there is no single criminal offence of abusing a child. Strategies to tackle domestic violence also remain presented as part of crime reduction policies rather than in terms of analyses of gender relations or of the nature of families (Saraga, 2001).

A constantly shifting balance between family privacy, support for parental authority and public recognition of familial violence continues to marginalize the issue of family crime in broader law and order agendas. It remains to be seen how far emergent discourses of human rights will be able to overcome such persistent ambivalence.

Esther Saraga and John Muncie

Associated Concepts: masculinities, radical feminism, victimology, violence

Key Readings

Biggs, S., Phillipson, C. and Kingston, P. (1995) *Elder Abuse in Perspective*. Buckingham, Open University Press.

Dobash, R.E. and Dobash, R.P. (eds) (1998) *Rethinking Violence against Women*. London, Sage.

Gordon, L. (1989) *Heroes of their Own Lives: The Politics and History of Family Violence, 1880–1960*. London, Virago.

Hotaling, G.T. and Straus, M.A. (eds) (1980) *The Social Causes of Husband–Wife Violence*. Minneapolis, University of Minnesota Press.

Morgan, J. and Zedner, L. (1992) *Child Victims*. Oxford, The Clarendon Press.

Saraga, E. (2001) 'Dangerous places: the family as a site of crime', in J. Muncie and E. McLaughlin (eds), *The Problem of Crime*, 2nd edn. London, Sage.

FEAR OF CRIME

Definition

Fear of crime is a rational or irrational state of alarm or anxiety engendered by the belief that one is in danger of criminal victimization.

Distinctive Features

Life in complex highly urbanized societies requires high levels of trust in others, especially strangers, and there is considerable evidence that 'strangers' are a potent source of fear in the public imagination. Particular forms of 'dangerous stranger' crime and/or high levels of crime can have a corrosive effect on everyday life because of the individual and public fear and anxiety they generate. A pervasive fear of crime encourages physical and psychological withdrawal from the community. It weakens informal social control systems and undermines the capacity of individuals and communities to respond to the problems that they face. As a consequence, it provides space for further crime and disorder. Public faith in the criminal justice system and the capacity of the state to protect its citizens is also damaged by fear of crime. This produces public calls for tougher law and order policies and creates the demand for high levels of private anti-crime security and self-protection.

Research suggests that the fear of crime is an ill-defined term that covers a variety of complex worries and anxieties. It relates to an individual's judgement about the amount and nature of crime in society and her/his own neighbourhood. Self-perceived vulnerability is also crucial to levels of individual fear. It also relates to a multitude of anxieties about the pace and nature of social and cultural change. For example, a sense of neighbourhood decline and shifts in racial and ethnic demographics seem to be particular sources of fear and anxiety. Conventional wisdom holds that the members of the public most afraid of crime are the ones who have been victimized. However, research in a variety of jurisdictions suggests that the relationship between the risk of victimization and fear of crime is not straightforward. Although it is true that among certain sections of the public fear of crime would seem to be out of all proportion to the actual risk of becoming a victim, this general statement about risk needs to be qualified. In-depth research among women in specific localities, for example, suggests that their fears and concerns are not exaggerated. On the contrary, women have a well-founded and precise understanding of their vulnerability with regard to sexual violence.

Fear of crime can escalate because of: direct experience; secondary knowledge from family, friends and acquaintances; the campaigning work of pressure groups representing victims; police officers and politicians who want to play the law and order card; the activities of private security firms looking for business; and insurance companies protecting their interests. Sections of the news media have a key role to play in circulating fear of crime through: over-reporting of violent and sexual crimes; personalization and sensationalization techniques; intense coverage of, and commentary on, crimes that grip the public imagination; and hard line and alarmist campaigns against particular types of criminals.

Evaluation

For criminal justice policy-makers in many jurisdictions tackling the fear of crime has become a priority. Government-sponsored advertising campaigns have been run in an attempt to persuade the public that many of their fears are irrational. Efforts have also been made to persuade the news media to be more responsible in their crime reporting activities. Situational crime prevention strategies have been used by administrative criminologists to target harden both potential victims and locations. Left realist inspired local authorities

in the UK have developed situational and community-based safety strategies that are intended to protect citizens from the criminal or anti-social behaviour of others and enable them to pursue their lives without the fear of victimization. These strategies specifically take account of the safety needs of vulnerable members of the community. Police forces have also developed aggressive, high profile operational strategies to shift the burden of fear from potential victims to offenders.

These policy developments and practical initiatives aside, there remains an urgent need to reach a more sophisticated theorization of such concepts as 'fear', 'risk', 'danger', 'security' and 'safety'.

Eugene McLaughlin

Associated Concepts: left realism, moral panic, personal safety, risk, situational crime prevention, victimology

Key Readings

Best, J. (1999) *Random Violence: How we Talk About New Crimes and New Victims.* Berkeley, University of California Press.

Davis, M. (1998) *Ecology of Fear: Los Angeles and the Imagination of Disaster.* New York, Metropolitan Books.

Ferraro, K.F. (1995) *Fear of Crime: Interpreting Victimization Risk.* Albany, State University of New York Press.

Hollway, W. and Jefferson, T. (2000) 'The role of anxiety in fear of crime in everyday life', in T. Hope and R. Sparks (eds), *Crime, Risk and Insecurity: Law and Order in Everyday Life.* London, Routledge.

Lewis, D.A. and Salem, G.W. (1985) *Fear of Crime: Incivility and the Production of a Social Problem.* New Brunswick, NJ, Transaction.

Schlesinger, P. and Tumber, H. (1994) *Reporting Crime: The Media Politics of Criminal Justice.* Oxford, The Clarendon Press.

FEMINIST CRIMINOLOGIES

Definition

Varied analyses using feminist or critical social theories that ask: what is the place of sex/gender in crime and justice? And what is the place of sex/gender in criminological and justice theories?

Distinctive Features

Feminist criminologies challenge the andro-centrism (or male-centredness) of the field of criminology and its explanations of crime and justice system practices in varied ways. Taking a broad and inclusive definition of feminist perspectives, two major axes are apparent: one drawing on liberal theory and the other on critical social theory (Daly and Chesney-Lind, 1988).

Liberal feminist criminologies assume that men and women are 'the same' but women are denied opportunities to do the same things as men, including participating in crime. This perspective typically ignores class and racial-ethnic differences among women, and defines gender either as the possession of masculine or feminine attitudes or as role differences between men and women. By contrast, feminist criminologies that draw on critical social theories assume that men and women are both the same and different, and they focus on gender power relations not role differences. They argue that traditional crim-inological theories are incapable of explaining the relationship of sex/gender to crime or justice system practices. This latter set of feminist criminologies is diverse; it includes scholars who focus exclusively on sex/gender, who are interested in the intersections of class, race and gender, and who analyse sex/gender as an active accomplishment or as a discursive field. They often draw from feminist work outside criminology, including post-struc-tural, post-colonial, critical race, philosophical, discourse and psychoanalytical theories.

Feminist criminologies are new, having emerged in the 1970s inspired by the women's movement. Beginning in the mid-1980s, they began to change, reflecting shifts in feminist thought more generally. Recent work attends to differences among women, to the impact of post-structuralist thinking in representing 'women', and to different epistemologies in producing feminist knowledge: empiricist, standpoint and postmodern. Whereas scholars in the 1970s and 1980s focused on depicting 'real women' and 'women's experiences', those in the 1990s became interested in prob-lems of representing 'women' in light of the discursive power of social, criminological and legal texts to contain sex/gender and women in ways that seemed obdurate to change (Smart, 1995).

During the 1990s, three modes of analysing sex/gender have emerged: class–race–gender, doing gender and sexed bodies (Daly, 1997). Class–race–gender focuses on the intersec-tions of different social relations on women's (and men's) lives; doing gender (and subse-quently doing masculinity) centres on the situations and social practices that produce gender; and sexed bodies focuses on sexual difference and on the relationship of sex and gender as corporeal and cultural categories. During this period there has been increasing interest to portray women victims and law-breakers as having choice and agency, rather than depicting women (or girls) as passive victims of male (or white) oppression (Daly, 1998).

Evaluation

Feminist perspectives in criminology are a very recent development, having only begun to appear in criminology or criminal justice texts in the early 1990s. As a set of perspec-tives, feminist criminologies make diverse claims about the relationship of sex/gender to crime and justice system practices. There is no one feminist criminology, and some suggest that the term *feminist criminology* should be abandoned. Over the past three decades, feminist perspectives in criminology have been applied most frequently to victimi-zation, especially to family violence and sexual assault. While developed feminist theories of victimization and men's violence toward women have emerged, feminist the-ories of crime are less evident.

Different sources of field expansion, one beginning with theories of crime and the other beginning with theories of gender, have created different types of knowledge about women, gender and crime. The first follows in the footsteps of traditional criminology and is liberal feminist in orientation; it seeks to devise a comprehensive theory that would explain gender differences in law-breaking (Steffens-meier and Allan, 1996). The second is the province of more critical feminist criminolo-gists, who begin with theories of sex/gender and with studies of women's (and men's) lives, and apply this body of knowledge to crime. This group is less interested in devising a comprehensive theory of gender and crime, and more inclined to identify the ways in which sex/gender structures men's and women's lifeworlds, identities and thinkable courses of action (Maher, 1997). Future work will likely reflect theory-building preferences structured not only by liberal and critical social theories, but also by the theorist's gender.

Kathleen Daly

Associated Concepts: critical criminology, hegemonic masculinity, liberal feminism, feminist research, masculinities, postmodern feminism, radical feminism, sexuality, victimology

Key Readings

Daly, K. and Chesney-Lind, M. (1988) 'Feminism and criminology', *Justice Quarterly*, 5 (4), pp. 497–538.

Daly, K. (1997) 'Different ways of conceptualizing sex/gender in criminological theories and their implications for criminology', *Theoretical Criminology*, 1 (1), pp. 25–51.

Daly, K. (1998) 'Gender, crime, and criminology', in M. Tonry (ed.), *The Handbook of Crime and Punishment*. New York, Oxford University Press.

Maher, L. (1997) *Sexed Work: Gender, Race and Resistance in a Brooklyn Drug Market*. Oxford, The Clarendon Press.

Smart, C. (1995) *Law, Crime and Sexuality*. London, Sage.

Steffensmeier, D. and Allan, E. (1996) 'Gender and crime: toward a gendered theory of female offending', *Annual Review of Sociology*, 22, pp. 459–87.

FEMINIST RESEARCH

Definition

The term 'feminist research' escapes any simple or ready definition. The questions: 'what makes research feminist?' and 'is it possible to speak of feminist methodology/ies or method?' have been the subject of continuing debate since at least the early 1980s.

Distinctive Features

Early debate centred on the assertion that feminist research was 'research about women, by women, for women'. Feminists recognized that women had been marginalized, stereotyped and sexualized in pre/non-feminist research. This 'absence' was first addressed by making women visible as autonomous subjects. However, the far-reaching nature of feminist critique generated complex methodological and epistemological questions to the extent that the feminist research project came to entail more than a simplistic adding of women to existing research agendas.

In criminology this is evident in a body of empirical studies examining women's relation to patriarchal institutions, for example in law, criminal justice and policing. As well as redressing absences in such research, these studies, consistent with feminism, advocated political and policy interventions designed to secure beneficial changes to the circumstances of those found to be experiencing oppression or discrimination. From the outset, feminist research aimed to both understand the nature of patriarchal oppression and to bring about change (Kelly et al., 2000).

Although the 'about women, by women, for women' formulation became something of an orthodoxy in the early 1980s, it has proved inadequate as a definition. Duelli Klein (1983) dismissed the notion that focusing on women as subjects is sufficient to define research as feminist, arguing that without a feminist framework, research about women can perpetuate dominant androcentric assumptions. The formulation was also limiting in its exclusion of research into the operation of male power, patriarchal institutions, men and masculinity, although these issues featured significantly in feminist research agendas. The early formulation also suggested that to be feminist, research had to be conducted by women, although it is clear from Duelli Klein that the significant factor is a commitment to feminism. As a result, the assertion that feminist research was 'for women', came closest to identifying what makes research feminist. Defined by Duelli Klein (1983, p. 90) as '. . . research that tries to take women's needs, interests and experiences into account and aims at being instrumental in improving women's lives . . .' the 'for women' tenet established feminist research as 'women-centred'.

Through its commitments to feminism and a women-centred research practice, feminist research presents a major challenge to the empiricist orthodoxy that social science research should strive for objectivity and be value-free. In relation to criminology, it is revealed that what previously passed as objective was imbued with masculinist misrepresentations of women. Recognizing that scholarship inevitably reflects the conditions of its production, including the gender standpoint of its producers, feminism rejects the possibility of objective knowledge. Rather, the subjectivity of the researcher is acknowledged as significant in the research process. Reflexivity at the personal level is a core methodological principle in feminist research. As Holland and Ramazanoglu (1994, p. 130) note, a key innovation of feminist research is 'the attempt to grasp the parts that experience, emotion and subjectivity play in the research process, rather than seeing these as weaknesses to be controlled'.

The critique of objectivity extended to research practice. Feminism demonstrated how the aim of objectivity resulted in the objectification of research participants. In contrast, feminist researchers respect participants as holders of valuable knowledge and experience. Being granted permission to gather and use this knowledge is considered a privilege. In accordance with feminist ethics is the commitment to developing research practices that ensure that women are not exploited or hurt by the research process. In contrast to the positivist commitment to 'objectivity', the 'women-centred' character of feminist research highlights the importance of subjectivity and meaning. MacKinnon (1987), for example, makes connections between feminist research, consciousness raising and the practice of sharing individual and personal experiences. Without structural and cultural location, subjectivity in itself is not a sufficient basis for theory-building, but when contextualized, it represents a significant starting point.

Placing women's experience at the centre of research carries the danger of exclusions in relation to marginalized groups, for example, black and minority ethnic women, lesbians and those belonging to minority faith groups. The question of 'which women?' must also be interrogated. This point has been emphasized in black feminist critiques and in research that is sensitive to issues of inclusion and exclusion.

Considerable emphasis was initially placed on qualitative methods in order to be sensitive to subjective experience and the meanings accorded to it. This approach also enabled power imbalances between the researcher and research subjects to be more readily negotiated. In fact, by the late 1980s, feminist research was often represented as synonymous with qualitative methodology. However, for feminists involved in activism, awareness of the strategic role of statistics in establishing a case for political intervention meant that quantitative research also became something of a necessary evil. But feminist attempts to develop more 'participant friendly', sensitive and accountable survey practices led to some creative innovations. Contrary to some academic representations, feminist research practice has demonstrated that all methods – surveys, discourse analysis, as well as autobiographical accounts and face-to-face interviewing – have been drawn on by feminists.

It is not the research methods that make research distinctively feminist. Rather, what distinguishes feminist research is its feminist commitment to producing research 'for women', the identification of women's experiences as a new empirical resource and the positioning of the researcher within the research processes. The distinctiveness of feminist research lies at these related levels of methodology and epistemology:

- Feminist research is explicitly positioned within the feminist project of understanding the nature of women's oppression with a view to ending it.
- The research agenda reflects women's concerns.
- Its underlying theory is feminist and its practice centres on women's experiences within a framework that acknowledges continuity and difference between women positioned differently in relation to other major power structures, significantly race, sexuality, culture and class.
- Its outcomes are presented accessibly and made available to those for whom they will be useful.
- It recognizes the significance of gender and gender power relations in all dimensions of social life.
- It accepts the importance of subjectivity and personal experience of the researcher.
- It minimizes or eliminates exploitative relations between researchers and participants.

These principles are embedded in practice at all stages of feminist research from theorizing the initial problem, its underpinning epistemologies, the data-gathering process, to the writing and publication of outcomes, including a strategic consideration of how to frame the issues and whether and where to publish.

Evaluation

Feminist research is not primarily about methods. It is a theoretical, empirical, interpretative, critical and engaged process, informed by the goal of ultimately eliminating the oppression of women. Acknowledging that feminist work is positioned within a struggle for change does not mean that it is biased, simply subjective and anecdotal. On the contrary, the development of strategies for change requires an accurate naming and analysis of the existing situation or problem.

Feminist research aims to produce outcomes that can be verified. Its openness regarding methodological and theoretical assumptions facilitates accountability and criticism. How feminist research is evaluated depends primarily on the standpoint of the reviewer. Those hostile to feminism criticize its overtly political standpoint, its emphasis on subjectivity and rejection of objectivity and its lack of a common method. Those more persuaded by feminism evaluate it against its own aims and achievements, including its usefulness in generating change.

Jill Radford

Associated Concepts: critical criminology, critical research, liberal feminism, radical feminism, reflexivity

Key Readings

Duelli Klein, R. (1983) 'How to do what we want to do: thoughts about feminist methodology', in G. Bowles and R. Duelli Klein (1983) *Theories of Women's Studies*. London, Routledge and Kegan Paul.

Holland, J. and Ramazanoglu, G. (1994) 'Power and interpretation in researching young women's sexuality', in M. Maynard and J. Purvis (eds), *Researching Women's Lives from a Feminist Perspective*. London, Taylor and Francis.

Kelly, L., Burton, S. and Regan, L. (1994) 'Researching women's lives or studying women's oppression? Reflections on what counts as feminist research', in M. Maynard and J. Purvis (eds), *Researching Women's Lives from a Feminist Perspective*. London, Taylor and Francis.

Kelly, L., Radford, J. and Scanlon, J. (2000) 'Feminism, feminisms: fighting back for women's liberation', in K. Atkinson, S. Orton and G. Plain (eds), *Feminisms on Edge: Politics, Discourses and National Identities*. Cardiff, Cardiff Academic Press.

MacKinnon, C. (1987) *Feminism Unmodified: Discourses on Life and Law*. Cambridge, MA, Harvard University Press.

FOCUS GROUPS

Definition

A form of interview which involves a number of individuals who discuss a particular topic under the direction of a facilitator who promotes interaction between individuals and assures that the discussion remains on the topic of interest. The data are not just the outcome of an exchange between the facilitator and the group but also the outcome of interactions between group members.

Distinctive Features

The term 'focus group' is derived from Merton and Kendall's (1946) work on the persuasiveness of wartime propaganda in the USA. Focus groups subsequently became a favoured tool within market research, for example, to examine product imagery. In the 1980s and 1990s they became widely used by social scientists and also by political parties to gather ideas regarding policy formation and presentation.

Social scientists use focus groups in three ways. First, they are used in an exploratory role, as a preliminary to more extensive research. For example, data collected from the groups can be used to identify issues which are crucial to the participants themselves, rather than what social scientists think are important; they may help to devise subsequent research design; and they can assist in the formulation of questions to be used in structured interviews. Secondly, focus groups can be employed as a method in their own right and as a central part of a research study, for example, to find out about how representatives of a community experience crime victimization and what views they have about strategies for prevention. Thirdly, focus groups can be used to triangulate or support findings from other forms of research. Focus groups can generate in-depth attitudes, opinions, examples and case studies which are often not obtainable from large-scale but shallow social surveys.

Typically, focus groups comprise between four and 12 participants, who will have been selected because they fit some criteria that are relevant to the research topic. Usually an attempt is made to ensure that the composition of the group is representative of the population to which the researchers wish the conclusions to apply. Discussion of topics is initiated by a facilitator who starts with introductions and general issues and then moves progressively to more focused questions. The role of facilitator is not solely to initiate an exchange with group members (as in-depth interviews) but to encourage interactions between group members which generate data not usually obtained in one-to-one interviews. The advantages of this interactive effect are that group members can be reminded of issues by others in the group; they can generate ideas new to the researcher; and they can give support to each other in discussing sensitive topics. For example, research involving a group discussion on domestic violence with a group of women from refuges found that they were prepared to share information of a personal and harrowing nature because they had had similar experiences. Once one group member began to talk, others were prepared to join in.

Evaluation

As with all methods of research there is a trade-off between strengths and weaknesses in relation to the topic of research. Focus groups are quicker and cheaper than detailed interviews with an equivalent number of individuals. They provide the depth and flexibility of approach of unstructured interviews but in addition provide insights into the effects of interactions between group members. In addition, group interviews can support individuals in discussing sensitive topics and also facilitate the brainstorming of original ideas. However, a good deal of skill is required of the facilitator in encouraging interactions, managing group dynamics and keeping discussion on the central topic. There can also be problems of generalizability and researchers should exercise caution in making inferences from a focus group to a wider population. This is one of the criticisms levelled at the use of focus groups by political parties to assist in the formulation of policy.

Victor Jupp

Associated Concepts: ethnography, feminist research, triangulation

Key Readings

Kreuger, R.A. (1994) *Focus Groups: A Practical Guide for Applied Research*. Thousand Oaks, CA, Sage.

Merton, R. and Kendall, P. (1946) 'The Focused Interview', *American Journal of Sociology*, 51, pp. 541–57.

Morgan, D.L. (ed.) (1993) *Successful Focus Groups*. Newbury Park, CA, Sage.

Stewart, D.W. and Shamdasani, D.N. (1990) *Focus Groups: Theory and Practice*. Newbury Park, CA, Sage.

FOLK DEVIL

Definition

A category of persons which becomes defined as a threat to societal values and interests and the embodiment of 'what is wrong with society'. Folk devils are presented in a stylized and stereotypical fashion by the mass media.

Distinctive Features

The concept of 'folk devil' is closely associated with Cohen's (1972) analysis of the ways in which confrontations between Mods and Rockers in an English holiday resort were reported in the media. The analysis owes much to the development of interactionist, labelling and new deviancy approaches within criminology during the mid to late 1960s. These approaches influenced the direction on Cohen's empirical work, which was essentially qualitative and ethnographic and involved an examination of the role of the media in reporting the events. His conclusions were that the media play a key role in symbolization in which key symbols, such as lifestyle, are portrayed as different from the norm and in a socially unfavourable light. Within symbolization a word, such as 'Mod', becomes symbolic of a certain status, such as delinquent or deviant. Objects, such as distinctive hairstyles and clothing, symbolize the word and the objects themselves become symbolic of the status, including the emotions attached to the status. Symbolization is crucial to the creation of folk devils.

The media also play an important part in the exaggeration and distortion of events, also in making predictions about future events, perhaps elsewhere, which are likely to be even worse than the exaggerations and distortions. This produces forms of societal reaction to the folk devils, such as greater police vigilance and surveillance and public campaigns to control or prohibit events. With regard to the Mods and Rockers, there was pressure for greater police vigilance and stronger action from the forces of law and order. The police reacted by intensifying foot patrols and greater levels of surveillance and intervention in seaside towns, dance halls and fairs, which were seen as potential areas of trouble. It is a fundamental element of Cohen's thesis that such societal reaction to folk devils increases rather than decreases subsequent deviance, a process known as deviancy amplification. The public and police react to the folk devils in terms of the images and symbols presented to them by the media. Individuals respond accordingly, thereby confirming their status as deviant and as a threat to what is viewed as normal.

The concept 'folk devil' is inextricably linked to another, namely 'moral panic'. The thesis is that societies go through periods of social change which instil feelings of uncertainty, fear and threat in their members and that during such periods folk devils emerge as the symbol, and even the cause of what is wrong. There is a middle range explanation for the emergence of folk devils in the media in terms of the need for 'news value' and 'good copy'. However, Cohen's thesis also suggests a much more fundamental explanation in the rapid social change which Britain was undergoing in the 1960s (decline of the traditional working-class community, increased permissiveness) and the dissipation of ensuing public anxiety by identifying folk devils as scapegoats and as symbols of what was wrong.

Hall et al. (1978) drew on Cohen's work in the analysis of the young-black-mugger-as-folk-devil. Their work was similar to Cohen's in the way in which it identified an increase in street mugging as a socially constructed phenomenon and traced its creation as a moral panic in the media during the 1970s. However, Hall and his colleagues linked the moral panic and the portrayal of young black muggers as folk devils to a crisis in hegemony during an economic recession in a capitalist system. It was argued that public concern about mugging served to distract attention away from the underlying causes and inherent problems of increasing economic decline. It thrust social anxieties on to black youths who were perceived as threats to ordinary (often old) citizens and to social order on the streets of inner city areas. Also, the threat from young black muggers was used to justify increased and heavier policing and a general drift towards a law and order society. In offering this analysis Hall et al. extended Cohen's thesis by adding a Marxist and critical slant to what was a predominantly interactionist and labelling approach to crime and deviance.

The concept 'folk devil' is capable of wide applicability but has been applied most forcefully in analysis of youth and of youth cultures (although often in couplets such as 'black youth', 'working-class youth', 'inner city youth'). A key reason for this is that youth are treated as a barometer of the current social health of society and as a means of forming a prognosis for its future.

Evaluation

'Folk devil' is a robust and enduring theoretical concept which has made important contributions to criminology by opening up fruitful lines of theorizing and empirical enquiry. It has facilitated the fusion of valuable aspects of interactionism and labelling theory with those offered by critical criminology and analysis at a social structural level. In doing so it has encouraged enquiry of micro and macro aspects of social life and interconnections between these. What is more, more recent applications of discourse analysis within criminology have embraced the concept of 'folk devil' in terms of addressing what types of people are portrayed as problematic within discourses at different levels of society, why, and with what effect.

Empirical enquiries, especially those based on ethnographic methods, have used 'folk devil' as a sensitizing device for guiding research. These include documentary analysis of media reports, police reports and public statements by politicians and judiciary; examination of the social construction of official statistics and of their role in creating crime waves and moral panics; observation of interactions between 'deviants' and law enforcement officers in terms of the application, receipt and amplification of deviant labels. The concept has also had some policy applications, for example in terms of introducing topics on the negative aspects of stereotyping into the education and training of criminal justice personnel and related professions.

Despite these contributions there is a danger that the discourse of 'folk devil' as an exaggerated and distorted image which is socially constructed and then used as a scapegoat for some other problems masks the fact that crime is a reality for those victims who have experienced it and for those who live in fear of it. Such a viewpoint is associated with those who come from a position of criminological realism and who emphasize the need to face up to the reality of crime.

Victor Jupp

Associated Concepts: criminalization, demonization, deviance, discourse analysis, ethnography, interactionism, labelling, moral panic, new deviancy theory, racialization, scapegoating, social reaction, stereotyping

Key Readings

Cohen, S. (1972) *Folk Devils and Moral Panics: The Creation of Mods and Rockers*. London, MacGibbon and Kee. (London, Paladin, 1973; new edition Martin Robertson, Oxford, 1980.)

Goode, E.R. and Ben-Yehuda, N. (1994) *Moral Panics: The Social Construction of Deviance*. Oxford, Blackwell.

Hall, S., Critcher, C., Jefferson, T., Clarke, J. and Roberts, B. (1978) *Policing the Crisis: Mugging, the State and Law and Order*. London, Macmillan.

Thompson, K. (1998) *Moral Panics*. London, Routledge.

FREE WILL

Definition

Within the discipline of criminology this concept generally refers to the ability to choose a certain course of action against another, one of which may be regarded as 'deviant'. Although this supposition does not presume that all behaviour is necessarily freely and rationally chosen, it implies that individuals can recognize rules and laws and decide which to obey. To what extent free will exists therefore facilitates discussions surrounding the motives and predictability of human behaviour. Rather than certain acts being determined, either by forces within, or external to, the individual, this allows crime to be viewed as a matter of personal autonomy.

Distinctive Features

The concept of free will has a number of important implications for the study of crime, criminality and penal policy. Within each of these three areas theorists have sought causal explanations, predictive models and the justification or effectiveness of modes of punishment. As autonomy underpins classicist criminological approaches and determinism is a central tenet of the contrasting paradigm of positivist criminologies, the notion of freely chosen behaviour is central to many disagreements within the discipline. Indeed, whether criminal acts are freely enacted or externally driven is the crux of this major area of debate. As the legal theorist Herbert L.A. Hart, known for his influential work on jurisprudence, argues, responsibility for most crimes relies upon certain 'mental elements'. Without proof that someone has the

knowledge and foresight to predict the consequences of their actions and their potential harm, then although negligence may be shown, criminal responsibility would not. He claims that for legal purposes 'an act is something more than a mere movement of the body: it must be willed' (1963: 41). To claim in the criminal courts, for example, that an individual is responsible and purposive in their actions may invalidate mitigating factors, which may have led to an accusation of murder being reduced to manslaughter. Conversely, if criminal intent or *mens rea* is not proven, if the accused is judged insane, provoked, or claims to have simply acted recklessly, then the concept of autonomous action may be disregarded. Being able to prove that the individual acted within the realm of freedom of choice is therefore linked to notions of justice and legitimacy, not only in theoretical debates but also in case law.

Evaluation

One of the assumptions underpinning the idea that individuals can exercise free will is that society, law and justice are based upon equality. Individuals within this broadly classicist approach may not be viewed as being free to choose whether to take part in the social contract, but they have faculties of reasoning and access to social justice. The problem with assuming that free will is enacted by individuals is that structures within society constrain different groups at different times in various ways, although as Bottoms and Wiles (1992/1996, p. 101) argue, 'it is dangerous to assume that place or design acts as a monocausal variable'. In paraphrasing Anthony Giddens's work on structuration theory (1984), they propose that although society enforces constraints, '[H]uman subjects are knowledgeable agents . . . [who] largely act within a domain of "practical consciousness"' (1992/1996, pp. 102–3). Finally, they quote Marx's famous dictum that human beings 'make history but not in circumstances of their own choosing' to illustrate the difficulties of explaining the constraints and choices surrounding the behaviour defined as criminal.

Similarly, in response to more individualist, psychological approaches in some cases it might be argued that the actor's behaviour was 'involuntary' due to a number of factors which are difficult to disprove. Instances of this include being subject to compelling internal psychological drives, the addiction to substances such as drugs, extreme provocation or automatous behaviour such as sleep-walking. More recent work on sociobiology, twin and adoption studies also suggests that 'some factor' (Mednick et al., 1987/1996) is transmitted genetically to children which increases their propensity to commit crime.

Other more recent advocates of this approach are Wilson and Hernstein (1986), who suggest that although individuals are free to choose a course of action that may be criminal, a combination of inherited traits and learned behaviour will influence their choice. Whether the act is outweighed by potentially negative outcomes is therefore influenced, according to this sociobiological approach, by a combination of nature and nurture.

                                        Louise Westmarland

Associated Concepts: classicism, determinism, neo-conservative criminology, rational choice theory

Key Readings

Bottoms, A.E. and Wiles, P. (1992) 'Explanations of crime and place', in J. Muncie, E. McLaughlin and M. Langan (eds) (1996) Criminological Perspectives. London, Sage.

Giddens, A. (1984) The Constitution of Society. Cambridge, Polity.

Hart, H.L.A. (1963) 'Acts of will and legal responsibility', in D.F. Pears (ed.), Freedom and the Will. London, Macmillan.

Mednick, S.A., Gabrielli, W.F. and Hutchings, B. (1987) 'Genetic factors in the etiology of criminal behavior', in J. Muncie, E. McLaughlin and M. Langan (eds) (1996) Criminological Perspectives. London, Sage.

Wilson, J.Q. and Hernstein, R.J. (1986) Crime and Human Nature. New York, Simon and Schuster.

FUNCTIONALISM

Definition

A structuralist perspective that argues that, although crime and deviance are problematic, they must also be understood as 'social facts' and analysed in terms of the possible manifest and latent functions that they perform in enabling the smooth running of the social system as a whole. Hence functionalism distances itself from those criminological perspectives that view crime and deviance as pathological and abnormal.

Distinctive Features

There is a long tradition of functionalist theorizing and explanation across the social sciences. It was introduced into sociology during the nineteenth century and developed and reworked within anthropology. From the 1920s through to the 1950s the functionalist paradigm dominated North American sociology and the approach was embodied most famously in the work of Talcott Parsons who developed a grand theory of social systems.

Functionalists argue that studying society as if it were a living organism is necessary if we are to understand its major structural institutions and be able to explain human behaviour. Society is viewed as a delicate system where the interdependent parts work in an integrated manner for the common good. Society is deemed to be an independent entity that is greater than the number of individual members. In order to survive and perpetuate itself, society has needs that have to be met and in certain instances these take priority over individual needs. Structures, institutions, practices, roles, values and norms exist because they contribute to the maintenance and proper functioning of society. Functions are assumed to be either manifest (intended) or latent (unintended or unrecognized). If an institution is unable to carry out its functions it will eventually cease to exist and be replaced by new institutional arrangements. According to Percy Cohen (1968, p. 167), functionalist theorizing is marked by the following basic assumptions:

- norms and values are the basic elements of social life;
- social life involves commitments to agreed norms and values;
- societies are necessarily cohesive;
- social life depends on solidarity and generates harmony;
- social life is based upon reciprocity and cooperation;
- social systems rest on consensus;
- society recognizes power as legitimate authority;
- social systems are integrated and stable;
- social systems tend to persist – conflict is temporary until equilibrium is re-established;
- change is functional adaptation.

Functionalists such as Daniel Bell and Talcott Parsons were attracted to the study of crime and deviance because in many respects it would provide the ultimate test of their theorizing. However, the social theorist most closely associated with the initial application of functionalist theorizing to crime and deviance was Emile Durkheim. His sociological positivism sought to identify and explain 'social facts': ways of thinking, feeling and acting that a society imposes upon its members to produce order. Even though he did not produce a systematic treatise on the subject, crime and deviance were of interest to Durkheim because his central political project was working out how social cohesion and solidarity can be secured in the face of rapid social and economic change.

Durkheim's contribution to functionalist criminology is two-fold. First, he argued that crime and deviance are normal (social facts) because acts that offend collective norms and expectations exist in all societies and their universal presence points to their systemic functionality. For Durkheim, crime and deviance, so long as they are not excessive, are functional because (i) the ritual of punishment is an expressive experience that serves to bind together members of a social group and establish a sense of community and (ii) they are useful in inaugurating necessary changes and preparing people for change. Even if society discovered the means for eradicating real crimes, it would have to elevate human weaknesses and petty vices to the status of crime. Albert Cohen (1966) built on Durkheim's position by clarifying the various ways that crime and deviance make positive contributions to society:

- deviance cuts through 'red tape';
- deviance acts as a safety valve for societal pressures and discontents and reduces strains;
- deviance clarifies the rules;
- deviance unites the group against the deviant(s) and provides commonality and solidarity;
- deviance defines and heightens conformity and normality;
- deviance acts as a warning signal to defects in society.

A classic example of functionalist theorizing on the positive contribution of crime and deviance to the social order remains Kingsley Davis's controversial analysis of the role played by prostitution in contemporary society. He argues that prostitution exists despite near universal condemnation and prohibition because it enables a small number of women to take care of the sexual needs of a large number of men: 'it is the most convenient sexual outlet for armies and for legions of strangers, perverts, and the physically repulsive in our midst. It performs a role which apparently no other institution fully performs' (1971, p. 351). Davis intimates that prostitution reinforces the norms and values and equilibrium of the family by providing a safety valve for married men's pent up sexual frustrations and deviant needs. Hence, prostitution allows the family to be a model of temperance and moderation and certifies the respectability of married women. Prostitution is functional for the women involved, according to Davis, because it enables them to earn more money than they would in other occupations. This led to the conclusion that there will always be a system of social dominance that provides the motive for commercial sex.

Durkheim's second contribution was his theorizing on anomie. Durkheim never spelled out how much crime and deviance are healthy and normal. For him, too little crime and deviance are indicative of an overly regulated society and excessive intolerance, whereas too much crime and deviance lower the levels of trust and interdependence that are necessary for the survival of society. It is this point that connects across to Durkheim's notion of the anomic society. This is a society in which the rules of behaviour and norms have broken down during periods of rapid social change and economic transition (recession, depression or economic boom). If a gap occurs between what the population expects and what the economic and productive forces of society can deliver, a situation of strain develops that can manifest itself in normlessness or anomie. A state of anomie undermines a society's capacity to exercise social control. Robert Merton (1957) subsequently reworked the concept of anomie in an attempt to illustrate how the USA's social structure exerted pressure on individuals to engage in non-conformist behaviour and could generate dysfunctionality. Durkheim viewed anomie as problematic and associated it with institutional normlessness and abnormality, but for Merton anomie resulted from the incongruity between culturally valued goals associated with the 'American Dream' and the number of legitimate opportunities available to pursue and achieve these goals. The resulting strain and frustration produce five 'modes of adaptation' – conformity, innovation, ritualism, retreatism and rebellion. Not surprisingly, the most common deviant response – innovation – was to be found among the lower classes. Many of the major sociological theories of delinquency are indebted to Merton's reworking of Durkheim's theorizing (as evidenced in sub-cultural theories and variants of control theory, for example).

Evaluation

Functionalist theorizing was attacked during the 1960s and stood accused of teleology and over-determinism. Its obsession with stability, consensus and social order, its emphasis on the self-governing nature of society and its lack of a theory of power also laid it open to the charge of being ideologically conservative and supportive of the status quo. Although it fell out of favour, it is possible to find examples of functionalist theorizing and logic across a variety of positivist, structural and materialist criminologies. Elements of what we might describe as a neo-functionalist

criminology retain a firm presence in much of North American criminology.

Eugene McLaughlin

Associated Concepts: anomie, determinism, positivism, social control theory, sociological positivism, strain theory, subculture

Key Readings

Cohen, A.K. (1966) *Deviance and Control.* Englewood Cliffs, NJ, Prentice–Hall.

Cohen, P. (1968) *Modern Social Theory.* London, Heinemann.

Davis, K. (1971) 'Prostitution', in R. Merton and R. Nisbet (eds), *Contemporary Social Problems,* 3rd edn. New York, Harcourt Brace Jovanovich.

Durkheim, E. (1964) *The Rules of Sociological Method.* New York, The Free Press.

Merton, R. (1957) *Social Theory and Social Structure.* New York, The Free Press.

Messner, S. and Rosenfield, R. (1996) *Crime and the American Dream.* Belmont, CA, Wadsworth Publications.

G

GATED COMMUNITIES

See Defensible space

GENETICS

Definition

A genetics-based criminology concentrates on attempting to identify the biological source or sources of criminal and anti-social behaviour.

Distinctive Features

Genetic determinism, in a variety of forms, has been a constant if largely hidden part of the Western criminological tradition. The best known early genetic approach to criminality was proposed by Cesare Lombroso (1835–1909) as part of his assertion of a positivist criminology that viewed crime as the product of physical and scientifically measurable variables that were beyond the control of the individual. Lombroso developed his theory of 'the criminal type', which depended on the identification of physical characteristics that indicated a biological reversion to a primitive or atavistic stage of evolution. The examination of the skull of a notorious Italian criminal led Lombroso to this discovery: 'At the sight of that skull, I seemed to see all of a sudden, lighted up as a vast plain under a flaming sky, the problem of the nature of the criminal – an atavistic being who reproduces in his person the ferocious instincts of primitive humanity and the inferior animals.' Even though Lombroso subsequently qualified his 'born criminal thesis', the conviction that crime was

hereditary generated studies such as those carried out in the USA by Hooton in the 1930s and Sheldon in the 1940s.

It must be noted that the Eugenics movement of the first 30 years of the twentieth century is largely written out of the history of criminology's flirtation with biology. The origins of Eugenics lie in Darwin's theory of evolutionary progress and it was defined by its originator, Sir Francis Galton (1822–1911), as 'the study of the agencies under social control that may improve or impair the racial qualities of future generations either physically or mentally'. The Eugenics movement – which both conservatives and progressives adhered to – was obsessed with the fear that those with negative genes such as low intelligence, insanity, pauperism and criminality, would swamp the human race. In order to reverse the imminent collapse of Western civilization, this movement argued that the biologically unfit and undeserving should be eliminated or limited in number and the biologically fit and worthy be encouraged to reproduce. This highly racialized scientific approach to 'social problems as diseases' resulted, in a variety of countries prior to the Second World War, in immigration restrictions, marriage laws, segregation of the mentally and physically handicapped, selective reproduction and the widespread practice of sterilization. Because the historical research has not been carried out we do not know how many criminologists were involved in the Eugenics movement. Eugenics was ideologically discredited, largely as a result of the Nazis' *Lebensborn* and 'racial self-defence' programmes, which took its core ideas to their logical conclusions.

Human genetics finally emerged as a cleansed discipline in the 1950s and it stayed well away from making pronouncements on controversial social problems such as criminality. This was also the period when socio-logical explanations of crime were dominant. However, during the 1980s crime was revis-ited by the sociobiologists and by those researchers who continued to carry out twin and adoption studies. Those presenting papers at controversial conferences on genet-ics and crime held in the UK and USA during 1995 rejected the search for the 'gene for crime'. However, they also stressed that the research capabilities were now available to enable scientists to untangle the genetic and environmental sources of crime and disorder and identify the temperamental traits and behavioural predispositions that may trigger some individuals to engage in specific forms of criminality and disorder. More recently, there has been renewed speculation that the human genome project will allow scientists to pronounce on the complex ways criminality and disorder are genetically encoded.

Eugene McLaughlin

Associated Concepts: biological criminology, individual positivism, positivism, racialization

Key Readings

Bock, G.R. and Goode, J. (eds) (1996) *Genetics of Criminal and Anti-Social Behaviour.* Chichester, John Wiley and Sons.
Burley, J. (1998) *The Genetic Revolution and Human Rights.* Oxford, Oxford University Press.
Jones, S. (1996) *In the Blood.* London, Harper Collins.
Lombroso, C. (ed.) (1911) *Criminal Man According to the Classification of Cesare Lombroso.* New York, Putnam.
Seldon, S. (1999) *Inheriting Shame: The Story of Eugenics and Racism in America.* New York, Teachers College Press.
Wilson, J.Q. and Herrnstein, R. (1985) *Crime and Human Nature.* New York, Simon and Schuster.

GENOCIDE

Definition

Acts organized and committed, in time of peace or war, with the intent to exterminate, in whole or in part, a national, ethnic, racial or religious group. It is distinguishable from all other crimes, including ethnic cleansing, because it is state organized.

Distinctive Features

In 1933, the Polish scholar Raphael Lemkin proposed that an international treaty be agreed to define aggression towards national, ethnic and religious groups as an international crime. In 1944, Lemkin, who was by then an advisor to the United States War Department, coined the term genocide because he believed that the terms 'mass murder' and 'war crimes' were inadequate to the task of describing and explaining what had happened in Nazi Germany. Existing criminal categories could not account for the motive for the crime, that is, acting on the principle that the victim is not human. Lemkin defined genocide as a coordi-nated plan to destroy the essential foundations of the life of national groups, with the aim of annihilating the groups themselves. Accord-ing to Lemkin, genocide had two phases: first, the destruction of the national pattern of the oppressed group; and secondly, the imposi-tion of the national pattern of the oppressor. What is significant to note from the original formulation is that physical extermination is only the most extreme form of genocide.

In the aftermath of the Nuremberg war crimes trials, the UN General Assembly adopted a resolution verifying that genocide was the most serious crime against humanity and that it was prohibited under international law irrespective of whether it occurred in peace or war. The 1948 UN Convention on the Prevention and Punishment of the Crime of Genocide defined genocide as 'acts committed with the intent to destroy, in whole or in part, a national, ethnical, racial or religious group'. Genocidal acts include: killing members of the group; causing serious bodily or mental harm to members of the group; deliberately inflict-ing on the group conditions of life calculated to bring about its destruction in whole or in part; imposing measures intended to prevent births within the group; and forcibly transfer-ring children of the group to another group. The 1948 Convention also outlawed conspi-racy to commit genocide, attempts to commit genocide and complicity in genocide. Cru-cially, the convention covers both individual and state responsibility for acts of genocide and imposed a general duty on all signatory states not only to punish but to prevent and suppress such acts. The convention ruled that those charged with genocide could be tried by court in the territory within which the act was committed or by a specially convened inter-national court. To facilitate extradition pro-ceedings between states, genocide was also decreed to be a non-political crime.

As a result of *realpolitik*, the 1948 Convention settled on a more limited definition of genocide than the one coined by Lemkin. It has been noted, for example, that the categories of 'politically defined groups' and 'economically defined groups' were deliberately omitted from the definition, as was the notion of cultural genocide, destroying a group through compulsory incorporation into a dominant culture. The principle of 'intentionality', which was embedded in the definition, has also been criticized by human rights activists because it allows governments and individuals to argue that their actions were accidental and/or unplanned, happening in the heat of battle.

There was also considerable disagreement about the acts of mass violence that could be covered by the definition. For example, in 1966, the year after General Suharto seized power in Indonesia, the military dictatorship is estimated to have murdered between 500,000 and one million people. After the Indonesian invasion and annexation of East Timor in 1975, an estimated 200,000 out of a total population of 700,000 were killed. During the Khmer Rouge's reign (1975–8) in Cambodia, it is estimated that between one and two million people died in the 'killing fields' as a result of the conditions of state-initiated massacres and prison-based execution programmes. However, the international community argued that these acts did not meet the definition of genocide laid down by the 1948 Convention since both perpetrators and victims were from the same ethnic/racial background. In part the hesitation to define these actions as genocidal also emanated from the desire not to over-use the term and thereby trivialize the nature and meaning of the Holocaust.

In 1993 the first international tribunal was established to prosecute those responsible for committing or ordering serious violations of international humanitarian law, including genocide, in the former Yugoslavia (ITY). A similar tribunal was established in 1994 for Rwanda (ITR) to investigate the murder of 800,000 people, mostly Tutsi minority by the Hutu majority. Both tribunals had to develop rules of procedure and establish principles to define the exact criminal nature of what had happened. In August 1998, the ITR produced a landmark decision in the history of international criminal law when it found Jean Kambanda, Rwanda's former Prime Minister, guilty of the crime of genocide. During 2000 the ITY heard the first charges of genocide to come before it. The indictment of senior officers of the Bosnian Serb army represented a breakthrough in international criminal law because it established that there was evidence that senior politicians and military leaders had planned the massacre of 7,000–8,000 Bosnian Muslims in the UN 'safe haven' of Srebrenica in 1995.

In 1998 120 nation-states signed a resolution calling for the establishment of a permanent International Criminal Court (ICC) with the power and organizational capacity to investigate and prosecute genocide, war crimes and crimes against humanity. If the resistance of powerful nations such as the USA and China can be overcome, the ICC will come into existence in 2002. In order to establish its credibility, the new court will have to end the 'culture of immunity' that was the hallmark of the twentieth century and establish punishments that are deemed to be appropriate to such criminality.

Eugene McLaughlin

Associated Concepts: critical research, crimes against humanity, denial, extraterritorial law enforcement, hate crime, human rights, obedience (crimes of), political crime, the state, state crime, transnational policing, torture

Key Readings

Ball, H. (1999) *Prosecuting War Crimes and Genocide: The Twentieth Century Experience*. Lawrence, KS, University of Kansas Press.

Destexhe, A. (1995) *Rwanda and Genocide in the Twentieth Century*. New York, New York University Press.

Gourevitch, P. (2000) *We Wish to Inform You that Tomorrow We Will Be Killed*. London, Picador.

Honig, J.W. and Both, N. (1996) *Srebrenica: Record of a War Crime*. Harmondsworth, Penguin.

Jonassohn, K. (1998) *Genocide and Gross Human Rights Violations*. Plymouth, Transaction.

GEOGRAPHIES OF CRIME

Definition

Geographies of crime address the complex of relationships constructed through crime, space and place.

Distinctive Features

Cartographic schools of criminology were established in various European countries during the nineteenth century, most notably in Belgium by Adolphe Quetelet (1796–1874) and in France by A.M. Guerry. Maps were drawn to plot regional patterns of crime, compare rural and urban differences and survey the relationship between crime and other socio-economic conditions. In an allied development, in England observational studies were undertaken within the newly industrialized cities by Mayhew and Booth to identify and examine 'criminal areas' such as the 'rookeries' of London. Many of these early surveys were undertaken to further the case for social and moral reform. An ecological approach to the study of urban crime was more fully developed by the Chicago School of social research during the 1920s. The guiding principle of the Chicago School was that cities were living organisms, composed of interconnected parts and the task of researchers was to understand how each part related to the overall structure of the city and the other parts. The zonal theory of city growth developed by Robert Park and Ernest Burgess enabled them to map the contours of crime more precisely and to offer an explanation as to why crime was concentrated in the zone of transition. Clifford Shaw and Henry McKay used this conceptual framework to construct their path-breaking study of the relationship between juvenile delinquency, gang membership and urban social disorganization. Versions of the ecological model and methodologies developed by the Chicago school dominated studies of urban crime undertaken between the 1920s and 1960s in cities across the United States and Europe.

As a result of theoretical and methodological developments in the 1980s and 1990s, environmental criminologies have given way to research on how crime is spatialized. A new generation of criminologists from a variety of disciplinary backgrounds became interested in theorizing the complex human public interactions and relationships associated with living in 'the city'. Contemporary spatial approaches to the study of crime can be grouped into four broad research areas:

- Studies concerned with identifying the spatial distribution of crime, criminogenic localities, vulnerable areas, defended spaces and sites of contestation and resistance.
- Studies of how and why the risk of crime victimization is distributed over space and the differential risks within and between different localities and various sections of the population.

- Studies of how and why the fear of crime is spatialized. This involves analysing the public's perception of where the crime problem is located and working through their mental mappings of safe and dangerous places.
- Studies of the flow and movement of particular crimes such as drugs and prostitution between different localities and countries.

Evaluation

Geographical research on crime and criminality has continued to play a central role in the development of crime prevention programmes, ranging from situational crime prevention strategies such as target hardening and crime prevention through environmental design (CPED). The underlying premise of these crime prevention efforts is that proper design and utilization of the built environment in conjunction with new surveillance technologies can lead to a reduction in the fear and incidence of crime and an improvement in the quality of urban life. *De facto* spatial policing is also taking place through the privatization of public space and the development of gated or 'crime-proof' communities. Sophisticated crime mapping techniques such as Geographic Information Systems (GIS) are also a logical, if controversial, outcome of spatial research into crime 'hotspots' (places where according to a variety of statistics the opportunities for certain forms of crime are highest). GIS consists of specialist database management systems, spatial analysis packages and sophisticated computer mapping systems which facilitate 'geocoded' proximity analysis, spatial clustering analysis and spatial correlation procedures. It is these features that have made GIS an invaluable tool not only for mapping crime 'hotspots' but for analysing crime trends and managing criminal investigations.

Eugene McLaughlin

Associated Concepts: Chicago School of Sociology, defensible space, fear of crime, situational crime prevention, social ecology, surveillance, victimology

Key Readings
Cohen, J. (1941) 'The geography of crime', *Annals of the American Academy of Political and Social Sciences*, 217, pp. 29–37.
Fyfe, N. (2001) *Geography of Crime and Policing*. Oxford, Blackwell.

Grescoe, T. (1996) 'The geography of crime', *Geographical Magazine*, 9, pp. 26–7.

Hirschfield, A., Brown, P. and Todd, P. (1995) 'GIS and the analysis of spatially referenced crime data: experiences in Merseyside UK', *International Journal of Geographical Information Systems*, 9 (2), pp. 191–210.

Longley, P.A., Goodchild, M., Maguire, D. and Rhind, D.W. (1999) *Geographical Information Systems*. London, John Wiley and Sons.

McLaughlin, E. and Muncie, J. (1999) 'Walled cities: surveillance, regulation and segregation', in S. Pile, C. Brook and G. Mooney (eds), *Unruly Cities*. London, Routledge.

GOVERNMENTALITY

Definition

The term applies to the characteristically 'modern' form of government that governs each individual and the 'population' through apparatuses of security (police, courts, health and welfare departments, etc.). The term also refers to an approach that focuses on the intellectual, linguistic and technical ways in which phenomena are constituted by government as governable problems. It is primarily in the latter sense that governmentality has a place in criminology.

Distinctive Features

Studying social relations from the point of view of governmentality means focusing on governance as a mentality or rationality of rule, stressing that phenomena have to be intellectually and linguistically represented as a certain kind of problem in order for them to be governed. For example, Simon (1997) has argued that American society increasingly is 'governed through crime', as more and more matters are represented as problems of 'criminality' and its effects, to be governed through criminal justice, crime prevention and so on. In turn, governmentality characteristically examines how such 'problematizations' are linked to practicable techniques for achieving their government. For example, crime is said increasingly to be governed through risk. This marginalizes therapeutic or punitive techniques for governing offenders, and valorizes such techniques as crime prevention, offender incapacitation and victim compensation and 'empowerment' (O'Malley,

1998). Governmentality thus focuses on questions of how government is planned as a practical exercise. Typical research has examined such issues as: how are the nature of offenders and the mainsprings of crime reimagined when we move from welfare states to neo-liberal government? How is this change linked to changes in the types of sanction that are deployed to deal with crime? What new 'problems' of crime emerge – for example: how to make potential victims more active in securing themselves and their property against crime? And how to make police more 'responsive' to public demands for security?

Governmentality also assumes the dispersal of governance in contemporary societies. 'The state' becomes merely one site – or, rather, a complex of sites – in which government is located. Governmentality work has examined how government of crime is practised, not simply by police and the criminal justice 'system', but also by the insurance industry, communities, potential victims, shopping centre managers and so on. Such work, it can be seen, avoids explanation, especially where this reduces government to a reflex of some other force, such as class interests or post-modernity. Rather, government is seen to be 'assembled' from available intellectual and material resources – and so is regarded as humanly contingent rather than theoretically determined. Governmental accounts are also characterized by a refusal to subject government to critique, rather seeing such evaluation as internal to government itself. These characteristics reflect a methodological suspension or denial of truth judgements – for understanding how government 'makes up' its truths is a key object of analysis. Governmentality denies an accessible 'real truth' from which critique and explanation are mounted.

Evaluation

Governmentality is an influential but still inchoate approach, and there are debates among its adherents about its nature and purpose (O'Malley et al., 1997). Consequently, making comment upon its strengths and shortcomings is subject to dispute. However, on the positive side, it has provided original and incisive analyses of the government of crime, especially related to risk techniques and neo-liberal politics. Perhaps this is because it breaks away from highly abstract theorizations, and focuses on detailed configurations of rule. Perhaps too it is because the refusal to engage in critique has generated a kind of non-committed analytic that has opened up many new insights. However, these possible sources of strength are also its most criticized features.

One of the most contentious features is its focus on the 'ideal knowledges' or mentalities of governance, rather than on 'what actually happens'. For many critics of this aspect of governmentality, it is 'essential to explore the real practices and processes in which these programs and rationalities and technologies are selectively and sometimes unexpectedly used, with all their compromised formations and unintended effects' (Garland, 1997). For some governmentality writers, however, this descends into familiar, realist, sociological terrain, unlikely to provide resources to think beyond what already exists, and – perhaps ironically – unlikely to destabilize rule. For others, however, this exercise may be essential, as part of the process of understanding government's key characteristic of failure.

Another contested feature is governmentality's rejection of 'critique'. Some criticize governmentality because it does not allow commentators to identify how malfunctioning institutions can be reformed, how authorities' explanations of crime are wrong, how and why programmes fail and so on (e.g. Garland, 1997). One response would argue that this criticism fails to escape the problematic of government – for like government, it sets for itself the task of making us into something else, to govern us better, on the basis of a superior regime of truth. This process of displaying the truth claims of government, and their contingent nature, is the operation of 'diagnosis' that displaces critique within governmentality. Diagnosis focuses on the question of 'how not to be governed thus?', rather than on that of 'how can we best be governed?'. Whether this is nihilistic, or promotes contestation of government, is the key evaluative issue; but it involves a political rather than methodological choice.

Pat O'Malley

Associated Concepts: discourse analysis, post-structuralism, risk, social constructionism

Key Readings

Dean, M. (1999) *Governmentality. Power and Rule in Modern Society*. London, Sage.

Garland, D. (1997) '"Governmentality" and the problem of crime', *Theoretical Criminology*, 1, pp. 173–214.

O'Malley, P. (ed.) (1998) *Crime and the Risk Society*. Aldershot, Dartmouth.

O'Malley, P., Weir, L. and Shearing, C. (1997) 'Governmentality, criticism, politics', *Economy and Society*, 26, pp. 501–17.

Rose, N. (1999) *Powers of Freedom*. Cambridge, Cambridge University Press.

Simon, J. (1997) 'Governing through crime', in G. Fisher and L. Friedman (eds), *The Crime Conundrum: Essays on Criminal Justice*. Boulder, CO, Westview Press.

H

HATE CRIME

Definition

A hate crime is a criminal act which is motivated by hatred, bias or prejudice against a person or property based on the actual or perceived race, ethnicity, gender, religion, or sexual orientation of the victim.

Distinctive Features

Certain criminal acts, if perpetrated because of hatred, hostility or negative attitudes towards the group or collectivity to which the victim is perceived to belong, are defined as hate crime. In jurisdictions where hate crime is recognized, the concept applies to crimes committed against individuals because of their real or perceived race, ethnicity, gender, religion or sexual orientation. Hence, in theory if not legislative practice, hate crime encompasses racist crime, sex crime, homophobia, anti-semitism and sectarianism and links across to ethnic cleansing and genocide. Campaigners have argued that hate crimes need to be acknowledged as different because they inflict distinctive collectivized harms upon their victims.

In the USA, hate crime laws have been passed by several states which enable the establishment of data collection systems to track the incidents of hate crime reported to the authorities and/or to increase the punishments set for criminal actions motivated by hate. In the UK, hate crime was officially recognized by the Metropolitan Police in the late 1990s in the aftermath of the publication of the report into the racist murder of Stephen Lawrence. The intention was to illustrate to minority communities that the police were taking their fears and concerns seriously and to persuade rank and file officers that these were serious forms of criminality worth targeting. The concept of hate crime has come under heavy criticism from right wing commentators in both the USA and the UK on the grounds that it will be used by minority groups to censor and criminalize those who oppose multi-culturalism and positive discrimination.

Eugene McLaughlin

Associated Concepts: genocide, institutional racism, racialization, violence

Key Readings

Bowling, B. (1999) *Violent Racism*. Oxford, The Clarendon Press.

Cuneen, C., Fraser, D. and Tomsen, S. (eds) (1997) *Faces of Hate: Hate Crime in Australia*. Annandale, Hawkins Press.

Hamm, M.S. (1993) *American Skinheads: The Criminology and Control of Hate Crime*. New York, Praeger Press.

Jacobs, J. and Potter K. (1998) *Hate Crimes: Criminal Law and Identity Politics*. Oxford, Oxford University Press.

Jenness, V. and Grattet, R. (2000) *Making Hate a Crime: From Social Movement Concept to Law Enforcement*. Berkeley, University of California Press.

Kelly, J.R. and Maghan, J. (eds) (1998) *Hate Crime: The Global Politics of Polarization*. Carbondale, Southern Illinois University Press.

HEDONISM

Definition

The pursuit of pleasure, sometimes considered as the subordination of reason to the play of desires and the attractions of the senses. Hedonism is also associated with risk-taking and excitement in criminality.

Distinctive Features

Hedonism is fundamental to the formation of classical criminology, especially in the work of Bentham (1823) and Beccaria. Defined as the desire to maximize pleasure and minimize pain, it was assumed to be the underlying mainspring of human behaviour. The rational choice criminal was imagined as weighing up the balance of pleasures and pains likely to result from the commission of a crime. Where this 'felicity calculus' indicated a positive balance of pleasures, criminal offending would result. As such, the assumption of hedonism underlies most punitive penology geared to deterrence. Bentham, himself, developed tables for the infliction of punishment based on the principle that the net calculus of pain had only marginally to outbalance the sum of pains. This principle, in turn, played a key intellectual role in the assault on the 'excessive' punishments of the eighteenth century.

By the 1930s, much academic criminology had dispensed with such thinking, arguing that few people lead such calculating lives, that most crimes are spontaneous acts of irrationality, and that many criminals are constitutionally incapable of performing the calculation of pleasures and pains. Despite this, the model of hedonistic behaviour persisted, albeit transformed. As crime increasingly came to be regarded as a pathology, hedonism too was pathologized – re-created as the inability to govern the desire for pleasure and excitement. This pathology was theorized as a cause of crime in a multitude of ways by positivist sociology and psychology.

Sociologically, hedonism was understood in Victorian terms as a universal, animalistic quality that socialization had to overlay with discipline. The middle classes were understood as 'normal' precisely because of such self-government: 'deferred gratification' became the norm against which hedonism was pathologized. Predictably, weak socialization emerged early as a cause of crime, and 'broken' and 'inadequate' working-class families were identified as failing to implant the necessary norms and techniques of self-discipline. More broadly, the breakdown of social control in the chaotic environment of inner city 'transitional zones' was seen as giving young people excessive licence for their

hedonistic desires. Other, cultural, theories of hedonistic pathology associated the boring, mundane and routine conditions of lower-class life with the emergence of criminogenic 'focal concerns' such as the search for 'excitement' or 'thrills' (Miller, 1958). As such models had trouble accounting for the gendered nature of working-class crime, subsidiary accounts suggested that the close familial governance of young women's (sexualized) hedonism gave women fewer opportunities to offend, and resulted in domesticated desires that immunized them against offending in later life (Cohen, 1954).

While most of these models linked crime to hedonism via social pathologies, the nexus is also found in psychological approaches. Thus Eysenck (1964) identified criminality especially with extroversion (outgoing impulsiveness) and neuroticism (behavioural instability). Extroverts, because of lower response thresholds in the brain's reticular formation, are said to require stronger stimuli to achieve excitation, and to respond weakly to rewards (pleasures) and punishments (pains). Therefore, they seek strong stimuli and learn conformity more slowly, and thus – it is argued – are more likely to commit crime. The familiar criminological formula of weak moral control coupled with strong desire for excitement is thereby retained: but the felicity calculus – the hedonistic attempt to achieve surplus pleasure over pain – has been translated into a neuro-psychological function of the brain.

More recently, this association between crime and excitement has been revived but taken in new directions (e.g. Bell and Bell, 1993). For example, rejecting rational choice models, Katz (1988) has argued that criminology has underestimated crime's emotional attractions. These extend hedonism beyond mere 'pleasures' to include other sources of excitement (righteous slaughter, sneaky thrills, doing stick-ups) that allow the subject to emotionally transcend the mundane nature of modern existence. Ironically, Katz's work, like most traditional sociological criminology, assumes a pathology (this time in the nature of modernity) that gives rise to a pressure to offend 'hedonistically'.

Such anti-rationalist developments coincide with the return of the rational choice felicity principle – embedded in the models of situational crime prevention and risk management that have become characteristic of *fin de siècle* administrative criminology. For the moment, at least, the latter has been the more influential.

Evaluation

Hedonism has proven almost impossible to avoid as an element in modernist (or with Katz, postmodernist) criminology – perhaps because the binary of pain and pleasure is so central to post-Enlightenment thought. It appears almost everywhere that rational choice models are deployed and, as with Katz or Eysenck, even where they are rejected. This suggests that hedonism is a category that can only be evaluated in relation to its particular criminological uses. For example, in some accounts it is limited because it is gendered (women's hedonism is sexualized), it is 'classed' (working-class hedonism is pathological and criminogenic), and it is 'aged' (youthful hedonism is virtually taken for granted as criminogenic). However, hedonism is also fundamental to the abstract and universal 'rational choice' criminology that ignores the causal impact of class, age and gender. Perhaps only those criminologies – for example, Marxist – that deny the category of human nature may escape this.

Pat O'Malley

Associated Concepts: carnival (of crime), cultural criminology, deviance, extroversion, free will, risk, subculture

Key Readings

Bell, N. and Bell, R. (eds) (1993) *Adolescent Risk Taking.* London, Sage.
Bentham, J. (1823) *An Introduction to the Principles of Morals and Legislation.* London, Pickering.
Cohen, A. (1954) *Delinquent Boys.* Glencoe, The Free Press.
Eysenck, H. (1964) *Crime and Personality.* London, Routledge and Kegan Paul.
Katz, J. (1988) *The Seductions of Crime.* New York, Basic Books.
Miller, W. (1958) 'Lower class culture as a generating milieu of gang delinquency', *Journal of Social Issues,* 14, pp. 5–19.

HEGEMONIC MASCULINITY

Definition

The set of ideas, values, representations and practices associated with 'being male' which is commonly accepted as the dominant position in gender relations in a society at a particular historical moment.

Distinctive Features

In an imaginative lateral shift, Bob Connell (1987, 1995) plucked the concept of hegemony from its original class setting in order to try to understand gender relations. Where Gramsci had sought to understand how a dominant class manages to legitimate its rule in societies characterized by class inequality, Connell set himself the task of understanding how an unequal gender order manages to reproduce itself: how hierarchies of dominance and subordination among men and between men and women come to be commonly accepted at any particular historical moment. The idea of hegemonic masculinity as the culturally dominant form of masculinity was the answer he proposed, which, following Gramsci, he saw as always historically contingent and contested. Hence, there are always subordinate masculinities. Given the widespread cultural ascendancy of heterosexuality, the idea of homosexual masculinities as subordinate is unsurprising. Given the long-standing, well-nigh general subordination of women, those masculinities that can be represented somehow as close to femininity will also be rendered subordinate.

In addition, Connell talks of 'complicit' and 'marginalized' masculinities. The former refer to those large numbers of men who do not themselves practise the hegemonic version of masculinity but do not challenge it either; they are its 'complicit' beneficiaries. Marginalized masculinities result from the interplay of gender with other structures such as class and race. Given the relations of domination/subordination between ethnic groups, for example, the masculinities of such subordinate groups will always be subject to the authority of the hegemonic masculinity of the dominant group, which has the power to marginalize or to authorize admission to the hegemonic project. Certain black US athletes, for example, may be 'authorized' exemplars of hegemonic masculinity, though this has no effect on the social authority of black men more generally.

Since Connell's original introduction of the term in the late 1980s, the idea of hegemonic masculinity has become almost ubiquitous in attempts to think through relationships among men, crime and masculinities. Perhaps the most common finding is how depressingly often hegemonic masculinity is implicated in the commission of crime and its control, a finding which testifies both to the strength and to the weakness of the concept.

Evaluation

Connell's introduction of the term hegemonic masculinity has inspired and influenced the whole range of contemporary writings on men and masculinity, including that currently being conducted within criminology. The strength of its appeal lies in its ability to recognize the diversity of men's lives, something that the early feminist writings on male violence failed to do, but without losing sight of the importance of power. The idea of power structuring relations among men has, for example, enabled the relationship between particular crimes and men's specific positions in gender/race/class hierarchies to be explored, something Messerschmidt does in *Masculinities and Crime* (1993). It also permits analysis of organizations and cultures as well as individual men since hegemonic masculinity, like hegemony generally, is not just a personal matter but is deeply embedded in institutional life across the society as a whole; hence the re-examinations of a variety of criminal justice institutions to reveal the masculinities embedded within them (Walklate, 1995). A final strength is the importance it attaches, in true Gramscian fashion, to contestation. Since hegemony is essentially about defending the indefensible – class inequality for Gramsci, gender inequality for Connell – it is always liable to challenge; it is never fixed nor absolute. Sometimes, only when it gets challenged by subordinate masculinities, in, for example, the idea of gay marriages or gay parenting, is hegemonic masculinity's commonly accepted, 'taken-for-grantedness' revealed for what it is: in this case, the imposition of one kind of sexuality, heterosexuality, through all kinds of powerful institutions from the Church to the State, as the common sense of the age, the norm, the culturally exalted, the ideal.

Despite the subtlety of Connell's theorizing, emphasizing the importance of diversity, power, institutions, and practice, and the greater gender awareness it has undoubtedly promoted within criminology, problems remain. There is a tendency to deploy the term masculinity as if it referred simply to a list of 'manly' attributes – competitive, aggressive, risk-taker, strong, independent, unemotional and so on – a tendency which, if anything, is heightened once the term 'hegemonic' is added, given the usual considerable overlap between the list and some cultural norm, ideal or stereotype of masculinity. (Students asked to write down what they understand by masculinity will tend to come up with very similar lists of 'hegemonic attributes'.) Within criminology, this has led to an accentuation of the negative dimension of these features in order to make the connections between masculinity and crime (and criminal justice), and to ignore the more positive, caring dimensions underpinning, for example, the father who protects and provides. Messerschmidt's (1993) catalogue of criminals may all be doing masculinity *differently*, depending on their place in gender, race and class relations, but they are all doing *bad* not good. Moreover, in reducing hegemonic masculinity to a set of traits or characteristics, the notion is rendered static, not the subject of constant contestation, as Connell's theoretical usage would suggest. However, the problem here may well reside partly in the original notion since, though Connell talks of a range of subordinate masculinities, hegemonic masculinity is always used in the singular. In other words, is there only ever one hegemonic strategy at any given historical moment, as Wetherell and Edley (1999) ask, or is hegemonic masculinity a much more contingent notion, always dependent on context? If this is the case, it poses a far more complex series of questions in understanding how masculinities and crimes are related than has been attempted hitherto.

A final problem is the oversocialized view of the male subject that users of the concept have generally taken, despite Connell's (1995) insistence that the depth and complexity of Freud's study of the Wolf Man constituted a challenge to all subsequent researchers interested in masculinity. Several writers have reiterated the importance of not ignoring the psychic or subjective dimension of masculinity, even though they have done so from very different theoretical traditions, and none is advocating a return to classical Freudianism (Jefferson, 1994; Wetherell and Edley, 1999). To the extent that some of these strictures are taken seriously, we can expect more complex and sensitive accounts of the relationships among men, masculinities and crime to emerge. However, we would do well to listen to Sandra Walklate (1995) when she warns us not to allow our interest in masculinity to obscure the role of other explanatory variables. Whilst hegemonic masculinity may well be implicated in certain crimes on certain occasions, to expect it to provide all the answers would be a serious mistake.

Tony Jefferson

Associated Concepts: critical criminology, feminist criminologies, hegemony, Marxist criminologies, masculinities

Key Readings

Connell, R.W. (1987) *Gender and Power*. Cambridge, Polity Press.

Connell, R.W. (1995) *Masculinities*. Cambridge, Polity Press.

Jefferson, T. (1994) 'Theorizing masculine subjectivity', in T. Newburn and E.A. Stanko (eds), *Just Boys Doing Business?* London, Routledge, pp. 10–31.

Messerschmidt, J.W. (1993) *Masculinities and Crime*. Lanham, MD, Rowman and Littlefield.

Walklate, S. (1995) *Gender and Crime*. London, Prentice–Hall/Harvester Wheatsheaf.

Wetherell, M. and Edley, N. (1999) 'Negotiating hegemonic masculinity: imaginary positions and psycho-discursive practices', *Feminism and Psychology*, 9 (3), pp. 335–56.

HEGEMONY

Definition

An unequal relationship between the ruling class (or alliance of classes) and the subordinate classes within a given social order which is based on authority or leadership achieved through the production of consent rather than through the use of coercion or force.

Distinctive Features

One of the earliest uses of the term hegemony appears in the writings of Lenin in the phrase 'hegemony of the proletariat'. Then it had the narrow meaning of political leadership within a class alliance, specifically the need for proletarian leadership in any alliance with the peasantry. In the writings of the Italian Marxist Antonio Gramsci (1971), the term achieves a far broader reach. Specifically, he expanded its meaning to include moral and intellectual leadership across society as a whole. He developed the idea as a way of conceptualizing how, in the aftermath of the Russian Revolution and the First World War, the industrial capitalist democracies of Western Europe and the USA managed to avoid the proletarian uprisings predicted for them by classical Marxism. Without ever abandoning the Marxist idea of the centrality of classes and class struggle, his key insight was that successful class rule entails the creation, through alliances, concessions, compromises and new ethico-political ideas and projects, of a collective will which was not narrowly class-based but had popular, national appeal. In short, a class wishing to become hegemonic had to 'nationalize' itself, had to become a 'popular religion'.

When such a 'national-popular' consensus is achieved, the dominant classes can be said to be ruling hegemonically: through authority or leadership rather than coercion or force. However, such an achievement is always fragile and temporary since it is contingent upon an ever-changing set of economic, political and ideological conditions, including, crucially, the constant challenges from the subordinate classes, whose goal, according to Gramsci, should be to win over the people to an alternative hegemonic project. Consequently, the achievement of hegemony in a particular historical moment, or conjuncture, could be followed by more coercive, less hegemonic moments: new legislation, tougher policing and, in extremis, the use of the army, to deal with dissent, unrest, conflict and, at worst, civil war.

Within criminology, Stuart Hall and colleagues used this Gramscian notion of hegemony to underpin their attempt, in *Policing the Crisis* (1978), to understand the state's response to mugging in the 1970s. One of the early examples of Marxist criminology in Britain, *Policing the Crisis* argued that the hegemony enjoyed by the ruling alliance in Britain in the 1950s entered into crisis in the 1960s as the conditions underpinning the postwar social democratic settlement proved impossible to sustain. Challenges to the existing consensus arose on multiple fronts, around issues to do with youth, drugs, sexual mores, race, women, students, industrial relations, crime and Northern Ireland. By the 1970s, the conditions for successful hegemonic rule had collapsed, signalled by an election-winning law and order crusade, new laws, the tougher policing of all kinds of protest and unrest, the entry of the army into Northern Ireland, and internment. Set within this context, the crackdown on mugging in 1972–3 by the police and the judiciary, to the accompaniment of media headlines and sermonizing editorials, was symptomatic of the collapse of hegemony. As one among several moral panics, the 'mugger' became a convenient folk devil, or scapegoat, for the new, more troubled and conflictual times.

Evaluation

The biggest single problem with Gramsci's concept of hegemony was its attempts to move beyond a class reductionist understanding of the reproduction of capitalism without ever losing sight of the concept's fundamental basis in economic class relations. This meant hanging onto the fact that for a class to become hegemonic it must move beyond its narrow class interests and construct a broad-based ethico-political project, whilst never overlooking the fact that hegemony had *necessarily* also to be 'economic'. For Chantal Mouffe (1979), one of Gramsci's most sympathetic commentators, this meant that only the two fundamental classes (bourgeoisie/proletariat) could be hegemonic and ultimately, since only the proletariat had an interest in finally ending exploitation, only a working-class hegemony could become genuinely successful. This lingering reductionism haunts her own attempt to work up Gramsci's concept of hegemony from the 'practical state' in which he left it in *The Prison Notebooks*. Having first established Gramsci's non-reductive conception of ideology, then the way elements within a hegemonic project must divest themselves of their class origins if they are to be capable of nationalizing themselves, and, finally, the importance of disarticulation-rearticulation to ideological struggle (rather than the confrontation of different, opposed, class-based world-views), she is forced to confront what it is that unifies the hegemonic project in a way that ensures its class character. At that point she suggests that this unity is supplied by the 'hegemonic principle', and this is always class-based.

Despite this difficulty, at the level of theory, of how to 'think' the structural basis of concepts without lapsing into structural determinism (a difficulty common to a whole raft of concepts in these post-structuralist/postmodernist times), when used to make sense of particular conjunctures, hegemony remains one of the most useful of Marxist concepts. Deployed by Stuart Hall (1988), it enabled a series of insightful and prescient readings of the rise and popular appeal of Thatcherism and the new right in the UK. Against those who stressed Thatcher's luck in becoming Britain's longest serving Prime Minister this century and pulling off an unprecedented transformation of the face of modern Britain, Hall always saw Thatcherism as something more profound; as a hegemonic project, albeit one based on a contradictory combination of nostalgic morality, ruthless modernization, authoritarian leadership and populist common sense. If 'Blairism' is the new common sense of the age, it is certainly inconceivable without the 'regressive modernization' and 'authoritarian populism' which Hall unerringly identified as typifying the project of Thatcherism.

Tony Jefferson

Associated Concepts: authoritarian populism, communitarianism, critical criminology, folk devil, hegemonic masculinity, Marxist criminologies, masculinities, moral panic, new criminology, radical criminologies, scapegoating, social reaction, the state

Key Readings

Gramsci, A. (1971) *Selections from the Prison Notebooks*. London, Lawrence and Wishart.

Hall, S. (1988) *The Hard Road to Renewal*. London, Verso.

Hall, S., Critcher, C., Jefferson, T., Clarke, J. and Roberts, B. (1978) *Policing the Crisis*. London, Macmillan.

Hall, S. and Jefferson, T. (eds) (1996) *Resistance Through Rituals*. London, Hutchinson.

Mouffe, C. (1979) 'Hegemony and ideology in Gramsci', in *Gramsci and Marxist Theory*. London, Routledge and Kegan Paul, pp. 168–204.

HIDDEN CRIME

Definition

At one level this refers to specific acts of crime which are not recorded in official crime statistics. At another level it refers to categories of crime which are either not represented in official statistics or which are significantly under-recorded. Sometimes it is also referred to as invisible crime.

Distinctive Features

Official statistics are known to massively under-record the true extent of crime. The reasons for this are numerous but one significant factor is that police rely heavily on victims and witnesses to report crime and on occasions they choose not to do so. The gap between the true extent of crime and crime recorded in statistics is known as the 'dark figure of unrecorded crime'. Estimates of this gap can be obtained by comparing official crime statistics with results derived from surveys of victims (whereby individuals are asked if they have recently been a victim of crime, and if so, whether they reported it to the police) and from self-report studies (whereby individuals are asked whether they have recently committed crimes and whether they were subsequently charged with the offence). The extent of hidden crime can vary according to the category of the crime but it is known to exist to some degree in relation to all such categories. Even in relation to so-called conventional crimes – for example street crimes, car crimes and house burglary – some proportion remain hidden.

Outside of so-called conventional crimes there are other types which, because of their nature, are not represented in official statistics or are massively under-represented. The range includes, first, crimes committed by employees against organizations for which they work, such as using an organization's facilities illegally and stealing work-based materials for personal use. Secondly, there are crimes perpetrated by organizations against their employees, including breaches of health and safety regulations resulting in workplace injuries, illnesses, accidents and sometimes deaths. A third example is fraudulent behaviour, including the use of another's money for personal or organizational gain without their knowledge or consent, and the use of 'sleaze' money to change the course of events, such as in political life or in the field of sport and leisure. Fourthly, the range encompasses hitherto neglected green crimes, including the pollution of the environment by industrial organizations and the smuggling of endangered species and products produced from them. A fifth category can be given the generic title 'cybercrime'. This includes computer crimes such as hacking, the illegal appropriation of image and likeness and the use of the Internet in order to sell drugs, to publish obscene materials or to advertise services in relation to paedophilia.

Seven features of hidden or invisible crimes can be identified (Jupp et al., 1999). First, *no knowledge*, that is, there is little individual or public knowledge that the crime has been committed. The ingenuity of the fraudster, the complexity of the act and the lack of knowledge and vigilance can all conspire to render a crime invisible. Even where individuals are aware that an act or event has taken place it can be taken for granted as normal rather than as criminal. For example, workers in hazardous industries may see themselves as doing a difficult job rather than as victims of illicit

health and safety practices. A second feature is that there are *no statistics*, that is official statistics fail to record or classify the crime. This may be because victims are unaware a crime has been committed, they may treat the crime as normal and not something to be reported, they may be frightened or intimidated or they may be unwilling to report the crime to the police because it is something in which they have colluded. Even where an action or event is reported to the police the complexity of some of the crimes, especially those relating to financial transaction, together with the ingenuity and specialist knowledge of those carrying them out, often means that the police are unable to satisfy themselves that a crime has been perpetrated and can therefore be recorded as such.

A third feature of hidden crime is *no theory*, that is, criminologists and others have neglected to explain the crime, its existence and its causes. Criminology has been heavily influenced by studies of sections of the population which are most visible in official crime statistics and by explanations which can be cast in terms of individual pathology. In the main, hidden crimes do not fit into these categories. Also, the sheer diversity of hidden or invisible crimes and of the sites at which they are committed – at the workplace, on the Internet, in the financial marketplace – probably militates against the development of any comprehensive theory of such crimes.

Fourthly, hidden crime is characterized by *no research*. There are a number of reasons for this, for example there are the mutually reinforcing effects of the paucity of knowledge, statistics and theory in relation to invisible crimes. Further, there are practical aspects of conducting social inquiry which restrict the feasibility and possibility of researching invisible crimes. One of these relates to access. There are often parties who have vested interests in relation to withholding information about their activities – parties who by one means or another are able to exercise power to deny researchers access to data with which to formulate and support conclusions. In the absence of such data either the research is not carried out or it is carried out by means that are not typically found in standard texts on research methods. Where the latter occurs, investigators are open to the, often unjustifiable, criticism of being non-scientific and biased.

Fifthly, there is the characteristic of *no control*, that is, there are no formal or systematic mechanisms for control of such crimes. This can be the result of blurring of boundaries between what is legitimate and illegitimate, because of the complexity of many crimes, for example, fraud, and also because of the diffusion of offenders. Further, where crime is international, especially in the context of increasing globalization and fewer barriers between nation-states, the possibility of detection, let alone prevention and control is made more difficult. Sixthly, hidden crimes are characterized by *no politics*, that is, such crimes as breaches of health and safety legislation do not typically appear as a significant part of the political agenda. Much more emphasis is placed on conventional and street level crimes and on law and order campaigns to combat them. Finally, there is *no panic*, that is, hidden crimes are not constituted as moral panics and their perpetrators are not portrayed as folk devils. There is a close connection between the formulation of the political agenda and the construction and amplification of moral panics and folk devils in the media. There has been increased awareness of financial irregularities, 'sleaze' and breaches of food safety regulations but these are invariably portrayed as scandals which are exposed rather than examples of sustained deviant or criminal activity. They are often treated as 'one-offs' and the fault of particular individuals at particular times rather than as deep-seated structural problems.

Evaluation

The above features help provide a means of categorizing and characterizing a wide range of acts and events which remain invisible in everyday life. Moreover, when combined, such features constitute a template with which to assess relative invisibility. The elements of this template (knowledge – statistics – theory – research – control – politics – panic!) can be viewed as independent of one another but there is also the potential for interaction and mutual reinforcement. For example, ignorance of victimization (no knowledge) often leads to non-recording in official statistics (no statistics) which in turn can have consequences in terms of under-theorizing (no theory), lack of policy-making at government level (no politics) and little consideration by the popular media (no panic).

Particular acts or events do not necessarily exhibit all of the above features nor will they exhibit them to the same degree at any given point in time. The relative invisibility of particular acts and events and their subsequent recognition and identification as crime

depends on whether the template fits (do the elements apply?), the degree to which it fits (to what extent does it apply?) and the power of interactive effects (to what extent do the elements reinforce one another?).

Victor Jupp

Associated Concepts: corporate crime, crime, cybercrime, family crime, official criminal statistics, self reports, social harm, state crime, victim surveys, white collar crime

Key Readings
Box, S. (1992) *Power, Crime and Mystification*. London, Routledge.
Davies, P., Francis, P. and Jupp, V.R. (eds) (1999) *Invisible Crimes: Their Victims and Their Regulation*. London, Macmillan.
Jupp, V.R., Davies, P. and Francis, P. (1999) 'The features of invisible crimes', in P. Davies, P. Francis and V.R. Jupp (eds), *Invisible Crimes: Their Victims and Their Regulation*. London, Macmillan.

HISTORICAL METHODS

Definition

In the last third of the twentieth century social historians increasingly turned their attentions to questions of crime and criminal justice institutions. Their principal aim was not to develop a better understanding of crime but rather to use the examination of crime and criminal justice as a means of broadening and deepening the understanding of past societies and of change through time.

Distinctive Features

The work grew out of the new social history of the 1960s and the fascination with 'history from below' typified by the work of E.J. Hobsbawm, George Rudé and E.P. Thompson. Initially the approach was rooted in a class-conflict perception of society. It was believed that an analysis of criminal justice records would bring the historian closer to the voices of those who seemed generally to have been ignored by historians. Much of the early work focused on periods of major economic upheaval, such as the eighteenth and early nineteenth centuries when, it was assumed, much 'crime' in the form of rioting and the appropriation of property was, in fact, a response to new concepts of private property, to new work practices and to new systems of payment for labour. More recently, and thanks largely to the growth of women's history, there has been a shift away from class to gender perceptions. This has tended to shift the focus away from property offences to interpersonal violence while, at the same time, generating questions about, first, the gender perceptions of agents of the criminal justice system, and secondly, about the extent to which notions of gender, particularly masculinity, have fostered aspects of criminality.

The historian's general concern with change through time has led to much work on the way in which different forms of criminality were constructed at different moments, notably the construction of the image of the juvenile delinquent, and of the 'dangerous' and subsequently the 'criminal classes'. A changing perception of the criminal during the nineteenth century has also been charted, from morally inferior to mentally deficient. Much of the early work had a strong statistical basis, with several historians constructing their own data from quarter sessions and assize records. The judicial statistics for the nineteenth century have been carefully assessed in conjunction with other social data to suggest, and subsequently to explain, a general levelling out of theft and violence during the Victorian and Edwardian periods. These conclusions have, however, been challenged by the suggestion that, from the mid-nineteenth century, the Treasury was imposing restrictions on the activities of the police and the courts through strict cash limits.

The concept of 'social crime' was developed to explain offending such as poaching, smuggling and wood theft, which, in many instances, had considerable community sanction. But it has also been challenged as too slippery to explain very much, especially since in some instances both poaching and wood theft were undertaken to meet the demands of the market, while eighteenth-century smuggling was often large-scale capitalist enterprise. The analysis of offending at the workplace, both pre-industrial and industrial, has thrown up similar complexities, and the early hypothesis of property crime as a response to industrialization and the capitalization of industry is now looking very tattered. Unfortunately, the extent to which such economic developments fostered white collar crime has been far less extensively researched.

Evaluation

The historian's desire to read and assess sources created by the agents of the criminal justice system has fostered new explorations of these agents and the institutions to which they belonged. There has, in consequence, been significant new work on the origins and development of police organizations and prisons – though the work of Michel Foucault and others has been an equally important intellectual stimulus here. There have also been important explorations of the impact of, and inter-relationship between, social norms and legal norms in police practice, and in the decision-making of both prosecutors and the courts.

Clive Emsley

Associated Concepts: critical criminology, moral economy, social constructionism

Key Readings
Arnot, M.L. and Usborne, C. (eds) (1999) *Gender and Crime in Modern Europe*. London, UCL Press.
Emsley, C. (1996) *Crime and Society in England, 1750–1900*, 2nd edn. London, Longman.
Emsley, C. and Knafla, L.A. (eds) (1996) *Crime History and Histories of Crime: Studies in the Historiography of Crime and Criminal Justice in Modern History*. Westport, CT and London, Greenwood Press.
Robb, G. (1992) *White-collar Crime in Modern England: Financial Fraud and Business Morality 1845–1929*. Cambridge, Cambridge University Press.
Taylor, H. (1998) 'Rationing crime: the political economy of criminal statistics since the 1850s', *Economic History Review*, LI, pp. 569–90.
Wiener, M.J. (1990) *Reconstructing the Criminal: Culture, Law and Policy in England, 1830–1914*. Cambridge, Cambridge University Press.

HUMAN RIGHTS

Definition

Throughout history various nation-states have made declarations that list certain elements considered to be basic human rights. These usually include civil and 'natural' rights ranging from the right to life, free speech, education, political freedom and family life. In addition, if citizens are accused of a criminal offence they are entitled to a fair trial, the presumption of innocence and humane punishment if convicted.

Distinctive Features

In general statements human rights act as a protection against the action and power of the state upon an individual. In times of war they also provide a set of rules of engagement for opposing sides in terms of their strategies and behaviour towards each other and treatment of prisoners. Various bodies and lists of rights and privileges exist, such as the United Nations Declaration of Human Rights and the European Convention for the Protection of Human Rights, the latter providing a basis for the European Court of Human Rights.

One of the significant aspects of the concept of human rights for criminology is associated with the definition of crime. If basic privileges provide the means by which individuals can fully participate within human society, then their deprivation could be regarded as criminal. As Schwendinger and Schwendinger (1970) argue, the institutions within any sociolegal system that lead to violations of these rights, resulting in racism, sexism or poverty for example, may be regarded as criminal.

Another area of interest for criminologists is the sphere of state crime and the enforcement, or more usually non-enforcement, of international conventions on war crimes, torture and the process of criminalization of certain groups who may be labelled political offenders or terrorists. As these groups often pose fundamental challenges to the state, again, debates about what is crime and who and why individuals or groups are criminalized, arise.

Furthermore, within the discourse of human rights, according to Stan Cohen (1993/1996), there are state crimes which are rightly classed as 'gross' violations. He argues that there are acts committed by regimes, which include genocide, mass political killings, state terrorism and torture and disappearances, which in terms of criminology would be defined as murder, rape, espionage, kidnapping and assault. Defining an agreed concept of human rights is problematic, he argues however, because the values underpinning these declarations vary according to the group or state's definition. Freedom fighters become terrorists when they endanger social order and enemies of the state can later become democratically elected leaders. Despite these problems Cohen argues that human rights has become a dominant narrative and an important issue for criminologists, especially through the growth of victimology surrounding the abuse of women and children.

Evaluation

Although the measures listed in declarations of human rights are designed to protect the individual from the state, and sometimes from other nations' actions, such as in times of war, in effect there are few enforceable international laws. A number of seemingly influential bodies have rules of engagement and supposed cooperation, such as the United Nations Declaration of Human Rights and the European Court of Human Rights, but as Jongman argues (1993), the 'rhetoric' of human rights is not supported by the power to prevent states committing crimes. It appears that these fundamental laws about human conduct are left to independent human rights organizations such as Amnesty International to highlight the behaviour of states that consistently violate their own citizens. Furthermore, only states who are signatories to a treaty such as the European Convention on Human Rights can be held accountable to its aims. Hurwitz argues that clauses such as 'national security, public safety or territorial integrity' (1981, p. 139) are often used to avoid its implementation.

Louise Westmarland

Associated Concepts: denial, genocide, natural justice, social harm, the state, state crime, torture

Key Readings

Cohen, S. (1993/1996) 'Human rights and crimes of the state: the culture of denial', in J. Muncie, E. McLaughlin and M. Langan (eds), *Criminological Perspectives*. London, Sage.

Hurwitz, L. (1981) *The State as Defendant*. London, Aldwych.

Jongman, A.J. (1993) 'Torture: definition and legal instruments', in R.D. Crelinsten and A.P. Schmid (eds), *The Politics of Pain: Torturers and Their Masters*. Leiden, Center for the Study of Social Conflicts.

Schwendinger, H. and Schwendinger, J. (1970) 'Defenders of order or guardians of human rights?', *Issues in Criminology*, 5 (2), pp. 123–57.

I

INCAPACITATION

Definition

A justification for punishment which maintains that the offender's ability to commit further crimes should be removed, either physically or geographically. In certain societies incapacitation can take the form of rendering criminals harmless through the removal of offending limbs (for instance, hands in the case of thieves), whilst in others the banishment of criminals to confined spaces, like prisons, curtails the possibilities for offending behaviour. The death penalty is the starkest form of incapacitation.

Distinctive Features

In contrast to other justifications of punishment, such as rehabilitation, the logic of incapacitation appeals to neither changing the offender's behaviour nor searching for the causes of the offending. Instead it advocates the protection of potential victims as the essence of punishment, as opposed to the rights of offenders. Many contemporary criminal justice strategies currently subscribe to the doctrine of incapacitation. In part, this is because it fills the void created by the collapse of rehabilitation and the associated argument that 'nothing works' in the 1970s, but also because it claims to offer a means of social defence through removing offenders from society and thereby eliminating their capacity to commit further crimes.

Examples of current criminal justice sentencing policy that are informed by the logic of incapacitation would include the 'three strikes and you're out' penalty and selective incapacitation, both of which usually involve long periods of incarceration. One of the distinguishing features of these approaches is that they are concerned with identifying offenders or groups of offenders who are likely to commit future crimes on the basis of the risk, or likelihood, of offending. The argument is that a small number of offenders are responsible for a significant proportion of crime in certain areas and if these individuals or groups were imprisoned then this would have a pronounced effect on the local crime rate. It is recognized that research carried out by the Rand Corporation in the USA provided the intellectual origins for contemporary incapacitative sentencing policies (Greenwood, 1983). More generally, the doctrine of incapacitation has become the main philosophical justification for imprisonment in countries that subscribe to the notion that 'prison works' as it takes many persistent and serious offenders off the streets and thereby, it is claimed, reduces the crime rate (Murray, 1997).

Evaluation

Incapacitation is essentially a strategy of containment and is frequently justified through a form of moral reasoning known as utilitarianism, which maintains that the financial and social benefits outweigh the costs of an ever expanding prison population. The model for this approach is what is known as the American 'prison experiment', where there has been a dramatic growth in the prison population over the past 30 years. For instance, in 1970 there were 196,000 prisoners in state and federal prisons in the United States, but by the mid 1990s the state and federal prisons were holding over 1.1 million prisoners on any given day (Currie, 1996).

An influential attempt to think through these changes is provided by Malcolm Feeley and Jonathan Simon (1992). Their argument is that a 'New Penology' has risen at the expense of an 'Old Penology'. For them, the 'Old Penology' was preoccupied with such matters as guilt, responsibility and obligation, as well as diagnosis, intervention and treatment of the individual offender. Whereas, they claim the 'New Penology' is radically different and actuarial in orientation as it is concerned with techniques for identifying, classifying and managing groups sorted by levels of dangerousness. The aim is not to intervene in offenders' lives for the purposes of ascertaining responsibility or rehabilitating them. It is instead a strategy of managing dangerousness, and incapacitation is part of this broader, apolitical displacement of individualized discipline and rehabilitation.

Critics of incapacitation, like Elliot Currie (1996), argue that whilst this strategy might have had some effect on the crime rate, this effect is distressingly small in relation to the huge costs involved. At best it can be argued that the effect of this massive experiment with imprisonment on the crime rate has been modest. For instance, whilst the overall crime rate declined by 3 per cent between 1993 and 1996 in the United States, it still remains at a very high level – with a homicide rate seven times that of England and Wales (Young, 1999). However, what is more alarming is the clear racial dimension to this strategy of containment, to the extent that one in nine African-American males aged 20–29 is in prison, whilst a staggering one in three is either in prison, on probation or parole (Mauer, 1997).

These figures raise fundamental ethical and moral questions on the nature of US society and the dangers posed by the wholesale importation of the incapacitation doctrine. For it is clear that the 'experiment' has been funded by the diversion of public expenditure from welfare to the prison, whilst the level of violence, particularly among the young and disadvantaged, continues to decimate life in many North American cities. Incapacitation as a penal policy amounts to little more than the 'warehousing' of prisoners, since there is scarcely any recognition of the human character of the offender nor are the reasons for offending addressed in any fundamental way as this is viewed as a pointless exercise.

Eamonn Carrabine

Associated Concepts: actuarialism, capital punishment, crime control model, deterrence, penality, penology, rehabilitation, retribution, social defence theory

Key Readings

Currie, E. (1996) *Is America Winning the War on Crime and Should Britain Follow its Example?* London, NACRO.

Feeley, M. and Simon, J. (1992) 'The New Penology. Notes on the emerging strategy of corrections and its implications', *Criminology*, 30 (4), pp. 449–70.

Greenwood, P. (1983) 'Controlling the crime rate through imprisonment', in J.Q. Wilson (ed.), *Crime and Public Policy*. San Francisco, Institute for Contemporary Studies.

Mauer, M. (1997) *Intended and Unintended Consequences: State Racial Disparities in Imprisonment.* Washington, DC, The Sentencing Project.

Murray, C. (1997) *Does Prison Work?* London, Institute for Economic Affairs.

Young, J. (1999) *The Exclusive Society*. London, Sage.

INCARCERATION

Definition

The process of confining and segregating deviant populations into specialist institutions for the purposes of punishment, treatment or care.

Distinctive Features

The eighteenth century marks a decisive moment in the history of social control in Northern Europe, as imprisonment became the dominant means of dealing with undesirable conduct and the preferred form of punishment. Up until this point the two main purposes of imprisonment were, first, to hold in custody those awaiting trial or execution of sentence and, secondly, coercing fine defaulters and debtors into making good their misfortune. Whilst custody could be used for punishment, it was primarily used for detention, and makeshift structures, like fortresses, castles, cellars and town gates, were deployed for this purpose. Instead the main forms of punishment were primarily corporal and included execution, mutilation, branding, whipping and other forms of public shaming (such as stocks and pillories).

However, as feudal systems of existence began to break down with the advent of mercantile capitalism and there were significant population migrations from rural areas to burgeoning towns and cities – as dispossessed peasants and labourers were forced to become urban scavengers – there emerged innovative responses to the anxieties provoked by this upheaval. From the 1500s galley slavery, transportation, bridewells and workhouses came to complement conventional forms of corporal punishment, as a means of distinguishing the 'deserving' poor from the 'undeserving' poor and fuelling colonial expansion.

Nevertheless, it is the Enlightenment that gave birth to incarceration as the generalized response to crime and deviance, as opposed to the myriad public spectacles of suffering, and proposed the architecture of segregation as the sole means of manufacturing virtue and communicating deterrence. But this was not an isolated event as whole populations became subject to processes of incarceration; not only were thieves consigned to prisons, but the mad became subjected to asylums, children were introduced to schools, workers came to exchange their labour power in factories, and the ill began to be treated in hospitals.

The question that needs to be answered is why did incarceration become the dominant response to crime from the end of the eighteenth century? Up until the 1970s the explanation would have been that imprisonment represents an enlightened, humanitarian, progressive response over the barbarism of earlier epochs. This Whig view of history emphasized how early forms of punishment, based on vengeance, irrationality and cruelty have been replaced by informed, professional and expert intervention and would celebrate the zeal of benevolent reformers in explaining why contemporary penal systems exist. However, this interpretation has been widely challenged by a range of 'revisionist' histories of the 'Great Incarcerations' (Cohen, 1985).

The earliest work that looked behind the rhetoric of reformers and asked why particular punishments gain prominence during certain historical periods is provided by Rusche and Kirchheimer (1968). Their argument is informed by a Marxist understanding of social relations and highlights the relationships between the form of punishment and the economic requirements of particular modes of production. For instance, they argue that the prison emerged with the advent of industrial capitalism as a means of creating a submissive and regulated workforce. Their account has been criticized for the way in which it provides a one-dimensional explanation of penal relations that prioritizes the significance of the labour market at the expense of other factors. A more sophisticated account is Ignatieff's (1978) analysis of the birth of imprisonment. He rejects economic functionalism and argues that incarceration was a response to the crisis in class relations wrought by the Industrial Revolution as it served to establish the legitimacy of the law and was understood as an element of a larger vision of securing popular consent in an increasingly unequal, class-divided society.

However, the most influential 'revisionist' history of imprisonment is Foucault's *Discipline and Punish* (1977), where he argues that the emergence of the prison does not mark a more humanitarian form of punishment. Instead, it represents an attempt to punish more efficiently and extensively to create a disciplined society, through the techniques of surveillance, classification and examination perfected in the new institutional spaces (e.g. Bentham's Panopticon). The originality of Foucault's argument lies in the importance he attaches to the relationship between power and forms of knowledge. The emergence of the prison is just one instance of the dispersal of new forms of knowledge and his project is to examine how domination is achieved and how individual subjectivity is socially constructed. The prison has always been a failure, as it does not reduce crime, yet the reason why it persists is because it stands at one end of a continuum in which surveillance and regulation have become normalized throughout society. Foucault employs the phrase 'carceral archipelago' to describe the chain of institutions that stretch out from the prison to imply that Western liberal democracies are intimately bound up with forms of oppression.

Evaluation

Whilst 'revisionist' histories continue to be influential, a number of critics have found fault with the way in which all social relations have been described in the language of domination, oversimplifying complex processes and overstating the instrumental aspects of punishment at the expense of the social support commanded by condemnation (Garland, 1990). Moreover, there is a failure to consider the punishment of women, which problematizes thinking on the role and development of incarceration. For instance, why women are more likely to be treated as 'mad' rather than 'bad' poses questions that conventional and revisionist histories are unable to answer.

Eamonn Carrabine

Associated Concepts: carceral society, decarceration, historical methods, normalization, panopticism, social control, transcarceration

Key Readings

Cohen, S. (1985) *Visions of Social Control*. Cambridge, Polity Press.

Foucault, M. (1977) *Discipline and Punish: The Birth of the Prison*. Harmondsworth, Penguin.

Garland, D. (1990) *Punishment and Modern Society: A Study in Social Theory*. Oxford, Clarendon Press.

Ignatieff, M. (1978) *A Just Measure of Pain: The Penitentiary in the Industrial Revolution*. London, Macmillan.

Rusche, G. and Kirchheimer, O. (1968) *Punishment and Social Structure*. New York, Russell and Russell (originally published 1939).

INDIVIDUAL POSITIVISM

Definition

A theoretical approach that views crime as being generated primarily by forces located within the individual. It usually takes one of two forms. Criminal predisposition is to be found either in biologically given constitutional factors or in the psychological make-up of particular individuals.

Distinctive Features

A key defining characteristic of individual positivism is that the fundamental predisposition to crime lies in the individual. Crime is determined by innate genetic or physiological incapacities or by inadequate child-rearing practices in dysfunctional families.

In the early twentieth century several attempts were made to isolate key physiological characteristics of known criminals. Goring (1913) studied more than 3,000 male prisoners in and around London and compared them with various control groups of non-prisoners. Using correlational analysis he found that the criminal tended to be shorter in height and weigh less. He explained such difference with reference to notions of 'inbreeding within a criminal class' which generated a lineage of mental deficiencies within certain families.

Such correlations of body build and behavioural tendencies reached their most sophisticated in the work of Sheldon (1949). His analysis suggested that the shape of the body correlated with individual temperament and mental well-being. Analysing and comparing 200 boys in a reformatory in Boston with 4,000 students, he concluded that most delinquents had a body shape of well-developed muscles and an athletic appearance. Their personalities were strong, active, aggressive and sometimes violent.

The earliest attempts to isolate a genetic cause of criminality involved analyses of the family trees of known criminals. Dugdale (1910), for example, traced more than 1,000 descendants of the Jukes – a New York family infamous for criminality and prostitution – and found 280 paupers, 60 thieves, 7 murderers, 140 criminals and 50 prostitutes. He concluded that 'undesirable' hereditary characteristics were passed down through families. Criminal families tended to produce criminal children. Criminals were born not made. Evidence from the Cambridge study in Delinquent Development in the 1970s continues to suggest that crime does indeed run in families. This study noted that of 397 families half of all convictions were concentrated in just 23. Convictions of one family member were strongly related to convictions of each other family member. Three-quarters of convicted mothers and convicted fathers had a convicted child.

More rigorous research directed at isolating a genetic factor has been carried out with twins and adoptees. These have concluded that children's behaviour is more similar to that of their biological parents than to that of their adoptive parents. Mednick concluded that some factor is transmitted by convicted parents which increases the likelihood that their children, even after adoption, would be convicted for criminal offences (Mednick et al., 1987). Further research has examined a wide range of bio-chemical factors (such as hormones, testosterone, adrenalin and blood sugar levels) in attempts to isolate an individual causal factor in the generation of deviant, anti-social, criminal or violent behaviour. However most current research in this tradition would not claim that biological make-up alone can be used as a sufficient explanation of crime. Rather, some biological factors may generate criminality, but only when they interact with certain other psychological or social factors. Nevertheless this type of research continues to attract significant research funding and publicity.

Another form of individual positivism, often termed the 'psychogenic school', has shifted the focus of analysis away from biologically given constitutional factors and towards more dynamic mental processes. Psychologists and psychiatrists have attempted systematically to associate particular personality traits with criminal behaviour. Much of this has depended on the construction of performance tests, personality scales and measurements of intelligence. From these a wide range of traits have been singled out as being indicative of delinquent and criminal propensities. They include extroversion, defiance, suspicion, low IQ, excitability and impulsiveness (Eysenck, 1964). Farrington (1996) details numerous risk factors including: being the child of a teenage mother, impulsive personality, low intelligence and poor performance in school, harsh or erratic parental discipline and parental conflict, as well as peer group influences and socio-economic status.

Evaluation

Individual positivism formed the bedrock of criminological studies for the first half of the twentieth century and regained importance in the 1990s. For some, because of advances in our knowledge of genetic structures it offers a way forward in understanding criminality which is free from a multitude of complicating social variables. For others it is little more than a dangerous political gambit to segregate those deemed to be physically or emotionally unfit. From within psychology, positivism has been attacked for its lack of attention to processes of human cognition and social learning in which individuals are viewed as capable of self-reflection and self-development, rather than as beings who simply act upon pre-given determinants. Whilst individual positivists tend to characterize deviant behaviour as pathological, it has also been argued that deviancy is a meaningful behaviour pattern which only becomes undesirable when judged and labelled by others. There are two major limitations of those theories which attempt to replicate principles of scientific determinism. First, the more that criminological research has developed, the more the number of variables thought to be important in crime has increased. Even if such variables were capable of adequate measurements, controlling for their relative effect is probably impossible. This leads to sampling variations between studies so that results are always difficult to replicate. A long list of correlations tends to be produced which, though interesting in themselves, shed no light on the question of causation. Secondly, psychological research may be capable of unearthing more and more variables, but then usually attempts to explain crime with reference to some existing psychological theory which is designed to account for some psychological abnormality.

Nevertheless, theories based on individual positivism continue to have widespread popular and political appeal. Notions of parental neglect, 'bad blood' and psychopathology all have their roots here. The search for the causes of crime by identifying a criminal type or a criminal personality will continue because of the general reluctance to believe that criminality is in any way 'normal'.

John Muncie

Associated Concepts: biological criminology, causation, conditioning, correlational analysis, determinism, dispositional theory, genetics, personality theory, positivism, somatotyping

Key Readings
Dugdale, R. (1910) *The Jukes*. New York, Putnam.
Eysenck, H.J. (1964) *Crime and Personality*. London, Routledge and Kegan Paul.
Farrington, D. (1996) *Understanding, and Preventing Youth Crime*. Social Policy Research Findings No. 93. York, Joseph Rowntree Foundation.
Goring, C. (1913) *The English Convict*. London, HMSO.
Mednick, S., Moffit, T. and Stack, S. (eds) (1987) *The Causes of Crime: New Biological Approaches*. Cambridge, Cambridge University Press.
Sheldon, W. (1949) *Varieties of Delinquent Youth*. New York, Harper.

INFORMAL JUSTICE

Definition

Informal justice refers to a variety of initiatives that are intended either to overcome the major limitations of formal criminal justice processes or replace the criminal justice system.

Distinctive Features

During the 1960s and 1970s socio-legal scholars campaigned for the move away from the formal criminal justice system and dependence on state-centred forms of law to alternative forms of dispute resolution. Considerable attention was paid to the applicability of non-Western practices and the need to do justice differently. Amongst more radical writers efforts were made to locate or imagine forms and processes of socialist justice that were built on different principles to those operating in Western capitalist societies. No one model of informal justice was developed but common features included advocacy of non-formal, non-adversarial, non-conflictual procedures and greater levels of direct community participation. The purpose of informal justice was defined as arbitration, mediation, reconciliation, reparation and restoration and would require decentralization, delegalization, deprofessionalization and deregulation. A critique of informal justice soon appeared pointing, for example, to the potential for reactionary and very coercive forms of community or popular justice. But perhaps more significant were evaluations of a variety of initiatives that suggested that 'alternatives' rather than replacing formal practices were in fact being added on to the existing unreformed system. The result was the blurring of the boundaries between formal and informal, the expansion of the overall system of social control and the creation of new forms of unaccountable governance. The remnants of the heated debates about informal justice now take place in relation to the possibilities for alternative forms of policing – dispute resolution and peacemaking initiatives and, perhaps most significantly, restorative justice projects. Those who are wary of the whole idea of 'informal justice' continue to focus on the logical outcome of such a process – spontaneous or organized vigilantism where self-appointed 'guardians' mete out justice. Lynchings in the southern states of the USA, 'burning tyre' justice in the townships of South Africa, punishment beatings in Northern Ireland can all be cited as disturbing examples of informal justice.

What is perhaps equally significant are ongoing examples of 'community justice' where specific types of dangerous or threatening offenders are, in the absence of decisive actions from the criminal justice system, hounded from neighbourhoods.

Eugene McLaughlin

Associated Concepts: abolitionism, community justice, peacemaking criminology, redress, restorative justice

Key Readings

Abel, R. (ed.) (1982) *The Politics of Informal Justice,* vols. 1 and 2. New York, Academic Press.

Cohen, S. (1985) *Visions of Social Control.* Cambridge, Polity Press.

Findlay, M. and Zvekic, U. (1988) *Analysing Informal Mechanisms of Crime Control: A Cross Cultural Perspective.* Rome, UNSDRI.

Matthews, R. (1988) *Informal Justice.* London, Sage.

Merry, S.E. and Milner, N. (1993) *The Possibility of Popular Justice: A Case Study of Community Mediation in the United States.* New Brunswick, Rutgers University Press.

Pavlich, G.C. (1996) *Justice Fragmented: Mediating Community Disputes Under Postmodern Conditions.* London, Routledge.

INSTITUTIONAL RACISM

Definition

Institutional racism refers to the processes – intentional and unintentional – by which criminal justice agencies systematically discriminate against certain social groups on grounds of race or ethnicity.

Distinctive Features

In the seminal text *Black Power: The Politics of Liberation in America*, Stokely Carmichael and Charles V. Hamilton distinguished between individual and institutional racism. They defined individual racism as overt acts carried out by individuals which cause death, injury and/or violent destruction of property. Classic examples of individual racism would include white people driving out black people from a particular neighbourhood or arson attacks on black property. Institutional racism 'is less overt, far more subtle, less identifiable in terms of specific individuals committing the acts' (1967, p. 4). It is equally, if not more, damaging in terms of its consequences as individual acts of racism. Because of its pervasive and insidious nature, they argue that it is institutional racism that denies black people proper welfare provision, health care amenities, education, access to proper jobs and traps them in slum tenements where they are exploited by landlords and loan sharks. And in terms of its outcomes institutional racism is remarkably similar to colonialism.

Carmichael and Hamilton used the term to present a devastating 'Black Power' critique of white liberal attitudes towards 'race' in the USA, arguing that although institutional racism 'relies on the active and pervasive operation of anti-black attitudes' because it originates 'in the operation of the established and respected forces in the society' it receives less attention and public condemnation. Institutional racism is maintained and perpetuated not just by the procedures and practices of white institutions but through indifference, inertia and ignorance on the part of white masses and officials. This led them to two primary conclusions. First, it is institutional racism that is at the root of the alienation of black people and causes of multitude of oppressive conditions for serious disturbances in black neighbourhoods. When these neighbourhoods do explode it is the residents who ae characteristically blamed for the criminality and in due course experts are appointed to prepare 'authoritative' reports which typically refuse to address deep-seated institutional racism. Second, race relations policies based on inclusion, assimilation and the adoption of white middle-class values tend only to incorporate black people into their own institutionalized oppression.

Evaluation

Because of its origins and its radical critique considerable efforts were made to discredit the value of the term by insistence amongst many social scientists that it was too sweeping and ill-defined and made it difficult for race relations bodies to 'prove' intention and causation. However, its potency for activists lay in its insistence that racism be addressed at an institutional or systemic level rather than concentrating efforts on identifying individual racists. Carmichael and Hamilton had also provided an intriguing explanation for how racism could persist in organizational settings despite the existence of official legislation geared to the removal of discriminary practices and equality of opportunity.

In the sphere of criminal justice in a variety of jurisdictions, a heated debate has taken place concerning the extent of racial discrimination, particularly the disproportionate application of discretionary police powers to black communities and the over-representation of young black men in the prison population. Black community groups insisted that institutional racism was at work, with young black men receiving less favourable treatment at every point between arrest and conviction. The cumulative effect was their disproportionate representation in the prison population. Community groups were also critical of the manner in which the criminal justice system discriminated against black victims of crime and the serious underrepresentation of black people in criminal justice agencies. However, official explanations such as those articulated by Lord Scarman in his report into the inner city riots in the UK in 1981, rejected allegations of institutional racism, focusing on the criminal tendencies of young black men and the overtly racist actions of a minority of front line police officers.

In the UK, the controversial and unresolved issue of institutional racism resurfaced during the official inquiry into the unsolved racist murder of Stephen Lawrence in South London in 1993. To the consternation of the Metropolitan Police, the inquiry team concluded that the police investigation 'was marred by a combination of professional incompetence, institutional racism and a failure of leadership by senior officers'. The final report also provided the UK government with an official definition of institutional racism: 'the collective failure of an organization to provide an appropriate and professional service to people because of their colour, culture or ethnic origin. It can be seen or detected in processes, attitudes and behaviour which amount to discrimination through unwitting prejudice, ignorance, thoughtlessness, and racist stereotyping which disadvantage minority ethnic people' (1999, paragraph, 6.34). The report emphasized that there must be unequivocal recognition and acceptance of the problem of institutional racism and commitment to fundamental organizational change. The government established an ambitious programme of reform to ensure that the policies, procedures and practices of the criminal justice agencies are consciously and actively anti-racist and promote racial fairness and equality. Whether the momentum for change will be sustained and the reform programme realized is open to question. As yet, there is little evidence that the criminal justice agencies have any understanding of how their policies and procedures and practices turn out to be 'racialized'. However, what is truly remarkable is that as a result of the Stephen Lawrence inquiry report, a version of a concept first coined by 'Black Panthers' now stands as the accepted centre of the race relations strategy of the UK criminal justice system.

Eugene McLaughlin

Associated Concepts: criminal justice, discretion, discrimination, disproportionality, racialization

Key Readings

Carmichael, S. and Hamilton, C.V. (1967) *Black Power: The Politics of Liberation in America*. London, Jonathan Cape.

Scarman, Lord (1981) *The Brixton Disorders, 10–12 April 1981*. London, HMSO.

Stephen Lawrence Inquiry (1999) *Report of an Inquiry by Sir William MacPherson of Cluny*. London, HMSO.

INTEGRATIVE CRIMINOLOGY

Definition

An interdisciplinary approach to understanding crime and crime control which incorporates at least two disciplinary (or non-disciplinary) bodies of knowledge. This incorporation of criminologies and other bodies of knowledge should ideally aspire to encompass any and all data, theories and methods that shed light on the production of crime, criminals and social control, including the field of criminology itself.

Distinctive Features

Unlike single perspectives or disciplinary approaches within criminology that assume that crime and crime control are the products of primarily biological, psychological, economic, political, social, or cultural factors, the emerging integrative paradigm argues that criminological knowledge should incorporate analyses that assimilate the realities from each of these areas of inquiry. Integrative criminology also assumes that the study of the causes or aetiology of crime and the study of the control or regulation of criminals are not separate but related phenomena. Together, these areas of criminology constitute the integrative parts of the whole of crime and social control. Thus, in order to understand criminals, crime control and prevention, or criminology, criminologists should not only study each of these in relationship to the other, but also as these are connected with other bodies of interdisciplinary knowledge such as cultural, media and gender/sex studies. Finally, integrative criminology endeavours to provide analyses that link the various bodies of knowledge that focus on the connections between the aetiology of crime, the behaviour of criminals, and the policies and practices of crime control.

C. Ray Jeffery made one of the earliest explicit cases for integration in his textbook *Criminology: An Interdisciplinary Approach* (1990, Prentice-Hall). In this work he argued that criminology had to integrate various bodies of knowledge from biology, psychology, sociology, law and other fields. Subsequently, he has argued that what is required is an integration of both a theory of crime and a theory of criminal behaviour. In order to accomplish this, Jeffery has maintained that criminology has to develop an interdisciplinary theory of behaviour and then apply it to the explanations of crime and criminal behaviour. Presently, the study of crime and crime control or of crime and justice reveals an assortment of integrative strategies (Barak, 1998a).

Integrating criminologies are expressed in a myriad of ways that may include the merging of the goals and objectives within or across the traditional and non-integrative approaches of classical, positivist and critical criminologies. Basically, however, there are three kinds of integrative approaches that may be adopted: (1) disciplinary perspectives that connect various explanations of crime and crime control from within one field of study, operating up and down, such as sociology, psychology, or anthropology; (2) multidisciplinary perspectives that partition the subject matter of crime and crime control into levels of analysis that are explained by different disciplines, operating side by side, such as sociology, psychology and anthropology; and (3) interdisciplinary perspectives that integrate crime and crime control, operating as holistic-interactive analyses, that incorporate the full range or varieties of knowledge from such diverse fields as the social sciences, natural sciences, and the humanities.

Essentially, there are two kinds of integrative criminology taking place today: 'modernist' and 'postmodernist' (Barak, 1998b). Both types of synthesis call for conceptual integration. However, modern forms emphasize the centrality of theory in scientific endeavours and the construction of 'causal models'. Postmodern forms emphasize the ever changing voices of plurality that provide meaning for the local sites of crime, justice, law and community and the construction of reciprocal, interactive or dialectical models of 'causality'. In comparison, the modern approaches are more concerned with integrating theories while the postmodern approaches are more concerned with integrating knowledges. Rather than pursuing the cause-effect predictions of theoretical integration within one or between a few disciplines like the modernists, postmodernists are developing explanatory models of crime and crime control that integrate the entire group of interdisciplinary knowledges.

An important distinction between the various models of integration hinges on the scope or range of deviance and criminality addressed by a specific approach. Usually, the causal logic of integrative theorization tends to be a composite of causal relationships taken from other theories that combine elements from social ecology theory, social learning theory, social control theory and subcultural theory. For example, Elliott, Huizinga and Ageton's (1985) integrated macro–micro theory of delinquency and drug use contends that social disorganization, strain and inadequate socialization cause a weakening of conventional bonding and a strengthening of delinquent bonding, which results in delinquent behaviour.

Other modernist formulations such as the social process-micro models tend to emphasize the integration of kinds-of-people explanations of human behaviour. For example, Wilson and Herrnstein (1985) have proposed an eclectic, social learning-behavioural choice formulation that relies on both positivist determinism and rational free will. This model of theoretical integration combines factors involving human agency, individual action and social process, while it omits considerations of social organization and culture. A third type of modernist integration includes the social structural-macro models, such as Quinney's (1977) structural theory which argues that all criminal activities are class-specific. In this formulation, the contradictions of capitalist development result in two interconnected sets of crime: the crimes of 'domination and repression' committed by the capitalists and agents of crime control; and, the crimes of 'accommodation and resistance' committed by workers and ordinary people.

Finally, there are the postmodernist efforts at integration. These argue that crimes are recursive productions, that is, routinized activities which cannot be separated from historically and culturally specific discourses and structures that have attained a relative stability over time and place. For example, Henry and Milovanovic's (1996) constitutive criminology argues, such discourses of difference and structured inequality become

courses of social action where criminals and crime-fighters alike represent excessive investors in the accumulation and expression of power and control. Similarly, Gregg Barak's *Representing O.J.: Murder, Criminal Justice, and Mass Culture* (1996, Harrow and Heston) argues that in order to understand the reactions of different groups of Americans to the O.J. Simpson trial, for example, an integration of the legal and cultural factors, such as the social and psychological group experiences that have helped to shape various peoples' attitudes and perceptions of crime and justice, must be adopted.

Evaluation

Although the field of criminology has always formally identified itself as an interdisciplinary exercise, most of its theoreticians and practitioners have worked primarily from narrow disciplinary frameworks. Hence, integrative or interdisciplinary criminology represents a challenge to the more traditional disciplinary approaches applied by the majority of criminologists. As an emerging paradigm within criminology, integration is relatively new; so the verdict is still out and pending. A number of criminologists today are sceptical of the ability of integrative criminology to deliver on its promises and possibilities. Some criminologists, such as Travis Hirschi, have already concluded that integrative criminology does not work and will not succeed. On the other hand, some criminologists, like John Braithwaite, believe that integration is the only way to proceed.

Gregg Barak

Associated Concepts: constitutive criminology, interactionism, social constructionism, social learning theory

Key Readings
Barak, G. (ed.) (1998a) *Integrative Criminology*. Aldershot, Ashgate.
Barak, G. (1998b) *Integrating Criminologies*. Boston, MA, Allyn and Bacon.
Elliott, D.S., Huizinga, D. and Ageton, S. (1985) *Explaining Delinquency and Drug Use*. Beverly Hills, CA, Sage.
Henry, S. and Milovanovic, D. (1996) *Constitutive Criminology*. London, Sage.
Quinney, R. (1977) *Class, State, and Crime*. New York, David McKay.
Wilson, J.Q. and Herrnstein, R.J. (1985) *Crime and Human Nature*. New York, Simon and Schuster.

INTERACTIONISM

Definition

A theoretical approach which focuses on interactions between individuals as symbolic and linguistic exchanges and as means of creative action. It views the social world as the product of such interactions. Sometimes this theoretical approach is also referred to as symbolic interactionism.

Distinctive Features

Interactionism is part of a broad strand of theorizing in the social sciences which seeks to integrate notions of purposeful and meaningful action into explanations of social phenomena such as crime and deviance. The writings of Max Weber were influential in building social meanings into theory but the specific formulation of symbolic interactionism emerged and developed during the interwar years, mainly at the University of Chicago and principally as a result of the work of the social psychologist George Herbert Mead. Mead did not systematically produce his theoretical ideas in written form. The published material is a compilation of lectures and notes and as a result there are a number of contradictions and areas for clarification in terms of fine detail (Mead, 1934). However, Mead's general thesis is as follows. Animal behaviour is largely determined and characterized by stimulus–response. Human behaviour, on the other hand, is flexible and dynamic and has the potential for creativity. An individual forms a concept and image of him or herself ('the self') by interacting with others and developing a reflexive awareness of how he or she is viewed by others. This is made possible through the significant symbols that people share. Human language is made up of symbols and it is through these that individuals can communicate meaningfully. This is what is known as symbolic interactionism. It is by such communication that the individual takes on the perspective of others and learns to act accordingly to them and to others. However, there is also an element of the self which has the potential for rejecting or changing the perspectives of others and for acting spontaneously and creatively.

Mead was especially interested in the development of 'the self' and in child development. These interests were encased in a general theoretical framework and set of insights which influenced other theorists, not just in social psychology but also in sociology (for example, Herbert Blumer, who made significant contributions in the 1960s). These insights were transferred and applied to a wide range of forms of social interaction, including those associated with crime and deviance.

Interactionism is not a grand theory in the sense of a set of integrated propositions. Rather, it is a framework which offers a set of assumptions about the nature of social action, the nature of the social world and relationships between them. It also comprises a set of key concepts. The main assumptions are that human action is characterized by free choice, flexibility and dynamism. It is forever changing according to types of interaction and types of context. Forms of social action are formed, adapted, refined or changed in interactions with others in micro-social contexts. Social order in such contexts and in society in general is not fixed and external, but the product of such interactions. Social order is not consensual; rather it is a plurality of perspectives, values and norms. Key concepts include 'interaction', 'meaning', 'social learning', 'negotiation', 'process', 'stereotyping', 'labelling' and 'career'.

The interactionist framework and the assumptions and concepts which comprise it provide a basis for seeking explanations of social phenomena (such as crime) which typically are non-positivist. Instead, explanations are cast in terms of processes and interactions rather than predispositions, pathologies, determinants and causes, especially where these are seen as located in the individual. Interactionism also provides a basis for empirical inquiry, often using the methods and practices of ethnography. Ethnography has a particular affinity with interactionism because they share an interest in 'capturing the actor's point of view' and also because methods such as participant observation are especially suited to the study of social interactions. The use of ethnographic enquiry, guided by interactionist concepts, to study criminal subcultures is sometimes referred to as appreciative criminology.

The interactionist perspective has influenced criminological thinking at various junctures since its emergence out of symbolic interactionism of the 1930s. It was particularly influential as part of the radical reaction, in the 1960s and early 1970s, to the dominance of positivism in criminology. It was typified by the labelling approach to deviance which emphasized that deviance is what people label as such. It encouraged many lines of enquiry. These included foci on: crime as the outcome of social interaction; crime as the result of negotiated processes involving rule violators and control agents as definers; changing definitions of crime in law enactment; police discretion in the enforcement of the law; crime as a meaningful act; and the consequences of being labelled deviant, for example in terms of further deviancy amplification.

Evaluation

An important element of social interaction is the exercise of power. Interactionists are interested in power, for example in the ways in which some categories of people are able to make deviant labels 'stick' and others are unable to cast them off. One of the challenges of interactionist-inspired criminological enquiry has been the ability successfully to demonstrate how the exercise of power in micro-social contexts has its source in wider, structural power inequalities in society. This requires criminologists to produce a synthesis of theorizing and empirical enquiry at micro and macro levels.

The contribution of the interactionist strand within criminology has been to challenge positivist approaches, with their emphasis on causality, by raising definitional issues (who gets labelled as deviant?) and by encouraging a focus on control agents as generators of crime (who does the labelling?). It has also produced a rich vein of ethnographic studies of deviant subcultures, criminal justice agencies and processes of social control.

Victor Jupp

Associated Concepts: appreciative criminology, ethnography, labelling, new deviancy theory, social learning theory

Key Readings

Becker, H. (1963) *Outsiders: Studies in the Sociology of Deviance*. New York, The Free Press.

Blumer, H. (1969) *Symbolic Interactionism*. Englewood Cliffs, NJ, Prentice–Hall.

Mead, G.H. (1934) *Mind, Self and Society*. Chicago, University of Chicago Press.

Sumner, C. (1994) *The Sociology of Deviance: An Obituary*. Buckingham, Open University Press.

J

JUST DESERTS

Definition

The proposition that the principles of proportionality, due process, determinant sentencing and non-discretional decision-making should be the central elements of systems of criminal justice.

Distinctive Features

The principles of 'just deserts' in sentencing are usually compared with those of rehabilitation, treatment or welfare. In the 1970s liberal lawyers and civil libertarians in the USA were becoming increasingly critical of rehabilitative sentencing. They argued that the 'need for treatment' acted as a spurious justification for placing excessive restrictions on individual liberty, particularly for young women, which were out of proportion either to the seriousness of the offence or to the realities of being in 'need of care and protection'. Indeterminate sentencing schemes, notably in California, meant that length of sentence was at the discretion of an Adult Authority (parole) board rather than a judicial body. Time in prison rested on psychological assessments of how far an offender had 'improved' rather than with reference to the actual crime committed. As a result minor offenders could serve longer sentences than those convicted of more serious offences, particularly if they declined the 'offer' of treatment. In a series of prison riots, most notably at Attica, a key grievance was the indeterminacy and lack of proportionality in sentencing. Probation, social work and welfare judgements were viewed as a form of arbitrary and discretional power. Many offenders, it was argued, were subjected to apparently non-accountable state procedures and their liberty often unjustifiably denied (American Friends Service Committee, 1972).

In the field of juvenile justice it was similarly argued that investigation of social background was an imposition: that social work involvement not only preserved explanations of individual pathology, but also undermined young persons' right to natural justice. Young people were placed in double jeopardy – sentenced for their background as well as for their offence – and as a result their movement up the sentencing tariff was often accelerated (Morris et al., 1980).

In the wake of these criticisms a new justice-based model of corrections emerged. Its leading proponent in America, von Hirsch (1976), proposed that the following principles be reinstated at the centre of criminal justice practice:

- proportionality of punishment to crime, or the offender is handed a sentence that is in accordance with what the act deserves;
- determinacy of sentencing and an end to indeterminate, treatment oriented sentences;
- an end to judicial, professional and administrative discretion;
- an end to disparities in sentencing;
- equity and protection of rights through due process.

The idea of punishing the crime, not the person, had clear attractions for those seeking an end to the abuses of discretional power.

Evaluation

However this liberal critique also coalesced with the concerns of traditional retributivists that rehabilitation was a 'soft option'. For them tougher sentencing would also enable criminals to get their 'just deserts'. For this reason Clarke (1985) maintained that the staking out of 'justice' as a strategy for reform is always liable to allow proponents of law and order to recruit the arguments of 'natural justice' for their own ends, although the former is more concerned with retribution and the latter with judicial equality and consistency. Within the political climate of the 1980s notions of 'just deserts' and 'anti-welfarism' were indeed politically mobilized by the right. The language of 'justice and rights' was appropriated by one of 'self responsibility and obligation'. Accordingly, Hudson (1987, 1996) has argued that the 'just deserts' or 'back to justice' movements that emerged in many Western jurisdictions in the 1980s were evidence of a 'modern retributivism' rather than necessarily heralding the emergence of new liberal regimes and sentencing policies.

John Muncie

Associated Concepts: disproportionality, due process model, natural justice, rehabilitation, retribution

Key Readings

American Friends Service Committee (1972) *Struggle for Justice*. New York, Hill and Wang.

Clarke, J. (1985) 'Whose justice? The politics of juvenile control', *International Journal of the Sociology of Law*, 13 (4), pp. 405–21.

von Hirsch, A. (1976) *Doing Justice: The Choice of Punishments*. New York, Hill and Wang.

Hudson, B. (1987) *Justice Through Punishment*. London, Macmillan.

Hudson, B. (1996) *Understanding Justice*. Buckingham, Open University Press.

Morris, A., Giller, H., Geach, H. and Szwed, E. (1980) *Justice for Children*. London, Macmillan.

JUSTICE

See Actuarialism; Crime control model; Criminal justice; Due process model; Informal justice; Just deserts; Natural justice; Popular justice; Restorative justice; Social justice

JUVENILE JUSTICE

See Bifurcation; Decarceration; Delinquency; Diversion; Just deserts; Multi-agency crime prevention; Net widening; Rehabilitation; Restorative justice; Social control theory

L

LABELLING

Definition

A sociological approach to understanding crime and deviancy which refers to the social processes through which certain individuals and groups classify and categorize the behaviour of others. On this basis labelled individuals are stereotyped to act in certain ways and are responded to accordingly. Such reaction tends to reinforce a self conception as deviant and has the unanticipated consequence of promoting the behaviour that it is designed to prevent.

Distinctive Features

Unlike traditional approaches which assume that the causes of crime and deviance lie either within individual offenders themselves or within their socio-economic circumstances, the labelling approach argues that criminological analysis should begin with how people come to be defined as deviant and examine the implications that such definitions hold for future offending behaviour. The approach is widely associated with the work of Howard Becker (1963), who famously claimed that deviance is not inherent in any action, but is created when rules and sanctions are applied to behaviour considered to be 'offending'. Behaviour only becomes deviant when it is labelled as such. Traces of such an approach can be found throughout the nineteenth century. The penal reformer and utilitarian philosopher Jeremy Bentham, for example, argued that certain social reactions to crime – the unreformed prison – are more likely to promote offending than curtail it. Henry Mayhew, the social commentator, considered that over-zealous policing was a significant factor in the creation of juvenile delinquency in the mid-nineteenth century. Such themes are widely repeated in the perennial claim that prisons are 'colleges of crime' and that they cement 'criminal careers'. In the 1930s Frank Tannenbaum (1938) argued that deviance was created through a process of social interaction. Whilst a majority commit deviant acts only a minority come to be known as deviant. The known deviant is then targeted, identified, defined and treated as such even though their behaviour may be no different from those who have not been so identified. As a result certain people 'become deviant' through the imposition of social judgements on their behaviour: they *become* the very essence of what is being complained of. In the 1950s Edwin Lemert further refined the approach by distinguishing between primary and secondary deviation. He argued that primary deviance is often a temporary waywardness and perpetrators have no conception of themselves as deviant. Secondary deviance is created through the reaction of others to the initial deviance. Through name-calling, stereotyping and labelling, a deviant identity is established and confirmed. Often deviants resolve this personal crisis by accepting their deviant status and by reorganizing their lives accordingly. They become more, rather than less, deviant. Lemert's conclusion that *social control causes deviancy* was a crucial turning point in the development of a radical criminological imagination that has flourished since the 1960s.

A fully fledged labelling approach emerged through the work of Howard Becker, Kai Erikson and John Kitsuse in the 1960s. For each, the key to understanding the origins of deviance lay in the reactions of a social audience, rather than in the behaviour of an individual actor. It is the audience which determines whether or not any behaviour comes to be defined as deviant. A number of studies were published in the 1960s and 1970s which revealed the processes of *becoming* a marijuana smoker, a prostitute, a homosexual, a prisoner and so on. In each it was the stigma attached to the label that was considered pivotal in informing future behaviour patterns. Defined as 'outsiders', it is such groups that come to epitomize what is considered to be criminal. A self-fulfilling prophecy ensues. Criminality is continually sought only in those identified as criminal. And the power of the label of 'criminal' ensures that 'criminal careers' are exacerbated.

To counter this process labelling theorists argue that only a diminution or absence of official reaction is able significantly to reduce offending. When no stigma, ostracism or exclusion is applied to a deviant act then delinquent 'careers' will not be established. In contrast to reactive 'get tough' approaches, decriminalization and a radical non-interventionism are called for.

By focusing on the processes whereby behaviour comes to be criminalized and by adopting a relatively non-judgemental or appreciative stance to primary deviance, labelling opened up whole new areas of interest in criminology, in which the concepts of stigma, social reaction and control were to become pivotal. Through labelling, the traditional behavioural questions – why do they do it? – were subordinated to a more critical line of enquiry – who defines another as deviant?, for what purposes? and with what implications for future deviant activity?

Evaluation

Labelling continues to offer an important challenge to traditional criminological approaches. By focusing on definitional issues it is able to reveal how the concepts of 'crime' and 'deviance' are not universally agreed upon, but are socially constructed, contingent and contestable. By drawing attention to the role of social reaction (and law and order enforcement in particular) it warns of the ways in which criminal justice may cause that which it is designed to curtail. However, a number of radical authors have subsequently argued that the logic of labelling is limited when employed without any analysis of the social and political structures and inequalities in which such labels are constructed and upheld. Labelling fails to explain *why* it is only *some* behaviours that come to be defined in a

historical and political context as deviant, whilst others do not. The key question – whose law and whose order is being protected? – was notably overlooked. As a result, some critical criminologists in the 1970s argued that the insights of labelling needed to be wedded to a Marxist model of society and the state. Only then could the subjective encounters of social reaction and social control be viewed as objective social processes set in particular social formations. As a result labelling has been critiqued as merely offering an *approach* and not meeting the requirements for a fully worked up criminological theory.

A different critique offered by positivist criminologists focuses on the lack of serious attention that labelling gives to primary deviance. By concentrating on such 'victimless' crimes as drug taking, homosexuality and so on, it has failed to recognize sufficiently the fundamental deviance attached to other 'serious crimes' such as murder, robbery and institutional violence. In addition, it has been suggested that the origins of a 'deviant identity' lie not in the processes of social reaction, but in local community and neighbourhood settings. The multiple sources and differential impacts of a range of negative labels are likely to be far more complex than that offered by the labelling perspective of the 1960s.

John Muncie

Associated Concepts: criminal careers, deviancy amplification, interactionism, radical criminologies, radical non-intervention, social constructionism, social reaction

Key Readings

Becker, H. (1963) *Outsiders: Studies in the Sociology of Deviance*. New York, The Free Press.

Erikson, K.T. (1966) *Wayward Puritans: A Study in the Sociology of Deviance*. New York, Wiley.

Kitsuse, J. (1962) 'Societal reaction to deviant behaviour', *Social Problems*, no. 9, pp. 247–56.

Lemert, E. (1951) *Social Pathology*. New York, McGraw–Hill.

Plummer, K. (1979) 'Misunderstanding labelling perspectives', in D. Downes and P. Rock (eds), *Deviant Interpretations*. Oxford, Oxford University Press.

Tannenbaum, F. (1938) *Crime and the Community*. New York, Colombia University Press.

LEFT IDEALISM

Definition

A sociological approach to crime and punishment whose roots lie in Marxist and neo-Marxist theory. This requires taking the problem of crime seriously while critically analysing the processes of criminalization, social construction and state power, which contribute to making crime and the responses to it a complex social process. Therefore, academic research should be critical and interventionist built on analysing the wider structures of power that reproduce the social divisions underpinning the social order of contemporary capitalist democracies.

Distinctive Features

Left idealism sits on the critical wing of criminology and is often contrasted with left realism. Both perspectives have their roots in the early 1970s and the shift towards a Marxist-oriented approach to the understanding of crime and deviance. In 1975 Jock Young argued in his influential essay 'Working Class Criminology' (in Taylor et al., 1975) that critical criminology was fragmenting into a number of distinct strands, two of which he identified as realism and idealism. By the mid-1980s the rise and consolidation of the New Right led realists such as Kinsey, Lea, Matthews and Young to call for a reappraisal of the role of criminology. In particular, they demanded that criminologists should reject the idealization of the criminal and the utopian romanticism they identified as central to idealist thought. Instead, they argued that criminologists should take crime and the fear of crime seriously, especially its impact on the powerless.

However, those labelled as idealists did not accept Young's argument:

> The critics of the new realists . . . reject their categorization as left idealists and argue forcefully that their interventionist work within critical criminology has responded to the realities of life under Thatcherism. Further, they challenge new realism on its misreading of history, under-theorization both of the structural contradictions under advanced capitalism and the advanced capitalist state form and its rule of law, and on its essentially superficial approach to the complexities of crime, crime control and the criminal justice process. (Sim et al., 1987, p. 39)

Thus British idealists such as Gilroy, Hillyard, Bunyan, Scraton, Sim and Gordon not only rejected a label which was, and is, identified with them but also they highlighted a series of key theoretical and political distinctions between their conceptualization of politics and criminology and that propounded by Young and his colleagues.

First, contrary to the theoretical 'straw man' that realists had established, those labelled as idealists did not see the state as an homogeneous entity incapable of change. This 'crude and simplistic' caricature (van Swaaningen, 1997, p. 201) seriously underestimated the idealist position that the state was a contingent and contradictory set of institutions. Critical criminologists should therefore exploit these contradictions through research whose results should be made available to those groups struggling to reform and radically change the criminal justice system. This 'criminology from below' (Sim et al., 1987, p. 7) led to a range of interventionist work in Britain throughout the 1970s and 1980s around prisons, the police, Northern Ireland, violence against women, institutionalized racism and deaths in custody. Like abolitionists, idealists understood political action as a hegemonic process which involved analysing the state both as a coercive set of institutions and as a site where dominant ideas could be fought over, challenged and resisted. Consequently, they supported community groups involved in official and unofficial inquiries into the operation of different criminal justice institutions to ensure that state definitions of 'truth' did not prevail and that alternative accounts from below were not marginalized. This remained a key aspect of left idealism in the 1990s.

Secondly, idealists maintained that crime and public concerns about it were complex phenomena which needed to be unpacked and understood. The realist's 'undifferentiated and abstract view of crime' was:

> Theoretically and politically problematic not only because it allows the already elastic concept of crime to become a catch-all category but also because it presents an idealized view of the working class community as a 'homogeneous group united by its fear of crime despite the everyday divisions of gender, race, craft, income and employment'. (Gilroy and Sim, cited in Sim et al., 1987, p. 45)

Thirdly, they argued that the state was concerned with the reproduction of an unequal social order rather than, as in the case of the police, offering a 'service' to the powerless.

This did not mean that its institutions defended processes of domination in every instance but that wider structures of power played a central role in the construction of criminal justice policies and the deployment of state personnel. Finally, like abolitionists, they contended that the state's response to crime should be deconstructed and replaced with an alternative set of democratically embedded policies and practices. This position contrasted with realists, who 'with their focus on the beginning of the "penal chain" (crime prevention and the police) . . . nearly forgot where this chain ends: in punishment' (van Swaaningen, 1997, p. 200).

Evaluation

Left idealism remains a central strand in critical criminological praxis. While the charge of utopianism is still leveled at them, idealists would say that the events of the 1990s have only underlined the strength of their thesis. The consolidation of the New Right, particularly in the UK and USA in the first half of the decade, coupled with an intensification in the authoritarian capabilities of the state, illustrates and reinforces their view that while crime should be taken seriously the state's primary focus is on the maintenance and reproduction of a social order that remains deeply divided along the fault lines of social class, gender, 'race', age and sexuality.

At the same time the moral panics around juvenile crime, single parents, asylum seekers and drug users during the decade illustrate how discourses surrounding conventional definitions of crime and deviance can still be mobilized ideologically to reproduce structures of domination and subordination. The election of New Labour in the UK in 1997, many of whose ideas on law and order can be traced back to left realism, has reinforced the idealist argument still further. While idealists would not support the sociologically reductionist position which contends that Labour has abjectly followed the policies of previous Conservative administrations, they would contend that many of the government's policies on law and order are built on a further consolidation of state power. This consolidation includes: a range of new powers for state servants; an ideological construction of particular groups as criminalistic and deviant; a failure to confront the issue of the democratic accountability of state institutions; and a reluctance to deal with crimes committed by the powerful, for example, in terms of deaths

at work and in custody. As Sumner (1990, p. 3) notes, tying theory and research to a social democratic agenda means that 'there is a grave danger of running into the cul-de-sac of a social democratic, parochial reformism which is not so far away from neo-positivist, administrative criminology'.

Realists maintain that idealists still conceptualize the state as a homogeneous entity which operates at all times and in all places for the benefit of those in power. Idealists would make two responses to this point. First, it remains necessary to scrutinize the state sociologically, its lack of democratic accountability and the institutional and personal accumulation of power that has underpinned its development since the beginning of the nineteenth century. Indeed, the trend towards post-structuralist and postmodernist thought in the social sciences has led to the state being airbrushed out of academic analysis. The state should therefore be brought back in as a focus for research and theorizing. This can be done without degenerating into a reductionist and instrumental view of state power.

Second, idealists would contend that the interventionist work of the 1970s and 1980s, built on exploiting the contingencies and contradictions in the state, continued into the 1990s. In a range of areas including deaths in custody, health and safety at work, violence against women and state behaviour in Northern Ireland, idealist academics have continued to work with community groups and others to change laws and state practices. Additionally, in the UK they have provided support to, and worked with, groups involved in major political issues such as the Hillsborough disaster and the Stephen Lawrence inquiry. They would also maintain that they have had an influence not only on public and political debate but, in working with particular pressure groups, have been instrumental in helping to achieve changes in the law, for example, around inquest procedures affecting deaths in custody.

In terms of future developments, idealists would argue for *greater* utopianism in social and criminological theory and that their alternative definition of crime and punishment remains central to their overall vision of a society devoid of the hierarchies of power that limit human capacities and capabilities. They would also agree with Stan Cohen that the choice for academics is not necessarily between scepticism and realism 'but to show in concrete situations where intellectual subversion might or might not lead'. For Cohen, this 'raises questions of strategy, tactics and alliances'. It follows from this that criminology has to try to satisfy:

> A *triple* loyalty: first an overriding obligation to honest intellectual inquiry itself (however sceptical, provisional, irrelevant and unrealistic); second, a political commitment to social justice; and third (and potentially conflicting with both), the pressing and immediate demands for short-term humanitarian help. We have to appease these three voracious gods. (Cohen, 1998, pp. 118–22; emphasis in the original)

Roy Coleman and Joe Sim

Associated Concepts: abolitionism, critical criminology, critical research, hegemony, left realism, the state

Key Readings

Cohen, S. (1998) 'Intellectual scepticism and political commitment: the case of radical criminology', in P. Walton and J. Young (eds), *The New Criminology Revisited*. Basingstoke, Macmillan.

Pearce, S. and Tombs, S. (1992) 'Realism and corporate crime', in R. Matthews and J. Young (eds), *Issues in Realist Criminology*. London, Sage.

Ryan, M. and Ward, T. (1986) 'Law and order: left realism against the rest', *The Abolitionist*, 22 (2), pp. 29–33.

Sim, J. Scraton, P. and Gordon, P. (1987) 'Introduction: crime, the state and critical analysis', in P. Scraton (ed.), *Law, Order and the Authoritarian State*. Milton Keynes, The Open University Press.

Sumner, C. (1990) 'Introduction: contemporary socialist criminology', in C. Sumner (ed.), *Censure, Politics and Criminal Justice*. Buckingham, The Open University Press.

Taylor, I., Walton, P. and Young, J. (eds) (1975) *Critical Criminology*. London, Routledge.

Van Swaaningen, R. (1997) *Critical Criminology: Visions From Europe*. London, Sage.

LEFT REALISM

Definition

A school of criminology which emerged initially in Britain in the early 1980s as a response both to the punitive and exclusionary policies of conservatism and to the utopianism of New Left radical criminologies.

Distinctive Features

Left realist criminology, as its name implies, is radical in its criminology and realistic in its appraisal of crime and its causes. It is radical in that crime is seen as an endemic product of the class and patriarchal nature of advanced industrial society. It is not a cosmetic criminology of an establishment sort which views crime as a blemish which, with suitable treatment, can be removed from the body of society, which is, in itself, otherwise healthy and in little need of reconstruction. Rather it suggests that it is within the core institutions of society (its relationships of class and of gender) and its central values (such as competitive individualism and aggressive masculinity) that crime arises. Crime is not a product of abnormality but of the normal workings of the social order. Secondly, it is realistic in that it attempts to be faithful to the reality of crime. This involves several tasks: realistically appraising the problem of crime, deconstructing crime into its fundamental components (the square of crime), critically examining the nature of causality, being realistic about the possibilities of intervention and, above all, fully understanding the changing social terrain in which we now live.

The particular political space in which left realism emerged was in the mid-1980s. The juxtaposition was with the emergence of conservative ('neo-liberal') governments in many Western countries which pursued an overtly punishment-oriented approach to crime control. At that time a liberal/social democratic opposition was on the defensive. The neo-liberals actively pointed to the rise in the crime rate and entered vigorously into law and order campaigns on behalf of 'the silent majority', holding offenders responsible for their actions and advocating punishment as the solution. The New Left position, which had its origins in the libertarianism of the 1960s, tended to resemble a mirror image of the right. That is, it denied or downplayed the level of crime, portrayed the offender as victim of the system, and stressed a multiculturalism of diversity and struggle where radicalism entailed the defence of the community against the incursions of the state, particularly the police and the criminal justice system. What was necessary was a criminology which could navigate between these two currents: which took crime seriously but which was radical in its analysis and policy.

It was, therefore, no accident that two key realist texts were published in the mid-eighties: *What is to be Done About Law and Order?* (by John Lea and Jock Young) in 1984 in Britain, and *Confronting Crime* (by Elliott Currie) in 1985 in the United States, whilst the first realist crime survey was carried out in 1985 by the Canadian Brian Maclean.

The evocation to 'take crime seriously' involved realists in large-scale local victimization studies directly and 'democratically' asking people about their problems of crime and their assessment of police effectiveness. These surveys, frequently funded by radical local councils, pointed both to the greater burden of crime on the poor, ethnic minorities and women and the extent of police abuses and inefficiency. Later surveys were widened out to include white collar crime and domestic violence (Mooney, 2000). In Britain such work has had considerable impact on the re-orientation of Labour Party policies towards a heightened concern with crime control issues. Although such quantitative work has become identified with realism, the need for qualitative research to make sense of the findings and provide clues to causality is constantly stressed.

A fundamental task of left realism is to deconstruct the concept of crime. First it is noted that crime is inevitably the product of action and reaction and that the failure of previous criminologies is that they have problematized one component and ignored the other. Thus positivism focuses on crime and tends to take the definition of crime for granted whereas constructionism (that is, labelling theory, abolitionism and much of critical criminology) problematizes the way in which crime is defined and constructed yet tends to ignore crime itself. The left realist critique argues that to explain crime necessitates a double aetiology of action and reaction and a corresponding denial of any essence of crime. Rather crime is viewed as a concept constantly changing over time and varying from the perspective of different groups. It occurs in the interrelationship between *offender* and *victim* within the varying definitional flux of *formal* and *informal* systems of control (Young, 1992). (Hence the *square of crime* between these four points.)

Realism stresses the need to seek the causes of crime but is critical of any positivistic notion of a mechanistic nature. A key causal concept is relative deprivation, which encompasses both the subjective and material nature of discontent. Such an emphasis on *both* the subjective and objective dimensions of human action is mirrored throughout realist analysis. Thus just as it is stressed that the causes of crime cannot be reduced to material deprivation alone, fear of crime cannot be understood as merely a reflection of risk rates and the rate of imprisonment cannot be simply correlated with crime rates. For all of these processes involve human evaluation and reflection upon material circumstances. And because of this double nature, the opposite reduction is equally invalid: for material inequality is the basis of crime, fear of crime cannot be dissociated from the risk of crime, and levels of punishment cannot be discussed without resort to the crime rates.

Realism is an integrated theory synthesizing theoretical traditions (particularly subcultural theory and labelling theory) and fuzing them together within a socialist feminist framework that stresses class and gender inequality (see Mooney, 2000).

Intervention to control crime is a central concern, involving multi-agencies and at different points in the natural history of a specific crime. Social crime prevention is stressed although situational crime prevention and deterrence from the criminal justice system play minor backing roles. The ultimate task is to make fundamental changes in the social order whilst at the same time intervening on a day-to-day basis to protect the public and push reform onwards. Like all radical politics the central problem is to remain committed to change without being merely utopian and to be immediately effective without being simply technocratic and pragmatic.

Evaluation

Left realism has moved in the last decade from a polemical position that stressed the need for radicals to take crime seriously to the foundation of an integrated theory that attempts to synthesize the major strands of criminological thought. What is now necessary is the development of a sociology that relates to the transition to late modernity and a politics that is in dialogue with contemporary feminist and social democratic theory. A start has been made in this direction, but much exacting and exciting work remains to be done.

Jock Young

Associated Concepts: fear of crime, left idealism, neo-conservative criminology, relative deprivation, social crime prevention, victim surveys

Key Readings

Currie, E. (1995) *Confronting Crime*. New York, Pantheon.
Currie, E. (1998) *Crime and Punishment in America*. New York, Metropolitan Books.

Lea, J. and Young, J. (1984) *What is to be Done About Law and Order?* Harmondsworth, Penguin.

Lowman, J. and Maclean, B. (eds) (1992) *Realist Criminology.* Toronto, University of Toronto Press.

Mooney, J. (2000) *Gender, Violence and the Social Order.* London, Macmillan.

Young, J. (1992) 'Ten points of realism', in J. Young and R. Matthews (eds), *Rethinking Criminology: The Realist Debate.* London, Sage.

Young, J. (1999) *The Exclusive Society.* London, Sage.

LIBERAL FEMINISM

Definition

Liberal feminism was the first of the theoretical feminist perspectives, developed in the 1920s from the work of Mary Wollstonecraft and J.S. Mill, and it greatly influenced the 'first wave' of modern Western feminism. Its emphasis is very much on the *equality* of men and women, especially with regard to their moral and intellectual characteristics, thus liberal feminists have argued for social and political changes in the educational and legal framework which they see as constraining women. In the sphere of criminal justice studies, liberal feminism has had a powerful impact on analyses of equity and discrimination.

Distinctive Features

Liberal feminism has claims to be the oldest and the original feminist theory, with its roots in eighteenth-century Enlightenment thinking and in the American Revolution (Banks, 1981). While the French Revolution did little to advance the emancipation of women, the intellectual ferment of ideas which it provoked inspired debate in England and America which did challenge the status quo, in which women had effectively no political rights. In 1792, Mary Wollstonecraft published *A Vindication of the Rights of Woman* in which she challenged notions of female inferiority and insisted that there should be equal educational opportunities for women with men and employment for single women. In 1869, J.S. Mill's *On the Subjection of Women* took up similar arguments in support of the contemporary campaigns for female enfranchisement: 'the legal subordination of one sex to the other – is wrong in itself . . . and that it ought to be replaced by a principle of perfect equality'. The American Declaration of Independence inspired the statement of feminist principles that emerged from the Seneca Falls Convention in 1848. This event, which marked the founding of organized feminism in the USA, laid claims to sexual equality and equal rights for women alongside men.

Thus both the early feminist writers and the campaigners whom they inspired, relied on an individualist notion of equality and on comparing women with men. Campaigns focused on formal recognition of females as free and equal individuals who could enjoy full legal and civil rights to vote, to enter into contracts, gain an education and membership of professions. Much effort in the USA and Britain went into the lengthy struggles to gain the vote, sometimes, as in certain US states, before all of the male population had been enfranchised. Nevertheless, insistence on rights-based claims to enfranchisement were successful in the early twentieth century in Australia, New Zealand and later in Britain and the USA.

In the later twentieth century, a second wave of feminism flourished, which had notably different aims. Nevertheless, there are clear links between this phase and the earlier one, chiefly through the modern version of liberal feminism. The central notion remains that of removing barriers and constraints to achieving equality. Equal rights and equal opportunities are key issues: sex discrimination must go, there must be more women in politics and positions of power, and in senior posts in industry and commerce, and sex stereotyping in the media, education and public attitudes should be combated (Dale and Foster, 1986). In the USA the National Organization of Women, in Britain the Equal Opportunities Commission are institutional examples of liberal approaches to women's rights.

In criminology, liberal feminists demonstrated many instances of inequitable treatment of girls and women: the extra penalties incurred by 'wayward' girls in the USA, or the more limited options available in prisons for women. However, some research has indicated that women may be less severely sanctioned than men and equalizing punishment (for example, through strict sentencing guidelines), may lead to the harsher, male norm being imposed (Chesney-Lind and Faith, 2000).

Evaluation

Liberal feminists have sought to play down biological differences between the sexes and to argue that women can achieve equality with men. These views have been criticized for ignoring structural differences between the power positions of men and women, especially in the family, and also for offering strategies that relate mainly to the interests of white, middle-class women and not to those of black or working-class women. This criticism has had particular relevance in criminology (Daly and Stephens, 1995) since women (and men) from some minorities are heavily over-represented in offender populations.

Campaigns mounted by first wave feminists to ensure the entry of women into policing, the legal and correctional professions were ultimately successful, although representation is still low in many countries. Nor has the small female presence achieved significant change, as earlier reformers had hoped (Chesney-Lind and Faith, 2000). Critics of liberal approaches have argued that institutions such as the law and the state are too imbued with patriarchal assumptions and sexist practices to enable real changes to be brought about. While liberal feminism clearly has its limitations, it has had influence and impact on much subsequent thinking and is the basis for later and more radical perspectives. Eisenstein (1981) had contended that because of its 'self-contradictory nature', liberal feminism logically leads to the development of much more radical approaches.

Frances Heidensohn

Associated Concepts: discrimination, feminist criminologies, radical feminism

Key Readings

Banks, O. (1981) *Faces of Feminism*. Oxford, Martin Robertson.

Chesney-Lind, M. and Faith, K. (2000) 'What about feminism? Engendering theory-making in criminology', in R. Paternoster and R. Bachman (eds), *Explaining Criminals and Crime: Essays in Contemporary Criminological Theory*. Los Angeles, Roxbury Publishing Co.

Dale, J. and Foster, P. (1986) *Feminists and State Welfare*. London, Routledge.

Daly, K. and Stephens, D. (1995) 'The "Dark Figure" of criminology: towards a black and multi-ethnic feminist agenda for theory and research', in N. Rafter and F. Heidensohn (eds), *International Feminist Perspectives in Criminology*. Milton Keynes, Open University Press.

Eisenstein, Z. (1981) *The Radical Future of Liberal Feminism*. London, Longman.

Wollstonecraft, M. and Mill, J.S. (1929) *The Rights of Women, The Subjection of Women* (ed. G. Catin). London, Dent.

LONGITUDINAL STUDY

Definition

A form of study in which observations are collected from the same people at different, sometimes key, points in their lifetime, often with a view to studying personal or individual development. Variants are sometimes also known as cohort studies and panel studies. In both cases there is repeated contact with the same individuals over a period of time.

Distinctive Features

With longitudinal cohort studies, a sample is drawn from a particular 'cohort', which is defined by membership of a particular group or category of individuals such as those born in a particular week or year, children entering school at the same time or offenders sentenced to imprisonment at the same time. The same sample members are contacted at regular intervals and over a much longer period of time than is typical of other forms of survey. In this respect, longitudinal surveys are also prospective designs (studying people as they develop) rather than retrospective designs (collecting observations about people's backgrounds retrospectively). Although it is not a necessary feature of longitudinal cohort studies, there is often an emphasis upon describing and explaining personal development, the progression of life events and the onset of behavioural patterns or physical illness. Sometimes these descriptions and explanations are used as a basis for making predictions about changes in other, but similar types of people, for example predictions about the kinds of people who are likely to embark on and pursue criminal careers.

Longitudinal surveys have been used in a wide range of areas, for instance psychiatry, paediatrics, child development and health. In criminology such surveys are associated with studies of the causes of delinquency and crime as typified by the Cambridge Study in Delinquent Development. In 1961 a sample of 411 working-class boys, aged about 8 years old, was selected from the registers of six state primary schools in an area of London. Girls were not included in the sample. The sample members were contacted at regular intervals up until the age of 21 and a subsample was interviewed. Finally, all sample members were contacted when they were 32 years old to examine which of them had continued a 'life of crime' into adulthood and why. Five key factors relating to the boys when they were 8–10 years old were identified as being statistically related to subsequent delinquency. These were low family income, large family size, parents with a criminal record, low intelligence and poor parental child-rearing practices (West, 1982). Six predictors of offending in later years, up to the age of 32, were also identified. These were poverty, poor parenting, family deviance, school problems, hyperactivity/impulsiveness/attention deficit and anti-social behaviour (Farrington, 1989).

The strategy of analysis used to explain delinquency and subsequent criminal careers owes much to the logic of the comparative method. At the point at which two subgroups were identified within the sample – those 'delinquent' and those 'non-delinquent' – these groups were compared on a range of variables to examine which were the best predictors of differences between them (in effect asking the question 'which factors do the delinquents share in common which are not shared to the same extent by the non-delinquents?'). This form of analysis is not only comparative but also multivariate in so far as a number of variables are introduced in order to explain the variables 'delinquency' and 'subsequent criminal careers'. These are not only explanatory variables but also predictors of delinquency and crime. Such predictors provide the basis for suggesting policy initiatives, such as introducing training in child-rearing methods for parents.

Although the distinction is not precise, panel studies differ from cohort studies in so far as they are based on representative samples of the population to be studied rather than cohorts based on birth or a particular entry point (for example, admission to a prison).

Longitudinal studies can also vary according to the period of time over which data are collected from the cohorts or panels. There may also be variations in the frequency of the intervals between data collection points (sometimes known as 'sweeps'). Birth cohort studies often extend over a lifetime and because they are usually interested in maturation and development (for example, of a criminal career) they collect data over longer time intervals than is typical for panel studies.

Evaluation

The strengths of longitudinal designs are as follows. First, unlike one-shot cross-sectional designs, longitudinal research is not dependent on the collection of retrospective data in seeking to relate past experiences to present day attitudes and actions. It can collect a wide range of data about a wide range of variables at different stages in an individual's life. Secondly, the collection of data at the stages in an individual's life to which they relate reduces the invalidity associated with the collection of retrospective data (for example, inaccuracies of memory). Thirdly, longitudinal studies can focus on individual development and can provide direct evidence of time-ordering of variable which gives credence to causal inferences that link contemporary attitudes and action to previous backgrounds, experiences and events.

On the negative side, however, longitudinal surveys are very costly and they produce their results very slowly, especially those relating to the later stages of development. Also, there is always a risk that members will change as a result of being part of the study, perhaps by responding in ways that they believe are expected of them. What is more, the sample runs the risk of being seriously depleted by drop-out over the years, something known as 'sample attrition'. A further problem is that variables about which data are collected at early stages may not anticipate theoretical developments at a later stage, with the result that crucial data relevant to such developments may not have been collected. This is sometimes referred to as the problem of 'fading relevancy'. A much more fundamental critique is of the causal and positivist assumptions of such surveys. Critical criminologists, for example, would argue that in placing emphasis on the causal agents in the early lives of individuals they distract attention away from contemporary inequalities and oppressions and also that they do not address 'crimes of the powerful'.

Victor Jupp

Associated Concepts: causation, cohort studies, comparative method, cross-sectional design, positivism, prediction studies, sampling

Key Readings

Farrington, D. (1989) 'The origins of crime: the Cambridge Study of Delinquent Development', in *Research Bulletin*, Home Office Research and Planning Unit, no. 27, pp. 29–33.

Magnusson, D. and Bergman, L.R. (eds) (1990) *Data Quality in Longitudinal Research*. Cambridge, Cambridge University Press.

Magnusson, D., Bergman, L.R., Rudinger, G. and Torestad, B. (1990) *Problems and Methods in Longitudinal Research*. Cambridge, Cambridge University Press.

Robins, L. and Rutter, L. (1990) *Straight and Devious Pathways from Childhood to Adulthood*. Cambridge, Cambridge University Press.

West, D.J. (1982) *Delinquency: Its Roots, Careers and Prospects*. London, Heinemann.

M

MANAGERIALISM

Definition

Managerialism is a set of techniques and practices which aim to fracture and realign relations of power within the criminal justice system in order to transform the structures and reorganize the processes for both funding and delivering 'criminal justice'.

Distinctive Features

Managerialism, or to be more specific, New Public Managerialism (NPM), is a set of post-bureau-professional knowledges, practices and techniques drawn from a wide variety of sources (reinventing government, new public administration, new wave management, human resource management, postmodern organizational theory). NPM is a hybrid theoretical and political construction whose purpose is to alter all aspects of the formulation and delivery of public services in an era of the smaller state. The UK has been in the vanguard of managerialization and it is possible to identify two waves of NPM that have enveloped the criminal justice system. Under successive Conservative administrations (1979–1997) managerialization of criminal justice was progressed through the quasi-marketization of certain criminal justice functions and the responsibilization of individuals and communities. The overall purpose of this first wave of managerialization was to create a cost-effective, efficient and unified criminal justice system which would work within nationally agreed sets of guidelines and standards to reduce the crime rate and the fear of crime to 'acceptable' levels.

New Labour's long-term programme of national renewal and governmental reform acknowledges that the managerial reform process of the late 1980s and early 1990s was a necessary act of modernization that improved productivity and delivered better value for money and enhanced quality of service. Under the guise of 'modernization', New Labour initiated a second wave of 'joined up' managerialization to entrench 'performance management' across the criminal justice system. This involves the: establishment of consistent and mutually reinforcing aims and objectives; installation of a 'what works'/'best practice' culture; development of an evidence-based approach to the allocation of resources; the institutionalization of performance management to improve productivity; and the establishment of 'partnerships'.

Thus, the UK is witnessing the intensification of the NPM disciplines of efficiency, effectiveness and economy that were already working their way, albeit unevenly, through the various parts of this intricate policy environment. In certain important respects, further managerialization is necessary if the contradictions and tensions generated by the Conservatives' uneven and unfinished reform project are to be 'resolved'. Virtually every Home Office policy document now stresses that 'modernization' will be achieved through constant auditing, priority and target setting, monitoring, evaluation and inspection.

Evaluation

There is considerable disagreement about what is driving managerialization. For some criminologists it is linked to neo-liberal forms of crime control, for example, privatization, commodification and actuarialism, neo-conservative criminology and/or administrative

criminology while for others managerialization is a relatively autonomous process and
needs to be analysed on its own terms. A
viable post managerialist vision of criminal
justice has yet to be articulated by critics.

Eugene McLaughlin

Associated Concepts: actuarialism, administrative criminology, neo-conservative criminology, risk

Key Readings

Clarke, J. and Newman, J. (1997) *The Managerial
State.* London, Sage.
James, A. and Raine, K. (1998) *The New Politics of
Criminal Justice.* London, Longman.
McLaughlin, E. and Muncie, J. (2000) 'The criminal
justice system: New Labour's New Partnerships',
in J. Clarke, S. Gewirtz and E. McLaughlin (eds),
New Managerialism, New Welfare. London, Sage.
McLaughlin, E. and Murji, K. (2001) 'Lost connec-
tions and new directions', in K. Stenson and R.
Sullivan (eds), *Neo-Liberalism and Crime Control.*
Cambridge, Willan Press.
O'Malley, P. (1997) 'Policing, politics and postmo-
dernity', *Social and Legal Studies*, 6 (3), pp. 363–81.

MARXIST CRIMINOLOGIES

Definition

A variety of criminological perspectives that
draw on the Marxian tradition in sociological
theory in order to explicate the dimensions of
crime and its control that revolve around class,
power and state.

Distinctive Features

Some social theorists have argued that Marxist
criminology is not possible, strictly speaking,
because Marxism, as a form of theoretical
system, specifies its own objects of analysis
(such as 'the mode of production', 'class
relations', 'alienation', 'ideology', 'hegemony')
and thus subsumes the analysis of crime
under much more general concerns (Bankowski et al., 1977). The bulk of Marx's vast
corpus of work did not concern itself with
crime. However, it is still possible to discover
something of his perspective on crime and its
control. In his early journalism Marx wrote an

extended essay based on the Proceedings of
the Sixth Rhine Assembly debates on The Law
on Thefts of Wood which was published in the
German paper the *Rheinische Zeitung* in
October of 1842. In this article, Marx discussed
how the peasants living in the Rhine Valley
had taken away their traditional right to
gather fallen wood (a primary source of fuel
for cooking and heating) as the framework of
the old feudal form of law was redrafted in
line with the needs of the emergent order
of industrial capitalism. This is an example of
criminalization, which contemporary criminologists would clearly recognize, and it had
negative consequences for those at the bottom
end of the 'class structure'.

'Property is Theft' is an aphorism frequently
associated with Marx. In truth that maxim was
Proudhon's (*La propriété, c'est le vol*) – Marx
was seldom so pithy. Still, that sort of revolutionary rhetoric, and the sympathies which
it represented, was vigorously articulated
during the recrudesence of student rebellion
of the late 1960s. May 1968 seemed to symbolize the possibility of revolutionary change
in affluent Western societies and in that
moment many academics who had been
inspired by, or were instrumental in developing, the sociology of deviance, were galvanized into a radical mode of enquiry that drew
heavily on the Marxian tradition. There are
many examples of work carried out in this
vein. They all exhibit a concern to illuminate
the 'class dimensions' of power insofar as they
relate to instances of crime and crime control.
Within this perspective, the 'capitalist order'
itself is held to be criminogenic, and the crime
panics that emerge from time to time are
analysed as being an attempt at the orchestra-
tion of a public consensus (in Marxian terms,
'hegemony') by the police, the media, the
judiciary and other elements of the 'state–
corporate apparatus': this not only deflects
public concern away from the central contradictions of capitalism (which emanate from
the 'wage–capital relation'), but also serves to
provide a justification for ratchetting up the
power of the system of social control which,
perversely, contributes to the intensification of
the conditions that produced the crime
phenomena in the first place. This reasoning
was employed to considerable effect in
Policing the Crisis (Hall et al., 1978), which
remains one of the seminal contributions of
British criminology. Focusing on a 'mugging
panic' in London during the early 1970s, the
denouement of their argument was that,
because crime is one of the few symbolic
sources of unity in an increasingly divided

and embittered class society and, moreover, because the traditional elements of consensus (especially deference to authority, the trappings of class power and the threat of external enemies) were exhausted, bringing the 'hegemony of the state' under threat, the 'war against crime' becomes the primary source of re-legitimation. The state's main concern, so the argument goes, is to define the elements of the crisis of capitalism away. The crisis is depicted in such a way that images of deviants (criminals, industrial dissidents, ethnic minorities, drug-takers, youth, welfare scroungers, political deviants etc.) are foregrounded. Thus confusion is created and the working class come to mis-recognize their enemy. The crisis is deflected on to youth, crime and race and away from capitalist class relations.

Evaluation

One of the earliest attempts to situate the study of crime within a Marxian problematic can be found in the work of Willem Bonger, but these works have had little lasting influence and were dismissed by latter progeny as 'not so much the application of a fully fledged Marxist theory as they are a recitation of a "Marxist catechism" in an area which Marx had left largely untouched' (Taylor et al., 1973, p. 222). The 'new criminologists' of the 1970s attempted to synthesize a 'fully social theory of deviance' and they did so very much through Marx's preferred style of intellectual labour. *The New Criminology* is largely a work of critique; the first eight chapters of the book are given over to a sustained criticism of liberal criminology, positivism, ecological and anomie theories, labelling theory, interactionism and phenomenology, classical Marxism (including the writings of Marx, Engels and Bonger), and, lastly, conflict theory. This *tour d'horizon* of early and mid-twentieth century criminological thinking remains a useful summary, even if the theoretical predilections of its authors are not widely shared. In the final chapter a 'synthesis' is presented which tries to salvage the useful elements of the theories that preceded 'the new criminology'. Briefly, this synthesis argues that it is axiomatic that capitalism is criminogenic and that a society based on 'socialist diversity' is the only social formation that, in principle, holds out any possibility of being crime-free. For the criminologist then, the goal should be the demise of capitalism and the transformation of society to one of socialist diversity. Anything else, by definition, implicates the

criminologist in 'correctionalism', that is: the coercive use of the criminal sanction to 'correct' behaviour on a personal basis when the roots of crime lie in the social structural inequalities of wealth and power. Their later work (Taylor et al., 1975) was not a significant departure from this line, but in it Jock Young did lay the basis for the argument that working-class control over policing should be greatly extended, an idea that presaged the school of left realism.

In *What is to Be Done About Law and Order?* (Lea and Young, 1984/1993) 'left realists' were to argue that the fatal flaw of the Marxist approaches to criminology had been their failure to offer any realistic solutions to crime, other than emphasizing 'changing the social order'. But Marxist-based criminologies do not succumb to realist criticisms so easily. Steven Box (1983, p. 3) pointed out that 'official crime' was real enough and that 'a radical criminology which appears to deny this will be seen as naive and rightly rejected', but 'before galloping off down the "law and order" campaign trail, it might be prudent to consider whether murder, rape, robbery, assault and other crimes focused on by state officials, politicians, the media and the criminal justice system do constitute the major part of our real crime problem'. He suggested that 'maybe they are only one crime problem and not *the* crime problem'. The clue to 'understanding most serious crimes', Box argued, 'can be located in power, not weakness, in privilege, not disadvantage, in wealth, not poverty'. Further, in another early contribution to the radical perspective, William Chambliss's work *On the Take: From Petty Crooks to Presidents* (1978, Bloomington, IN, Indiana University Press) charted the social composition of racketeering in Seattle showing that the 'hidden hands' in American organized crime were leading lights of the political and economic elite. Extensive field work allowed Chambliss to piece together the links between the front-line operators and the shadowy entrepreneurs who ultimately controlled the crime networks: key personnel in the police force, the legal profession, business, local government and the prosecutor's office. Writing in the late 1970s, Chambliss was able to assert that these connections extended to the highest office in the land. Presidents Nixon and Johnson were said to have substantial dealings with men 'whose business profits derived at least in part from illegal business'. Evidence of the pervasive connections between the 'underworld' and the 'upper world' of the capitalist order seemed ample enough to indicate that criminality was indeed an endemic feature of American capitalism.

Criminologists who follow the lead of Durkheim might maintain that Marxist analyses represent an unnecessary narrowing of concern to the criminogenic properties of capitalist society; 'crime is a normal social fact', it is a feature of *any* social order. Those who wish to draw on insights from the Marxist tradition might argue in turn that, in the contemporary period when free-market liberalism has become hegemonic (to use a Marxist term) globally, this narrowing is not so much the product of theoretical blinkers (that is, the result of idealist assumptions), but rather is the realistic basis on which criminology must inevitably build. In this regard it would do to cite W.G. Carson's *The Other Price of Britain's Oil* (New Brunswick, Rutgers University Press, 1982). Carson's book took as its starting point the unacceptable level of fatal and non-fatal accidents that occurred during the United Kingdom's scramble to develop its off-shore oil and gas reserves. He was moved to remark that it was conditions in the capitalist world economy that 'explain why successive governments would opt to get their hands on the new-found wealth of the Continental Shelf as rapidly as possible and at almost any cost'. It is only by seeing the development of Britain's petroleum extraction industry in the context of global capitalism that 'the troubles endured by those who have been killed or injured in the North Sea can be viewed in terms of the "historical change and institutional contradiction" which earns them anything more than a coincidental place in "the course of world history"'.

The crimes of the powerful remain a significant blind spot for conventional criminology. Yet, if there is any sense in the notion that 'property is theft', there is much criminological work to be done. A significant new frontier is being opened up through the institution of intellectual property. Patent law has been extended in such a way as to allow the ownership of DNA and other biological materials. It has become possible for multinational corporations to 'own' DNA sequences. 'Biopiracy' is a term that has been given to the practices of some companies who have asserted the right of ownership over genetic materials taken from living organisms (Manning, 2000). If the roots of Marxist criminologies can be said to lie in the article on *The Law on Thefts of Wood*, it would seem that the crimes of capitalist accumulation continue to

provide fertile ground for critical scholarship in this field.

James Sheptycki

Associated Concepts: conflict theory, corporate crime, criminalization, critical criminology, labelling, left realism, new criminology, new deviancy theory, radical criminologies

Key Readings
Bankowski, Z., Mungham, G. and Young, P. (1977) 'Radical criminology or radical criminologist?', *Contemporary Crisis*, 1 (1), pp. 37–51.
Box, S. (1983) *Power, Crime and Mystification*. London, Tavistock.
Greenberg, D. (1980) *Crime and Capitalism*. Palo Alto, CA, Mayfield Publishing Company.
Hall, S., Critcher, C., Jefferson, T., Clarke, J. and Roberts, B. (1978) *Policing the Crisis: Mugging, the State and Law and Order*. London, Macmillan.
Lea, J. and Young, J. (1984/1993) *What is to be Done About Law and Order?* Harmondsworth, Penguin.
Manning, P.K. (2000) 'Policing new social spaces', in J.W.E. Sheptycki (ed.), *Issues in Transnational Policing*. London, Routledge.
Taylor, I., Walton, P. and Young, J. (1973) *The New Criminology*. London, Routledge and Kegan Paul.
Taylor, I., Walton, P. and Young, J. (eds) (1975) *Critical Criminology*. London, Routledge and Kegan Paul.

MASCULINITIES

Definition

Variable sets of ideas, values, representations and practices associated with 'being male' which structure relations among men as well as between men and women, and produce effects on individuals, organizations and cultures.

Distinctive Features

The traditional idea of masculinity (in the singular) as a set of psychological attributes was developed to understand differences between the sexes. In its classical psychoanalytic variant, naturally bi-sexual infants are precipitated into sexed identities through the difficulties of coping with the entry of the father into the mother–child dyad. Rather than continue an unequal struggle to take the place of the father, boy children, fearful of the potentially castrating father, forsake desire for the mother and settle for becoming like the father (and hence the culturally masculine he embodies) through identifying with him (which, for Freud, was a difficult and never-completed process). The social psychological variant married research into differences between the sexes (which always found remarkably few) with role theory (how social positions, like father, get reproduced), to produce the idea of male and female sex-roles (or masculinity and femininity), the successful learning of which ensures the cultural reproduction of sexual difference.

Second wave feminists concerned with understanding the oppression of women introduced the importance of power, the idea that the key difference between men and women was the greater power men systematically enjoyed. When the spotlight was turned specifically onto violence, and the maleness of the perpetrators was noticed and named, the notion of masculinity began to enter criminology's field of vision. Men's violence against women was seen as part of the system of male power and a key to its reproduction – hence explaining why domestic violence and rape were often not taken seriously. The early interest in male psychology, whether based in biology, early relationships or the social learning of sex-roles, had shifted to an interest in the social structures of male domination (or patriarchy). This provided the basis for a less individually based understanding of masculinity, but the conception of masculinity informing the work (where there was one) was still a singular one.

The emergence of feminist-inspired, gender-aware historical and ethnographic work on men revealed not only the diverse forms masculinity has taken over time and cross-culturally, but also the co-existence of different forms of masculinity within particular cultures; thus was born the idea of masculinities. And, just as power affects the relations between men and women and masculinity/femininity, so it was seen to affect relations among masculinities. Masculinities were argued to be 'structured in dominance', with the most powerful (or valued), culturally speaking, in any given social order, being 'hegemonic'.

In attempting to understand the complex, contradictory and uneven nature of male domination and thus move beyond the reductiveness of the idea of 'the structure of patriarchy', certain feminist writers had begun to posit several structures underpinning gender relations, each with their own specific forms of oppression and particular historical trajectory. Building on this idea, Connell (1987, 1995), the most influential contemporary writer on masculinities, suggested the existence of three distinct but inter-related structures: labour (to do with work and the division of labour); power (to do with authority, control, coercion and violence); and cathexis (to do with sexuality, emotional relationships and desire). None of these was accorded primacy and all were to be understood as the outcome of practice (albeit always taking place within structured, or constrained, situations). Collectively, the product of these manifold structured practices at any given time was the historical pattern of gender relations: the 'gender order'.

Within criminology, Messerschmidt (1993) has developed these ideas and applied them to thinking about crime. He utilizes Connell's notions of a tripartite structure of gender relations and hegemonic and subordinated masculinities, as well as the importance of practice. In addition, he addresses the structures of race and class by conceptualizing all structures as implicated simultaneously in any given practice, and practice as situationally constrained by the need to 'account' for our actions to normative conceptions (of appropriate gender/race/class conduct). In different situations class, gender or race 'accounting' may be more or less salient. Within this schema, crime becomes a resource for certain men in certain situations for accomplishing masculinity. Its salience for particular men as such a resource will depend on other resources at their disposal, which, in turn, will be a product of their position in class, gender and race relations and the sorts of situations they find themselves in.

Evaluation

Freud thought the concept of masculinity was one of the most 'confused' in science. Unfortunately, pluralizing the term has not eliminated all confusions. In particular, there is a constant tendency to elide men and masculinities, to reduce the latter to lists of attributions, what men do ('take risks', compete, etc.) or should do (be strong, stoical, etc.), as opposed to what women do/should do, rather than use the term consistently in relational terms: as places within gender relations that *only* exist in contrast to femininities. No femininities, no masculinities. No doubt this attributional tendency stems in part from our desire to concretize, to turn abstract relations into definable objects, as well as from the sorts of observable differences between men and women which we encounter daily.

One development of a strictly relational approach has been to see masculinity purely as an ideology developed to help people make sense of the continuation of sexual inequality in an age of formal equality (MacInnes, 1998). Others, like Collier (1998), influenced by debates about embodiment, have attempted to develop relational accounts in a way that puts back the 'sexed' body, but without reverting to a biological essentialism. The relentlessly sociological nature of most contemporary accounts has reawakened an interest in the psychological dimension of masculinity, influenced this time by post-structuralism and the 'object relations' school of psychoanalysis (Jefferson, 1997). Critics of Messerschmidt's attempts to explain the 'doing' of all kinds of crime, from varieties of work-based crime to diverse forms of street crime, as different ways of 'doing' masculinity, have begun to question whether this key idea of his is always *necessary* to explain a particular crime, and, more generally, whether it is *sufficient* as an explanation of *any* crime. The idea of masculinity as a key concept in understanding why most crimes are committed by men was an exciting, post-feminist development. Whether the spate of new writings this idea has generated can surmount the many theoretical confusions intrinsic to it time alone will tell.

Tony Jefferson

Associated Concepts: feminist criminologies, hegemonic masculinity, hegemony, psychoanalytic criminology, radical feminism

Key Readings

Collier, R. (1998) *Masculinities, Crime and Criminology*. London, Sage.
Connell, R.W. (1987) *Gender and Power*. Cambridge, Polity Press.
Connell, R.W. (1995) *Masculinities*. Cambridge, Polity Press.
Jefferson, T. (1997) 'Masculinities and crimes', in M. Maguire, R. Morgan and R. Reiner (eds), *The Oxford Handbook of Criminology*, 2nd edn. Oxford, The Clarendon Press.
MacInnes, J. (1998) *The End of Masculinity*. Buckingham, Open University Press.
Messerschmidt, J.W. (1993) *Masculinities and Crime*. Lanham, MD, Rowman and Littlefield.

MEDIATION

See Reparation; Restorative justice

MORAL ECONOMY

Definition

The concept of the moral economy, in the context of criminal offending, was developed by E.P. Thompson as a means of analysing and explaining eighteenth-century crowd action.

Distinctive Features

Dissatisfied with social tension charts and the reductionist argument that food shortages and high prices led to hunger which, in turn, led to food riots, Thompson looked for the notions that legitimated rioting in the eyes of the participants, the communities that supported them, and the authorities who, for much of the eighteenth century, gave them a measure of licence. He concluded that the men and women in the crowds were motivated by beliefs that they were defending customs or traditional rights. They were not entirely helpless or hopeless, but sensed that they had some power to help themselves and ensure food of decent quality at a fair price. Eighteenth-century rioters rarely took food without payment of some kind, and they would destroy grain or bread to punish a double-dealing farmer, miller or baker, rather than simply taking them. For much of the century landed gentry, eyeing middlemen as profiteering interlopers, were sympathetic to such crowds. A gradual change began with the increasing acceptance of Smithian economics, particularly the importance of the freedom of the marketplace, towards the end of the century, particularly by a government fearing itself threatened by a radicalism that appeared to advocate French revolutionary models.

Evaluation

Criticism was levelled at Thompson's concept of the moral economy, particularly for failure to appreciate nuances in Adam Smith's work and the way in which the market works. After 20 years Thompson replied with customary panache and Swiftian wit. During those 20 years, and subsequently, the idea of the moral economy was also developed by those more sympathetic to his perspective, perhaps most significantly by David Arnold and John Bohstedt. The former traces similar patterns of rioting to that of eighteenth-century England in early twentieth-century India. The latter described how eighteenth-century rioting might be construed as 'community politics'. According to Bohstedt, horizontal and vertical relationship networks within communities were brought into play at different moments of crowd action, and with different results depending on a community's structure. In 1985, following the Broadwater Farm riots in London, Bohstedt published a letter in *The Times* suggesting how these disturbances also needed to be considered in such terms. No historian can now approach crowd action without some acknowledgement of the moral economy concept, yet, as Mark Harrison has warned, there is danger in the way in which crowd and riot have often been conflated in social history, and in seeking to impose a moral economy legitimation to every riot. Disorders, he insists, on occasions looked backward to traditional rights for legitimacy; on others they looked forward to a vision of how society might be in the future, but they could also be spurred by demands to meet changing expectations.

Clive Emsley

Associated Concepts: historical research, Marxist criminologies, primitive rebellion, social justice

Key Readings

Arnold, D. (1979) 'Looting, grain riots and government policy in South India, 1918', *Past and Present*, 84, pp. 111–45.

Bohstedt, J. (1983) *Riots and Community Politics in England and Wales, 1790–1810*. Cambridge, MA, Harvard University Press.

Harrison, M. (1988) *Crowds and History: Mass Phenomena in English Towns, 1790–1835*. Cambridge, Cambridge University Press.

Thompson, E.P. (1991) *Customs in Common*. London, Merlin Press.

MORAL PANIC

Definition

Disproportional and hostile social reaction to a condition, person or group defined as a threat to societal values, involving stereotypical media representations and leading to demands for greater social control and creating a spiral of reaction.

Distinctive Features

Since it appeared in the title of Cohen's (1972) book, the term moral panic has been ubiquitous in criminology and the sociology of deviance. Its many uses to characterize social reaction are too numerous to catalogue but include media coverage of youth, sex, drugs, juvenile crime, single parents, child abuse and diseases of humankind and animals (such as HIV/AIDS, as well as BSE or 'mad cow' disease).

Cohen's work on the moral panic around Mods and Rockers in Britain examines media coverage in the 1960s and the pronouncements of various authorities or experts who defined the 'youth problem' as a symptom of the state of society and social decline. Cohen uses the analogy of a disaster to identify various stages of social reaction. The inventory involves taking stock of what happened, a time at which media descriptions and definitions are crucial since they are the main source for most people's information. Cohen categorized the media inventory of Mods and Rockers in three parts: first, the media exaggerated the numbers involved, the extent of the violence and the amount of damage caused. Distortion of the events was multiplied by the use of sensational headlines and the adoption of a dramatic reporting style, especially in the use of words such as 'orgy of destruction', 'mob' and 'siege'. Secondly, media coverage contained many predictions that there would be more conflict and violence. Thirdly, Cohen argued that media coverage served to re-code or to symbolize deviance through associating the word 'Mod' with particular expressions of style such as clothes and hairstyles. Symbolization leads on to sensitization so that other events that may otherwise have been seen as isolated or un-connected ones are linked into a pattern and understood as symptomatic of the same underlying malaise. Both processes produce an increase in social control responses and Cohen saw this control culture as containing three common elements:

- *Diffusion*, in which events in other places are inter-connected with the initial event.
- *Escalation*, in which there are calls for 'strong measures' to counter the threat.
- *Innovation*, referring to increased powers for the police and courts to deal with the threat.

Various moral entrepreneurs who call for action to be taken against the outbreak of lawlessness usually also proclaim that current controls are inadequate. As Cohen shows, entrepreneurs exaggerate the problem in order to make local events seem ones of pressing national concern, and an index of the decline of morality and standards. The stepping-up of controls leads to further marginalization and stigmatization of deviants which, in turn, leads to more calls for action, more police action and so on into a deviancy amplification spiral. Cohen's analysis located the nature and extent of reaction to Mods and Rockers to the social context of Britain in the 1960s. In particular, ambivalence about social change in the postwar period, the new affluence and freedom of youth cultures and their apparent rejection of traditional forms of incorporation such as work and families are used to contextualize the panic.

The social context of moral panics was developed by Hall et al.'s (1978) analysis of social reaction to 'mugging' or street crime. Working within a Marxist framework, they argued that mugging achieved the prominence it did because its themes of 'race', crime and youth meshed with or crystallized political and economic shifts in the 1970s. Economically, this was a period of crisis in Britain. Politically, Britain's standing in the world continued to decline and, domestically, trade unions, left wingers and the welfare state were blamed for much of the state of 'sick Britain'. New racial discourses were emerging that identified blacks as part of the problem of British society. Concerns about sexual permissiveness and a lack of controls on young people continued from earlier times. In this climate racialized crime statistics were used to draw attention to the problem of disproportionate amounts of street crime committed by young blacks and drove discourses for more law and order to stem the rising tide of crime and to protect innocent victims. Hall et al. argued that this moral panic underscored the development of authoritarian populism in Britain in the 1970s.

Moral panics have been seen as inevitable and periodic occurrences for societies undergoing a reaffirmation or re-definition of moral boundaries. Functionalism has been a recurring feature of moral panic theory, even in its radical applications. In a crude version the reaction is seen as akin to a form of mass delusion where the public is 'duped' into panicking. This tends to over-state the extent of social consensus and to assume a straightforward correspondence between the inten-

tions of an elite and outcomes. In seeking to move beyond this, Goode and Ben-Yehuda (1994) distinguish between three theories or approaches. The grassroots model is where a panic originates from the general public and expresses a genuinely felt, even if mistaken, concern about a threat. The elite-engineered approach is where an elite deliberately and consciously generates concerns and fears. The interest-group theory is where rule-creators and moral entrepreneurs launch crusades for controls. Goode and Ben-Yehuda have distilled five key characteristics of a moral panic:

• disproportionality of reaction;
• concern about the threat;
• hostility to the objects of the panic;
• widespread agreement or consensus that the threat is real;
• volatility, that is, moral panics are unpredictable in terms of scale and intensity.

Evaluation

A moral panic entails simplification, stigmatization and heightened public feeling about an individual, group, or event. Calling this a moral panic draws attention to exaggerated and distorted media coverage and the ways in which it may be seen as symbolizing diffuse social anxieties in particular conjunctures. A wide battery of arguments has been raised against the conceptualization and utilization of moral panics as a way of capturing social reaction. Criticizing Hall et al. (1978) in particular, left realism maintains that crime and the fear of crime should be taken seriously and not dismissed as 'just' an expression of media over-reaction or panic. Waddington (1986) took issue with the empirical basis of *Policing the Crisis*. He argued that, contrary to the view presented in that book, mugging was rising and questions the view that media coverage was disproportionate. Waddington and others have asked what a 'proportionate' reaction would be. The scale of media reaction can rarely be measured or judged in terms of either proportionality or seriousness, as the highly uneven coverage of wars around the world indicates. This casts doubt on one of the central tenets of moral panics.

Problems have also been identified with the use of the concept of moral panic to capture reaction to diverse themes or issues. There is a problem in reducing all episodes of over-reaction to the catch-all notion of 'panickiness'. A more detailed understanding of different types of social reaction, as well as to the very different conditions that seem to constitute moral panics has been called for. Watney (1987), for example, questioned those who used it to characterize media and policy reactions to HIV/AIDS. He argued that moral panic theory is unable to deal with the entire field of representations because it operates with a distinction between exaggerated media representations and the 'reality' of a particular issue, the latter being treated as standing outside the field of representations. Furthermore, there is a problem with the implicit or explicit contrast between the 'irrational' panic and the supposedly 'rational' analysis of it.

McRobbie and Thornton (1995) argued that the idea of moral panic needs to be re-thought in an environment with multiple media outlets and where folk devils are accustomed to presenting alternative frameworks for understanding or explaining an issue or problem. Moral panics, they add, have become routine not exceptional. In an environment where there may be an institutionalized need for the media to generate 'good stories', moral panics can easily become part of a promotional culture that 'ironically' uses sensationalism for commercial purposes.

Karim Murji

Associated Concepts: authoritarian populism, deviance, deviancy amplification, folk devil, labelling, left realism, Marxist criminologies, new deviancy theory, social constructionism, social reaction, stereotyping

Key Readings

Cohen, S. (1972) *Folk Devils and Moral Panics*. London, MacGibbon and Kee. (New edition Oxford, Martin Robertson, 1980.)

Goode, E. and Ben-Yehuda, N. (1994) *Moral Panics: The Social Construction of Deviance*. Oxford, Blackwell.

Hall, S., Critcher, C., Jefferson, T., Clarke, J. and Roberts, B. (1978) *Policing the Crisis*. London, Macmillan.

McRobbie, A. and Thornton, S. (1995) 'Rethinking "moral panic" for multi-mediated social worlds', *British Journal of Sociology*, 46 (4), pp. 559–74.

Waddington, P.A.J. (1986) 'Mugging as a moral panic: a question of proportion', *British Journal of Sociology*, 32 (2), pp. 245–59.

Watney, S. (1987) *Policing Desire: Pornography, Aids and the Media*. London, Methuen.

MULTI-AGENCY CRIME PREVENTION

Definition

The planned, coordinated response of several social agencies to the problems of crime and incivilities. The movement to multi-agency prevention implies that probation/corrections services, education, employment, family services, health and housing, and private bodies such as charities and business, and at times the 'community', as well as the police, all have a role to play in crime prevention.

Distinctive Features

Such initiatives are, for the most part, elements of a 'top-down', managerialist project emanating from neo-liberal states in the past two decades of the twentieth century. This project has also involved the 'local delivery' of crime prevention by means of multi-agency partnerships between statutory agencies, private business and, at times, 'community' initiatives in various 'watch' schemes. In both the academic literature and in policy circles, the terms 'multi-agency' and 'community' crime prevention are often used interchangeably. This is understandable on a number of counts. First, the term 'community' retains its feel-good factor and is thus a useful legitimating, rhetorical device in crime prevention discourses. Secondly, and less cynically, some multi-agency prevention initiatives have sought to adopt a *social* crime prevention approach and attempt to involve members of local communities in their work. However, the key feature to multi-agency crime prevention is that it is chiefly a 'top-down', neo-corporatist strategy from both central and local state regimes.

Multi-agency crime prevention now has the status of a taken-for-granted 'fact of life' in the crime control business across many contemporary states. Popular examples of such multi-agency interventions across the world include both local government- and privately-run CCTV initiatives, play/sports schemes during school holidays, activity-based projects with (potential) young offenders, educational projects on drugs and so on. However, the exact contours of multi-agency crime prevention, not to mention the 'success' of such approaches, remain somewhat unclear. It is impossible to discuss multi-agency crime prevention, or what is increasingly termed 'community safety', without engaging in a debate about the changing modalities of state power in relationship to civil society and 'the public'. Indeed, notions of 'local' and 'central' state are becoming increasingly problematic with the rise of what is often termed 'governance at a distance'. This development is well illustrated by the example of state power being exercised through indirect rather than direct agency, as in the fad for local, preventive 'partnerships against crime'. In this new era, responsibility for setting up and running multi-agency crime prevention initiatives at the local level is increasingly put out to 'tender', inviting bids from rival competitors.

Alongside the emotionally expressive politics of popular punitiveness, the discourse of managerialism has come to play an increasingly important part in the restructuring of criminal justice in most mature capitalist democracies. The managerialist discourse suggests that the organization and coordination of public services are best realized by means of the processes of marketization and the replacement of professionals and bureaucrats by managers. It assumes that better management will prove an effective and economical solution for a wide range of economic and social problems. Indeed it has come to affect the organization and operational work of the police and other agencies of criminal justice and prevention in novel and unprecedented ways. In most multi-agency crime prevention initiatives a managerialist ethos is increasingly to the fore as evidenced in the obsession with 'mission statements', 'performance indicators', measurable 'objectives', 'customer surveys', 'audits' and 'evaluation' and so on, all of which reflect the governmental pressure to be able to count 'what works' in crime and disorder reduction.

Evaluation

Supporters argue for the superiority and success of such corporate and managed approaches over traditional, single-agency prevention approaches. However, academic research has been more circumspect about the success of multi-agency partnerships in crime reduction, highlighting the lack of clarity and conflict about shared goals between the participating agencies and limited, tangible evidence of successful outcomes (Graham and Bennett, 1995). Research has also pointed to the centrality of power differentials between the major agencies involved and the importance of sectional differences within existing communities 'subject' to such multi-agency

cooperation. Furthermore, the conceptual boundaries of multi-agency social crime prevention are particularly vague, encompassing a diversity of schemes under the label. Despite or perhaps because of this 'catch-all' quality to such initiatives, the appeal of multi-agency crime prevention partnerships across contemporary states, faced by both growing rates of crime and disorder and declining trust in traditional crime control responses, is unlikely to wane in the foreseeable future.

Gordon Hughes

Associated Concepts: community crime prevention, community safety, crime prevention, evaluation research, managerialism, realist criminologies, situational crime prevention, social crime prevention

Key Readings

Crawford, A. (1997) *The Local Governance of Crime.* Oxford, The Clarendon Press.

Graham, J. and Bennett, T. (1995) *Crime Prevention Strategies in Europe and North America.* New York, Criminal Justice Press.

Hughes, G. (1997) 'Strategies of crime prevention and community safety in contemporary Britain', *Studies on Crime and Crime Prevention*, 5, pp. 221–44.

O'Malley, P. and Sutton, A. (1997) *Crime Prevention in Australia: Issues in Policy and Research.* Sydney, Federation Press.

Pearson, G., Blagg, H., Smith, D., Sampson, A. and Stubbs, P. (1992) 'Crime, community and conflict: the multi-agency approach', in D. Downes (ed.), *Unravelling Criminal Justice.* London, Macmillan.

MULTIVARIATE ANALYSIS

Definition

Multivariate analysis is, quite simply, the explanation of variation in a dependent variable using more than one independent/explanatory variable. It has three main uses:

1 determining the overall effect of several independent variables on a dependent one;
2 determining the *independent* effect of one variable on another, controlling for the overlapping effects of other variables;
3 statistical control of alternative explanations for the observed effect, for example, control for sampling inadequacies.

Table 1   Age, gender and previous convictions in a mythical survey

Convictions during next year	Total	Age Younger (%)	Older (%)	
Total sample				
None	2450	55.0	75.0	
One	600	17.5	15.8	$\chi^2 = 195.62\ p < 0.001$
Two	480	17.5	12.6	$\phi = 0.31$
More than two	270	10.0	3.9	
Males				
None	1000	40.0	60.0	
One	500	30.0	22.0	$\chi^2 = 159.94\ p < 0.001$
Two	480	17.5	12.6	$\phi = 0.40$
More than two	270	10.0	3.9	
Females				
None	1450	83.3	76.3	
One	100	5.0	5.6	$\chi^2 = 63.30\ p < 0.001$
Two	200	15.0	10.5	$\phi = 0.25$
More than two	150	10.0	5.6	

Distinctive Features

A (zero-order) correlation coefficient estimates the amount of the variation in a dependent variable which is 'explained' by a single independent variable. A multiple correlation coefficient shows the amount 'explained' by a number of variables taken together (in statistics 'explanation' means adequate prediction; it does not necessarily imply and certainly does not prove the identification of a causal mechanism.) A variant of the correlational technique is *partial correlation*, which establishes the amount of variation in a dependent variable explained by an independent one with the effects of one or more other variables held constant – the *independent* effect of the independent variable on the dependent one. Techniques such as multiple regression (see below) allow us to establish the minimum number of variables needed to make as good a prediction of the dependent variable's values as can be achieved with the information that has been collected – the point at which adding more variables to the prediction yields no new information. They also allow us to assess the effect of leaving a given variable out of the prediction – by how much the proportion of variance explained falls – and so to establish the independent effects of each variable and its share in the overall prediction.

The simplest multivariate procedure is tabular analysis, illustrated in Table 1. The first four rows show the relationship between age and criminal conviction for the total sample, and we can see that older people in this mythical sample are less likely than younger people to be convicted during the next year: 75 per cent of older people have no such convictions, compared with 55 per cent of younger people, and 10 per cent of younger people have more than two convictions but only 3.9 per cent of older people. The χ^2 figure on the right is a measure of how far the pattern in the table departs from a random one, and $p < 0.001$ indicates that the relationship is statistically significant – there is less than one chance in a thousand of obtaining a departure as extreme as this by chance alone. ϕ is a correlation coefficient, a measure of the strength of the relationship. The remainder of the table looks at males and females separately. We may note:

1   that women have fewer convictions than men – many more of them have none at all;
2   the relationship of age and conviction rate is significant for both genders; but
3   the ϕ coefficient is much smaller for women than for men, suggesting that the relationship with age is much stronger for men than for women. Tabular analysis is the easiest kind of multivariate analysis to interpret. However, it is relatively crude and insensitive, and it becomes very cumbersome when dealing with more than three or four variables. Other commonly encountered varieties of multivariate analysis include:

- Multiple regression, which combines the effects of different variables into a single predictor of a dependent variable, making allowance for their overlap. Statistics generally produced are the multiple correlation and its statistical significance, the significance of each component variable's contribution and estimates of their independent effects (beta coefficients). Multiple regression needs an interval or ratio-level variable as dependent variable (one where it makes sense to talk about some values as being twice or half others – like money or age or number of previous convictions). Dichotomies (variables with only two values – such as gender) or interval/ratio variables may be used as independent variables.
- Discriminant function analysis, which works in a similar way to multiple regression but will allow categorical variables (e.g. type of crime) as dependent variables.
- Analysis of variance works on categorical independent variables and on an interval/ratio dependent one. It provides an estimate of each variable's independent contribution to the explanation of variance and a similar estimate for each interaction effect (each combination of variables working together).
- Logistic regression permits the sophisticated prediction of categorical variables, combining the strengths of discriminant function analysis, analysis of variance and tabular analysis, but it is sometimes difficult to interpret.

All of these methods, adapted to different kinds of data, are used for the same purposes: to assess the overall effect of several variables on a dependent variable, to assess the independent effect of variables that may be related to each other as well as to the dependent, and/or to control for alternative explanations to the one proposed.

Evaluation

Caution should be taken in interpreting multivariate analyses, however.

- Most of such analyses work by taking account first of the variable which explains the greatest amount of variation, then of the variable that explains the greatest amount of what is left, and so on. The effect of the first variable is therefore sometimes exaggerated because all of the overlap with other variables is attributed to it.
- It is always possible that apparent causal relationships are in fact spurious and due to the effect of some other variable which has not been measured. Statistical control is never as effective in eliminating alternative explanations as control by the design of the study.
- While correlation is necessary for causation, it is not sufficient. There is always a tendency in these analyses to move from prediction to causal explanation, and this is seldom appropriate without additional evidence and argument which cannot be supplied by the analysis itself.

Roger Sapsford

Associated Concepts: causation, correlational analysis, experiments, prediction studies

Key Readings
Hood, R. (1992) *Race and Sentencing*. Oxford, The Clarendon Press.
Sapsford, R.J. (1999) *Survey Research*. London, Sage.

N

NATURAL JUSTICE

Definition

A concept of natural justice emphasizes basic principles necessary to ensure fairness in legal proceedings; principles of justice deriving from the nature of humanity; and principles of justice which would obtain in a state of nature and which are independent of social relationships.

Distinctive Features

Natural justice entails practical applications in law of principles to ensure procedural fairness, in civil as well as criminal proceedings. That is, that no one should be judge in their own cause; and that no one should be condemned without representation.

The first principle has led to procedural rules about vested interests and about the independence of the judiciary; the second mandates a right to legal representation, if necessary paid for by the state.

Is it illogical or nonsensical to describe formally constituted laws as 'unjust'? Officials enforcing pass and residence laws in apartheid South Africa were applying laws enacted by the recognized legislative body, but this does not make the laws 'just'; similarly the rules affecting treatment of Jews in Nazi Germany were passed by parliamentary process and so were 'laws', but we would none the less have no hesitation in describing them as 'unjust'. It follows, therefore, that there must be some quality of 'justice' which is not simply that which is prescribed by law; a quality which can act as a standard by which existing laws and legal systems can be assessed.

Philosophers from the ancients onwards have pondered the essence of natural justice.

To be natural, justice must be derived from characteristics all persons have in common, and which are not derived from the culture and institutions of particular societies; to be natural, justice must be based on characteristics persons have independent of their status, relationships, or individual biographies. Aristotle thought natural justice was revealed by universality: all known societies have some common laws, for example a law of murder. Religious philosophers such as St Thomas Aquinas have seen natural justice as a reflection of the wisdom of God; modern religious theorists have pointed to the common elements in all the major faiths as revealing the divine source of natural justice.

Secular theories have sought the origin of natural justice in the nature of human beings, and have nominated *reason* as the characteristic possessed by all human beings just in virtue of being human. Humans possess reason, and they seek to pursue their own goals. Since the eighteenth century, natural justice theories based on irreducible human characteristics have usually been formulated as rights theories. These have been expressed in idealistic proclamations such as the United States Declaration of Independence in 1776 and the French Declaration of Rights in 1789. More recently, after the Second World War the founding of the United Nations was marked by the Universal Declaration of Human Rights, echoed by the European Convention on Human Rights. Most declarations of rights are embellishments on the common elements of 'life, liberty and the pursuit of happiness'.

Evaluation

Theories of natural justice have been unfashionable for several decades. Awareness of differences in societies' conceptions of rights and justice led to the rise of 'relativism' in social science and 'legal positivism' or 'legal realism' among legal theorists. These perspectives emphasize the social embeddedness of moral rules and the role of legislators and judges in defining justice for any society. In legal theory there is perhaps not so much distance between natural justice and legal positivism positions as between relativists and universalists in social science. The best-known contemporary theorist of natural justice, Finnis (1980), places importance on context and interpretation, while Hart (1994), a leading legal realist, says that valid legal systems necessarily contain some minimum content of natural law.

Natural justice is undergoing a revival in the form of increased adherence to human rights theory and politics. Desire to help those living under oppressive regimes has led to championing of the claims of human rights against inviolability of sovereignty; feminists and those seeking to remove discrimination against ethnic and religious minorities have also drawn on the idea of human rights. Even communitarian theorists and critics of 'cultural imperialism' acknowledge the necessity of universal commitment to fundamental human rights.

Barbara Hudson

Associated Concepts: communitarianism, human rights, social justice

Key Readings

Dworkin, R. (1977) *Taking Rights Seriously*. London, Duckworth.
Finnis, J. (1980) *Natural Law and Natural Rights*. Oxford, Oxford University Press.
Hart, H.L.A. (1994) *The Concept of Law*, 2nd edn. Oxford, Oxford University Press.
Reiman, J. (1990) *Justice and Modern Moral Philosophy*. New Haven, CT, Yale University Press.
Sandel, M. (1998) *Liberalism and the Limits of Justice*, 2nd edn. Cambridge, Cambridge University Press.

NEO-CONSERVATIVE CRIMINOLOGY

Definition

Neo-conservative criminology treats criminality as one of a group of social pathological phenomena, the prevalence of which is due to the corrosive influence of the liberalist modern culture. In terms of criminal justice policy, neo-conservative criminology is oriented on the one hand to the preservation of traditional values and norms and on the other to the promotion of a technocratic rationality that decouples the control of crime from its social and economic aetiology.

Distinctive Features

The term neo-conservative criminology signifies the existence of a close causal relationship between specific theoretical positions on crime and crime control and the neo-conservative political convictions of their authors. The main exponent of neo-conservative criminology is the American James Q. Wilson, a political scientist who has nevertheless greatly influenced criminal justice policy through his widely read writings (for example, he co-authored along with George Kelling (1982) the influential theory of Broken Windows), and his numerous advisory roles during the Reagan and Bush administrations.

Neo-conservative criminology does not amount to a criminological theory. It should rather be understood as a specific application of a broader social engineering perspective that utilizes theoretical, and particularly applied, knowledge in the service of the functional exigencies of the state and the economy. Whilst according to neo-conservative political thought, the economic, technical and managerial achievements of modernity should be safeguarded and further extended, the same does not apply to its ethical and cultural components. Indeed, modernist culture with its emphasis on 'subjective value orientations' and 'expressive self-realization' is held out as undermining the motivational requirements of an 'efficient economy and a rational state administration', namely the individual's willingness to achieve and to obey (Habermas, 1989). In place of such subversive modernist culture, neo-conservatives ask for a revival of tradition and call for 'courage for the past' in the state, schools and family.

The functional logic which lies behind their justification of traditionalism in terms of its beneficial effects for the system can also be discerned in certain other central features of neo-conservative thinking. Neo-conservatives urge the state to withdraw to activities it can effectively control – so as to lessen legitimation problems. They, moreover, recommend a greater detachment of administration from public will-formation so as to minimize the burden of democratic participation on controversial issues concerning socio-political goals.

The influence of neo-conservative political thinking can be easily traced in the specific understanding of crime and deviance that is characteristic of neo-conservative criminology. The latter elevates the moral culture of a society to a key (if not *the* key) variable for the explanation of long-term changes in the levels of criminality and disorder. A central proposition of neo-conservative criminology is that the propensity of people to commit crimes varies in accordance to the extent to which they have internalized a commitment to self-control. This in turn depends on the level of a society's investment in promoting self-control (through its socialization mechanisms) as well as on the (not necessarily unchangeable) genetic and biological characteristics of individuals, which determine the effectiveness of the conditioning process in specific cases. Existing high levels of criminality and disorder are thus causally linked to the weakening strength of the sources of social authority, namely family, schools, religion and so forth, and even more so to the corrosive influence of the surrounding culture which 'emphasizes rights rather than rightness of behaviour' and which celebrates self-expression – to the point of self-indulgence – instead of promoting self-control and self-restraint.

In view of the detrimental effects of this expressive individualism neo-conservatives attempt to redefine what properly constitutes the private sphere. Forms of behaviours and individual choices that have broader social ramifications cannot, in their opinion, be treated as wholly private matters, but instead call for a public response. The use of drugs, disorderly behaviour, specific choices concerning the family structure (single mothers, and the ways children are raised) should accordingly not be dealt with on the basis of the liberal principle of moral neutrality but require an affirmative moral stance. Hence neo-conservative strong opposition to the decriminalization of 'victimless crimes', the espousal by them of a 'zero tolerance' approach to disorderly behaviour, their proposals about introducing specific disincentives for single mothers, and so on.

The rather comprehensive conception of the good which this neo-conservative stance embodies reflects 'a healthy appreciation of tradition', that is, the need to exploit those traditional values and institutions on which the public order and stability of the social and economic structure depend.

However, the 'functional traditionalist' streak of neo-conservative criminology should not allow us to overlook its strong technocratic orientation which is apparent in its attempts to rationalize the administration of the criminal justice system. Efficiency and effectiveness in the pursuit of clearly prescribed and realistic goals is the main, if not the sole, criterion for the choice amongst alternative policies of crime control. If the curbing of drug use is the goal, then one should concentrate on the drug users that 'can be saved' with less cost (that is, the first time users). To 'avoid wasted resources and dashed hopes' attention should, moreover, be concentrated to those areas 'where the public order is deteriorating but not unreclaimable' as well as to the careful selection of high-risk repeat offenders 'for arrest, prosecution and incarceration'.

However, as Wilson, the author of the above quotes, points out, existing criminological theories are generally of little use for the specification of the precise points and methods of effective intervention. Being preoccupied with causal analysis, (with the identification of the root or ultimate causes of crime), these theories draw our attention to factors that cannot be changed at all or can only be changed with great difficulty. The development of reasonable policy alternatives is instead thought to require 'patient trial and error, accompanied by hard-headed and objective evaluations' (Wilson, 1985, pp. 253–4). The implicit identification of social and policy analysis with policy-making entails a shift of focus away from the pursuit of the 'utopian' goal of tackling the root causes of crime and towards the achievement of 'marginal gains' (gains that are compatible with the existing constraints of the contemporary social and economic system).

Evaluation

Neo-conservative criminology undoubtedly contributes to the rationalization of the criminal justice system. It does so by placing a heavy premium on the efficient handling of urgent 'policy' problems and by advocating a kind of social analysis that is of direct relevance to the resolution of such problems. However, the instrumental type of (applied) analysis they advocate leaves no room for a serious probing of the normative questions involved in the development of criminal justice policy. 'Political' policies tend to be treated as managerial ones and to be evaluated in terms of their effectiveness with respect to certain goals: namely goals that are derivable from factual 'needs' and are thus essentially beyond choice.

The tendency, furthermore, of neo-conservative criminology to clearly demarcate causal analysis from policy analysis and policy-making leads to a lowering of expectations with regard to crime prevention and control, to the pursuit of marginal gains primarily through a fight against symptoms and to the abandonment of attempts to tackle the root causes of crime. The extent to which the latter is necessary or unavoidable remains an open question. Attempts to remove the root causes of criminality are portrayed by neo-conservative criminology as utopian in view of a variety of more or less 'objective' biological, social, economic, political and technical constraints. However, many of such constraints may themselves be manufactured and thus are in principle solvable. Causal analysis can direct our attention to new possible fields of intervention and change, which policy-related research, inextricably linked – as it is – to the requirements of the policy-maker, is bound to exclude from its agenda.

Finally, the selective attention of neo-conservative criminology to the moral culture of contemporary society as a major cause of existing levels of crime, as well as an appropriate field of intervention, is open to serious criticism. The importance attached to culture as a causal factor – largely on the basis of speculation rather than firm evidence – is dictated by the same functional logic which runs through neo-conservative writings. Modernist culture is examined by the neo-conservatives solely from the point of view of its functional role as an element of the 'pattern maintenance' of the system. But attempts to restore traditional values and norms are themselves utopian. Traditional (familial) values (to take only one example), cannot be restored without 'turning back the clock of modernization' (for example, by undoing the social, political and economic processes, which have historically led to a change of the female role and family relationships). As has succinctly been pointed out: 'precisely the fact that today tradition must be invoked shows that it has lost its power' (Horkheimer, 1974, cited in Habermas, 1989, p. 44).

An important question is, moreover, raised concerning the extent of the legitimation of the particular normative preferences of neo-conservative criminology. The functional understanding and use of values does not necessarily provide the legitimation for them being imposed on society's members. There have to also be other, morally philosophically valid, reasons for attempting the refurbishing of fading values.

Tonia Tzannetakis

Associated Concepts: actuarialism, administrative criminology, 'broken windows', managerialism, rational choice theory, realist criminologies, situational crime prevention, underclass

Key Readings
Habermas, J. (1989) *The New Conservatism*. Cambridge, Polity Press.
Wilson, J.Q. (1985) *Thinking about Crime*. New York, Vintage.
Wilson, J.Q. and Herrnstein, R.J. (1985) *Crime and Human Nature: The Definitive Study of the Causes of Crime*. New York, Simon and Schuster.
Wilson, J.Q. (1991) *On Character: Essays by James Q. Wilson*. Washington, DC, A.E.I. Press.
Wilson, J.Q. and Kelling, G. (1982) 'Broken windows', *Atlantic Monthly*, March, pp. 29–38.
Young, J. (1994) 'Incessant chatter: recent paradigms in criminology', in *The Oxford Handbook of Criminology*. Oxford, The Clarendon Press, pp. 69–124.

NET WIDENING

Definition

The processes whereby attempts to prevent crime and develop community-based corrections act to expand the criminal justice system and draw more subjects into its remit.

Distinctive Features

In the 1970s diversion became a widely acclaimed strategy for reducing the numbers of offenders, particularly young offenders, from appearing in court and thereby avoiding the stigma and labelling of judicial processes. Sentencing alternatives such as probation and community supervision were also intended to reduce the use and cost of custody. However, it was repeatedly found that while 'alternatives' have burgeoned, so have prison populations. Moreover, the very existence of apparently benign and welfare-based options has increased the numbers subject to some form of official, rather than informal, intervention. In California, for example, increasing the proportion of offenders placed on probation was encouraged by providing state funds (a subsidy) to the counties for not committing cases to state institutions. However Lerman's (1975) assessment of the subsidy programme found that many probationers were subsequently sent into custody for probation violations. Moreover, those not recommended for probation were receiving longer sentences. He suggests that the creation of new 'diversionary' measures achieved no long-term decarceration and ultimately expanded the numbers subject to various forms of official surveillance and detention. This resulted not just from courtroom decisions but from an increased willingness on the part of social workers to use their discretionary power to intervene on the offender's behalf. A Canadian study, which examined the effects of community corrections programmes introduced in Saskatchewan from 1962 to 1979, concluded that not only had these failed to reduce the size of the prison population, they actually resulted in a three-fold increase in the proportion of persons under formal state control. Similarly, the National Evaluation of the Deinstitutionalization of Status Offenders project in the USA reported that the programmes were so clearly biased to heighten the intake of less serious offenders, that many more were caught up in the referral network than if the project had not been established.

Stanley Cohen (1979) described such processes as 'thinning the mesh' and 'widening the net'. Allied to his wider 'dispersal of discipline' thesis, Cohen contended that as control mechanisms are dispersed from custody into the community they penetrate deeper into the social fabric. A blurring of boundaries between the deviant and non-deviant and between the public and the private occurs. A 'punitive archipelago' is expanded as new resources, technology and professional interests are applied to an increasing number of 'clients' and 'consumers'. Entrepreneurs are drawn into the control enterprise in search of profits. Communities are mobilized to act as voluntary control agents in their own right. But, throughout, the prison remains at the core of the system. The rhetoric of diversion and community camouflages what is really going on. Rather, alternatives to prison and crime prevention policies have failed to reduce the reach of criminal justice and tend to draw more people into the mesh of formal control:

- Petty or 'potential' delinquents are subject to more intrusive and disguised control in the name of diversion or prevention.
- As the soft end of the system appears more and more benign, so the hard core appears more hopeless and becomes a target for such policies as selective incapacitation.
- Whole populations are subjected to further and subtler involvement in the business of social control. They are made the object of preventive social control before any deviant act can take place.

For Cohen (1985, p. 37) and Austin and Krisberg (1981) the real effect of diversion and decarceration is to increase the reach and intensity of state control:

- The criminal justice system expands and draws more people into its reach (net widening).
- The level of intervention, involving individualized treatment and indeterminate sentencing, intensifies (net strengthening).
- Institutions are rarely replaced or radically altered but supplemented by new forms of intervention (different nets).

Evaluation

These readings of criminal justice reform have been challenged in various ways as one-dimensional, unduly pessimistic and nihilistic. Indeed Cohen's (1985) later reflection on this 'nothing works' mentality concedes that the intentions of 'doing good' are not automatically misguided. Specific policies at particular times may have a positive and progressive effect – that there remains some possibility 'for realizing preferred values'. He eventually argues for a slightly different reading of net widening which would allow 'sensitivity to success (however ambivalent)'. McMahon (1990, p. 144) also points out that the concept only directs attention towards expansionary trends and draws attention away from 'any moderation of penal control which may have taken place and from the superseding of some previous forms of penal control by preferable ones'. Nevertheless, the concept continues to serve as a reminder of the unintended consequences of some criminal justice reform, particularly when that reform is couched in terms of 'zero tolerance', the need for early (pre-criminal) intervention or as acting in the 'best interests' of others.

John Muncie

Associated Concepts: bifurcation, carceral society, community corrections, decarceration, diversion, social control

Key Readings

Austin, J. and Krisberg, B. (1981) 'Wider, stronger and different nets: the dialectics of criminal justice reform', *Journal of Research in Crime and Delinquency*, 18 (1), pp. 165–96.

Cohen, S. (1979) 'The punitive city: notes on the dispersal of social control', *Contemporary Crises*, 3 (4), pp. 341–63.

Cohen, S. (1985) *Visions of Social Control*. Cambridge, Polity Press.

Lerman, P. (1975) *Community Treatment and Social Control*. Chicago, University of Chicago Press.

McMahon, M. (1990) 'Net-widening: vagaries in the use of a concept', *British Journal of Criminology*, 30 (2), pp. 121–49.

NEUTRALIZATION, TECHNIQUES OF

Definition

A distinctive set of justifications that enables individuals temporarily to drift away from the normative rules and values of society and engage in delinquent behaviour. This social psychological 'social control' perspective was developed by Gresham Sykes and David Matza to challenge overly deterministic, positivistic subcultural theories of crime which denied agency and rationality.

Distinctive Features

Delinquents, according to Sykes and Matza, rather than forming a subculture that stands in opposition and antagonism to the dominant social order, 'drift' in and out of deviant activity. The division between 'deviant' and 'respectable' is not hard and fast and delinquents are conceived of as choice-makers who move between and have to negotiate these two interconnected worlds. The proof of this is the fact that delinquents often voice a sense of guilt and/or shame about their actions; frequently convey respect for law-abiding citizens; and regularly draw the line between those who can be victimized and those who cannot. Delinquents are not immune to the demands of the dominant social order; are not delinquent all of the time; and do not necessarily conceive of themselves as criminals.

Because they are intimately connected to a normative value system that is flexible and provides 'qualified guides for action', delinquents can develop a set of techniques or rationalizations to neutralize and temporarily suspend commitment to these values and construct the freedom to engage in deviant acts to cope with the moral dilemmas posed by their actions, and to retain their self esteem and non-criminal self-image. For Sykes and Matza learning the following techniques of neutralization lessens the effectiveness of social controls and enables the individual to become delinquent or justify her/his delinquency:

1 The denial of responsibility ('I did not mean to do it').
2 The denial of injury ('No one was hurt').
3 The denial of the victim ('She started it').
4 The condemnation of the condemners ('They are just as bad').
5 The appeal to higher loyalties ('I was helping my friends').

These techniques assert the rightfulness and normality of the behaviour and are extensions of commonly accepted motivational accounts that are in use in everyday life. Matza subsequently incorporated this thesis into his 'drift' theory of juvenile delinquency, proposing that the techniques of neutralization are the means through which individuals get 'episodic release' from established moral constraints and can drift into and out of delinquency.

Evaluation

There have been remarkably few empirical evaluations of neutralization theory. The thesis has been developed generally by Agnew (1994) whilst Coleman (1994) has reworked it conceptually in the context of researching white collar criminality. Stan Cohen (1993) has provided criminology with one of the most innovative applications of Sykes and Matza's techniques in his argument that they are present in official state discourses concerning human rights violations and state crime. Critics of Sykes and Matza, such as Katz (1987), continue to insist that certain types of committed criminals have different values and that neutralization is unnecessary. There is also still a major debate about whether delinquents and criminals engage in neutralization (before the event) or ad hoc rationalization (after the event).

Eugene McLaughlin

Associated Concepts: appreciative criminology, rational choice theory, subculture

Key Readings

Agnew, R. (1994) 'The techniques of neutralization and violence', *Criminology*, 32, pp. 555–79.

Cohen, S. (1993) 'Human rights and crimes of the state', *Australian and New Zealand Journal of Criminology*, 26 (2), pp. 97–115.

Coleman, J.W. (1994) *The Criminal Elite: The Sociology of White Collar Crime*. New York, St Martins Press.

Katz, J. (1987) *Seductions of Crime: Moral and Sensual Attractions in Doing Evil*. New York, Basic Books.

Matza, D. (1964) *Delinquency and Drift*. New York, Wiley.

Sykes, G.M. and Matza, D. (1957) 'Techniques of neutralization: a theory of delinquency', *American Sociological Review*, 22, pp. 664–70.

NEW CRIMINOLOGY

Definition

A form of radical criminology which first came to fruition in the UK in the early 1970s. It was designated 'new' because of its then novel attempt to fuse an interactionist approach to deviance focusing on personal meaning with a structural approach grounded in the analysis of political economy, class relations and state practices. It is widely cited as marking the beginnings of a critical criminology.

Distinctive Features

The term originates from a book of the same name authored by Ian Taylor, Paul Walton and Jock Young and published in 1973. It was the product of discussions and developments inspired by the National Deviancy Conference established in 1968 as a forum for critical analysis. Much of the book is a sustained critique of classical and positivist criminologies as well as of interactionism, labelling and classical Marxism. A final chapter, however, attempts a synthesis of several of these different theoretical traditions under the rubric of a fully social theory of deviance. The new criminology advocates that such a theory must include the connections between:

- *the wider origins of the deviant act* (the economic and political contingencies of advanced industrial society);
- *the immediate origins of the deviant act* (the interpretation and meaning given to deviance by individuals);
- *the actual act* (the rationality of individual acts and the social dynamics surrounding them);
- *the immediate origins of social reaction* (the contingencies and conditions crucial to the decision to act against the deviant);
- *the wider origins of deviant reaction* (the political and ideological concerns of the state);
- *the outcome of social reaction on the deviant's further action* (the conscious decisions made by an individual to respond to sanctions);
- *the nature of the deviant process as a whole* (the necessity to integrate all elements of the deviant process while being alive to the conditions of social determination and self-determination).

However, *The New Criminology* was not only an attempt to develop the parameters of an adequate criminological theory; it was also designed to promote a form of radical politics. Its insistence that inequalities and divisions in material production and ownership are intrinsically related to the social factors producing crime, brought notions of the possibility of a crime-free society to the fore: a society based on principles of socialist diversity and tolerance. The intention, then, was also to construct the parameters of a radical praxis. Any criminology not committed to 'the abolition of inequalities of wealth and power' was bound to be ultimately reducible to the interests of the economically and politically powerful. Above all, the new criminology sought to illustrate how crime was politically and economically constructed through the capacity and ability of state institutions within the political economy of advanced capitalism, to define and confer criminality on others. The study of crime could no longer be compartmentalized in a world of pathologies, deviances and otherness, but was to be used as a means through which the exploitative machinations of the state could be exposed. The new criminology opened a door through which valuable insights could be made, not into crime *per se*, but into how society works, how social order is maintained and how such order could be subjected to political challenge.

Evaluation

This politicization of criminology was in many ways a logical extension of the critical questioning of social science and its role in research, teaching and policy-making that had emerged in the 1960s. Becker (1967) brought such questioning directly into criminology and the sociology of deviance by asking social scientists: 'Whose side are you on?' Social science in general, and individual positivism in particular, were charged with lending the state a spurious legitimacy and functioning as little more than a justification for oppressive power. What the new criminology managed to achieve was a radical reconstitution of criminology as part of a more comprehensive sociology of the state and political economy, in which questions of political and social control took precedence over behavioural and correctional issues. By the mid-1970s such reflections on the construction of crime became pivotal in the formulation of a *critical criminology*. When the task of criminology was defined as one of creating a society 'in which the facts of human diversity are not subject to the power to criminalize' (Taylor et al., 1973, p. 282), it was clear that criminology was being transformed from a science of social control and into a struggle for social justice.

Such critical analysis was indeed influential in awakening interest in analysis of the role of the law in capitalism, in particular spawning a series of revisionist histories of the relationships between what counted as 'crime', class position and systems of punishment. Such complexities could not be addressed, for example, by an uncritical adoption of the economic and material determinism of Marxism. A major stumbling block in the synthesis of Marxism, interactionism and labelling was that the concerns of criminology and its continuing observance of the concept of 'crime' do not represent a theoretical field of study within Marxism. Rather crime is an ideological category generated by state agencies and intellectuals. For many Marxist scholars the new criminological agenda was limited because there could be no such thing as a Marxist criminology. Retaining the concept of crime as the key referent inevitably laid open the possibility of collusion with state-sponsored definitions of undesirable behaviours. It was noticeable too that the new criminology retained a gender-specific mode of analysis and failed to encompass the then emergent field of gender studies or to include any reference to women and crime in its analysis. From a left realist perspective, subsequently developed by one of the original authors of the new criminology, it has been further claimed that the pursuit of structural change and a tolerance of diversity are idealist and utopian. A lack of political pragmatism and failure to be policy prescriptive offer little

of practical help to those on the receiving end of repressive control systems or to those members of the working class who suffer most from the effects of everyday criminal actions. Nevertheless the new criminology's programme of focusing on agency and structure, and on the micro as well as the macro social world, arguably created a vital space from which a whole range of critical, feminist and left realist positions could subsequently emerge.

John Muncie

Associated Concepts: critical criminology, left idealism, left realism, Marxist criminologies, new deviancy theory, radical criminologies

Key Readings

Becker, H. (1967) 'Whose side are we on?', *Social Problems*, 14 (3), pp. 239–47.
Taylor, I., Walton, P. and Young, J. (1973) *The New Criminology*. London, Routledge.
Taylor, I., Walton, P. and Young, J. (eds) (1975) *Critical Criminology*. London, Routledge.
Walton, P. and Young, J. (eds) (1998) *The New Criminology Revisited*. Basingstoke, Macmillan.

NEW DEVIANCY THEORY

Definition

A theoretical position which emphasizes micro-sociological explanations of the ways in which deviance is generated in interactions between individuals and law enforcement agents, with particular reference to the process of labelling and deriving from symbolic interactionism.

Distinctive Features

New deviancy theory emerged in the 1960s and early 1970s as part of a radical response to the positivist domination of criminology. New deviancy attempted to recover the 'meaning' in human behaviour denied in positivism. It had a number of influences and strands including interactionism (derived from George Herbert Mead's writings on symbolic interactionism), labelling theory and the ethnographic tradition of social research.

The main features of new deviancy theory are as follows. There is emphasis on social action as free, creative and spontaneous rather than something which is determined by individual predispositions or by external and all-constraining social reality. Social interactions, institutions and structures do have a limiting influence on individuals but at one and the same time they are the constructions of these individuals. Individuals and categories of individuals have the capacity to bring their own meanings to interactions, institutions and structures and there is the potential – indeed, certainty – that there will be a multiplicity of meanings and interpretations. Social order is therefore characterized by plurality rather than a naturally occurring consensus. Different groups and sections of society will have their own norms and values and there may be conflict between these. Such conflict may be characterized by the exercise of power by one group over another in order to impose its value system. This may be done via repressive institutions such as the police and the penal system and more subtly by ideological apparatus such as the media.

The influence of labelling theory within new deviancy can be seen in terms of conceptions of what is, and is not, crime and deviance. A favoured dictum is that crime and deviance are that which is labelled as such. This can happen at a societal level in terms of law enactment and the definitions in legislation of certain kinds of acts as 'criminal'; and it can happen at street level in terms of the ways in which law is enforced by individual police officers. The latter involves a consideration of the meanings officers attach to others' actions and of the ways in which they lie within or outwith the law, as they interpret it, and in the particular circumstances of the time.

New deviancy theory does not have a conception of crime as a distinct and separate phenomenon which is perpetrated by a category of people who are 'criminals'. Nor does it explain the criminality of such people by reference to individual predispositions to crime or other causal determinants. Rather, crime is ubiquitous and criminals are evenly distributed across society. In order to explain crime and its distribution and to understand how and why categories of people become criminal it is necessary to examine definitional and labelling processes. For new deviancy theorists this involves a focus on agents of social control and institutions of criminal justice and not a sole preoccupation with the offender and his or her antecedents. In this endeavour key concepts from interactionist perspectives are enlisted such as 'meaning', 'social definition', 'label', 'stereotype', 'social reaction' and 'deviancy amplification'.

Methodologically, new deviancy typically employs ethnographic methods of research on the grounds that they are much more compatible with such concepts. Ethnographic research can facilitate direct and natural observation of interactions between would-be offenders and law enforcers and can employ unstructured methods of interview and documentary analysis to uncover the meanings, labels and stereotypes employed in the everyday practices of criminal justice personnel.

Policy implications of new deviancy flow from the assumptions that there can be a plurality of equally valid perspectives: that crime is what is labelled as such; and that social reaction and social control are what generate crime. Such implications can include increased tolerance of the diversity and plurality of cultural values and forms of action in society: official de-bunking of popular but inaccurate stereotypes of crime and criminals; decriminalization of certain forms of action; and non-intervention in events and actions on the part of control agencies.

Evaluation

The contributions of new deviancy theory are numerous. For example, in its emphasis on interactions, labelling and social construction it offers a reminder that crime is a social concept rather than something which is 'fixed' and 'given'. It also encourages an examination of definitional issues in law enactment *and* in the enforcement of law and criminal justice personnel. Methodologically it provides an alternative perspective on official crime statistics to that provided by positivist approaches. This perspective encourages a view of crime statistics as the outcome of criminal justice policies and practices rather than valid indicators of the 'true' extent of crime.

One key danger of adopting a new deviancy framework is that of treating the notion of social construction of crime as a universal 'covering law' (that is, one which covers or explains all forms of action deemed to be criminal). There are certain kinds of crimes, such as rape and paedophilia, where individual pathologies are likely to have a great deal of credence as explanations. What is more, the victims of these and other crimes are unlikely to take kindly to offences committed against them being treated as mere social constructions (within which the *offender* may be treated as the victim). The critique that new deviancy theory fails to face up to the fact that crime, and fear of crime is experienced as a reality by many, tends to come from those who advocate realist criminological thinking.

Victor Jupp

Associated Concepts: deviance, ethnography, interactionism, labelling, radical criminologies, social constructionism

Key Readings

Becker, H. (1963) *Outsiders: Studies in the Sociology of Deviance*. Glencoe, IL, Free Press.
Sumner, C. (1994) *The Sociology of Deviance: An Obituary*. Buckingham, Open University Press.
Young, J. (1990) 'Thinking seriously about crime: some models in criminology', in M. Fitzgerald, G. McLennan and J. Pawson (eds), *Crime and Society: Readings in History and Theory*. London, Routledge in association with The Open University Press, pp. 248–310.

NEWSMAKING CRIMINOLOGY

Definition

The processes whereby criminologists use mass communication for the purposes of interpreting, informing and altering the images of crime and justice, crime and punishment, and criminals and victims.

Distinctive Features

Gregg Barak (1988) first used the term 'newsmaking criminology' to explore the relationships between the study and production of crime news and the interaction by criminologists and others involved in the processes of mass communication. Like students of crime and media generally, students of newsmaking criminology are concerned with the degrees of distortion and bias in the news, or with the distance between the social reality of crime and the newsmaking reality of crime. Like other analysts of the news media, newsmaking criminologists are similarly interested in seeing that the news media 'tell it like it is', and better yet, 'like it could be' or 'like it should be', based on an informed scientific view of crime and justice (Barak, 1994).

The concept of newsmaking criminology refers to criminologists' conscious efforts and activities in interpreting, influencing, or shaping the presentation of information or of 'newsworthy' items about crime and justice. Newsmaking criminology attempts to demystify images of crime and punishment by locating these in the context of all illegal and harmful behaviour; it strives to affect public attitudes, thoughts and discourse about crime and justice so as to affect social policies of crime control; and it encourages criminologists to find their public voices and to come forth and share their knowledge of crime and justice as creditable spokespeople. In short, newsmaking criminology is about analysing, participating and ideally impacting the mass-mediated, socially constructed and collectively consumed images of crime and justice. Several styles of newsmaking criminology have been identified, including: (1) disputing data; (2) challenging journalism; (3) self-reporting; and (4) confronting media (Henry, 1994). Each of these styles possesses strengths and weaknesses for newsmaking criminologists. As newsmaking criminology continues to develop, its strategies have been fine-tuned (Barak, 1996) and its methods have expanded. For example, as the World Wide Web grows in the dissemination of mass communication, it is changing the manner in which we both offer and seek information on a daily basis. Today, news groups, political organizations, criminal justice agencies, criminology associations and individual criminologists, all make use of the Web in order to influence and shape public knowledge and attitudes about crime and justice (Greek, 1997; Greek and Henry, 1997).

Evaluation

The ultimate value of newsmaking criminology still remains to be seen. In terms of criminologists having a strong influence over the social construction of crime and justice, this appears to vary by nation-state and the role of public intellectuals in particular societies. At the same time, newsmaking criminology has already raised the consciousness of criminologists about the processes of newsmaking and about their interactive roles with the mass-mediated images of crime and justice, whether these be in the areas of researching, teaching, or newsmaking *per se*.

Gregg Barak

Associated Concepts: constitutive criminology, cultural criminology, social constructionism

Key Readings

Barak, G. (1988) 'Newsmaking criminology: reflections on the media, intellectuals, and crime', *Justice Quarterly*, 5 (4), pp. 265–87.

Barak, G. (ed.) (1994) *Media, Process, and the Social Construction of Crime: Studies in Newsmaking Criminology*. New York, Garland.

Barak, G. (1996) 'Media, discourse, and the O.J. Simpson trial: an ethnographic portrait', in G. Barak (ed.), *Representing O.J.: Murder, Criminal Justice, and Mass Culture*. Guilderland, NY, Harrow and Heston.

Greek, C. (1997) 'Using the Internet as a newsmaking criminology tool'. Paper presented at the annual meetings of the American Society of Criminology, San Diego.

Greek, C. and Henry, D.B. (1997) 'Criminal justice resources on the Internet', *Journal of Criminal Justice Education*, 8, pp. 91–9.

Henry, S. (1994) 'Newsmaking criminology as replacement discourse', in G. Barak (ed.), *Media, Process, and the Social Construction of Crime: Studies in Newsmaking Criminology*. New York, Garland.

NORMALIZATION

Definition

Implicit in the term is the idea of the normal. Whilst the normal has meaning in statistical terms it is inflected with ideas of what is traditional and cultural. It conflates what is with what ought to be. A normal distribution suggests a spread around the mean but it also predicts values at and beyond standard deviations either side of the mean. Thus a standardized deviance is expected yet normal comes to be associated with the 'mean'. A conservative might speak of normalization meaning a return to order after a temporary and unexpected disorder. A radical take on the same process might emphasize the price paid by the 'normalized'. Military humour mixes the two in the abbreviation SNAFU – Situation Normal, All Fucked Up!

Within criminology theoretical usage of the term is derived from Foucault's 'dispositifs de normalization'. However, the term is also used in a variety of contexts, including in the debate about whether drug use has become normalized or in describing attempts to bring prison regimes into line with human rights outside the prison.

Distinctive Features

For Foucault (1975) the disciplines of psychiatry, medicine and criminology produce knowledge about and exercise power over the subject. That power may sometimes be to incarcerate or exclude but it works most effectively when internalized and acted upon by the self-policing, docile body – bio-politics. We know it is 'normal' to be sane, non-criminal, heterosexual, slim, hard-working and so on. It is this knowledge as much as – and often more than – the power that renders the subject docile. However, just as the disciplines produce – rather than simply attempt to repress – deviance as a category they also create resistance. Thus the 'criminal' and the 'homosexual' are brought into being. Their resistance may take the form of denying that they are deviant through 'techniques of neutralization' or by embracing and flaunting the disciplinary norms – black pride, gay pride.

In a self-report study of criminologists and criminal justice practitioners, Robinson and Zaitzow (1999) found 66 per cent reported driving under the influence of alcohol or drugs at some time and 35 per cent within the past year. Only slightly fewer (60 per cent) had used illegal drugs at some time, with 27 per cent reporting recent use. One-third had bought drugs and 11 per cent admitted to selling them. Thus crime can be seen to be normal – statistically expected and measurable. However, it is more arguable whether crime is normalized. It is from this position of complicity that criminologists have, for example, engaged in the debate – with politicians and practitioners – about whether drug use in society or amongst young people has become normalized.

Evaluation

Britain may have waged war in the past with China to force the opium trade on them, but now – like the USA – it sees itself at war with drugs. Or, at least, this is the official line. Shiner and Newburn (1999) open their discussion of the issue by noting the furore in January 1997 over the comments of a number of pop stars about drug use. Noel Gallagher, of the UK rock group Oasis, declared in the *New Musical Express* (29 January 1997) that 'the majority of people in this country take drugs ... like getting up and having a cup of tea'. This confirms the claim of Parker et al. (1995) that for young people taking drugs has become the norm and that non-drug-taking can be seen as deviant. Yet Shiner and Newburn draw on UK and USA data to argue convincingly that whilst drug taking was common amongst young people it was not the norm and that substantial numbers continue to 'say no to drugs' and disapprove of their use.

However, it could be argued that Shiner and Newburn accept too readily the distinction between legal and illegal drugs and fail to take sufficient account of cultural aspects. Using figures for both prescribed and over-the-counter medicines it is possible to argue that there is a cultural expectation of using a 'pill for every ill' amongst the whole population. In this scenario tea, coffee, alcohol, Prozac, Ecstasy and aspirin are all used to get people through their life. Moreover, popular culture and the media are saturated with references to drug use and culture. For instance, a bicycle advertisement punningly asks, 'what's he on?'.

The debate about normalization of drugs often turns on definitional issues about what is *or* should count as normal. Similarly, the argument for the normalization of prison regimes (Feest, 1999) or of policing (Mulcahy, 1999) assumes the normality of the comparator being used. Thus, in a carceral society – returning to Foucault – can we simply compare regimes inside prison with those obtain-ing outside? Is the policing, say, of London normal enough for that of Belfast to be compared to it?

Nic Groombridge

Associated Concepts: deviance, neutralization (techniques of), pathology

Key Readings

Feest, J. (1999) 'Imprisonment and prisoners' work: normalization or less eligibility', *Punishment and Society*, 1 (1), pp. 99–107.

Foucault, M. (1975) *Surveiller et punir*. Paris, Gallimard.

Mulcahy, A. (1999) 'Visions of normality: peace and reconstruction of policing in Northern Ireland', *Social and Legal Studies*, 8 (2), pp. 277–95.

Parker, H., Measham, F. and Aldridge, J. (1995) *Drugs Futures: Changing Patterns of Drug Use amongst English Youth*. London, Institute for the Study of Drug Dependency.

Robinson, M.B. and Zaitzow, B.H. (1999) 'Criminologists: are we what we study? A national self-report study of crime experts', *The Criminologist*, 24 (2), pp. 1, 4, 17–19.

Shiner, M. and Newburn, T. (1999) 'Taking tea with Noel: the place and meaning of drug use in everyday life', in N. South (ed.), *Drugs: Cultures, Controls and Everyday Life*. London, Sage.

O

OBEDIENCE, CRIMES OF

Definition

Harmful acts committed by a subordinate in obedience to the orders of a superior.

Distinctive Features

Explaining 'crimes of obedience' took on a renewed significance as a result of the return of ethnic war and genocide in the late twentieth century. The International Criminal Tribunals for the Former Yugoslavia and Rwanda established in the 1990s continue to grapple with issues of individual responsibility and obedience to orders, as did the Nuremberg Tribunal before them.

In the immediate aftermath of the Second World War, social scientists also sought explanations for crimes of obedience, as represented, in particular, by the Holocaust, through an analysis of the personality traits of the perpetrators. Perhaps the most notable work in this area was Theodore Adorno's analysis of the 'authoritarian personality' in the 1950s. In later analysis, however, by Hannah Ahrendt (1964) and Stanley Milgram (1974), the focus shifted to the social processes that enabled such crimes, rather than the psychological predispositions of individual perpetrators.

In a series of laboratory experiments, Milgram (1974) found that a majority (65 per cent) of apparently normal people could be induced to harm others if instructed to do so by a person in authority. In these experiments, Milgram investigated the willingness of research subjects, who had been asked to play the role of a 'teacher' in a learning experiment, to administer what they were told would be painful electric shocks to another subject on the instructions of the person in charge of the experiments. Despite apparent evidence that the pain administered was becoming progressively more severe and dangerous, the majority of the research subjects ('teachers') were prepared to continue administering shocks when urged to do so by the authority. Milgram found that the greater the distance between the research subjects giving the shocks and the 'victims', the greater was their willingness to obey instructions to continue. Conversely, the greater the distance between the research subject and the 'authority', the less was their willingness to continue.

Milgram described the research subjects who obeyed orders to inflict pain on others as having entered an 'agentic state', one in which upon entering the experimental authority system they had relinquished their sense of personal responsibility for their harmful actions by transferring responsibility to their superiors. Importantly, according to Milgram, this was a function not of individual propensities so much as a specific social condition explicable in terms of culturally generated deference to authority.

Ahrendt (1964), writing about the Nazi war criminal Adolf Eichmann, argued that it becomes possible (though not inevitable) for ordinary people to do evil when the wrongdoing is 'banalized' – that is, when it is made routine and morally neutral. More recently, in their work on war crimes in Vietnam, Kelman and Hamilton (1989) argued that crimes of obedience are more likely to be committed where there has been a 'weakening of moral restraint'. Kelman (1995), in his later work on the social context of torture, suggests that this weakening of moral restraints against wrongdoing is brought about by three interrelated social processes which simultaneously *authorize* (the harm is sponsored, expected or tolerated by those in authority) and *routinize* the harmful acts and also *dehumanize* their victims. The process of authorization is one in which the situation is redefined in such a way that normal moral principles do not apply and the individual is 'absolved of the responsibility for making moral choices'. The process of routinization structures the (harmful) action so that there is no opportunity for raising moral questions or making moral decisions. Finally, the process of dehumanization ensures that the 'perpetrator's attitudes towards the victim become structured in such a way that it is neither necessary nor possible for him to view his relationship with the victim in moral terms' (Kelman, 1995, pp. 29–32).

Evaluation

Social scientific work on 'crimes of obedience' is important for the way it highlights the different social contexts and social processes that are associated with the production of what otherwise might simply be dismissed (and therefore not explained) as immoral, evil or pathological acts. In his writing on the Holocaust, for example, Zygmunt Bauman has emphasized the inescapable importance of understanding the processes through which immoral regimes are institutionalized and given a 'normal' authority (Bauman, 1989). Thomas Scheff's work on emotions, nationalism and war is a good example of a social scientist trying to make sense of the ways in which ethnic division, rage, humiliation and the cultural devaluation of the fate of individual human beings may combine to produce the conditions of genocide and other war crime (Scheff, 1993). The laboratory-based experimental work conducted by Milgram did not in itself identify – and did not try to identify – any of these processes or the factors that influenced the behaviour of the 35 per cent of his subjects who refused to obey. Milgram's 'agentic state' model of obedience failed also to explain the temporal dimension of obedience. People are often caught up in sequences of demands for obedience, in which the degree of harm escalates from one moment to the next. Once they have committed their first crimes of obedience, they may become entrapped into continuing to obey.

Overwhelmingly, the concept of a crime of obedience has been applied to activities conducted in circumstances of war. There is, of course, no in-principle reason why the concept might not be applied, to useful analytic effect, in many other areas of human life of interest to students of crime – for example, in respect of the collective collusion of middle-range employees of large corporations involved in systematically fraudulent activity or in crimes against the environment. The exploration of the utility of the concept in these areas will be an important future task both for criminal lawyers involved in specific litigation and for social scientists involved in the analysis of 'criminal behaviour' in these areas, as much as in respect specifically of crimes committed in circumstances of war.

Ruth Jamieson

Associated Concepts: genocide, social control theory, state crime, torture

Key Readings
Ahrendt, H. (1964) *Eichmann in Jerusalem*. Harmondsworth, Penguin.
Bauman, Z. (1989) *Modernity and the Holocaust*. Cambridge, Polity Press.
Kelman, H.C. (1995) 'The social context of torture: policy process and authority structure', in R. Crelinson and A. Schmid (eds), *The Politics of Pain*. Oxford, Westview Press.
Kelman, H.C. and Hamilton, V.L. (1989) *Crimes of Obedience*. New Haven, CT, Yale University Press.
Milgram, S. (1974) *Obedience to Authority*. New York, Harper and Row.
Scheff, T. (1993) *Bloody Revenge: Emotions, Nationalism and War*. Boulder, CO, Westview Press.

OFFICIAL CRIMINAL STATISTICS

Definition

Statistical data compiled by the police and the courts and routinely published by governments as indices of the extent of crime.

Distinctive Features

Most countries annually collect data which are a count of the volume of particular categories of crime as recorded by the police. In the USA data are submitted voluntarily by local police departments to the FBI and published as *Uniform Crime Reports*. In the UK similar statistics are produced by the Home Office (*Criminal Statistics England and Wales* and the biannual *Statistical Bulletins*). Each includes data on offences (from which trends in crime over time are charted) and on offenders who have eventually been found guilty or cautioned (from which details of the sex and age of offenders are derived).

The first national crime statistics were produced in France in the early nineteenth century (Quetelet in 1842). In England and Wales crimes recorded by the police have been published since 1876 and in the USA since 1930. Both of these latter countries have witnessed a dramatic rise in the crime rate since the mid 1950s, with the only sustained fall occurring in the mid to late 1990s. A similar long-term upward trend has been a feature of most Western democracies, with the notable exception of Switzerland (Maguire, 1997, p. 159).

Breaking down this overall rate into *offence groups* reveals that the 'crime problem' is predominantly one of crimes against property (theft, burglary, criminal damage) and above all theft of, or from, vehicles. Crimes of violence appear small in comparison. Turning to the data on *offenders*, it is first notable that their numbers are dramatically lower than the total number of offences recorded. Whilst some of this disparity may be attributable to those committing more than one offence, it is clear that in the vast majority of cases nothing is officially known about those responsible (Maguire, 1997, p. 173; Coleman and Moynihan, 1996, p. 43). The data on 'known offenders', however, produce a picture of the 'typical offender' as male and young. For example in England and Wales the official criminal statistics have consistently found that over 80 per cent of offenders are male and almost half are under the age of 21.

Criminologists have long debated the reliability of these statistical measures. Self evidently they only measure those offences reported to and recorded by the police. As a result these basic data are now regularly added to by nationwide victim surveys. In 1972 the US Bureau of the Census began collecting information about rates of victimization by asking random samples of the population to recall crimes committed against them in the past year. In 1982 Britain followed this lead with its own *British Crime Survey* (BCS). Both in the USA and in Britain it was consistently revealed that only about 50 per cent of crime is in fact reported to the police.

Evaluation

The official criminal statistics do not provide any straightforward answers to the questions of: How much crime? How many criminals? How many victims? The 'true facts' of crime are probably unknowable. They depend not only on what we define as crime, but also on the *validity* of statistical measures, no matter how they are produced. Most academic analysts, the media, politicians and the public rely on official statistics as 'hard facts', but they are both partial and subjectively constructed.

- In the USA the Uniform Crime Report distinguishes between index crimes and non-index crimes. It constructs crime trends from tabulating eight index crimes – those the FBI believes to be the most serious. The list does not include fraud, embezzlement, offences against family or children, drug abuse, vagrancy and so on. In England and Wales the official statistics do not include offences recorded by the British Transport Police, Ministry of Defence Police and UK Atomic Energy Authority Police, who collectively record about 80,000 offences per year (Maguire 1997, p. 149). Tax evasion (recorded by the Inland Revenue) and VAT evasion (recorded by Customs and Excise) will only appear in official criminal records if they are subsequently brought to court.
- Crime statistics are based on those crimes reported to and subsequently recorded by the police. But some offences may not be reported because of ignorance that a crime has been committed (for example, tax evasion, computer fraud); there appears to be no victim (for example, certain drugs offences, prostitution, sexual offences between consenting adults, illegal abortion); the victim is powerless (for example, child abuse); ambivalence towards or distrust of the police (for example, certain youth cultures); the offence may be considered trivial (for example, thefts from work, vandalism, minor shoplifting, brawls); the victim may be concerned that the offence will not be taken seriously (for example, some cases of rape); or the victim has no faith that the police will act to protect his or her interests (for example, racial intimidation and harassment). Measurements of crime rest initially and critically on the extent to which the public perceives and interprets behaviour as 'criminal' (Walker, 1983, p. 292).
- Not all offences reported are recorded as such by the police. The amount of resources available to the police and courts is limited and thus subjective

and/or administrative decisions are made concerning which crimes to act against. It is only recorded crime which enters the official statistics. Walker (1983, p. 286) notes that, although the police in England and Wales have a statutory obligation to record crimes, considerable discretion remains about whether it is considered sufficiently serious to warrant their attention. Violent disputes between neighbours or members of a family may, for example, be classified as 'domestic – advice given' and the alleged 'offence' not recorded. Similarly, how a recorded offence is classified by the police – as 'theft from a person' or 'robbery'; as 'burglary, no loss' or 'vandalism'; as 'wounding' or 'common assault' for example – will affect the rate at which certain crimes appear to be committed. Problems inherent in recording, and variations due to local police 'targeting', will also affect our understanding of the extent of particular crimes.

- Changes in law enforcement and in what the law counts as crime also preclude much meaningful discussion over the extent of historical increases and decreases in crime. Legislative changes may mean that existing categories are redefined, thus rendering historical comparison meaningless. Some increases in crime can be artificially constructed solely by economic and administrative circumstance: inflation provides a perfect example of such a bias. The law is not index linked and so acts of criminal damage, officially defined in England and Wales as damage exceeding £20 in value, shot up from 17,000 in 1969 to 124,000 in 1977. Inflation shifted many thousands of previously trivial incidents of damage into the more serious crime bracket.

- Changes in police practices, priorities and politics will also have a dramatic effect on such headline statistics as 'crimes recorded by the police'. What is remarkable for example about long-term historical trends in crime rates in England and Wales is their consistently low level during the nineteenth and early twentieth centuries followed by a consistent doubling in every decade (except the 1950s) until the 1990s. By examining police inspectorate and committee reports at the time, Taylor (1998) argues that the increases in crime between 1914 and 1960 can be largely accounted for by senior police officers 'playing the crime card' in order to improve their establishment. By

recording large numbers of minor property offences which were traditionally 'cuffed' (not recorded) chief constables were able to persuade their police authorities to increase funding. The crime rate is then more a reflection of police lobbying and politics, than of criminal behaviour.

- Changes in the number of arrests, trials and sentences may not represent actual changes in the amount of crime, but rather changes in the *capacity* of the criminal justice system to process individual cases. Increases or decreases in the number of police, judges, courtrooms and prison places will inevitably affect these statistics. More police, more judges and more prisons appear to have a nearly infinite capacity to increase the amount of officially recorded crime. This is partly because there is a forever-present unlimited well of unrecorded criminal behaviour which can be tapped when and if the political will and the resources for law enforcement are sufficiently activated. It is also because there exists a huge potential to perceive and redefine actions as 'crimes' as the technological ability to implement forms of mass surveillance increases.

Collectively, such processes of data collection inevitably mean that notions of crime waves and of perpetual increases in offending have to be interpreted with extreme caution. Nevertheless, the pictures they create of crime, criminals and offending remain some of the key means through which academic, political, media and public knowledge is gained. The statistics cannot be dismissed as simply meaningless. They can provide valuable insights into police and court definitions of crime and the operation of social, legal and organizational constraints and priorities. They cannot, however, be expected to aid our understanding of the 'independent entity of crime' for, by its nature, no such fact exists.

John Muncie

Associated Concepts: crime, hidden crime, self-reports, victim surveys

Key Readings

Coleman, C. and Moynihan, J. (1996) *Understanding Crime Data*. Buckingham, Open University Press.

Maguire, M. (1997) 'Crime statistics, patterns and trends: changing perceptions and their implications', in M. Maguire, R. Morgan and R. Reiner (eds), *The Oxford Handbook of Criminology*, 2nd edn. Oxford, The Clarendon Press.

Taylor, H. (1998) 'The politics of the rising crime statistics of England and Wales 1914–1960', *Crime, History and Societies*, 2 (1), pp. 5–28.

Walker, M.A. (1983) 'Some problems in interpreting statistics relating to crime', *Journal of the Royal Statistical Society, Series A*, No.146, part 3, pp. 282–93.

OPPORTUNITY THEORY

Definition

An approach to explaining criminal behaviour that sees crime as a function of the characteristics of situations that offer the opportunity, to those inclined to take it, to benefit from an illegal act.

Distinctive Features

Historically, theories of crime took either a 'dispositional' stance, with a focus on the individual offender, or a 'sociological' approach, with emphasis on the social conditions associated with crime. A rather different approach began to emerge following the work of Cohen and Felson (1979) and the advent of 'routine activities theory'. The core of this theoretical approach is that crime will occur when three elements combine: a specific situation (i.e., a time and location), a target, and the absence of effective guardians. The combination of these three elements provides the *opportunity* for successful offending.

The beginnings of views about crime based on routine activities and opportunity are to be found in research broadly concerned with the environmental correlates of crime. These studies are concerned with the specific environmental conditions that might account for patterns of crime. For example, rising numbers of burglaries can be explained by the greater proportion of empty houses as more people go out to work leaving homes unguarded and offering the opportunity for undetected crime. Similarly, it can be seen that more street parking leads to higher rates of car theft; street violence is more likely in dimly lit areas of towns and cities; and the probability of vandalism to property is increased when there is no one with direct responsibility for the safety of buildings and utilities.

The concept of opportunity began to come under increasing scrutiny, with various dimensions of the three critical elements being described in the literature. With respect to the target, Bottoms and Wiles (1997) note the importance of 'target attractiveness'. Target attractiveness has several dimensions: financial value is obvious, but other factors such as being simple to sell and easily transported can be important in making a target attractive. It is also the case, of course, that the same target will not be equally attractive to all potential offenders.

The critical elements of the situation might, as Bottoms and Wiles (1997) suggest, be seen in terms of 'accessibility'. Accessibility refers to the physical qualities of the situation such as visibility, ease of access, and lack of observation at the scene of the crime. The latter factor, lack of observation, may be linked with the third dimension of opportunity, absence of a responsible guardian. A reasonable guardian may, for example, be a neighbour, an official such as a car park attendant, or a police officer.

In considering accessibility and guardianship, it is difficult to disentangle the environment and the individual. For example, an individual might need specialist knowledge to recognize the environmental cues that signal an attractive target. Thus, burglars may be aware of cues, such as type of lock or window catch, that signal easy entry to a property. Similarly, a guardian may be present but it is the guardian's perceived effectiveness that is the critical dimension with respect to the potential offender's decision-making and eventual actions.

As the concept of opportunity is stretched to include a wider range of factors, so the associated models of crime become more complex. Clarke (1995) presents a model of the opportunity structure for crime that incorporates such diverse elements as socio-economic structure, perception, physical environment, and information processing. Such deepenings also begin to overlap with the view, reminiscent of classicism, of criminals as motivated by self-interest. Owing more to economics than human science, the basis of human action is seen in terms of 'expected utility'. A quotation from Van Den Haag (1982) illustrates this approach in its most stark form: 'I do not see any relevant difference between dentistry and prostitution or car theft, except that the latter do not require a license . . . The frequency of rape, or of mugging, is essentially determined by the expected comparative net advantage, just as is the rate of dentistry and burglary' (p. 1,026).

Like an accountant reckoning a balance sheet, the offender considers the net gains and losses then, as it were, moves into the market to make a profit. The offender is seen as a rational decision-maker, as a 'reasoning criminal', with personal benefit a prime motivation for crime. This theme of the criminal as a rational decision-maker was developed to significant effect by Cornish and Clarke (1986). Cornish and Clarke are clear that while social factors, such as family and peer group, may be part of an individual's growing up to be involved in crime, the 'event decision', the making of a rational choice, at the point of committing the offence, is critical.

Evaluation

The development of concepts such as opportunity, routine activities and rational decision-making has had a profound practical impact in the form of situational crime prevention (Clarke, 1992). This approach to crime prevention takes the broad approach that by changing elements of the situation, such as target availability and levels of surveillance, it is possible to impact significantly on the opportunities for crime and the offender's decision-making. There are criticisms of this approach at theoretical and practical levels, particularly with regard to the rationality of some offending and the issue of displacement. However, there is little doubt that the overall approach has taken criminological theory into new areas of research and practice.

Clive Hollin

Associated Concepts: classicism, defensible space, free will, geographies of crime, rational choice theory, routine activity theory, situational crime prevention, surveillance

Key Readings

Bottoms, A.E. and Wiles, P. (1997) 'Environmental criminology', in M. Maguire, R. Morgan and R. Reiner (eds), *The Oxford Handbook of Criminology*, 2nd edn. Oxford, The Clarendon Press.

Clarke, R.V. (ed.) (1992) *Situational Crime Prevention: Successful Case Studies*. New York, Harrow and Heston.

Clarke, R.V. (1995) 'Situational crime prevention', in M. Tonry and D.P. Farrington (eds), *Building a Safer Society: Strategic Approaches to Crime Prevention*. Chicago, University of Chicago Press.

Cohen, L.E. and Felson, M. (1979) 'Social change and crime rate trends: a routine activities approach', *American Sociological Review*, 44, pp. 588–608.

Cornish, D.B. and Clarke, R.V. (eds) (1986) *The Reasoning Criminal: Rational Choice Perspectives on Offending*. New York, Springer-Verlag.

Van Den Haag, E. (1982) 'Could successful rehabilitation reduce the crime rate?', *Journal of Criminal Law and Criminology*, 73, pp. 1,022–1,035.

ORGANIZED CRIME

Definition

This concept emerged first in the United States in the 1920s but is now used internationally, for example, by the United Nations and G8 countries, as shorthand to describe a range of serious crimes that are deemed especially difficult to control. It may be defined as the ongoing activities of those collectively engaged in production, supply and financing for illegal markets in goods and services.

Distinctive Features

There are two main analogies employed in the description and analysis of organized crime: the market and government. In the first, a distinction is commonly drawn between 'ordinary' criminals, even if in gangs, whose crimes are 'predatory', that is, concerned with the illegal redistribution of already existing wealth, and criminal organizations committing 'enterprise' crime: the production and distribution of new, though illegal, goods and services (Naylor, 1997). This is not a hard and fast distinction: the more opportunistic the criminal organization the more likely it is to be involved in both types of crime.

This basic idea of 'enterprise' crime is central to most contemporary accounts of the concept, both official and academic, but crucially different approaches emerge once analysis proceeds. In the official discourse criminal enterprises *penetrate* otherwise lawful business, thus undermining and corrupting it, for example, offering counterfeit supplies or protection including threats. Such activities do happen but they represent only a partial account. A fuller examination of the interaction between organizations and markets shows that under certain conditions the relationship between legal and illegal organizations is *symbiotic*. For example, the study of corporate crime examines the extensive illegal behaviour of organizations that are formally legal. Similarly, Smith (1980) develops a model of enterprises being situated on a spectrum between legality and illegality and explains how the interaction of entrepreneurs and customers leads to 'stratified marketplaces', for example, entrepreneurs may prefer to borrow money from a bank but, if unable to do so, may go to a loan shark.

Overall, the enterprise model is at the heart of the common metaphor of the criminal 'firm'; for some, however, what is particularly significant about criminal organizations including, for example, the Mafia, is not their marketplace activities so much as their 'governmental' behaviour. At one level, this may reflect attempts by criminal organizations to corrupt government in general, for example, contractual bid-rigging, and law enforcement in particular, paying-off police, prosecutors and judges for favourable decisions. However, more fundamentally, criminal organizations have been characterized as threatening the state's monopoly of functions such as coercion, protection and extraction (Naylor, 1997, pp. 15–16). These functions are all central to the legitimacy claims of modern states and to the extent that other organizations deploy violence, offer protection and benefits and extract 'taxation', then they may be seen as challenging that central claim. Post-Soviet Russia is seen as an example of this. Indeed, taking a longer historical view, the struggles between rivals to establish monopolies can be seen as the central feature of 'state-making' (Tilly, 1985).

Evaluation

Considerable controversy has surrounded the use of this concept, much of it centring on the nature and extent of the organization of crime. Work carried out for the US President's Crime Commission in the 1960s presented the Italian-American Mafia as the core manifestation of organized crime; specifically that it resembled a corporate *hierarchy* with the associated features of ranks and division of labour. Critics argued that this image resulted from the over-reliance of researchers on files and other evidence from a law enforcement community that was anyway predisposed to describe their targets in the same hierarchical terms as they were themselves organized. Alternative models, based more on the idea of *networks*, for example, based on families or more broadly, friends and business connections (e.g. Hobbs, 1998) are a more accurate depiction.

Further impetus has been given to this controversy by the identification of transnational organized crime as a major problem during the 1990s. The reasons for this are clear: the end of the Cold War and collapse of the former regimes of the Soviet bloc has seen a re-orientation not just of security intelligence agencies and military forces but also of academic departments of international relations to the analysis of 'new' security threats. Coinciding as it has with the era of globalization, the result has been an outpouring of official concern at national and international level that organized crime is not just a 'serious problem' but that it actually constitutes a threat to national security. Further, the threat is normally presented as if it were primarily an *external* one in much the same way as 'ordinary' crime is normally represented as crimes of 'the other'. Therefore discussion is of 'Russian-', 'Asian-', 'Nigerian-organized crime' and so on and unreliable estimates of the values of cross-border crime are often given. Actually, more careful analysis indicates that crime remains predominantly local in origin and carried out by national citizens.

Thus, great care must be taken with the use of the concept: organized crime is an issue on which governments feel strongly the need to reassure insecure populations that 'something can be done' and there is consequently much rhetoric of 'wars' on crime and drugs. In reality, organized criminality is so deeply embedded within the operation of domestic and global markets that the most that can be achieved is to ameliorate somewhat its most damaging effects.

Peter Gill

Associated Concepts: corporate crime, critical criminology, extraterritorial law enforcement, Marxist criminologies, state crime, transnational organized crime, white collar crime

Key Readings

Abadinsky, H. (1997) *Organized Crime*, 5th edn. Chicago, Nelson-Hall.

Hobbs, D. (1998) 'Going down the glocal', *The Howard Journal of Criminal Justice*, 37 (4), pp. 1–19. (See also other articles in this special edition.)

Naylor, R.T. (1997) 'Mafias, myths and markets', *Transnational Organized Crime*, 3 (3), pp. 15–30.

Smith, D. (1980) 'Paragons, pariahs and pirates', *Crime and Delinquency*, 26 (July), pp. 45–57.

Special Issue on Transnational Crime (1998) *International Journal of Risk, Security and Crime Prevention*, 3 (2).

Tilly, C. (1985) 'War making and state making as organized crime', in P. Evans (ed.), *Bringing the State Back In*. Cambridge, Cambridge University Press.

P

PANOPTICISM

Definition

Panopticism is a theoretical concept associated with the French philosopher Michel Foucault (1977). Foucault uses Jeremy Bentham's eighteenth-century design for a prison – the Panopticon (which was never actually built) – as a starting point to analyse the general 'exercise of power' in society as a whole.

Distinctive Features

The central feature of Bentham's unused prison design for the Panopticon was visibility and inspection. In the words of Foucault (1977, p. 200):

> We know the principle on which it [i.e. the Panopticon] was based: at the periphery, an annular building; at the centre, a tower; this tower is pierced with wide windows that open onto the inner side of the ring; the peripheric building is divided into cells, each of which extends the whole width of the building; they have two windows, one on the inside, corresponding to the windows of the tower; the other, on the outside, allows the light to cross the cell from one end to the other. All that is needed, is to place a supervisor in a central tower and to shut up in each cell a lunatic, a patient, a condemned man, a worker or a pupil. By the effect of backlighting, one can observe from the tower, standing put precisely against the light, the small captive shadows in the cells of the periphery. They are like so many cages, so many small theatres, in which each actor is alone, perfectly individualized and constantly visible. The panoptic mechanism arranges spatial unities that make it possible to see constantly and to recognize immediately. In short, it reverses the principles of the dungeon; or rather of its three functions – to enclose, to deprive of light and to hide – it preserves only the first and eliminates the other two. Full lighting and the eye of a supervisor capture better than darkness, which ultimately protected. Visibility is a trap.

In a chapter entitled 'Panopticism', Foucault argues that institutions other than prisons begin to use the same forms of power – visibility and inspection – to exercise control in factories, schools, hospitals and so on. The Panopticon 'must not be understood as a dream building; it is the diagram of a mechanism of power reduced to its ideal form; its functioning, abstracted from any obstacle, resistance or friction, must be represented as a pure architectural and optical system: it is in fact a figure of political technology that may and must be detached from any specific use' (Foucault, 1977, p. 205).

Despite using the Panopticon as a historical metaphor for the seventeenth and eighteenth centuries, the application of the theoretical principles of the disciplinary power of visibility and the idea that inspection or observation affects behaviour which Foucault develops have numerous contemporary resonances. In particular, the increasing use of closed circuit television (CCTV) in our cities, in both public and private spaces, has precisely the same disciplinary functions that Foucault suggested lay at the heart of the Panopticon, and is linked to the idea of the 'carceral society'.

Evaluation

What makes Foucault so interesting and challenging is his almost poetic use of language. Like a true poet or philosopher he makes connections between seemingly unconnected events. Alternatively, what makes him frustrating is his failure to cite sources, and his endless willingness to push his materials beyond the point at which they can be sustained. Panopticism benefits and suffers from these strengths and weaknesses in almost equal measure. It should be remembered, for example, that Bentham's design was never accepted, and the Panopticon never built. On the other hand, as a basis for analysing our contemporary preoccupation with security surveillance, panopticism offers many interesting insights.

David Wilson

Associated Concepts: carceral society, electronic monitoring, penality, penology, surveillance

Key Readings

Bozovic, M. (ed.), (1995) *The Panopticon Writings of Jeremy Bentham*. New York, Verso Press.

Foucault, M. (1977) *Discipline and Punish: The Birth of the Prison*. London, Allen Lane.

PARTICIPANT OBSERVATION

Definition

The collection of information through active participation in the social world that is under study.

Distinctive Features

Pioneered by the Chicago School of Sociology in the 1920s, the key aim of participant observation is to view the social world, as far as possible, from the actor's own point of view. Typically this involves becoming a part of the group under study, learning its culture and observing its behaviour. The key aim is to gain access to the meanings actors themselves make of their own personal and social situations. It facilitates data collection on situations as they occur rather than in artificial situations (as in experimental research) or through constructs of reality provided by the researcher (as in survey research). The promise is held that such observations can help to make sense of behaviour that may appear to be irrational and paradoxical to those 'on the outside'. As a result, it is most

closely associated with interactionism and appreciative forms of criminology. The participant observer becomes immersed 'in the field' by emphasizing:

- the study of groups in their natural surroundings, with the minimum of disturbance;
- empathy and understanding;
- the direct observation of interactions and in particular the meanings they have for participants; and
- descriptions in terms of the everyday understandings of actors in a situation.

Gold (1969) distinguished four forms of such research: 'observer-as-participant', 'participant-as-observer', 'the complete observer' and 'the complete participant'. In full participant observation, the researcher identifies an area worthy of study and enters the field without much preconception about what is to be found. Typically the observer also conceals their identity as a researcher from those being studied.

In the 1960s and 1970s the development of explicitly anti-positivist approaches to the study of crime and deviance, for example in labelling and new deviancy theory, provided the political and theoretical inspiration for what was arguably the heyday of participant observation research. Polsky's (1971) research into poolroom hustlers in New York and Parker's (1974) study of a group of male 'street kids' in Liverpool came closest to Gold's notion of 'complete participant' in that their position as researcher and as participant was often indistinguishable. Both carried out their research covertly, and in order to gain trust engaged in deviant activities themselves – a position that some ethnographers have described as having 'gone native'. However, each provided invaluable insights into the complexity of subcultural codes and behaviour that previous researchers had been unable to, or failed to, acknowledge. As a result each was also able to offer a damning critique of 'orthodox' research masquerading as 'science'.

On the other hand, participant observation has also been used to improve understandings of the internal workings of the criminal justice system, as in Holdaway's (1983) study of the British police. This study was carried out covertly and was able to reveal the extent to which police work was framed by the everyday meanings and definitions that officers themselves had constructed to make sense of their role and the people that they policed.

Fully developed, covert participant observation research is necessarily time-consuming, difficult, long-term, potentially risky and can in some circumstances raise serious ethical questions. It is probably no surprise, in a criminology that had by the 1990s become dominated by technicist, evaluative and administrative concerns, that such research has become increasingly rare. But it remains one of the few means through which a humanization of the subjects of criminological research can be achieved.

John Muncie

Associated Concepts: appreciative criminology, Chicago School of Sociology, ethnography, interactionism, new deviancy theory

Key Readings

Adler, P.A. (1993) *Wheeling and Dealing: An Ethnography of an Upper Level Drug Dealing and Smuggling Community*. New York, Columbia University Press.

Burgess, R.G. (1984) *In the Field*. London, Unwin Hyman.

Gold, R. (1969) 'Roles in sociological field observation', in G. McCall and J. Simmons (eds), *Issues in Participant Observation*. London, Addison Wesley.

Holdaway, S. (1983) *Inside the British Police*. Oxford, Blackwell.

Parker, H. (1974) *View from the Boys*. Newton Abbot, David and Charles.

Polsky, N. (1971) *Hustlers, Beats and Others*. Harmondsworth, Penguin.

PATHOLOGY

Definition

Within bio-medical discourse – the study of disease; by extension and common usage – the abnormal (that which is not normal), an unhealthy deviation from the norm, degenerate. For those who follow individualistic explanations of crime, pathology will be located in the individual at the level of the genes, hormones or psyche. For sociologists, the pathology might be located in the family, peer-group, area or social formation.

Distinctive Features

Durkheim (1895, 1964) devotes a chapter to the 'Normal and the Pathological'. However, the greater part of his discussion is given over to bio-medical analogy. Moreover the term morbidity is sometimes used – again emphasizing the organicism of his argument. Famously, Durkheim used suicide to illustrate the utility of sociological method even in the most seemingly individual act. Similarly, he claims 'if there is any fact whose pathological character appears incontestable, that fact is crime. All criminologists are agreed on this point. Although they explain this pathology differently.' He then proceeds to make his oft-quoted claim about crime being normal (even amongst a 'society of saints'). However, he allows some crime to be pathological. He acknowledges that a person may commit crime for individual pathological reasons *and* sociologically that a rate of crime may be pathologically higher than predicted for social types and levels of society. This too he calls morbidity or abnormal. However, contrary to the general positivism of his arguments, he recognizes – and foreshadows the labelling perspective – 'that, among these divergences, there are some with a criminal character. What confers this character upon them is not the intrinsic quality of a given act but that definition which the collective conscience lends them' (1895, 1964, p. 70).

It is a mark of the extent to which sociological criminology has advanced that Durkheim's claim that all criminologists agree on the pathological character of crime strikes the modern reader as odd. Durkheim was able to overturn the narrow bio-medical definition of pathology and give it a sociological face. However, despite Durkheim's influence 'pathology' has not usually been the nomenclature favoured by those who followed in his footsteps. It can be argued that it appears in various disguises in the sociology of deviance, such as differential association, social disorganization and strain. It might also be argued that some positivistic readings of both Marxism and feminism see class society and patriarchy as pathological or responsible for the 'pathologies' of the working class or of men.

Evaluation

It can be argued that pathology no longer has any place in sociology. However, as psychopathology, it has been elevated in criminal justice discourse and popular cultural representation – note the character of Hannibal Lecter in *Silence of the Lambs* – to prime importance once again as an explanation of crime. Sumner (1994) claims that the field of study that Durkheim opened up was killed off in 1975. Sumner proposes replacing deviance with censure as the field of study. In this, the term pathology, including psychopathology, can be seen as the censure of the different by those with the power to define it. This can be seen in Durkheim's terms as functional, in labelling terms as misguided or counterproductive or in Foucauldian terms as productive. The disciplines of medicine and the psy-sciences employ the nexus of power/knowledge to produce – and offer to control – pathology, as they have done with madness, crime and sexual dissidence.

Administrative criminology has sought to side-step the issue of pathology within the individual or society but replaces it with the fear or risk of other's pathology, which is to be managed. In this way the gated community might be seen as a *cordon sanitaire* and security guards as white blood corpuscles and T-cells mobilizing to neutralize pathogens. 'Sterilizing' urban spaces in the nineteenth century was the job of the 'new police'. Now it falls to the martian ray of CCTV. Staying with the medical metaphor, society seems uncertain whether to swallow up (a cannibalistic response) or vomit out (a bulimic response) the pathologized 'other' (Young, 1999).

Nic Groombridge

Associated Concepts: demonization, deviance, individual positivism, normalization, sexuality, social censure, sociological positivism

Key Readings
Durkheim, E. (1895, 1964) *The Rules of Sociological Method*. London, The Free Press of Glencoe.
Lemert, E. (1967, 1972) 'Forms and pathology of drinking in three Polynesian societies', in *Human deviance, social problems and social control*. Englewood Cliffs, NJ, Prentice–Hall, pp. 218–33.
Sumner, C. (1994) *The Sociology of Deviance: An Obituary*. Buckingham, Open University Press.
Young, J. (1999) *The Exclusive Society: Social Exclusion, Difference and Crime in Late Modernity*. London, Sage.

PEACEMAKING CRIMINOLOGY

Definition

The study of the processes and ways of relating that leave people safer, more trusting and less guarded with others. The science and art of weaving people, including those called 'offenders' and 'victims' in conventional 'war-making' criminology, into social networks secure from violence. Peacemaking criminology is the opposite of the prevailing 'war-making' paradigm in criminology, which is the science and art of identifying, isolating and subduing offenders or would-be offenders.

Distinctive Features

Like all spiritual and religious and political or cultural traditions, all social science, including criminology, can be divided into two competing paradigms on how to belong in social order. The war-making paradigm presupposes that we are born ignorant and need to learn to obey instruction from our properly constituted earthly superiors, from whose might right is made. In this paradigm the key dependent variables are negative – such as crime, violence, criminality, punishment, deterrence and risk. In the peacemaking paradigm, social relations become stronger and richer insofar as they are built on mutual respect. Dependent variables in a peacemaking paradigm are positive, such as compassion, love, empathy, respect, dignity, mutuality and trust.

Within the peacemaking paradigm, punishment itself is presumed to be a social problem rather than a social solution. It is common to see those identified as doing peacemaking criminology belonging to corollary groups. Some, for example, draw upon Gandhian principles of non-violence. Some, including those who note that 'penal servitude' is the one kind of 'slavery' explicitly allowed by the Thirteenth Amendment to the United States Constitution, call themselves 'penal abolitionists'. Some advocate 'restorative' or 'transformative', rather than 'retributive justice'. Some call for 'compassion' in Buddhist terms, others for 'love' and 'mercy' in Judaeo-Christian-Muslim terms. Traditional ways of responding to personal and structural violence, from indigenous peoples around the world, are especially prominent in peacemaking literature and in criminal justice practice, as in the New Zealand parliament's adoption of the Maori practice known worldwide today as family group conferencing, in Canadian sentencing circles, or in growing Anglo legal recognition of, and admiration for, the Navajo peacemaking court in the United States.

Criminologists who are drawn to peacemaking commonly report that their spirits are lifted by studying what people value in others and how to elicit what we like from each other, in contrast to the despair and discouragement that they had come to feel studying what we want people not to do and how to get people to stop doing things. It feels better to learn how to get what we do want and value with others than to learn how to crush human miscreants.

Whether secular or deist, peacemaking criminology is explicitly concerned with the spiritual attitude we bring to bear in our social relations, while war-making criminology tends to embrace Enlightenment dualism between spiritual value and social fact-making. Much peacemaking criminology is critical of value neutrality in retributive criminology. Indeed, one theory of the causes of violence and punitiveness, notably as stated by renegade German psychoanalyst Alice Miller, is that all violence and punishment presuppose personal dissociation of one's feelings from one's action. When you pull the switch to punish a transgressor, your feeling for the transgressor's suffering is cut off by messages from authority figures as to what you *ought* to do to the offender for some higher good. In peacemaking criminology, there is no higher good than empathy, or, as some like US war resister A.J. Muste and criminologist Richard Quinney have put it, 'peace is *the* way'. In radical feminist terms, in peacemaking criminology power over others is violence itself, and the building of safe community lies in power sharing and in participatory democracy.

Evaluation

The three main criticisms of peacemaking criminology are that it is not a theory, that it is impractical and that it is privileged.

Peacemaking criminology is not a theory. Like retribution, peacemaking is more an attitude or definition of the situation. On the other hand, peacemaking criminology includes theories of how peace is made.

Practicality is a paradigmatic matter. Peacemaking criminology is not prophecy. Peacemaking theory only purports to predict whether people will be safer or more at risk as a result of this or that intervention, not whether people will actually do what makes them safer. There is in peacemaking criminology a rich body of empirically tested propositions as to what brings people together or separates them.

The realist criticism is that peacemaking criminology is concocted by people who do

not understand just how bad oppression is, the urgency of supporting those who even take up arms to resist and subdue their oppressors, nor the progress that has been made through militant class struggle. Other than prisoners, it is by and large true that peacemaking criminologists and their critics are privileged. This issue recurs in all theological and political debate over whether to be hard-hearted or to let our hearts bleed.

Some texts have taken to calling 'peacemaking criminology' a 'school'. In recent history, 'peacemaking' became an operative word in criminological circles when the title of an edited book – *Criminology as Peacemaking* – caught on after its publication in 1991. Criminologists who say they are doing 'peacemaking' encompass a wide range of criminological individualists, which surely includes those who would be loath to accept the definition of 'peacemaking' set forth here. In peacemaking criminology, as in everyday life, it pays not to take for granted that one knows any criminologist by the label 'peacemaking' alone.

Hal Pepinsky

Associated Concepts: abolition, anarchist criminology, human rights, labelling, restorative justice, social reaction

Key Readings

Anderson, K. and Quinney, R. (eds) (2000) *Erich Fromm and Critical Criminology: Beyond the Punitive Society*. Urbana, IL, University of Illinois Press.

Consedine, J. (1999) *Restorative Justice: Healing the Effects of Crime*. Lyttleton, NZ, Ploughshares Press.

Fuller, J.R. (1998) *Criminal Justice: A Peacemaking Perspective*. Boston, MA, Allyn and Bacon.

Miller, A. (1990) *For Your Own Good: Hidden Cruelty in Child-Rearing and the Roots of Violence*. New York, Noonday Press.

Morris, R.M. (1993) *Penal Abolition: The Practical Choice*. Toronto, Canadian Scholars' Press.

Pepinsky, H.E. and Quinney, R. (eds) (1991) *Criminology as Peacemaking*. Bloomington, IN, Indiana University Press.

PENALITY

Definition

A term introduced from the French *pénalité* and owing its current salience primarily to the influence of Foucault. It designates not only the institutions and agencies composing the penal system but also their surrounding economic, political, intellectual and cultural conditions.

Distinctive Features

The use of the term penality often intends to strike a conscious difference from the traditional concerns either of normative penal theory on the one hand or the instrumental and pragmatic preoccupations of conventional penology on the other. Whereas the former is devoted to discussion of the proper aims of penal action (their basis in legal theory, their moral implications, their coherence) and the latter has historically been taken up with ameliorating penal institutions and refining their effectiveness, 'penality' denotes an attempt to historicize penal questions and to situate them in terms of their sociological and political connections and surrounding conditions. Thus, in an important early instance of the English-language use of the term, Garland and Young argued that conventional penology had become 'marginal to any attempt actually to explain the nature of the penal system' (1983, p. 5). In place of such descriptive, meliorist and politically compromised exercises, Garland and Young proposed a more intellectually ambitious enterprise which would reconceive the penal realm as a 'specific *institutional site* . . . traversed by a series of different social relations' (p. 21).

Although the translation of Foucault's *Discipline and Punish* was the single event that gave most impetus to such attempts at reconsideration, the social analysis of penality in fact has much longer and more extensive intellectual antecedents. These flow in part from the legacies of Durkheim, whose social theory reserved an important place for punishment among the ritual affirmations of social solidarity. Durkheim's influence is also visible, if sometimes more remotely, in the work of anthropologists such as Mary Douglas and of historical sociologists such as Kai Erikson. Such studies made available an awareness that practices for the maintenance and application of conduct norms and rules and for the imposition of sanctions, censures and blame were culturally and historically variable and specific. They thereby also facilitated a recognition that the penal arrangements so familiar to the citizens of contemporary Western societies might similarly be subjected to a more sceptical and critical appraisal.

A comparable shock of 'defamiliarization' resulted from the appearance of a number of 'revisionist' histories of penal systems and institutions, especially prisons. The foundational text here is unquestionably Rusche and Kirchheimer's *Punishment and Social Structure* (first published in 1939 and influentially republished in 1968). Rusche and Kirchheimer's basic contention, flying in the face of much philosophical effort to distil the proper or intrinsic nature of punishment, was that 'there is no such thing as punishment, but only concrete systems of punishment'. This thesis might be taken as a motto for the revisionist historians. Whatever their differences (for example the explicitness of their debt to Marxist theory or to specific varieties thereof) the latter had in common a concern to locate the development of the 'modern' form of penitentiary imprisonment, around the turn of the eighteenth and nineteenth centuries, to the emergence of industrial capitalism, and the deployment of penal power by the state to the management of the conflictual social relations over which it presided (see Garland, 1990, chapters 4 and 5).

In this context, the primary distinctiveness and originality of Foucault's contribution lay not so much in his view of the broad outlines of chronology, nor even in any particular new empirical discovery, but rather in his anatomization of the styles and techniques of penal discipline characteristic of modernity. Foucault saw the prison not as *sui generis* but rather as standing within a continuum of disciplinary institutions (schools, hospitals, workhouses, barracks) whose common aspect was the minute regulation of daily conduct and whose object lay not merely in the suppression or subjugation of the unruly but rather in the positive production of 'docile yet capable bodies'. In Foucault's account, the emergence of modern penality is unintelligible without reference to the new varieties of specialist knowledge (such as psychology, psychiatry, social statistics and epidemiology) that provided its classifications, and which guided, supported and authorized its strategies of intervention – its 'discursive practices' (see Garland, 1990, chapter 6; Howe, 1993, chapter 3).

In subsequent work elements of each of these conceptual resources have been revised and put to diverse uses. For example, David Garland in *Punishment and Welfare* (Gower, 1985) traces the emergence of a form of penality characteristic of twentieth-century welfare states and especially the development of hybrid forms of 'welfare sanction'. Pat

Carlen in *Women's Imprisonment* (Routledge and Kegan Paul, 1983) identifies the modes of discipline specific to the carceral control of women. Jonathan Simon in *Poor Discipline* (Chicago, 1993) follows the rise, decline and re-engineering of parole and the supervision of offenders. Adrian Howe (1993) proposes a thoroughgoing feminist re-evaluation of penality in terms of the multiple modes of discipline governing the lives of girls and women. Garland (1990) offers an ambitious synthesis which accommodates not only the longstanding preoccupations with the powers of the state and the Foucauldian concern with the 'micro-physics' of penal practice but also a wider interest in the place of the penal in modern culture, especially in its expressive and emotive aspects.

Evaluation

In view of the complexity and scale of contemporary penal systems, their endless changeability (yet the obdurate and intractable nature of many of their central problems) and the intense political controversy and sensitivity that surround them, the social analysis of penality has become a necessary and highly active field of criminological enquiry. The emergence of new modes and techniques, for example around the assessment and calculation of risk, in conjunction with some ostensibly very old themes in populist political rhetoric, together with the grossly unequal weight of penal action that falls on specific sections of the population – especially along the fault-line of race (Wacquant, 2000) – makes for a penal landscape that demands a continuous effort of understanding and critical evaluation.

Richard Sparks

Associated Concepts: carceral society, governmentality, penology, risk, social control

Key Readings
Foucault, M. (1977) *Discipline and Punish*. London, Allen Lane.
Garland, D. (1990) *Punishment and Modern Society*. Oxford, Oxford University Press.
Garland, D. and Young, P. (eds) (1983) *The Power to Punish*. Aldershot, Gower.
Howe, A. (1993) *Punish and Critique: Towards a Feminist Analysis of Penality*. London, Routledge.
Rusche, G. and Kirchheimer, O. (1968) *Punishment and Social Structure*. New York, Russell and Russell.
Wacquant, L. (2000) 'The fourth peculiar institution: the prison as surrogate ghetto', *Theoretical Criminology*, 4 (3), pp. 377–90.

PENOLOGY

Definition

A term which (although arguably in less common usage now than formerly) covers the application of clinical, managerial or social scientific methods or expertise to the disciplined study and evaluation of penal institutions, especially prisons.

Distinctive Features

In its older and narrower sense 'penology' designates the attempt to reform or rationalize penal conditions and regimes so as to maximize their corrective effectiveness. In recent times (roughly since the middle of the twentieth century), its sense broadens to include any form of systematic enquiry into the characteristics of penal systems – including, at its radical edge, arguments for their abolition.

It is conventional, and probably appropriate, to date the inception of modern penological thinking from the reform projects undertaken by John Howard, Jeremy Bentham and others from the later eighteenth century onwards. Mention of these two very different thinkers, the former an impassioned advocate of Christian charity and the latter a utilitarian rationalist, betrays a duality that has since recurred many times in the historical development of penology between motivations grounded in humanitarian magnanimity or the desire for the religious reformation of the offender and those directed more instrumentally at the refinement of techniques of behavioural control. To the extent that these ambiguities attended the birth of penology it is unsurprising that the subsequent activities of penologists have often produced ambiguous, hybrid and sometimes perverse or contradictory results, as historians of the subject have often demonstrated (see, for example, Ignatieff, 1978; McGowen, 1995). Suffice here only to note that the particular histories of prison architecture and disciplinary regimes, as well as the minutiae of medico-psychiatric services, religious observance, diet and other aspects of the material infrastructure and social relations of penal institutions are largely unintelligible without reference to the intellectual inputs of the various penologies that have successively informed them. In that penology has been throughout most of its history a reform-minded subject with practical goals, it has been characterized by the repeated inventiveness (and as often the repeated failures) of projects for the improvement, if not indeed the utopian perfectibility, of prisons and other penal arrangements.

For much of the twentieth century two major foci of penological effort are apparent. The first is the monitoring of variations in sentencing and of the manipulation of penal regimes (both in prisons and in non-custodial settings) for evidence of their impact on offending and re-offending, whether on grounds of rehabilitation, deterrence or incapacitation. In the hands of its more sophisticated practitioners (for example Norval Morris, Michael Tonry or Franklin Zimring and Gordon Hawkins for the United States; Nigel Walker or Anthony Bottoms for the United Kingdom), this concern necessarily shades into legal theory and the philosophy of punishment. If penology has a disciplinary identity which is distinguishable from these normative and theoretical matters it lies in its rigorous application of empirical procedures. For a representative survey of work in these traditions see von Hirsch and Ashworth (1998).

The second major focus of enquiry is the systematic study of penal institutions themselves – their social organization, routines and characteristic relationships; the experience of confinement and of custodial or supervisory work; the recurrent problems of imprisonment (riots, violence, suicide and self-harm); and, more especially in the last three decades, questions of discriminatory or disparate treatment on grounds of race, gender and age. Such work arguably enjoyed a heyday in the middle decades of the twentieth century when the prison aroused the fascination first of functionalist (Clemmer's 'prison community', Sykes's 'society of captives') and later of symbolic interactionist (Goffman's 'total institutions') sociologies (see Sparks et al., 1996, chapter 2 for a short survey).

The subsequent relative decline both of therapeutic penology and of prison sociology, especially in the United States, would seem to flow in large part from a diminished confidence, increasingly evident from the 1970s onwards, in the capacities of penal interventions to reduce reoffending (the so-called 'loss

of the rehabilitative ideal', or in its more extreme formulation the 'nothing works' position). For many observers this coincides with a shift, again most pronounced in the United States, towards primarily incapacitative rationales for punishing or, more critically understood, a move towards a 'warehousing' approach to imprisonment. These developments are summed-up by Garland (1990) as constituting a 'crisis of penal modernism'. The irony for penology is that whereas the latter developments tend to increase the scale of imprisonment this is met by a reduced intensity of scholarly interest in what goes on in prisons, or more generally in the lives and fates of offenders beyond a merely supervisory concern with risk management and case-processing (for an account of the outworkings of this view see Simon, 2000).

Evaluation

Penology has not, however, come to a full stop. For its more practically oriented practitioners there is now a sense that 'nothing works' always was an over-reaction and a resurgent interest (albeit in more modest but more technically sophisticated vein) in 'what works?'. For others there is also the sobering awareness that however much penologists have historically claimed to stand on the progressive side of every engagement, the subject cannot evade complicity in or responsibility for the disciplinary apparatuses erected in its name and especially their regressive consequences for stigmatized and dispossessed people.

Richard Sparks

Associated Concepts: deterrence, incapacitation, incarceration, penality, rehabilitation

Key Readings

Garland, D. (1990) *Punishment and Modern Society*. Oxford, Oxford University Press.

von Hirsch, A. and Ashworth, A. (eds) (1998) *Principled Sentencing: Readings on Theory and Policy*, 2nd edn. Oxford, Hart Publishing.

Ignatieff, M. (1978) *A Just Measure of Pain*. Harmondsworth, Penguin.

McGowen, R. (1995) 'The well-ordered prison: England, 1780–1865', in N. Morris and D. Rothman (eds), *The Oxford History of the Prison*. Oxford, Oxford University Press.

Simon, J. (2000) 'The "society of captives" in the era of hyper-incarceration', *Theoretical Criminology*, 4 (3), pp. 285–308.

Sparks, J.R., Bottoms, A.E. and Hay, W.T. (1996) *Prisons and the Problem of Order*. Oxford, Oxford University Press.

PERSONAL SAFETY

Definition

The daily, often taken for granted, routines, that human beings engage in as a way of feeling safer at home, on the street and in the workplace.

Distinctive Features

The concept is primarily associated with the radical feminist response to the fear of crime debate. Radical feminists argue that that debate constructs a passive image of (female) victims of crime and renders their fears irrational by pursuing an understanding of criminal victimization which focuses on the threat posed by random violence from a stranger. The radical feminist response to the fear of crime, however, focuses attention on the threat of danger from people (men) that are known and consequently is concerned to understand how women (and men) manage danger in their routine everyday lives. Hence a concern with the active construction of strategies for the management of personal safety. It is a concept that emphasizes the active participation by individuals in their everyday lives rather than presuming that human beings are passive recipients of events that just happen to them. Work informed by this concept has demonstrated that men and women work with different languages of personal safety. For example, women's strategies are much more likely to be informed by the threat of sexual danger, whilst men's strategies are much more likely to be informed by the threat of physical danger, though the subsequent experience of vulnerability can be felt in very similar ways. In addition, age and sexuality also appear to contribute to individual personal safety strategies.

Evaluation

This concept constituted an important interjection into the fear of crime debate and has contributed to a more careful and considered approach to understanding the way in which crime routinely impacts upon the everyday life of individuals. It challenges the image of the individual paralysed by the fear of crime and encourages an understanding of the ways in which people manage what they know may or may not happen to them. In particular it has contributed to an appreciation of understanding women as experts in their own safety and to the difficulties of separating the public from the private: the fear of the unknown from the fear of the known.

As a concept it has become absorbed by the crime prevention literature in which setting it has lost some of its feminist resonance. Nevertheless, as an idea, it does encourage practitioners to work with an active rather than a passive image of the human being.

Sandra Walklate

Associated Concepts: community safety, crime prevention, fear of crime, left realism, radical feminism, victimology

Key Readings
Goodey, J. (1997) 'Boys don't cry; masculinities, fear of crime, and fearlessness', *British Journal of Criminology*, 37 (3), pp. 401–18.
Stanko, E. (1990) *Everyday Violence: How Women and Men Experience Sexual and Physical Danger*. London, Pandora.
Stanko, E. (1997) 'Safety talk: conceptualizing women's risk assessment as a "technology of the soul"', *Theoretical Criminology*, 1 (4), pp. 479–99.
Walklate, S. (1998) 'Excavating the fear of crime: fear, anxiety or trust?', *Theoretical Criminology*, 2 (4), pp. 403–18.

PERSONALITY THEORY

Definition

Personality theory is a central feature of mainstream psychology. The term personality is generally taken to refer to a relatively stable set of distinguishing psychological characteristics. It is the combination of such features that defines a particular type of personality. Personality theory is therefore concerned with understanding the constituents of personality, its development and, ultimately, its measurement.

Distinctive Features

The core of personality theory lies in attempting to understand the behavioural variance that can be ascribed to factors internal to the person, as opposed to the effects of the environment. Thus, personality can be thought of as the stable structure and pattern of an individual's thoughts and feelings which, in turn, are related to distinctive styles of behaviour. Personality theorists might look for basic dimensions, or *types*, of personality that can be ascribed to distinctive psychological factors such as beliefs or emotions. The idea of types of personality is not new: Hippocrates, for example, described four basic types of temperament as Sanguine (Optimistic), Melancholic (Depressed), Choleric (Irritable) and Phlegmatic (Calm).

If, as personality theory suggests, there are particular personality *types*, then what are the constituents of the type? Some personality theorists argue that *traits* are the building blocks of a personality type. A consistent grouping of particular traits, is then said to constitute a type. For example, a personality test might show that an individual scores highly on the traits of competence, self-discipline, dutifulness and reliability. This grouping of traits might then be said to define a conscientious type of personality.

The distinction between a type and a trait can be thought of as the distinction between a category and a dimension. Gordon Allport (1897–1967) summed it up in a comment that a person can be said to *have* a trait but to *fit* a type.

As in any broad theoretical approach, personality theorists differ in their views about the distinctions between traits, the nature of types, and the complex biological and psychological processes that must be involved. From the standpoint of criminology, it is the personality theory of Hans Eysenck (1916–97) that is of greatest interest.

Eysenck's theory is, in essence, a control theory, beginning from the perspective that everyone has the potential to behave in a criminal manner: the issue is why does everyone not commit crimes? In other words, what are the forces that *control* the common propensity to crime? Eysenck (1959) defined two personality types, *extroversion* (E) and *neuroticism* (N); later work (Eysenck and Eysenck, 1968) described a third dimension, *psychoticism* (P). Each of these basic types is conceived as a continuum, with most people falling in the middle range, and, it follows, with comparatively few people at the extremes of each scale. Extroversion runs from high (extrovert) to low (introvert); similarly neuroticism runs from high (neurotic) to low (stable); as also does psychoticism.

Eysenck's theory of personality proposes that, principally through our genetic endowment, we are born with cortical and autonomic nervous systems that directly affect our ability to learn from, or more properly to *condition* to, environmental stimuli. Biologically, the extrovert is cortically *under*-aroused and so seeks stimulation to maintain cortical arousal at an optimal level. The extrovert will display traits such as being impulsive, seeking excitement and social contact, and being assertive. The introvert is cortically *over*-aroused and tries to avoid stimulation to keep arousal down to a comfortable level: introverts are characterized by a quiet, reserved demeanour. In terms of conditioning, that is learning by Pavlovian conditioning or association rather than operant conditioning, the theory maintains that extroverts condition less efficiently than introverts.

Neuroticism, sometimes called emotionality, is said to be related to the functioning of the autonomic nervous system (ANS). Individuals at the high extreme of this continuum are characterized by a very labile ANS, which causes strong reactions to any unpleasant or painful stimuli: high N individuals display moody, anxious behaviour. Low N individuals have a very stable ANS and so display calm, even-tempered behaviour even when under stress. As with E, N is also linked with conditionability: high N leads to poor conditioning because of the vitiating effects of anxiety; low N leads to efficient conditioning. Each individual will manifest both E and N and, as conditionability is related to levels of E and N, it follows that stable introverts (Low N–Low E) will condition best; stable extroverts (Low N–High E) and neurotic introverts (High N–Low E) will be at some mid point; while neurotic extroverts (High N–High E) will condition least well.

The third personality dimension, psychoticism (P), is less well formulated than E and N: while maintaining a genetic basis for P, its biological basis has not been described in detail. P consists of traits such as a preference for solitude, a lack of feeling for others, sensation-seeking, toughmindedness and aggression.

The relationship between personality and crime has been further described and refined (for example Eysenck, 1977; Eysenck and Gudjonsson, 1989). But the principal assumption informing the theory remains that children learn to control antisocial behaviour through the development of a 'conscience': this conscience, Eysenck maintains, is a set of conditioned emotional responses to environmental events associated with the anti-social behaviour. For example, the child who misbehaves receives a parental reprimand, the fear this brings is associated with the anti-social act, and over time this conditioning determines the child's level of socialization. The speed and efficiency of social conditioning will mainly depend upon the individual's personality in terms of E and N. As the High E–High N combination leads to poor conditionability then such individuals will be least likely to learn social control and therefore, it is predicted, will be over-represented in offender populations. Conversely, Low E–Low N would lead to effective socialization, so that these individuals would be predicted to be under-represented in offender groups. The remaining two combinations, High E–Low N and Low E–High N, fall at some intermediate level and so would be expected in both offender and non-offender groups. The third personality dimension, P, is also argued to be strongly related to offending, particularly with crimes that involve hostility towards other people.

Evaluation

Eysenck's theory of crime (or more properly *anti-social behaviour*) has generated a great deal of empirical research. The broad position is that there is unanimous support for the contention that offenders will score highly on P; the majority of studies show that offender samples score highly on N; and the evidence is mixed for E. In seeking to account for the discrepant findings for E, Eysenck suggested that E might be split into two components, Sociability and Impulsiveness, with only the latter related to offending. A study by Eysenck and McGurk (1980) confirmed that an offender sample scored higher than a non-offender sample on Impulsiveness, with no difference between the two samples on a measure of Sociability.

Evidence in support of the theory is presented in a study by McGurk and McDougall (1981), which conducted a cluster analysis of the P, E and N scores of 100 delinquents and 100 non-delinquent college pupils. The analysis showed four personality clusters in each group: both groups contained Low E–High N and High E–Low N clusters, but the clusters predicted to be related to criminal behaviour – High E–High N and High P–High E–High N – were, indeed, found only in the delinquent sample. The Low E–Low N group, which the theory would predict to be highly socialized, was found only in the non-delinquent group. However, not all studies using cluster analysis have produced such clear findings.

The weight of empirical evidence lends some support to Eysenck's thesis that there is a relationship between personality (as he defines it) and crime. A number of reservations, as Eysenck acknowledges, need to be made. The theory does not explain all crime and, with its concentration on the high and low extremes of the personality types, is clearly not applicable to all offenders. Further, one of the theoretical bases of the theory, the link between classical conditioning and socialization, remains to be established satisfactorily. Still further, the theory demands acceptance of a trait theory of personality which is only one of a number of ways of conceptualizing personality, and one that has come under fierce attack from proponents of other theoretical approaches to understanding human behaviour.

Clive Hollin

Associated Concepts: biological criminology, conditioning, extroversion/introversion, social control theory

Key Readings

Eysenck, H.J. (1959) *Manual of the Maudsley Personality Inventory*. London, University of London Press.

Eysenck, H.J. (1977) *Crime and Personality*, 3rd edn. London, Routledge and Kegan Paul.

Eysenck, H.J. and Eysenck, S.B.G. (1968) 'A factorial study of psychoticism as a dimension of personality', *Multivariate Behavioural Research* (Special Issue), pp. 15–31.

Eysenck, H.J. and Gudjonsson, G.H. (1989) *The Causes and Cures of Criminality*. London, Plenum Press.

Eysenck, S.B.G. and McGurk, B.J. (1980) 'Impulsiveness and venturesomeness in a detention centre population', *Psychological Reports*, 47, pp. 1299–1306.

McGurk, B.J. and McDougall, C. (1981) 'A new approach to Eysenck's theory of criminality', *Personality and Individual Differences*, 2, pp. 338–40.

POLICING

See 'Broken windows'; Community policing; Problem oriented policing; Self-policing; Social control; Surveillance; Transnational policing; Zero tolerance

POLITICAL CRIME

Definition

Political crime has been defined in a number of different ways but, apart from a broad definition which sees all crime as political, most seek to make a distinction between political crime and ordinary crime either because of the different *motivations* or *ideology* of the individuals involved or the different *context* in which the crime takes place.

Distinctive Features

All crime is political in the sense that it is a violation of the criminal law, which itself derives from a political process and defends some value system. Two early materialist proponents of this position, who have been much neglected by criminologists, were Godwin and De Sade (Jenkins, 1984). Godwin rejected all claims that could be made in favour of the state and criminal law and De Sade argued that the criminal law was developed to safeguard property, much of which the powerful had acquired themselves through violence and theft. Property was simply theft. Radical criminology also considered that crime was political in the sense that the processes of 'crime-creation are bound up in the final analysis with the material basis of contemporary capitalism and its structures of law'. Most writers, however, make a distinction between political crime and ordinary crimes because there are important differences in form, context and motivation.

There are a number of definitions that emphasize the *conviction* or *motivation* of the actor. Schafer (1971, 1974), for example, distinguished between the convictional and the conventional criminal. The former commits crime because he or she is convinced about the truth or justification of their own altruistic beliefs. Hagan (1997) defines political crime as criminal activity which is committed for ideological purposes rather than by private greed or passion. He provides a list of different types of motivation and examples of individuals who expressed these: socio-political (Robin Hood), religious (Martin Luther), moral or ethical (anti-abortion activists), science (Copernicus or Galileo), political causes (Nathan Hale, Benedict Arnold). For Hagan, political crime can take two forms: crime by the government or crime against the government. But some argue (for example, Turk, 1982) that political crime should not also include crimes committed by the state.

Closely related to the debate about the definition of political crime is the question of how those who commit these types of offence should be treated when punished. The activities of both the Fenians and the Suffragettes, who both broke the law for political objectives, led to considerable discussion in the late nineteenth and early twentieth centuries over whether the political offender should have special status in prison. Anglo-American law, in general, has, since the early twentieth century consistently refused to allow a distinction between political and ordinary criminals (Radzinowicz and Hood, 1981).

One exception was the granting of special status category to prisoners in Northern Ireland under emergency legislation in 1972. When the government tried to abolish it, IRA prisoners went on hunger strike in 1980/81. The Prime Minister of the United Kingdom, Mrs Thatcher, expressed the government's position in the now famous aphorism: 'A crime, is a crime, is a crime'. In short, no crimes can have political origins and no criminal would be recognized as a political criminal. Notwithstanding this position, subsequently an official government inquiry into the emergency legislation acknowledged a distinction that most people made in Northern Ireland between political criminals and what were euphemistically described as 'ordinary decent criminals'.

Evaluation

The concept of political crime, however defined, is a key notion in criminology. As Schafer (1974, pp. 8, 22) has pointed out, it is 'pivotal to the understanding of criminology and the whole normative system of society'. It has been a relatively neglected concept. Few criminology textbooks discuss it or provide historical or contemporary examples. Yet the concept challenges a number of taken-for-granted assumptions about crime and its causes. To begin with, it challenges definitions of crime that assume crime to be a relatively unproblematic concept possessing some ontological reality. Events or activities that are defined as criminal are only one set of a range of harms captured in the criminal law. A notion of political crime draws attention to the politics involved in deciding what should or should not be embraced by the criminal law. Secondly, the concept draws attention to the fact that crime and criminal behaviour are not always negative phenomena. Many people commit crimes for altruistic purposes, just as people give blood, and as a direct result of their activities many progressive reforms have been introduced. Thirdly, when defined in terms of illegal activities of states or governments, it forces a comparison between the extent of harm from political criminals and ordinary decent criminals. In many regions of the world the harm produced through state crime is far greater than through ordinary crime. One problem, however, with the concept when defined in terms of motivation is its relativity. A political criminal today may be a government minister tomorrow.

Paddy Hillyard

Associated Concepts: crime, emergency legislation, genocide, human rights, new criminology, primitive rebellion, radical criminologies, the state, state crime

Key Readings

Hagan, F.E. (1997) Political Crime: Ideology and Criminology. Boston, MA, Allyn and Bacon.
Jenkins, P. (1984) 'Varieties of Enlightenment criminology: Beccaria, Godwin, de Sade', British Journal of Criminology, 24 (2), pp. 112–30.
Radzinowicz, L. and Hood, R. (1981) 'The status of political prisoners in England: the struggle for recognition', The Virginia Law Review, 65 (8), pp. 1421–81.
Schafer, S. (1971) 'The concept of the political criminal', Journal of Criminal Law, Criminology and Police Science, 62 (3), pp. 380–7.
Schafer, S. (1974) The Political Criminal: The Problems of Morality and Crime. New York, The Free Press.
Turk, A. (1982) Political Criminality. London, Sage.

POPULAR JUSTICE

See Informal justice

POSITIVISM

Definition

A theoretical approach that emerged in the early nineteenth century which argues that social relations and events (including crime) can be studied scientifically using methods derived from the natural sciences. Its aim is to search for, explain and predict future patterns of social behaviour. In criminology it straddles biological, psychological and sociological disciplines in an attempt to identify key causes of crime – whether genetic, psychological, social or economic – which are thought to lie largely outside of each individual's control.

Distinctive Features

The key characteristic of positivism is the application of the methods of the natural sciences to the study of social behaviour. It has generally involved the search for cause and effect relations that can be measured in a similar way to which natural scientists observe and analyse relations between objects in the physical world. Positivism does not concern itself with the abstract and the unproven, but with the tangible and quantifiable. Through gaining 'objective' knowledge about how behaviour is determined by physiological, psychological and environmental conditions, it is assumed that most social problems can be understood and treated through the 'positive application of science'.

Whilst it is difficult to identify the precise moment when a positivist criminology emerged, one of the first attempts to apply positivist principles to crime emerged through the work of French and Belgian statisticians in the 1820s. Adolphe Quetelet, for example, found that crime and crime rates, rather than being random and unpredictable, were remarkably constant. He inferred that crime seemed to obey the same law-like irregularities as physical phenomena. However, it is widely assumed that a modern scientific criminology began with the advent of a criminal anthropology associated with the work of the Italian physician Cesare Lombroso in the 1870s. By studying the body shapes of executed criminals, Lombroso attempted to prove scientifically that those who broke the law were physically different from those who did not. Such notions were in direct contrast to the prevailing judicial doctrine which was grounded in principles of neo-classicism and which maintained that, with few exceptions, behaviour was a matter of free will and individual choice. People broke laws because they anticipated that the benefits would outweigh any loss. They acted largely out of hedonism, choosing behaviour that was pleasurable and avoiding that which would give pain. For much of the eighteenth and nineteenth centuries this meant that no defences of criminal acts could be entertained. The arrival of Lombroso's theory remained a significant challenge to the judicial orthodoxy. For if criminality was determined by factors other than rational choice, then surely it made little sense to punish offenders. Rather their condition should be treated.

By the early 1920s the development of a criminological science – positivism – was to become influential, not only in physiology, but also in medicine, psychiatry, psychology and sociology. Offending came to be thought of as being determined by biological and/or cultural antecedents. It was no longer viewed as simply self-determining. By searching for the specific causes (or aetiology) of criminal behaviour, positive criminology assumes that criminality has a peculiar set characteristics. Accordingly, most research of this type has tried to isolate key differences between criminals and non-criminals. Some theorists have focused on biological and psychological factors, thus locating the sources of crime primarily within the individual and bringing to the fore questions of individual pathology and abnormality. This approach is central to individual positivism. In contrast, sociological positivism argues that the key causative factors lie in the social contexts external to the individual. Here crime is more a matter of social pathology.

Evaluation

Many of the basic principles of positivism came to be questioned during the 1960s. In particular positivism was criticized for:

- Denying the role of human consciousness and meaning in social activity.
- Assuming that there is an underlying consensus in society, of which crime is a key violation.
- Presenting an over-determined view of human action.
- Equating crime with *under*-socialization or social *dis*-organization rather than accepting the validity of different forms of socialization and of social organization.

- Ignoring the presence and relevance of competing value systems, cultural diversity or structural conflict.

Nevertheless, positivism maintains a strong presence in contemporary criminological studies. Since the 1970s work has continued in examining the role genetic structures play in determining patterns of individual behaviour (including crime). Evidence from the Cambridge Study in Delinquent Development suggests that crime runs in particular families. Poor parenting, low intelligence, hyperactivity and anti-social behaviour have been cited as key predictors of future criminality. Similarly, research of long-term trends in crime has concluded that property crime increases at times of economic depression whilst personal crime increases at times of economic boom. Positivism also retains popular and political appeal (in both its individual and sociological variants) because of a general reluctance of governments to accept that crime lies beyond their control. However, it also remains the subject of controversy. Some would argue that the use of the scientific method remains superior to conjecture or polemic, but such methodology carries no automatic guarantee of uncovering the 'truth'. Inaccurate assumptions, misinterpretations, misapplication of findings and inadequate measures for testing can all conspire to produce not only misleading but dangerous conclusions. Assumptions are likely to be made about exactly which factors, from a myriad of the potentially relevant, are worthy of study. In this, the selection of particular variables will depend on a priori assumptions the scientist holds about the nature of human behaviour. Positivist modes of study tend to discover various *correlations* between crime and extraneous conditions but can rarely if ever claim to have specified direct *causes*. Above all, the concept of crime is accepted uncritically.

John Muncie

Associated Concepts: biological criminology, causation, determinism, dispositional theories, genetics, individual positivism, rehabilitation, sociological positivism, somatotyping

Key Readings

Ferri, E. (1901) *Criminal Sociology*. Boston, MA, Little, Brown.

Lombroso, C. (1876) *L'Uomo Delinquente*. Milan, Hoepli.

Lombroso, C. (1913) *Crime: Its Causes and Remedies.* Boston, MA, Little, Brown.

Quetelet, A. (1842) *A Treatise on Man.* Edinburgh, Chambers.

POST-COLONIAL CRIMINOLOGY

Definition

At its most simple, the term 'post-colonial' refers to the historical period after colonialism and is linked to anti-colonization and de-colonization. A much broader conceptualization of the term would include the analysis of the on-going relationship between the colonial and post-colonial and the signalling of new ways of thinking which have emanated from heterogeneous sources. In this sense the post-colonial is both a condition and a space. Although at the time of writing there is no fully fledged post-colonial criminology, there is a convincing case for such an emergent field of study.

Distinctive Features

The concept post-colonial is most fully developed in the humanities and it refers to the interdisciplinary work of a body of scholars such as Edward Said, Gayatri Spivak and Homi Bhabha, who are involved in a political project of both remembering and promoting new forms of literature from those countries colonized by European imperial powers, particularly England. These new and not so new literatures have the vital role of challenging and disrupting the Western sense of where the 'centre of important things' lies. They also analyse what was left behind in terms of the cultural residues of race and empire. Hybridity, subaltern, interstices, otherness, alterity, double awareness, in-betweenness, rootedness and diaspora are among the key words that mark out the complexities of post-colonial analysis. The post-colonial is vitally important for understanding the shifting cultural relationships between different parts of a thoroughly globalized world. As a mode of critique and challenge, it provincializes much of what passes for general theory and points to its Eurocentrism.

So what work would a post-colonial criminology do? Its initial work would consist of:

- analysing criminology's historical complicity in techniques of colonial governance;
- exposing its practices of interiorization and exteriorization;
- revealing the racialized subjects and categories constructed within and through criminological discourses;
- centring what has been denied, ignored and marginalized;
- working within or in relation to non-European/non-Western criminological 'writings from elsewhere';
- identifying and inscribing what has been silenced by 'the canon' and 'founding gestures' of Western criminology;
- reinterpreting the 'classics' of Western criminology through application of post-colonialism's key concepts and methodologies;
- acknowledging that the point of departure for understanding Western criminal justice practices might be 'elsewhere';
- producing alternative conceptualizations of 'self-evident' issues;
- deploying strategic essentialism to generate new oppositions;
- formulating discourses of resistance to neo-colonial criminological practices.

Evaluation

Post-colonialization would involve the re-thinking and re-writing of criminology's past and present with the overall intention of de-colonizing the disciplinary space. This involves interrogating Western criminology not only from the outside but from within. In the case of 'British' criminology this would involve problematizing its unacknowledged core English identity and reference points. Reading a contemporary post-colonial criminology one would, for example, be conscious of the plurality of cultural meanings attached to words such as 'crime', 'criminal', 'state', 'law and order', 'culture' and 'justice'.

Eugene McLaughlin

Associated Concepts: constitutive criminology, postmodernism, post-structuralism

Key Readings

Chambers, I. and Curtis, L. (eds) (1996) *The Post-Colonial Question: Common Skies and Divided Horizons.* London, Routledge.

Gilroy, P. (1986) *There Ain't No Black in the Union Jack.* London, Hutchinson.

Hall, S., Critcher, C. Jefferson, T., Clarke, J. and

Roberts, B. (1978) *Policing the Crisis: Mugging, the State, and Law and Order*. London, Macmillan.

Shohat, E. (1992) 'Notes on the "post-colonial"', *Social Text*, 31/32, pp. 99–113.

Spivak, G. (1993) *Outside in the Teaching Machine*. London, Routledge.

Sumner, C. (1986) *Crime, Justice and Underdevelopment*. Aldershot, Gower.

POSTMODERN FEMINISM

Definition

A strand of feminism informed by postmodernism, post-colonialism and post-structuralism which rejects the notion of the essentialist 'woman', arguing the term is culturally constructed in relation and opposition to 'man' and can be deconstructed and reconstructed due to its fluidity.

Distinctive Features

Influenced by poststructuralist theorists such as Derrida and Foucault, postmodern feminists reject not only the notion of 'woman' but also patriarchy and women's subordination. Also referred to as 'post-feminism', this term is misleading, however, as it is often used by the media to define a period of time when feminism is no longer deemed relevant.

Postmodern feminism rejects binary opposites, for example male/female, objectivity/subjectivity, arguing concepts are culturally constructed in relation to one another and are therefore unstable. The production of knowledge is questioned, and claims to objectivity and the notion of a universal 'truth' are rejected. Postmodern feminists have criticized standpoint theorists, claiming neither women nor men can ever have total knowledge as all knowledge is partial and situated, and although all standpoints are conflicting, none is privileged (Haraway, 1991).

Criticisms of postmodern feminism come most strongly from radical feminists who argue that destroying the concept 'woman' will result in less collective activism. There is also concern that postmodern feminism is too 'academic' and will further widen the gap between feminist activists and academics resulting in a form of elitist feminism. It is also accused of dressing up in philosophical (male?) language what feminism has been saying for years, for example the questioning of 'malestream' knowledge and claims to objectivity originated from other strands of feminism in the early 1980s. These criticisms, along with the rejection of the existence of patriarchy have led some feminists to classify postmodern feminism as part of the growing backlash against feminism.

Evaluation

Few feminist criminologists accept postmodern feminism as being useful in its entirety, although it is also worth noting that intellectual autobiographies are increasingly offered in acknowledgement that a researcher's work to some degree reflects who and what they are. The notion that 'woman' is culturally created through power and language draws parallels with feminist objections to how women are portrayed in court in sexual assault cases. However, the influence that postmodern feminism had in recognizing this is debatable.

While postmodern feminism has been useful in terms of theory, it has limited use in view of the key aims of second-wave feminism, and although epistemological debates have been widely accepted it remains the case that few feminists are able to accept a feminism without sisterhood; a feminism without 'women'. Until criminology is ready to depart from 'modernity' and embrace 'the postmodern', there is little future for a postmodern feminism within criminology, or vice versa.

Nicole Westmarland

Associated Concepts: deconstruction, postcolonialism, postmodernism, post-structuralism, radical feminism

Key Readings

Barrett, M. (2000) 'Postfeminism', in G. Browning, A. Halcli and F. Webster (eds), *Understanding Contemporary Society: Theories of the Present*. London, Sage.

Brooks, A. (1997) *Postfeminisms – Feminism, Cultural Theory and Cultural Forms*. London, Routledge.

Haraway, D.S. (1991) *Simians, Cyborgs and Women: The Reinvention of Nature*. London, Free Association Books.

Riley, D. (1988) *Am I That Name? Feminism and the Category of 'Women' in History*. New York, Macmillan.

Smart, C. (1990) 'Feminist approaches to criminology, or postmodern woman meets atavistic man', in A. Morris and L. Gelsthorpe (eds), *Feminist Perspectives in Criminology*. Milton Keynes, Open University Press.

Young, A. (1996) *Imagining Crime*. London, Sage.

POSTMODERNISM

Definition

Postmodern theory in criminology arose in the early 1990s out of the disenchantment with modernist and Enlightenment thought. It privileges non-linear developments, orderly disorder, extreme sensitivity to initial conditions, disproportionate effects, fractal geometry, chance factors, contingency, irony, local knowledge, the decentred subject and the effects of language in the constitution of the subject. It situates its critique and suggestions for reconstruction, or transpraxis, in political economy.

Distinctive Features

Postmodern thought can be traced to French theorists in the 1970s and 1980s. Several theorists formed the kernel of the first wave: Baudrillard, Cixous, Deleuze, Derrida, Foucault, Guattari, Irigaray, Kristeva, Lyotard, Moi. Many were influenced by Nietzsche and more recently Jacques Lacan, a revisionist Freudian who integrated the works of Benveniste, Jakobson, Kojeve, de Saussure, Strauss and topology theory. He was to give Freud's early work a linguistic spin (the 'unconscious structured like a language'). Second wave theorists have emerged in the late 1980s and 1990s who have applied this body of theory to law, criminology, cultural and media studies, the clinical and literary criticism.

Postmodern thought differs from modernist thought along several dimensions (Milovanovic, 1997).

- *Society and social structure*. Modernist thought, such as typified by the works of Durkheim, Parsons and Luhmann, privileges order, stability, linear developments, equilibrium and homeostatic analysis. Postmodern analysis privileges order *and* disorder (orderly disorder), far-from-equilibrium conditions, non-linear change, chance, indeterminacy, contingency and

irony. Rather than rigid structures such as bureaucracies, postmodern analysis privileges 'dissipative structures', which are very sensitive and responsive to their environment.

- *Social roles*. Modernist thinkers often rely on a Parsonian notion of the person whereby s/he is seen as a role player on various stages, reading specific scripts. Through socialization one is cast into various roles. For postmodernists, roles are unstable constructions; a person is always a role-maker.

- *Subjectivity/agency*. Modernists celebrate the notion of the individual (the centred subject) best typified in *Cogito, ergo sum*. This is the conscious, determining, reflective, rational and unitary person, epitimized in the notion of the juridic subject, the 'reasonable man in law'. Postmodernists offer the idea of the decentred subject, a person who is less in control, more located in various languages and what they allow.

- *Discourse*. Modernist thought assumes language is neutral; it is but an instrument for use in verbalizing a person's desire. Postmodernists argue that discourses are rather linguistic coordinate systems, and language is always already populated with voices. It is never a neutral medium.

- *Knowledge*. Modernist thought privileges global knowledge and foundational truths that can be arrived at through the scientific method. Postmodernists see knowledge as always partial, fractured, fragmented and contingent. They focus on Pathos (suffering, struggle, overcoming) over Logos (logic and rationality).

- *Space/time*. Modernist thought situates itself in Newtonian physics of space and time and in Euclidean geometry. Privileged is linearity, stasis, determinism and stability. Postmodernists privilege quantum mechanics, non-Euclidean geometry, topology theory, fractal geometry, 'striated space,' irreversibility of time among others.

- *Causality*. Modernist thought privileges determinism, linear causality and the inherent potential for discovering all laws of nature. Postmodernists, however, say 'God plays dice'. Quantum and chaos theories indicate the centrality of chance and indeterminacy as well as disproportionate effects.

- *Social change*. Modernists assume linear development in historical change, whether Hegelian (Absolute Spirit), Marxian (dialectical materialism), Weberian (rationalization), or Durkheimian (a Darwinian driven division of labour). Postmodernists identify non-linear change, orderly disorder, continuity and discontinuity existing side by side, singularities which are moments in which accurate understanding breaks down, and disproportionate effects (small changes may have large, unanticipated results).

The emerging perspective has several prominent threads, some of which have been integrated, some not.

- *Discourse analysis*. The most significant form has been Lacanian psychoanalytic semiotics. It assumes the interconnectedness of the subject and discourse. The subject of desire finds her/his coordinates of being in various discourses which 'speak the subject'. Lacan has offered the notion of the decentred subject in a static form (Schema L) and in more dynamic forms (Graphs of Desire, Schema R, Schema I, Borromean Knots). In criminology, discourse analysis is important for realizing how various social realities get constructed and how some become more stable and privileged. In postmodern society a new reality has been constructed through the media, the 'hyper-real', which has become the coordinate for social action.
- *Chaos theory*. Chaos theory has offered several novel conceptualizations that challenge modernist ideological constructions. They offer the notion of attractors (points toward which dynamic systems tend), iteration (continuous feedback loops which lead to disproportionate effects), sensitive dependence on initial conditions (small changes may, after iteration, produce disproportionate and unexpected results), fractal geometry (in-between dimensions exist beyond the integer space that is privileged in modernist thought), far-from-equilibrium conditions (dynamic states that refuse closure), and dissipative structures ('structures' that are extremely sensitive to initial conditions, which take on only tentative, contingent stable forms and are always in process of becoming). Criminological theory has seen several recent approaches applying these conceptualizations (see the collection of essays in Milovanovic, 1997).
- *Catastrophe theory*. This approach, pioneered by Thom (1975), argues for discontinuities appearing in otherwise continuous systems. It provides a topology of various generic forms of catastrophe, depending on the number of variables that are relevant. It identifies bimodal behaviour in each at the 'fold' region, which represents discontinuous change. For an application to explaining 'seductive' forms of crime ('edgework') see Milovanovic (1996); and to insights on developing alternative conflict resolutions, Milovanovic (1999).
- *Topology theory*. Perhaps least understood, topology is referred to as a 'rubber math'. Only recently, perhaps through Lacan's extensive use, is it beginning to emerge in situating behaviour on more complex, interacting planes for expository purposes. It is more useful as a discovery principle in indicating some insight on complex dynamics. For an application in explaining non-material forms of crime see Milovanovic (1996) and for general theorizing in criminology, Arrigo (1998).

Two approaches have been at the cutting edge in integrating various of these threads into criminology:

- *Constitutive criminology*. Constitutive theory argues for the interconnectedness of phenomena and co-production in the manifestation of phenomena. It offers the notion of COREL sets in indicating historical specificities of configurations of coupled iterative loops that have often unexpected effects. Thus alternative notions of 'cause', 'harms', 'reduction' and 'repression' have been conceptualized.
- *Postmodern feminism*. Several theorists have spearheaded postmodern analysis in criminology and law. They have offered an 'ethical feminism' as opposed to a hate politics, 'contingent universalities' and new understandings of the subject in law, textual constructions of the female offender, and concepts for a social justice.

Evaluation

Postmodern criminology began to bloom in the late 1990s. Early forms (prior to 1990) were heavily criticized for their nihilism, fatalism and relativism, best identified in battle cries for 'reversal of hierarchies' and 'anti-foundationalism'. This is called the 'nihilistic form of postmodernism'. More mature forms are 'affirmative postmodernism', which is rooted not in reaction-negation dynamics but in a Nietzschean call for the affirmative. This is called transpraxis; in other words, not just reaction and criticism (negation) of what is, but also visions for a possible better society must be offered simultaneously. At the minimum, postmodernist thought has brought much debate in criminology in re-thinking causation, subjectivity, responsibility and forms of organization. The work that is appearing is beginning to integrate the various dimensions of postmodern analysis and to apply it to difficult issues in criminology. More recently, critical race theory has begun to utilize and develop the conceptual tools provided by postmodern theorizing.

Dragan Milovanovic

Associated Concepts: chaos theory, constitutive criminology, deconstruction, discourse analysis, integrative criminology, postmodern feminism, post-structuralism, praxis, psychoanalytic criminology

Key Readings

Arrigo, B. (1998) 'Theories of crime and crimes of theories: on the topological construction of criminological reality', *Theory and Psychology*, 8 (2), pp. 219–53.

Henry, S. and Milovanovic, D. (1996) *Constitutive Criminology*. London, Sage.

Milovanovic, D. (1996) 'Postmodern criminology', *Justice Quarterly*, 13 (4), pp. 567–609.

Milovanovic, D. (1997) *Chaos, Criminology and Social Justice*. New York, Praeger.

Milovanovic, D. (1999) 'Catastrophe theory, discourse, and conflict resolution', in B. Arrigo (ed.), *Social Justice/Criminal Justice*. Belmont, CA, Wadsworth.

Thom, R. (1975) *Structural Stability and Morphogenesis*. Reading, MA, Benjamin.

POST-STRUCTURALISM

Definition

Post-structuralism refers to a variety of theoretical perspectives that succeeded structuralism in France. Indebted to Nietzsche's critique of reason and rationality, post-structuralists look for the tensions and contradictions and the irrational in discursive formations. In criminology, post-structuralism remains most closely associated with the work of Michel Foucault.

Distinctive Features

Structuralism originated in the linguistic studies of language undertaken by Ferdinand de Saussure (1857–1913). It was subsequently taken up by Lévi-Strauss, Lacan and Althusser who applied structural-linguistic concepts to the humanities and social sciences in an attempt to construct a more coherent mode of analysis. Structuralists favoured holistic forms of analysis that characterized phenomena in terms of parts and wholes, defining structure as the interrelation of parts of a common system. Revealing the underlying codes, rules and functions that organized phenomena into a social system was the purpose of structuralist analysis. Structuralists believed in objectivity, logic, unity, coherence, self-sufficiency, rigour and truth, and claim social scientific status for their theorizing. In doing so they rejected humanist approaches such as phenomenology and existentialism, with their stress on the subject and subjectivity. Meanings are constituted not by conscious subjects but by relations among the parts of a system. Criminology has always been home to structuralist approaches such as structural functionalism and structural Marxism. Both of these share a belief in their social scientific ability to identify underlying causes that generate particular patterns of criminal behaviour and emphasize materiality and the primacy of structure over agency. Although French structuralist debates had little impact on criminology, Althusser's writings on scientific Marxism, with its emphasis on structural causality, and his reading of ideology did resonate within left-wing criminology in the UK in the late 1970s.

Post-structuralism is both a reaction against and complication of structuralist insights and can be found in the work of writers such as Derrida, Foucault, Deleuze and Kristeva. Post-structuralists question the assumption that systems are self-sufficient structures and that theorists can somehow position themselves outside and independently of that which they are analysing. For post-structuralists there is no 'outside' position (whether in language or politics) from which to critique. The world, rather than existing independently of the ways we talk about it, is constructed in discourse. Post-structuralists also challenge the structuralist claim to scientific status, preferring to view science as a discourse that is constituted through and embodies social relations of power that underpin its claims to truth. It is worth noting that the post-structuralists are also dismissive of structuralism's claims to clarity, opting for a mode of address and argumentation marked by density, impenetrability, ambiguity and incoherence. Post-structuralism not only re-centres the subject but constructs a subject that is fragmentary and contradictory. Consequently, it also stresses the importance of differences over unity. As a result of post-structuralism's anti-essentialism, considerably more attention was paid to theorizing subjectivity, agency and power. Post-structuralism has had a major influence on feminist and postmodernist theorizing.

Derrida developed deconstruction as a method of destabilizing and decentring modern philosophy's claims to truth. Deconstruction involves looking at a system, examines how it was built, identifies the keystones and the defining angles which support the structure. By moving the component pieces around, one can free oneself from the authority and logics of the system. In its analysis of texts, deconstruction identifies the key processes of signification, looking for the incoherences, instabilities and ambivalences within texts, locating the traces of oppositional elements and reversing the normal patterns of interpretation. Deconstruction is radically disruptive because it first of all reverses and then seeks to replace 'natural' oppositions such as nature/culture, male/female and object/subject. For Derrida these oppositions are restrictive substitutes for thinking.

Post-structuralism impacted on criminology via Michel Foucault's anti-realist and anti-essentialist *Discipline and Punish*. In this book he presents not a history but an 'archaeology' or 'genealogy' of the transformation of the notion of punishment and the birth of the prison. Foucault's intention is to lay to rest those congratulatory histories of the modern prison which tell a story of progress, reform and enlightenment. For Foucault, what is significant in the transformation of a mode of punishment that depended on the infliction of bodily pain and public theatrical spectacle to one organized around incarceration, regulation, surveillance and reformation of the mind is not whether it is better or more humane but how it represents the re-organization of disciplinary knowledge/power. For Foucault, the techniques and rationales embedded in Bentham's proposed 'Panopticon' – surveillance, classification, examination – were the embodiment of this shift to a new modality of control. The prison was but one representative institution of the carceral society where disciplinary power/knowledge is exercised within a multitude of institutional practices.

Foucault's analysis of the prison also provides us with an answer to the question of why the new model prison failed to reform offenders. Discussions that focus on the 'success' or 'failure' of the prison are inappropriate. The prison cannot fail because 'it is not intended to eliminate offences, but rather to distinguish them, to distribute them, to use them'.

Evaluation

A post-structuralist Foucauldian perspective on the constitution of power/knowledge has provided criminologists with a vital set of conceptual tools for analysing official texts in a wide range of criminal justice settings and for undertaking histories of the present. The work of feminists writers such as Vikki Bell (on incest), Carol Smart (on law) and Alison Young (on postmodern criminology) signifies the intellectual power of post-structuralist ideas.

Eugene McLaughlin

Associated Concepts: deconstruction, discourse analysis, essentialism, panopticism, postmodern feminism, postmodernism, social control

Key Readings

Bell, V. (1993) *Interrogating Incest: Feminism, Foucault and the Law*. London, Routledge.
Berman, A. (1996) *From the New Criticism to Deconstruction: The Reception of Structuralism and Post Structuralism*. Urbana, IL, University of Illinois Press.
Foucault, M. (1977) *Discipline and Punish*. Harmondsworth, Penguin.
Smart, C. (1995) *Law, Crime and Sexuality*. London, Sage.
Young, A. (1995) *Imagining Crime*. London, Sage.

PRAXIS

Definition

Praxis refers to the link between theory and practice, and the struggle that exists in all intellectual movements to transform existing (oppressive or marginalizing) societal conditions into meaningful reflection, action and change. Praxis is a complicated and intricate phenomenon because it entails a re-constitution of culture, institutions, relationships and social interaction, such that a more humane, emancipatory climate of pro-social civic life prevails. Moments of praxis, then, redirect our entire way of being from the alienating constraints of identity politics to the unifying dynamics of a pluralistic society. Self-determination, intentionality, sociality and creativity are cornerstones of praxis and the new social order it endorses.

Distinctive Features

The notion of praxis has its roots in the work of Karl Marx. Marxism is a dialectical and historical theory of human progress, that responds to the economic and social problems associated with (advanced state-regulated) capitalism. For Marx (1868) praxis was that moment in which 'the free development of each [was] the free development of all'. According to Marxist thought, praxis is a political and economic effort designed to change the conditions that give rise to psychological alienation and social oppression. Indeed, during the period in which Karl Marx lived and wrote, people were alienated from their labour, from their fellow workers, and from themselves. Under such conditions, change was necessary and inevitable. The source of this change was a blend of scholarly enquiry and political action; namely, praxis.

Others have contemporized Marx's notions on praxis and applied his insights in different social science contexts. For example, the dialogical and liberation pedagogy of Paulo Freire (1985, p. 50) calls for *conscientization*. The purpose of conscientization is for the oppressed to 'exercise the right to participate consciously in the socio-historical transformation of their society'. Freire was particularly interested in how the oppressed (such as the poor, the illiterate, the disenfranchised) could function as cultural revolutionaries. The key to transformation is reflection and dialogue in which the subjugated speak 'true words' about themselves, about the conditions in which they live, and about the necessary and inevitable process by which change (an alternative, emancipatory reality) can materialize.

Feminists, especially Marxist and socialist feminists, have appropriated Marx's notion of praxis. Both claim that the conditions in which women find themselves are related to the state of malestream praxis and the culture of patriarchy and capitalism. Women's liberation is rooted in transforming the sexual division of labour, reconstituting society's notions of masculinity, femininity, competition, hierarchy

and production. Feminist praxis entails endorsing such interventions as consciousness-raising, connectivity, the primacy of relationships, and the personal is political.

Postmodernists have further refined the Marxist notion of praxis by utilizing the concept of 'transpraxis.' Transpraxis retains the Marxist conviction that theory and practice need to be linked to produce change; however, it also addresses the role of language in such transformations. Transpraxis involves the dialectics of linguistic struggle in which the new, reconstituted order does not re-create conditions of alienation and oppression. Transpraxis is a deliberate and affirmative attempt not to reverse hierarchies but, instead, to affirm those who victimize, marginalize and criminalize while renouncing their victimizing, marginalizing and criminalizing practices. Transpraxis is an effort to validate the act of resistance. The key to transpraxis is speech, words, grammar and how we talk about (and then act upon) emancipation.

Evaluation

Praxis (or transpraxis) symbolizes efforts to alter and improve the conditions in which people live, work and engage others. Critical and radical criminology have been more closely linked with the Marxist notion of praxis. Socialist feminist criminologists have similarly relied upon the Marxist concept, infusing it with a sensitivity to gender politics. Postmodern criminologists (particularly constitutive criminologists) have appropriated the idea of transpraxis in their explanation of crime, criminals and criminal behaviour.

Bruce Arrigo

Associated Concepts: constitutive criminology, critical criminology, feminist criminologies, Marxist criminologies, political crime, postmodernism

Key Readings

Eisenstein, Z. (ed.) (1979) *Capitalist Patriarchy and the Case for Socialist Feminism*. New York, Monthly Review Press.
Freire, P. (1972) *Pedagogy of the Oppressed*. New York, Herder and Herder.
Freire, P. (1985) *The Politics of Education*. South Hadley, MA, Bergin and Garvey.
Henry, S. and Milovanovic, D. (1996) *Constitutive Criminology: Beyond Postmodernism*. London, Sage.

Marx, K. (1868) *Capital*, 3 vols. New York, International Press.

Marx, K. and Engels, F. (1845–6) *The German Ideology*. New York, International Publishers.

PREDICTION STUDIES

Definition

The aim of prediction studies is to find the variables (risk factors) that most accurately predict the likelihood of offending (or more usually) reoffending. It is held that knowledge of accurate predictors of offending is important theoretically and practically valuable, as, for example, in informing parole decisions.

Distinctive Features

Prediction studies are characterized by two elements: first, the definition of the *criterion* of concern; secondly, identification of the *predictors* (or risk factors) for the specified criterion. For example, prediction studies may be concerned with the specific criterion of *violent* offending by males. The aim of the research would therefore be to find the specific predictors of male violent offending. There are two types of predictors: *static* predictors are risk factors that cannot change, such as criminal history, family background and employment record; *dynamic* predictors are risk factors that can change, such as level of drinking, employment or relationships.

There are also two main styles of conducting prediction studies. *Actuarial prediction* seeks to analyse statistically data gathered across a range of potential predictors to identify which predictors perform best in predicting the given criterion. *Clinical prediction* relies on individuals, teams, or case conferences to make predictions as to the likelihood of future offending. The generally accepted position, dating from Meehl's (1954) seminal text, is that statistical prediction is superior to clinical prediction.

Attempts at predicting risk can have various outcomes, each of which has very different implications for those involved. Strong predictors for a given criterion will produce high levels of *true positive* and *true negative* outcomes. In other words, the predictors will correctly predict either the occurrence or absence of the criterion. These 'true' outcomes, positive and negative, are known as 'hits'. A

false positive outcome arises when the presence of the predictors indicates the outcome will occur but it does not arise; while a *false negative* refers to the situation when, in the absence of predictors, the criterion of risk actually does occur. 'False' outcomes are generally called '*misses*'.

The first attempts at prediction of reoffending were made by criminologists in the 1920s (e.g., Burgess, 1928). These mainly relied on measurement of a range of potential static risk factors for reoffending, typically information gleaned from demographic and criminological records, followed by statistical calculations to determine the factors that best predicted the outcome (that is, recidivism). This tradition has continued into more recent times with the development of several actuarial prediction instruments based on static factors for use with general offender populations.

Examples of actuarial scales used to predict offending include the California Base Expectancy Scale, the Salient Factor Scale, and the Offender Group Reconviction Scale. The Salient Factor Scale, developed and refined in studies conducted within the US Parole Commission, is an actuarial scale that contains only static risk factors. It is a six-item checklist that produces a score from 0 to 10 points: the higher the score, the lower the likelihood of reconviction, with bands of scores used to categorize risk. Hoffman (1994) has reported a long-term follow-up of the Salient Factor Score on three samples of prisoners released from prison and concludes that the scale has retained its predictive accuracy over the 17-year period in which the various samples of offenders were released.

While prediction scales based on static factors can be accurate, by definition they cannot give any indication of a change in risk. However, the new generation of 'risk–need' scales are designed to include dynamic as well as static risk factors. For example, the Level of Supervision Inventory-Revised (LSI-R) is completed through file review and interview, and assesses a range of risk factors, including 'static' factors such as previous convictions, and 'dynamic' factors such as drink problems and employment. The pattern of scores identifies specific areas of offender need (informing service providers), while the total score can be translated into a risk band for future offending (Andrews and Bonta, 1995). The empirical evidence supporting the LSI-R as a measure of risk and needs is strong: Gendreau et al. (1996) conclude their review of predictors of adult recidivism with the view that the LSI-R is the current measure of choice.

Evaluation

It is plain that in risk assessment the stakes can be high for all concerned: in working with offenders, assessment of risk can influence sentencing decisions, type of disposal, appropriate level of security, parole, breach of probation order, and level and intensity of interventions. Research aiming to produce a valid and reliable method to estimate the likelihood of an individual reoffending depends on measurement of two variables. The first necessity is for accurate measurement of offending; the second is for accurate measurement of the predictors of risk, whatever they may be, for type of offence under consideration. It is plain that there is considerable room for error of measurement with these variables. It follows that any scales produced should be sufficiently tried and tested to be as robust as possible.

Clive Hollin

Associated Concepts: evaluation research, risk

Key Readings

Andrews, D.A. and Bonta, J. (1995) *LSI-R: The Level of Supervision Inventory-Revised*. Toronto, Multi-Health Systems.

Burgess, E.W. (1928) 'Factors determining success or failure on parole', in A.A. Bruce, A.J. Harno, E.W. Burgess and J. Landesco (eds), *The Workings of the Indeterminate Sentence Law and the Parole System in Illinois*. Springfield, IL, Illinois State Board of Parole.

Gendreau, P., Little, T. and Goggin, C. (1996) 'A meta-analysis of predictors of adult offender recidivism: what works', *Criminology*, 34, pp. 401–33.

Hoffman, P.B. (1994) 'Twenty years of operational use of a risk prediction instrument: the United States parole commission's salient factor score', *Journal of Criminal Justice*, 22, pp. 477–94.

Meehl, P.E. (1954) *Clinical Versus Statistical Predictions: A Theoretical Analysis and a Review of the Evidence*. Minneapolis, MN, University of Minnesota Press.

PRIMARY DEVIATION

See Labelling; Social reaction

PRIMITIVE REBELLION

Definition

In Eric Hobsbawm's original (1959) formulation, primitive rebellion is defined as a form of social movement or social agitation that is 'pre-political' in the sense that the protagonists 'have not yet found, or only begun to find, a specific language in which to express their aspirations about the world'.

Distinctive Features

Primitive rebellion as used by Hobsbawm referred to 'pre-political' social agitation in the nineteenth and twentieth centuries, particularly millenarianism, labour sects, the city mob, Mafia and the 'social bandit'. It is in relation to social banditry, and his related notion of 'social crime', that this work on primitive rebellion has produced the most impact on criminology. Hobsbawm himself restricted social banditry to peasant societies, on the grounds that it was a backward-looking protest, fighting for a traditional vision of a just world, having next to no organization and being 'totally unadaptable' to modern social movements. In his later treatment of social banditry (Hobsbawm, 1969) he developed this view to stress that social banditry may operate as a surrogate for a social movement through its symbolic representation of peasant discontents. In this way, many 'less than ideal' bandits have been raised to the status of social bandit, simply because they provided the poor with the only available overt symbols of resistance.

The notion of primitive rebellion proved attractive to conflict and class oriented radical criminologists of the 1960s and 1970s, particularly those sharing Hobsbawm's Marxist leanings. Thus, Australian work focusing on the 'Kelly Outbreak' of the 1880s developed the nexus between crime and class struggles over land, locating the critical feature of social banditry in the social support that the rural poor provided bandits – food, shelter, and information, but also non-cooperation with authorities. Such work also confirmed Hobsbawm's views that when organized political movements emerged to take up the cause of the downtrodden, social bandits would be deprived of their conditions of existence (O'Malley, 1979).

Bringing together rebellion and political 'primitivism', not only in the form of social banditry but also in the category of the urban 'mob', provided a foundation for criminologists and historians seeking to understand crime among the poor and minorities. Such work focused on social crime in the eighteenth and nineteenth centuries, including poaching, smuggling, luddism, haystack burning and other crimes interpreted as upholding the old 'moral economy' and traditional rights of the poor. It sought to give voice to poor criminals whose offences were related to resisting egregious exploitation associated with early capitalist development. Much of this work echoed Hobsbawm's caution that such criminals would not simply appear as heroic and attractive, but often bloody, reactionary and barbarous. Even so, the characterization of contemporary urban street crime as primitive rebellion and 'social crime' by some criminologists in the 1970s, led others to become highly critical of tendencies to 'romanticize' hoodlums and thugs.

Nevertheless, an attempt recently has been made to revive this line of analysis. Citing the emergence of new, urban 'dangerous classes', their exclusion from capitalist relations, and their participation in alternative economies, Lea (1999) suggests that Hobsbawm's notions of primitive rebellion and social crime may once again enter criminological currency.

Evaluation

Primitive rebellion sensitized a generation of social historians and critical criminologists to the nexus between popular crime and politics, by broadening the notion of politics to include the expressions of the inchoate and ignorant, and by linking these to 'criminal' acts of resistance where criminal law operated as a means of oppression. Equally important, it provided an important stimulus for developing a critical historiography within criminology. The historical analyses associated with E.P. Thompson and his colleagues, that owed much to Hobsbawm's pioneering work, remain one of the most lasting, scholarly and elegant contributions to criminology. Such work added considerable sophistication to a radical criminological theory that had become prone to rather literal and unsubtle translation of Marxist theory. However, the concept of primitive rebellion has occupied a limited and diminishing place in criminology in the past two decades, and it seems unlikely to recover the high profile it held during the 1970s. Its decline is probably linked to the crystallization of anti-romanticism into left realism during

the 1980s. Additionally, the current theoretical environment has rather turned its back on class oriented accounts and related forms of radical theory – in particular Marxist theory. Nevertheless, especially if Hobsbawm's own cautions about romanticism are heeded, primitive rebellion still seems to promise much for analysis of the inchoate politics of some forms of contemporary crime among the underclass and the excluded. Its implications for feminist criminology have yet to be explored.

Pat O'Malley

Associated Concepts: critical criminology, left idealism, Marxist criminologies, moral economy, political crime

Key Readings

Hay, D., Thompson, E. and Linebaugh, P. (eds) (1975) *Albion's Fatal Tree. Crime and Society in Eighteenth Century England*. London, Allen Lane.

Hobsbawm, E. (1959) *Primitive Rebels: Studies in Archaic Forms of Social Movement in the 19th and 20th Centuries*. Manchester, Manchester University Press.

Hobsbawm, E. (1969) *Bandits*. Harmondsworth, Penguin.

Lea, J. (1999) 'Social crime revisited', *Theoretical Criminology*, 3, pp. 307–26.

O'Malley, P. (1979) 'Class conflict, land and social banditry. Bushranging in nineteenth century Australia', *Social Problems*, 26, pp. 271–83.

Thompson, E. (1977) *Whigs and Hunters. The Origins of the Black Act*. London, Allen Lane.

PRIVATIZATION

See Managerialism

PROBATION

Definition

Supervision of offenders in conditions of freedom by designated officers of the court (sometimes called probation officers or community corrections officers). Nowadays regarded as an 'alternative to prison', though, historically, has been viewed as an 'alternative to punishment'.

Distinctive Features

Probation emerged towards the end of the nineteenth century as a reaction against the austere uniformity of penal institutions. Rooted in humanitarian concerns for the poor and a growing awareness of the contaminating influence of imprisonment, probation represented the move towards the individualization of sentencing – the tailoring of punishment to the needs of the individual offender. The underlying assumption was that the criminal would benefit from developing a close relationship of trust with a law-abiding citizen who would use their experience, wisdom and professional training to reclaim and rehabilitate them. The role of the probation officer was to offer advice and guidance on social problems such as employment, money and accommodation, as well as counselling for personal and relationship problems. Some jurisdictions (including England and Wales) even expected the probation officer to 'befriend' the offender.

According to Hamai et al. (1995) the concept of probation appears to imply four key elements in most countries where it exists: selection (following an assessment that the offender is 'suitable'), a conditional suspension of punishment (or, more commonly, nowadays, of imprisonment), personal supervision and, finally, guidance and/or treatment. Beyond that basic definition, probation may mean many different things depending on the social and economic framework within which it has to function.

Offenders are selected for probation through a process of assessment by a probation officer who advises, or writes a report for, the sentencing court. Probation orders require the offender to maintain contact with their supervising officer and to tell their supervisor about changes in their circumstances. Failure to comply with these conditions constitutes a breach of the probation order and the offender can be re-sentenced, usually to a period of imprisonment.

Evaluation

Historically, probation has been orientated towards the welfare of the offender and probation officers have been required to undergo training as social workers. With the demise of the rehabilitative ideal in the 1960s and 1970s, however, traditional approaches to probation were discredited (Brownlee, 1998; Worrall, 1997). Critics with socialist views on welfare provision argued that traditional probation was patronizing and coercive; pragmatists argued that it simply did not 'work'; those of a conservative persuasion argued that it was too lenient and should be replaced by more punitive sentences. As a result, probation supervision has been increasingly 'strengthened' by the addition of various conditions, mainly relating to where an offender is required to live, with whom s/he may associate and what 'programmes' s/he is required to undertake.

The nature of probation intervention has also changed. Personal counselling, based on psychotherapeutic approaches, has been replaced by cognitive-behavioural programmes, based on social learning theory. Rather than attempting to change the whole personality or circumstances of an offender, cognitive-behavioural programmes focus on specific unacceptable behaviours and seek to modify these by correcting distortions in the way offenders think about their crime. Offenders are required to accept full responsibility for their actions (instead of blaming the victim or their circumstances), empathize with the victim of their offences and expand their repertoire of responses to those situations that have previously triggered a criminal response. Programmes cover a range of specific problem behaviours such as anger management, drunken driving and sex offending.

These programmes collectively form the 'What Works?' agenda. The etymology of this phrase lies in a famously pessimistic remark made in 1974 by the criminologist Robert Martinson to the effect that 'nothing works' in penal interventions. The disillusion which followed this conclusion (supported by research findings at the time) led to a loss of confidence in probation which lasted until the early 1990s when the 'discovery' of cognitive-behavioural programmes (initially in North America) gave rise to a series of conferences entitled 'What Works?' (McGuire, 1995). The phrase caught the imagination of politicians and professionals and now dominates probation intervention in the English-speaking world. Evaluation research gives cause for cautious optimism in respect of the effectiveness of such programmes in reducing reoffending (Vennard and Hedderman, 1998) but critics have argued that enthusiasm for the cognitive-behavioural approach should not result in the neglect of other provision such as basic literacy skills and social skills. Nor should the wider social problems that may lead people into crime be overlooked.

Anne Worrall

Associated Concepts: community corrections, community sentences, evaluation research, rehabilitation, social learning theory

Key Readings

Brownlee, I. (1998) *Community Punishment: A Critical Introduction.* Harlow, Addison Wesley Longman.

Hamai, K., Ville, R., Harris, R., Hough, M. and Zvekic, U. (1995) *Probation Round the World: A Comparative Study.* London, Routledge.

McGuire, J. (1995) *What Works? Reducing Reoffending.* Chichester, John Wiley.

Ruggiero, V., Ryan, M. and Sim, J. (eds) (1995) *Western European Penal Systems: A Critical Anatomy.* London, Sage.

Vennard, J. and Hedderman, C. (1998) 'Effective interventions with offenders', in P. Goldblatt and C. Lewis (eds), *Reducing Offending: An Assessment of Research Evidence on ways of Dealing with Offending Behaviour.* Research Study 187. London, Home Office.

Worrall, A. (1997) *Punishment in the Community: The Future of Criminal Justice.* Harlow, Addison Wesley Longman.

PROBLEM ORIENTED POLICING

Definition

Problem oriented policing is a deceptively simple and sensible idea. It requires police forces to analyse the problems that they are routinely called upon to deal with and to devise more effective ways to respond to them.

Distinctive Features

Problem oriented policing was first developed by Herman Goldstein in the late 1970s and represents an attempt to persuade the police that it is in their interests to adopt a different operational philosophy. He is critical of the traditional incident-driven policing strategies, where the organization responds to individual calls for assistance as they happen and attempts to cope with the demand. Officers or their colleagues repeatedly revisit the same localities and social settings to deal with the repetitive, all too predictable, behaviour of individuals and groups. This is demoralizing for officers, a waste of organizational resources and unsatisfactory for members of the public. Goldstein is also critical of police work, which concentrates on law enforcement

and crime control. The majority of incidents with which police officers have to deal are non-criminal in nature and police methods should reflect this fact. The prioritization of the law enforcement function disproportionately influences the operational practices, structure, training and recruitment policies of police forces. It can also compound rather than resolve problems because it leads police officers to think that the solution to the problems they face is more legal powers. For Goldstein, police forces need to accept that good police work requires the development of the most effective means for dealing with a multitude of troublesome situations. Equally crucially, these means will very often, but not always, require the invocation of criminal law.

The reactive, law enforcement based model of police work should be replaced by proactive 'bottom-up' approaches which emphasize getting to grips with the underlying conditions that create the problems police officers have to deal with. They can do this because many of the incidents that take up police time are recurring rather than random in nature. Police forces should analyse patterns of crime incident clusters to identify underlying causes and problems and formulate appropriate responses. To do so requires disaggregating vague and overly general categories such as 'crime', 'disorder', 'violence' and so on into particular problems. It is not good enough to break them down into 'robbery', 'theft', 'assault', for example, because these concepts are framed by the criminal law. There should be as detailed a breakdown of problems as possible from the outset and the identification of key characteristics (location, time, participants' behaviour and so on). In addition, information should be gathered from a range of police and non-police sources. Only then can specific plans and imaginative strategies be developed to reduce or eradicate these recurring problems. In this way police officers will concentrate not on organizational matters but the ends of their police work and the quality of the police product. Problem-solving policing is more rewarding for officers and enables the organization to manage the demands made upon it more effectively because police work is geared towards resolving the root causes of related problems.

Evaluation

In many respects problem oriented policing makes common sense, and yet for police forces to embrace this model requires them to engage in a fundamental re-examination of what they do and why and how they do it. It requires police officers, at all levels of the organization, to focus on the substantive outcomes of police work and stop thinking of themselves as law enforcement officers. Forces have to commit themselves to address complex and sensitive problems and harms that are normally over-looked or ignored by officers. It also demands that officers are trained in problem-solving techniques and empowered to work with and be accountable to local communities. Forces must also develop reliable incident data in a form that is open to external evaluation and public discussion.

Eugene McLaughlin

Associated Concepts: 'broken windows', community policing, geographies of crime, situational crime prevention

Key Readings

Brodeur, P. (1998) *How To Recognize Good Policing: Problems and Issues.* London, Sage.

Eck, E. and Spelman, W. (1987) *Problem Solving: Problem Oriented Policing in Newport News.* Washington DC, US Department of Justice, National Institute of Justice.

Goldstein, H. (1977) *Policing a Free Society.* Cambridge, MA, Ballinger.

Goldstein, H. (1979) 'Improving policing: a problem-oriented approach', *Crime and Delinquency*, 25, pp. 236–58.

Goldstein, H. (1990) *Problem-Oriented Policing.* New York, McGraw–Hill.

Leigh, A., Read, T. and Tilley, N. (1998) *Brit Pop II: Problem Oriented Policing in Practice.* London, Home Office, Police Research Series, Paper 93.

PROPORTIONALITY

See Discrimination; Disparity; Disproportionality; Due process; Just deserts

PSYCHOANALYTIC CRIMINOLOGY

Definition

This neologism is misleading if it is taken to designate a discrete sub-genre of criminological scholarship. No such entity as psychoanalytic criminology in this sense exists.

However, it is possible to talk of the vicissitudes of relationships between psychoanalysis and criminology over the past century.

Distinctive Features

We can make a start by reversing the two terms that together compose the neologism. Criminological psychoanalysis? Psychoanalysis has always been criminological. In making this claim, I have in mind the dynamic role accorded to criminal wishes and fantasies within the broad spectrum of psychoanalytic theories of mental processes. For instance, the psychoanalytic terms pertaining to neurosis convey a primitive and talionic penal code within the unconscious. Psychoanalytic theory makes no qualitative distinction between normal and pathological and its account of the character of human subjectivity attributes significance to the traces of unconscious taboos and violent wishes and fantasies that persist throughout life. These are seen in phenomena such as the dream, parapraxes and the losing of objects. There is a conception of human nature or identity within every criminological theory or philosophy of punishment, however implicit. Psychoanalysis challenges these in various ways.

Relationships between psychoanalysis and criminology are not reducible to the study of the emotional aspect of offending behaviour and of punishing. Psychoanalysis presents criminology with a number of epistemological questions. Clearly the psychoanalytic appreciation of methodological rigour is quite different to that favoured by empirical criminology. A psychoanalyst would contend that the happy analysis of an isolated dream fragment can reveal far more than a large-scale survey on delinquency. Further, psychoanalysis problematizes the relationship between fantasy and reality.

Freud's brief insight 'Criminals from a sense of guilt' of 1916 presented his reflection on the dynamic role of mental conflict in the origins of criminality. This piece suggested a wholly new approach in criminology and penology. How far has this been developed? Writing about France, Laurent Mucchielli (1993) argued that the history of connections between psychoanalysis and criminology has been marked by suspicion. Yet for a time aspects of psychoanalytic thought exercised a major influence within British criminology. What can be made of this difference?

Over the past century, psychoanalysts have been prominent among those arguing for the reform of criminal law and penal policy; for example, British psychoanalysts gave testimony to the Royal Commission on Capital Punishment of 1952. These activities were informed by a literature on the unconscious motivations of legal punishment, which foregrounded the aggression and ambivalence of subjective investments in punitive practices. A general statement of this view is of the order of: 'punishment of the criminal is punishment of something which the individual feels to be present in themself.'

Psychoanalysis accords a central place to gender and sexuality in its exploration of psyche. From the early days, analysts pointed up the significance of troubles with masculinity to the origins of men's criminality. A recent example of this kind of scholarship can be seen in Tony Jefferson's (1996) use of Kleinian concepts such as projection to think about the case of Mike Tyson in terms of the relationship between the constitution of black masculine subjectivity and the crime of which the boxer was convicted.

An understanding of the contemporary as the locus of a 'risk society' or 'actuarial society' has recently attained prominence in theoretical criminology. An alternative way of looking at this question of our actuality employs the idea of an affective society. Such a picture is offered by Hollway and Jefferson (1997), who employ a psychoanalytic conception of anxiety to think about the fear of crime, and by Mark Watson (1999), in his essay on the paranoiac structure of police discourse. Key respects in which the subject of a society construed as affective differs from the subject of a risk society include the retrospective temporal orientation of the former and his/her emotional and unconscious reflexivity, which predominates over the cognitive and rational.

Evaluation

Psychoanalytic thought exercised a considerable influence upon the British criminology of the inter-war and postwar periods (Valier, 1998). In the sphere of penal practice, probation became reconceived as a process of emotional re-education, and the role of the probation officer therein that of a caseworker. From the 1970s, radical, conflict and feminist criminologies with a commitment to political critique denounced the psychoanalytic study of the criminal as positivistic, normative and biologically deterministic. The rejection of the rehabilitative ethos in penality under the aegis of the slogan 'nothing works' also contributed

to a fall from favour for psychoanalytic thought in criminology. The extent to which psychoanalysts had engaged from the outset upon a complex and sometimes heated debate concerning the ethics of their practice and the efficacy of their techniques was overlooked, as was the profound disagreement between different genres of psychoanalysis.

Over the past century there have been many contentious debates among psychoanalysts. The expulsion of various individuals from particular circles of affiliation and professional bodies, as well as the emergence of rival schools of thought and of clinical practice, is one lasting manifestation of the degree of divergence. In addition to division pertaining to institutional structures and doctrinal preferences, a proliferation of different cultures of psychoanalysis influenced by local socio-political contexts has been marked.

The most intentionally provocative and self-consciously political culture of psychoanalysis emerged in France with the impetus of the 'return to Freud' undertaken by Jacques Lacan. Lacan repeatedly differentiated his work from the genre of American ego-psychology, which emphasized adaptation to dominant socio-cultural structures and mores. In his address to the second international congress on criminology of 1950, he asserted that 'the denunciation of the morbid Universe of the misdeed cannot have for its corollary, nor for its aim, the ideal of an adaptation to a reality without conflicts' (Lacan, 1984, p. 24). Lacan emphasized the emotional ambivalence occasioned by the dialectical negativity by which the ego is formed through an identification with the other. Two of his earliest works discussed the cases of certain criminal women. Lacan's doctoral thesis of 1932 described the case of Aimée, who had attempted to stab a famous actress. Lacan rejected organic explanations of psychosis and saw her act as springing from conflicts within her personality. Her delusional system had turned these conflicts into external persecutors. The wish behind the delusions was one of unconscious self-punishment. This was followed by a paper on the Papin sisters, two maids who had murdered their employers in 1933. Lacan's reflection on these criminal cases was crucial to the elaboration of his concepts of the imaginary and the mirror phase, the latter theorizing the alienation that resides at the heart of all human subjects and initiates in an act of self-misrecognition.

Lacanian thought has now exercised considerable influence in areas such as literary and cultural criticism. There is a rich literature extant which employs psychoanalytic thought in the analysis of the plethora of visual and literary representations of crime and punishment with which we are daily confronted.

The psychoanalytic understanding of the criminal cannot be simply condemned as a correctionalist, normalizing discourse. A more nuanced account of the kinds of psychoanalysis taken up by criminology, and of the changes to classical technique thought necessary to the treatment of criminals, as well as an engagement with the extensive critical literature on many aspects of psychoanalysis, are prerequisites to any assessment of relationships between psychoanalysis and criminology. Further, the comfortable assimilation of psychoanalytic thought into criminological theory is both unlikely and undesirable. For this eventuality to take place, a considerable domestication of psychoanalysis would have to occur.

Claire Valier

Associated Concepts: hegemonic masculinity, masculinities, postmodernism, risk, sexuality

Key Readings
Hollway, W. and Jefferson, T. (1997) 'The risk society in an age of anxiety: situating the fear of crime', *British Journal of Sociology*, 48 (2), pp. 255–66.

Jefferson, T. (1996) 'From "little fairy boy" to "the compleat destroyer": subjectivity and transformation in the biography of Mike Tyson', in M. Mac an Ghaill (ed.), *Understanding Masculinities: Social Relations and Cultural Arenas.* Buckingham, Open University Press.

Lacan, J. (1984) 'Psychanalyse et criminologie. Résumé', *Ornicar*, 31, pp. 23–7.

Mucchielli, L. (1993) 'Le sens du crime: histoire des r(apports) de la psychanalyse à la criminologie', in L. Mucchielli (ed.), *Histoire De La Criminologie Française.* Paris, L'Harmattan.

Valier, C. (1998) 'Psychoanalysis and crime in Britain during the inter-war years'. The British Criminology Conferences, Selected Proceedings. Electronic journal at the website of the British Society of Criminology: http://www.lboro.ac.uk/departments/ss/bsc/bccsp/vol01/VOL01_12.HT

Watson, M. (1999) 'Policing the affective society: beyond governmentality in the theory of social control', *Social and Legal Studies*, 8 (2), pp. 227–52.

PUNISHMENT

See Capital punishment; Penality; Penology

Q

QUEER THEORY

Definition

Queer theory or, in activist parlance, simply 'queer', is a short-hand for gay, lesbian, bisexual and transgendered experience applied to literature, politics, the arts and social sciences; and presents a challenge to both homophobic heterosexism and to affirmative homophilic theories of homosexuality. Applied to crime and criminal justice it exposes the heterosexism of criminal justice practice and of much criminological theory *and* the homoeroticism of its focus on the bodies of young men. The early fusion of criminology and sexology also placed the woman criminal both outside the law and also outside the heterosexual norm.

Distinctive Features

To be or to render odd. Queer theory perversely both resists and invites a variety of definitions. Definitions vary depending on whether given by activists or academics. Part of the argument is in respect of identity politics – the possibility or desirability of a gay or lesbian movement, culture, sensibility, standpoint or perspective – and part concerned with the debate about modernism and postmodernism. Healy's summation that 'Queer was lesbian and gay politics catching up with postmodernism' (1996, p. 175) addresses both aspects. The academic roots of queer theory lie in the humanities, but Seidman (1996) convincingly argues for the relevance to sociology and Groombridge (1999) argues for its significance to criminology and to the sociology of deviance. An activist queer politics addressing discrimina-tion on grounds of sexuality or reactions to AIDS may employ direct action which may offend public sensibilities and break the law. Metaphorically it may seek to bash the gay-bashers through 'camp' and 'drag'.

Its activist roots noted the white, middle-class, Western orientation of gay and lesbian politics and lifestyles which appeared to exclude other identities much as women of colour and lesbians had noted the exclusionary appeal of feminism to 'sisterhood'. Moreover, academic commentators, drawing on Foucault, noted the disciplinary features of, even transgressive, identities and lifestyles. Psychology, sexology and criminology had for a long time insisted – sometimes by silence – on the normality of heterosexuality and the pathology of other sexualities. Gay activism and human rights campaigners were able to secure some rights for gays and lesbians but through insisting on a foundational gay identity (of choice or disposition). Queer theory threatens the stability of both a foundational gay and straight identity by insisting on the fluidity and performativity of identity. The fluidity of queer theory – like much postmodernism – threatens to violate the modernist theories of normative heterosexuality and of an oppositional homo-sexuality.

Thus whilst an empirically minded and sympathetic researcher might seek to under-stand homosexuality, a gay or lesbian one might want to document and understand homophobia. A polemical inversion might call homophobia deviant or seek its criminaliza-tion. This can be seen in the pressure in some jurisdictions to accept or widen the ambit of 'hate crime' legislation. A gay standpoint might want to take such empirical work and campaign around it in the way that radical feminism sought to do with research by women on women and for women. Cam-paigns against homophobic violence, the use of the 'gay-panic defence' and for equal ages of consent can be seen in this light. The logic of queer theory, however, is that you need not be homosexual in practice or identity to be queer. Whilst this makes political mobilization more difficult it should also be remembered that you don't have to be gay to suffer homophobia. 'Doing' masculinity often involves the rejection of the feminine and the queer. Thus many men operate under the fear of being thought queer as the fewer openly gay men operate under the fear of being bashed. The political task facing all men is to remove the distal fear of being called a 'poof' or 'faggot' and the proximate fear of being bashed like one. Whilst gay liberation specifically aimed to improve the lot of gay men and lesbians, queer theory opens up the possibility of a wider liberation.

Evaluation

Whilst the queer take on sexualities (hetero, homo, bi and transgendered) could be sociologically and criminologically productive (as argued above), there is little evidence outside of socio-legal studies that queer theory has made the progress in the social sciences that it has in the humanities. Moreover, given the disputes over definition and applicability (whether being gay is essential or merely helps), it seems likely that further progress will be uneven. However, homosexuality has haunted criminology from the pathologizing positivism of Lombroso to the appreciative ethnographies of the sociology of deviance. A radical victimology and increasingly criminal justice practice recognize attacks on the 'gay community' but still require the 'victim' to 'out' themselves to receive due recognition. Given the limited extent to which criminology

has embraced feminism it seems that any serious consideration of sexualities as important to criminology – whether purely empirical, standpoint or queer – may take decades. However, without such consideration, even apparently simple issues – like what do we mean by the expressions 'going straight' and 'bent copper' – will elude criminology. Queer theory seeks to find the odd within the normal or render the normal odd – as in the mention of 'straight' and 'bent' above. It is this sort of sub(per)version that will render it unpalatable to the criminological mainstream. Moreover, queer practice and culture – camp to kitsch – long predates the turn to theory and may, like some feminisms, wish to keep its distance from criminology.

Nic Groombridge

Associated Concepts: deviance, hate crime, hegemonic masculinity, masculinities, normalization, pathology, postmodernism, sexuality

Key Readings

Groombridge, N. (1999) 'Perverse criminologies: the closet of Doctor Lombroso', *Social and Legal Studies*, 8 (4), pp. 531–48.

Hart, L. (1994) *Fatal Women: Lesbian Sexuality and the Mark of Aggression*. London, Routledge.

Healy, M. (1996) *Gay Skins: Class, Masculinity and Queer Appropriation*. London, Cassell.

Seidman, S. (ed.) (1996) 'Introduction', *Queer Theory/ Sociology*. Oxford, Blackwell.

Stychin, C. (1995) *Law's Desire: Sexuality and the Limits of Justice*. London, Routledge.

Tomsen, S. (1997) 'Was Lombroso a queer? Criminology, criminal justice and the heterosexual imaginary', in G. Mason and S. Tomsen (eds), *Homophobic Violence*. Sydney, The Federation Press, Australian Institute of Criminology.

R

RACIALIZATION

Definition

The process by which a particular group, or its characteristics or actions, is identified as a collectivity by its real or imagined phenotypical characteristics, or 'race'. More broadly, the ways in which social structures and ideologies become imbued with 'racial' meanings.

Distinctive Features

The concept of racialization emerges from historical work which shows that the idea of 'race' is a social construction that emerged at a particular time in European history and, since then, has been used to refer to divisions of the world's population in terms of supposedly fixed biological characteristics. In contrast, racialization draws attention to the ways in which ideas about 'race' have been and are constructed, maintained and used as a basis for exclusionary practices. In its more general sense, the concept of racialization refers to cultural or political processes or situations where 'race' is invoked as an explanation or a means of understanding. Thus, suggestions of distinctly 'Irish', 'Italian' or 'Jewish' forms of criminal activity and association could be understood as instances of racialization. A more specific usage analyses the ideological processes through which 'race' is given significance.

Examples of racialization in criminology include:

- The role of the media and authorities, such as the police, in defining street crime or 'mugging' – as well as 'steaming' and 'wilding' – as activities characteristic of young black men.

- The police's continuing use of racialized statistics on street crime to mount media campaigns against any diminution in their powers, such as stop and search.
- Analysis of discourses of 'race', crime and nation in which criminality is seen as distinguishing black people of African and Caribbean origins as 'other' and as standing outside the boundaries of 'Britishness'.
- Accounts of 'black crime' and public disorders that rely on 'culturalist' explanations such as a matriarchy, a lack of a father/authority figure, or most crudely, a simple disrespect for English traditions of civility.
- Racialization within fields of social policy – including education, employment and crime – that have variously served to construct the 'problem of black youth'.
- The connections between 'race' and place that underlie police racializations of particular communities and areas (or 'symbolic locations').
- Racialization and criminalization as twinned processes in the development of disciplinary strategies of governance and policing.
- The stigmatization of particular black subcultural styles.
- The identification and construction of particular groups, activities and commodities, for example connections between crack-cocaine and 'yardies' or 'posses'.
- Media and police constructions of a distinctively 'Asian' criminality.
- Racialization within organizations and occupational cultures.
- The racialization of 'whiteness' through ideas of a white criminal underclass, or 'white trash'.
- The demonization of 'Islamic terrorists'.
- Racialization as a process of visualization, through which the beating of Rodney

King by Los Angeles police officers, for example, could be redefined as a situation where he was seen as endangering the police.

Evaluation

Unlike the term race relations, racialization always highlights the constructed nature of 'race'. It shifts the focus of attention away from black people to questions about how racialization structures and defines social relations. Connections between 'race' and, among many other things, locality, masculinity and sexuality could all be developed further. The contingent and constructed nature of 'race' implies that other constructions are possible, though the extent to which some associations endure indicates how deeply rooted racialization is. The multiplicity of racial constructions transversing across biology, culture, politics and nationality indicates how flexibly racialization can operate.

Karim Murji

Associated Concepts: criminalization, demonization, essentialism, institutional racism, social constructionism, stereotyping, stigma

Key Readings

Butler, J. (1993) 'Endangered/endangering: schematic racism and white paranoia', in R. Gooding-Williams (ed.), *Reading Rodney King/Reading Urban Uprising*. New York, Routledge.

Gilroy, P. (1987) *There Ain't No Black in the Union Jack*. London, Hutchinson.

Hall, S., Critcher, C., Jefferson, T., Clarke, J. and Roberts, B. (1978) *Policing the Crisis: Mugging, The State and Law and Order*. London, Macmillan.

Keith, M. (1993) *Race, Riots and Policing: Lore and Disorder in a Multi-racist Society*. London, UCL Press.

Solomos, J. (1988) *Black Youth, Racism and the State*. Cambridge, Cambridge University Press.

Webster, C. (1997) 'The construction of British "Asian" criminality', *International Journal of the Sociology of Law*, 25, pp. 65–86.

RADICAL CRIMINOLOGIES

Definition

There is no one radical criminology. The term is used to delineate a series of distinct theoretical positions whose main common characteristic is one of anti-positivism. Rather than viewing crime as determined by individual or social pathology, radical criminologies assume humans are active agents in the construction of their own biographies. They are more concerned with discovering the meaning of criminal behaviour than trying to isolate specific causes.

Within the broad classification of 'radical criminology' there is a diverse range of theories that contest the behavioural questions posed by positivist criminologies. Crime is to be found less in particular individual characteristics and environmental conditions and more in relations of power and selective processes of criminalization. In labelling this is expressed in terms of a 'society' that creates rules. Within Marxism and critical criminology it is expressed in terms of 'a capitalist state' that has the power to criminalize those behaviours which are deemed 'threatening'. In some feminist perspectives it is expressed in the social construction of 'hegemonic masculinities' within patriarchal societies. All such notions have shifted the criminological agenda away from popular ideas about causation.

John Muncie

Associated Concepts: critical criminology, feminist criminologies, interactionism, labelling, Marxist criminologies, new criminology, new deviancy theory

RADICAL FEMINISM

Definition

Radical feminism offers a systematic analysis of the nature of women's oppression, including the ways it is sustained through law and criminal justice processes. Its aim is not only to understand male dominance and control of women and children, but also to end it. It defines what have been named variously as 'violence against women', 'sexual violence' and 'gender violence' as key elements in the power relations of patriarchy: that is, the maintenance of male power and control over women and children. Sexual violence has become a central concept in radical feminist theory and women throughout the world have organized in a variety of ways to highlight, respond to and campaign against it.

Distinctive Features

- Its central foci are male supremacy, men and masculinity as structured through the power relations of patriarchy: a universal social formation, characteristic of almost all known societies. Its analysis locates women's oppression in patriarchy: a systematic expression of male domination and control over women which permeates all social and political and economic institutions. Patriarchal oppression is conceptualized as fundamental and pervasive. Crossing public and private spheres, it impacts at the level of the state, law, culture and religion and reaches into the intimacy of the home, family and sexuality.

- Often conceptualized solely in terms of gender relations, radical feminism recognizes that, based on a familial model of power, patriarchy is also defined by generational gender power relations. In the traditional notion of 'rule by the father', its gender dimension facilitates understanding of the power of men over women, and its generational element, power hierarchies between men, between women and over children. The generational dimension of patriarchy further provides a framework for understanding difference and change through time, at both societal and individual levels. This accords dynamism to the concept of patriarchy, enabling analysis of continuity, difference and change through time and between and within societies.

- Radical feminism is a women-centred theoretical perspective and political practice constructed by and for women, inspired by the 1970s Women's Liberation Movement. As a politics of resistance, radical feminism, through the notion of 'praxis', insists theory and activism are inseparable. As well as theorizing sexual violence (MacKinnon, 1987; Kelly, 1988), it has also been at the forefront of activism as demonstrated in England by Women's Aid, the Rape Crisis Federation and campaigning groups like Justice for Women.

- Radical feminism is broad based. Within it exists a range of concerns and controversies adding to its richness. For example, while most radical feminist analysis holds a social constructionist position in relation to human nature, there are traces of biologistic arguments in early accounts (for example, Firestone's (1970) *The Dialectic of Sex* and Brownmiller's (1975)

Against Our Will). The diversity of radical feminism is also illustrated in its range of concerns, which include sexuality, health, education, language and the facilitation of autonomous women's spaces, women-centred culture and women's communities in rural and city areas.

- Through its focus on the victimization of women and children, radical feminism has significantly impacted on criminology – by exposing the extent of victimization and by improving the treatment of female survivors of violent relationships and rape by police and criminal justice processes. It has also informed criminology and jurisprudence through its analysis of law as a patriarchal institution reflecting and reproducing male dominance. Man-made law is exposed as shaped by male norms and interests and structured around the situations and circumstances they, rather than women, commonly encounter. Through its failure to effectively sanction male sexual violence or provide protection for women and children, the law acts as a form of male control. MacKinnon (1987) developed the analysis beyond the substance of law to include also its style, form, ritual and language. The law creates an illusion of fairness and impartiality to mask its inherently masculinist nature.

Evaluation

For complicated reasons, ultimately linked to its critique of male power, there are difficulties in the representation of radical feminism. As a politics of resistance, it is virtually unrecognizable in academic accounts, where it is often presented as an American phenomenon, little changed since the 1970s. Its critique of heterosexuality as an institution predicated upon patriarchal gender power relations, enforced by sexual violence and the stigmatization of alternatives to sexual relationships with men (Rich, 1980), has also led to its being defined primarily in terms of lesbian separatism.

It is frequently claimed that radical feminism is based on an ahistorical and universalist model of patriarchy. While this may be true of some early US radical feminist theory, recent writings are more nuanced to reflect difference, change and historical specificity (Radford et al., 2000).

Of specific relevance to criminology, radical feminism has been criticized for constructing women as 'victims'. This is misplaced. Radical feminism rejects the concept of 'victim' for that of 'survivor', while not denying the reality of victimization (Kelly, 1988). More recent writings recognize both concepts as problematic at the level of identity, as both are defined by unchosen experiences of violence. Radical feminism accords agency to women and men. At the individual level it recognizes that men are responsible for their own actions and the diversity of resistance, coping and survival strategies adopted by women. The presence of a vital radical feminist activism against male violence further points to the power of women's agency.

A more difficult question relates to radical feminist strategies relating to law as a site (albeit one of many) of struggle for change. Radical feminism identifies law and criminal justice as patriarchal institutions, complicit in oppression of women and children, and identifies sexual violence as a defining characteristic of patriarchal societies. Yet it campaigns for changes in law within a patriarchal social order. This may appear contradictory. However, radical feminism holds that law is too significant an institution to neglect. For example, tens of thousands of individual women by necessity resort to the law annually, to make best use of the limited protection it offers. Politically, struggle through law in campaigns for gender justice can play a significant awareness-raising role, at times securing some beneficial change. Nevertheless, radical feminism is not unaware of the limits or ironies of reformism. Whereas sociological theory has perceived irresolvable tensions between working for long-term structural change and short-term reform, more creative approaches to this dilemma have been explored by radical feminism. Consequently, rather than adopt simplistic reformism, radical feminist strategies have more in common with a transformative approach to law, that is, one that involves the transformation of male categories and concepts to address women's experiences.

Radical feminist interventions in relation to violence against women are definitively one of the more successful areas of feminist practice:

At the very least, their efforts have provided support for tens of thousands of women throughout the world and brought this issue into the public arena from which it cannot now be removed. This has provided a vehicle for change within institutions of the state as well as within wider society. Perceptions, discourses and reactions have all been challenged. (Dobash and Dobash, 1992, p. 298)

Nevertheless, the achievements of radical feminism do not represent a non-controversial model of linear development or progress. Patriarchy has not been overthrown, violence against women has not been eliminated. Law and criminal justice systems still fail effectively to sanction or prosecute this violence or accord effective protection to women and children victimized. The radical feminist project is not yet concluded.

Jill Radford

Associated Concepts: family crime, hegemonic masculinity, liberal feminism, violence

Key Readings

Dobash, R.E. and Dobash, R.P. (1992) *Rethinking Violence Against Women*. London, Sage.
Hester, M., Kelly, L. and Radford, J. (eds) (1996) *Women, Violence and Male Power*. Buckingham, Open University Press.
Kelly, L. (1988) *Surviving Sexual Violence*. Cambridge, Polity Press.
MacKinnon, C. (1987) *Feminism Unmodified: Discourses on Life and Law*. Cambridge, MA, Harvard University Press.
Radford, J., Friedberg, M. and Harne, L. (eds) (2000) *Women, Violence and Strategies for Action: Feminist Research, Policy and Practice*. Buckingham, Open University Press.
Rich, A. (1980) 'Compulsory heterosexuality and lesbian existence', *Signs*, 5 (4), pp. 631–60.

RADICAL NON-INTERVENTION

Definition

A criminal justice strategy which advocates a minimalist approach to instances of law-breaking in order to reduce the range and depth of state intervention. The least amount of criminal justice processing as possible is viewed not only as humanitarian, but as effective in preventing the development of criminal careers. Tolerance is preferred to moral indignation.

Distinctive Features

The phrase 'radical non-intervention' is widely attributed to Edwin Schur. It is the logical policy implication of a labelling approach to understanding crime and deviance. If, as labelling theorists suggested, social reaction does not prevent offending but establishes deviant identities and careers then the reach of reaction should be reduced. If state intervention causes crime and is a significant agency in the creation of the crime problem, then steps must be taken to limit its powers. In particular, Schur (1965) argued that a range of 'victimless crimes' should be removed from the remit of criminal law. Drug use, gambling, juvenile status offences (truancy, promiscuity), pornography and so on, it is argued, may be undesirable, but tackling them with the full weight of the law is not only expensive, but also generally ineffective. Criminalizing drug users, for instance, not only creates new classes of criminals, but may also drive them to commit further offences to support their habits, encourages the development of organized crime and law enforcement corruption and redirects resources away from health and treatment programmes. In short, the removal of many troubling behaviours from criminal law sanction has the potential to be a highly effective measure of crime reduction.

Radical non-intervention (and the labelling approach in general) grew in popularity during the 1960s and was in part a reflection of an emergent distrust of institutional intervention that developed throughout that decade. It has had a profound impact on social policy (Empey, 1982). A series of measures – decriminalization, diversion and deinstitutionalization – designed to limit the extent of the state's intrusion into offenders' lives, have been implemented to varying degrees and with varying success in most Western criminal justice systems.

John Muncie

Associated Concepts: decriminalization, diversion, labelling, tolerance, victimless crime

Key Readings

Empey, La Mar T. (1982) *American Delinquency: Its Meaning and Construction*, 2nd edn. Chicago, Dorsey Press.

Schur, E.M. (1965) *Crime Without Victims*. Englewood Cliffs, NJ, Prentice–Hall.

Schur, E.M. (1974) *Radical Non-Intervention: Rethinking the Delinquency Problem*. Englewood Cliffs, NJ, Prentice–Hall.

RATIONAL CHOICE THEORY

Definition

The starting point of rational choice theory is that offenders seek advantage to themselves by their criminal behaviour. This entails making decisions among alternatives. These decisions are rational within the constraints of time, ability and the availability of relevant information.

Distinctive Features

Rational choice theory is the perspective on offender behaviour which underpins situational crime prevention. Ronald V. Clarke is the leading proponent both of the theory and the situational prevention approach with which it is consistent. Demonstration that crime is distributed *as if* offenders were rational (Mayhew et al., 1976) predated full presentation of the theory (Cornish and Clarke, 1986) by almost a decade. The Clarke and Cornish view dealt both with a person's initial decision to become involved in crime, and the decisions leading up to a crime, the general decision to commit it having been made. The theory has been used more in its second area of application, with the 'choice-structuring' properties of pre-crime situations being the topic of most research in this tradition. Ways of thinking about choice-structuring properties focus increasingly on 'offending scripts'.

Rational choice theory has many similarities with routine activity theory. The latter focuses on the necessary conditions for a crime to occur, namely the convergence in time and place of a motivated offender and a suitable victim in the absence of a capable guardian (Felson, 1997). The two perspectives hold in common a focus on the crime event. They are both concerned with how the press of circumstances shapes individual acts (rational choice) or acts of a particular class (routine activities). Rational choice theory appears to make no differential predictions that would allow a critical test against routine activity. Routine activity theory supposes that, in the aggregate, trends will look as if there were (limited) rationality at the individual level. What rational choice theory adds is twofold. First, a more precise exploration of what counts in people's heads as capable guardianship and victim suitability. And second, offender-specific departures from presumptive rationality, and thereby a theoretical platform for offender profiling.

Since Ron Clarke and Marcus Felson are now frequent collaborators, we may see the theories being consolidated. Indeed, the process has already begun and their collaboration is increasingly concerned with ethical issues in crime control (Clarke and Felson, 1993). The more explicit application of rational choice theory to the practice of offender profiling would almost certainly prove fruitful.

Evaluation

Rational choice theory frees us from considering pathologies of offender motivation. It should find favour with many of those opposed to the demonizing of offenders as 'different'. It enables rationality to be applied to the design, distribution and maintenance of products and services to limit their vulnerability to crime (the essence of situational prevention), because the behaviour of rational offenders is predictable by other rational people in possession of the same information. One effect has been research in which offenders are questioned about their precautions and methods while offending, research which has proved remarkably fruitful.

It has been suggested (Trasler, 1993) that rational choice theory is more applicable to crime for gain than to 'expressive' crime. Arguably the theory is also liable to criticism on grounds of circularity, in that the choice-structuring properties nominated by offenders are deemed rational in the absence of precise awareness of situations in which there may have been less risky and more profitable alternatives to hand. Thus, from a distance and without any counter-evidence, rationality is inferred wrongly. No such attack has yet been mounted in print.

Ken Pease

Associated Concepts: administrative criminology, neo-conservative criminology, opportunity theory, routine activity theory, situational crime prevention

Key Readings

Clarke, R.V. and Felson, M. (eds) (1993) *Routine Activity and Rational Choice*. London, Transaction.
Cornish, D. (1994) 'The procedural analysis of offending and its relevance to situational prevention', in R.V. Clarke (ed.), *Crime Prevention Studies 3*, Monsey, NY, Criminal Justice Press.
Cornish, D. and Clarke, R.V. (eds) (1986) *The Reasoning Criminal: Rational Choice Perspectives on Offending*. New York, Springer-Verlag.
Felson, M. (1997) *Crime and Everyday Life*, 2nd edn. Thousand Oaks, CA, Pine Forge Press.
Mayhew, P.M., Clarke, R.V., Sturman, A. and Hough, J.M. (eds) (1976) *Crime as Opportunity*. Home Office Research Study No. 34. London, HMSO.
Trasler, G. (1993) 'Conscience, opportunity, rational choice and crime', in R.V. Clarke and M. Felson (eds), *Advances in Criminological Theory*. New Brunswick, NJ, Transaction.

REALIST CRIMINOLOGIES

Definition

In contemporary criminology realist theorizing is most closely associated with the rejection of utopian solutions to crime and the advocacy of pragmatic policies to pursue crime reduction. It originally surfaced as a right-wing critique of sociological positivism and radical criminologies in the USA in the mid-1970s which maintained that it was fruitless to search for the causes of crime and that sole attention be returned to designing effective measures of crime control. A left-wing variant subsequently developed in Britain in the mid 1980s in order to formulate social democratic policies that would both take crime seriously and implement accountable programmes of crime control. Realist criminologies, of whatever ideological persuasion, are primarily concerned with developing responses to a perceived intensity in the public's fear of crime, notably of street crime, violence and burglary.

John Muncie

Associated Concepts: administrative criminology, crime prevention, deterrence, fear of crime, left idealism, left realism, neo-conservative criminology, relative deprivation

RECIDIVISM

Definition

Recidivism is concerned with the reconviction rates of offenders released from custody.

Recidivist rates are generally used to test whether a term of imprisonment can reduce future re-offending; whether different programmes undertaken within prison contribute towards re-offending; or whether other forms of community-based punishment are more effective at reducing further re-offending.

Distinctive Features

The most typical form of recidivist rate measures the proportion of offenders who have been re-convicted within a two-year period following release. However, this measure has to be used with some caution, as for example, it will reflect only those offences that have been reported, recorded and successfully prosecuted. Figures from a variety of criminal justice systems demonstrate that being sent to prison is likely to be related to future re-offending. For example, *Prison Statistics – England and Wales, 1997* (Home Office, 1998, p. 156), reveals that of all the prisoners who were discharged in 1994, 56 per cent were re-convicted within two years. This figure can be further broken down to demonstrate that women showed the lowest rate of re-conviction, with 46 per cent re-convicted within two years, whereas young offenders had the highest rates of re-conviction, with 75 per cent re-convicted within a two-year period.

The high rates of re-conviction of young offenders sent to prison were given formal recognition by a government Green Paper in England and Wales – *Punishment, Custody and the Community*, which stated that with regard to young offenders even a short period of custody was likely to confirm them as 'criminals', particularly if they acquired new criminal skills from more sophisticated offenders. They see themselves labeled as criminals and are likely to behave accordingly (Home Office, 1988, para. 2.15).

Recidivist rates have thus also been used to affirm Robert Martinson's originally rather pessimistic analysis of the effectiveness of treatment programmes for the rehabilitation of offenders. Despite Martinson himself re-assessing his evidence more favourably, the analysis gave rise to the infamous view that 'nothing works' in terms of treatment programmes within prisons.

None the less, whilst it is clear that prisons stigmatize rather than re-socialize offenders, attempts have also to be made to prevent prison further de-socializing offenders, and therefore to provide opportunities in prison for education, work and to accept self-responsibility. As a consequence, prompted by research in Canada into the impact of 'cognitive skills' training on recidivist rates, a new debate has begun to consider 'what works' in a penal setting (Correctional Service of Canada, 1996). Research into 'what works' in reducing further offending would suggest that the following principles apply.

- That the greater the seriousness of the offending and risk of re-offending the more intensive and extensive any treatment programme should be.
- That any programme should target the needs of offenders which are directly related to their offending.
- That programmes that encourage the participation of the offenders are more effective.
- That once a programme has been started it should be completed as planned, and the results evaluated.

This has meant that specific programmes have been introduced into a variety of penal settings to help offenders overcome problems with, for example, drugs and alcohol, or to improve their educational or social skills. These interventions can be taken further, and are sometimes targeted at specific types of offenders, and in England and Wales, for example, a specific programme has been introduced to deal with sex offenders (Home Office, 1996). Great claims are made for some of these programmes, and a Home Office research study, entitled *Reducing Reoffending*, suggests that 'larger percentage point reductions in recidivism (typically around 20 per cent of points lower than control groups) have been reported' (Goldblatt and Lewis, 1998). However, of late, concerns have been expressed as to whether forcing prisoners to engage in treatment programmes presents other ethical problems.

More promisingly, research into the efficacy of HMP Grendon in England, which accepts only volunteers and operates as a therapeutic community, has also recently indicated success in relation to recidivist rates (Marshall, 1997). This research suggests that reconviction rates for those prisoners who stayed at HMP Grendon for at least 18 months were lower by as much as one-fifth to one-quarter, based on a prediction of the likely number of future offences which would have been committed by the group under consideration had they not gone to HMP Grendon. This predictive use of recidivist rates is becoming increasingly common.

Whilst most figures demonstrate that going to prison is likely to be related to future offending, they also demonstrate that non-custodial sanctions – whilst substantially cheaper – are not much better at reducing the likelihood of future re-offending (cf. Kershaw et al., 1999). What this suggests is that sentencing decisions, whether that decision is to incarcerate or punish in the community, have little to do with those factors that influence offending behaviour.

Evaluation

Recidivism is clearly related to being sent to prison. Except in certain circumstances prison stigmatizes rather than rehabilitates, and as such any sentencing decision should be based on factors other than the possible beneficial consequences of a period of imprisonment. Some positive interventions can be offered to prisoners who have been incarcerated. The key word here is 'offered', and ethical considerations such as the desirability of forcing prisoners to engage in treatment by, for example, making treatment a condition of early release, which have rarely featured in the 'What Works?' debate, should be more clearly acknowledged.

David Wilson

Associated Concepts: evaluation research, incarceration, prediction studies, rehabilitation, reparation

Key Readings

Correctional Service of Canada (1996) *The Impact of Cognitive Skills Training on Post Release Supervision among Canadian Federal Offenders*. Ottawa, Correctional Service of Canada.
Goldblatt, P. and Lewis, C. (eds) (1998) *Reducing Reoffending*. London, Home Office Research Study No. 187.
Home Office (1988) *Punishment, Custody and the Community*. London, HMSO, cm 424.
Home Office (1998) *Prison Statistics – England and Wales, 1997*. London, HMSO, cm 4017.
Kershaw, C., Goodman, J. and White, S. (1999) *Reconviction of Offenders Sentenced or Released from Prison in 1995*. Home Office Research Findings No. 101. London, HMSO.
Marshall, P. (1997) *A Reconviction Study of HMP Grendon Therapeutic Community*. Home Office Research Findings No. 53. London, HMSO.

REDRESS

Definition

According to the *Concise Oxford Dictionary*, 'redress' can mean: to put right or in good order again, to remedy or remove trouble of any kind, to set right, repair, rectify something suffered or complained of like a wrong, to correct, amend, reform or do away with a bad or faulty state of things, to repair an action, to atone a misdeed or offence, to save, deliver from misery, to restore or bring back a person to a proper state, to happiness or prosperity, to the right course, to set a person right by obtaining or (more rarely) giving satisfaction or compensation for the wrong or loss sustained, teaching, instructing and redressing the erroneous by reason (Sixth Edition, 1976, p. 937).

Distinctive Features

This seemingly 'obsolete' concept carries an elaborate set of different meanings which is why the notion of 'redress' provides such a useful alternative to the key concepts of both 'punishment' and 'crime'. Traditional criminological discourse and, more specifically, deterrence theory support the myth of a direct causal relationship between crime and punishment. The complex notion of 'redress' offers a perspective in which problematic events, normally calling forth punitive intervention by the criminal justice system, are not automatically subsumed under universalistic categories, but rather established through a process of understanding and creative response. As such, the notion of 'redress' can be seen as part of a more comprehensive 'replacement discourse' 'that begins the deconstruction of crime and crime control, the correction of corrections and the ultimate criminal justice policy that denies itself' (Henry and Milovanovic, 1994, p. 130).

Evaluation

Advantages of the notion of 'redress' are, briefly:

- It includes almost every conceivable reaction to an event – individual, collective – which causes material or immaterial harm.

- It implies that response is mandatory, without pre-defining the event as a crime, an illness, or whatever.
- It invites analysis of the event before deciding or choosing a proper response.
- As a concept with ancient origins, it invokes the consideration of historical and anthropological forms of dispute settlement and conflict resolution for possible clues to rational forms of response.

To claim redress is merely to assert that an undesirable event has taken place and that something needs to be done about it. It carries no implications concerning what sort of reaction would be appropriate; nor does it define reflexively the nature of the initial event. Since it invites an open discussion about how an unfortunate event should be viewed and what the appropriate response ought to be, it can be viewed as a rational response *par excellence*. It puts forth the claim for a procedure rather than for a specific result. Punitive claims already implied in defining an event as a 'crime' are opened up to rational debate. Thus, to advocate 'redress' is to call for 'real dialogue' (Christie, 1982) at every level of 'crime' control proceedings.

In this way, the notion of 'redress' is put forth in order to reconceptualize the familiar concepts of 'crime' and 'punishment' and generate a critical and constructive alternative to the politics of crime, punishment and penal reform. It is an approach which is ambitious and modest at the same time. The politics of 'redress' tries to combine principles of generalizability and universality with those of contextuality, solidarity and care – not as a blueprint, but as a perspective and a commitment, enabling criminology to liberate itself from the punitive logic of exclusion.

Willem de Haan

Associated Concepts: abolitionism, constitutive criminology, peacemaking criminology, restorative justice, shaming

Key Readings

Christie, N. (1982) *Limits to Pain*. Oxford, Martin Robertson.
de Haan, W. (1990) *The Politics of Redress. Crime, Punishment and Penal Abolition*. London, Unwin Hyman.
Henry, S. and Milovanovic, D. (1994) 'The constitution of constitutive criminology: a postmodern approach to criminological theory', in D. Nelken (ed.), *The Futures of Criminology*. London, Sage, pp. 110–33.
Van Swaaningen, R. (1997) *Critical Criminology. Visions from Europe*. London, Sage.

REFLEXIVITY

Definition

The process of monitoring and reflecting on all aspects of a research project from the formulation of research ideas through to the publication of findings and, where this occurs, their utilization. Sometimes the product of such monitoring and reflection is a reflexive account which is published as part of the research report.

Distinctive Features

Although important in all areas of social research, reflexivity has an especial role in ethnography in which the investigator is close to the subjects and to the data. What is more, the whole process of formulating ideas, collecting observations, analysing and reaching conclusions is part of the role of the investigator *vis-à-vis* those who are the objects of enquiry. It is for this reason that ethnographers see reflexivity as part of research in its own right and not as a collection of afterthoughts on how a project has been accomplished.

At one level, a reflexive account will be descriptive in terms of providing an account of, for example, how interviews were carried out, what methods of recording data were used and so on. However, at another – much more important – level a reflexive account should be evaluative in terms of providing some assessment of the likely validity of the conclusions that have been reached. This might, for example, involve a consideration of whether respondents selected for interview are typical of the group about which conclusions are to be made; whether there is a possibility that responses to questions were the outcome of exaggeration or even downright falsification; and whether the method of recording data resulted in only a partial or even distorted, account of reality. These are what are known as 'threats to validity'. A researcher may not be able to anticipate and rule these out. However, s/he should be aware of them and provide some assessment of their potential effects on the validity of conclusions. At a minimum, the expectation is that the researcher will provide sufficient detail about the research process – and decisions taken within it – to allow the reader to make some judgement by him/herself.

Ethnographic research on criminal subcultures has produced some classic and colourful reflexive accounts of 'how it was done'. These include William Foote Whyte's account of *Street Corner Society*, Clifford Shaw's life history of *The Jack Roller* and Karl Klockars' interviews with *The Professional Fence*. To take the latter as one example, Klockars describes how he used different data sources – such as letters, newspaper articles, bills, sales receipts and stock certificates – with which to triangulate his conclusions and thereby improve their validity.

On occasions reflexivity involves not just monitoring and assessing validity (to what extent are conclusions credible and plausible?) but also questions of ethics (has anyone been harmed by the research?) and questions of politics (whose side am I on, if any?). Validity, ethics and politics can impact one on another. For example, a decision not to publish interview material collected from corrupt policemen, for fear of exposing them, will not result in a full and valid account of the realities of police subcultures. Therefore, reflexivity often involves the researcher in reaching a personal standpoint in relation to trade-offs that often have to be made between validity, politics and ethics.

Evaluation

Reflexivity is concerned with the social production of knowledge. It involves reflecting on the various social roles, interactions and processes which resulted in the kinds of observations and conclusions that emerged. It is possible to consider reflexivity in a sense wider than that of monitoring and assessing the validity of a particular research project. This wider perspective involves viewing critical reflection as a form of research in its own right, and as part of the school of critical thinking and theorizing in the social sciences in general. A critical research agenda could include a consideration of why particular (say, punitive) law and order discourses take the form that they do and come to be accepted as 'truth' when they do. What is more, it could consider the role of criminological research in the production and dissemination of such 'truths'. This would involve reflecting on the criminological enterprise as a whole and

asking the questions what gets studied, when, by whom, what gets published, and with what effect?

Victor Jupp

Associated Concepts: appreciative criminology, Chicago School of Sociology, critical research, ethnography, participant observation, triangulation

Key Readings

Hughes, G. (2000) 'The politics of criminological research', in V. Jupp, P. Davies and P. Francis (eds), *Doing Criminological Research*. London, Sage.

Jupp, V.R. (1996) *Methods of Criminological Research*. London, Routledge.

Klockars, C.B. (1974) *The Professional Fence*. London, Tavistock.

Shaw, C.R. (1930) *The Jack Roller*. Chicago, University of Chicago Press.

Whyte, W.F. (1943) *Street Corner Society* (2nd edn 1955). Chicago, University of Chicago Press.

REGULATION

See Governmentality

REGULATORY AGENCIES

Definition

The determination of bodies of law and the establishment of some agency, usually a state agency, for enforcing and overseeing compliance with such laws.

Distinctive Features

While social scientific concern with regulation is long-standing – the first regulatory agency (the British factory inspectorate) was documented by Marx in *Capital* – this became prominent in the USA in the so-called Progressive Era of 1900–16, and then again during the New Deal of the 1930s, as part of a general concern with the activities of 'big business'. Bernstein's (1955) path-breaking work on regulation constituted a searing critique of the contemporary state of regulatory enforcement, and set out a 'Capture Theory' of regulation, positing that regulatory agencies are not able to maintain themselves as representatives of 'public interest'; even if this is why they are formed, an inevitable life-cycle of enthusiasm, the provocation of reaction from the regulated, and the demise of original agency zeal, ensure that the interests of some generalized public become subsumed to the demands of a regulated industry (Bernstein, 1955). Such a view of regulation continues to have some force. For some (instrumental) Marxists, a regulatory agency is subordinated to a state which is itself simply an instrument of capital or a ruling class; for some neo-liberal thinkers, regulatory agencies are inevitably captured by organized interests to distort 'free' markets. The common feature of these (different) perspectives is that regulatory agencies operate in a biased fashion. Capture Theory has been challenged by other Marxists and some critical criminologists who argue that regulation is the outcome of class conflict and compromise; the role of regulatory agencies is thus to mediate conflicts between competing class interests as part of the process of maintaining hegemonic domination.

In the 1970s, studies of the enforcement of new social regulation – for example, around occupational safety and health and environmental legislation – began to emerge in various nation-states, though particularly in the USA. Simultaneously, the new social regulation also prompted (largely neo-liberal) critics to call for the removal of these laws and the bodies designed to enforce them. These latter deregulatory arguments have assumed increasing importance across advanced capitalist economies – albeit variably – in the past quarter of a century. The dominant strand in regulatory concern within and around criminology has contributed to this 'debate' between regulation and deregulation, focusing in particular upon the issue of enforcement; that is, how do and how should regulatory agencies enforce law?

The distinction between compliance-oriented and punitive modes of enforcement is a key one within the literature on regulatory enforcement. While the aim of the latter is said to be to apply a punishment for breaking a rule and doing harm, the goal of a compliance strategy is to prevent a harm rather than punish an evil. Enforcers advise, educate, bargain, negotiate and compromise with the regulated. Whilst there are, of course, important national differences in enforcement strategies, and in enforcement strategies across different spheres of business activity (for example, financial regulation has generally been stricter than that

pertaining to occupational health and safety), it is fair to say that compliance-oriented enforcement techniques dominate (Pearce and Tombs, 1998, pp. 229–45). There now exist a mass of studies – mostly nationally based, though with some useful cross-national comparative studies also – regarding the practices of a whole range of regulatory bodies. In general, non-enforcement is the most frequently found characteristic. Enforcement activity tends to focus upon the smallest and weakest individuals and organizations, and sanctions following regulatory activity are light (Snider, 1993, pp. 120–4). Hutter has recently pointed to a body of evidence from Australia, Britain, the Netherlands, Sweden, and the USA, indicating that regulators increasingly favour compliance-based methods, an emerging preference which extends to financial regulation and certain areas of 'conventional' policing (Hutter, 1997, p. 243).

Evaluation

Much work on regulation not only documents a compliance-oriented approach as that which regulators adopt, but tends to endorse (some version of) this as the most appropriate enforcement approach (Pearce and Tombs, 1998, pp. 223–46). This endorsement is based upon a combination of a recognition of the power of business *vis-à-vis* regulators, and thus a concern not to provoke counter-productive tendencies through punitive enforcement, and also the claim that business offences call for different forms of regulation than other kinds of law breaking, a view reducible to the claim that business crime is not real crime, differing substantially from 'conventional' crime.

Linked to such claims are arguments around the potential of (enforced) self-regulation, a form of enforcement where the onus for compliance with the law is placed upon the regulated themselves, but distinct from deregulation, the latter term usually referring to the removal of laws designed to regulate the corporation. Increasingly allied to arguments around enforced self-regulation are claims regarding the utility of 'goal-oriented' (reflexive) over prescriptive (command and control) legislation. While the latter is said to specify the means of securing compliance, the former entails an agency negotiating 'the substantive regulatory goal with industry, leaving the industry discretion and responsibility of how to achieve this goal' (Ayres and Braithwaite, 1992, p. 38).

Regulation raises an enormous range of complex issues which go to the core of debates about the nature and role of law, corporations, contemporary economies and states. Current debates around the need or otherwise for international regulatory structures seem to become more pressing given the increasing momentum of claims regarding the demise of the nation-state, the internationalization of business activity, and the proliferation of social harms associated with these processes.

Steve Tombs and Dave Whyte

Associated Concepts: criminalization, corporate crime, deterrence, extraterritorial law enforcement, self-policing, social harm, the state, transnational policing, white collar crime

Key Readings

Ayres, I. and Braithwaite, J. (1992) *Responsive Regulation. Transcending the Deregulation Debate.* Oxford, Oxford University Press.

Baldwin, R., Scott, C. and Hood, R. (eds) (1998) *A Reader on Regulation.* Oxford, Oxford University Press.

Bernstein, B.H. (1955) *Regulating Business by Independent Commission.* Princeton, NJ, Princeton University Press.

Hutter, B. (1997) *Compliance: Regulation and the Environment.* Oxford, The Clarendon Press.

Pearce, F. and Tombs, S. (1998) *Toxic Capitalism: Corporate Crime and the Chemical Industry.* Aldershot, Dartmouth.

Snider, L. (1993) *Bad Business. Corporate Crime in Canada.* Toronto, University of Toronto Press.

REHABILITATION

Definition

The rehabilitation model takes the stance that crime is best prevented by addressing directly the factors – economic, social, or personal – believed to be the cause of crime. The treatment model is a special case of the rehabilitation model in that it seeks to work directly with the individual offender in order to bring about a reduction in offending.

Distinctive Features

The basis of the rehabilitation model is that if the factors that bring about crime can be addressed then it is possible to reduce crime.

For example, it is clear from the research literature that there is an association between unemployment and crime. A rehabilitative solution would therefore attempt to enhance the prospects of offenders gaining employment. This aim might be achieved through legislation, or through working with employers, or through working with offenders to give them skills suited to the job market. Similarly, poor educational achievement is another factor associated with crime. A rehabilitative solution might be to improve school conditions and so raise educational standards, or to have educational schemes specifically aimed at offenders. As Cullen and Gilbert (1982) note, the rehabilitative ideal stands directly opposed to ever-escalating levels of punishment as a response to crime. The ethos of rehabilitation holds that not all members of society are equal and that when crime arises from that inequality the constructive response is to redress that inequality. Some agencies within the criminal justice system, such as the probation service, have historically had the rehabilitative ideal as their driving force. In other cases it is voluntary agencies, such as the National Association for the Care and Resettlement of Offenders (NACRO), that seek to put rehabilitation into effect.

The *treatment model* is a special case of the rehabilitative model in that is has as its focus the individual offender. Historically, the development of psychological theories of criminal behaviour led to attempts to turn theory into practice. As new treatment methods followed theoretical advances, so a range of therapeutic approaches began to be applied to work with offenders. The earliest treatments aimed at offenders worked within a psychoanalytic tradition. For example, August Aichhorn (1925/1955) articulated a psychoanalytic formulation within which delinquent behaviour was seen as the product of a failure in psychological development; from this position Aichhorn developed therapeutic methods to work with young offenders. From the 1930s through to the 1970s, treatment with offenders was dominated by psychodynamic theory and practice, with counselling and group therapy being particularly popular. Educational programmes were also widespread during that period: a trend that is still evident today. While treatment within a psychodynamic tradition continues, the decades since the 1970s have seen a rise in treatment programmes based on behavioural and cognitive-behavioural theory.

Jeffery (1960) notes, there are three assumptions inherent within a rehabilitation, and particularly a treatment, philosophy: *determinism*, *differentiation* and *pathology*. Each of these assumptions sets advocates of rehabilitation in potential conflict with a criminal justice system that is built on principles of individual responsibility.

First, determinism maintains that factors outside of the individual's control – biological, psychological, social, or a combination of all three – bring about the individual's behaviour. Secondly, the logical conclusion from a deterministic position is that criminals must, in some way, be different from non-criminals. The origin of this differentiation may be biological, psychological, or social, but it remains the case that criminals are different from those who are not criminals. Thirdly, the notion of pathology, the logical step from differentiation, is that the difference between criminals and non-criminals is one of abnormality. The cause of the abnormality may be individual to the offender (biological or psychological) or social through learning from an abnormal environment.

As a net result, we arrive at a position in which the offender is portrayed as a victim of circumstance, with some level of individual or social 'wrongness' or abnormality as the root cause of their behaviour. There are cases where the legal system makes due allowances, as for example with mentally disordered offenders, but in the main determinism, differentiation and pathology stand in direct conflict with a justice system based on the notions of free will and individual agency in making choices. A deterministic position, in which the individual is compelled to offend by forces beyond their control, is not in accord with the classical concept of rational hedonism as the basis for dispensing justice.

During the 1970s and 1980s the rehabilitative ideal fell heavily from favour as the notion that 'nothing works' gathered momentum. However, the 1990s saw a remarkable resurrection of rehabilitation, certainly in Canada and Britain and also in parts of the USA. The return to grace of rehabilitation within the criminal justice system can be directly traced to the impact of a string of meta-analytic studies of the effects of offender treatment (see for example Redondo et al., 1999). The message that emerged from these studies was that treatment with offenders can have a small but significant effect in terms of reducing re-offending. Further, when certain treatment factors are combined, the meta-analyses suggest that this small effect can be amplified. This research gave rise to the movement known as 'What Works?' (McGuire,

1995). Current concern is with the design, implementation and evaluation of 'high impact' treatment characteristics of programmes for offenders. While practical success might be achievable, there remains the issue of rethinking the conceptual assumptions of determinism, differentiation and pathology (Hollin, 1999).

Clive Hollin

Associated Concepts: behaviour modification, conditioning, determinism, pathology, positivism, probation, social learning theory

Key Readings

Aichhorn, A. (1955) *Wayward Youth* (trans.). New York, Meridian Books. (Originally published 1925.)

Cullen, F. and Gilbert, K. (1982) *Reaffirming Rehabilitation*. Cincinnati, OH, Anderson Publishing.

Hollin, C.R. (1999) 'Treatment programmes for offenders: meta-analysis, "what works", and beyond', *International Journal of Psychiatry and Law*, 22, pp. 361–72.

Jeffery, C.R. (1960) 'The historical development of criminology', in H. Mannheim (ed.), *Pioneers in Criminology*. London, Stevens.

McGuire, J. (ed.) (1995) *What Works?: Reducing Reoffending*. Chichester, Wiley.

Redondo, S., Sánchez-Meca, J. and Garrido, V. (1999) 'The influence of treatment programmes on the recidivism of juvenile and adult offenders: a European meta-analytic review', *Psychology, Crime and Law*, 5, pp. 251–78.

REINTEGRATIVE SHAMING

See Shaming

RELATIVE DEPRIVATION

Definition

A concept, latterly most associated with left realism, by which it is maintained that it is not necessarily absolute deprivation or poverty that causes crime but discontent arising from perceptions of disadvantage and injustice.

Distinctive Features

First coined by Sam Stouffer and his associates in their wartime study *The American Soldier* (1949), relative deprivation was rigorously formulated by W.G. Runciman in 1966. Its use in criminology was not until the 1980s, by theorists such as S. Stack, John Braithwaite and particularly the left realists, for whom it is a key concept. Its attraction as an explanatory variable in the postwar period lies in the rise of crime in the majority of industrial societies despite the increase in living standards: that is, where material deprivation in an absolute sense declined and the old equation of 'the more poverty the more crime' was clearly falsified.

Relative deprivation occurs where individuals or groups subjectively perceive themselves as unfairly disadvantaged over others perceived as having similar attributes and deserving similar rewards (their reference groups). It is in contrast with absolute deprivation, where biological health is impaired or where relative levels of wealth are compared based on objective differences – although it is often confused with the latter. Subjective experiences of deprivation are essential and, indeed, relative deprivation is more likely when the differences between two groups narrow so that comparisons can more easily be made, than where there are caste-like differences. The discontent arising from relative deprivation has been used to explain radical politics (whether of the left or the right), messianic religions, the rise of social movements, industrial disputes and the whole plethora of crime and deviance.

The usual distinction made is that religious fervour or demand for political change are a collective response to relative deprivation whereas crime is an individualistic response. But this is certainly not true of many crimes – for example, smuggling, poaching or terrorism – which have a collective nature and a communal base and does not even allow for gang delinquency, which is clearly a collective response. The connection is, therefore, largely under-theorized – a reflection of the separate development of the concept within the seemingly discrete disciplines of sociology of religion, political sociology and criminology.

The use of relative deprivation in criminology is often conflated with Merton's anomie theory of crime and deviance and its development in subcultural theory by Cloward and Ohlin. There are discernible, although largely unexplored, parallels. Anomie theory involves a disparity between culturally induced aspirations (for example, success in terms of the American Dream) and the opportunities to realize them. The parallel is clear: this is a subjective process wherein discontent is transmuted into crime. Furthermore, Merton, in his classic 1938 article *Social Structure and Anomie*, clearly understands the relative nature of discontent by explicitly criticizing theories that link absolute deprivation to crime by pointing to poor countries with low crime rates in contrast to the wealthy USA with a comparatively high rate. But there are clear differences. In particular, Mertonian anomie involves an inability to realize culturally induced notions of success. It does not involve comparisons between groups but individuals measuring themselves against a general goal. The fact that Merton, the major theorist of reference groups, did not fuse this with his theory of anomie is, as Runciman notes, very strange but probably reflects the particular American concern with 'winners' and 'losers' and the individualism of that culture. The empirical implications of this difference in emphasis are, however, significant: anomie theory would naturally predict the vast majority of crime to occur at the bottom of society amongst the 'losers', but relative deprivation theory does not necessarily have this overwhelming class focus. Discontent can be felt anywhere in the class structure where people perceive their rewards as unfair compared to those with similar attributes. Thus crime would be more widespread, although it would be conceded that discontent would be greatest amongst the socially excluded.

Evaluation

The future integration of anomie and relative deprivation theory offers great promise in that relative deprivation offers a much more widespread notion of discontent. Its emphasis on subjectivity insures against the tendency within anomie theory of merely measuring objective differences in equality (so called 'strain' theory). Anomie theory, on its part, offers a wider structural perspective in terms of the crucial role of differential opportunity structures and firmly locates the dynamic of deprivation within capitalist society as a whole.

Jock Young

Associated Concepts: anomie, left realism, strain theory, subculture

Key Readings

Box, S. (1987) *Recession, Crime and Punishment*. London, Macmillan.

Lea, J. and Young, J. (1993) *What is to be Done About Law and Order?* London, Pluto.

Runciman, W.G. (1966) *Relative Deprivation and Social Justice*. London, Routledge.

Stouffer, S.A. (1949) *The American Soldier*. Princeton, Princeton University Press.

Young, J. (1999) *The Exclusive Society*. London, Sage.

REPARATION

Definition

Actions that aim to repair the damage caused by crime. These can include restitution to the victim.

Distinctive Features

Although the terms 'reparation' and 'restitution' are often used interchangeably, a distinction can be drawn between them. Restitution implies the restoration of goods or monetary compensation for loss or injury to the victim. Reparation has the wider aims of recognition of the social rights of victims and repairing the social damage caused by crime, in which restitution may play a part.

Principles of reparation and restitution emphasize the right of victims to obtain redress for the loss or harm they have suffered. Modern Western criminal justice systems, by contrast, give primacy to the punishment of offenders in the general interest, reflecting principles of retribution (the offender should pay a debt to society) or the prevention of future crime. The rights of victims to seek redress have become, at best, marginal in the course of what Christie (1977) famously described as the 'theft' by the state of conflicts between victims and offenders.

More recognition of the rights of victims has been a feature of criminal justice systems in recent decades, largely as a result of the growth of social movements to promote victims' interests. One manifestation of this has been a widening of the powers of courts to order offenders to make some form of restitution (compensation orders) to the victim, either in addition to punishment or as an alternative to it. One of several problems with these schemes (Ashworth, 1986) is that compensation of this type is analogous to civil damages and thus lacks penal value: that is, payment of compensation does not necessarily meet other penal aims (such as the prevention of future crime). Moreover, the use of such orders by the criminal courts means that compensation for individual victims becomes dependent upon the particular offender being caught and convicted and being willing and able to pay. State compensation schemes, which have been established in several jurisdictions, may give better assurance of compensation to victims (although eligibility and levels of payment are often restricted), but, since they require nothing from the offender, they cannot meet either the traditional aims of punishment or the broader aims of restoration. Advocates of the restitution and reparation principle often argue that state compensation provision is necessary as a back-up, but that restitution should come from the offender wherever possible

The idea of reparation (and restitution in its wider sense) implies more than the provision of compensation for victims. Repairing the social damage of crime requires that offenders should acknowledge the wrongfulness of their actions. Part of this involves making amends to the victim (through monetary compensation or, especially in the case of poor offenders, the performance of some service) and/or the community (for example, through community service, especially when there is no identifiable victim). It also entails the active participation of both victim and offender in the process, giving both a chance to explain their position and to resolve their own conflict. Since formal court procedures do not allow these voices full expression, particularly that of the victim, informal justice procedures, particularly mediation, are seen as appropriate. The purpose is to address the full impact of crime on the victim (for example, increased fear) and to identify a way in which the offender can do something positive for them. Realization of the harm caused and the making of positive amends may also facilitate the social re-integration of the offender.

Evaluation

Principles of reparation and restitution have assumed greater importance in recent years, as shown by the growth of state-sponsored compensation, compensation ordered by criminal courts and of victim–offender mediation schemes at pre-prosecution, pre-sentence and post-sentence stages of the criminal justice process. However, traditional principles of punishment remain dominant. From some critical penological perspectives (notably abolitionism but also other communitarian theories such as 're-integrative shaming'), it is seen as desirable that reparation, rather than punishment, should become the organizing principle of justice: reparative or restorative justice. Other commentators, whilst recognizing the importance of addressing the rights and needs of victims, have noted various problems with reparative justice. These focus upon the issue of whether reparation involves adequate recognition of the harms to the wider community and whether it has adequate 'penal value' to control crime.

Maggie Sumner

Associated Concepts: abolitionism, communitarianism, informal justice, redress, restorative justice, shaming, victimology

Key Readings

Ashworth, A. (1986) 'Punishment and compensation: victims, offenders and the state', *Oxford Journal of Legal Studies*, 6, pp. 86–122.
Barnett, R.E. (1977) 'Restitution: a new paradigm in crime control', *Ethics*, 87, pp. 279–301.
Christie, N. (1977) 'Conflicts as property', *British Journal of Criminology*, 17 (1), pp. 1–15.
Hudson, J. and Galaway, B. (1980) *Victims, Offenders and Alternative Sanctions*. Lexington, MA, Lexington Books.
Wright, M. (1991) *Justice for Victims and Offenders*. Buckingham, Open University Press.
Zedner, L. (1992) 'Reparation and retribution: are they reconcilable?', *Modern Law Review*, 37, pp. 228–50.

REPEAT VICTIMIZATION

Definition

Repeat victimization occurs when the same location, person, business, vehicle or household suffers more than one crime event over a specified time period. The offence may be of the same or a contrasting type.

Distinctive Features

Crime is preventable insofar as it is predictable in time and place. 'Sting' operations by the police engineer such predictability, for example by setting up a shop and making it

known that it will deal in stolen goods, or leaving a frequently stolen vehicle type in a high crime area, modified to trap a would-be thief inside. Such operations are liable to the charge of entrapment (literally, in the latter case). A less contentious approach involves targeting people and places at high risk of crime. Recent crime victimization is a good predictor of future victimization, almost certainly the best such predictor available without any additional analysis being necessary (Pease, 1998). An officer attending a crime scene needs no extra information to alert him or her to the elevated risk of future victimization. Targeting prior victims for crime prevention help is an attractive option, for several reasons:

- It requires no analysis; it is light on resources.
- It combines crime prevention help and victim support, since both are required by the same people at the same time.
- The deployment of help can be time-limited, since repeat crime against the same target *tends* to happen quickly.
- There is emerging evidence that prolific offenders are disproportionately responsible for repeat offending against the same target, so incapacitation of those inflicting repeat victimization may be especially productive in crime reduction.

There are two basic reasons for repetition of crime against the same target. These are known formally as risk heterogeneity and event dependence, and colloquially as flag and boost accounts. Examples will be taken from the offence of burglary. *Risk heterogeneity* occurs because the same attributes that *flag* a place or person as a good target at time 1, continue to do so at time 2. Thus lace curtains and porcelain ladies in crinolines as window ornaments alert the passer-by to the likely age of the householder, and her possible vulnerability to burglary by deception. It will flag the same message to every passer-by. *Event dependence* occurs when experience during the first offence *boosts* the attractions of coming back and doing it again. This may be because much cash is found, and may well be found again. It may be because electronic goods will be replaced by insurers, and the replacement goods may be stolen. Being new, they will fetch a higher price. Research evidence, notably offender accounts, suggest that both flag and boost accounts are relevant to repeat victimization (Ashton et al., 1998; Lauritsen and Davis Quinet, 1995).

An important virtue of the concept and associated research programme is that it picks apart the crude notion of crime incidence, defined as the number of crime events per population at risk. Incidence can be seen to be a function of crime prevalence (the number of those victimized within a population at risk) and crime concentration (the number of victimizations per victim). Thus, in a population of 100 homes, a total of 20 burglaries may be suffered. Thus, 0.20 is the burglary incidence. This may be a result of 20 homes being burgled once (i.e. a prevalence of 0.20 and a concentration of 1) or of one home being burgled 20 times (i.e. a prevalence of 0.01 and a concentration of 20), or any intermediate pattern. Research carried out within a repeat victimization framework shows that the extent to which areas differ in crime rate is to a surprisingly large extent a function of area differences in crime concentration (Trickett et al., 1992). Only when one can unpick the contribution of prevalence and concentration to an area's crime problem can a solution be intelligently formulated.

The prevention of repeat victimization has been the means whereby some successful crime reduction programmes have achieved their effect (Chenery et al., 1997; Forrester et al., 1988). No doubt the mechanisms involved are complex and varied, but repeat victimization does have the central advantage of directing crime prevention effort to individuals at high risk of crime, in areas with high rates of crime. The first part of the advantage is something which hot spot analysis lacks. The emerging link between prolific offenders and repeat victimization affords a means of targeting prolific offenders through the kinds of crime which they are likely to commit, and avoiding personal surveillance, with all its civil rights ambiguities.

Evaluation

Recent work is developing a more subtle view, invoking the notion of 'virtual repeats' whereby repetition is not against physically the same object or person, but against functionally identical objects, such as the same model of Ferrari or homes with the same floor plan. In this way, repeat victimization is set to merge with the study of offender targeting practices, along the dimension of similarity.

Ken Pease

Associated Concepts: community crime prevention, crime prevention, defensible space, geographies of crime, situational crime prevention, social crime prevention, victim surveys, victimology

Key Readings

Ashton J., Senior, B., Brown, I. and Pease, K. (1998) 'Repeat victimization: offender accounts', *International Journal of Risk, Security and Crime Prevention*, 3, pp. 269–80.

Chenery S., Holt, J. and Pease, K. (1997) *Biting Back II: Reducing Repeat Victimization in Huddersfield*. Crime Detection and Prevention Paper 82. London, Home Office.

Forrester D., Chatterton, M. and Pease, K. (1988) *The Kirkholt Burglary Prevention Project, Rochdale*. Crime Prevention Unit Paper 13. London, Home Office.

Lauritsen, J.L. and Davis Quinet, K.F. (1995) 'Repeat victimization among adolescents and young adults', *Journal of Quantitative Criminology*, 11, pp. 143–66.

Pease, K. (1998) *Repeat Victimization: Taking Stock*. Crime Detection and Prevention Paper 90. London, Home Office.

Trickett, A., Osborn, D., Seymour, J. and Pease, K. (1992) 'What is different about high crime areas?', *British Journal of Criminology*, 32, pp. 81–9.

REPLACEMENT DISCOURSE

See Constitutive criminology

RESTITUTION

See Reparation

RESTORATIVE JUSTICE

Definition

The idea has connotations traditionally of returning things to the state 'as they were'. It is a capacious concept which generally stands for the repair of harms and of ruptures to social bonds resulting from crime; it focuses on the relationships between crime victims, offenders and the community.

Distinctive Features

The last decades of the twentieth century witnessed the contemporary 're-surfacing' of appeals to traditional non-statist, communitarian modes of justice, ironically alongside the simultaneous renaissance of incapacitation and a retributive model of justice. According to the idea of restorative justice, justice is primarily a process of reconciling conflicting interests and healing rifts in communities resulting from harms committed. The restorative justice movement is a body of work which has gained much momentum in societies that have managed in part to 're-discover', to varying degrees, the systems of justice of their indigenous peoples, such as Canada and New Zealand (see Braithwaite, 1989). And social theologians have also sought to recover what may be a rich but largely suppressed tradition of communally based restorative justice when crime is understood as an interpersonal harm rather than as a violation of an abstract legal rule (Zehr, 1990). These harms are viewed as creating obligations and liabilities which have to be put right by the parties concerned themselves, with the state and its agents only minimally involved. Zehr argues that justice (now generally interpreted narrowly as due process, fairness or impartiality in modern Western legalism) needs to be re-entwined with conceptions of respect, love, peace and community.

There is also a much wider 'abolitionist' body of literature on restorative justice (Christie, 1977; de Haan, 1990), which has criticized the workings of the formal criminal justice system across a whole gamut of fronts. Abolitionists are keen to remind us that the events and behaviours that are criminalized make up only a minute part of the events and behaviours that can be so defined. They suggest that crime is not the object but the product of crime control philosophies and institutions. More particularly, social problems, conflicts and troubles are an inevitable part of everyday life and therefore cannot, or rather should not, be delegated to professionals and specialists claiming to provide 'solutions'. When professionals and state agencies intervene, the essence of social problems and conflicts are 'stolen' and re-presented in forms that only perpetuate the problems and conflicts. Traditional state-based, adversarial justice thus makes both the victim and the offender passive spectators, at formal and legalistic court proceedings. It is suggested that the abolition of the 'crime control industry' would also revitalize the social fabric by allowing other forms of conflict resolution, peacemaking and community safety to be imagined and properly resourced.

Supporters of the restorative justice movement argue that it is not a soft option for offenders. Instead, they point to the stress on personal responsibility for harms done, from which offenders cannot hide. The emphasis on using the techniques of reintegrative shaming, mediation and reparation in turn are meant to work on the conscience of the harm-doer in ways that formal legal procedures do not. In accord with the general drift of communitarian thought, Braithwaite, as the most famous theoretician and proponent of reintegrative shaming, does not flinch from arguing that society's response to crime must be moralizing (but not rejecting). Examples are offered of community conferences (or Family Group Conferences) for young offenders in New Zealand which are 'based' on Maori traditions conducive to reintegrative shaming, involving kin and significant others of both the victim and the offender. In acting as a form of 'communion', it is further contended that such conferences are de-professionalizing, empowering of women, oriented to flexible community problem-solving and for the most part, narrowing the nets of social control.

Evaluation

Great claims have been made for reintegrative shaming and family group conferences as concrete examples of the workings of restorative justice. However, it is wise to remain circumspect about their potential for creating the conditions for a radical, non-discriminatory approach to justice. Significant questions also remain about the theory and practice of reintegrative shaming as a form of restorative justice. For example, it has as yet to be shown that reintegrative shaming will not be mobilized against the most vulnerable sections of the society and indeed be employed for trivial offenders without any reduction in the use of traditional custodial sentences. Furthermore, the lack of accountability and the absence of protection for the offender in terms of appeals to legality and due process remain major areas of concern associated with most forms of restorative justice. In terms of criminal justice system practice, restorative justice is viewed as a set of alternatives *within* the system to formal justice, for example siphoning off less serious cases and providing opportunities for victims and offenders to meet and perhaps make amends (Daly and Immerigeon, 1998). For the most part, practices are contained by formal criminal justice. There is also the question of the extent to which restorative justice initiatives, administered in a governmental context – and subject to bureau-professional capture – may extend the net of social control deeper into the community. At the same time, it is questionable whether any of the above criticisms negate the progressive potentialities of restorative justice *per se*. Rather, such criticisms demonstrate in part both the pitfalls of poor implementation and the subversion of restorative justice's principles in specific 'projects'. A more general difficulty with restorative justice concerns its assumption – alongside retributivism – that individuals are autonomous, rational individuals able to make free moral choices for which they may be held to account. However, restorative justice continues to provide an alternative to punishment, violence, exclusion and coercive power to effect change in our lives and our social institutions (Sullivan et al., 1998).

Gordon Hughes

Associated Concepts: abolitionism, communitarianism, community justice, peacemaking criminology, redress, reparation, shaming

Key Readings

Braithwaite, J. (1989) *Crime, Shame and Reintegration*. Oxford, Oxford University Press.
Christie, N. (1977) 'Conflicts as property', *British Journal of Criminology*, 17, pp. 1–15.
Daly, K. and Immerigeon, R. (1998) 'The past, present, and future of restorative justice: some critical reflections', *Contemporary Justice Review*, 1, pp. 21–45.
de Haan, W. (1990) *The Politics of Redress*. London, Unwin Hyman.
Sullivan, D., Tifft, L. and Cordella, P. (1998) 'The phenomenon of restorative justice', *Contemporary Justice Review*, 1, pp. 7–20.
Zehr, H. (1990) *Changing Lenses: A New Focus for Crime and Justice*. Waterloo, ON, Herald Press.

RETRIBUTION

Definition

Punishment inflicted upon offenders in consequence of their wrong-doing. Retributivism is the view that the moral justification for punishment is that the offender deserves it.

Distinctive Features

The term 'retribution' originally referred to the repayment of a debt (Walker, 1991), an idea which is easily seen in the very old notion of 'an eye for an eye, a tooth for a tooth', *lex talionis* (the law of the scale). The principle is that it is morally right and good that offenders should suffer: punishment is deserved and should also be proportionate to the amount of harm done. The offender 'owes a debt', not just to the victim (where restitution might be appropriate) but to the wider society.

Strict retributivists hold that society has a moral *obligation* to punish wrong-doers. By choosing to break the law individuals are deemed to have disturbed a moral equilibrium which must then be restored through legal denunciation and/or punishment. Individuals must be treated as rational moral agents and so held responsible for their actions (as in classicism). According to the philosopher Immanuel Kant, offenders therefore have a *right* to punishment as a mark of respect for their human autonomy and membership of society. It follows that (i) only offenders *can* be punished and (ii) all offenders *must* be punished.

The punishment should 'fit the crime', being proportionate to the harm done rather than being tailored to the individual offender, for example to the likelihood of re-offending. In sentencing practice, retribution appears as a 'tariff system', a more or less fixed scale of penalties for particular offences.

Punishment is therefore justified by reference to past action and, for the strict retributivist, it is a natural consequence of human law-breaking (hence retributivism is referred to as a *deontological* theory: punishment follows from the nature of the human action to which it is related). Punishment is seen as morally right in itself, regardless of any other effects it may or may not have. Retributivism thus stands in contrast to consequentialist justifications for punishment (rehabilitation, deterrence, incapacitation) which focus upon the future effects that might be achieved (being concerned with outcomes, such theories are described as *teleological*).

Evaluation

Retribution remains an important principle in contemporary penal practice. However, there are a number of problems associated with it. First, the moral philosophical basis for the claim that offenders deserve punishment (rather than, for example, mercy or forgiveness) has been found wanting (e.g. Honderich, 1989; Walker, 1991). Retributivism can appear as no more than a primitive demand for vengeance. A related criticism is that retributivism requires that punishment be inflicted even where no positive good will be achieved, for example, in the case of a remorseful offender who is unlikely to commit further crime. The infliction of punishment on grounds of the harm done, regardless of the circumstances of the individual offender, may be not only pointless but also lead to social injustice. It is also difficult to translate the principle of proportionality, the idea that punishment should reflect the degree of harm done, into practice. Two problems arise. The first is how to determine in absolute terms what *quantum* or amount of punishment is proportionate to a particular offence (the problem of *cardinal proportionality*): there is a vast range of offences to which the 'eye for an eye' principle is not very easily applied. A second problem, that of *ordinal proportionality*, is how different offences and the penalties attached to them are to be ranked (whether, for example, a rape merits more or less punishment than a muti-million pound fraud).

Although strict retributivism is largely discredited on these grounds, the 1970s saw a resurgence in the form of 'just deserts' theory. This was in response to the alleged failings of the then dominant principle of rehabilitation. Right-wing critics of rehabilitation saw it as a 'soft option' and called for more traditional punitive responses. Liberal and more radical critics saw it as leading to injustice in the form of disparities in sentencing, as well as the use of long and indeterminate sentences, in the name of preventing future crime. They advocated a 'justice model' (as opposed to a treatment model) of sentencing, drawing upon retributivism.

In contrast to pure retributivists, 'just deserts' theorists argued that there is no moral *obligation* to punish offenders: whether the power to punish is exercised in a particular case can be decided on consequentialist grounds. However, punishment can be given *only* when it is deserved: people should be punished for what they have done and not what they might do, for past rather than future crimes (von Hirsch, 1985). The desert principle acts as a limit on the distribution of punishment. Similarly, the principle of proportionality provides a ceiling on the amount of punishment. The severity of the punishment does not always have to match the gravity of the offence: something less (though nothing more) is permissible. Arguments in which desert and proportionality are employed as limiting principles are sometimes referred to as 'negative retributivism'.

A number of jurisdictions, influenced by the just deserts movement, have introduced systems of mandatory or presumptive sentences either through legislation or in the form of guidelines for sentencers. Whilst these may have led to increased consistency, the difficulties of determining levels of proportionality have often led to greater severity of punishment, contrary to the implicit aims of the neo-retributivist 'just deserts' advocates (Hudson, 1987).

More fundamental criticisms of retributivism, even in its modified form, concern the continued focus on the punishment of the individual offender, without questioning the nature of criminal justice and its relationship to social justice (e.g. Braithwaite and Pettit, 1990; Hudson, 1987).

Maggie Sumner

Associated Concepts: classicism, deterrence, incapacitation, just deserts, proportionality, rehabilitation

Key Readings

Braithwaite, J. and Pettit, P. (1990) *Not Just Deserts: A Republican Theory of Criminal Justice*. Oxford, The Clarendon Press.
von Hirsch, A. (1985) *Past and Future Crimes*. Manchester, Manchester University Press.
Honderich, T. (1989) *Punishment: The Supposed Justifications*. Cambridge, Polity Press.
Hudson, B. (1987) *Justice through Punishment: A Critique of the Justice Model of Corrections*. London, Macmillan.
Walker, N. (1991) *Why Punish? Theories of Punishment Reassessed*. London, Opus.

RIGHT REALISM

See Administrative criminology; Neo-conservative criminology; Rational choice theory

RISK

Definition

In criminology, risk refers to the probability of harm, the role of its calculation or assessment in making decisions about whether to perform criminal actions, and its role in criminal justice decision-making.

Distinctive Features

Risk has a foundational role in modern criminology, in classical criminology's focus on the calculation of probable gains and losses in projected offending, and – as well – much current research focuses on crime as risk-taking, especially where taking risks is a source of excitement that brings people into trouble with criminal justice. Today, risk increasingly refers to governing crime through official discourses and techniques of risk management, especially 'actuarial justice' (Feeley and Simon, 1994), a term that refers to the displacement of individually based justice by decision-making based on the statistical probability of re-offending.

However, actuarial justice is only one risk managerial response to crime. For example, English 'Sex Offender Orders', under the Crime and Disorder Act 1998, allow for restraints on former offenders on the basis of 'reasonable' fears that they represent risks to the community. Such judgements are made by police, using traditional means of discretionary assessment rather than statistical data or processes. Similarly, requiring community notification about resident former sex offenders is the focus of 'Megan's Laws' in the USA, even though it is not clear this leads to risk reduction (Simon, 1998). As these examples also suggest, risk refers not only to statistical probabilities of harm but also to other forms of estimating probability, and to harm's moral magnitude: 'high risk' may refer to intolerable risk of incalculable or uncalculated probability (Beck, 1992). Thus, much 'risk' legislation of this sort arises out of community pressure rather than sound foundations in actuarial evidence. 'Risk talk' has also entered other areas of criminal justice without necessarily implying statistical risk assessment. Decision-making about risk in areas such as inmate security, pre-sentencing reports and prison parole decisions usually reflects expert evaluation of individual cases, rather than actuarial classification. In all these instances, the spread of risk appears as a matter of governmental fashion and popular consciousness that extends well beyond actuarialism's power to predict (Beck, 1992). But they also indicate that discourses and practices of risk are multiple, not just statistical, and are mobilized in different ways in different parts of criminal justice (O'Malley, 1998).

Crime risk thinking reaches well beyond criminal justice. Under the banner of governing crime risks, streetscapes, house design, 'gated communities' and the planning and operation of shopping centres are being organized around crime prevention. In the government of illicit drug use, criminal justice may be deliberately marginalized in favour of preventative, risk-reducing programmes such as needle exchanges and safe injecting facilities, and police may be instructed not to enforce the law against drug users. Indeed, for some writers the development of a 'risk society' implies a new governmental principle in which the place of criminal justice, not merely its organization, changes dramatically (Simon, 1987).

Many fears have been raised about the spread of risk frameworks in criminal justice. First, is the potential for net-widening, as 'unacceptable risks' become subjects of justice. Secondly are fears concerning the marginalization of individualized justice, abandoning the proportionality of offence and punishment, and diminishing judicial discretion. Such fears generate considerable resistance to risk-based justice, particularly by the judiciary. More generally, however, the development of risk technologies and practices may create a society that is increasingly insecure: fear of crime may be exaggerated by high profile crime prevention initiatives, social isolation and divisiveness may spread with the rise of 'gated communities', and fears of 'Big Brother' surveillance are increased as invasive technologies preventatively govern crime 'in the community' (Ericson and Haggerty, 1997).

These observations raise the issue of a politics of risk. Some argue that the emergence of risk in government reflects the rise of neo-liberalism (O'Malley, 1992). Such politics have shaped the character of risk, making citizens and communities (neighbourhoods, women, home-owners, etc.) more 'responsible' for managing their own crime exposure – for example, by forming 'partnerships' with police and avoiding high-risk situations. Likewise, they foster a rational-choice 'risk-taking' image of offenders, who calculate the risks and benefits of their offending and thereby become more criminally 'responsible' than under therapeutic regimes of rehabilitation. Risk, in this view, is being politically reshaped, rather than actuarialized, in current politics of crime risks.

Evaluation

There is no doubt that crime risk discourses are becoming more prevalent. The theoretical and political implications of theses changes are considerable. Like all models, however, it is prone to exaggeration. While many illustrations are provided, there is no systematic evidence of risk's relative increase or dominance. Certainly, outside certain US jurisdictions, actuarial sentencing has remained marginal. Little research has been carried out on the variety of risk discourses and techniques, leading to some misleading characterizations of risk-oriented justice as 'actuarial'. There is also a tendency to ignore the continuity of long-established risk techniques (e.g. in parole decisions), perhaps giving exaggerated impressions of risk's 'rise'. Explanations of risk's ascendancy are also impressionistic rather than solidly grounded. Most accounts rely on largely speculative and poorly evidenced accounts that link risk-based justice with mega-crises of modernity (Ericson and Haggerty, 1997) or with the rise of postmodernity (Feeley and Simon, 1994), or simplistically reduce a wide diversity of changes to a single effect of neo-liberalism (O'Malley, 1992). At present, despite the apparent importance of justice through risk, we have no more than descriptive accounts, possibly selective, conceptually varied, and of debatable generality.

Pat O'Malley

Associated Concepts: actuarialism, defensible space, fear of crime, hedonism, net widening, opportunity theory, rational choice theory, situational crime prevention, surveillance

Key Readings

Beck, U. (1992) *Risk Society*. London, Sage.

Ericson, R. and Haggerty, K. (1997) *Policing the Risk Society*. Toronto, Toronto University Press.

Feeley, M. and Simon, J. (1994) 'Actuarial justice. The emerging new criminal law', in D. Nelken (ed.), *The Futures of Criminology*. London, Sage.

O'Malley, P. (1992) 'Risk, power and crime prevention', *Economy and Society*, 21, pp. 252–75.

O'Malley, P. (ed.) (1998) *Crime and the Risk Society*. Aldershot, Dartmouth.

Simon, J. (1987) 'The emergence of the risk society', *Socialist Register*, 95, pp. 61–89.

Simon, J. (1998) 'Managing the monstrous: sex offenders and the new penology', *Psychology, Public Policy and the Law*, 4, pp. 452–67.

ROUTINE ACTIVITY THEORY

Definition

According to Marcus Felson, mainstream criminology has devoted the majority of its attention to 'the criminal', investigating why certain individuals are more criminally inclined than others. As a consequence of this fixation, criminology has given very little thought to either the context or nature of criminal acts or the role of victims as active participants in crime production and prevention. His writings represent one of the most significant attempts to redress this imbalance, and he does so from a rational choice perspective. Crime, for Felson, is first and foremost a physical act and the product of the recurrent, routine activities and structuring of everyday life. This means that the potential for crime is inevitable and constant. A utilitarian motivation to commit crime is taken as given. It also means that criminologists can contribute in a practical manner to criminal justice policy debates by shifting the focus from detection and punishment of the criminal to reduction and prevention of the criminal event.

Distinctive Features

The original formulation of routine activities postulated that the volume and distribution of 'predatory crime', that is those direct contact crimes in which one or more individuals attacks the person or property of another, are closely related to three variables. First, motivated offenders, usually young males, must be in attendance. Secondly, 'suitable targets', in the form of person or property, must be available. Routine activity theory prefers to use the term 'target' instead of 'victim' because it emphasizes that the majority of criminality is geared towards acquisition of property. Suitability is characterized by four attributes (VIVA):

- **V**alue calculated from the offender's perspective,
- **I**nertia – the physical aspects of the person or property that hinder or interrupt its suitability as a target
- **V**isibility, which marks out the person or property for attack
- **A**ccessibility which increases the risk of attack.

The third variable is the absence of 'capable guardians' against crime. According to Felson, individuals looking after a household, family members, colleagues in the workplace, friends or indeed strangers on the street, are more likely to act as 'capable guardians' than police officers.

It is the physical coming together of these three variables that produces the opportunity for a predatory crime to occur. To put it succinctly, a predatory crime is most likely to occur when an offender meets in time and space with a viable target in the absence of a capable guardian. Crucially, the convergence transpires because of the routine practices of everyday life. Hence, criminal acts are intimately related to and feed off normal behaviours associated with work, school, transportation, recreation, shopping, production of consumer goods and so on. Changes in routine activities and the rhythms of life have placed more people in particular places at specific moments, which increases their accessibility as realistic targets of crime. People are also more likely to be away from their homes, thus reducing their ability to act as capable guardians of their property and opening up new opportunities for crime through the ever increasing number of portable possessions. For Felson, contemporary society invites high crime rates by generating a huge number of illegal opportunities.

Routine activity theory was subsequently developed by Felson and applied to four other types of crime: exploitative (robbery, rape); mutualistic (gambling, prostitution, selling and buying illegal drugs); competitive (fighting) and individualistic (individual drug use, suicide). In so doing he identified a fourth element that allows a criminal event to happen – the absence of an 'intimate handler', a significant other who can impose informal social control on the offender. A potential offender must break free of the 'intimate handler' then find a target for crime, unmonitored by a 'capable guardian'.

More recently Felson in conjunction with Ron Clarke has claimed that the principles underpinning routine activity can provide criminology with a new general opportunity-based theory of crime that forces criminologists to move away from using vague criminological concepts to formulating precise research questions.

Evaluation

Routine activity theorizing has opened up an important debate about the context within which crime takes place. The crime prevention implications focus on changing routine activities and practices to frustrate potential offenders and prevent easy victimization. Thus, it underpins situational crime prevention and personal risk assessment strategies such as defensible space and target hardening and arguments for increasing the presence of 'capable guardians' and 'eyes on the street'. Critics argue that it overlooks the offender and cannot answer the question why some individuals are more motivated to commit criminal acts than others. It also carries with it a tendency to blame the victim. Also, in its original focus on 'predatory crime', it reproduced stereotypical representation of the problem of crime. Although it makes increasing claims to be enriching criminological theory, its primary concern remains producing practices that help policy-makers.

Eugene McLaughlin

Associated Concepts: defensible space, opportunity theory, rational choice theory, situational crime prevention, surveillance

Key Readings

Birkbeck, C. and La Free, G. (1993) 'The situational analysis of crime and deviance', *Annual Review of Criminology*, 19, pp. 113–37.

Cohen, L.E. and Felson, M. (1979) 'Social change and crime rate trends; a routine activity approach', *American Sociological Review*, 44, pp. 588–608.

Felson, M. (1986) 'Routine activities, social controls, rational decisions and criminal outcomes', in D. Cornish and R.V. Clarke (eds), *The Reasoning Criminal*. New York, Springer-Verlag.

Felson, M. (1987) 'Routine activities and crime prevention in the developing metropolis', *Criminology*, 25, pp. 911–31.

Felson, M. (1998) *Crime and Everyday Life*, 2nd edn. Thousand Oaks, CA, Pine Forge Press.

Felson, M. (2000) 'The routine activity approach as a general social theory', in S. S. Simpson (ed.), *Of Crime and Criminality: The Use of Theory in Everyday Life*. Thousand Oaks, CA, Pine Forge Press.

S

SAMPLING

Definition

The process of selecting a sub-set of cases from a wider population with a view to making inferences from the sample to the wider population.

Distinctive Features

The cases sampled from a population are largely determined by the focus of research, and can include documents, interactions, institutions, communities and societies. However, in social surveys the basic sampling unit is usually the individual (for example, offender, victim, police officer, magistrate). The term population is used in the statistical, rather than geographical, sense and refers to the total category or group of cases about which the researcher wishes to reach conclusions. However, the statistical population in which the researcher is interested may correspond with a geographical area, for example, 'all victims of house burglary living in London, 1990–2000', but that is not a requirement.

The basis of making inferences from samples to populations is sampling theory, which is a set of assumptions and mathematical deductions. One key assumption is that samples are selected from the population at random. This means that every case in the population must have an equal and non-zero chance of being selected as part of the sample. In order to carry out random sampling it is necessary to have a sampling frame, which is a listing of all cases in the population (for example, a list provided by the police of all

victims of house burglary in London, 1990–2000). It is rarely, if ever, possible to produce completely accurate estimates of population values, perhaps due to errors in the process of sampling. Fortunately, provided the sample has been selected using random techniques, it is possible to estimate sampling error (which provides a calculable margin of error).

In many instances it is not desirable or feasible to collect findings from random samples. For example, tracing each member of a sample can be a costly and time-consuming business. Therefore where results are required quickly and cheaply, researchers often use quota sampling, whereby the population to be studied is divided into categories that are relevant to the topic of investigation (for example, categorized by gender, age and ethnicity). Interviewers are given quotas of types of people to interview. The quotas are often proportionate to the significance of the categories in the population as a whole, and the interviews usually take place after stopping people in public areas. Quota sampling is typically used to obtain a cheap and quick estimate of public opinion on a recent issue or event (for example, the introduction of a new policing strategy).

For some topics of study a sampling frame is not available and therefore random sampling is not feasible. In such instances researchers may turn to 'volunteer sampling', whereby respondents volunteer to be part of a study, or 'snowball sampling', whereby the researcher makes an initial contact with one person and then is introduced to others in 'chain-letter' style. Both types of sample have been used in research involving drug-takers.

Quota, volunteer and snowball samples share the feature of not having been selected by random procedures. This means that, in contrast with random samples, it is not possible to estimate sampling errors.

Evaluation

Where researchers are interested in reaching conclusions about reasonably sized populations it is fairly rare to investigate every case in that population (which is known as a census). The advantages of sampling over a census are that it is cheaper, quicker and there is potential for greater efficiency per unit of analysis. However, such advantages need to be balanced against the desirability of deriving accurate estimates of population values from samples. A key factor in this is the degree to which samples are representative of the populations from which they are drawn, especially in relation to the central topic of the research.

Although sampling is typically associated with quantitative, especially social survey, approaches to criminological research, some qualitative approaches employ what is often termed 'theoretical sampling'. Theoretical sampling is much less technical and much more flexible than statistical sampling. It involves selecting groups or cases as the research develops in order to discover meaningful categories and to develop theory. For this reason, theoretical sampling is often closely associated with the development of grounded theory. Groups or cases may be selected so as to maximize or minimize their differences on some features whilst seeking to make comparisons between them on other features. For example, 'rookie' and 'old stager' police officers may be selected and compared with regard to their attitudes towards young offenders. The research may progress by making further selections in terms of male rookie police officers. When new ideas and theoretical revisions are no longer emerging, the point of theoretical saturation has been reached and the process of theoretical sampling is terminated.

Victor Jupp

Associated Concepts: comparative method, ethnography, longitudinal study, social survey, victim surveys

Key Readings

Arber, S. (1993) 'Designing samples', in N. Gilbert (ed.), *Researching Social Life*. London, Sage.

Sapsford, R. (1999) *Survey Research*. London, Sage.

Schofield, W. (1996) 'Survey sampling', in R. Sapsford and V. Jupp (eds), *Data Collection and Analysis*. London, Sage.

SCAPEGOATING

Definition

To cast blame or guilt on to an innocent person, group or object.

Distinctive Features

The biblical scapegoat was an animal onto which the sins of the people were transferred and erased through the expulsion of the goat. In anthropology the role of the scapegoat has usually been analysed as a purification ritual or ceremonial process through which evil is dealt with. In racial and ethnic studies, particular groups – such as blacks and Jews – have commonly been seen as being scapegoated for wider social and economic problems such as unemployment. These examples indicate that blame or guilt for social problems is attached to groups that may have little or no responsibility for an event; in fact, a strict definition of scapegoating would require that the scapegoated should be innocent of any responsibility for events. This is similar to the process of 'victim blaming'. Scapegoating processes include the identification of relatively powerless individuals or groups who can easily be blamed for a condition and amplification by the media through representing particular groups as a threat, probably in a stereotypical way. The objects or victims of scapegoating are thought to be chosen because they are identifiably 'different', for example due to external markers such as skin colour or some bodily sign, which connects scapegoating to both racialization and stigmatization. However, not all instances of scapegoating involve visibly different individuals or groups, or the powerless. The powerful can also be scapegoated, for instance when army commanders and politicians are held responsible for particular defeats or, more generally, for national decline.

Scapegoating is said to be a product of a universal societal requirement for some 'other' or 'out group' that serves the needs of groups to foster and maintain integration. Scapegoating is a social process that can be observed historically and cross-culturally, which has been taken to indicate that it is an expression of a deep human need to transgress and to reaffirm boundaries to maintain group solidarity. Indeed, for Erikson (1966) deviants have a maintenance function, so groups need to induce and sustain deviant behaviour in order to help them maintain and restore social equilibrium. Strategic scapegoating describes the use of tactics to deflect blame by an individual or group fearing exposure. Scapegoating is therefore a diversionary process that serves to demonize particular groups and may result in a moral panic. In this view, scapegoating is a form of mystification that obscures the real or essential problem. Nevertheless, no uniform motivations of scapegoaters have been identified. Their actions could be seen as rational or irrational. Explanations suggested are that scapegoaters act out of frustration, aggression, or to displace certain feelings (the frustration–aggression hypothesis), or projection and psychic discomfort (a reaction to, or denial of, tension), or a general hostility to others. The latter has been associated with the idea of the authoritarian personality (Douglas, 1995).

Scapegoating entails the drawing of a boundary between good and evil. It is something that is usually seen as pre-criminological superstition. However, Tannenbaum (1938) argued that criminological theories have persistently reproduced this distinction, so that terms such as normal and abnormal stand in exactly the same relation as good and evil. Instead of 'demonic possession', classical criminology employed the idea of rational choice to do evil; positivism differentiated the abnormal through various bodily manifestations as predictors or determinants of criminality; while functionalists see the criminal as socially maladjusted. Each involves the dramatization and symbolization of difference and, in the process, the deviant is tagged or stigmatized.

Evaluation

The idea that a group or individual is a scapegoat for some wider ill is in common use. The term is frequently and loosely used so that its many applications defy an overall definition of its usages. This wide utilization makes it difficult to evaluate or assess its veracity, particularly since there is room for debate on how far the scapegoated are 'innocent' or totally blameless, whether scapegoating can be explained in functionalist terms of serving group needs, and whether expurgation or purification actually occurs. Individuals, groups and both animate and inanimate objects (animals, financial markets), as well as nation-states, have been regarded, and sometimes defined themselves as, scapegoats. For instance, in the Balkans war the Bosnian

government asserted that it was made a scapegoat to justify US military action. Similar claims have been made by Iraq following the Gulf War. At another level, the blaming of individuals and/or paediatricians and social workers for being perpetrators of or uncovering child abuse has been seen as a mode of scapegoating for a society that could not accept such transgressions of family norms, or to accept that there might be widespread abuse in society.

The idea of scapegoating as a mode of boundary maintenance is basically functionalist. This is problematic when boundaries have been transgressed, or at least become blurred. The objects of scapegoating may also be much more able to challenge images and representations and this too indicates that understanding and accounting for scapegoating is a far from straightforward process.

Karim Murji

Associated Concepts: demonization, folk devil, labelling, moral panic, stigma, stereotyping

Key Readings

Douglas, T. (1995) *Scapegoat*. London, Routledge.
Erikson, K.T. (1966) *Wayward Puritans*. New York, Wiley.
Jenkins, P. (1992) *Intimate Enemies*. New York, Aldine de Gruyter.
Tannenbaum, F. (1938) *Crime and the Community*. New York, Colombia University Press.

SECONDARY DEVIATION

See Labelling; Social reaction

SELF-POLICING

Definition

A criminal justice concept that draws attention to the capacity of members of the community to make decisions about the appropriate level and means of control response without necessarily invoking criminal law agents.

Distinctive Features

There is a real sense in which society is self-policing. Formal policing measures are most often the result of calls for action from members of the public. Crime surveys tend to show that about one-half of the most common types of crime are not reported to the police. This suggests that members of the public judge that formal invocation of the law enforcement machinery is not necessary, even though the instance in question is understood to be a crime or otherwise somehow answerable to police action. Even quite serious issues can be negotiated without recourse to the criminal law. Extended family, religious organizations, friendship and neighbourhood networks can all be drafted in to control forms of rule-breaking, disorder and conflict that otherwise might become the object of the criminal justice process.

Evaluation

There are several limitations to the notion of society as self-policing that are worth noting. First, although crime surveys do indicate that a large proportion of scenarios that people regard as in some sense criminal are not reported to the police, an unquantified proportion of them may be due to pessimism about the effectiveness of formal criminal justice responses. In such instances, it is not so much self-policing, as it is non-policing. Secondly, perhaps one-quarter of indictable crimes are discovered by the police themselves; proactive policing, particularly in such areas as drink driving, illicit drug markets and other forms of vice, shows that a significant proportion of policing activity comes about as a result of priorities set by control agencies. This raises knotty questions about the relationship between policing and society that the notion of self-policing cannot wholly clarify. This leads to a third difficulty with the idea of society as self-policing: some police and/or control functions are tangential to the awareness of most citizens. The activities of the Serious Fraud Office might be an example here, but policing (in the sense of maintaining peace, order and good government) also extends to the activities of inspectorates for pollution, fire, health and safety as well as many of the tasks undertaken by the uniformed public police. Of course, the public may make reactive demands of such governmental services in some fraught circumstances, but the routine activity of such agencies largely lies outside of common perceptions of policing (as simply crime control) and yet it has become an indispensable aspect of social ordering and the

maintenance of the 'health of the social body'. Fourthly, the idea of society as self-policing may lend legitimacy in some instances of the social reaction to alleged criminal wrong-doing, which would be better characterized as vigilantism.

James Sheptycki

Associated Concepts: community policing, criminal justice, informal justice, redress, social control, social justice

Key Readings

Ashworth, A. (1994) *The Criminal Process: An Evaluative Study*. Oxford, The Clarendon Press.
Brown, R.M. (1969) 'The American vigilante tradition', in H.G. Graham and T.R. Gurr (eds), *The History of Violence in America*. New York, Bantam Books.

SELF-REPORTS

Definition

The self-report method is a means of collecting information about aspects of an individual's personal experience – such as involvement in offending – using a structured interview. The method can generate both statistical and qualitative data, but has most commonly been used to quantify rates of self-reported crime and drug use.

Distinctive Features

Self-report methods have been used to investigate forms of behaviour as varied as alcohol and drug use (both legal and illegal), tobacco smoking, sexual experiences, diet and other aspects of physical health. Respondents are asked to describe an aspect of their behaviour or life experience, and often to give views and opinions about a particular topic, either in a face-to-face interview, by completing a questionnaire or, increasingly, using a computer. Of most relevance to criminology are the self-report *offending* surveys that have a history in criminology dating back to the 1940s (Coleman and Moynihan, 1996). The method has been used to estimate rates of offending in the general population, among university students, 'persistent offenders' and those in prison or on probation orders. Recently, in the UK, self-report offending surveys have been suggested for evaluating crime reduction strategies, as an alternative to re-conviction studies. The method has also been used for comparative analysis of crime and deviance.

Surveys using this method have contributed to knowledge about deviance, often producing a picture that contradicts 'conventional wisdom'. For example, self-report studies indicate that drug use and crimes including theft, violence and fraud are much more widespread among the general population than commonly imagined, most of which goes undetected. Self-report offending survey rates among males in one cohort study exceed 95 per cent by the time of early middle age, many more than the one in three who were convicted in court of a non-motoring offence (Farrington, 1997). Self-report offending surveys conducted in the USA, UK and continental Europe also suggest that gender, ethnic and class differences in offending are much smaller than the picture painted by arrest and imprisonment statistics. Despite methodological weaknesses (see below), this finding lends weight to the evidence that suggests that selective enforcement and discrimination in criminal justice processing explain the disproportionate rates of imprisonment among particular ethnic groups.

The self-report method offers the possibility of attempting to explain offending from the offender's perspective and to discover the personal and social factors that can be identified as the 'correlates' of offending. This lends itself to 'control theories' of offending, focusing on aspects of the life of the 'admitted offender', their social bonds to family and friends, school and work experiences, and attitudes towards life in general. The statistical correlations that emerge from self-report studies cannot be taken as causative, however, because so little light is shed on the mechanisms and processes required to explain deviance and the process by which labels are attributed and acquired.

A method that relies on the honesty of interviewees to disclose dishonest and violent acts is obviously vulnerable to a challenge to its validity. How can we be sure that respondents are not lying, or (more charitably) saying what they think the interview wants to hear? Attempts to test the extent to which self-report studies generate valid and meaningful information about crime and deviance have included the use of polygraph ('lie detector') tests, the use of questions designed to identify exaggeration or embellishment (such as questions about fictitious drugs),

and back-checking what interviewees have said against police records. (In some studies, this back-checking has been done without the interviewee's consent, raising ethical concerns.) In general, surveys have tended to show greater levels of concealment than exaggeration and given that the extent of self-reported offending is often much higher than many people assume, it seems reasonable to accept that they are a useful alternative measure of people's unrecorded delinquent behaviour. The method has been shown to be reliable using various tools such as 'test–retest' and through the use of repeated measurement.

Self-report offending and drug surveys uncover a very large number of people who have committed unlawful acts, some of which would result in harsh penalties in the event that they were caught, prosecuted and convicted. However, self-report surveys capture a great deal of less serious offences, laying the method open to the charge that it places excessive emphasis on trivial offences. Care has to be taken to identify the minority of more serious offenders among the great number of people (the majority of the population) who admit to committing minor offences.

Self-report studies have been limited by a more or less exclusive focus on descriptive quantification of offending rates. They can also be criticized for seeking to explain patterns at the population level, rather than shedding much light on what happens in individual lives or on the dynamics of communities. To overcome these limitations, some surveys have combined self-report offending and victimization into one questionnaire (Anderson et al., 1994). Others have conducted follow-up qualitative interviews to illustrate the dynamics of offending and desistance (Graham and Bowling, 1995).

Evaluation

In sum, the self-report method provides a helpful, but limited, alternative to recorded crime statistics and victimization surveys. It is, arguably, the only way to estimate the extent of 'primary deviance' in the general population (Box, 1981). Certainly, self-report studies uncover forms of behaviour that can be quantified using no other means – including 'victimless' deviant acts (such as drug use), those that have a low likelihood of detection (such as handling stolen goods and fraud), and undetected offences in general. The method has tended to focus on the crimes of the powerless, whereas it could have a wider application in estimating the extent of corporate and white collar crime.

Ben Bowling

Associated Concepts: hidden crime, labelling, official criminal statistics, social reaction, social survey, victim surveys, victimology

Key Readings

Anderson, S., Kinsey, R., Loader, I. and Smith, C. (1994) *Cautionary Tales: Young People, Crime and Policing in Edinburgh.* Aldershot, Avebury.

Box, S. (1981) *Deviance, Reality and Society*, 2nd edn. London, Holt Rinehart and Winston.

Coleman, C. and Moynihan, J. (1996) *Understanding Crime Data.* Buckingham, Open University Press.

Farrington, D. (1997) 'Human development and criminal careers', in M. Maguire, R. Morgan and R. Reiner (eds), *The Oxford Handbook of Criminology.* Oxford, The Clarendon Press.

Graham, J. and Bowling, B. (1995) *Young People and Crime.* Home Office Research Study No. 145. London, HMSO.

Ramsay, M. and Spiller, J. (1997) *Drug Misuse Declared in 1996. Key Results from the British Crime Survey.* Home Office Research Findings No. 56. London, HMSO.

SERIAL KILLING

Definition

Stranger perpetrated murders – usually by men – which often appear motiveless and are characterized by gratuitous violence. Though rare, serial killing stands at the apogee of a popular fascination with crime, fuelling both a robust mythology and demands for retribution to be at the heart of criminal justice, particularly in the USA – the 'natural' habitat of such criminals.

Distinctive Features

Criminologists are in broad agreement that the serial killer is different from the 'normal' single incident murderer and other types of multiple killer, for example the *'mass murderer'* and the *'spree murderer'*. The serial killer is said to exhibit some or all of the following definitional characteristics. First, the killings are repetitive or 'serial' and, because the murder is in itself the motive, they will continue until the serial killer is caught. Secondly, the majority of serial killers like to work on their own and this is why they are so difficult to track down. There are, of course, well-known 'killer couples', 'partnerships' and 'groupings', but they run a greater risk of detection. Thirdly, there is little personal connection between the perpetrator and the victim. These are classic stranger perpetrated murders and a significant number are 'motiveless'. There is nothing personal in the choice of victim, other than s/he may belong to a particular cultural/social grouping. Fourthly, very few display a clearly defined or rational motive. It may not become apparent until a killer is arrested that a series of unsolved murders/attempted murders may be related. Fifthly, increased spatial mobility and social fragmentation enable a serial killer to extend and intensify his killing capacity. And because the communication flows between different police forces are haphazard and uncoordinated, serial killers can escape detection. Sixthly, there is often a high degree of gratuitous violence. Experts argue that this is because of the motivation for the crime. The killing is not the means to another end but an end in itself. Finally, because the majority of serial killers are men, we need to consider the complex relationship between particular forms of *masculinity* and violent criminality.

Studies suggest that there are four main motivational typologies:

- Visionaries: Included in this typology would be those killers who claim to be reacting to or directed by 'voices' and *alter egos*, where the 'instructions' received justify and legitimize the murders.
- Missionaries: Included in this category are 'clean-up' killers, who are quite willing to accept responsibility for 'cleansing' society of its 'undesirable' or 'unfit' elements. Any 'group' could become a target for the 'missionary' killer. However, the majority of targets are chosen from 'deviant' groupings such as prostitutes, homosexuals or drug addicts. The killer can justify her/his actions on the grounds that s/he is acting on behalf of decent people. In doing so, s/he can utilize a classic 'technique of neutralization'.
- Hedonists: A broad category which includes the types of killer for whom 'pleasure' is the 'reward' of murder. This category includes lust killers, fantasy killers and thrill killers.

- Power seekers: Domination is the strong motive force but these killers are aware of their behaviour and can describe their motivational state.

In response to the inadequacy of traditional techniques of murder investigation, the FBI began to develop a system of analysing evidence, both tangible and intuitive, collected by law enforcement officers from the scene of the crime. A 'psychological profile' is built through a contextual analysis of (a) victim traits, (b) witness reports, and (c) the method of killing. A detailed list of physical and psychological characteristics is built up until a portrait of the killer and her/his behavioural patterns appears. Included in the list would be: age, sex, marital status, occupation, race, criminal record, class, sexual preferences etc. A considerable amount of intuitive guesswork is involved, but this does not seem to damage the investigative procedure because, as David Canter argues (1992), a criminal leaves evidence of his personality through his criminal actions. An individual's behaviour, according to Canter, exhibits characteristics unique to that person, as well as patterns which are typical of the subgroup to which s/he belongs. Law enforcement agencies throughout the world have realized that they also need to develop sophisticated information collection systems which can coordinate, analyse and review reports from different agencies and identify early serial killing patterns. These developments have allowed law enforcement agencies to compile personality profiles, which enhance the early identification of a potential or 'emergent' serial killer. Psychologists and psychiatrists working in this field argue that there are significant levels of childhood violence, abuse and neglect present in the backgrounds of some of the most notorious serial killers that may provide a clue to their subsequent actions. Such connections lend weight to their arguments that efforts and resources should be focused on the early identification of violent behaviour that could escalate into murderous thoughts and deeds. This will necessitate monitoring the child-rearing practices of families for signs of maladjusted relationships and pathological dynamics.

Others argue that there are very clear links between alcohol dependency and violence, and pornography and violence, and that their availability should be proscribed and policed more rigorously. Yet others point to testimony from serial killers that it was fictional representations of violence that 'triggered' their actions. Psychologists argue that in order to kill, a person must dehumanize their victim, reducing the victim to the status of an object. Constant exposure to graphic, highly glamorized violence desensitizes viewers and readers to the human pain and suffering and paves the way for certain individuals to view murder as a 'normal' course of action. For certain serial killers, it is clear that they view themselves as 'actors' in a Hollywood film scripted by Quentin Tarantino or Oliver Stone. Again, such connections have brought forth a chorus of demands for tighter regulation and control of the entertainment industry.

Evaluation

The mythological status of the threat posed by the serial killer to American society has led to civil liberties objections being neutralized. In the twenty-first century, it seems as if there will be only one answer to the following question. Which are more important, the civil liberties of law-abiding innocent citizens or those of a potential killer?

Eugene McLaughlin

Associated Concepts: masculinities, neutralization (techniques of), personality theory, victimology

Key Readings
Canter, D. (1992) *Criminal Psychology*. London, Routledge.
Egger, S.A. (1998) *The Killers Among Us*. New York, Prentice–Hall.
Fox, J.A. and Levin, J. (1994) *Overkill: Mass Murder and Serial Killing Exposed*. New York, Plenum Press.
Holmes, R.M. (1987) *Serial Murder*. Beverly Hills, CA, Sage.
Leyton, E. (1988) *Hunting Humans*. New York, Pocket Books.
Seltzer, M. (1998) *Serial Killers: Death and Life in American Wound Culture*. New York, Routledge.

SEXUALITY

Definition

Literally being sexual, possessing the capacity for sex or sexual feelings. However, within lesbian and gay movements sexuality has become a cornerstone of identity and political campaigning around it. Some gay activists welcome 'gay gene' research as affirming the 'normality' of all sexualities; for most, sexuality has been seen as defining of one's identity and self-hood. That is, gay liberation could be achieved by gay identification. 'Coming out' came to be seen as revealing a 'true' self to oneself, family, friends and wider society. Both identity politics and popular prejudice might concentrate on homosexuality and bisexuality – in often opposing ways – but heterosexuality needs to be considered too. Katz (1995) argues for the invention of 'heterosexuality' by the discipline of sexology, which also discursively produced 'homosexuality'. Smart (1996) argues that probably only the male heterosexual was conceived as possessing a sexuality. In criminology, generally sexuality is normatively and implicitly heterosexual and often only explicitly possessed by the young or black. Sexuality is often seen as pathological.

Distinctive Features

Typically, sociology has ignored sex and sexuality, leaving the debate and discourse to a variety of sexologies which derive their methods and concerns primarily from medicine and psychoanalysis. Early criminology shared practitioners with medicine so some mention of sexuality as pathology can be found in early works. For instance, Lombroso favoured light punishments for those deprived of heterosexual outlets, but long-term incarceration for the congenital homosexual. The effect of this would be to deprive the offender of 'homosexual outlets'. Moreover much homosexual – and some heterosexual – activity is illegal and therefore falls within the ambit of criminology. The conflation is evident in the UK Wolfenden Committee's remit to study both homosexuality and prostitution.

The 1970s onward have shown small but steady advances by feminism into sociology and eventually criminology. This has raised the interest in and knowledge of gender as an issue in studies of crime and criminal justice. With that recognition has grown an interest in masculinities – the acceptance that whilst the problem may still be men, men still had problems. However, this emphasis on gender has continued to obscure the cross-cutting issues raised by sexuality. There are sexist gay men but the main complaint of women and feminism has been against heterosexual men – their sexual, domestic and economic violence. However, much of that feminism assumed a unified 'sisterhood' which simply aggregated the problems faced by educated, middle-class white wives with those of lesbians, women of colour and so forth.

Apart from early criminology's assumption of the pathology of homosexuality (maintained by psychology until the 1970s), issues of sexuality have been downplayed as purely personal or left to other disciplines. However, under the banner of the sociology of deviance a number of sensitive studies have been carried out. Humphreys' (1970) study of men who have sex with men in public toilets found that many men lived ostensibly heterosexual lives, and Reiss (1961/1968) explored the extent to which young 'delinquents' were prepared to receive oral sex from gay men without peer group damage to their heterosexual identity.

Evaluation

In as much as criminology is concerned about order it should be concerned with issues of sexuality. Plummer argues that a 'central problem for sociologists is that of order and control, and sexuality is sometimes seen as playing an important part in this order. Either it is argued that through sexuality our social order is channelled, or it is argued that through social order our sexuality is channelled' (1975/1980). Yet, other than the 'commonsense' criminology that sees homosexuality as 'symptomatic of treason and political deviancy' (Collier, 1995, pp. 97–8), sexuality has been treated poorly in criminology. However, just as gender has begun to make an impression within criminology, it is argued that sexuality must too. Empirically it has already begun (and largely remained) outside the discipline with activists contesting homophobic violence and policing priorities. Left realist victimology should be able to take this on board without adopting a specifically gay standpoint or perspective. It remains to be seen whether a full blown – possibly queer – consideration of sexuality is possible within criminology. Much of the work on male heterosexuality has been carried out by feminists – as a problem to be explained – and is now carried forward under the banner of the 'masculinities' literature. Much of that literature fails to acknowledge the work of lesbian feminists or gay men's attempts to explain heterosexuality.

Nic Groombridge

Associated Concepts: feminist criminologies, hegemonic masculinity, masculinities, pathology, queer theory, victimology

Key Readings

Collier, R. (1995) *Masculinity, Law and the Family*. London: Routledge.

Humphreys, L. (1970) *Tearoom Trade: Impersonal Sex in Public Places*. London, Duckworth.

Katz, J.N. (1995) *The Invention of Heterosexuality*. New York, Dutton.

Plummer, K. (1975/1980) 'Sexual stigma: an interactionist account', in R. Bocock, P. Hamilton, K. Thompson and A. Walton (eds), *An Introduction to Sociology*. London, Fontana.

Reiss, Albert J. Jr (1961/1968) 'The social integration of queers and peers', in E. Rubington and M.S. Weinburg (eds), *Deviance: The Interactionist Perspective*. London, Macmillan.

Smart, C. (1996) 'Collusion, collaboration and confession: on moving beyond the heterosexuality debate', in D. Richardson (ed.), *Theorizing Heterosexuality*. Buckingham, Open University Press.

SHAMING

Definition

The mode of punishment stigmatizing deviant individuals or groups which turns them into identifiable outcasts, either on a temporary or permanent basis. Shaming may take both disintegrative and reintegrative forms.

Distinctive Features

There is a long tradition of the use of shaming as one component of stigmatizing punishments in pre-industrial and traditional communities. However, processes of shaming also continue into modern times. Doubtless, everyone has encountered some form of shaming at some point in their lives, especially in the micro-interactions between people in both formal and non-formal settings, such as in school or in the family. But shaming has not been generally recognized as a legitimate and explicit criminal justice strategy in most modern systems of justice and punishment. There are, of course, some notable exceptions to this tendency. In particular we may note the cultural embeddedness and acceptance of the legitimacy of shaming in Japan, where there is widespread use of shaming techniques for offenders in its system of criminal justice.

Furthermore, shaming was crucial to the punishment by public disgrace in 'community courts' of the Soviet Union and Maoist China. And, of course, there has also been a recent growth and rebirth of the appeal to public shaming in the contemporary campaigns and movements to 'name and shame' offenders in many contemporary Western countries. In the USA, for example, current shaming techniques include the forced carrying of sandwich boards announcing 'I am a criminal': a throwback to kinds of public shaming that were standard practice in the North American English colonies of the seventeenth century. We should note then the danger of shaming in practice degenerating into vindictiveness. The latter development appears in part to be influenced by the conservative communitarian impulse over 'community' justice and punishment and the emotive politics of popular punitiveness, as well as being indicative of the lack of trust in the workings of the formal criminal justice system.

The recognition of the importance of shaming to modern criminological thinking and its potentially positive role in the workings of social control has largely been the result of John Braithwaite's (1989, 1993) important work. He has noted that shaming may take both disintegrative and reintegrative forms. The former stigmatizes people and turns them into outcasts (as in the examples of punitive exclusion through imprisonment and the use of banishment in pre-modern societies). Disintegrative shaming is the norm in modern Western states, as a result of which there is labelling and stigma and the creation of a class of outcasts. By way of contrast, reintegrative shaming offers gestures of re-acceptance.

According to Braithwaite, reintegrative shaming is a form of disapproval dispensed within an ongoing relationship with the offender based on respect. It is a shaming that focuses on the evil of the deed rather than on the offender as an irredeemably evil person. In turn, degradation ceremonies are followed by ceremonies to decertify deviance, where forgiveness, apology and repentance are culturally important (Braithwaite, 1993, p. 1). Reintegrative shaming also expresses society's disapproval of the act by bringing the wrong-doer, the victim and close associates of each party together in a group setting. It is argued that much of its preventive success lies in its work on the offender's conscience. However, such preventive processes will only work in situations where loss of respect counts heavily. Braithwaite thus acknowledges that it is 'communitarianism that makes shaming possible' (Braithwaite, 1993, p. 2). Unlike modern Western systems of justice and punishment, which isolate and stigmatize the guilty through exclusionary disposal (such as custody), reintegrative shaming therefore aims to accept the guilty back into the community and so help prevent future offending through a process of active re-integration.

There are obvious risks with this strategy, of which Braithwaite is well aware. As he notes, shaming can become the principal weapon of the tyranny of the majority over vulnerable minorities (Braithwaite, 1989, p. 158). This concern has led Braithwaite to argue that the securing of liberty must lie at the centre of what he terms civic republican justice. Despite claims that shaming is unlikely to work in the complex, anonymous societies of the modern era, Braithwaite has made a strong argument for its continuing salience as a crime prevention approach today. Indeed, it may be argued that today's proliferation of roles makes us all more vulnerable to shame in a way that is peculiar and specific to a world of such proliferation of roles. According to proponents of reintegrative shaming, this mode of restorative justice is far from being reactionary and targeted at the most vulnerable minorities. Instead, it is viewed as a crucial communitarian resource in mobilizing against those offenders who brutalize (such as abusers) and exploit (such as corporations) as well as restraining those who would wish to trample on the rights of citizens who wish to be (harmlessly) deviant. However, the extent to which reintegrative shaming is employed routinely against powerful individuals and agencies, not least shaming intolerable criminal justice practices, needs to be given critical attention.

Evaluation

Significant and worrying questions remain with the theory and practice of shaming, whether disintegrative or reintegrative. It has as yet to be proven that shaming will not be used and mobilized against the most vulnerable, deviant sections of the population with little concern for their legal and human rights. Given the previous history of other community justice-based initiatives, it is also quite possible that (reintegrative) shaming will be used chiefly for trivial offences and young offenders without any reduction in the use of traditional, disintegrative custodial sentences. Indeed, critical authors, such as Blagg (1997), have noted that the 'product' of reintegrative

shaming being franchised in Australia is being targeted at Aboriginal people, and may intensify rather than reduce police controls over this already victimized population. More general criticisms may be made of the notion that shaming is a universal trait in all human cultures. If shaming is a forced and ingenuine process imposed on the offender, its reintegrative efficacy may be open to question and instead result in the more traditional consequence of stigmatizing criminalization.

Gordon Hughes

Associated Concepts: communitarianism, community justice, restorative justice, stigma

Key Readings

Blagg, H. (1997) 'A just measure of shame: aboriginal youth and conferencing in Australia', *British Journal of Criminology*, 37 (4), pp. 481–501.

Braithwaite, J. (1989) *Crime, Shame and Reintegration*. Oxford, Oxford University Press.

Braithwaite, J. (1993) 'Shame and modernity', *British Journal of Criminology*, 33 (1), pp. 1–18.

SITUATIONAL CRIME PREVENTION

Definition

Crime prevention as a whole can be defined as reducing the risk of occurrence and the potential seriousness of criminal events, by intervening in their causes. Situational crime prevention (SCP) intervenes in those causes which the offender encounters, or seeks out, in the immediate circumstances of the criminal event.

Distinctive Features

SCP methods aim to reduce a wide range of crimes. They commonly involve the design of products, services, environments or systems to make them crime-resistant – a strategy implemented alone or in combination with certain social activities, such as surveillance and response to crimes by people in various roles: householder, passer-by, employee or security personnel, and the more strategic managers of places. The methods range from supplying toughened drinking glasses to reduce injury from fights in bars, to establishing rules for acceptable behaviour in shopping centres and football matches; from traffic enforcement cameras to anti-climb paint; from encryption of financial data to CCTV in banks; from better laid-out housing estates to hard-to-forge holographic labels to discourage counterfeit vodka; from airport metal detectors and security guards to Farm Watch and similar community-based schemes.

SCP does not rely on past improvements in society, treatment regimes for offenders or early interventions in children's socialization to reduce current criminality; nor on the sheer aversive intensity of sanctions anticipated at some remote point in the future to deter or incapacitate present offending. It does not directly aim to change *offenders'* propensities or motives for crime at all. It takes these as given and, proceeding from an analysis of the circumstances engendering particular crimes, it introduces specific changes to influence the offender's *decision* or *ability* to commit these crimes at given places and times. These interventions usually act on the here-and-now of the immediate crime situation, removing or altering some of its components or preventing them coming together. The generic components of the crime situation include a human, material or informational target of crime; a target enclosure, such as a safe or a building; a wider environment, such as a housing estate or town centre; and people or institutions playing two opposing roles – preventers, who make crime less likely, and promoters, who carelessly or deliberately make it more likely. The interventions may sometimes act on prior '*scenes*' (Cornish, 1994), in which offenders prepare, or become primed for, crime (such as acquiring weapons, getting drunk or engaging in disputes over parking). Interventions may be implemented indirectly – for example, helping people protect their own homes, or naming and shaming manufacturers of insecure vehicles so *they* are motivated to make them harder to steal.

SCP methods are widely adopted in society, shading into common-sense 'routine precautions' (Clarke, 1997). But only in the past 20 years has the 'official' world of government and police taken them seriously. In the USA, the approach developed through the Crime Prevention through Environmental Design movement (National Crime Prevention Council, 1997). In the UK, a programme of practical research directed by Ron Clarke at the Home Office inspired the search for a more theoretical foundation built around the concept of crime as opportunity. This was based (at a time of 'nothing works') on dissatisfaction with the limited effectiveness of crime prevention through conventional means, particularly

attempts to change the disposition of the offender; and growing academic awareness of the general limits of 'personality' in explaining behaviour. Two main theoretical approaches now underlie SCP. Both take offender characteristics, including motivation, as given.

The *rational choice* perspective sees the fundamental causal mechanism of SCP as making the commission of specific sets of crimes more risky (deterrence), requiring of more effort and less rewarding (discouragement), or less comfortable (removing excuses) (adapted from Clarke, 1997). For SCP to work – at least in the short term – deterrence and discouragement need only be *perceived* barriers.

Routine activity theory (Felson, 1983) takes a wider causal view. Here, criminal events stem from the conjunction of a likely (motivated) offender, a suitable target and the absence of capable guardians. SCP is about changing the last two. A related approach, which attempts to understand and predict what brings these ingredients together in terms of spatial arrangements, patterns of travel etc., is *environmental criminology* (Brantingham and Brantingham, 1995).

Evaluation

The main practical criticism of SCP centres on *displacement*, that is where an offender, blocked by an SCP measure, seeks a similar target at another time or place, changes methods or changes target altogether. Clarke (1997) has, however, shown displacement to be limited in effect and sometimes even reversed (*diffusion of benefit*, where cautious offenders avoid more than just the officially protected site); but the possibility of displacement can never be ruled out in any specific circumstances.

Aesthetic criticisms centre on fears of 'fortress society', and ethical ones on loss of privacy or freedom. According to advocates of SCP, both can be minimized through good design of products, environments and procedures to reconcile security with these potentially conflicting requirements. Some practitioners – and criminologists – whose primary interest is in offenders and their motives find SCP trivial; some situationalists in their turn regard offender-oriented approaches as over-optimistic or misguided. Having 'two cultures of prevention' blocks practical and theoretical progress.

Theoretical criticisms highlight the limits to offenders' rationality – but these are neither fatal to SCP, nor contested by its protagonists.

More recently (e.g. Ekblom, 2000) there have been attempts to integrate SCP with a wider understanding of offenders – their criminal predispositions, immediate motives to offend and resources for offending (tools, weapons, knowledge and skill). From this perspective, the concept of *opportunity* for crime is not simply a property of the crime situation, but is conjointly dependent on the offender's resources to exploit it and cope with the risks (an open window three floors up is only an opportunity to someone with agility, courage and maybe a ladder).

Paul Ekblom

Associated Concepts: carceral society, community safety, crime prevention, defensible space, geographies of crime, rational choice theory, routine activity theory, surveillance

Key Readings

Brantingham, P. and Brantingham, P. (1995) 'Criminality of place: crime generators and crime attractors', *European Journal on Criminal Policy and Research*, 3 (3), pp. 5–26.

Clarke, R.V.G. (1997) *Situational Crime Prevention: Successful Case Studies*, 2nd edn. Albany, NY, Harrow and Heston.

Cornish, D. (1994) 'The procedural analysis of offending and its relevance for situational prevention', in R. Clarke (ed.), *Crime Prevention Studies, 3.* Monsey, NY, Criminal Justice Press, pp. 151–96.

Ekblom, P. (2000) 'The conjunction of criminal opportunity – a tool for clear, "joined-up" thinking about community safety and crime reduction', in K. Pease, S. Ballintyne and V. McLaren (eds), *Key Issues in Crime Prevention, Crime Reduction and Community Safety*. London, Institute for Public Policy Research.

Felson, M. (1983) 'Linking criminal choices, routine activities, informal control, and criminal outcomes', in D. Cornish and R. Clarke (eds), *The Reasoning Criminal*. New York, Springer-Verlag.

National Crime Prevention Council (1997) *Designing Safer Communities: A Crime Prevention through Environmental Design Handbook*. Washington, DC, NCPC.

SOCIAL CENSURE

Definition

To censure is to blame, criticize, express disapproval, or condemn. A social censure is a category expressing cultural disapproval, or a sign of blame.

Distinctive Features

The process of blaming and stigmatizing others in general is of core interest to criminology, but the social patterns of censure are of particular concern to sociologists. Psychologists are interested in the censorious personality or the roots of individual prejudice; sociologists in the political uses and social functions of scapegoating.

The concept of social censure refers to those censures which are common within a culture and which reflect the dominant or key relationships or structures of the society. Censures mostly reinforce the established order and its institutions – for example, the social censure of bastardy reinforces the normative reverence for procreation within marriage. Some can be seen as master-censures in that they are so deep-rooted within the culture and its forms of thought that they permeate many other forms of censure. However, some are counter-censures, expressing the opposition or criticism of subordinate social groups to the social system or its institutions.

The concept of social censure differs from that of the label because the latter belongs to a theoretical standpoint, which emphasizes conscious blaming practices using ideas as a kind of stick to beat people with. This is a liberal 'voluntarist' approach which supposes all is rational choice – and that categories of blame are not generated by the social structure nor creep quietly into our unconscious minds loaded with ideological or cultural baggage. Censure theory, as developed by Sumner (1990, 1994, 1997), is lodged within a theoretical analysis that emphasizes that feelings of disapproval are as much unconscious and emotional as they are conscious and rational, that social structures by their very nature imply, and predispose us to, certain categories of blame, and that social censures come to us already steeped and rooted within the structures and events of social history and thus coated with acquired meanings and implications.

The concept draws upon the idea of a vote of censure in Parliament or Congress to imply that even everyday social censures have a political, organized, dimension – something which reflects the fact that most practices and institutions in modern 'disciplinary' societies are deeply permeated, and even structured, by normative judgements and judgemental or inspectorial practices and that the interests of the state have been inserted into most dimensions of private morality (Foucault, 1967, 1975). Governance cannot evade moral propriety and custom has long lost its virginity to state interference. Public and private worlds were linked up by the seventeenth-century European city-states concerned with the conservation of healthy populations (see Shakespeare's *Measure for Measure*) but they were fully merged in the formation of the welfare state and have never been de-coupled. This linkage was a vital part of the imperialist expansion into and creation of the 'Third World', leading later critics to observe that the cultural colonization of the mind was the most debilitating aspect of being colonized.

In European and New World societies of the twentieth century, the dominant social censures were probably those of property crime and communism, both censures of activities directed at the fundamental structures of private property. These were, arguably, closely followed by the social censures of women, homosexuals and immigrants, groups whose existence and self-expression constantly challenged the established order of white, patriarchal, power in the home and the local community.

Designed as a replacement for the concept of social deviance, which is itself a social censure favoured by sociologists in the twentieth century, the concept of social censure signifies the way that notions of the disapproved or immoral have over time acquired surplus associated meanings, such as stereotypes, which specify likely offenders, appropriate emotional responses to the act, contexts of commission and possible consequences. It thus designates cultural packages of blame which, insofar as they reflect social-structural needs, partisan interests, belief-systems and traditional assumptions, amount to ideological formations that target groups or acts or styles perceived by the dominant culture to be its enemies. As such, their function is usually to denounce and regulate rather than to explain or understand. They demarcate the regulator from the offender, the normal from the abnormal, the healthy from the unhealthy, and the good from the bad.

Since social censures are cultural, or even ideological formations tied to a will to punish or to social control, they are not good foundations for open-minded or scientific analysis. Social scientists do not begin with the idea that, for example, terrorism is a neutral, descriptive category; they take it as an object whose significance needs to be explored for its variety of meanings, functions and roles for different groups at different historical moments. Censures are objects of study not tools of enquiry. Social research using the concept of social censure has found it valuable in analysing culturally and politically loaded data and attempting to distinguish social attributions from ontological realities.

Colin Sumner

Associated Concepts: deviance, labelling, racialization, stereotyping

Key Readings

Foucault, M. (1967) *Madness and Civilization: A History of Insanity in the Age of Reason*. London, Tavistock.
Foucault, M. (1975) *Discipline and Punish: The Birth of the Prison*. London, Allen Lane.
Sumner, C.S. (ed.) (1990) *Censure, Politics and Criminal Justice*. Milton Keynes, Open University Press.
Sumner, C.S. (1990) 'Foucault, gender and the censure of deviance', in L. Gelsthorpe and A. Morris (eds), *Feminist Perspectives in Criminology*. Milton Keynes, Open University Press.
Sumner, C.S. (1994) *The Sociology of Deviance: An Obituary*. Buckingham, Open University Press.
Sumner, C.S. (ed.) (1997) *Violence, Censure and Culture*. London, Taylor and Francis.

SOCIAL CONSTRUCTIONISM

Definition

A perspective that explores the assumptions embedded in the labelling of people and places and emphasizes the importance of social expectations in the analysis of taken-for-granted or apparently natural social processes.

Distinctive Features

A naturalistic or realist perspective in the social sciences treats social problems as though they are given: phenomena about whose existence we can all agree. The social constructionist perspective insists on the necessity of taking a step back from this view and asks instead, who says this is a social problem – and what sort of social problem do they think it is? This perspective draws on a very different sociological inheritance, one that treats society as a matrix of meaning. It accords a central role to processes of constructing, producing and circulating meanings. Within this perspective, we cannot grasp reality (or empirical phenomena) in a direct and unmediated way. Reality is always mediated by meaning. Indeed, some of its proponents argue that what we experience is 'the social construction of reality' (Berger and Luckman, 1966). How something (or someone) is named, identified and placed within a 'map' of the social order has profound consequences for how we act towards it (or them). There cannot be 'social problems' that are not the products of processes of social construction – naming, labelling, defining and mapping them into a place – through which we can 'make sense' of them.

The crux of this argument was established by Howard Becker (1963) in relation to deviant behaviour. Realist explanations attempt to account for deviance by identifying differences between those who behave 'normally' and those who behave in an 'abnormal' way. Becker pointed to a number of problems with this approach. First, it assumed the accurate and unproblematic knowledge of who was normal and who was deviant. But, said Becker, the distinction is socially constructed. It involves the exercise of judgement by social actors, located in social institutions, applying social norms. Secondly, deviance is context-specific rather than universal. Behaviour that is viewed or classified as deviant varies between and even within societies, and shifts over time. As a result, Becker argued, it is analytically and methodologically incorrect to pursue the explanation of deviance in terms of discovering the 'deviant characteristics' of the 'deviant' person, when deviance is a product of a process of labelling some behaviours as deviant and others not. In short, deviance is socially constructed.

This basic social constructionist view has been subjected to a wide range of criticisms, some of which have attempted to refute its claims, while others have tried to develop and enhance the approach. Many of these developments centre on three key issues: the social context of social constructions; the conflictual or contested character of social constructions; and the unstable or changeable character of social constructions. In particular, attempts at developing social constructionism have hinged around issues of power (Bacchi, 1999, pp. 50–64). This interest in social constructionism and its potential development is part of wider shifts in the social sciences in which a

cluster of concerns with culture/meaning/language have come to occupy a more central place (Clarke, 1999). Social constructionism is one tributary that flows into this wider movement, intersecting with questions of ideology, discourse and the articulation of power in a range of ways (Burr, 1996; Saraga, 1998).

Evaluation

The social constructionist perspective has been subject to criticisms that challenge its value for the study of crime in particular and social problems in general. Social constructionism is sometimes seen as trivializing the reality of social problems – implying that such issues are *merely* social constructions. It may be that the emphasis on language, meaning, imagery and so on involved in social constructionist analyses foregrounds what we are used to seeing as peripheral or epiphenomenal matters (compared with the gritty stuff of 'real life'). But if we can only apprehend and act on 'real life' through language, then social constructions matter profoundly. Constructions, ideologies and discourses become institutionalized. They become the 'taken-for-granted' wisdom about the way of the world and what can be done in it. They define the thinkable (and attempt to dismiss alternatives as unthinkable, utopian, politically motivated and the like). In the process, dominant constructions become 'solidified' – apparently immovable and irresistible ways of thinking and acting that sustain existing patterns of social arrangements. They are supported by knowledges and become embedded in institutional arrangements and embodied in social practices that attempt to realize their 'truth claims' in practice. These solidifications – patterns of institutionalized habit and repetition – are not insubstantial and nor are they 'just words'. A social constructionist perspective, however, insists that such solidity is still a social accomplishment – it is not natural, it is not universal, and it is not eternal. Social constructionism insists, abstractly, that all social practices have the potential to be deconstructed and reconstructed – however inert and immovable they may appear. What the perspective reveals is how the density and solidity of social reality has been constructed and how many layers of habit, everyday wisdom, institutionalized norms, and forms of social power have been built up to keep things that way. But such conditions are always in need of being reproduced – they do not carry on without the expenditure of social energy. They may, then, be reproduced differently through conflict, contestations and challenge.

John Clarke

Associated Concepts: crime, deconstruction, deviance, discourse analysis, interactionism, labelling, left realism, social reaction

Key Readings

Bacchi, C. (1999) *Women, Policy and Politics: The Construction of Policy Problems*. London, Sage.

Becker, H. (1963) *Outsiders: Studies in the Sociology of Deviance*. New York, The Free Press.

Berger, P. and Luckmann, T. (1966) *The Social Construction of Reality*. New York, Doubleday.

Burr, V. (1996) *An Introduction to Social Constructionism*. London, Routledge.

Clarke, J. (1999) 'Coming to terms with culture', in H. Dean and R. Woods (eds), *Social Policy Review 10*. London, Social Policy Association.

Saraga, E. (ed.) (1998) *Embodying the Social: Constructions of Difference*. London, Routledge/Open University.

SOCIAL CONTROL

Definition

A poorly defined concept which has been used to describe all means through which conformity might be achieved – from infant socialization to incarceration. It has been employed in various guises within interactionism, labelling, control theory, feminism, critical criminology and post-structuralism.

Distinctive Features

The precise parameters of 'social control' escape any straightforward demarcation. The standard definition simply describes all the means and processes through which social conformity is achieved, ranging from primary socialization, through informal mechanisms (such as peer group pressure) to formal methods associated with the police and the legal system. Within interactionism the key concern is with how cooperation and social integration are achieved, usually without recourse to a coercive and authoritarian discipline. Interactionists broadly conclude that the key to the maintenance of social order lies in the realm of informal and primary socialization processes through which core social values are transmitted and internalized. This benign reading of 'social control' as a functional and political necessity was mirrored in traditional positivist criminology. Within such readings it is widely assumed that a consensus exists in society, that primary socialization is largely successful in achieving a widespread and uncontested conformity and that external agencies are only called upon to 'mop-up' those deviants who have suffered a failure or lack of adequate socialization.

In the late 1960s an alternative view of social control came to the fore. Generated by the protest movements in America (civil rights, Vietnam, Counterculture) and the emerging utopian and personal politics of the New Left in Britain, arguments concerning the essential consensual nature of society became harder to sustain and social control came to be seen as organized repression. In particular, the labelling perspective argued that social control was not simply a reactive and reparative exercise, but an active force in the identification and creation of the deviant. In effect, labelling challenged notions of 'social control' as 'doing good' and replaced them with notions of 'doing bad'.

Such a premise became particularly influential in critical readings of a wide range of purportedly reformist and welfare-related practices. The coercive – but often hidden – aspects of control entailed in the professional practices of youth training, social work, law, probation, medicine, schooling and psychiatry were highlighted and analysed as part of a burgeoning social control culture. An image of society as moving incessantly towards more sophisticated means of repressive control was created. The intrusion of the state into the private and familiar, the capacity for behaviour to be continually subjected to surveillance, monitoring and regulation and the spectre of mind control constructed a powerful portrayal of a one-dimensional society in which 'social control has become Kafka-land' (Cohen, 1985, p. 6).

Whilst moving the concept of social control from its benign underpinnings, this new interpretation maintained that social control, whether weak or strong, informal or formal, remained all-pervasive. But the key neglected issues remained of how and why such control operated differently in different social contexts. It was also often in danger of caricaturing all police, social workers and teachers as agents of repression. Lacking any precise definition and consistent use, the concept was aptly described by Cohen (1985, p. 2) as

'Mickey Mouse' and by Lowman et al. (1987, p. 4) as 'a skeleton key opening so many doors that its analytic power has been drained . . . a spectral category which becomes all things to all theorists'.

It was only following the work of Foucault that the term 'social control' was resurrected in the 1980s as a means through which analytical justice could be done to the complex and contradictory means by which order is achieved in democratic societies. Foucault's recognition of processes of diffuse societal power (or the 'microphysics of power') significantly broadened the concept of social control to include not only institutional practices, but the realms of discursive construction, ideology and the production of meaning. For example, Foucault refers to a continuous disciplinary discourse, in which no one source is given privileged attention, which informed and was intertwined with all forms of social control in the late eighteenth century. Thus the reform of prisoners, confinement of the insane and supervision of industrial workers as well as the training and education of children, all formed part of an emerging carceral society, in which it was not only deviance or crime that was controlled, but also every irregularity or the least departure from the norm. This power emanates not simply from the state or a mode of production but, for Foucault, from forms of knowledge that inform all social relations. It is because of this broad canvas that Foucault's work remains influential in historical and contemporary readings of social control. It allows for a greater sensitivity to the interrelations of social structure with processes of power, knowledge and governance. It is more attuned to processes of domination and enablement; of constraint and resistance. As a result terms such as 'regulation', 'knowledge', 'normalization', 'governmentality' and 'discipline' have come to hold a central place in a 'revisionist' literature of social control.

Of note is Cohen's (1979, 1985) 'dispersal of discipline' thesis which contends that as control mechanisms are dispersed from custody into the community they penetrate deeper into the social fabric. A blurring of boundaries between the deviant and non-deviant, the public and the private occurs. A 'punitive archipelago' is expanded as new resources, technology and professional interests are applied to an increasing number of 'clients' and 'customers'. Entrepreneurs are drawn into the control enterprise in search of profits. Communities are mobilized to act as voluntary control agents in their own right.

But throughout, the growing invisibility and diversification of the state's role does not mean it has withered away. The prison remains at the core of the system.

Lowman et al. (1987, p. 9) argue that these developments can best be captured in the concept of transcarceration. They argue that as the old institutions of control remain and the new are created, we are now confronted with a 'peno-judicial, mental health, welfare and tutelage complex . . . for delinquents, deviants and dependants this means that their careers are likely to be characterized by institutional mobility as they are pushed from one section of the help–control complex to another. For control agents, this means that control will essentially have no locus and the control mandate will increasingly entail the "fitting together" of subsystems.' This formulation of control continues to acknowledge its versatility: infiltrating many levels of discourse and 'arenas of action' and serving and constituting a diversity of interests. Of particular note is how, by the 1990s, much of this control had become privatized – that is, removed from direct state control and activated by communities, voluntary agencies and private security companies. It is in this context that Cohen (1994, p. 74) begins talking of social control as a commodity: as something to be purchased and sold.

David Wilson

Associated Concepts: carceral society, governmentality, labelling, net widening, social control theory, social reaction, the state, transcarceration

Key Readings

Cohen, S. (1979) 'The punitive city: notes on the dispersal of social control', *Contemporary Crises*, 3 (4), pp. 341–63.

Cohen, S. (1985) *Visions of Social Control*. Cambridge, Polity Press.

Cohen, S. (1989) 'The critical discourse on "social control": notes on the concept as a hammer', *International Journal of the Sociology of Law*, 17, pp. 347–57.

Cohen, S. (1994) 'Social control and the politics of reconstruction', in D. Nelken (ed.), *The Futures of Criminology*. London, Sage.

Cohen, S. and Scull, A. (eds) (1983) *Social Control and the State: Historical and Comparative Essays*. Oxford, Martin Robertson.

Lowman, J., Menzies, R.J. and Palys, T.S. (eds) (1987) *Transcarceration: Essays in the Sociology of Social Control*. Aldershot, Gower.

SOCIAL CONTROL THEORY

Definition

A sociological approach to understanding the causes of conformity that focuses on the ability of society and its institutions (parents, peers, schools, spouses and jobs) to restrain human behaviour. From this theoretical perspective, human nature is assumed to be essentially anti-social – a view borrowed directly from Thomas Hobbes's (1985 [1651], p. 188) description of life in a world without externally imposed control as a 'war of every man against every man'. Thus, the central question is, 'What is it about society that restrains individuals from deviance?' The basic premise is that conformity results when societal ties are strong.

Distinctive Features

Social control theory includes a number of related sociological explanations that variously explain how social institutions restrain individuals to societal norms. While human behaviour is the result of both motivations and restraints, social control theorists find it more fruitful to focus on variations in restraints to explain orderly behaviour. Thus, various approaches to social control theory all explain why individuals conform to societal norms rather than why they deviate.

Early social control theorists speculated that juvenile delinquency (the primary area of study) was caused mainly by a weak ego or poor self-concept. Reiss's (1951) theory of personal and social controls described how weak egos of juvenile delinquents lacked the requisite personal controls to produce conforming behaviour. Similarly, Briar and Piliavin (1965) believed that adolescents who feared getting caught for delinquent activities were the most likely to conform to society's rules because it could damage their self-image. A positive attitude purportedly helped the adolescent to resist negative influences, especially delinquent peers. Similarly, Reckless (1967) argued that a good self-concept helped boys to insulate themselves from negative influences while growing up in criminogenic areas. Certain internal (e.g., positive self-concept) and external (e.g., positive peer support) factors or 'containments' helped to insulate youths from delinquency-promoting situations.

Other control perspectives explain conformity by variations in basic 'ties' or 'commitments' to the conventional social order. Nye (1958) identified four types of social control: (1) direct control, based on the threat of punishments and rewards to gain compliance to societal norms; (2) indirect control, based on affectional attachments to conventional persons; (3) internalized control, based on the development of the individual personality, self-concept, or conscience; and (4) control over opportunities for deviant and conventional activities.

Among the various social control perspectives, however, Hirschi's (1969) 'social bond' version is probably the most widely known and cited. It is relatively explicit, well developed and amenable to empirical tests. The social bonds have four components (attachment, involvement, belief and commitment), which are positively related to conformity (and to each other) and are thought to have independent effects on delinquency.

'Attachment' refers to the affective ties that adolescents form with significant others – especially parents, peers and school. The central principle is that adolescents who are only weakly attached to others are also insensitive to their opinions, thereby 'freeing' the child to deviate in response to situational demands and peer pressures. Thus, attachment is essentially a social-psychological concept, involving the motivational value of social approval. 'Involvement' refers to the idea that juveniles may get so caught up in conventional activities that they do not have the time for delinquent behaviours. 'Commitment' is synonymous to the idea of 'stakes in conformity' in that deviation jeopardizes chances for success. For example, those adolescents committed to a college education are less likely to commit delinquency because such behaviours (if caught and punished) can jeopardize chances for future success and accomplishments. 'Belief' refers to respect for society's laws. If children have been socialized to respect the law, they should be less inclined to commit legal violations of the law.

Hirschi's (1969) concepts of attachment and belief correspond conceptually to Nye's concepts of indirect and internalized controls, except that Hirschi locates the conscience in the social bond to others rather than making it part of the individual personality. Also, Nye's concept of direct control and Hirschi's concept of involvement have some conceptual overlap, but they are clearly not identical. The premise behind involvement is time ('idle hands are the devil's workshop'), while direct controls are more indicative of physical restriction, surveillance, monitoring and punishment of behaviours. Both Nye and Hirschi argued that the utility of direct monitoring and supervision by parents is probably limited, since adolescents are relatively autonomous from their parents. The inference is that the major controlling mechanisms will be through attachments or indirect controls.

Evaluation

On the one hand, much of Hirschi's theory has been corroborated by empirical research, indicating that delinquents often feel detached from typical societal bonds. Indeed, research generally supports Hirschi's basic proposition that weak school and parental attachments increase the probability of delinquency. On the other hand, various measures of belief and especially involvement (e.g., sports activities, hobbies, extracurricular school activities) have revealed few statistically reliable associations with delinquency. In addition, evidence suggests that strong attachments to *delinquent* peers actually increase deviance rather than having a beneficial effect, as suggested by Hirschi. Research also has indicated that direct parental controls should not be dismissed as theoretically and empirically irrelevant, as suggested by both Nye and Hirschi. Empirical evidence indicates that direct parental controls (such as monitoring, rewards, punishments) are just as effective as indirect controls or attachments in controlling delinquency.

Furthermore, Agnew (1985) suggests that the temporal ordering of the variables in Hirschi's model should be reversed. Rather than weak social bonds being a cause of delinquency (as suggested by Hirschi), Agnew's research indicates that delinquent behaviour may actually lead to weakened social bonds. While plausible, this criticism can be levelled against virtually all theories tested by means of empirical research that is cross-sectional (rather than longitudinal) in design.

Generally, however, social control theory is probably more incomplete than it is incorrect; thus, researchers have sought to extend, clarify and refine its basic tenets. Most of this research has led to modifications in the operational measures and conceptual qualifications in the empirical interpretation of the perspective rather than to an outright rejection or overhaul of the entire theory. For example, researchers have interpreted the actual measurement of parental attachments in a variety of ways, including indicators of affection and love, interest and concern, support, encouragement, desire for physical closeness and positive communication. Although all are correlated with delinquency to about the same degree, they may reflect different dimensions of parental attachment.

Furthermore, there is a lack of conceptual development by social control theorists about the interactive effects of various variables. Indeed, there is a tendency to predict the impact of one measure of social control quite independently from other variables, implying a simple additive model. For example, what is the probability of delinquency under the condition that attachment to both parents is strong, while simultaneously the adolescent is strongly attached to delinquent peers? Similarly, what is the conjunctive impact of both direct (monitoring) and indirect (attachment) parental controls on delinquency? A child may place little value on parental approval but conform to parental expectations out of a belief that they monitor his or her behaviours closely and will punish any deviation. On the other hand, some children may behave solely because they desire parental acceptance. Generally, explications of social control theory have failed to predict behavioural outcomes beyond the bivariate level. Because little theoretical and empirical attention has been directed toward the examination of such effects, many questions remain unresolved.

In sum, empirical research has generally supported the core concepts of Hirschi's version of social control theory. While some critics question its validity, few would question that it has been the most influential theory of delinquency over the past 30 years.

Joseph Rankin and Roger Kern

Associated Concepts: conditioning, containment theory, cross-sectional design, delinquency, longitudinal study, neutralization (techniques of)

Key Readings

Agnew, R. (1985) 'Social control theory and delinquency: a longitudinal test', *Criminology*, 23, pp. 47–61.

Briar, S. and Piliavin, I. (1965) 'Delinquency: situational inducements and commitment to conformity', *Social Problems*, 13, pp. 35–45.

Hirschi, T. (1969) *Causes of Delinquency*. Berkeley, CA, University of California Press.

Hobbes, T. (1985 [1651]) *Leviathan*. New York, Viking Penguin.

Nye, F.I. (1958) *Family Relationships and Delinquent Behavior*. New York, John Wiley.

Reckless, W. (1967) *The Crime Problem*. New York, Appleton–Century–Crofts.

Reiss, A.J. (1951) 'Delinquency as the failure of personal and social controls', *American Sociological Review*, 16, pp. 196–207.

SOCIAL CRIME PREVENTION

Definition

Measures to prevent crime which are aimed at the social causes of crime rather than those concerned with the mechanical reduction of opportunities (situational crime prevention) or with deterrence (the criminal justice system).

Distinctive Features

The distinction between social and situational revolves around the focus on causes (Crawford, 1998). Both situational crime prevention and deterrence explicitly disavow causality (hence their designation as administrative criminology). The difference does not hinge on the social – for situational crime prevention can have social aspects, for example, the increase in the facilitation of surveillance in neighbourhood watch and in environmental design of housing estates. The emphasis on social causes, therefore, relates social crime prevention to any causal theory of crime (for example, whether strain, relative deprivation, control, labelling or criminal careers are highlighted as causative factors). In common with crime prevention strategies in general, it is aimed at intervention before the offence has occurred rather than after (for example, in the arrest and punishment of offenders and victim support). Interest in both situational and social crime prevention has risen concomitantly with the postwar rise in crime in industrial societies and the recognition of the strained resources and limits of efficacy of the criminal justice system. In general, situational crime prevention has been predominant in neo-liberal political contexts and social crime prevention in those that have a stronger social democratic setting (see Hughes, 1998). Social crime prevention is seen as being expedited by multi-agency initiatives outside of the criminal justice system – the precise forms of intervention and the major institutions involved depending on whether causality is located primarily in employment, the family, education or community. Both situational and social crime prevention form part of most community safety programmes, although Elliott Currie (1988) makes the useful distinction between those projects that view crime as an outside threat to the community (in which situational crime prevention is paramount) and those where crime is sees as a product of the institutions and structure of the community (in which social crime prevention is seen as appropriate).

Social crime prevention is viewed by left realists as the key platform for tackling crime (Currie, 1998; Young, 1991), although both situational crime prevention and the criminal justice system are accorded supporting roles.

Jock Young

Associated Concepts: communitarianism, community crime prevention, community safety, crime prevention, left realism, situational crime prevention

Key Readings

Crawford, A. (1998) *Crime Prevention and Community Safety*. London, Longman.

Currie, E. (1988) 'Two visions of community crime prevention', in T. Hope and M. Shaw (eds), *Communities and Crime Reduction*. London, HMSO.

Currie, E. (1998) *Crime and Punishment in America*. New York, Metropolitan Books.

Hughes, G. (1998) *Understanding Crime Prevention*. Buckingham, Open University Press.

Walklate, S. (1996) 'Community and crime prevention', in E. McLaughlin and J. Muncie (eds), *Controlling Crime*. London, Sage.

Young, J. (1991) 'Left realism and the priorities of crime control', in K. Stenson and D. Cowell (eds), *The Politics of Crime Control*. London, Sage.

SOCIAL DEFENCE THEORY

Definition

A penal philosophy developed in the early twentieth century that adhered to the 'protection of society' by the neutralization and resocialization of the offender, whereby fixed penalties were set aside for individualized punishment.

Distinctive Features

The development of a 'social defence theory' has been accredited to the Belgian jurist

Adolphe Prins following the publication of his book *La Défense sociale* in 1910 (see Ancel, 1965). As a penological concept, however, its origins are to be found in the early nineteenth century. In 1831, the Italian jurist Carmignani argued that the rigid administration of crimes and punishments should be replaced with a new penal theory based on the concepts of 'social offence' and 'social defence' (see Pasquino, 1980). Its origins are clearly European, notably Italian, German, French and Belgian. Carmignani's vision of a social defence doctrine gathered momentum and acceptance during the positivist revolt of the late nineteenth century. Radzinowicz describes the place of social defence within positivist ideology:

> It was not the business of the criminal justice system to assess and to measure the moral guilt of an offender but only to determine whether he was not the perpetrator of an act defined as an offence and then to apply to him one of the measures of 'social defence' so as to restrain him from committing further crimes. (Radzinowicz, 1961, p. 17)

Social defence is a phrase that has been subject to widespread interpretation and distortion (Ancel, 1962). During the late nineteenth and early twentieth centuries some social theorists and penal philosophers in Europe, such as Tarde and Signorel, argued that social defence was the repression of crime by the criminal law and the administration of 'stern' punishment, thus reflecting classicist doctrine or principles of the *ancien régime*. However, the positivists of this era adopted an alternative interpretation that was more widely adopted into criminal science rhetoric. For them, social defence centred on the protection of society from dangerous and habitual criminals (see Ancel, 1965). Enrico Ferri used the term 'social defence' to describe the purpose and justification of punishment as an indeterminate treatment reflecting the needs of the individual rather than moral culpability and retribution.

The Italian positivist school at the end of the nineteenth century referred to the failures of social defence, as expressed by the repressive criminal law and deterrent-based punishments of the nineteenth century. In its place, they argued that a doctrine of social defence should no longer focus on individual and moral responsibility but be replaced with preventative measures that would address the criminal's 'dangerous condition' (Ancel, 1962, p. 498). Pratt (1997) argues that a 'new penality' emerged in Europe in the late

nineteenth and early twentieth centuries, one that classified criminals into categories (insane, habitual, degenerate, weak-minded etc.) and subsequently tailored punishment on an individual basis. For Pratt 'the individualization of punishment' served a broader social purpose. He argues, '[the penal process] would now be a form of social defence, providing insurance against the risks that the habitual criminals presented, alongside the other strategies that the emerging welfare state had introduced to protect its citizens from risk and ensure their security' (Pratt, 1997, p. 47).

As a concept, social defence in the first half of the twentieth century received much criticism because of its suppression of the individual in favour of social protection, or as Radzinowicz (1999, p. 38) has argued 'social defence [sliding] into social aggression'. Individual freedoms were viewed as subsidiary to those justified measures that aimed to protect the moral and legal fabric of society. Social defence has also been interpreted as a form of social hygiene. The International Union of Penal Law founded in 1889 comprised an alliance of European penal reformists. It adopted an interventionist approach to penology and interpreted social defence to mean 'social hygiene', involving the 'mopping-up of the social breeding grounds of crime' (Pasquino, 1980).

Marc Ancel (1965) describes the more extreme applications of social defence expressed through repressive governmental regimes such as those of Communist Russia, Nazi Germany and Fascist Italy, where social defence was viewed as a form of 'community protection' and completely eroded human rights and civil liberties.

Evaluation

The earliest usage of social defence is, therefore, founded on broad and changing interpretations. Its 'modern' definition and application are, however, applied with greater consistency. The United Nations resurrected the term in 1948 as 'the prevention of crime and the treatment of offenders'. This definition has focused on positivist explanations of criminality and penal solutions that serve to protect society whilst addressing the criminogenic characteristics of the offender. Nowadays, social defence theory is rarely used within criminal justice rhetoric. However, its underlying principles of protecting society through individualized punishment, for example, indeterminate sentences, preventative detention, dangerousness legislation, have re-emerged in late modernity as important facets of penal and criminal justice policy and realist criminological thinking.

Reece Walters

Associated Concepts: crime control model, crime prevention, deterrence, positivism, risk

Key Readings
Ancel, M. (1962) 'Social defence', *The Law Quarterly Review*, 78, pp. 497–503.
Ancel, M. (1965) 'Social defence', in *A Modern Approach to Criminal Problems*. London, Routledge and Kegan Paul.
Pasquino, P. (1980) 'Criminology: the birth of a special saviour. Transformations in penal theory and new sources of right in the late nineteenth century', *Ideology and Consciousness*, 7, pp. 1–17.
Pratt, J. (1997) *Governing the Dangerous. Dangerousness, Law and Social Change*. Sydney, The Federation Press.
Radzinowicz, L. (1961) *In Search of Criminology*. London, Heinemann.
Radzinowicz, L. (1999) *Adventures in Criminology*. London, Routledge.

SOCIAL DISORGANIZATION

See Chicago School of Sociology; Geographies of crime; Social ecology

SOCIAL ECOLOGY

Definition

Social ecology explanations of crime are a variant of sociological positivism. They imply that crime is not caused by aberrant individuals but by the 'pathological' conditions of particular areas or communities. They draw upon modes of analysis developed within human geography and biology to argue that one outcome of the structuring of space is a patterned distribution of crime.

Distinctive Features

Crime is always subject to uneven geographical distribution. Urban areas appear to have higher recorded crime rates than rural areas and within cities there are presumed to be 'criminal areas' or 'hot spots' of crime. To explain these patterns of crime distribution analogies have been made between the ecology of plant life and human organization. Cities are viewed as akin to living and growing organisms, with individuals growing together over time and declining when superseded by other individuals with different forms of social organization. In the 1920s and 1930s sociologists at the University of Chicago embarked on a systematic study of all aspects of their local urban environment. Park, a newspaper reporter turned sociologist, and Burgess, his collaborator, were particularly influential. They noted that, like any ecological system, the development and organization of the city of Chicago was not random but patterned, and could be understood in terms of such social processes as invasion, conflict, accommodation and assimilation. They likened the city to a living and growing organism and viewed the functions of various areas of the city as fundamental to the survival of the whole. The city's characteristics, social change and distribution of people were studied by use of Burgess's concentric zone theory. The city was divided into five areas: zone 1, the central business district; zone 2, a transition from business to residences; zone 3, working-class homes; zone 4, middle-class homes; zone 5, commuter suburbs. Zone 2 – the zone in transition – was a particular focus of study. Here the expansion of the business sector continually meant that residents were displaced. It became the least desirable living area. It was characterized by deteriorating housing stock, poverty, pawn shops, cheap theatres, restaurants, casual workers, new immigrants and a breakdown in the usual methods of social control. It was hypothesized that it was in zone 2 that crime and vice would flourish. Shaw (1929) and Shaw and McKay (1942) set out to test this hypothesis by using juvenile and adult court and prison statistics to map the spatial distribution of the residences of delinquent youths and criminals throughout the city. They were eventually to conclude that as this particular zone maintained a regular crime rate even when its populations completely changed, then there must be something about particular places that sustains crime.

Evaluation

Such early social ecology theory has subsequently been critiqued for its denial of human choice; its reliance on official definitions and statistics as 'true' indices of crime; and its inability to account for contra evidence, such as high rates of crime in stable communities or low rates in areas of high social disorganization. Nevertheless, the approach experienced something of a revival in England in the 1970s and in the USA in the 1980s. These have added spatial analysis, victimization data and accounts of political economy to the original formulation. For example, Morris (1957) found that the areas of peak crime rates in Croydon, South London were two of the inter-war council housing estates and two older residential areas noted for slum housing and physical deterioration. From this he argued that the political decision by local authorities to concentrate certain of their tenants in less desirable housing was central to the creation of distinct 'criminal areas'.

Later studies widened the focus further to include not only the study of differential access to housing space and of the effects on people compelled to live in low-grade housing in 'rough' areas, but also the relevance of social *class* and differential access to *power* for understanding the continuing 'competitive struggle for space'. New versions of spatial analysis (Bottoms and Wiles, 1992; Brantingham and Brantingham, 1984) have succeeded not only in substantiating that crime is spatially as well as socially defined, but that it is a natural and normal expression of social interaction given the organization of particular localized communities. In particular, it is how individuals recognize the role of space in their own biographies and how space mediates the relationship between individual and environment that creates different *opportunities* for crime.

John Muncie

Associated Concepts: Chicago School of Sociology, defensible space, geographies of crime, sociological positivism

Key Readings

Bottoms, A. and Wiles, P. (1992) 'Explanations of crime and place', in D.J. Evans, N.R. Fyle and D.T. Herbert (eds), *Crime, Policing and Place*. London, Routledge.

Brantingham, P.J. and Brantingham, P.L. (1984) *Patterns of Crime*. New York, Macmillan.

Morris, T. (1957) *The Criminal Area: A Study in Social Ecology*. London, Routledge.

Park, R.E. (1936) 'Human ecology', *American Journal of Sociology*, 42 (1), p. 15.

Shaw, C.R. (1929) *Delinquency Areas*. Chicago, University of Chicago Press.

Shaw, C.R. and McKay, H.D. (1942) *Juvenile Delinquency and Urban Areas*. Chicago, University of Chicago Press.

SOCIAL EXCLUSION

Definition

Social exclusion refers to the dynamic, multidimensional process of being shut out, fully or partially, from the various social, economic, political or cultural systems which serve to assist the integration of a person in society. When combined, acute forms of exclusion are created that find a spatial and concentrated expression in particular localities and communities.

Distinctive Features

Social exclusion can be best thought of as a dynamic and fluid process rather than as a static and clearly defined condition. It refers to marginalization, social isolation and dislocation, disaffiliation and vulnerability. More than simply the circumstances of the poorest individuals, social exclusion describes a pattern of profound changes in social arrangements and the ever-increasing growth in inequalities and insecurities produced by those changes. Thus the concept of social exclusion has to be understood within the context of the transition from modernity to late modernity. It covers not only the unemployed and economically inactive but also the 'working poor' and those sections of the economically active increasingly affected by the 'structural insecurity' generated by the new 'flexible' labour market. It is an extended concept that includes situations of distress, discrimination and disadvantage that are largely, although not exclusively, socio-economic in nature. Social exclusion occurs primarily on three levels: the economic and material exclusion of individuals denied access to paid, full-time employment; the isolation from relationships produced by social and spatial segregation, and the ever-increasing exclusionary policies and practices of the criminal justice system.

During the 1960s and 1970s the cultural revolution of individualism and the economic crisis and subsequent restructuring of the labour market signalled the beginning of the transition from modernity to late modernity. Three discernible and interrelated trends indicative of this shift are of particular relevance. First is the economic crisis of the 1970s and the 'hollowing out' and the 'rolling back' of the state. The more important aspects of this transformation have involved the abandonment of attempts to provide the social 'rights' of citizenship, including full employment, and a significant reduction in 'welfare' assistance. Thus the influence of neo-liberalism and its conception of freedom as the absence of state control and intervention has changed the relationship between citizens and the state. Subsequently a deconstruction of the previous consensus on social and political values has taken place.

Secondly, the transition to late modernity has also led to radical changes in the mode of production and in the organization of the workforce. The full employment of modernity has been replaced by the structural unemployment, the casual/part-time (under-) employment and the insecure employment of late modernity. The most significant products of these changes are unpredictability, uncertainty, precariousness and insecurity. What we have witnessed is a tripartite division of society made up of a securely employed or wealthy minority, an increasingly squeezed middle of insecurely employed, and the part-time/casually employed and unemployed poor. Thus work is a much-decreased means by which risk is managed, identities are formed and maintained and citizenship and participation achieved.

Thirdly, profound changes in the meanings of inclusion and citizenship have occurred. Social citizenship and identity are increasingly constructed around levels of consumption and lifestyle choice as opposed to work and one's relationship with the state. The state now argues that the inclusion of individuals is not its proper role and instead it is the responsibility of the individual to gain inclusion via choices made in the market place. However, given structural unemployment and job insecurity, a section of the population remains constantly surplus to the requirements of advanced capitalism. The resulting lack of access to material resources via paid work combined with the reduction in state welfare means that the market and lifestyle choices of an increasing number of individuals and families are severely constrained.

In relation to crime, social exclusion is an inevitable by-product of the activities and operations of an increasingly punitive criminal justice system. Prison is the definitive form of exclusion and the imprisoned are a distinctly excluded population. Fear of crime has produced perceptions of the late modern city as an uneven patchwork of safe and unsafe, high- and low-risk areas and has resulted in social and spatial segregation. In public places a whole series of exclusionary technologies and practices have been generated and designed to provide consumer security and crime prevention. In the interests of increasing consumption levels, business is increasingly excluding non-consumers, particularly youth who are perceived as a threat to the efficient flow and activity of legitimate consumers. The privatization of public space, and the creation of 'mass private property', is set to continue, and with it the exclusion of youth and other marginalized groups from the very locations in which their market and lifestyle choices are made. Finally, the new 'social' crime prevention policies of government are themselves exclusionary in that they entail a process of categorization, a separating out of the population according to actuarially based calculations of risk.

Evaluation

Social exclusion is increasingly coming to replace the more pejorative concept of 'underclass' in debates about the poor. Social exclusion, unlike underclass, implies that the process of exclusion is the result of society-wide forces beyond the control of the individual who is in some way responsible for his/her own exclusion.

Critics of the concept argue that it glosses over inherent divisions within capitalist societies. In referring to the shift from modernity to late modernity, critics claim that the concept implies some 'golden age' where social consensus and growing equality were achieved and, therefore, the term fails to acknowledge the ongoing poverty- and class-based divisions in society. Finally, social exclusion may have become the preferred term in political debate because it can depoliticize poverty in relation to income distribution. Political leaders can speak of social exclusion while denying the existence of poverty. Thus social exclusion can have two forms, a weak and a strong: 'Weaker' versions seek solutions in altering the characteristics of the excluded. 'Stronger' versions emphasize the uneven patterns of resource and income distribution and the role of the excluders and aim to address these patterns and thereby reduce the power of the excluders.

Trevor Bradley

Associated Concepts: left realism, risk, social crime prevention, underclass

Key Readings

Byrne, D. (1999) *Social Exclusion*. Buckingham, Open University Press.

Donnison, D. (1998) *Policies for a Just Society*. London, Macmillan.

Finer, C. and Nellis, M. (eds) (1997) Special Edition: 'Broadening perspectives on social policy: crime and social exclusion', *Social Policy and Administration*, 31 (5).

Jordan, B. (1996) *A Theory of Poverty and Social Exclusion*. Cambridge, Polity Press.

Madanipour, A., Cars, G. and Allen, J. (eds) (1998) *Social Exclusion in European Cities*. London, Jessica Kingsley.

Young, J. (1999) *The Exclusive Society*. London, Sage.

SOCIAL HARM

Definition

Injury or damage inflicted on society or social institutions either intentionally or unintentionally.

Distinctive Features

The concept of social harm is closely associated with notions of crime and immorality but is not reducible to them. While many socially harmful acts are immoral and criminal there are some actions which may be considered to be socially harmful but are neither criminal nor immoral.

Edwin Sutherland in 'Is "White Collar Crime" Crime?' (1945) claimed that the defining features of a criminal act were that there was a 'legal description of an act as socially injurious and a legal provision of a penalty for the act'. By employing this definition of crime Sutherland sought to show that illegal actions committed by corporations and persons of high social status in breach of civil or administrative law were qualitatively little different from those actions committed by individuals of low social status in breach of criminal laws.

Sutherland's position was criticized by Paul Tappan on the grounds that regulatory offences are inherently different from criminal offences, that they are *mala prohibita* rather than *mala in se* – that is, acts that are 'illegal but not immoral' rather than acts that are 'wrong in themselves'. According to this view criminologists needed to restrict their focus to the criminal law or risk undermining their academic objectivity by defining anything they disapproved of as criminal.

Sutherland countered Tappan's argument by showing how these 'technical violations' were in fact distributed along a continuum with *mala prohibita* at one extreme and *mala in se* at the other. Furthermore, he showed how such regulatory laws were adaptations of common law prohibitions against theft and assault and thus not qualitatively different from criminal sanctions.

The extent to which the state *ought* to enforce morality and thus attempt to prevent socially harmful actions was the subject of a debate between Patrick Devlin and H.L.A. Hart. Lord Devlin claimed that the law exists for the protection of society and the individuals within it from harm. 'Society' consists of not just the individuals who make it up, but also of a shared moral code without which society cannot exist. Any attack on this moral code threatens the viability of society and the state is therefore justified in defending society by using criminal sanctions. For Devlin 'The suppression of vice is as much the law's business as the suppression of subversive activities; it is no more possible to define a sphere of private morality than it is to define one of private subversive activity'.

Hart countered Devlin's position by arguing that although society could not exist without *some* shared morality, a deviation from a part of that moral code was in no way tantamount to a destruction of society. There was no reason to assume that a person who rejected *part* of the shared morality would in any other manner be 'hostile to society'.

The debate between Devlin and Hart highlights the difficulty in drawing boundaries between the individual and society. While social harm is by definition an injury to society and *may* therefore become encompassed within the criminal law, harms that affect only individuals are seen as being more appropriately dealt with in civil litigation as torts. However, the boundary between the individual and society is not easily drawn. There is a very real sense in which 'no man is an island' and any injury inflicted on an individual has a wider impact on the society to which this individual belongs. As Keith Bottomley (1979, p. 35) observed,

> Whether we look at socially injurious acts from the point of view of the victim (if any), the intentions of the actor, or in the light of the nature of the harm done, it seems clear that there is no hard and fast distinction between torts, crimes and non-criminal harm. In practice there is a very blurred demarcation line between those acts or omissions which are the concern of the civil law and of the criminal law – or no law at all.

Evaluation

The relationship between social harm, crime and immorality is a complex one. Not all that is socially harmful falls within the domain of criminal or civil law. Inadequate health care, unemployment, overcrowded housing and insufficient educational opportunities are all socially harmful but attempting to alleviate such social problems by the use of criminal sanctions would be fraught with difficulties both practical and ethical. Natural disasters such as earthquakes and volcanic eruptions are undoubtedly socially harmful but obviously fall outside of the scope of the criminal law, while actions that are racist or sexist may or may not, depending on particular jurisdictions. Similarly, activities that result in unforeseen and unpredictable harm to society cannot be condemned as immoral. There is little doubt that the manufacturing and distribution of CFCs has led to widespread social harm through the depletion of the ozone layer and the resultant health defects which this has caused, but these adverse consequences were not at the time predictable and it therefore may not be appropriate to attribute moral turpitude.

Conversely, unjust laws may be deemed socially harmful, such as the 'apartheid' laws of South Africa. Victimless crimes such as some sexual acts between consenting adults, drug taking and prostitution are also often cited in this context. Civil disobedience, including law-breaking, when opposing such laws has been justified on the grounds that the law-breaking is less socially harmful than the law that is opposed. Criminal acts do not therefore always necessarily cause harm to society. There is no clear unequivocal standard for determining whether a particular action is socially beneficial or harmful. Such judgements are informed by political and ethical theories concerning what constitutes 'the good life' for both individuals and society.

But a concept of social harm does hold some advantages over that of crime to the extent that it enables the criminological gaze to go beyond legal and state definitions of injurious practices (Tifft, 1995) and to recognize certain legal behaviours as harms in themselves.

Mark Thornton

Associated Concepts: constitutive criminology, corporate crime, crime, deviance, natural justice, political crime, proportionality, redress, state crime

Key Readings
Bottomley, K. (1979) *Criminology in Focus.* Oxford, Martin Robertson.
Devlin, P. (1968) *The Enforcement of Morals.* London, Oxford University Press.
Hart, H.L.A. (1963) *Law, Liberty, and Morality.* London, Oxford University Press.
Sutherland, E. (1945) 'Is "white collar crime" crime?', *American Sociological Review*, 10, pp. 132–9.
Tappan, P. (1947) 'Who is the criminal?', *American Sociological Review*, 12, pp. 96–102.
Tifft, L. (1995) 'Social harm definitions of crime', *Critical Criminologist*, 7 (1), pp. 9–12.

SOCIAL JUSTICE

Definition

Fair distribution of opportunities, rewards and responsibilities in society. Principles and institutions for the distribution of meaningful social goods – income, shelter, food, health, education, freedom to pursue individual goals.

Distinctive Features

Theories of social justice focus on two main questions. First, how rules for a fair distribution of meaningful social goods can be determined; secondly, how much or how little inequality is permissible in a socially just society.

Over the past few decades, the most influential theory of social justice has been John Rawls's (1972) notion of *justice as fairness.* He draws upon social contract theory and the Kantian philosophical tradition of justice as impartiality, stating that for people to devise rules that are fair to all, they must be unaware of their own position in society. A rich person, or someone who confidently expects to become rich, for example, would favour rules that advantage the rich, such as low taxation and low public spending, whereas someone who is poor or expects to be poor would probably favour high taxation and high public expenditure. Only someone unaware of their own position or expectations would come up with levels of taxation and spending fair to all. Rawls therefore says that rules and institutions of a just society can only be arrived at by people acting in an 'original' (pre-social) position, or from behind a 'veil of ignorance' in which they are unaware of their own actual or potential social position. He realizes, of course, that people deciding actual rules for actual societies are not in this position; he is suggesting that fair distribution can only be arrived at by procedures designed to secure impartiality as far as possible.

Rawls's answer to the question of degrees of inequality is his *difference* principle: social and economic inequalities are just to the extent that they benefit everyone. This principle allows some inequality, but protects the least well-off, and because of this protection his theory is often classified as welfare-liberalism.

Rawls tries to strike a balance between equality and freedom; alternative theories prioritize one or the other. Marxist theories prioritize equality, whereas libertarian and neo-liberal theories prioritize freedom. Libertarians argue that governments should not involve themselves in the distribution of social goods. A just distribution, for libertarians and neo-liberals, arises from individual decisions to give or exchange goods which they legally hold. Any state interference with distribution, beyond establishing property laws, is unwarranted interference with individual freedom.

A variant of welfare-liberalism is put forward by Michael Walzer (1983). Walzer argues that Rawls was mistaken in trying to suggest one principle of distribution for all social goods. For Walzer, the principle of distribution and the amount of inequality in its distribution that is socially just, arise from the nature of the good in question. With medical care, for example, distribution should be on the basis of need, and there should be no inequality of access; for education, the principle should be that each should have as much education as s/he desires and can derive benefit from. For Walzer, the key issue is *domination*: the distribution of no one good should dominate the distribution of others. In capitalist society, the distribution of money can dominate the distribution of other goods;

in communist societies the dominant good may be political influence.

Evaluation

Social justice is relevant to criminology in several ways. Rawls's justice as fairness is reflected in contemporary just desert theories of punishment, and a major point of contention between desert theorists and their critics has been the extent to which criminal justice should take account of social injustice. It is also suggested that high levels of social injustice bring into doubt the legitimacy of law and criminal justice.

High rates of social inequality are associated with high crime rates and high imprisonment rates, and criminologists have criticized reliance on penal policy rather than social policy to combat crime in the UK and USA (Young, 1999). Some criminologists explicitly advocate social justice as a value-base for criminology, and have argued that penal, crime prevention and community safety policies need to be mindful of the rights and opportunities of those at whom they are targeted (Arrigo, 1999; Van Swaaningen, 1997).

Barbara Hudson

Associated Concepts: criminal justice, human rights, just deserts, natural justice, social exclusion

Key Readings

Arrigo, B. (ed.) (1999) *Social Justice/Criminal Justice.* Belmont, CA, Wadsworth.

Bouchier, D. and Kelly, P. (eds) (1998) *Social Justice: From Hume to Walzer.* London, Routledge.

Rawls, J. (1972) *A Theory of Justice.* Oxford, Oxford University Press.

Van Swaaningen, R. (1997) *Critical Criminology: Visions from Europe.* London, Sage.

Walzer, M. (1983) *Spheres of Justice: A Defense of Pluralism and Equality.* New York, Basic Books.

Young, J. (1999) *The Exclusive Society.* London, Sage.

SOCIAL LEARNING THEORY

Definition

A theory of learning that maintains that to understand behaviour it is necessary to account for the reciprocal relationship between the person and their environment.

Its defining characteristic as a learning theory is the role it gives to cognitive variables.

Distinctive Features

As originally formulated, behavioural theory concentrated on the relationship between the environment and observable behaviour. The contribution of social learning theorists was to attempt to incorporate more explicitly the role of cognition into an account of human behaviour (Bandura, 1977, 1986). The beginnings of the departure from mainstream behavioural thinking came with research that focused on the phenomenon of learning by observation. Traditionally, the accepted position within learning theory was that behaviour developed through the individual's experience of the rewarding or punishing consequences, contingent on their actions, that were delivered by the environment. Social learning theorists departed from this position in that, while continuing to acknowledge the role of external reinforcement, they suggested that learning could also take place purely at a cognitive level. Thus, behaviour could be acquired simply through observing models in the social world. Bandura suggested that there are three potent sources of modelled behaviour: these models are family members, members of one's peer group, and symbolic models as, for example, in the popular media.

Further, Bandura advanced the concept of 'motivation' to supersede reinforcement. In social learning theory terms motivation is held to take three forms: *external reinforcement*, in the traditional sense that the term is used in behavioural theory; *vicarious reinforcement*, where actions are based on observing what happens to other people who behave in a particular way; and actions that produce *self-reinforcement*, as in a sense of personal pride or achievement. As social learning theory stimulated interest in the role of cognition within an overarching behavioural framework, the term *cognitive-behavioural* became more widely used.

One of the consequences of the rise of social learning theory was an upsurge in interest in cognition and cognitive processes. The notion of *social information processing* seeks to develop an understanding of the cognitive processes when we interact with other people. The basis of this approach is that when we interact socially, there is a flow of verbal and non-verbal information between those involved. This flow of information communicates details of emotional state, level of interest in the other person, and so on. The social tasks facing those engaged in an interaction are first to be sensitive to this social information, then to decode or understand the information, and finally to use this information to inform their own behaviour. It is argued that biases at any of these cognitive stages can result in socially dysfunctional behaviour, particularly aggressive behaviour (Akhtar and Bradley, 1991).

Social learning theory has been applied to the study of criminal behaviour by psychologists (e.g., Nietzel, 1979); and interventions based on the principles of social learning have also been developed for use with offenders (e.g., Hollin, 1990). These interventions might include working with offenders to help improve levels of social ability, as with social skills training and social problem-solving skills training; or to challenge offenders' thinking by, for example, increasing awareness of the effects of victimization, or beliefs about, say, sexual acts with young children.

Criminologists have also attempted to develop a mainstream theory of crime using differential association theory, reinforcement theory, and social learning theory (e.g., Akers, 1990). In a social learning theory account, the acquisition of criminal behaviour (that is, attitudes and skills as proposed by differential association theory) is via direct reinforcement from the environment, as in operant terms, or through modelling and imitation. The models for all behaviour, including criminal behaviour, are to be found directly in the behaviour of friends and family and more abstractly in cultural forces such as visual images and the written word. (This is close to Sutherland's differential association theory articulated before the theoretical advances of social learning theory.) In terms of its maintenance and in line with traditional learning theory, criminal behaviour is reinforced by the external rewards that it produces: these rewards include tangible, often financial, gain, along with social rewards such as peer group status. However, social learning theory would add personal, internal rewards as factors that maintain criminal behaviour: these rewards might be the excitement of stealing a car and joyriding; or a sense of personal pride in avoiding detection for a theft.

Further, the meaning (or definitions in differential association terms) of criminal behaviour for the offender should be taken into account as they give some level of understanding of criminal behaviour for the individual concerned. Thus, the offender's definition of their actions may be positive, so that offending is seen as desirable: for example, sex offenders against children may say that their actions are desirable because in reality children enjoy sex and early sexual encounters act for the child's benefit in later life. Alternatively, the offender's definition of their actions may be neutralizing, negating the impact of what society sees as intolerable behaviours: for example, burglars may say that stealing from people's homes is defensible because their victims are insured and so no real loss is caused.

Evaluation

The criticism of social learning theory, or more accurately the *application* of social learning theory, is that it focused on the individual and their close social world, but has failed to take into account large-scale sociological factors. The development of a theoretical model to take such broad factors into account is a project waiting to happen.

Clive Hollin

Associated Concepts: behaviour modification, conditioning, differential association, differential reinforcement

Key Readings

Akhtar, N. and Bradley, E. J. (1991) 'Social information processing deficits of aggressive children: present findings and implication for social skills training', *Clinical Psychology Review*, 11, pp. 621–44.

Akers, R.L. (1990) 'Rational choice, deterrence, and social learning theory in criminology: the path not taken', *Journal of Criminal Law and Criminology*, 81, pp. 653–76.

Bandura, A. (1977) *Social Learning Theory*. Englewood Cliffs, NJ, Prentice–Hall.

Bandura, A. (1986) *Social Foundations of Thought and Action: A Social Cognitive Theory*. Englewood Cliffs, NJ, Prentice–Hall.

Hollin, C.R. (1990) *Cognitive-Behavioral Interventions with Young Offenders*. Elmsford, NY, Pergamon Press.

Nietzel, M.T. (1979) *Crime and its Modification: A Social Learning Perspective*. Oxford, Pergamon Press.

SOCIAL REACTION

Definition

The social process characterizing media, public, political and criminal justice responses to crime and deviancy. These responses often stereotype, stigmatize, label, criminalize, scapegoat and/or amplify the behaviours of certain individuals and groups.

Distinctive Features

Historically, some authors referred to social reaction (or societal reaction) as a theoretical perspective, using it interchangeably with interactionist, labelling and transactional perspectives. However, social reaction is more usefully viewed as a theoretical concept central to these perspectives, and to a broader understanding of the nature and impact of societal responses to crime and deviance.

The theoretical legacy of social reaction and the labelling perspective derived from it lies in the work of symbolic interactionists, notably Charles Horton Cooley and George Herbert Mead. In the tradition of Mead, Tannenbaum (1938) acknowledged that crime and deviance were created through processes of social interaction, especially through societal responses like tagging, definition, identification and segregation. This culminated in a person becoming what they were described as, separating the 'criminal' from the group in a process that Tannenbaum called the 'dramatization of evil'. However, it was Lemert's (1951) theory of sociopathic behaviour which undertook a systematic analysis of societal responses to deviation. His basic premise was that social control created deviance. Distinguishing between original causes and effective causes, he argued that there were many original causes of initial or 'primary' deviance, but that importantly this deviance was of little consequence to one's self-concept. Societal reaction, however, was seen as the effective cause of 'secondary' deviance, whereby an individual used their deviant behaviour or status to defend, attack or adjust to the problems created by societal responses to primary deviance. Lemert suggested that responses to deviation ranged from strong approval to indifference to strong disapproval, but that sociopathic behaviour was that which was effectively disapproved. Furthermore, one's deviant identity was shaped by the level of deviation engaged in, its social visibility, and the exposure, nature and strength of societal reaction. Recognizing both formal and informal responses to crime and deviance, he argued that formal agents of social control extended and formalized informal responses.

The 1960s witnessed further development of these ideas by Kitsuse (1962), Becker (1963) and Erikson (1966). In what came to be known as the labelling perspective, the concept of social reaction was pivotal. Following their theoretical predecessors, proponents of this perspective focused on the social processes by which persons and behaviour come to be defined as deviant, and on who has the power to confer such a label. As the most famous advocate of labelling suggested, 'social groups create deviance by making the rules whose infraction constitutes deviance, and by applying those rules to particular people and labelling them as outsiders. From this point of view, deviance is not a quality of the act the person commits, but rather a consequence of the application by others of rules and sanctions to an "offender"' (Becker, 1963, p. 9). Thus, nothing was inherently criminal and social reaction created deviance.

While interactionism and labelling are the key theoretical perspectives associated with social reaction, there are also a number of interrelated theoretical concepts crucial to illustrating the nature and impact of societal responses to crime and deviance. As Lemert suggested '[m]ythologies, stigma, stereotypes, patterns of exploitation, accommodation, segregation, and methods of control spring up and crystallize in the interaction between the deviants and the rest of society' (1951, p. 55). Indeed, the crux of social reaction is that behaviour that is subjectively stigmatized, stereotyped, labelled and criminalized, may create moral panics and 'folk devils' (Cohen, 1972), facilitate 'criminal careers' and self-fulfilling prophecies of deviance amplification and scapegoating.

Up until this point, social reaction has been examined as an 'active' concept. However, in some instances social reaction may also be 'inactive' or lacking, for example, in terms of the lack of negative societal responses to white collar and corporate crime, as compared to 'conventional' crime.

Evaluation

Together with interactionist and labelling perspectives, and related theoretical concepts, social reaction shifted the focus of sociological enquiry from causes and explanations of crime and deviance to societal responses. In doing so

it presented crime and deviance as social constructs. Furthermore, it examined the unintended consequences of media, public, political, and criminal justice responses to crime and deviance, providing impetus for non-interventionist criminal justice strategies. Overall, social reaction has proved a valuable theoretical concept for explaining processes of marginalization, especially where gender, ethnicity, mental illness and youth are concerned. Indeed, in the case of young people, social reaction has highlighted the continued association between 'youth' and 'crime', which has contributed to the criminalization of youth and non-criminal behaviour, and perceptions of youth as 'other'.

Many of the criticisms of labelling apply to social reaction, including that it does not explain the causes of primary deviance (although advocates argue they did not seek to explain them). Furthermore, the extent to which social reaction to crime and deviance is wholly subjective is questionable, for example, in the case of societal responses to murder. Finally, the extent to which social reaction causes deviance is surely unmeasurable, and thus unknowable.

Anna Duncan

Associated Concepts: criminal careers, criminalization, deviancy amplification, folk devil, interactionism, labelling, moral panic, scapegoating, social constructionism, stereotyping, stigma

Key Readings

Becker, H. (1963) *Outsiders: Studies in the Sociology of Deviance*. New York, The Free Press.

Cohen, S. (1972) *Folk Devils and Moral Panics*. New York, St Martins Press.

Erikson, K. (1966) *Wayward Puritans: A Study in the Sociology of Deviance*. New York, Macmillan.

Kitsuse, J. (1962) 'Societal reaction to deviant behaviour', *Social Problems*, 9, pp. 247–56.

Lemert, E. (1951) *Social Pathology: A Systematic Approach to the Theory of Sociopathic Behavior*. New York, McGraw–Hill.

Tannenbaum, F. (1938) *Crime and the Community*. New York, Columbia University Press.

SOCIAL SURVEY

Definition

A research design which, first, collects and assembles a structured set of data about a large number of cases (or units of analysis) and, secondly, involves a form of statistical analysis that seeks to describe the characteristics of the set of cases and sometimes also seeks to provide explanations of such characteristics.

Distinctive Features

Surveys can embrace a wide range of activities involving a wide range of types of cases. However, the case or unit analysis about which data are collected is often the individual, although that is not an essential requirement. For example, it is possible to survey police–public interactions to describe them in terms of, say, 'friendliness' or 'hostility'; incidents may be surveyed to count how many of them are recorded as crimes; and newspaper articles may be analysed to count how many argue for 'justice through punishment'.

All of the cases in a given population may be surveyed, in which instance it is usual to use the term census. For example, the British Census has taken place every ten years since 1801 and provides a count of the population of England and Wales on one particular day and describes the population in terms of basic characteristics. Most developed countries carry out a census. For example, the Census of Population of the United States has been held every ten years since 1790. It is much more common to study only a sample of the population. This is done on the grounds of cost and time and also because the principles of statistical inference can permit accurate estimates of the population to be obtained (with calculable margins of error) from relatively small samples. It is because most surveys involve some form of selection that the term social survey is often taken as being synonymous with a sample survey rather than census. What is more, as indicated above, although a wide range of units may be surveyed the most common is the individual.

As a result, in the narrow sense, social surveys are often taken to refer to the selection of individuals drawn from some wider population with the aim of making inferences from the sample to the wider population. In such instances data are collected either by interview, usually structured interview, or by respondents completing a questionnaire by themselves.

There are two broad strategies for selecting individuals to be members of samples. The first is known as random or probability sampling, whereby everyone in the designated population is given an equal chance of selection. The other is known as purposive or non-probability sampling whereby individuals are deliberately selected for inclusion in a sample because they have some distinctive features which are relevant to the research (for example, some specialist knowledge, particular background attributes or willingness to participate). Both random and purposive samples can have variations in terms of design, for example to make them more or less representative of the wider population. In order to make reasonably precise and calculable estimates about characteristics of a population it is advisable to select random, but more importantly, representative samples.

Data may be collected from samples of individuals at one particular point in time, in which case it is common to refer to one-shot or cross-sectional designs. A crime survey that involves interviewing a sample of the population of a town during, say, January in order to estimate the total amount of victimization during that month is a cross-sectional survey. Sometimes researchers are interested in trends and patterns over time and may interview an equivalent but different selection of people each January over a 10-year period. This is known as a time series design. The British Crime Survey is an example of a time series survey (Mayhew, 2000). Where the same group of people are interviewed at different periods of time, perhaps to study their personal development, it is common to refer to them as longitudinal studies or cohort studies. Longitudinal studies have been used to follow up a cohort of individuals into early adulthood to see which ones engage in criminal careers, and why. An example is the Cambridge Study of Delinquency Development (West, 1982).

Evaluation

Social surveys are valuable instruments of criminological research because they provide means of collecting a good deal of information about a lot of cases over a relatively short period of time (with the exception of longitudinal surveys) and at a reasonable cost per unit of analysis. They are means by which the main features of populations can be described, usually statistically, by studying relatively small samples. What is more, forms of statistical analysis – especially those based on correlations – allow the researcher to search for patterns in the populations and to seek to explain one set of characteristics in terms of another set. For example, a researcher may move beyond estimating the number of victims of crime towards explaining victimization in terms such as age, gender, ethnicity and lifestyle.

It is, however, necessary to recognize the limitations of social surveying. There are many potential sources of bias, for example, in the ways in which interviewers ask questions and the ways in which respondents interpret them and answer them. The questionnaires or interview schedules may force answers that do not truly reflect the ways in which individuals wish to respond, and samples may be so unrepresentative as to make inferences drawn from them worthless. Such matters can be addressed in careful planning and research design. However, more fundamental issues have been levelled at surveys. One is that by their very nature (for example, collecting data from large numbers of cases) they are shallow and superficial and do not allow researchers to capture the depth of meaning which criminological understanding requires. Typically, such an argument comes from those who advocate an appreciative criminology. Other viewpoints are that social surveys have certain in-built quantitative and positivist assumptions and also tend to be favoured research instruments of the 'official' criminology of government departments and other state institutions such as the police and prison services. As such, they do not address fundamental issues of criminal justice such as inequality, power and oppression. Typically, such an argument comes from those who advocate a critical criminology.

Victor Jupp

Associated Concepts: appreciative criminology, cross-sectional design, longitudinal study, sampling, structured interviews, time series design, victim surveys

Key Readings
Jupp, V., Davies, P. and Francis, P. (eds) (2000) *Doing Criminological Research*. London, Sage.
Mayhew, P. (2000) 'Researching crime and victimization: the BCS', in P. Davies, P. Francis and V. Jupp (eds), *Victimization: Theory, Research and Policy*. London, Macmillan.
Sapsford, R. (1999) *Survey Research*. London, Sage.
de Vaus, D.A. (1995) *Surveys in Social Research*, 4th edn. London, UCL Press, and Sydney, Allen and Unwin.

West, D.J. (1982) *Delinquency: Its Roots, Careers and Prospects*. London, Heinemann.

SOCIO-BIOLOGY

See Biological criminology

SOCIOLOGICAL POSITIVISM

Definition

Sociological positivism stresses the importance of social factors – such as anomie, social disorganization and economic recession – as causes of crime. The broad aim is to account for the *distribution* of varying amounts of crime within given populations.

Distinctive Features

A sociological form of positivism was first developed by philosophers such as Comte and Saint-Simon in the early nineteenth century. Comte's insistence that society both predates and shapes the individual psychologically provided the foundation for sociological criminology. This mode of analysis can be traced back to the work of the French statistician Guerry and the Belgian mathematician Quetelet, in the 1830s. They analysed official statistics on variables such as suicides, educational levels, crime rates and age and sex of offenders, within given geographic areas for specific time periods. Two general patterns emerged: types and the amount of crime varied from region to region, but within specific areas there was little variation from year to year. Because of this regularity it was proposed that criminal behaviour must be generated by something other than individual motivation. Quetelet (1842) found that the factors most strongly tied to criminal propensity were gender, age, occupation and religion. Fluctuations in crime rates were explained with reference to changes in the social, political and economic structures of particular societies, while crime itself was viewed as a constant and inevitable feature of social organization.

At the turn of the century its most influential advocate was Emile Durkheim (1895). He argued that in any given social context, the predictability of crime rates must mean they are social facts, and thus a normal phenomenon. Crime is rarely abnormal – it occurs in all societies, it is tied to the facts of collective life and its volume tends to increase as societies evolve from mechanical to more complex organic forms of organization. Above all, crime and punishment perform a useful function for society because they maintain social solidarity, through establishing moral boundaries and strengthening the shared consensus of a community's beliefs and values. Crime, then, is positive – an integrative element in any healthy society. In other words, Durkheim reasoned that societies without crime must be extremely repressive and incapable of adapting to social change.

One of the most influential forms of sociological positivism was developed by the Chicago School in the 1920s. Their early work argued that crime rates were determined by certain economic, environmental and spatial conditions. They noted that rates of truancy, delinquency and adult crime tended to vary inversely in proportion to their distance from the city centre. The closer to the city, the higher the rate of crime. These rates reflected differences in the physical make-up of different communities. High crime rates occurred in areas characterized by deterioration and declining populations. Moreover, relatively high rates of crime persisted in certain areas even when the composition of their population had changed significantly.

These observations suggested that it was the nature of neighbourhoods, and *not* the nature of the individuals who lived there, that determined levels of criminality. As a result, this line of reasoning has also been termed 'environmental determinism'. The concentration of crime and delinquency in particular areas was also viewed as indicative of processes of *social disorganization*. As industry and commerce invaded, and transient populations entered such areas, community ties were destroyed and resistance to deviance lowered.

Evaluation

Sociological positivism views the individual as a body that is acted upon, and whose behaviour is determined, by external forces. Little or no role is given to the processes of choice, voluntarism or self-volition. While Durkheim argued that crime is a normal social fact, he also acknowledged that in given contexts its rate might be abnormal. Thus crime is also regarded in terms of some form of pathology:

if not the abnormality of individuals, then dysfunctions in social systems. The study of crime remains in the tradition of scientism, essentialism and positivistic method: that is, it can be measured and evaluated by means of statistical methods and empirical data. It also assumes that there must be something distinguishable about crime that differentiates it from normal behaviour. A consensus, or in Durkheim's terms, a 'collective conscience' exists which marks out the criminal from the non-criminal. The role of social conflict between individuals and among competing groups is downplayed. Compared to individual positivism, sociological theories appear less interested in crime as a particular pattern of behaviour and more in *probabilistic* accounts of variations in crime rates given particular social, geographical and economic circumstances. They focus on general patterns of criminality rather than on individual motivations. Nevertheless, the concern remains to isolate key causal variables, such as social disorganization and criminal area, and to infer that such conditions *determine* rates of criminality. Crime remains a violation of a social order that is considered to be based on a consensus of legal and moral codes. Little room is given for the contrary positions that crime may be a freely chosen course of action and that it may be due to *different* forms of socialization, rather than lack of socialization.

John Muncie

Associated Concepts: anomie, Chicago School of Sociology, geographies of crime, positivism, social ecology

Key Readings

Durkheim, E. (1895/1964) *Rules of Sociological Method*. New York, The Free Press.
Quetelet, A. (1842) *A Treatise on Man*. Edinburgh, Chambers.
Shaw, C.R. (1929) *Delinquency Areas*. Chicago, University of Chicago Press.

SOMATOTYPING

Definition

A means of measuring variations in body types through which certain physiological features have been claimed to be causative of crime and delinquency.

Distinctive Features

The classifying of criminal types by physiological characteristics was the hallmark of early biological criminology, in particular the work of Lombroso, Goring and Hooton. The Harvard anthropologist Earnest Hooton, for example, studied over 17,000 criminals and non-criminals and reported that criminals tended, amongst many other characteristics, to have sloping foreheads, thin lips, long necks and sloping shoulders (Hooton, 1939). He maintained that tall thin men tended to commit fraud, short heavy men to commit sex crimes and men of moderate physique to have no crime speciality.

Despite the obvious over-generalized nature of the conclusions to such research, work into body types continued in the mid-twentieth century. The German psychiatrist Ernst Kretschmer (1925) identified three major types: thin (asthenic), heavy (pyknic) and muscular (athletic). The American psychologist William Sheldon (1949) expanded on this model by correlating body build with behavioural tendencies. His analysis of somatotyping suggested that the shape of the body correlated with individual temperament and mental well-being. A person's somatotype is made up of three components: endomorphy, ectomorphy and mesomorphy.

- *Mesomorphs* have well-developed muscles and athletic appearance. Body shape is hard and round. Personality is strong, active, aggressive and sometimes violent.
- *Ectomorphs* have small skeletons and weak muscles. Body shape is fragile and thin. Personality is introverted, hypersensitive and intellectual.
- *Endomorphs* have heavy builds and are slow moving. Body shape is soft and round. Personality is extrovert, friendly and sociable.

Analysing and comparing 200 boys in a reformatory in Boston with 4,000 students, Sheldon concluded that most delinquents tended towards mesomorphy. Ectomorphs had the lowest criminal tendencies. Glueck and Glueck (1950), using large samples of delinquent and non-delinquent boys, found similarly that there were twice as many mesomorphs among delinquents than could have occurred by chance. Sixty per cent of delinquents were mesomorphic, while only 14 per cent were ectomorphic, compared with 40 per cent of non-delinquents. The Gluecks contended that strength and agility might enable boys to fill a delinquent role. Endomorphs were too clumsy, and ectomorphs too fragile, to be successful delinquents. On reviewing a number of such studies, Wilson and Herrnstein (1985, p. 89) feel confident to conclude that criminals do differ in physique from the population at large. Physique, however, does not cause crime, but it does correlate with temperaments that are impulsive and given to uninhibited self-gratification.

However as is common with such studies, it is not *causes* that are revealed but *correlations*. Being athletic in stature may be correlated with delinquency, but this does not mean that either is the cause of the other. Both are probably influenced by other factors, including the adequacy of nutrition, extent of manual labour and social class position. Similarly, what Hooton and Sheldon were measuring were not the characteristics of the criminal *per se* but of the identified and processed criminal, who is most likely to be of working-class origin. Above all, any association between body type and crime remains in need of explanation. Are mesomorphs biologically predisposed to crime or is their criminality simply more socially visible? Such questions continue to plague physiological research, but it is clear that its assumptions continue to impact on popular conceptions of crime. Research undertaken in the 1970s showed that members of the public and the police readily and consistently put the same faces to particular crimes even when the individuals involved had not been convicted of any crime at all.

John Muncie

Associated Concepts: biological criminology, causation, correlational analysis, determinism, genetics, individual positivism

Key Readings

Glueck, S. and Glueck, E. (1950) *Unravelling Juvenile Delinquency*. New York, Harper and Row.
Hooton, E. (1939) *Crime and the Man*. Cambridge, MA, Harvard University Press.
Kretschmer, E. (1925) *Physique and Character*. New York, Harcourt Brace.
Sheldon, W. (1949) *Varieties of Delinquent Youth*. New York, Harper.
Wilson, J.Q. and Herrnstein, R.J. (1985) *Crime and Human Nature*. New York, Simon and Schuster.

THE STATE

Definition

The state is a set of historically variable, macro institutions and organizations charged with the maintenance of order over a given terrain. This heterogeneity within the state form – its traversing of public/private boundaries – implies disunity as well as unity, conflict and consensus within and between state organs. States display a balance between the use of coercive and consensual means to maintain social order. In that states attempt to provide a focus for leadership in society, they are always implicated in articulating the parameters of the general social interest. Thus state institutions are involved in constructing and maintaining, not always successfully, a popular legitimacy for the state form itself.

Distinctive Features

The relationship between state institutions, crime, deviance and social order has been the subject of fierce dispute within criminology. Whether the state merely responds to problems of crime and disorder or is active in their precipitation is one such contention. Furthermore, in its dealings with 'the problem of crime' the state has been conceived of in relatively neutral terms in that institutions intervene to preserve a notion of order based on a given social consensus. On the other hand, the state has been drawn in more partial terms in that its actions, interventions and legal prescriptions can only be understood as serving to promote particular interests within societies based on division, inequality and conflict.

The early attempts at establishing a scientific positivistic criminology in the late nineteenth century framed its terms of reference and objects of enquiry in such a way as to make it compatible with penal administration, structures of law and political ideology. In order to make itself a policy-relevant discipline, criminology for much of its growth and development did not problematize state processes and instead searched for the causes of criminality as located within individual and environmental processes.

It was with the turbulent changes associated with developments in industrialism, urbanization and technological advances that the state began to emerge as an object of social scientific analysis. Writing at the end of the nineteenth century, Emile Durkheim was concerned with the seemingly fragmentary, amoral and uncivilizing effects of these rapid social and economic changes that undermined traditional sources of control and social bonding found within families and community structures. He saw the increases in crime and conflict as inevitable features of a fragmenting social order. The decline of traditional forms of solidarity had encouraged normlessness, which for Durkheim would be best countered by a state that operated on and through the 'public interest' to foster unity and consensus via a combination of law, punishment and community organizations. The modern state according to Durkheim, through law and punishment based on restitution, reflected popular sentiment and morality, which dictated what was to be punished, and at what level of severity.

This view of the state as standing above social antagonisms and reflecting the greater 'social good' was developed in the writings of the 'Chicago School' in the 1920s and by Parsons' structural functionalism which dominated social science in the 1950s. Essentially, the state was depicted in conservative and/or pluralist terms: a preserver of an already existing moral order, divorced from particular powerful social interests. State institutions were seen as disinterested referees in times of social conflict whose policies reflected the 'general interest'. Thus laws and policies were enacted on this basis. Max Weber's conception of the state extended these formulations, depicting it as imbued with a rational, bureaucratic set of procedures while holding a monopoly of the legitimate use of physical force.

These liberal, essentially benevolent, views of the state were challenged in the 1960s with the new control culture theories emerging out of the labelling perspective. Although writers within this perspective such as Becker did not provide a clear conceptualization of the state they did focus attention on the agents of social control whose actions, through the application of labels, constructed 'crime' and 'deviance' in the interests of the control culture. Thus the notion of agents of social control acting in the 'public interest' was challenged. Questions remained, however: in whose *specific* interests were deviant labels applied and *why* were they applied to particular groups at particular times? These questions led to a shift towards a more radical analysis – a Marxist account – which linked crime and the state to the dynamics of the political economy of capitalism.

Marxist accounts sought to conceptualize the state in more substantive and specific terms. Quinney straightforwardly argued that the state and rule of law served to secure the interests of the dominant class. This instrumentalist view developed out of the writings of Marx and Engels who depicted the state as an arena for the material and ideological organization and continued dominance of the ruling class. Ralph Miliband continued this perspective through his examination of the formal and informal connections between those in positions of power within the state and ruling class fractions. For others in the Marxist tradition this was a crude model of state processes tainted with a 'functionalist' gloss. Poulantzas was particularly critical of Miliband's functionalism and pointed to the shift towards a more authoritarian state form that was emerging in Western Europe in the 1970s. This he termed 'authoritarian statism'. Althusser, another structural Marxist, also expanded the analysis by focusing on the different sites where the authority of capitalist social relations were maintained and reproduced. These he termed 'ideological state apparatuses' (family, school and media) and 'repressive state apparatuses' (police, courts, prisons and army).

Other neo-Marxist studies followed. Thompson, Hay and Linebaugh's work on the eighteenth-century state as a social relationship pointed to its position both as a site of class struggle and its role in the formation and reproduction of the new bourgeois social order. Hall et al. (1978) developed a model of the capitalist state derived from the work of the Italian Marxist Antonio Gramsci. Here the state is conceived of as a historically specific set of institutional arrangements whose 'independent' stance becomes untenable in times of crisis and whose leadership or hegemony is a matter of struggle within and outside of state institutions. The work focuses on the structural economic crisis of British capitalism which underpinned the social, political, cultural and moral crisis of authority signalled by youth rebellion, industrial militancy, anti-racist and anti-sexist movements, student protest and the rise of permissiveness in the 1960s and1970s. In times of crisis the 'spontaneous consent' for state rule becomes exhausted and the more coercive character of state rule becomes visible. In this context, the state: 'is progressively drawn . . . down into the arena of struggle and direction, and exhibits more plainly than it does in its routine manifestations what it is and what it must do to provide the cement which holds a ruptured social formation together' (Hall et al., 1978, p. 217).

This line of thinking led to an analysis of the ideological aspects of state power: how popular consent for state coercion was produced and struggled over; how the hegemony of ruling economic and political alliances was established through negotiation and compromise; and how, ultimately, in times of economic crisis, the popular masses come to support processes of criminalization in the construction of social consensus. Hall termed this 'authoritarian populism'. Thus state institutions are very much at the centre of social struggles and through the process of criminalization construct discourses of censure and moral culpability – particularly aimed at the powerless – in the attempt to order and lead the society in a particular direction. This process reinforces the interests of the powerful, the majority of whose own crimes and illegal activities are not subject to scrutiny, sanctioning or punishment. Importantly, when the consensus fragments, coercion will be mobilized to restore order. However, unlike earlier Marxist formulations the state does not always 'win' this struggle in every instance. Instead, the state was itself characterized as an arena of struggle where definitions prescribing what is criminal and the responses to crime could be challenged, resisted and occasionally overturned, as in the case of feminist struggles around the law on rape and marriage.

Feminist perspectives that emerged in the 1970s and 1980s questioned the view that depicted state institutions in class terms and as always repressive in their actions. Feminist writers pointed to what the state omitted to do as much as what it did. Thus it was not so much a case of *over-regulation* but the *under-regulation* of crimes against women – for example, in areas of domestic and sexual violence. The state was reconceptualized as a gendered set of apparatuses, serving the aims of a patriarchal order. It is not only that state institutions are overwhelmingly staffed by men but that masculinist ideologies inform the policy and decision-making process. This analysis has focused on the differential treatment of women within state criminal procedures and how regimes of control are as much about the penalization of behaviours that step outside of ascribed feminine boundaries as about the control of crime (Hester et al., 1996). This work also emphasized engaging with the state in order to generate social change for women. This perspective was particularly evident in the work of a number of Australian feminists, such as Sophie Watson.

More recently, under the impact of privatization and managerialist discourses some writers have identified a fragmentation of the state both in practical and theoretical terms. Thus policies of decentralization, partnership and the growth of private policing in theme parks and retail centres has led some to argue that the state monopoly on policing and justice is being eroded. Corporations and other private interests are increasingly defining and responding to problems of order without any recourse to the public interest. Following the work of Michel Foucault, this has led to a move away from the state as a privileged centre of power relations. This perspective is particularly critical of Marxist theorists and what is regarded as their homogeneous and economically reductionist views of state institutions. Much of this work has focused on 'neo-liberalism' as a form of rule that traverses and empowers a range of non-state agencies that 'seek to employ forms of expertise in order to govern society at a distance, without recourse to any forms of direct repression or intervention' (Barry et al., 1996, p. 14). Thus a range of expertise is at work in the assessment and containment of risks from crime which moves beyond so-called modernist views of the state as a clearly defined set of institutional mechanisms with precise boundaries. The state's decline in power and influence has been depicted in terms such as the 'lean' state, the 'hollowed out' state and the 'stretched' state.

Other writers, particularly in the Marxist and neo-Marxist traditions, continue to develop and refine a concept of the state that does not presuppose fragmentation, ideological coherence, institutional unity or functionality. These writers include: Jessop (1990), with his emphasis on contingency and contradiction inherent in state practices; Clarke and Newman (1997), on the state as a managerial set of institutions; and Coleman and Sim's (1998) analysis of the dialectical inter-relationship between 'old' forms of state power (e.g., the police) and 'new' forms of state control (e.g., CCTV cameras). Writers working around the human rights group *Statewatch* have argued that the state is becoming increasingly authoritarian and increasingly internationalized through the interpersonal and ideological connections of those working within different nation-states. Consequently, Europe is witnessing the emergence of a pan-European, minimally accountable state designed to manage an increasingly unmanageable detritus comprising conventional criminals, asylum seekers, drug users, single parents (particularly

women) and the homeless. At the same time, crimes committed by the powerful including the state's own servants remain effectively beyond scrutiny and punishment. In different ways such writers have helped maintain a critical focus on the processes of state formation (its shifting boundaries, central–local relations) and the exercise of state power in the arena of crime control (its targets, legitimating discourses and impact on social divisions and inequality).

Roy Coleman and Joe Sim

Associated Concepts: authoritarian populism, critical criminology, hegemony, radical criminologies, radical feminism, social control, state crime

Key Readings

Barry, A., Osborne, T. and Rose, N. (eds) (1996) *Foucault and Political Reason*. London, UCL Press.

Clarke, J. and Newman, J. (1997) *The Managerial State*. London, Sage.

Coleman, R. and Sim, J. (1998) 'From the dockyards to the Disney store: surveillance, risk and security in Liverpool city centre', *International Review of Law, Computers and Technology*, 12 (1), pp. 27–45.

Hall, S., Critcher, C., Jefferson, T., Clarke, J. and Roberts, B. (1978) *Policing the Crisis*. London, Macmillan.

Hester, M., Kelly, L. and Radford, J. (1996) 'Introduction', in M. Hester, L. Kelly and J. Radford (eds), *Women, Violence and Male Power*. Buckingham, Open University Press.

Jessop, B. (1990) *State Theory*. Cambridge, Polity Press.

STATE CRIME

Definition

State crime covers forms of criminality that are committed by states and governments in order to further a variety of domestic and foreign policies.

Distinctive Features

State crime is one of the most serious forms of criminality for the following reasons. First, the monopoly of violence enjoyed by the state means that it has the potential to inflict massive violations of human rights on its own citizens and foreign nationals. Secondly, the state is the primary source of laws and this provides it with the ability to define what is criminal. Thirdly, the state's control of the institutions and personnel of the criminal justice system enables it to target and neutralize its economic, social or political enemies. Finally, the state is in the strategic position to conceal its criminality. To date, state crime has been broken down into four categories:

1 Acts of political criminality, for example, corruption, intimidation, manipulating the electoral process and censorship.
2 Criminality associated with the security and police forces, for example, war-making, genocide, ethnic cleansing, torture, disappearance, terrorism, assassination.
3 Criminality associated with economic activities, monopolization practices, violations of health and safety regulations, illegal collaboration with multinational corporations.
4 Criminality at the social and cultural levels, which includes the material immiseration of sections of the community, institutional racism, cultural vandalism.

Although there are national and international laws and conventions which regulate the state and protect citizens, the principle of national sovereignty makes it extremely difficult for these protections to be accessed.

Eugene McLaughlin

Associated Concepts: political crime, the state, war crimes

Key Readings
Fredrichs, D.O. (ed.) (1998) *State Crime*, vols 1 and 2. Aldershot, Gower.

STATUS FRUSTRATION

Definition

The concept of status frustration is used to explain crime and delinquency by strain theorists. Individuals who cannot achieve their status goals through legitimate channels become frustrated, and they may (a) try to achieve their status goals through illegitimate or criminal channels, (b) vent their frustration at others, (c) make themselves feel better through illicit drug use, or (d) focus on alternative status goals that they can achieve, with these goals sometimes involving crime.

Distinctive Features

Some strain theorists, such as Robert Merton (1938) and Richard Cloward and Lloyd Ohlin (1960), argue that people in the USA are most concerned with their monetary status. That is, they desire a lot of money. They are encouraged to desire money by the people around them and the larger culture, and they are regularly exposed to all the wonderful things that money can buy. Many people, however, are unable to achieve monetary success through legitimate channels – like getting a good education and then a good job. This is especially true of lower-class individuals, although many higher-class individuals may also have trouble achieving their monetary goals. Such people become frustrated and may turn to crimes such as theft, prostitution and drug selling in order to achieve their monetary goals.

Other theorists, such as Albert Cohen (1955), argue that individuals have a more general desire for middle-class status. They not only want money, but also want to be viewed and treated with respect by others. Once again, lower-class individuals often have difficulty achieving this goal through legitimate channels. Unlike money, middle-class status is not something that one can easily obtain through crime. Some lower-class individuals, however, respond to their status frustration by setting up an alternative status system in which they can successfully compete. Their hostility toward the middle-class, among other things, may lead them to set up a status system that values behaviours like fighting and theft in certain conditions.

Still other theorists, like James Messerschmidt (1993), focus on the desire of males for 'masculine status'. While there are different views of what it means to 'be a man', most such views emphasize traits like independence, dominance, toughness, competitiveness and heterosexuality. Certain people – especially juveniles, lower-class individuals, and members of minority groups – may have trouble exhibiting these traits through legitimate channels. They may engage in crime to demonstrate their dominance and toughness and to coerce others into giving them the respect they feel they deserve as real men.

Finally, several theorists argue that many adolescents desire adult status – particularly the autonomy or freedom associated with being adult. Delinquency may be a means to assert or achieve autonomy (for example, sexual intercourse, under-age drinking, stealing to gain financial independence from parents) or to vent frustration against those who deny autonomy.

Evaluation

The effect of status frustration on crime and delinquency has not been well tested, although several observational studies suggest that the above types of status frustration do contribute to crime. And limited survey data suggest that individuals high in status frustration may be more likely to engage in crime, although status frustration does not lead to crime in most cases.

Robert Agnew

Associated Concepts: anomie, masculinities, strain theory, subculture

Key Readings

Agnew, R. (1992) 'Foundation for a general strain theory of crime and delinquency', *Criminology*, 30, pp. 47–87.

Cloward, R.A. and Ohlin, L. (1960) *Delinquency and Opportunity* New York, The Free Press.

Cohen, A.K. (1955) *Delinquent Boys.* New York, The Free Press.

Merton, R.K. (1938) 'Social structure and anomie', *American Sociological Review*, 3, pp. 672–82.

Messerschmidt, J.W. (1993) *Masculinities and Crime.* Lanham, MD: Rowman and Littlefield.

STEREOTYPING

Definition

The process of applying condensed images to a group or category of people. These images represent over-simplified and over-generalized abstractions regarding such people, their values, behaviour and lifestyle. Stereotyping not only involves categorizing and classifying people but also acting towards them in particular ways.

Distinctive Features

As a theoretical concept stereotyping has a disciplinary base in both social psychology and sociology. Social psychologists focus on stereotyping as part of unconscious and conscious thought processes and explore its link with perception (how individuals give

coherence and unity to sensory inputs, such as observing the actions of others) and also with prejudice (negative attitudes towards a group of persons based not on individual qualities but on traits assumed to be uniformly shared by all members of the group). In addition to exploring the negative aspects of stereotyping, especially in its connection with prejudice, they also examine its positive functions as a means by which individuals can bring order to a potentially complex – even chaotic – social environment, thereby facilitating ease of communication and interaction.

Sociologists have located stereotyping within interactionist, labelling and new deviancy approaches. All of these share a concern with examining the ways in which rounded images are applied so as to define some people as 'deviant' or 'other' and others as 'normal'. They emphasize the tendency for stereotypes to be structural, that is embedded in key criminal justice agencies and also in the everyday practices of their personnel. Although stereotypes are expressed in interactions between individuals, they are not idiosyncratic nor applied randomly: rather they exhibit patterns and regularity in the ways in which they are generated and applied. A sociological approach seeks to explore the relationship between such patterns and the exercise of power by one group of people over another. In this respect, sociologists tend to focus on the process of negative stereotyping by one group and its effect on another group.

The concept 'stereotype' is relatively imprecise and there can be variations in the ways in which it is applied. In some cases it is restricted to negative, unfavourable imagery whereas for others it can embrace positive portrayals of categories of people. Stereotypes may be viewed as relatively fixed, rigid and enduring or subject to manipulation and change. There are also differences as to whether stereotypes necessarily involve biased and inaccurate as opposed to valid – although simplified – portrayals. Finally, stereotypes are sometimes conceptualized as representing a universally shared set of beliefs: alternatively they are viewed as means by which one group characterizes and acts towards another group with adverse consequences for the latter. This formulation links the process of stereotyping to the exercise of power.

There are overlaps between the concept 'stereotype' and others used within an interactionist perspective such as 'label', 'symbolic representation' and 'folk devil'. The notion of folk devil was central to Cohen's (1973) analysis of violence at an English seaside resort and the creation of rounded images of 'Mods' and 'Rockers'. This analysis generated a wider thesis that society goes through periodic moral panics during which 'folk devils' are constructed and portrayed as the essence of 'what is wrong with society'.

The media play an important role in the formation and transmission of stereotypes. In doing so they are often influenced by primary definers such as the police, who give information to the press and provide initial stereotypes. Such stereotypes are fed into the public domain and also back into formal and informal police culture.

The use of stereotypes by police in their interactions with others can generate actions that fit the stereotype. In this way they can become amplified and self-fulfilling. Sometimes this is known as deviancy amplification.

Evaluation

Along with other concepts deriving from an interactionist perspective, stereotyping has contributed to criminology in terms of highlighting the social construction of crime and the process of criminalization as opposed to explanations cast in causal terms. However, it runs the risk of contributing to explanations that suggest crime and criminality are the outcome of stereotyping by the media and police, rather than a reality for those who are victims.

Victor Jupp

Associated Concepts: deviance, deviancy amplification, folk devil, interactionism, labelling, moral panic, racialization, scapegoating, social constructionism, social reaction, stigma

Key Readings
Cohen, S. (1973) *Folk Devils and Moral Panics.* London, Paladin.

STIGMA

Definition

A sign of disgrace imposed upon certain identified individuals as a means of marking them out as different, deviant or criminal.

Distinctive Features

The term stigma derives from the practice in ancient Greece of marking the body of individuals with cuts or brands to signify them as morally inferior, blemished or polluted and to be avoided, especially in public places. Goffman (1963) distinguishes between three types of stigma: physical deformity, blemishes of character (dishonesty, criminality, radical politics, unemployment, mental disability and so on) and the 'tribal' stigma of race, nation and religion. In his sociological and interactionist analysis stigma is derived less from a particular attribute (stigmata) and more through a social process in which particular attributes are discredited at particular times and in particular places. It is described as a discrepancy between virtual and actual social identity. The normal and the stigmatized are not persons but rather perspectives. Stigma is a relational phenomenon. For example, having a university degree may be a sign of success in one social context but a sign of oddity in others. In some contexts killing is heroism, in others it is murder. The meaning of stigma also varies across gender and class. Sexual promiscuity may be condemned for women (sluts) but may be a source of esteem for men (studs). Goffman observed that there is no possibility of objectively defining stigma. There is no clear and universal distinction between the normal and the deviant. In pluralistic and heterogeneous societies we continually move from one to the other. Stigma is a 'two-role social process in which every individual participates in both roles, at least in some connections and in some phases of life' (Goffman, 1963, p. 138).

However, he also noted that certain people, such as in-group deviants, those engaged in a collective denial of social order, minorities and the lower classes, are all likely to find themselves functioning as stigmatized individuals at some time. This is because the actual identity of such groups is more likely to confront a virtual middle-class ideal. Difference is translated into undesirability or inferiority. The stigmatized are cast as not quite human. Reactions against such castings are likely to be viewed as confirming the original defect. The stigmatized individual may attempt to correct the condition, but it can also affect self-esteem, self-concept and future behaviour. The stigmatized may come to resist their classifiers as unjustly exercising their power to deny them their full humanity.

It is in these senses that the concept has been most widely employed in criminology. In Becker (1963) and Lemert's (1967) labelling analysis the stigma process cements rather than prevents the onset of deviant careers. Applied to prisoners and inmates of mental hospitals, the stereotyping of them as 'spoiled' precludes their ability to return to a mainstream life. Further deviance is entertained when opportunities are foreclosed by persistent readings of character as negative and by related feelings of estrangement, self-doubt or resistance. Schwartz and Skolnick's (1964) study on legal stigma found consistent discrimination by employers when considering job applications from unskilled workers with a criminal record. However, stigma also varies according to social status. Examining the subsequent careers of doctors who had been accused of malpractice this research found almost no subsequent negative effect. As a result, only a partial and distinct population of deviants emerges: a direct result of the stigma of imprisonment and of collective intolerance to the relatively powerless. Stigma, too, can also be used for wider political purposes through which moral entrepreneurs engage in moral crusades (or 'stigma contests') to manipulate public opinion against specific groups, such as youth subcultures, asylum seekers, working mothers, teenage mothers, drug users and so on (Schur, 1980).

John Muncie

Associated Concepts: deviance, deviancy amplification, labelling, moral panic, radical non-intervention, recidivism, scapegoating, social censure

Key Readings

Becker, H. (1963) *Outsiders*. New York, The Free Press.

Goffman, E. (1963) *Stigma*. Englewood Cliffs, NJ, Prentice–Hall.

Lemert, E. (1967) *Human Deviance, Social Problems and Social Control*. Englewood Cliffs, NJ, Prentice–Hall.

Schur, E. (1980) *The Politics of Deviance: Stigma Contests and the Uses of Power*. Englewood Cliffs, NJ, Prentice–Hall.

Schwartz, R. and Skolnick, J. (1964) 'Two studies of legal stigma', in H. Becker (ed.), *The Other Side*. New York, The Free Press.

STRAIN THEORY

Definition

Strain theory argues that people are more likely to engage in crime when they cannot get what they want through legitimate channels. They become frustrated or angry, and they may (a) try to get what they want through illegitimate or criminal channels, (b) strike out at others in their anger, or (c) make themselves feel better through illicit drug use. Strain theories describe the types of strain that contribute to crime, and the factors that influence whether one responds to strain with crime.

Distinctive Features

Robert Merton (1938) developed the first major strain theory of crime. He argued that people in the USA are encouraged to pursue the goal of monetary success, but that lower-class individuals are often prevented from achieving such success through legitimate channels – like getting a good education and then a good job. The inability to achieve economic success creates much frustration, and individuals sometimes respond to this frustration by engaging in crime. Most notably, they may try to achieve economic success through illegitimate channels, like theft, prostitution and drug selling. Some individuals may also deal with their frustration through drug use.

Albert Cohen (1955) and Richard Cloward and Lloyd Ohlin (1960) drew on Merton's strain theory to explain the origin of juvenile gangs in the lower-class. Cohen argues that lower-class boys desire middle-class status, which includes both money and respect from others. Many lower-class boys, however, are unable to achieve such status through legitimate channels. For example, they have not been taught the skills and attitudes necessary to perform well in school. As a consequence, they cannot live up to the expectations of their middle-class teachers or compete effectively against middle-class students. If these strained boys are in contact with one another, they may cope with their frustration by setting up an alternative status system in which they can successfully compete. Their hostility toward the middle class, among other things, leads them to set up a status system that values criminal acts like fighting and theft. Thus, the gang is born.

Cloward and Ohlin, like Merton, argue that most lower-class boys want to achieve monetary success. They realize that they will not be able to achieve such success through legitimate channels and so are ripe for delinquency. But, like Cohen, Cloward and Ohlin argue that juveniles are unlikely to violate the law unless they receive support from others. They then discuss the conditions that influence whether strained individuals will form delinquent gangs. Among other things, strained individuals must blame their strain on the larger social system and be in contact with one another. The gangs that arise support and help justify the juvenile's crime.

The strain theorists mentioned above focus on the inability to achieve the goal of monetary success or middle-class status. More recent strain theorists, such as David Greenberg (1977) and Delbert Elliott and associates (1979), have expanded strain theory by arguing that juveniles may pursue a variety of goals in addition to money. Such goals include autonomy from adults, positive relations with family members, and popularity with peers. Further, they note that middle-class as well as lower-class juveniles may have trouble achieving certain of these goals. They thus provide an explanation for middle-class delinquency.

Most recently, Robert Agnew (1992) has further expanded strain theory. Like his predecessors, Agnew argues that strain may result from the failure to achieve a range of goals, including financial goals, autonomy and status goals – especially the desire of certain males to be viewed and treated like 'real men'. Agnew, however, goes on to argue that the failure to achieve positively valued goals is only one type of strain. Strain may also result from the loss of positive stimuli (for example, the death of a relative or friend, the break-up with a romantic partner, moving to a new community) and from the presentation of negative stimuli (for example, physical assaults, verbal insults, unreasonable demands). Agnew also discusses the factors that influence whether people respond to strain with crime. A criminal response is said to be more likely when individuals blame their strain on the deliberate actions of others, have poor coping skills and resources, have little social support from conventional others, are in situations where the costs of crime are low and the rewards are high, and are disposed to crime. The disposition to crime is influenced by the individuals' traits (such as, impulsivity, irritability), level of social control, and extent to which they have been taught to engage in crime.

Evaluation

The effect of goal blockage on strain has not been well examined. Researchers typically examine whether juveniles expect to achieve their educational and occupational aspirations (or ideal goals). Researchers ignore the monetary and other goals emphasized by strain theorists. And the inability to achieve one's aspirations or ideal goals is unlikely to result in much strain, since ideal goals have something of the utopian in them and are probably not taken seriously in most cases. It is not surprising, then, that studies indicate that the failure to achieve one's ideal educational or occupational goals is not related to delinquency. Limited data, however, suggest that crime is more common among people who are dissatisfied with their monetary situation – with such dissatisfaction being higher among people who are lower-class and who state that they want 'a lot of money'. There are also some data to suggest that the failure to achieve autonomy and 'masculinity' goals may contribute to crime.

Data also indicate that the other two types of strain – the loss of positive stimuli and the presentation of negative stimuli – may contribute to crime. In particular, crime and delinquency are associated with child abuse and neglect, criminal victimization, physical punishment by parents, negative relations with peers, neighbourhood problems, homelessness and a wide range of stressful life events – like the divorce/separation of a parent, parental unemployment and changing schools. Further, there is some, limited, evidence that at least certain of these types of strain affect crime, partly through their effect on the individual's level of anger/frustration.

At the same time, strain theory does suffer from certain problems. While some types of strain are related to crime, other types are not. Strain theory does not currently offer a good explanation as to why only some types of strain contribute to crime. Also, studies examining the factors that influence the effect of strain on crime have produced mixed results. So we currently do not have a good idea of why some people are more likely to respond to strain with crime than others. So strain theory may be described as a promising theory in need of further work.

Robert Agnew

Associated Concepts: anomie, status frustration, subculture

Key Readings

Agnew, R. (1992) 'Foundation for a general strain theory of crime and delinquency', *Criminology*, 30, pp. 47–87.

Cloward, R.A. and Ohlin, L. (1960) *Delinquency and Opportunity* New York, The Free Press.

Cohen, A.K. (1955) *Delinquent Boys*. New York, The Free Press.

Elliott, D.S., Ageton, S.S. and Canter, R. (1979) 'An integrated theoretical perspective on delinquent behavior', *Journal of Research in Crime and Delinquency*, 16, pp. 3–27.

Greenberg, D.F. (1977) 'Delinquency and the age structure of society', *Contemporary Crises*, 1, pp. 189–223.

Merton, R.K. (1938) 'Social structure and anomie', *American Sociological Review*, 3, pp. 672–82.

STRUCTURED INTERVIEWS

Definition

Research interviews in which questions are asked in accordance with precisely defined instructions and the answers are recorded in pre-determined categories. Such interviews are usually facilitated by a formal interview schedule for the collection and analysis of data. Structured interviews are in contrast to other forms of interviewing which give much greater freedom to the respondent to answer in his or her own terms, such as life histories, oral histories and conversational analysis.

Distinctive Features

Structured interviews are used to collect observations from respondents in – usually large-scale – social surveys. The same questions are asked of every respondent, in the same way. The range of answers is usually pre-set and may even be pre-coded. The interviewer should be able to categorize the responses to any questions into a set of mutually exclusive and exhaustive categories. As far as possible, the context in which the interview is carried out, and the procedures which are followed, should be standardized. In some cases the role of the interviewer is reduced to a minimum by respondents interacting with a laptop computer. An example of a structured interview is a battery of questions that collectively measure or 'scale' the attitudes of respondents, such as attitudes towards the police or attitudes towards rehabilitation as opposed to punishment. A number of established techniques exist to measure attitudes, such as the Thurstone scale, the Likert scale and the Guttman scale.

The principle underlying structured interviews is that different individuals should be presented with 'equivalence of stimulus', thereby facilitating comparability of responses across the sample in the belief that the procedures of the research have not affected the responses. The aim is to keep what is known as procedural reactivity to a minimum. In addition, structured interviews seek to reduce personal reactivity in the form of interview bias. The latter can occur when responses are affected by the attitudes or the behaviour of the interviewer as expressed in the ways in which he or she asks questions, probes or interprets answers.

Evaluation

Despite these advantages, structured interviews can have weaknesses. For example, they can be too shallow, especially where the researcher is seeking to examine the variety and depth of meanings or attitudes which respondents hold. For this reason some argue that structured interviews are only appropriate to the collection of responses on factual matters. A further problem is that structured interviews can result in data degradation, that is, the irretrievable loss of data as a result of reducing the breadth of responses to a few categories. What is more, the imposition of structure may produce distortion of the ways in which respondents would want to respond, for example because the range of categories offered is inappropriate or not sufficiently exhaustive. One way of trying to overcome this is by exploratory in-depth research, for example by using in-depth interviews or focus groups to uncover a range of issues and of responses that are valid in so far as they are grounded in the frames of reference of the subjects themselves rather than those of the researchers. Such exploratory research with small, but representative groups can provide a basis for the design of valid and meaningful questions for use in structured interviews with large samples. Even after this has been done, structured questionnaires or interview schedules should be 'tested' for their appropriateness in pilot surveys.

Victor Jupp

Associated Concepts: conversational analysis, focus groups, self-reports, social survey

Key Readings

May, T. (1997) *Social Research: Issues, Method and Process*. Buckingham, Open University Press.
Oppenheim, A.N. (1973) *Questionnaire Design and Attitude Measurement*. London, Heinemann.
Wilson, M. (1996) 'Asking questions', in R. Sapsford and V. Jupp (eds), *Data Collection and Analysis*. London, Sage.

SUBCULTURE

Definition

First used by anthropologists, the concept of subculture was applied to the study of delinquency in the mid 1950s. It was used to understand social deviance, and delinquency in particular, by referring to distinctive sets of values that set the delinquent apart from mainstream or dominant culture. It made sense of the apparently senseless by arguing that delinquency was a solution to the structural and cultural problems facing marginalized groups.

Distinctive Features

American in origin, a theory of *youth subculture* gained criminological prominence through Albert Cohen's (1955) research into the culture of the gang in Chicago. Cohen viewed the gang as a subculture with a value system different from that of mainstream American culture, distinguishable through special vocabulary, shared internal beliefs and specialized ways of dressing and acting. He attempted to account for the working-class gang in terms of a lower-class adaptation to a dominant and discriminatory middle-class society. According to Cohen, subcultures of delinquency are characterized by working-class membership, masculinity, group loyalty, short-term hedonism, non-utilitarianism and a lack of specialism in delinquent acts. He developed the notion of *status frustration* to explain how the subculture acts as a means for working-class boys to find a solution to a lack of status in middle-class life. The development of specialized vocabulary, internal beliefs and innovative ways of dressing and acting, he argued, represented an inversion of dominant

values. Status frustration becomes visible in negative forms of behaviour whereby the dominant goals of ambition and achievement, deferred gratification and respect for property are rejected and reversed. By a process of *reaction formation*, dominant values are inverted to offer a collective solution to restricted opportunity in which 'the delinquent conduct is right by the standards of his subculture precisely because it is wrong by the norms of the larger culture' (Cohen, 1955, p. 28).

Similarly Cloward and Ohlin (1961) explained working-class deviancy as a collective, rather than an individual solution. In this version, however, the problem for the delinquent is to achieve a high status position in terms of lower-class, rather than middle-class, criteria. They distinguished three types of delinquent subculture relative to the differential availability of legitimate and illegitimate means to gain material and status success. A *criminal subculture* develops mainly in lower-class neighbourhoods where the successful criminal is not only visible to young people, but is willing to associate with them. Denied access to conventional role models of success, these youths access criminal success models instead. However, in more disorganized neighbourhoods when access to a criminal subculture is denied, a *conflict subculture* is more likely to arise in which the lack of legitimate *and* illegitimate opportunities for material success is solved by achieving status through fighting and violence. A *retreatist subculture* arises where neither of these options is available and the gang resorts to hustling and drug usage.

Evaluation

These formative subcultural theories were influential because they showed that delinquency resulted not from psychologically damaged individuals but through a series of collective, local and cultural solutions to the blocked opportunities and inequalities of the American class structure. Such theory underpinned a variety of crime prevention programmes in the USA in the 1960s. The most famous was *Mobilization for Youth*, which was designed to open up new opportunities for working-class youth through educational and employment support. However, subcultural theory in general came to be critiqued because of its almost sole concern to explain high rates of delinquency within the male lower classes. Criminal law and statistical representations of offending rates were taken as given. Subsequent studies, based in particular on self-reports, found that most people, irrespective of gender and class position, commit acts for which they could be adjudicated criminal or delinquent. In ignoring both the ubiquity of crime, and its white collar variants, it conveys the impression that lawlessness is exclusively a lower-class and male phenomenon. The degree to which behaviour is determined by structure and class position and the sharp separation of delinquent and non-delinquent values on which these studies were based has also been heavily criticized.

For example David Matza's (1964) research found that individual members of a gang were only partially committed to subcultural norms. Rather than forming a subculture that stands in antithesis to the dominant order, he argued that the delinquent *drifts* in and out of deviant activity. This is made possible because there is no consensus in society – no set of basic and core values – but rather a plurality in which the conventional and the delinquent continually overlap and interrelate. Instead of delinquent acts being conceived as a direct expression of delinquent norms and thus system-determined, Matza was more concerned to illustrate how their diversity was dependent on particular individuals and situations. He insisted that *pluralism* rather than consensus and *interaction* rather than determinism provided more adequate means of studying deviant behaviour.

Downes's (1966) research in Britain also found little evidence of Cohen's 'status frustration' among the working-class boys of East London, either in school or work. Rather they *dissociated* themselves from the labour market and deflected their interests, achievements and aspirations into leisure pursuits. As such, leisure, rather than delinquency, provided working-class youths with a collective solution to their problems. The connection between leisure and delinquency only becomes apparent if leisure aspirations also remain unfulfilled. Some working-class youths reached a 'delinquent solution' by 'pushing the legitimate values of teenage culture to their logical conclusion' (Downes, 1966, p. 134). Neither did this research find any evidence of structured gangs in Britain. Whilst definitions of the 'gang' are often loose and variable, the term implies some form of identifiable leadership, membership criteria and organizational structure. Contemporary and classic subcultural studies of white, black, Chinese and Puerto Rican gangs in America paint a picture of neighbourhood groups, organized largely along racial lines, with a strong sense of local territory, mutual obligations and, latterly, direct involvement in extortion, trafficking and the drugs trade. However, in the British version of subcultural theory, criminal activity is not a key concern. Rather it is argued that leisure and delinquency combine to provide the conditions in which aspects of subcultural behaviour can become *criminalized*. Indeed, in Britain, Downes's study was influential in various respects. Not only did it shift the debate away from discourses of crime and delinquency and towards discourses of leisure and entertainment as a means of securing 'cultural space', but it also recognized how subcultural experiences and opportunities were structured by class-based material and economic conditions.

These twin concerns were elaborated by various subcultural studies published by 'the Birmingham School' at the Centre for Contemporary Cultural Studies in the UK during the 1970s. On the one hand, the meaning of subcultural style was examined through various ethnographic and semiological analyses; on the other, the political implications of deviancy were explored through investigations of the structural and class position of various subcultures and their propensity to create 'moral panics' (Hall and Jefferson, 1976). By drawing on the work of the Marxist author Gramsci, subcultures were located not just in relation to their parent cultures, but in relation to structures of class conflict. The British working class, it was argued, has developed its own historical cultures and the relations between these and the dominant culture are always negotiable. Working-class culture is always in a position to win 'space', for the hegemony of the dominant culture is never completed. It is always in the process of being contested and fought for. Subcultures contest this space through their 'focal concerns' and in the moments of originality created by the formation of deviant subcultural styles. Above all, subcultures were viewed as symbolic representations of social contradictions and as offering a symbolic critique of the established order: they were viewed as *oppositional* rather than simply deviant formations.

John Muncie

Associated Concepts: anomie, delinquency, differential association, neutralization (techniques of), new deviancy theory, status frustration, strain theory

Key Readings

Campbell, A. and Muncer, S. (1989) 'Them and Us: a comparison of the cultural context of American gangs and British subcultures', *Deviant Behaviour*, 10, pp. 271–88.

Cloward, R. and Ohlin, L. (1961) *Delinquency and Opportunity: A Theory of Delinquent Gangs*. London, Routledge.

Cohen, A. (1955) *Delinquent Boys: The Culture of the Gang*. New York, The Free Press.

Downes, D. (1966) *The Delinquent Solution*. London, Routledge.

Hall, S. and Jefferson, T. (eds) (1976) *Resistance through Rituals*. London, Hutchinson.

Matza, D. (1964) *Delinquency and Drift*. New York, Wiley.

SURVEILLANCE

Definition

The ability to monitor public behaviour for the purposes of crime and population control. Associated, in the main, with measures to reduce the opportunities for crime within the rubric of situational crime prevention.

Distinctive Features

In 1778 Jeremy Bentham coined the term 'Panopticon' to describe a prison design which allowed for uninterrupted inspection, observation and surveillance of prisoners. He envisaged the replacement of the old dark and dank prison by a light, visible architectural form in which inmates would be separated off from each other and placed permanently in full view of a central but unseen observer. Prisoners would never know when they were being observed but would be forced to behave at all times as if they were. A state of conscious and permanent visibility would assure the automatic functioning of self-control and self-discipline. In this way, Bentham was first and foremost championing a new conception of surveillance. He dreamed of entire cities being reorganized along panoptic lines. He believed that the principle of continual surveillance would be applicable to any establishment where a number of persons were meant to be kept under restriction, no matter how different or how opposite their purpose. In other words, the notion of perpetual surveillance could be applied not just to prisons but to workhouses, factories, asylums, hospitals and schools. Although the panoptic prison was never built, as Foucault (1977) pointed out, many of the emergent urban institutional arrangements of the early nineteenth century began to work on the principle that populations could be ordered through surveillance.

By the late twentieth century a range of surveillance techniques, such as CCTV and biometric scanning devices (smart cards, fingerprinting, iris scans, hand geometry scans, voice recognition, DNA testing and digitized facial recognition) were rapidly being removed from the realm of science fiction. The potential for national and international systems of intimate monitoring to classify individuals into appropriate spaces and times where they 'belong' was rapidly being realized. Retina scanning of prison inmates is in operation in Cook County, Illinois. Frequent travellers between Canada and Montana use automated voice recognition to enable speedier clearance through border controls. A national DNA database operates in the UK for tracking criminals. Commercial DNA databases are raising the prospect of gene tests to underpin surveillance systems in the health insurance industry, excluding those recorded as 'abnormal' or 'high-risk'. By the mid 1990s the UK had the highest penetration of CCTV cameras in the world. Pictorial databases of such groups as hooligans, political demonstrators, bank robbers, suspected illegal immigrants and environmental campaigners have been established.

All these developments have potentially enormous consequences for population control and urban regulation in the twenty-first century. Bentham's original conception of the Panopticon was of the use of architecture to control prison populations. Modern forms of social panopticism extrapolate from the 'unseen eye' of the penal realm and apply its logic to entire populations. Control is accomplished by unobtrusive but pervasive means through which notions of public or private space become increasingly blurred. The information collected by the new technologies of surveillance allows for the systematic categorization of whole populations. Gandy (1993) refers to this as a 'panoptic sort': a process whereby individuals in their daily lives as citizens, employees and consumers are continually identified, classified and assessed and the information then used to coordinate and control their access to goods and services. In an age of electronic networks, virtual memory and remote access to information and data, the disciplinary surveillance of the Panopticon identified by Bentham and Foucault is increasingly being dispersed beyond architectural boundaries and walls. Observation is no longer limited to what the eye can see. As Gandy (1993, p. 15) argued, this is not just a vision of the future. Rather the 'panoptic sort' has been institutionalized: 'It is standard operating procedure. It is expected. It has its place. Its operation is required by law. And where it is not, people call out for its installation. Its work is never done. Each use generates new uses. Each application justifies another.' It has become a system of power on which the survival of corporate capital exists. It endlessly seeks for the norm and disregards those who are classified as 'abnormal'. It selectively allocates privilege on the basis of information stored, perpetuating inequality and a mistrust which leads to further surveillance: 'each cycle pushes us further from the democratic ideal' (Gandy, 1993, p. 230).

A similar vision is offered by Bogard's (1996) notion of a 'telematic society'. For Bogard the surveillance capacities of late modern societies are characterized by:

- The application of military initiated simulation technologies and command and control communications.
- The comodification of spaces of cities and spaces of information.
- Globalization, whereby corporate state interests depend on global words of digitally interconnected control systems.

Surveillance and simulation have become increasingly interwoven. Telematic technologies, such as virtual reality and image databases, continually produce electronic data which is then taken to be 'reality' by dominant institutions. The key to understanding modern social control, Bogard argues, lies not simply in the extension of surveillance but in the generation of *simulated* notions of order/disorder. Social relations are reduced to a 'space between keyboard and the screen'. People are known and situated only as they are reproduced in the hyper-real space generated by electronic data banks, electronic communities or genetic algorithms. It is surveillance without limits.

These visions of a dystopian future (and present) rely on a reading of Foucault which promises the 'disciplinary society'. But Foucault's work can also be read as allowing for resistance. Strategies of power and knowledge are never pre-determined but always con-

tested and contingent and may enable as well as constrain. Lyon (1994), for example, considers that modern surveillance brings real benefits as well as real harms. By linking the expansion of surveillance to a simultaneous growth in citizenship, he argues that it is the very improvements in civic and political entitlement which have generated demand for a greater documentary identification, which in turn depends on a growing sophistication in methods of recording and surveillance. As a result he identifies no single omnipotent Big Brother, but a variety of dispersed 'little brothers'. Panoptic power is partial, contingent and unevenly developed. The sheer volume of new data becoming available is always likely to create contradictory and contingent simulations of people and places. Its meaning becomes ever less verifiable and forever open to contestation.

These macro political economic visions also need to be balanced with finer-grained analyses of how surveillance impacts differently on different populations, at different times and in different places. *Selective* surveillance has clearly played a role in furthering processes of spatial segregation and social polarization. There are obviously different risks involved in the entrenchment of 'suspect populations' in outcast under-protected ghettos and of 'innocent populations' in over-protected consumerist citadels and residential enclaves. A measured response to modern regulation and surveillance probably requires neither outright acceptance nor paranoia. Subtle distinctions need to be made to unravel the complexities involved in addressing whether the future holds a nightmare vision of zones of exclusion and zones of safety or whether surveillance can allow us to re-imagine the urban as rejuvenated, repopulated and more secure.

John Muncie

Associated Concepts: defensible space, governmentality, panopticism, risk, situational crime prevention, social control

Key Readings
Bogard, W. (1996) *The Simulation of Surveillance: Control in Telematic Societies.* Cambridge, Cambridge University Press.

Foucault, M. (1977) *Discipline and Punish.* London, Allen Lane.

Gandy, O. (1993) *The Panoptic Sort.* Boulder, CO, Westview Press.

Lyon, F. (1994) *The Electronic Eye: The Rise of Surveillance Society.* Cambridge, Polity Press.

Norris, C., Moran, J. and Armstrong, G. (eds) (1999) *Surveillance, Closed Circuit Television and Social Control.* Aldershot, Ashgate.

SYMBOLIC INTERACTIONISM

See Interactionism

T

See Defensible space; Repeat victimization; Situational crime prevention; Surveillance

TARGET HARDENING

TIME SERIES DESIGN

Definition

A research design in which measurements of the same variables are taken at different points in time, often with a view to studying social trends. For this reason such designs are sometimes also known as trend designs and are distinguishable from 'one shot' cross-sectional designs in which measurements are taken only once.

Distinctive Features

Time series designs can be used in conjunction with official data, for example by plotting crime rates for the same area but for different points in time (monthly, quarterly, annually). This acts as a basis for making statements about trends in levels of crime. When this is done it is known as univariate time series analysis. It is possible to plot the trends for different variables at one and the same time with a view to making inferences about their relationship. This is known as multivariate analysis and involves comparing one variable with another or others in the context of believing that there are strong theoretical reasons for the variables concerned being causally connected. It is possible, for example, to map unemployment rates against crime rates for England and Wales, 1990–2000 to consider whether changes in one rate coincide with changes in the other. Although such analysis may provide evidence of association, that is, that changes in crime rates are correlated with changes in unemployment rates, it does not by itself provide a sufficient basis for making inferences about causality (that is, that changes in crime rates are *caused* by changes in unemployment rates). It would be necessary, for example, to have evidence that changes in one variable consistently preceded change(s) in the others.

The term 'time series' is sometimes also used to refer to a form of survey design in which equivalent samples of the population are taken at different points in time and data collected about them, usually by interviewing sample members. The samples are equivalent because they are collected by the same principles and using the same criteria but that does not mean that the same individuals are selected (although in statistical terms that is a theoretical possibility). The British Crime Survey (BCS), carried out under the auspices of the Home Office, is an example of a time series sample survey. The first BCS was carried out in 1982 and has been repeated at regular (usually 4-year) intervals. Although there are variations, at each point in time sample members are asked if they have recently been a victim of crime, and if so, to specify the type of crime; and also asked to indicate whether the crime was reported to the police. Adjustments are made to the number of crimes reported by sample members to facilitate comparisons with crime officially recorded in the publication *Criminal Statistics*. In this way an estimate of the 'dark figure' of unrecorded crime is obtained.

The BCS also provides evidence of trends in crime levels, and because of recognized deficiencies in official recorded data it is usually viewed as the more reliable indicator.

Evaluation

Time series designs are predominantly descriptive rather than explanatory. For example, victim surveys such as the BCS are descriptive studies which measure crime at particular points in time, and look for trends, but make no great claims to provide explanations. There is the potential, as with all trend designs, to theorize about why changes in trends have occurred, but surveys do not by themselves provide sufficient evidence as to causality.

The value of time series surveys is that they can be used to map changes and trends in society (or a sub-section of it). However, as indicated earlier, they are based on equivalent, not identical, samples, in terms of including the same individuals. Therefore they should not be used as a basis for making inferences about individual development (for example, development of criminal careers). For this, some variant of a longitudinal cohort survey is required.

Victor Jupp

Associated Concepts: causation, cohort studies, cross-sectional design, longitudinal study, multivariate analysis, official criminal statistics, victim surveys

Key Readings

Jupp, V.R. (1996) *Methods of Criminological Research*. London, Routledge.
Magnusson, D. and Bergman, L.R. (1990) *Data Quality in Longitudinal Research*. Cambridge, Cambridge University Press.

TOLERANCE

Definition

As a criminal justice concept, tolerance is a form of partial non-intervention. It is based on the acknowledgement that (1) a dominantly moralistic approach is unsuited to actually solve social problems; (2) not all (legal) norms can be upheld and enforced; and (3) in many cases subtle problem-management or non-intervention is socially less damaging than repression.

Distinctive Features

Four centuries before the emergence of the labelling approach in criminology, the idea

that deviance is partly created by the social reactions to it and that a tolerant attitude is a more pragmatic way to control deviance was already in existence (Gijswijt-Hofstra, 1989). The cradle of this idea of tolerance is often sought in the Reformation and the Dutch revolt against the Spanish occupation and the Inquisition in the sixteenth century. In this era, tolerance is a philosophical argument in the plea for freedom of religion and a political argument against the intolerant Spanish ruler. Already in 1525, when Erasmus was asked to advise on how the religious peace could be best guaranteed, he argued that both Protestant and Roman Catholic services should be allowed, because tolerance would be the best ruler. Spinoza has contributed largely to the theoretical development of tolerance, in his book *Tractatus theologico-politicus* of 1670, by separating philosophy from religion. In Britain, John Locke defended a political concept of 'tolerance'. In his *Epistola de tolerantia* of 1689, he calls 'tolerance' the starting point of every reasonable morality.

David Downes (1988) has used the term 'tolerance' to describe the cultural phenomena that have accompanied a period of decarceration, that is, in the Netherlands from 1950 to 1975. Downes focuses in this respect on tolerant outcomes, rather than on an inherent, principled tolerance. Tolerance in social control is rooted in the Eliasian civilization process. If the citizen is expected to control himself, external control becomes less necessary. Tolerance implies both a moral appeal for self-control and a pragmatic *modus vivendi* to keep things as quiet as possible by not provoking unnecessary unrest in society. In line with Herbert Marcuse's model of repressive tolerance – people are given a wide range of 'innocent' freedoms in order to avoid protest against more structural confinements – Nils Christie (1993, pp. 41–6) has described the Dutch mode of social control as *tolerance from above*; that is, a tolerance that depends on the definitory power of a changing group of dominant professionals. In this sense, tolerance does not imply a real acceptance of difference on an equal basis, but implies a kind of moral superiority of those who can tolerate deviations from their own normal standard. It is quite nice to be tolerant, but it is much less enviable to be tolerated.

A policy of tolerance does not imply that authorities think of certain practices as being without problems. It shows a realist appraisal of the modest possibilities of social engineering through penal means, as well as an awareness of the counter-effects of penal intervention as an effective form of control. A tolerant penal approach (1) is a product of pragmatic considerations of control – often combined with an ideology of benevolence and humanism – and (2) goes together with a tight net of other forms of social control – like health care, social work and so on. An example of how tolerance functions as a criminal justice concept is the decriminalization of so-called victimless offences without actually taking these formally out of the criminal code. Law and morality are treated as separate fields. In Dutch legal practice, limited penal intervention is pursued in cases where no individual victim makes a claim for state intervention – such as (soft) drug-taking, abortion, euthanasia, pornography, prostitution and so on. These morally loaded issues are subjects of eternal public debate, which ensures that the policy of tolerance (*gedoogbeleid* in Dutch) adopted in these fields is carried by a rather wide consensus in society (Blankenburg and Bruinsma, 1991). The major advantage of a policy of tolerance is the practicability by which law and practice can be attuned. The dangers are, first, that law derails into an opaque political instrument ruled by administrative opportunism, and secondly, that it becomes a synonym for indifference.

René van Swaaningen

Associated Concepts: decriminalization, labelling, radical non-intervention, restorative justice, shaming

Key Readings

Blankenburg, E. and Bruinsma, F. (1991) *Dutch Legal Culture*. Deventer, Kluwer.

Christie, N. (1993) *Crime Control as Industry: Towards Gulags Western Style?* London, Routledge.

Downes, D. (1988) *Contrasts in Tolerance: Post-War Penal Policy in the Netherlands and England and Wales*. Oxford, The Clarendon Press.

Gijswijt-Hofstra, M. (ed.) (1989) *Een Schijn van Verdraagzaamheid. Afwijking en tolerantie in Nederland van de zestiende eeuw tot heden*. Hilversum, Verloren.

Marcuse, H. (1971) 'Repressive tolerance', in R.P. Wolff, B. Moore and H. Marcuse (eds), *A Critique of Pure Tolerance*. Boston, MA, Beacon.

Schur, E. (1965) *Radical Non-Intervention; Rethinking the Delinquency Problem*. Englewood Cliffs, NJ, Prentice–Hall.

TORTURE

Definition

Torture is the infliction of severe physical and/or mental pain or suffering as punishment and/or as a means of persuasion and confession. It is the ultimate form of individualized terror and is universally prohibited by international human rights conventions. However, its use remains commonplace and, as a consequence of the lucrative global market in 'internal security' and 'law enforcement' technologies, it is undergoing constant refinement.

Distinctive Features

The 1948 United Nations Declaration of Human Rights proclaims unambiguously that no one should be subject to torture. It is one of the few human rights that may not be derogated – there can be no excuse for torture nor mitigating circumstances which can be cited. Despite the fact that a variety of United Nations, regional and national conventions and statutes have reiterated that torture is illegal, human rights groups report that its use remains widespread across every continent.

Research suggests that torture is practised by state security and policing institutions for a variety of logistical reasons: to elicit information; to prepare enemies for public trials; to terminate the political effectiveness of the victim; and to create a 'culture of terror' permeating every milieu of society. In this last scenario, torture is being utilized intentionally as a mode of social control and governance. And because torture is being used to intimidate and silence the general population and deter opposition, innocent surrogate victims are as effective as political activists. In parts of the world where states are at war or in conflict with sections of their own citizenry, criminal justice and military agencies have been transformed into bureaucratic instruments of terror, complete with networks of clandestine torture and death centres with routine operating procedures and professionals whose specialist knowledge and methods are employed to keep people alive for as long as is deemed either useful or necessary.

Research into the 'world of the torturer' indicates that, although popularly depicted as psychopaths, more often than not torturers are state employees who undergo specialist training and group socialization and who, by and large, regard their work with a degree of professional detachment. In essence, torture becomes a form of state sanctioned routine activity. The making of a torturer would appear to have less to do with 'individual psychology' and more to do with the social and political order in which the torture is licensed to take place. A number of studies make it clear there is no one 'type of person' who is more likely to become a torturer. If the appropriate learning procedures are applied in the right context, a significant number of individuals have the potential to be torturers.

Because of the existence of various human rights conventions and the campaigns of pressure groups, torture is constantly being 'modernized' and sanitized by the state. For example, evidence from Israel suggests that there is a very thin dividing line between psychological modes of torture and sophisticated 'interrogation' techniques which have as their intention breaking the will of a detainee. This is posing a problem for human rights campaigners because the stereotypical representations of torture they have been working with may no longer apply.

Eugene McLaughlin

Associated Concepts: human rights, state crime

Key Readings

Basoglu, M. (ed.) (1999) *Torture and its Consequences.* Cambridge, Cambridge University Press.
Cassese, A. (1996) *Inhuman States: Imprisonment, Detention and Torture in Europe Today.* Cambridge, Polity Press.
Conroy, J. (2000) *Unspeakable Acts, Ordinary People: The Dynamics of Torture.* New York, Alfred A. Knopf.
Duner, B. (ed.) (1998) *An End to Torture: Strategies for its Eradication.* New York, St Martin's Press.
Feitlowitz, M. (1999) *A Lexicon of Terror: Argentina and the Legacies of Torture.* Oxford, Oxford University Press.

TRANSCARCERATION

Definition

The movement of offenders between different institutional sites, state agencies and correctional programmes, so that the network of social control is expanded rather than reduced.

Distinctive Features

The concept of transcarceration provides an important reworking of the decarceration thesis, as it argues that the 'clients' of institutions are not returning to the community, rather they are experiencing an institutionally mobile career (Lowman et al., 1987). For instance, offenders can move between local prisons, half-way houses, sheltered accommodation, or in some cases to high security prisons or large mental hospitals. Their institutional location depends not so much on their actual behaviour but on whether it is defined as ill or criminal. The move from understanding drug addiction as sickness to crime provides a good example of how constructions of deviant behaviour can shift from medical to penal responses, and the 'War on Drugs' is one of the main reasons for the recent increases in US prison populations.

The intellectual origins of transcarceration lie in Cohen's (1985) application to the community corrections movement of Foucault's (1977) account of incarceration. He argues that the movement represents an extension of the disciplinary project identified by Foucault. Whilst social control had initially focused on the concentration and segregation of deviant populations into specially designed institutions, like prisons and asylums in the nineteenth century, the community corrections movement represents the dispersal of discipline and surveillance deeper into civil society. The overall effect is that more people are caught in the web of control and that the boundaries between liberty and confinement have become so blurred that it is difficult to identify the differences between the prison and the community.

The concept of transcarceration builds on these insights to account for the expansion, rather than decline, of prison populations as community sanctions have proliferated. It also intimates that deviant destinations are not just restricted to the realm of criminal justice but can also encompass mental health and social welfare systems. For instance, the criminalization of homelessness and mental illness are examples of how social policy has been replaced by penal regulation in recent years. Yet in order to account for these processes, the dispersal of discipline thesis needs to be complemented by an analysis that directs attention to the ways in which particular groups become ideologically vilified and the targets of repression. It is no coincidence that transcarceration, as a theoretical concept, rose to prominence in the 1980s, when the New

Right came to power and mounted attacks on health, education and welfare spending whilst instigating authoritarian, punitive campaigns against populations marginalized from economic well-being. The important point is that the prison remains the focal point and organizing principle of this project.

Eamonn Carrabine

Associated Concepts: carceral society, community corrections, decarceration, incarceration, social control

Key Readings

Cohen, S. (1985) *Visions of Social Control.* Cambridge, Polity Press.

Foucault, M. (1977) *Discipline and Punish: The Birth of the Prison.* Harmondsworth, Penguin.

Lowman, J., Menzies, R. and Palys, T. (eds) (1987) *Transcarceration: Essays in the Sociology of Social Control.* Aldershot, Gower.

TRANSNATIONAL ORGANIZED CRIME

Definition

Transnational organized crime (TOC) refers to certain types of criminal activity that transgress national boundaries. TOC is usually associated with illicit markets, for example in weapons, drugs, products made from endangered species and so forth. Smuggling of licit goods so as to avoid import duties may also come under the concept. This may include the smuggling of tobacco, alcohol and luxury goods such as jewellery, coins, art, antiques and other high-value items, whether stolen or legally acquired. Fraud may be perpetrated transnationally, but corruption and white collar type crime are seldom presented under this rubric. Immigration controls create market opportunities for criminal entrepreneurs; the sex industry and other low paid and low skill occupations which provide employment opportunities in the 'developed world' for workers from less developed countries are exploited in this manner. Moral campaigners have also tried to raise the profile of a transnational trade in human organs, as well as children and babies sold for adoption, as issues related to TOC.

Distinctive Features

Transnational organized crime is often said to be the product of criminal networks or criminal organizations that consciously employ national jurisdictional boundaries so as to avoid criminal law enforcement efforts. It is uncertain to what extent these criminal enterprises arise because of the presumed weakened ability of criminal justice agents to act transnationally, and to what extent they arise simply because illicit transnational trade is profitable in its own right. It seems likely that profitability provides the basis for criminal markets in the first instance, and that some criminal entrepreneurs then use the potential of jurisdictional fragmentation to insulate themselves from arrest and protect their accumulated capital from asset forfeiture (via the process of money laundering).

Evaluation

There is no accurate or independent measure of the extent of TOC. Pronouncements about the 'threat' posed by its manifestations are based on control agency estimates, which imply the same caveats (with due alteration of detail) that are placed on police statistics relating to more conventional types of crime. The concept undoubtedly refers to negative features of the global free-market economy, which may in fact be more amenable to control through economic regulation than by criminal law enforcement. However, there are additional issues which complicate criminological understanding of TOC. The TOC concept came into use after the end of the Cold War. According to some, the 'threats to international security in the 1990s are less direct and apocalyptic than they were during the Cold War . . . one of the most serious of these threats is that posed by transnational organized crime' (Williams and Savona, 1995, p. vii). The control of TOC by police agencies (the FBI in America, the RCMP in Canada, the NCIS in the United Kingdom, Europol in Europe, etc.), has become entwined with the control efforts of Secret Service-type institutions (the CIA and the NSA in America, MI5 and MI6 in the UK, the DST and the RG in France, etc.). The CIA has been implicated in drug and weapons smuggling uncovered as a result of investigations that followed the Iran–Contra scandal, and in 1985 the French Secret Service planted a bomb on the Greenpeace ship *Rainbow Warrior*, sinking the vessel in

Auckland Harbour, causing the death of one person. There are also documented cases of transnational actions by ordinary police agencies that involve illegalities.

While the TOC concept draws attention to criminal activity that is difficult for traditional police agencies to address, by virtue of their embeddedness in nation-states (which raises questions about extraterritorial law enforcement), it also tends to elide the possibility of state agents themselves committing criminal acts. TOC discourse has also largely been framed in such a way that crime perpetrated by multinational corporations (for example despoliation of the environment) is left out of the picture. Some criminologists argue that 'state crimes' and other 'crimes of the powerful' require a degree of organization that makes the TOC label an apt one, but these concerns have largely been left to one side by law enforcement practitioners.

Despite the conceptual difficulties posed for academic criminology, transnational organized crime, and the illicit markets associated with it, has been placed high on the agenda of the United Nations. It is evident that the international community will, over the foreseeable future, continue to build up systems of transnational police cooperation in response to it.

James Sheptycki

Associated Concepts: extraterritorial law enforcement, governmentality, organized crime, state crime, transnational policing

Key Readings

Beare, M.E. and Naylor, T. (1999) *Major Issues Relating to Organized Crime within the Context of Economic Relationships*. York, ON, Nathanson Centre for the Study of Organized Crime and Corruption, presented to the Law Commission of Canada.

Block, A. (1994) *Space, Time and Organized Crime*, 2nd edn. New Brunswick, NJ, Transaction.

Naylor, T. (1999) *Patriots and Profiteers: On Economic Warfare, Embargo Busting and State-Sponsored Crime*. Toronto, University of Toronto Press.

Pearce, F. and Woodiwiss, M. (1993) *Global Crime Connections; Dynamics and Control*. London, Macmillan.

Williams, P. and Savona, E.U. (1995) 'The United Nations and transnational organized crime', *Transnational Organized Crime Special Issue*, 1 (3), (London, Frank Cass).

TRANSNATIONAL POLICING

Definition

Policing activity involving systems of cooperation that cross national boundaries. Such activity need not be restricted to law enforcement, but may be extended to take in the whole range of police functions including crime prevention activity, social service provision, training, risk assessment and management, and state security.

Distinctive Features

Policing is a modern institution which grew up during the period of state-building, at first in Europe and then, through the processes of colonialism, elsewhere. As such, policing is an expression of sovereignty understood as a governmental activity intended to secure the peace, prosperity and good order of territorially bounded states. Since policing has been conceived of as an activity that is geographically circumscribed, difficulties arise when such action extends across national borders. Transnationalization of policing is profoundly effected by the doctrine of sovereignty, which suggests that jurisdiction for criminal law enforcement is strictly territorial. Transnational policing therefore involves and requires reciprocal arrangements for the exchange of criminal intelligence, police expertise, evidence and so on so that jurisdictional boundaries are not an impediment to the policing function. Jurisdictional fragmentation characterizes the legal landscape for transnational policing and concomitant worries about jurisdiction shopping raise questions about 'due process' constraints on transnational policing activity.

Interpol is the most famous instance of institutionalized reciprocity between police organizations across national boundaries. The Interpol system provides a channel of communication between police forces, but strictly speaking it is not 'operational': the 'man from Interpol' never arrested anyone. Interpol's primary role is the exchange of messages between police forces and judicial authorities of its member countries. This is facilitated by the system of 'coloured notices': red notices are in effect international arrest warrants, blue notices are requests for information on a specific individual, green notices contain information on suspected criminals intended for circulation, yellow notices contain details of missing persons, and black notices concern the finding of unidentified bodies. Additionally, there is circulation of information about stolen goods and notifications regarding the *modus operandi* of criminals and criminal groups. Interpol has developed databanks relating to drugs importation and manufacture and has developed systems of crime analysis to mine this data, which signal the priorities for international law enforcement. The organization also holds conferences on a range of matters such as counterfeiting, fraud, drug smuggling and money laundering. It is thus through the circulation of information, and by shaping the interpretation of that information, that Interpol influences the nature of transnational policing.

At first sight it seems that this organization would be the obvious choice to develop as the institution for coordinating transnational policing in Europe as well as more globally. It provides an established international infrastructure and communication network and has an accumulation of relevant expertise. Yet it has been displaced as the transnational policing institution in Europe by the development of Europol. One reason for this is the uncertainties caused by the unusual legal position of the organization. Importantly, Interpol was not established by any international treaty but rather was developed by police agencies themselves. At present there is no method of making Interpol democratically accountable, the organization publishes no financial records (despite, ultimately, being funded by taxpayers' money), and there is only limited provision in respect of data protection (despite the organization's accumulation of large amounts of data). There are also lingering doubts about the organization's efficiency and concerns about its lack of security.

The idea of Europol was first put forward by Helmut Kohl in 1991. Then Chancellor of West Germany, Kohl envisaged an agency akin to the Federal Bureau of Investigation in the USA. However, while the FBI could be fostered in the context of the US federal system (in order to overcome the logistical problems of policing inter-state crimes), in the European context the lack of harmony between national criminal justice systems and the concurrent effects of the doctrine of sovereignty have, thus far, limited the development of the new institution. The consequence is that Europol has evolved to be primarily concerned with the acquisition, analysis and dissemination of criminal intelligence pertaining to transnational crimes. The

agency was first put under way in January 1994, with a brief to support member states of the European Union in drug-related law enforcement, including money laundering. In July 1999 Europol took up its activities under the Europol Convention with specific competence over a range of criminal activities. These include: illegal immigration and 'human smuggling' – especial mention is made of child pornography and the sex industry in this regard – trafficking in stolen vehicles and nuclear materials, the counterfeiting of currency – especially the new Euro – money laundering and terrorism. Like Interpol, Europol officers have no powers of arrest, but instead depend on domestic police acting within their respective national jurisdictions to undertake this aspect of police operations. The difference between Europol and Interpol is not so much in the way that the agencies are organized (both are essentially institutions that process knowledge about criminals and criminal activity), but rather in their legal constitution. Europol has recognition under the Treaty of European Union. Further, under the terms of the Europol Convention, the Council of Ministers is accorded executive, but not legislative, authority while two other institutions, the European Commission and the European Parliament, are also accorded formal, although limited, oversight. While mechanisms of accountability for Europol can be characterized as meagre (Anderson et al., 1995, p. 253), there is not the degree of ambiguity that surrounds Interpol.

The role of the 'liaison officer', an officer seconded to another force in something akin to a 'diplomatic capacity', has been developed internationally since the 1970s. These officers also facilitate the smooth transnational flow of police information, but, in comparison with the Europol and Interpol frameworks, this information exchange is much less formal and, hence, it is much less visible. The development of training schools and the exporting of policing expertise should also be considered a transnational activity, but very little systematic attention has been given to these programmes to date. Increasing attention is being paid to the transnational activities of private security providers.

Evaluation

Overall, outside of academic circles debates about the accountability of transnational policing enterprises have been muted. While academic criminology has maintained an interest in comparative police systems for many years, the study of transnational police activity is quite new. As such, evaluation studies have not yet produced a measure of efficacy or effectiveness and the doubts that have been raised about the accountability of the transnational police enterprise have yet to be comprehensively articulated.

James Sheptycki

Associated Concepts: extraterritorial law enforcement, transnational organized crime

Key Readings

Anderson, M., de Boer, M., Cullen, P., Gilmore, W.C., Raab, C. and Walker, N. (1995) *Policing the European Union*. Oxford, The Clarendon Press.

Sheptycki, J.W.E. (1995) 'Transnational policing and the makings of a postmodern state', *British Journal of Criminology*, 35 (4), pp. 613–35.

Sheptycki, J.W.E. (1997) 'Transnationalism, crime control and the European state system: a review of the scholarly literature', *International Criminal Justice Review*, 7, pp. 130–40.

Sheptycki, J.W.E. (1998) 'The global cops cometh', *British Journal of Sociology*, 49 (1), pp. 57–74.

Sheptycki, J.W.E. (1998) 'Policing, postmodernism and transnationalization', *British Journal of Criminology*, 38 (3), pp. 485–503.

TREATMENT MODEL

See Rehabilitation

TRIANGULATION

Definition

The use of different methods of research, sources of data or types of data to address the same research question.

Distinctive Features

The term triangulation was first propounded in the context of social research by Campbell and Fiske in 1959 but became much more widely known after the publication in 1966 of *Unobtrusive Measures: Non-reactive Research in the Social Sciences* by Eugene Webb and others. The concept emanates from an analogy with

navigation and with surveying, whereby one 'fixes' a position in relation to two or more landmarks or objects. The rationale is that the position will be more accurate and precise than it would be if located in relation to only one landmark or object. When transferred to the context of social research, the argument is that if the same conclusions can be reached by using different methods of research there can be a stronger belief in the validity of these conclusions than if they were founded on the use of only one method. There is, therefore, a strong link between triangulation and validity, which is the extent to which conclusions are believed to be plausible and credible. At the heart of this argument is the viewpoint that different methods of research have different strengths and weaknesses and that triangulation – in theory at least – can serve to 'trade-off' the weaknesses of one method against the strengths of another. In this way the convergence of methods or of data produces 'value-added' in terms of validity.

There is a much less bold and precise claim for triangulation, namely that the use of different methods can assist in examining different aspects or dimensions of the same problem. For example, victim surveys which use structured questionnaires are able to measure the extent of victimization in a community but they would need to be supplemented with in-depth semi-structured interviews with individuals (such as narrative interviews) in order to gain some appreciative understanding of the experience of victimization for those individuals. Similarly, quasi-experimental methods can be used to assess the efficiency of criminal justice policies but would need to be combined with qualitative methods such as observation or interviews to understand the social processes by which policies do or do not work.

It is common to distinguish different types of triangulation. Data triangulation refers to the collection of different types of data on the same topic, for example statistical indicators of fear of crime complemented with appreciative, qualitative accounts collected from individuals. These different types of data may be collected at different phases in the fieldwork, for instance, qualitative data collected in focus groups or by in-depth interviews may be used to uncover the dimensions of the concept 'fear of crime' (such as psychological dimensions and social dimensions or fear of different types of crime such as personal crimes and property crimes). This is known as the process of elaborating a concept into dimensions. Such qualitative work can act as a precursor to the development of formal questions structured around such dimensions which, when combined together, produce a statistical scale or index of 'fear of crime'.

Investigator triangulation refers to the collection of data by more than one researcher. This is especially useful in ethnographic studies of institutions, communities or social groupings which are fragmented and where entry into one part of the social field precludes entry to another (for example in prison research, which requires participation in both inmate and prison officer subcultures).

Method triangulation involves the collection of data by different methods so as to counterbalance the different threats to validity which each entails. For example, official statistics on crimes recorded by the police play an important part in criminological research. They are detailed, readily available and there are no fieldwork costs to collect them. However, other deficiencies are well known. In order to counteract some of these deficiencies, especially those relating to under-reporting, victim surveys are used. A sample of the general population is selected and individuals are asked whether they have recently been a victim of crime and whether they reported the crime to the police. The results of such surveys give some measure of the extent of unreported crime (and of crimes of different kinds).

Evaluation

The previous example illustrates one way in which a convergence of methods can make a contribution to the validity of measurements of crime. However, not all combinations of methods work in this way. Different methods of research, for example qualitative ethnographic methods in contrast to highly statistical social surveys, are often founded on different assumptions about the nature of the social world and the nature of explanation. In such cases it is not possible to think in terms of contrasting methods being combined in a simple additive way which provides 'value-added' in terms of validity.

The notion of triangulation is very plausible in principle but in practice it is necessary to be explicit about the ways in which different data and methods can support each other, especially in relation to improvements in validity.

Victor Jupp

Associated Concepts: appreciative criminology, self-reports, structured interviews, victim surveys

Key Readings

Campbell, D.T. and Fiske, D.W. (1959) 'Convergent and discriminant validation by the multitrait-multimethod matrix', *Psychological Bulletin*, 56, pp. 81–105.

Denzin, N. (1970) *The Research Act*. London, Butterworths.

Jupp, V.R., Davies, P. and Francis, P. (2000) *Doing Criminological Research*. London, Sage.

Webb, E.J., Campbell, D.T., Schwarz, R.D. and Sechrest, L. (1966) *Unobtrusive Measures: Non-Reactive Research in the Social Sciences*. Chicago, Rand McNally.

U

UNDERCLASS

Definition

In its contemporary guise, underclass refers not to the especially poor but to the cluster of pathological and destabilizing cultural attitudes and lack of moral values associated with a particular section of the poor – the 'feckless', 'the undeserving', 'the disreputable', 'the depraved' and 'the criminal'.

Distinctive Features

The idea of an 'underclass' has been around in various popular discursive forms, for example, the dangerous classes, since the late eighteenth century. However, during the 1980s and 1990s in the USA and UK the term was 'rediscovered' and popularized by neo-conservative commentators, such as Charles Murray. His central argument is that postwar liberal and social democratic social and criminal justice policies have produced a growing population of work-age, healthy people who inhabit a 'different world' to decent, respectable citizens. The pathological core values and attitudes of this emergent underclass are contaminating not only their own children but spreading through neighbourhoods. For Murray the three interconnected defining features of the underclass are illegitimacy, criminality and refusal to participate in the formal labour market. The massive increase in illegitimacy, which is concentrated in the poorest neighbourhoods, is having a devastating impact on child-rearing practices and social controls, especially on male children. Crime is also disproportionately

located in underclass neighbourhoods because, at a very early age, young males are being socialized to view criminal activity as a normal activity. The presence of high levels of criminal victimization also has a demoralizing impact on these neighbourhoods. Equally alarming, as far as Murray is concerned, is the drop out in underclass neighbourhoods of a large number of young males from the labour market. For Murray, young males are 'essentially barbarians' who need the disciplines and routines associated with the work ethic to make the transition to responsible adulthood. In the absence of this they find other ways of proving their masculinity, impressing young women and surviving economically, for example, violence and criminality. These three defining features produce pathological neighbourhoods in which children are encultured into an anti-social set of norms and have young single mothers and violence obsessed young males as their role models. In a subsequent elaboration of his thesis, Murray re-named the underclass 'the new rabble', arguing that we could identify them through high levels of illegitimacy, child neglect and abuse, drug use and crime and welfare fraud.

In terms of solutions to this predicament, Murray argues that a radical departure from the status quo is needed if we are to reverse the drift into the 'underclassization' of significant sections of the lower class. Not surprisingly, he blames postwar welfare policies for creating and perpetuating this underclass and advocates policy initiatives that change incentives. Policy needs to distinguish between respectable and disreputable and he supports a punitive approach to single mothers, draconian cuts in welfare support and the stigmatization of illegitimacy. Murray has also allied himself with right realist prison-centred law and order policies to restore lawfulness and take criminal young males off the streets. As far as he is concerned, crime levels are low when criminals realize that crime does not pay.

Evaluation

Murray has been heavily criticized for individualizing and racializing the problem of poverty, pathologizing the poor, absolving the state of welfare responsibilities and demonizing young single mothers. However, despite the intensity of the criticism, it is important to note that many of his core ideas have found 'softer' moral expression in 'workfare' policies in the USA and 'social exclusion' policies in the UK. They also continue to echo in the UK in New Labour's highly moralistic 'tough on crime' discourses on anti-social behaviour, incivility and public disorder.

Eugene McLaughlin

Associated Concepts: 'broken windows', demonization, neo-conservative criminology, racialization, social exclusion

Key Readings

Levitas, R. (1998) *The Inclusive Society? Social Exclusion and New Labour.* London, Macmillan.
Murray, C. (1989) 'Underclass; a disaster in the making', *Sunday Times*, 26 November, pp. 26–45.
Murray, C. (1994) 'Underclass: the crisis deepens', *Sunday Times*, 22 May, pp. 10–11.
Murray, C. (ed.) (1997) *Does Prison Work?* London, Institute of Economic Affairs.
Murray, C. (2000) The British underclass', *Sunday Times*, 13 February, News Review section, pp. 1–2.
Young, J. (1999) *The Exclusive Society.* London, Sage.

UTILITARIANISM

See Classicism; Deterrence; Rational choice

V

VICTIM SURVEYS

Definition

In differing ways, surveys of victims are concerned with crime measurement and reasons for the under-reporting of crime; the correlates of victimization; the risk of victimization; the fear of crime and its relationship to the probability of victimization; the experience of crime from the viewpoint of victims; and the treatment of victims in the criminal justice system.

Distinctive Features

In part, victim surveys developed as a result of recognized deficiencies of official crime statistics as valid measures of the extent of crime in society. For example, crimes recorded by the police rely to a great extent on members of the public reporting such crimes. There are several reasons for not reporting crime, for example the sensitivity of the criminal act, triviality of offence or distrust of the police. Victim surveys collect data on the occurrence of criminal acts irrespective of whether such acts have been reported to the police and, thereby, gain some measure of the extent of the 'dark figure' of unreported crime. A further impetus came from a direct concern for the victim within criminology and also within criminal justice policy. This coincided with the formation of victim support schemes and the publication of victims' charters.

Four broad patterns in victim surveys are discernible. These are local cross-sectional sample surveys; 'appreciative' surveys; national trend sample surveys; and cross-national surveys. In local cross-sectional studies a representative sample of the population of a particular area or district is selected and sample members are asked if they have been the victim of a crime within a specified period of time and also whether they reported such crimes to the police. Sometimes they are asked about their experiences of, and relationships with the police in that particular area. In the United Kingdom such surveys are exemplified by research associated with left realist criminology (which, in general terms, is concerned with facing up to the reality of crime from a social democratic standpoint). Realist surveys pay particular attention to the experiences of vulnerable groups within a particular locality. There is the opportunity for such cross-sectional surveys to be repeated, as with the first and the second Islington Crime Survey in London, thereby facilitating some comparison over time (see, for example, Crawford et al., 1990; Jones et al., 1986).

Typically, appreciative studies are less concerned with seeking precision in estimates of victimization in the community and more with the qualitative descriptions of the experience of crime from the victim's point of view. They may also seek to examine victims' experiences of being processed within the criminal justice system, for example by the police and by courts. Research design is typically based on purposive rather than random sampling. Appreciative victim studies are likely to be associated with victim support groups and feminist approaches within criminology (especially in relation to women as victims of sexual crimes). In some cases such studies are closely related to social and political action to reduce victimization of vulnerable groups and to improve the treatment of victims in the criminal justice system.

Large-scale national trend victim surveys were given impetus by their use in the United States in the 1960s, specifically in relation to

President Johnson's war against crime as expressed in the Commission on Law Enforcement and Administration of Justice, established in 1965. There was recognition of the need to supplement official crime statistics with data collected at first hand from victims. After a number of pilot studies, the National Crime Survey was carried out in 1972. It comprised three parts: commercial surveys, city surveys and a large-scale National Crime Panel survey. This last is the only remaining part of the US National Crime Survey.

In the UK national trend studies are typified by the British Crime Survey (BCS), sponsored by the Home Office. The BCS is an example of what is known as administrative criminology because of its close association with government and with official policy-making. The first survey was conducted in 1982 and subsequent surveys have been carried out at regular intervals. Different independent samples are selected at each sweep and therefore a panel element is missing. For example, in 1994 a sample for England and Wales of 15,000 adults over 16 years of age was chosen. Respondents were interviewed and asked about their experience of crimes committed against them as individuals and against their household since the beginning of the previous year (Mayhew et al., 1994). The BCS facilitates an examination of trends in the extent of crime, the risk of crime and the fear of crime (Mayhew and Hough, 1991). This examination is for the country as a whole or for sub-categories and local areas. The lack of a panel element does not permit such analysis for particular individuals. A major flaw with the BCS is that it is believed that it does not capture sufficiently the extent of sensitive crimes, especially sexual crimes and domestic violence. A Computer Assisted Personal Interviewing (CAPI) system of self-completion was introduced in 1998 to alleviate this.

A fourth type of study is concerned with cross-national comparisons of rates of victimization. For example, the International Crime Survey (ICS) is a large-scale survey of experiences of crime in 17 countries. A standardized interview schedule, translated into different languages, is administered to respondents by telephone using a method of random dialling of private phone numbers (van Dijk et al., 1990). The survey provides a valuable source of data in victimization among different groups and areas within countries and between countries. It does not, however, consider the experiences of victims in relation to the economic and social conditions of each country nor to the varying

institutional arrangements for dealing with crime and with victims in particular.

Evaluation

Victim surveys have played an important role in criminology and in policy-making especially, in providing better estimates of the extent of crime than those provided by official criminal statistics and by giving insights into victims' experiences of crime and of the criminal justice system. However, they do have deficiencies, for example in not being able to provide estimates of 'victimless' crimes such as drug-taking, in not addressing crimes affecting large populations, such as mass pollution, and in not providing measures of crimes, for example fraud, of which individuals are not aware.

Victor Jupp

Associated Concepts: appreciative criminology, cross-sectional design, hidden crime, left realism, official criminal statistics, self-reports, victimology

Key Readings

Crawford, A., Jones, T., Woodhouse, T. and Young, J. (1990) *Second Islington Crime Survey*. London, Centre for Criminology, Middlesex Polytechnic.

van Dijk, J.J.M., Mayhew, P. and Killias, M. (1990) *Experiences of Crime Across the World: Key Findings of the 1989 International Crime Survey*. Deventer, Gower.

Jones, J., Maclean, B. and Young, J. (1986) *The Islington Crime Survey*. Aldershot, Gower.

Mayhew, P. and Hough, M. (1991) 'The British Crime Survey: the first ten years', in G. Kaiser, H. Kury, and H.-J. Albrecht (eds), *Victims and Criminal Justice*. Freiburg, Max-Planck Institute for Foreign and Penal Law.

Mayhew, P., Mirrlees-Black, C. and Aye Maung, N. (1994) *Trends in Crime: Findings from the 1994 British Crime Survey*. Home Office Research and Statistics Department, Research Findings No. 14. London, HMSO.

O'Brien, R. (1985) *Crime and Victimization Data*. London, Sage.

VICTIMIZATION

See Victimology; Repeat victimization; Victim surveys; Victimless crime; Violence

VICTIMLESS CRIME

Definition

A victimless crime is a form of behaviour that is illegal but is consensual in nature and lacks a complaining participant.

Distinctive Features

In conventional forms of crime it is possible for the police and courts to establish the harm that has been done and the respective status, identity and roles of perpetrator, victim and complainant. However, victimless crimes or 'crimes without victims' or 'public morality crimes' normally involve participants in illegal but consensual activities. Because no criminal victimization is occurring the participants have no reason to complain to the police. Classic victimless crimes include the use of illegal drugs, gambling, homosexuality and prostitution. The notion that these activities are victimless is used to further campaigns for legalization and decriminalization.

This concept has been criticized on the grounds that it works with simplistic notions of 'consensus', 'harm' and 'victimization'. Many feminist criminologists, for example, argue that prostitution is not a victimless crime for the majority of the women involved. They are forced to engage in prostitution because of economic circumstances or because of the coercion of individual men or criminal gangs. The women run the risk of physical and sexual violence at the hands of clients and are open to blackmail by police officers. There is also the distinct possibility that if they do report a crime to the police they will not be taken seriously. Society is also affected by the crime because it reinforces stereotypical representations of women. Similar criticisms have also been made of those who argue that illegal drug-taking is a victimless crime. All drugs are addictive and drug addiction affects the health of individuals and their families. At a macro level, the production of illicit drugs diverts scarce resources from more productive activities and fuels organized criminal activity. Thus, many criminologists would argue that closer inspection indicates that there is no such thing as a victimless crime and that the very use of the term constitutes a process of denial and revictimization.

Eugene McLaughlin

Associated Concepts: decriminalization, denial, tolerance, victimology

Key Readings

Gusfield, J. (1986) *Symbolic Crusade: Status Politics and the American Temperance Movement*, 2nd edn. Urbana, IL, University of Illinois Press.

Schur, E.M. (1965) *Crimes Without Victims: Deviant Behavior and Public Policy*. Englewood Cliffs, NJ, Prentice–Hall.

Schur, E.M. and Bedau, H.A. (1974) *Victimless Crimes: Two Sides of a Controversy*. Englewood Cliffs, NJ, Prentice–Hall.

VICTIMOLOGY

Definition

There is some dispute as to who first coined the term 'victimology' but what is not in dispute is that its usage first appeared in the late 1940s. As a term it was originally used to designate an area of study concerned to address the relationship between the victim and the offender, though since the late 1970s it has been used to delineate a more general concern with the victim of crime. Often referred to as a sub-discipline of criminology, it has paralleled the development of its parent discipline in demonstrating an early concern with victim typologies and the responsibility of the victim for the creation of a criminal event to a more recent focus on the structural dimensions of criminal victimization.

Distinctive Features

There are different theoretical and conceptual strands within the sub-discipline of victimology reflecting different definitions of who constitutes the victim of crime (from the victim of street crime to the victim of state crime). Understanding the nature and impact of criminal *victimization* has been one of the key concerns of victimology. This concern has manifested itself in different ways. Early victimologists endeavoured to understand victimization through the construction of 'victim typologies', that is, by looking for a way to identify different types of victims. For example, von Hentig (1948) constructed a typology based on an understanding of 'victim proneness', that is, some people were more prone to victimization than others; whilst Mendelsohn's (1956) typology was more concerned with 'victim culpability', that is, the extent to which the victim could be held responsible for the events that had occurred. This latter concept has been particularly influential in articulating one way of understanding the process of victimization: the notion of victim precipitation. The use of this concept as a way of explaining cases of rape led those associated with the feminist movement to see victimology as shorthand for victim blaming.

Later victimologists looked to less individual and more structural understandings of the process of victimization by understanding the impact of patterns of lifestyle on patterns of criminal victimization – the lifestyle exposure model (Hindelang et al., 1978). This concept has underpinned much of the thinking associated with, and has contributed to the development of, the criminal victimization survey. Hence the inclusion of questions concerning routine patterns of behaviour such as use of public transport or drinking habits. This understanding of victimization, however, whilst structural in its approach, remained focused on understanding patterns of criminal victimization largely associated with crime as it is conventionally understood, that is, street crime and household crime. In order to incorporate an understanding of other forms of victimization, for example, that which occurs behind closed doors (child abuse, domestic violence), Mawby and Walklate (1994) articulate a view of victimization as structural powerlessness. This view of victimization recognizes that the impact of criminal victimization is mediated and rendered more complex by factors such as age, sex and race.

Evaluation

Whilst it can be seen that, at an analytical level, victimization can be understood as an individual or a collective attribute of powerlessness, experientially there are different ways in which individuals might respond to such powerlessness. The uneasy relationship that exists between victimology and feminism articulates some of the tensions between analysis and experience. Feminism's preference for the term survivor rather than victim is not just a matter of semantics; though it is the case that the genealogy of the term victim connotes the sacrificant, who was more often than not female. Indeed when the word is itself gendered, as in French, it is denoted as female. Feminists, recognizing the power of linguistics, object to the term victim because of its

emphasis on passivity and powerlessness and prefer instead to focus on ways in which women actively resist the oppression of their personal and structural locations. However, whilst these terms are presented as oppositional, in experiential terms such oppositions are much more difficult to identify. It is possible to think in terms of both active and passive victims and active and passive survivors in relation to experience. This is more than an argument of semantics. Understanding victimization as a process in which individuals express different feelings at different points and make choices about what to do or not to do as a consequence, is as important as understanding victimization as a structural location. Both differently inform policy responses and the appropriateness of support services.

Sandra Walklate

Associated Concepts: family crime, fear of crime, left realism, repeat victimization, victim surveys, victimless crime, violence

Key Readings

Davies, P., Francis, P. and Jupp, V. (2000) *Victimization: Theory, Research and Policy.* London, Macmillan.

Hentig, H. von (1948) *The Criminal and his Victim.* New Haven, CT, Yale University Press.

Hindelang, M.J., Gottfredson, M.R. and Garofalo, J. (1978) *Victims of Personal Crime: An Empirical Foundation for a Theory of Personal Victimization.* Cambridge, MA, Ballinger.

Karmen, A. (1990) *Crime Victims: An Introduction to Victimology.* Pacific Grove, CA, Brooks Cole.

Mawby, R. and Walklate, S. (1994) *Critical Victimology.* London, Sage.

Mendelsohn, B. (1956) 'Une nouvelle brouche de la science bio-psycho-sociale: victimologie', *Revue Internationale de Criminologie et de police technique.* pp. 10–31.

VIGILANTISM

See Informal justice

VIOLENCE

Definition

Our thinking about what constitutes 'violence' is distorted by the traditional way violence is treated as a phenomenon in law and in criminology. Framed by criminal statute, legal definitions of violence emphasize the outcome – how badly the person was hurt – injury, proof of identity of the particular assailant and so forth – and the intention, *mens rea* of the violent act. Its impact and the motivation of the offender are influential in defining its seriousness. When a court of law considers a case of criminal assault, most of us assume that these are the most serious forms of violence. However, crime surveys show quite clearly that most violence is kept away from the purview of the criminal justice system. Research shows that individuals largely manage the violence of others without the aid of so-called expert systems, such as the criminal justice system. Those who are its victims are most likely to seek advice from family and friends first when searching for ways of minimizing the impact of violence. Feminist researchers, and those studying other forms of hatred such as racist or sexualized hatreds, also consistently demonstrate that many very serious acts of violence fail to be reported to the police.

Distinctive Features

Violence is 'rarely' random or without a purposeful target (Stanko, 1998). Violence typically (although not exclusively) takes place between those who are familiar with each other. Harris and Grace's (1999) report on rape found that so-called stranger rapes only constituted 12 per cent of rape complaints in the 1990s, as opposed to 30 per cent in 1985. Whether the very low conviction rate (only 6 per cent in the 1990s) for rape in the criminal justice system in England and Wales is linked to judges' and juries' difficulty in understanding sexual violence between those who are known to each other is difficult to say. However, this study leads one to ask how familiarity and sexual violence might pose difficulties to criminal justice decision-makers who might link rape to the actions of strangers. Thus, even if violent acts are reported to the police, considerations other than the seriousness of the act may also influence whether law mediates an act of violence.

The complexities of the way violence dovetails with social relations continue to show us that the criminal law is a blunt instrument when it comes to intervening into violence and threat. In order to think about minimizing its impact, violence must first be understood as part of the wider social foundations of everyday life. Its use has meaning to victims and to offenders in terms of people's grounded social knowledge about the way the social world 'works' to maintain personal and institutional power. This understanding is used by those who threaten and hurt – either as individuals acting alone, on behalf of a collective group or on behalf of the state. Violence and its threat can be mobilized on behalf of institutions or the state to keep particular people 'in line'. The brutality of a police officer or a prison officer, for instance, has additional impact on people's lives because the individual meting out violence is authorized to do so. Even if unauthorized, it is up to the victim of the violence to demonstrate that such brutality was 'outside' the official remit of the person who committed the act on behalf of the state. Victims of violence also understand that its use is woven into the basic fabric of social relations. Depending on the circumstances (or lack) of intervention, together with the meanings individuals give to such threats and acts, violence may be treated as acceptable, unacceptable, lawful or unlawful.

Perhaps a more adequate description of violence would include the following. It involves any form of behaviour by an individual that intentionally threatens or does cause physical, sexual or psychological harm to others or to her/himself. It is not a phenomenon framed only through/by criminal statute. It is framed through and by the perceptions of and actions of those directly involved as well (Cretney and Davis, 1995). It is then re-framed through and by institutionally based decision-makers, witnesses and commentators (Harris and Grace, 1999; Hoyle, 1999; Stanko, 1985). How authorities and individuals label acts as *violence* and assess its impact depends on the situational contexts within which violence occurs. The institutional circumstances, which intersect both, affect this process of labelling acts 'as violence'. How the parties involved and institutional decision-makers make judgements about violence has consequences. As Stanko (1990) argued, many of our experiences of threat and physical harm are considered ordinary and routine parts of everyday life.

The way in which people define violence and institutional responses to it remains highly contested ground. Work on bullying, sexual harassment, racist abuse and so forth specifies a whole range of interactions and actions, implicit and explicit verbal abuse that people interpret as threatening and hurtful. The wide range of types of threatening behaviour may include name calling, stalking, vandalism and other forms of intrusive behaviour that make people feel uncomfortable and unsafe, that is, feeling under intimidation of violence. Such a continuum of harm not only contains elements of physical, sexual and psychological damage. People's wider social contexts exacerbate or minimize the psychological and social consequences of violence. Such differential damage is evidence that individual violent behaviour has varying impacts on people. People's vulnerability to violence and its effects are rooted in individual and social resources. For instance, sexual abuse and threat, by all research findings, impact women's lives more than men's lives. The consistent evidence of higher levels of sexual harassment, abuse and threat women experience, feminists argue, underpin gendered discrimination. Similarly, higher levels of racist abuse reported by minority groups demonstrate the way in which inequalities founded in the hierarchies of 'raced' social privilege impinge on many people's everyday lives. Such abuse based on and in racialized knowledge of the way threats intimidate different people who have differential social capital (so to speak), holds a unique but often hidden place in the way people understand their social worlds. This is one way to link violence to other structures of social exclusion. One interesting observation from research on violence is that actual physical harm is not necessary to demand and to receive compliance from people. Threats 'work' because people do not wish to experience physical harm. Debate about how social differences are maintained through violence and intimidation can be found in the scholarly discussions of gender, race, age, religious and ethnic social exclusion, poverty and social assistance, employment discrimination, homelessness and so forth. These are often linked to the naming of violence and fear of violence as a serious problem for many categories of people simply because of who they are.

In this way, debates about forms of violence often challenge institutions to recognize their role in the perpetuation of violence and how it creates and maintains social disadvantage in contemporary society. To a large extent, violence as a phenomenon has been made more visible through these challenges to institutional practices. For example, the debate about the high levels of violence met by Health Service staff is as much about the potential for experiencing physical harm as it is about being expected to work under conditions that are dangerous. In a similar vein, the debate about bullying at school is presented as a problem of the working conditions for teaching staff as well as for the education of students. Alongside this impediment to learning that bullying poses are the detrimental consequences of such intimidation to the health and development of children. But what is important here is how many forms of violence that were once treated as part and parcel of everyday life are now elevated to social problems. The harassment of women, for instance, was considered a routine part of being female. However, when it was problematized as a condition of being female, the consequences of such harassment for women's feelings of safety become the evidence of gender discrimination.

Evaluation

What continues to hamper our understanding about violence is the persistence of a framework that has long outlived its usefulness, but not its popularity. Violent offenders are still imagined as people 'out-of-control', psychologically disturbed, distant and different from the rest of us law-abiding folk. An emphasis is placed on people's psychological motivation for committing acts of violence. The result of looking to biology or psychology to explain any violent act overlooks many common features of violence. Because most violent acts are committed by men against other men, such violence is explained as part of men's nature. When violence occurs between women and men, this violence is assumed to flow from men's right to control women. And when women commit violence, they are often treated as if they have stepped beyond the respectable boundaries of non-violent femininity. The common explanations about violence dominate popular culture and media representation.

The use of violence, how victims, offenders and institutions define it, and its public imagery show the complex set of social relations embedded in hierarchies of the distribution of power in society. Its impact is not only limited to the personal consequences for individuals linked to their own health and well-being. Its impacts are firmly rooted in social structures and social privileges of individuals and social groups. Those who assess the impact of violence on behalf of institutions and in particular on behalf of the criminal justice apparatus display their knowledge of such social relations when deciding when, how and why intervening in violence is important for the health and well-being of the nation as a whole.

Elizabeth Stanko

Associated Concepts: crime, family crime, hate crime, hegemonic masculinity, masculinities, personal safety, social harm, victimization

Key Readings

Cretney, A. and Davis, G. (1995) *Criminalizing Assault.* London, Routledge.

Harris, J. and Grace, S. (1999) *A Question of Evidence: Investigating and Prosecuting Rape in the 1990s.* Home Office Research Study No. 196. London, HMSO.

Hoyle, C. (1999) *Negotiating Domestic Violence.* Oxford, The Clarendon Press.

Stanko, E.A. (1985) *Intimate Intrusions.* London, Routledge.

Stanko, E.A. (1990) *Everyday Violence.* London, Pandora.

Stanko, E.A. (1998) *Taking Stock: What Do We Know about Violence in the UK?* ESRC Violence Research Programme, Royal Holloway, University of London, Egham, Surrey, TW20 OEX.

W

WAR CRIMES

Definition

War crimes are acts that retain their essential criminal nature even though they are committed by individuals in time of war and/or under official military orders.

Distinctive Features

By the outbreak of the First World War, European nation-states had accepted that certain breaches of the laws of war were crimes. The International Military Tribunal at Nuremberg (1945–6) opted for a criminal justice, rather than political or military, approach to produce the basic definition of what constituted a war crime. This, according to the Tribunal, comprised: the murder, ill-treatment or torture, or deportation to slave labour or for any other purpose, of civilians of or in occupied territory; the murder, ill-treatment or torture of prisoners of war; the killing of hostages; the plunder of property; the wanton destruction of human settlements; and devastation not warranted by military necessity. Members of the armed forces and civilians who violate these laws are guilty of committing war crimes and can be individually judged and, where appropriate, punished by international or national courts and military tribunals. This is the case whether or not such war crimes have been ordered by a political leader or by commanding officers. Individuals accused of war crimes cannot absolve themselves of criminal responsibility by citing an official position or that they obeyed superior orders – that is, the crime of obedience. Conversely, commanding officers are responsible for violations carried out by their troops unless they self-evidently attempted to suppress them. The 1949 Geneva Conventions codified the set of war crimes settled on by the Nuremberg trial and subsequent protocols have expanded the protection available to combatants and civilians in times of war. For human rights campaigners, the crucial issue is not the existence of a body of laws covering war crimes but the willingness to enforce them. Although nation-states have the legal right to prosecute war criminals, the dominant pattern is either impunity or administrative punishment.

Eugene McLaughlin

Associated Concepts: crimes against humanity, genocide, obedience (crimes of), state crime, torture

Key Readings

Gutman, R. and Reiff, D. (eds) (1999) *Crimes of War: What the Public Should Know.* New York, W.W. Norton.

Neier, A. (1998) *War Crimes: Brutality, Genocide, Terror, and the Struggle for Justice.* New York, Times Books.

Ratner, S.R. and Abrams, J.S. (1997) *Accountability for Human Rights Atrocities in International Law: Beyond the Nuremberg Legacy.* Oxford, Oxford University Press.

Roberts, A. and Guelff, R. (2000) *Documents on the Laws of War.* Oxford, Oxford University Press.

Robertson, G. (2000) *Crimes Against Humanity.* Harmondsworth, Penguin.

WHITE COLLAR CRIME

Definition

A heterogeneous group of offences committed by people of relatively high status or enjoying relatively high levels of trust, and made possible by their legitimate employment. Such crimes typically include fraud, embezzlement, tax violations and other accounting offences, and various forms of workplace theft and fiddling in which the organization, its customers or other organizations are the victims.

Distinctive Features

In developing the concept of 'white collar crime' – 'a crime committed by a person of respectability and high social status in the course of his [sic] occupation' (Sutherland, 1945, 1949) – Sutherland challenged the stereotypical view of the criminal as typically of lower class, arguing that the powerful routinely commit crimes. Some individual white collar offenders avoid criminal prosecution because of the class bias of the courts, but more generally they are aided by the power of their class to influence the implementation and administration of the law. Thus the crimes of the upper and lower classes differ mainly in the implementation of the criminal laws that apply to them. Given that 'upper-class' criminals often operate undetected, that if detected they may not be prosecuted, and that if prosecuted they may not be convicted, Sutherland argued that the criminally convicted are far from the closest approximation to the population of violators.

Sutherland produced a more encompassing and abstract version of 'crime', defined through the 'legal description of an act as socially injurious and legal provision of a penalty for the act' (1949, p. 46). While retaining reference to law, he seeks to encompass acts beyond those proscribed by criminal law; the content of laws and the nature of legal distinctions are social products, and 'crimes' are illegalities which are contingently differentiated from other illegalities by virtue of the specific administrative procedures to which they are subject. Sutherland's arguments regarding the nature and significance of 'white collar' crime were part of a much broader theoretical project which sought to redefine the scope and substance of criminology, organized around the explanatory concept of differential association, through which he sought (highly imperfectly) to provide an explanation for lower-class and upper-class crime.

In his article 'Who is the criminal?' (1947), Paul Tappan developed a systematic criticism of Sutherland's work, focusing first on Sutherland's sociological definition of crime, and seeking to provide a 'rigorous' (legalistic) definition, organizing this around intention, the criminal law and successful prosecution following due process. In Tappan's view, it is illegitimate to describe people as criminal when they have not been successfully prosecuted for a crime; this is to engage in normative reasoning, or moralizing. Ironically, Tappan went on to argue that much of what Sutherland wants to label crime constitutes 'normal business practice', and in so doing argues that those offences typically committed by business people are inherently different from criminal offences, a view held by many academics who comment upon white collar and corporate crime (Pearce and Tombs, 1998).

Evaluation

These – and other – aspects of the dispute between Sutherland and Tappan have endured and remain pertinent for contemporary attempts to define and understand white collar crime. These disputes entail disagreements about values, politics, theory, epistemology and methodology.

Amongst recent debates around white collar crime, perhaps the most significant has been that which distinguishes between occupational and organizational crimes. Thus, one view is that the term white collar crime should be restricted to the study of crimes by the individually rich or powerful which are committed in the furtherance of their own interests, often against corporations or organizations with, for or within which they are working. These occur when individuals or groups of individuals make illegal use of their occupational position for personal advantage and victimize consumers or their own organization, for example, either directly through theft or indirectly by damaging its reputation. Such acts or omissions are distinct from organizational illegalities or corporate crimes, designed to further organizational ends.

This indicates that opportunity structures are important in understanding the incidence of white collar crime. Some criminologists have begun to shift from a focus upon the status of the offender to the nature of the crime; Shapiro (1990), for example, focuses upon the (differential) levels of opportunity and temptation to commit crime in different social situations, her central concern being the way that trust is differentially distributed throughout occupational hierarchies.

For others, white collar crime is an illusory concept. Thus, for example, Hirschi and Gottfredson have argued that as with conventional crime, the white collar offender seeks personal benefit (short-term gratification), and that the setting of the offence or the status of the offender is simply not relevant to the cause of crime and criminality.

White collar crime, then, is certainly a contested concept. In that the term emphasizes the social characteristics of individual offenders, it invariably leads us into inadequate attempts to characterize certain forms of criminality in terms of respectability, status, trust, and so on. Moreover, it subsumes within one category what are a heterogeneous group of phenomena with different rationales, methods, effects, likelihood of detection, and so on. Indeed, while Sutherland 'named' white collar crime, his own, fundamental concern was with what is now commonly known as corporate crime. The value of retaining a focus on white collar crime is perhaps that this topic 'illustrates the possibility of divergence between legal, social and political definitions of criminality [and] . . . in so doing it reminds us of the artificiality of all definitions of crime' (Nelken, 1994, p. 84).

Steve Tombs and Dave Whyte

Associated Concepts: anomie, crime, corporate crime, criminalization, critical criminology, deviance, differential association, governmentality, social control theory, social harm

Key Readings

Friedrichs, D. (1996) *Trusted Criminals. White Collar Crime in Contemporary Society*. Belmont, CA, Wadsworth.

Nelken, D. (1994) 'White collar crime', in D. Nelken (ed.), *White Collar Crime*. Aldershot, Dartmouth.

Pearce, F. and Tombs, S. (1998) *Toxic Capitalism*. Aldershot, Dartmouth.

Shapiro, S. (1990) 'Collaring the crime, not the criminal: reconsidering the concept of white collar crime', *American Sociological Review*, 55, pp. 346–65.

Sutherland, E.H. (1945) 'Is "white collar crime" crime?' *American Sociological Review*, 10, pp. 32–9.

Sutherland, E.H. (1949) *White Collar Crime. The Uncut Version*. New Haven, CT, Yale University Press.

Tappan, P. (1947) 'Who is the criminal?', *American Sociological Review*, 12, pp. 96–102.

Z

ZERO TOLERANCE

Definition

Zero tolerance policing is a high profile, proactive maximum enforcement street policing strategy that requires police officers to pursue even the most minor offences with the same vigour as more serious forms of criminality. This policing style is intended to send a signal to criminals and law-abiding citizens that the police have the capacity and motivation to tackle the spectrum of anti-social and petty criminal behaviours that make a city or neighbourhood feel and look unsafe.

Distinctive Features

During the late 1990s the term zero tolerance policing was the subject of considerable media attention, with proponents of this particular policing style elevating it to the status of a miracle treatment for crime. It can be defined in a number of ways but primarily involves strict, aggressive enforcement of laws irrespective of the circumstances on the grounds that eradicating minor crime can contribute to a notable reduction in serious crime. Zero tolerance policing is most closely associated in the public imagination with the innovative policing strategies developed by William Bratton in the aftermath of his appointment as commissioner of the New York Police Department by Mayor Rudolph Giuliani in 1994. Prior to taking control of the NYPD, Bratton, a strong supporter of 'broken windows' theory as developed by George Kelling and James Q. Wilson, had already tested zero tolerance policing tactics on the New York Transit system and as commissioner of the Boston Police. Bratton promised New Yorkers

that the NYPD 'were going to fix broken windows and prevent anyone from breaking them again'. In order to heighten their visibility, New York's police officers were put back on the beat and encouraged to look for the signs of crime and take an interventionist stance. They were directed to focus on low-level infringements of the law, public nuisance violations and incidents of incivility such as pan handling, fare dodging, public drinking, jay walking and the activities of graffiti artists and squeegee merchants, on the grounds that these are the forms of behaviour that make citizens feel unsafe in public places. Suspects were stopped, frisked and questioned about a range of criminal activity occurring in a given neighbourhood to access information about more serious forms of crime and deter offenders. Officers on the beat were also encouraged to arrest suspects and process them through the criminal justice system and to break away from the idea that certain forms of crime were the preserve of specialist squads. Organizational re-engineering of the NYPD also accompanied zero tolerance policing. William Bratton decentralized the management structure by pushing authority and responsibility down to precinct commanders and introduced new technologies, such as COMPSTAT, to monitor and map crime events and make commanders focus on emergent patterns and results. This technology also allowed the NYPD to update their data base on the city's population and crime flows across and within neighbourhoods.

Evaluation

This policing strategy scooped up honours both within the USA and internationally because it was represented as being responsible for a dramatic decrease in the crime rate

– particularly the murder rate – across New York boroughs and reclaiming the main thoroughfares and parks of 'Gotham City' from the criminal and disorderly elements. A central attraction for police chiefs in various parts of the world was that zero tolerance policing provided badly needed proof that order maintenance policing was central to effective crime control and to garnering support amongst both the general public and rank and file officers. However, critics of zero tolerance policing insisted that as a result of the relentless PR activities of Bratton and Giuliani zero tolerance policing had been given more credit than it deserved for reductions in serious crime. There is evidence that the crime rate was falling in New York before zero tolerance policing was introduced and that the downward trend in the murder rate across the USA was related to the waning of the crack epidemic of the early 1990s and broader demographic shifts. There was also mounting evidence that the strategy was: promoting an aggressive attitude amongst police officers; encouraging discriminatory and insensitive policing; resulting in the harassment and criminalization of powerless groups who were already disproportionately represented in the criminal justice system; and enflaming racial divisions. The zero tolerance policing philosophy came into disrepute as a result of a sharp rise in complaints and public protests about the torture of Abner Louima, a Haitian security guard, by officers from the 70th precinct in Brooklyn in August 1997 and the murder of Amadou Diallo, an unarmed West African street vendor, in February 1999 by the NYPD's renowned Street Crimes Unit. The police brutality associated with these incidents provided evidence that 'letting the cops off the leash' had given licence to certain officers to over-ride civil liberties and human rights. In the aftermath of these cases, William Bratton and senior police officers in other countries who were converts to his aggressive policing philosophy became considerably more cautious in their use of the term 'zero tolerance policing', preferring to emphasize the value of community and problem oriented policing strategies and policing by consent.

Eugene McLaughlin

Associated Concepts: 'broken windows', community policing, problem oriented policing

Key Readings

Bratton, W.J. and Dennis, N. (eds) (1997) *Zero Tolerance: Policing a Free Society*. London, IEA Publications.

Bratton, W.J. and Knoblach, P. (1998) *Turnaround: How America's Top Cop Reversed the Crime Epidemic*. New York, Random Books.

Chua-Eoan, H. (2000) 'Black and blue: cops, brutality and race', *Time*, 6 March, pp. 24–8.

Human Rights Watch (1998) *Shielded from Justice: Police Brutality and Accountability in the United States*. New York, Human Rights Watch.

Kelling, G. and Coles, C. (1996) *Fixing Broken Windows*. New York, The Free Press.

Silverman, E.B. (1999) *NYPD Battles Crime*. Boston, MA, Northeastern University Press.

ZONAL THEORY

See Chicago School of Sociology; Social ecology

SUBJECT INDEX

Note: Page numbers in *italics* indicate main article.

NAME INDEX